Money, Banking, Financial Markets & Institutions

Michael W. Brandl

The Ohio State University

Max M. Fisher College of Business

Department of Finance

CENGAGE

Australia • Brazil • India • Mexico • Singapore • United Kingdom • United States

CENGAGE

Money, Banking, Financial Markets & Institutions

Michael W. Brandl

ISBN-13: 978-93-5350-223-2
ISBN-10: 93-5350-223-3

Registered Office:
Cengage Learning India Private Limited
T-303, 3rd Floor
DAV Complex, Plot 3
Mayur Vihar Phase 1
Delhi-110091
Email: asia.infoindia@cengage.com

Cengage Learning is a leading provider of customized learning solutions with office locations around the globe, including Andover, Melbourne, Mexico City, Stamford (CT), Toronto, Hong Kong, New Delhi, Seoul, Singapore, and Tokyo. Locate your local office at: **www.cengage.com/global**

Cengage Learning Products are represented in Canada by Nelson Education, Ltd.

For product information, visit our website at **www.cengage.co.in**

Printed in India
First Indian Reprint 2019

Disclaimer:
This book contains link to resources which are a part of the US edition. The same may not be available with the Indian edition. The buyer needs to purchase a copy of the US edition to have full access to those resources. In no event the publisher shall be liable for any limitation or performance due to unavailability of these resources.

Brief Contents

Contents

Part 1
Money and Its Prices

Part 2
Money and the Overall Economy

CHAPTER 5

CHAPTER 6

CHAPTER 7

Part 3
Central Banks

CHAPTER 8
Central Banks 159

CHAPTER 9
Monetary Policy Tools 183

CHAPTER 10
The Money Supply Process 213

Part 6 Global Financial Markets

CHAPTER 19 Foreign Exchange Markets 381

CHAPTER 20 Global Financial Architecture 403

Part 7 Financial Institutions

CHAPTER 21 Thrifts and Finance Companies 429

Preface

Note from the Author

My goal in creating what you are about to experience was to show students that money, banking, and financial markets and institutions are fascinating and exciting things. I wanted to create something that students will actually read and enjoy. By going on this intellectual journey, you will see the application of these important concepts. My objective is to teach students to critique what is actually happening around them and what has happened to the economy in the past. I want to encourage students to discuss and debate among themselves what is going on and why.

This book and all of the digital technologies that go along with it are designed to be used in almost all economics departments that offer money and banking courses. It allows economics faculty members to delve into topics that are usually only discussed in business schools, which illustrates to students how economics is truly applicable to what they are seeing happen in the economy. The book is also well suited for financial institutions or financial markets courses taught in business schools; the text focuses on creating an important link between the economics courses students have taken and the finance courses they may be currently taking or will be taking in the future.

For Instructors

Your students are, most likely, of a different generation. You are probably teaching Millennials (born roughly between 1981 and 1995) or members of Generation Z (born roughly between 1996 and 2010). These two generations are technologically savvy, globally connected, and very well versed in multitasking. They like their information in quick, small bits, and they appreciate humor. They use Twitter and Snapchat, they get their news from *The Daily Show* and HBO's *Last Week Tonight*, and they are in many ways different learners than those in previous generations. They also like to engage each other when given the chance. This text is aimed at them. It is designed to get students to think, discuss, and debate. It was not designed to encourage the simple regurgitation of facts; thus, the structure of this book is different. Traditional "chapters" are now broken up in to small chunks and are sprinkled with digital assets. The end-of-section review questions are designed to get conversations and discussions flowing. However, while the structure of the text is different, academic rigor has not been sacrificed. The issues discussed are too important to be watered down. Instead, we delve into a wide variety of issues, many of which you will not have time to discuss in class. That's okay. Allow the students to learn on their own and to learn from each other. That is what this text is designed to do.

For Students

Important issues and concepts do not need to be presented in boring ways. Can't we discuss, debate, even argue, and learn while also having a bit of—dare I say it—fun? That's what "this" is about. I hate to use the word *textbook* because it conjures up big, thick tomes of

50- to 75-page chapters that drag on and on and on. Instead, I have created something that is designed to get you to think, to contemplate, and to discuss with your friends and colleagues. The point, after all, is not to merely get the exam question right; the point is for you to learn and to have fun along the way. So get ready to discuss and debate some very important issues that concern money, banking, and financial markets and institutions. ICYMI, follow me on Twitter @MichaelBrandl.

Features of *Money, Banking, Financial Markets & Institutions*

AN APPROACHABLE, STUDENT-ORIENTED WRITING STYLE. This book reads much more like a conversation than a lecture. It presents the content in a unique way to foster discussion, contemplation, and debate as opposed to simple memorization and regurgitation.

SECTION REVIEW QUESTIONS. Every section ends with Section Review questions to make sure students understand the concepts before moving on. There are two short-answer questions and one multiple-choice question.

TYING CONCEPTS TOGETHER. Throughout the chapters are "Tying Concepts Together" boxes that help bring together various concepts in the chapter as well as from other chapters.

IN THE NEWS. At the end of every chapter is an article from the current news that brings the concepts to life for the student. Also included are questions to spark discussion and debate.

Teaching Materials

Instructor's Manual

The Instructor's Manual, available on the Instructor's Support Site at www.cengagebrain.com, includes special features to enhance class discussion and student progress.

PowerPoint Lecture Slides

PowerPoint slides are available for instructors to use with their lectures. Download these slides online at www.cengagebrain.com.

For more information about any of these ancillaries, contact your Cengage Learning Consultant for more details, or visit the *Money, Banking, Financial Markets & Institutions* website at www.cengagebrain.com.

Acknowledgments

Writing a first edition book is a huge undertaking, and it would not be possible without the contributions of many people. Numerous colleagues reviewed portions of this book in various stages and drafts; I am grateful to each of them for their time and insightful comments and suggestions.

The talented people at Cengage have provided me with spectacular support and insight. I am most grateful to Mike Worls for all of his encouragement and support. Thank you to Tara Slinger, Kristen Meere, and Colleen Farmer who kept me on task and did just a wonderful job in editing and producing this project.

Special thanks also go to Cengage's Mike Roche and Clara Goosman for their encouragement throughout this project.

Kris Maxwell and the folks at Evil Cyborg did a wonderful job in creating a variety of digital assets you will find throughout this text.

A variety of former students helped out on this project especially Rashee Raj, Kelly Stowe, and Lemuel Anaejionu. Thanks to all my former students who provided feeback on the manuscript at University of Texas-Austin, University of Wisconsin-Madison's Department of Economics, and at The Ohio State University. I could not have done this without all of your help, insights, and support.

Dedication

To S.H., my wife and best friend

About the Author

Dr. Michael Brandl received his BS degree in Economics from the University of Wisconsin at Madison and his PhD in Economics from the University of Houston. His research interests include economic growth, financial economics, and labor economics. His teaching focuses on the application of economic theory to management decision making as well as global financial markets.

Dr. Brandl was previously on the faculty at University of Texas at Austin McCombs School of Business and has held visiting positions at University of Wisconsin–Madison Department of Economics, University of Houston Department of Economics, and Aalto University School of Business (Helsinki, Finland). As a consultant, he offers custom training for numerous entities, including 3M, LG Electronics, Motorola, Texas Instruments, Frito-Lay, Texas Association of Counties, and the American Public Power Association. He also serves as an economic consultant with the Magee & Magee consulting firm, where he has provided economics analysis in a variety of antitrust, patent infringement, intellectual property, and economic damage litigation cases.

He has won more than 40 teaching awards over his career.

1

Introduction

1-1 Why Study This Stuff?

Can we talk? Money, banking, and financial markets are a fascinating subject full of unresolved issues, questionable incentives, and controversial issues. Yet all too often this incredibly interesting topic is presented in dry, dull, boring tones that could put the most ardent insomniac to sleep in no time. I will be honest: This kind of presentation baffles me.

It baffles me because instead of getting students excited about this subject, many of my esteemed colleagues want to examine the issue only in the most rigid "scholarly" (read: boring) manner. In doing so, students are bored. Students want to learn about what happened during the global financial crisis that started in 2008. They want to know why it happened: Could it have been avoided? Could it have been anticipated?

Instead of addressing these interesting questions, we usually inundate students with confusing terminology, a myriad of facts and figures, and a mind-numbing number of equations and graphs. Then, at the end of it all, we wonder why students walk away dissatisfied. It's time for a different approach.

This book is much more of a conversation than a lecture. I want this to be the start of discussions, debates, even arguments you will have with your friends and colleagues. I want you to talk about this stuff, to think about it, and, yes, even argue about it. The futures of not just our financial system but our economic system, and ultimately our way of life, are at stake. That is why this stuff matters.

This stuff matters not just because you are going to be asked about it on your exams. It also matters because it brought about the worst economic slowdown since the Great Depression of the 1930s. This stuff matters because it affects the lives of so many people who will never fully understand how it works.

But let me warn you: This stuff is complicated. It involves complex concepts that span the world and across time. To fully master these concepts and have intelligent, well-informed discussions, we have to do some heavy intellectual lifting. But the effort you put forth in mastering this stuff will be worth it. By the end, you may find you have raised more questions than you answered. Welcome to life. As Aristotle so brilliantly put it: The more you know, the more you know you don't know. Are you ready for the challenge?

The Key Components 1-2

To understand our financial system and the issues it faces, we need to understand the major components and the major players.

1-2a Money and Financial Assets

Remember, assets are things of value or things that are useful. Money, which is anything that is generally acceptable in exchange for goods and services, is clearly an asset because anything that functions as money is useful for attaining other things. Financial assets, then, are intangible assets whose value is derived from a contractual claim.

As we will learn, the concept of money is much more complex than the scraps of currency we carry around in our pockets. We will spend a bit of time digging further into what we mean by "money" and the important "prices of money": interest rates and exchange rates.

In addition to money, financial assets also include stocks and bonds. Stocks represent part ownership of a corporation and are thus a contractual claim on the corporation's assets. Equity also generally means ownership. This is why the terms *equity* and *stock* often are used interchangeably. We will refer to both the "stock market" and the "equity market" or to "stocks" and "equities" and mean the same thing.

Financial assets also include bonds, which are the promise of the issuer (either corporations or governments) to pay interest and principle, or the amount borrowed, over a specific time period. Thus a bond is a contractual claim to a flow of funds in the future. Because bonds represent the debt of the issuer, we will use the terms *bond market* and *debt market* interchangeably. An important type of debt is one that is entered into when someone finances the purchase of real estate. Mortgages, or loans where real estate is used as security or collateral on the loan, play a key role in global financial markets. In fact, these mortgages were at the heart of the financial crisis that began in 2008.

Another important financial asset is that issued by depository institutions such as banks. Thus bank accounts such as checking accounts and savings accounts are also financial assets because they are contractual claims on funds on deposit with the depository institution, or bank.

1-2b Financial Markets

Many of the financial assets mentioned in the previous section are traded in financial markets. While the popular and business press spend a great deal of time discussing the stock market or the market for equities, the bond or debt market is just as important, if not more so. There is a big market for mortgages and mortgage-backed securities, but the largest financial market is the foreign exchange market, where currencies are bought and sold. Financial markets essentially bring savers, called surplus units, together with borrowers, called deficit units. Households, firms, governments, and the rest of the world are both savers and borrowers.

These savers and borrowers initially meet in the primary market, where financial instruments or financial assets are initially sold. Over time, the saver who purchased a financial instrument or asset may want to resell it. This reselling and buying takes place in the secondary market. The existence of a secondary financial market is necessary so that the holder of a financial asset can easily convert it into another financial asset such as cash. Liquidity is the ease with which a financial asset can be converted into another financial asset. Some assets, such as checking accounts, are very liquid; that is, they are easy to turn into another financial asset such as cash. Other financial assets are less liquid, or are more difficult to convert into another financial asset.

The prices determined in these financial markets turn out to be extremely important. One of the most significant prices of money is interest rates. Changes in interest rates can have dramatic effects on the survivability of firms and thus on the level of employment, prices, and the health of the entire economy. The bond market helps to determine these critical interest rates; thus understanding the various aspects of the bond market is critical. Understanding price determination in the stock market and the foreign exchange market also is insightful because changes in prices in these markets have widespread effects.

These financial markets tend to be so vital to the overall economy that oversight and regulation are deemed necessary. Central banks are often one of the main regulators, and monetary policy uses these financial markets to guide the overall economy.

1-2c Central Banks

While the **Federal Reserve** is the central bank and monetary authority of the United States, it is, naturally, not the only central bank in the global economy. In fact, the Federal Reserve is one of the youngest central banks. It certainly plays a major role in global financial markets, but to gain a better understanding of how these markets function, our study of central banks must reach beyond only the Federal Reserve.

The European Central Bank is the youngest of the major central banks, and in many ways it is based on the structure of the Federal Reserve. Yet the European Central Bank is vastly different from the Federal Reserve in other ways. While students often learn a great deal about the Federal Reserve, their knowledge of the European Central Bank is much more limited. This lack of knowledge can create obstacles to understanding the problems the EuroZone faces.

Other critical central banks around the world include the Bank of Japan, the Bank of England, and the Bank of Canada. Much about our global financial markets can be learned by understanding how these significant central banks function and how they responded to the recent crisis that began in 2008. This brought to light the important link between our banking system and other financial institutions.

1-2d Banking System and Financial Institutions

Banks face many risks, or the potential for losses. Their ability to manage this risk is pitted against their drive to earn an accounting profit and satisfy the demands of their shareholders. The push for profits, however, can lead bank management to undertake actions that can put their bank—and thus, by extension, the entire financial system—at risk. This problem, called systemic risk, is one that bank regulators need to monitor closely.

Commercial banks are facing more and more competition from other financial institutions. These institutions perform some, but not all, of the tasks that banks do. Finance companies, insurance companies, mutual funds, investment banks, and private equity partnerships often are referred to as part of the "shadow banking industry." These financial institutions came out of the shadows during the recent global financial crisis that helped push the global economy into a deep recession.

These entities are so important that they are not allowed to operate purely on their own. Instead, these markets and institutions are some of the most regulated entities in a market-based economic system. Yet, as we will see, these regulations often don't work the way they are designed. Some argue that these regulations failed to stop the financial crisis that began in 2008. Others believe that these regulations actually contributed to the crisis, which led to the worst economic slowdown since the Great Depression.

So, it is with money that we start. Let's first understand what exactly we mean by "money" and how the price of money is determined. Next we examine how money affects the entire economy and has done so over time. Then we examine the central banks: what they do, how they do it, and why they remain so controversial. We then delve into banks more in depth and move on to financial markets in general. We conclude by considering other types of financial institutions.

Enjoy the ride.

2

Money, Money Supply, and Interest

2-1 The Concept of Money

One of the hit songs from the Broadway musical *Cabaret!* is the catchy tune "Money." The refrain from the song goes "Money makes the world go around, the world go around, the world go around. . . ." It's a catchy little phrase that may get your foot tapping, but what does it really say? What does one really mean by *money*? How exactly does it "make the world go around"?

The concept of money is something everyone, including songwriters, seems to think they know exactly what it means—until you ask them to define it. As it turns out, the definition of money is anything but straightforward. Many things can function as money and have done so over time. As we shall see, in today's modern economy many things function as money, and different assets can have different levels of "moneyness."

One of the reasons money does, in fact, make the world go around is because the growth rate of the money supply is very important to the proper functioning of a modern-day market economy. Here we examine why this is the case and how difficult it actually is to measure the money supply.

Finally, one thing we will come back to again and again is the "price of money." One, but not the only, price of money is interest rates. We take a look at why interest rates exist and how they are used in calculating the value today of money we will receive in the future, as well as the value of money in the future that we have today. The changes in the price of money can have a large impact on just how fast, or slow, the economic world goes around and around.

2-1a Money Defined

Whenever you begin studying a new concept, it is often best to start with a formal definition. A formal definition of **money** would read something like this:

Money: Anything that is generally acceptable in exchange for goods and services and/or repayment of debt.

What does that really tell us? First, notice it says "anything"; there is no mention that money has to come from the government or the central bank, or even from banks in general. Money is something that people "generally accept" in exchange for goods and services.

Note that just because a government or central bank issues currency does not mean it will be accepted as money. For example, leading up to the Russian Ruble Crisis of 1999, people in Russia stopped using the official, government-issued ruble in exchange for goods and services. Thus the ruble was ceasing to be money because it was no longer "generally accepted" by the Russian people.

Later in this chapter we look at how a wide variety of things, including vodka during the Russian Ruble Crisis, has functioned as money over time. At this point, don't get hung up on the idea that money must be those little scraps of paper issued by the central bank that you are carrying around in your wallet. Remember, money is anything that is *generally acceptable* in exchange for goods and services and/or repayment of debt.

Let's think more about the next part of the definition: "generally acceptable." It is this portion of the definition that perplexes economists the most. Why will people accept certain things in exchange for goods and services and not others? Think more about those currencies issued by central banks. When is that considered money? All the time? No—remember the Russians in 1999. Currencies can stop being money if people don't accept them in exchange for goods and services.

To understand why this might be an issue in a different setting, consider the idea of dollarization that occurred in many Latin American countries over the past several decades. Let us again start with a formal definition.

Dollarization can be official or "full" dollarization, where a country legally accepts another country's currency as their **legal tender** (assets accepted for repayment of debt to the government as well as private transactions), and contracts and prices are stated in this currency. In 2001 Ecuador officially and legally started using the US dollar as its currency. Thus, since 2001 Ecuador has been officially dollarized.

Dollarization: The situation when market participants use another country's currency as money.

Legal tender: Assets accepted for repayment of debt to the government as well as private transactions.

Dollarization can, however, also be de facto, where "in fact" the people use another country's currency as their own money. This is also referred to as "unofficial dollarization" or the even more vague "currency substitution." In these cases people use another country's currency in private transactions, but the local currency remains legal tender and continues to circulate.

For example, for most of the last 30 years the US dollar has been used as money in Bolivia, even though Bolivia has its own currency, the Boliviano. There was nothing "official" that stated that the US dollar would be used as money—it just sort of happened.[1] It was the people who decided the US dollar would now be money in Bolivia.

Between full dollarization and de facto dollarization is "official semi-dollarization," whereby another country's currency *is* legal tender but the country also issues its own currency, which can also be used to repay debts to the government. For example, the US dollar has been legal tender in Haiti since 1919, as has the Haitian currency the gourde.

One thing to note about this terminology: Even though the term *dollarization* is used, do not falsely believe that the "other currency" is always the US dollar. The dollar is often used, but not always. For example, the Vatican City in Rome was dollarized to the Italian lira and now the Euro.

How is it that the dollar became money in Bolivia? Or, more generally, how does any currency become money? For any asset to function as money, it has to perform three very important functions. Let's look at these three functions next.

2-1b Functions of Money

Medium of Exchange

An asset that is going to function as money first must be generally accepted by all sides in a transaction. This is what we refer to as a **medium of exchange**. The concept of medium of exchange may seem obvious to those of us living in a modern economy: Of course when I take my dollar bill to the convenience store, the clerk will exchange it for goods and services.

Medium of exchange: A good that is accepted by both sides in a transaction.

To understand why the concept of medium of exchange is so important, think of what would happen if we did not have a money. Without a money we would then have to rely on barter: trading a good or service for another good or service. Now, barter is fine as long as your economy is small—say, a family or a small social group like a church or fraternity/sorority. In these cases one member of the group simply has to find someone else in the group who has what they want and also wants what they have. This is what economists call the **double coincidence of wants.**

Double coincidence of wants: The situation where each party wants what the other has to offer for sale.

1 Bolivia suffered from extremely high rates of inflation, especially during the 1980s. The worst inflation was between 1984 and 1986, with the peak being a monthly inflation rate of 183%. The people of Bolivia wanted a currency that would not continuously lose its value as a result of hyperinflation.

The double coincidence of wants, however, becomes a huge problem once the size of the economy grows to be more than just a few people. In a barter economy among a population of a few million people, the double coincidence of wants problem becomes daunting because in a barter economy the number of "prices" you need is equal to the number of paired goods you have. Thus, the number of prices you need is

$$\{N(N-1)\}/2$$

So, if you have five goods, you need

$$(5[5-1])/2 = (5[4])/2 = 20/2 = 10$$

or 10 prices.

Creating 10 prices may be doable. Sure, price tags may be relatively lengthy since each and every good needs (N − 1) prices or here four different prices, but it certainly is not out of the question.

But if you have 5,000 goods, you need

$$(5{,}000[5{,}000-1])/2 = (5{,}000[4{,}999])/2 = 24{,}995{,}000/2 = 12{,}497{,}500$$

or approximately 12.5 million prices. That is, you must have 12.5 million prices, or each good would need 4,999 prices! What a mess.

Within a barter economy, a great deal of time, effort, and energy is expended trying to line up wants. Thus, in a barter economy there are very high search costs—costs expended to find the appropriate good or service to satisfy the want. Because these search costs can become so large, people often simply stop trading. They start producing goods themselves instead of spending huge amounts of time searching for someone who has what they want and at the same time wants what they have. As you remember from microeconomics, however, this autarky, or lack of trading, is inefficient and results in a misallocation of resources.

This is also why barter is untenable once the economy grows to any significant size. The economy will almost collapse. Instead of this catastrophic outcome, we thankfully have a medium of exchange—a money—that allows us to specialize and reduce our search costs. This medium of exchange also allows us to reduce the number of stated prices that we need.

Hopefully, you are convinced that in a modern day economy we need money. That is, we need something that functions as a medium of exchange so we do not have to rely on bartering.

Remember, being a medium of exchange is only one of the important characteristics of money. Next we look at another: a unit of account.

Unit of Account

The concept of **unit of account** is another one of those things we take for granted. Think of a convenience store: When you go into the store and you see the price for a gallon of milk at $3.00 and the price of a loaf of bread at $1.50, you know that two loaves of bread are equal to one gallon of milk. The dollar is functioning as a unit of account.

Unit of account: An agreed-upon method of placing relative value on assets.

But imagine there is no unit of account. Now you go into the convenience store and the price on the gallon of milk is 857 whopwinks, while the price on the loaf of bread is 679 linkspinks. What are whopwinks and linkspinks? You have no idea. Is the bread cheap or is it expensive? You can't tell because you have no way to place a relative value on these different goods. Since you can't compare the prices, you cannot make a rational decision. How can you equate marginal utility to a price if you can't figure out the price?

Thus, without a unit of account, or without money, microeconomics fails. We need a unit of account for a market economy to function. How lucky we are to be part of a modern economy that has a money—a unit of account.

Store of Value

The last characteristic of money has to do with time called the **store of value.**

Store of value: A money must retain some of its purchasing power over time.

Store of value is another one of those concepts that we take for granted in a modern economic system. For example, suppose you buy a sandwich for lunch and you get three dollar bills as change. You cram the three bills in your jeans pocket and leave the shop. At night you throw the jeans in your clothes hamper, completely forgetting about the three dollar bills in the pocket. Then, two weeks later, when it is time for you to do laundry, you empty the pockets of your jeans, and to your pleasant surprise you come across the forgotten three dollar bills. You think, "Great! Now it's time for an unexpected Starbucks coffee."

Now imagine when you go to pay for your coffee at Starbucks, the barista behind the counter looks suspiciously at your three crumpled dollar bills. The barista looks up at you then returns to staring at your green dollar bills. In a low, slow voice she says, "These are green dollar bills. We don't accept green dollar bills anymore, only red dollar bills." You stammer in frustration: "but . . . I just found these, I mean, I was given these as change just two weeks ago." The barista just shrugs and slides back your crumpled, now worthless three green dollar bills.

Thank goodness this does not happen today in the United States. Why not? The answer is because the dollar is a store of value—it maintains some of its purchasing power over time. Thus for any asset to be money, it must retain some of its purchasing power over time.

How does some "money" lose its store of value? Most often the cause is inflation.

Think about what inflation—the continuous ongoing increase in the general level of prices—means in terms of money. When there is inflation, you have to give up more units of a currency to buy the same amount of goods. Therefore as an economy suffers from inflation, the currency is losing its store of value.

Thus for an asset to function as money it must perform three important functions: medium of exchange, unit of account, and be a store of value. However, we also need to consider questions about the amount of money. That is, is there an optimal amount or growth rate of money? We turn our attention to this important issue in the next section.

SECTION REVIEW

Q1) What is the difference between money and currency? When are they the same? Why might they be different?

Q2) How many prices must a barter economy have if the economy has four goods? What if it has 400 goods? Explain why having a money in the second case is beneficial.

Q3) You read a news story about a country that is suffering from rapid, ongoing increases in the cost of living. Which characteristic of money is being directly negatively impacted in that economy?

a. Unit of account

b. Medium of exchange

c. Store of value

d. Double coincidence of want

2-2 Amount of Money and Money Through Time

Hopefully you are convinced that a modern economic system needs money to allocate resources in a reasonably efficient way, and for an asset to function as money it must be a medium of exchange, be a unit of account, and have a store of value. Next we want to consider why the amount or growth of the money supply matters. Then we will examine how different assets have served as money over time.

2-2a The Amount of Money Matters

While the content presented in the previous section makes a compelling argument for why money is important, most modern economists, and professionals working in financial markets, worry more about the *quantity* of money as opposed to what actually functions as money. To understand why the quantity of money is such an important concept, let's think more about the growth rate of the money supply.

In 1811 David Ricardo published a widely read book called *The High Cost of Bullion* in which he argued that inflation occurs when the money supply grows too quickly. In the 1960s Milton Friedman offered a corollary to this, arguing that the Great Depression of the 1930s came about because the money supply contracted in the early days of the Depression.

These two ideas can be summarized as follows:

> If the money supply increases too quickly, you have too much money chasing too few goods. On the other hand, if the money supply does not grow fast enough, there will not be enough money for transactions to take place and the economy will slide into a recession or a depression.

To see why this is the case, imagine a classroom with 45 students. Let's assume everyone in the room is thirsty and no one is allowed to leave the room. Let's further assume that the professor has a pristine, chilled bottle of water that she is going to auction off to the members of the class. Let us finally assume everyone in the room has one dollar in their pockets—and no collusion is allowed.

The professor begins the bidding. Someone bids \$0.50, someone else bids \$0.75, someone else, \$0.85, and then someone bids \$1.00. The bidding stops. The person who bids \$1.00 gets the bottle of water. The price of the bottle of water is therefore \$1.00.

Now imagine into the room walks the dean. The dean has access to a "keep students happy fund," and she decides the best way to keep students happy is to give the students \$5.00 of their tuition money back. So the dean proceeds to give every student in the room a five-dollar bill. Then the dean leaves the room.

Let's now suppose the professor is going to auction a second bottle of cool water. Everyone in the room wants the bottle of water and now everyone has \$6.00. The bidding begins: Someone bids \$0.50, someone else bids \$1.25, yet another bids \$3.75, and another bids \$6.00. The bidding stops at \$6.00. The person who bids \$6.00 gets the bottle of water. The price of the bottle of water is \$6.00.

What happened?

The price of a bottle of water went from \$1.00 to \$6.00. Why? The amount of money in "the economy" (i.e., the room) increased "faster" that the amount of stuff the economy was producing, ceteris paribus, or all things held constant.

Take this perhaps overly simplistic but illustrative example and expand it to an entire economy and you come to the general conclusion that if the money supply increases too quickly, you have too much money chasing too few goods. Thus, the general level of prices increases, that is, inflation occurs. See this illustrated in Figure 2-1.

Figure 2-1 Money Supply and Inflation

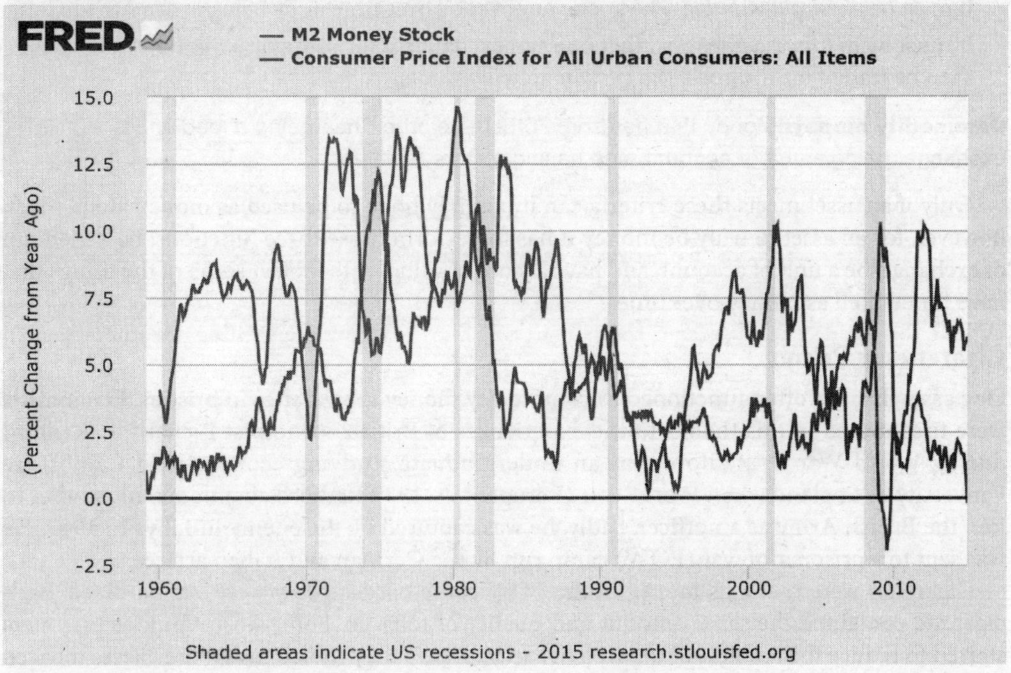

Source: Copyright 2014 by the Federal Reserve Bank of St. Louis.

Conversely, think about what might happen in the other extreme. If the money supply does not increase fast enough, there may not be enough money for transactions to take place. Thus, because few transactions take place, output decreases and the economy contracts. These contractions in the economy can lead to an economic recession or, as Milton Friedman pointed out, even economic depressions.

Thus we care about the growth rate of the economy's money supply because "too much" money can lead to inflation, whereas "not enough" money can lead to economic recessions and depressions.

This should convince you that the growth rate of the money supply is what matters the most. But this also raises the question, What functions as money? Next we look at the issue of the different types of money used today and how the money supply is actually measured.

2-2b Money Through Time

Financial historians tell us that through time a wide variety of assets have functioned as money. Centuries ago commodities—things such as fur pelts, wheat, or gold—were used as money. **Commodity money** is an asset that is used as money but also has another, or different, use. For any asset to function as money, it must meet certain criteria. These criteria include the following:

- It must be *easily standardized* so that the prices of two units can be easily compared. That is, the good that is functioning as money has to be homogenous or the same. For example, if gold is to be used, a purity standard must be agreed to, such as 99% pure gold per ounce. If a bushel of wheat is to be used as a money, the weight, quality, color, and so on of the wheat that makes up that bushel need to be agreed to.
- It must be *easily divisible*. Not all goods are going to have their value stated in nice round amounts; sometimes you have to "make change."

- It must be *easy to carry around*. The good functioning as money has to be portable. Steel I-beams would obviously not make a good currency.
- It must be *physically durable*. The good cannot spoil over time or by being in the sun too long.
- It must be in *broad demand* so that one can exchange it for some other good, which can then be traded for the good the person actually wants.

Commodity money: Money that has some other use other than being a medium of exchange, being a unit of account, and having a store of value.

Only if an asset meets these criteria can it possibly hope to be used as money. Remember, however, for an asset to truly be money it has to perform those three functions: be a medium of exchange, be a unit of account, and have a store of value. Let's look at some of the things that have functioned as money over time.

Cigarettes in Prison

One asset that has often functioned as commodity money is cigarettes in prisons. Economists were first alerted to this thanks to the experiences of British economist Richard A. Radford during World War II. Radford was an undergraduate studying economics at Cambridge University in England when World War II erupted. In 1939 Radford abandoned his studies to join the British Army as an officer. Sadly, he was captured by the enemy in Libya in 1942. He was sent to a prisoner of war (POW) camp run by the German and Italian armies.

Cigarettes were useful as money in the POW camp because they were standardized. Each cigarette contained the same amount and quality of tobacco. Some unscrupulous prisoners started to reduce the amount of tobacco in the cigarettes they traded, using the excess tobacco to roll their own cigarettes and thus cheat the system. This debasement, as economists call it, did not last long, however, as the altered cigarette quickly traded at a discount. So, for the most part, the cigarettes used in trading were standardized.

Cigarettes also were useful as money because they were easily divisible. A pack contained 20 cigarettes, so "making change" in transactions was relatively simple and straightforward. Cigarettes also were easy to carry around (portable). In terms of durability, cigarettes also fit the bill as a money. As long as they were kept dry, cigarettes had a relatively long shelf life. Finally, in terms of being in demand, prisoners would often smoke the cigarette as a source of tension relief. Thus, cigarettes in the POW camps were always in demand.

This is why Radford's article is so intriguing: It demonstrates that any asset that is able to be standardized, divisible, durable, and in demand could be a currency, as long as it is a medium of exchange, is a unit of value, and has a store of value. Thus, in the POW camps cigarettes were money.[2]

But, as Radford recognized, cigarettes have another use: They can be smoked. Thus cigarettes are an example of commodity money.

Other Commodity Money

Cigarettes in POW camps are not the only type of commodity money. For example, leading up to the Russian Ruble Crisis of 1999, the Russian people turned away from using the ruble as money and started using many different forms of commodity money.

David Woodruff, a political scientist at the London School of Economics, has spent a great deal of time studying Russian monetary systems—or the lack of them. Woodruff notes that as of early 1998, 50% to 75% of "exchange in industry" was in the form of some type of commodity money, including Russian vodka. However, industries were not the only ones turning away from using the ruble in Russia. Woodruff also reports that "in 1997, at least a quarter of revenues collected for the Federal budget took a non-monetary form."[3]

---

2 Radford, R.A. "The Economic Organisation of a P.O.W. Camp" Economica, New Series, Vol. 12, No. 48. (Nov., 1945), pp. 189–201.

3 For Woodruff's study of the political economy of the Russian monetary system, see his book, *Money Unmade: Barter and the Fate of Russian Capitalism*. Ithaca, NY: Cornell University Press, 1999.

Political scientists such as Woodruff are often as interested in "money" as economists are because a link can be drawn between the collapse of a people's faith in a currency issued by the government and their support of the government itself. In his 1999 book Woodruff argues that the failure of the Russian ruble to function as money was directly tied to the failure of the political system in Russia.

Challenges with Commodity Money

Of course, one of the biggest challenges with commodity money is getting the amount just right. There has to be enough of it for transactions to occur, but not too much. To understand why this is such a big issue, think of two of the most widely used types of commodity money through time: gold and silver.

For an economy that uses gold and silver as money, there has to be enough gold and silver coins in circulation so that all of the transactions people want to undertake can occur. If some people start to hoard the gold or silver coins, or if other people take their gold and silver coins to another country, there may not be enough money, and the economy could slide into a recession or an economic depression.

On the other hand, if the amount of gold and silver coins increases too rapidly, the economy can suffer from inflation. This is exactly what happened in the sixteenth century in Europe. During this time period, money in Europe was made up almost exclusively of gold and silver coins. The Spanish conquest of Latin America resulted in a huge influx of gold and silver into Europe. This Latin American gold and silver was quickly minted into new coins, thus rapidly increasing the money supply. As mentioned earlier, if the money supply increases too rapidly, the economy can suffer from inflation because too much money chases too few goods. In sixteenth-century Europe, the rapid increase in commodity money—gold and silver coins—resulted in periods of devastating inflation.

It is in great part because of these problems of controlling the amount of commodity money that the use of fiat money became more and more popular as time went by. **Fiat money** is an asset that has no intrinsic value, nor can it be directly exchanged for any precious metal or commodity. Most money today is fiat money; of that, most of the money supply is not little scraps of paper. What, then, constitutes modern-day money and the money supply? These are the questions to which we next turn.

Fiat money: An asset that functions as money but has no intrinsic value.

SECTION REVIEW

Q1) Bobby is confused. He states: "Since prisoners are not allowed to smoke in prisons any longer, Radford's examples of cigarettes in POW camps no longer applies." How would you explain to Bobby how Radford's story demonstrates the concepts of the criteria of money, as well as the importance of changes in the money supply?

Q2) Proponents of the Gold Standard, or using gold as money, often argue that it will keep inflation under control. How does the experience of Europe in the sixteenth century raise doubts about that claim?

Q3) Ricardo and Friedman agree that if the money supply increases "too quickly" the following happens:

a. The rate of inflation decreases.

b. The rate of real economic growth increases.

c. The rate of inflation increases.

d. The level of employment decreases.

2-3 Money Supplies

Fiat money has become more popular in large part because of problems of controlling the amount of commodity money in an economy at any given point in time. What exactly do we mean by fiat money and how do we measure it?

Think of fiat money as scraps of paper issued by a bank, or a government or central bank, that is not "backed up" by anything. That is, fiat money does not have its value stated in direct relationship to a precious metal such as gold or any other asset. One distinguishing feature about fiat money is it is often legal tender; by law, a creditor must accept it in repayment of debt. Most modern-day currencies are, in fact, fiat money. They are "money" that is not backed up by anything but is legal tender. The issuance of fiat money usually falls to central banks, and the fiat money represents the liabilities, or promises to repay, of the central bank. Fiat currency is not, however, the only type of money. Think about writing a check. When you write a check—or, more likely, swipe your debit card—isn't that "generally accepted in exchange for goods and services and/or repayment of debt?" Sure it is. So your checking account, in the form of checks and/or debit transactions, is also a type of money, isn't it? Expand on the idea of your debit card, and you can see where a wide variety of electronic accounts can act as money or have a certain level of "moneyness" to them. Money is the most liquid of assets; that is, it is the easiest and least expensive way to transform one asset into another asset. But different financial assets have different levels of liquidity, or, stated differently, they have different levels of moneyness.

Think about a savings account at a bank. If you can access that account with a debit card, then isn't it a type of money? Or, think about a money market account you might have at a depository institution. These money market accounts allow you to make a limited number of withdrawals each month, usually around six, including checks you can write on the account, so aren't they also a type of money? Yes, they are.

Economists have come up with various measurements of the money supply. These different measurements—some are very narrow, whereas others are very broad—contain assets with varying degrees of "moneyness." Some of the assets are very close to being what we consider cash: very liquid assets that are easily converted to cash without cost. These assets have a high level of moneyness. Other assets are less liquid but can still be considered a form of money and are thus included in some measurements of the money supply. These various measurements of the money supply are called money supplies or sometimes **monetary aggregates**. These monetary aggregates are a way to measure the money supply and, more importantly, the growth rate of money supply. As we will see, measuring the monetary aggregates is more difficult than it may seem.

Monetary aggregates: Broad measurements of the total amount of money within an economic system. Also referred to as the money supply or money supplies.

2-3a Monetary Aggregates[4]

Over the years economists have developed a number of different monetary aggregates, or measurements of the money supply. Let's look at what these different measurements are and why so many have been developed.

M1

One of the narrowest measurements of the money supply is given the fancy name M1. This measurement includes the things we most often think of as "money." M1 includes currency held by the public and transaction accounts at depository institutions:

- Currency held outside the vaults of depository institutions, the Federal Reserve Banks, and the US Treasury

4 For a more detailed discussion of monetary aggregates and their current levels, refer to "Monetary Trends," published monthly by the Federal Reserve Bank of St. Louis (https://research.stlouisfed.org/publications/mt/).

- Demand deposits and other checkable deposits, except those due to the Treasury and depository institutions (basically checking accounts)
- Traveler's checks
- Less cash items in the process of collection

For many decades M1 worked fairly well as a monetary aggregate or a measurement of the money supply. If M1 increased too quickly, that is, faster than the growth rate of the economy, inflation rates increased. On the other hand, if M1 increased too slowly, the economy slowed down, sliding into a recession and even long depressions. So, M1 worked the way we wanted it to—it was a nice measurement of the money supply.

Then things changed.

M1 Falls Apart Starting in the late 1960s and continuing throughout the 1970s, the U.S. economy suffered from increasing rates of inflation. As the FRED chart in Figure 2-2 shows, inflation, measured by the Consumer Price Index, or CPI, starts creeping up after 1965, recedes during and after the 1970–71 recession, but then begins shooting up drastically starting in 1973.

Figure 2-3 shows what is happening to the growth rate of M1 during the same period. Except for a brief period in about 1967, as the M1 growth rate (in red) increases, the inflation rate (in blue) increases. When the M1 growth rate decreases, the economy slides into a recession right after; the 1970–71 recession is indicated by the gray bar. Therefore, M1 works very well as a monetary aggregate.

But look what starts to happen around 1974 and 1975: The growth rate of M1 declines but the rate of inflation actually increases! At this point, M1 was failing as a monetary aggregate to warn us of inflation. What happened?

Financial market innovation is what happened. Specifically, the creation of money market mutual funds (MMMFs) rendered the M1 statistic utterly useless. Why? It goes back to the Great Depression of the 1930s.

Figure 2-2 Consumer Price Index in the U.S.

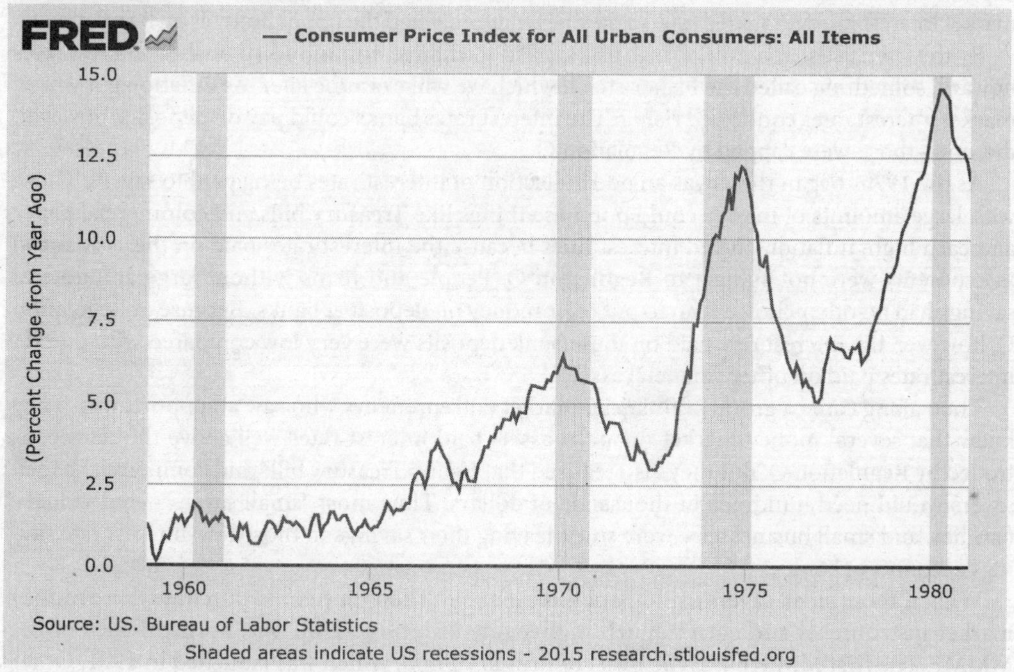

Source: Copyright 2014 by the Federal Reserve Bank of St. Louis.

Figure 2-3 U.S. Inflation (CPI) v. Money Supply Growth (M1)

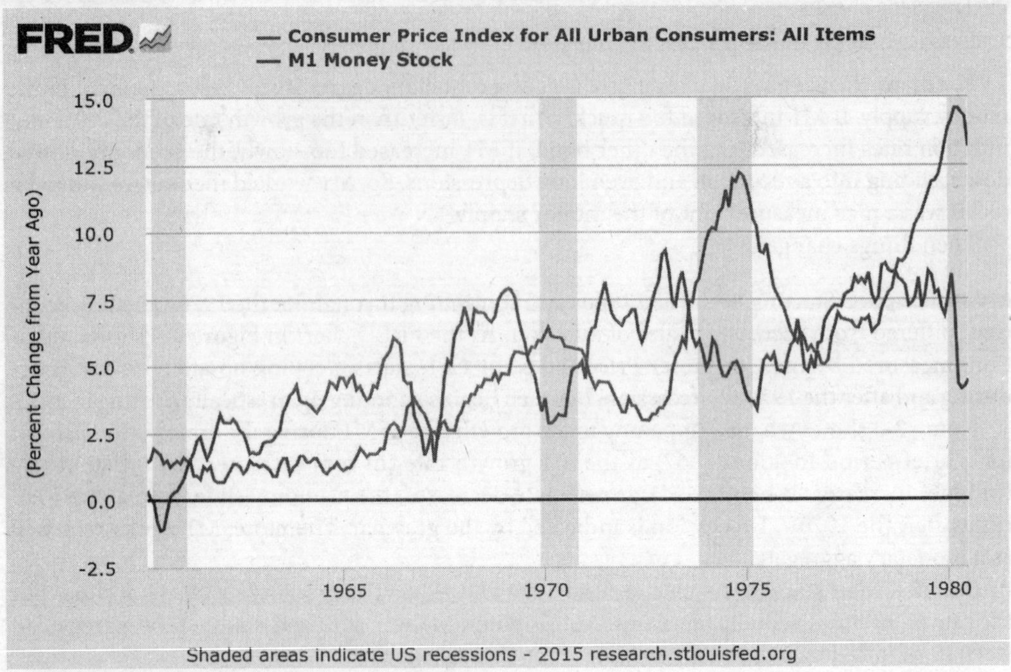

Source: Copyright 2014 by the Federal Reserve Bank of St. Louis.

M1, MMMFs, and Disintermediation Coming out of the Great Depression of the 1930s, Regulation Q was a law that, among other things, stated the maximum interest rate banks could pay on deposits. For much of the time from the 1930s to the 1960s, Regulation Q didn't have much impact; market interest rates remained low, so they never approached the upper limit set by Regulation Q.

By the late 1960s, however, things had started to change. Inflation had pushed interest rates upward, something called the Fisher effect, which we will examine later. As inflation got worse, market interest rates continued rising. The interest rates banks could pay on deposits, however, did not—those were capped by Regulation Q.

As the 1970s began there was an odd collection of interest rates being paid to savers. Those with large amounts of money could purchase things like Treasury bills and commercial paper and earn high, inflation-fueled interest rates because the interest rates paid on these financial instruments were not subject to Regulation Q. People and firms without large amounts of savings had no other choice than to put their money on deposit at banks. Because of Regulation Q, however, the interest rate paid on these bank deposits were very low compared with market interest rates paid on other financial assets.

Then along came a group of financial market entrepreneurs who saw an opportunity. They knew that several money market financial assets paid interest rates well above the rates controlled by Regulation Q. But they also realized that to buy Treasury bills and commercial paper, savers would need hundreds of thousands of dollars. Thus most "small savers"—individuals, families, and small businesses—were stuck leaving their savings in those low-interest rate savings accounts at banks.

What if these small savers could pool their money? Then they could purchase these money market instruments and earn a much higher rate of return. Thus was born the idea of the MMMF. The first MMMF was the Reserve Primary Fund, which was launched in 1971. Other MMMFs quickly followed, and by 1974 large amounts of savings started to flow out of the bank accounts with low interest rates and into MMMFs.

This flow of funds is sometimes called **disintermediation**, the removal of funds from a financial intermediary, such as a bank, to invest them directly, for example, through a mutual fund. This disintermediation caused the growth rate of M1 to decrease. Money was flowing out of demand deposits and thus out of M1. But the money supply growth rate was not decreasing; the measurement of the money supply was too narrow. Therefore economists had to come up with a better measurement of money supply.

Disintermediation: The removal of funds from a financial intermediary (e.g., a bank) to invest them directly, as through a mutual fund.

M2

M2 is a broader measurement of the money supply that builds on M1 (Table 2-1). (Economists come up with very creative names.) M2 includes:

- All of M1
- Savings deposits, including money market deposit accounts
- Small (<$100,000) time deposits
- Shares in retail MMMFs, net of retirement accounts

For a while, M2 worked well as a monetary aggregate. Reviewing Figure 2-4, notice that from 1983 to about 1987, as the rate of M2 declined the inflation rate declined, and before the 1990 recession, as M2 growth increased, inflation rates increased. Then in the early 1990s the growth rate of M2 decreased dramatically, but the inflation rate remained about the same. This is *not* how a monetary aggregate is supposed to work.

By 1993 the Board of Governors of the Federal Reserve had downgraded M2 as a reliable indicator. Looking again at Figure 2-4, as the 1990s goes on we can see the growth rate of M2 increase but the inflation rate remain rather stable. Then, in the first decade of the twenty-first century, the growth rate of M2 and the inflation rate actually go in the opposite direction of each other!

Many economists argue that, again, it was changes in financial markets—financial innovation and changes in the way banks operate—that led to the decline in the usefulness of M2 as a monetary aggregate.

Table 2-1 Monetary Aggregates

Aggregate	Component	Amount, Seasonally Adjusted*
M1	Currency in the hands of the public	1,239.8
	+ Traveler's checks	3.0
	+ Demand deposits	1,128.3
	+ Other checkable deposits	481.7
		2,852.8
M2	All of M1	2,852.8
	+ Small time deposits	524.0
	+ Savings deposits, including MMDAs**	7,557.3
	+ Nonretirement retail money market accounts	627.8
		11,561.9

* In billions of dollars as of November 2014.

** MMDA, money market deposit account.

Source: Board of Governors of the Federal Reserve.

Figure 2-4 U.S. Inflation (CPI) v. Money Supply Growth (M2)

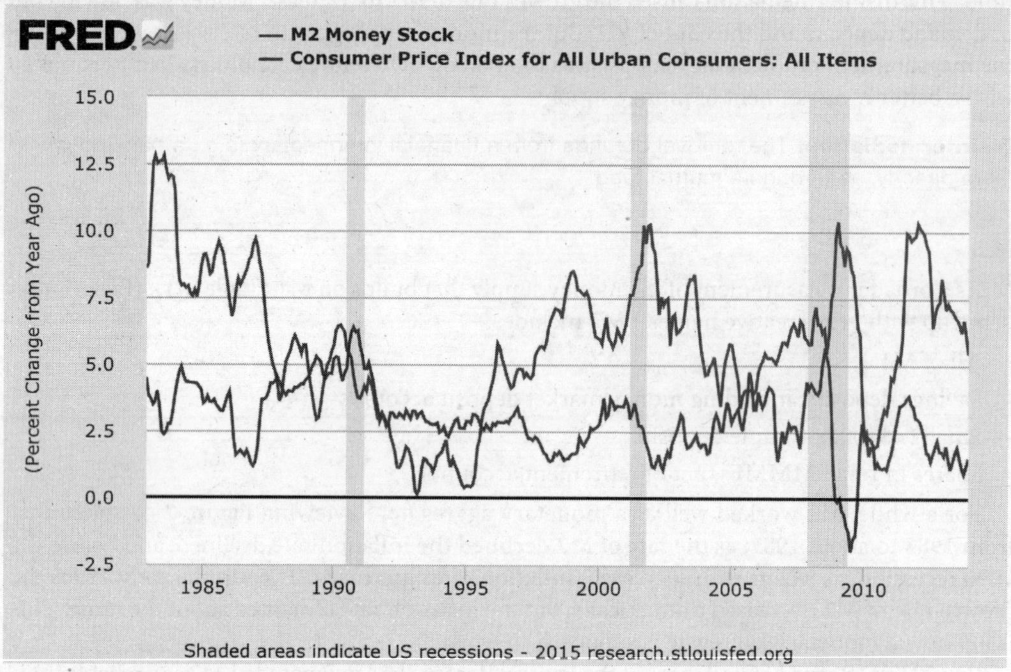

Source: Copyright 2014 by the Federal Reserve Bank of St. Louis.

Economists have tried to use other monetary aggregates, including M3, which the Federal Reserve no longer even bothers to report; Divisa, which was a weighted average used by the Bank of England; and others. They all basically have the same outcome: None consistently work well as a measurement of the money supply.

So, accurately measuring the money supply may not be an easy thing to do. But, in addition to the amount of money or the money supply, we also are interested in the prices of money: interest rates and exchange rates. We discuss exchange rates in Chapter 19, but next let's think more about this important price of money: interest rates.

SECTION REVIEW

Q1) A critic of money economics once stated, "if you cannot measure the money supply accurately, it is not worth discussing at all." How would you refute this statement?

Q2) Economists are searching for a "good" measurement of the money supply. What constitutes a good measurement of the money supply?

Q3) Which of the following is the most broad or most inclusive measurement of the money supply?

a. M1

b. M2

c. M3

d. M0

The Price of Money: Interest Rates

2-4

One of the most important prices of money is interest rates. We hear interest rates being discussed almost constantly by the business press. It seems as though the talking heads on CNBC, Fox Business, Bloomberg, and other media outlets are always talking about interest rate movements or the potential for interest rate movements. In this book we spend a lot of time talking about interest rates. Very seldom, however, does anyone ask the question, Why do interest rates exist?

2-4a Time Value of Money

The simple answer to the question of why interest rates exist is the time value of money. But what does that mean?

The **time value of money** means, everything else being constant, people would prefer to consume today as opposed to in the future because life is uncertain. Think about it this way: Imagine I say, "Please lend me $100 today and I will pay you back tomorrow." You might ponder this for a moment and retort, "Well, you are kind of old, Mr. Professor, and you might not be nimble enough to move out of the way of a high-speed bicyclist zipping across campus. If that happens and the bike runs over one of your old feet, you could be laid up in the hospital for a while and I won't get my $100 back." Being old, I have a hard time refuting your concerns.

Time value of money: Money received today has a higher value than money received in the future.

People don't like putting off consumption until the future because they don't know what the future holds. If you greatly prefer current consumption to future consumption, you have "high time preference." If, on the other hand, you are indifferent between consuming now or in the future, you have a "low time preference."

Thus, because of **time preference**—the preference to consume now as opposed to in the future—when I ask you to defer your consumption to the future (something you don't want to do), I have to compensate you. The compensation I pay you is called interest. The higher your rate of time preference, the higher the rate of interest I must pay you to defer your consumption.

Time preference: The rate at which a person will prefer to consume today as opposed to consuming in the future. A high time preference implies a person wants very much to consume now as opposed to in the future. A low time preference implies a person is indifferent between consuming now or in the future.

So, because of the time value of money we have interest and interest rates. That is, because people have a time preference, money and the ability to consume now has more value than money in the future.

2-4b Present Value

Let's think about how the idea of the time value of money works in reality. Suppose someone lends you $1,000 for one year. Since you are asking that person to defer their consumption for one year, they are going to charge you $100 in interest on the loan, that is, an interest rate of 10%. So, at the end of the year you will have to pay back the $1,000 plus $100 in interest. The interest rate (i) is

$$i = \frac{\$100}{\$1,000} = 0.10, \text{ or } 10\%$$

So, you have to pay back at the end of the year

\$1,000 plus 10%, or

$$\$1{,}000 \times (1 + 0.10) = \$1{,}000(1.10) = \$1{,}100$$

Now, let's further suppose that at the end of year one you ask to roll over the loan for another year. The nice person lending you the money agrees: They will lend you the \$1,100 for another year. That \$1,100 is the amount you originally borrowed, that is, the \$1,000 plus the interest you owe at the end of the first year. Now you have to pay the initial amount plus interest, plus interest on the new amount. This is called **compound interest**.

Compound interest: Interest earned on the principal plus interest.

Now, at the end of the second year you owe

$$\$1{,}100 \times (1 + 0.10) = \$1{,}100(1.10) = \$1{,}210$$

Going back to the original loan amount, this can be written as

$$\$1{,}000 \times (1.10) \times (1.10)$$

Or, we can simply write

$$\$1{,}000(1.10)^2 = \$1{,}210$$

If you want to roll over the entire amount for a third year, you would owe

$$\$1{,}000(1.10)^3 = \$1{,}331$$

You can see how fast the debt burden increases when you simply keep rolling over that debt. This is one of the reasons why people who allow their debts to accumulate can quickly get into financial difficulty.

We can generalize this to the end of n years and any initial or present value amount PV, which results in a **future value** (FV) of debt burden, by writing

$$PV(1 + i)^n = FV$$

Future value: The nominal value of an asset, such as money, at some point in time in the future.

But this doesn't have to be a depressing story of increasing debt burden. We can use the concepts of the time value of money to show why saving is such an important thing to do when you are young.

Imagine by some good fortune a relative leaves you \$15,000, and you wisely decide to save this money. Let's suppose you lend your \$15,000 to some government agency that will pay you 4% a year to borrow your money for the next 10 years. Remember,

$$PV(1 + i)^n = FV$$

Therefore, at the end of the 15 years, you would have

$$FV = \$15{,}000(1.04)^{10} = \$22{,}203.66$$

Pretty nice, isn't it? Suppose instead you lend that \$15,000 to the government agency for 30 years, and the government agency agreed to pay you 6% a year. Then, at the end of the 30 years you would have

$$FV = \$15{,}000(1.06)^{30} = \$86{,}152.37$$

How sweet is that? The present value formula is powerful: It shows the power of savings as well as how destructive debt can become.

Getting the Time Periods Right

Up to this point we have been doing our calculations in nice round years. But life usually isn't so simple. Financial agreements involving saving and lending often are defined in months, not years. When this is the case, you have be careful to make sure all of the variables are stated in the same measurement of time.

For example, let's say you are going to borrow $20,000 to buy a new car. The loan will last 50 months, and the annual interest rate is 9%. We have the term or length of time of the loan in months, but we need to convert the annual interest rate (i^{annual}) into a monthly interest rate ($i^{monthly}$). Because there are 12 months in a year, the monthly interest rate is

$$i^{monthly} = \frac{i^{annual}}{12} = \frac{0.09}{12} = 0.0075$$

So, the FV will be

$$\$20,000(1.0075)^{50} = \$20,000(1.45296) = \$29,059.14$$

This can also be calculated by figuring out daily interest rates. Suppose the annual interest rate is now 8.5%, and you want to figure out the FV in 65 days. The daily interest rate would be

$$i^{daily} = \frac{i^{annual}}{365} = \frac{0.085}{365} = 0.00023288$$

So, the FV of $20,000 in 65 days would be

$$\$20,000(1.00023288)^{65} = \$20,0000(1.01525) = \$20,305.01$$

We have seen how interest, determined by the time value of money, is really the price of money. In the next chapter we examine how these concepts of money and interest rates are used in financial markets, especially in the pricing of bonds. We also discuss how these interest rates actually come about by using a simple framework called the loanable funds model.

SECTION REVIEW

Q1) Each person might have a different time preference. Explain why an older person might have a higher or lower time preference than a young person.

Q2) What is the future value of $500 in two years if the interest rate is 4%? How would you explain this to someone who has no training in economics?

Q3) If the annual interest rate is 2%, what is the quarterly interest rate?

a. 0.0204

b. 0.0166

c. 0.005

d. 0.001

2-5 Conclusion

No matter how you define it, money certainly does seem to make the world go around, doesn't it? As we have seen, however, even defining money is a difficult thing to do. A wide variety of assets can function as money, as long as they perform three important functions. But it's not just the type of money a society has that is important; it is how fast, or slow, that money supply changes over time that matters. If the money supply grows too quickly, the economy can suffer from inflation; but if the money supply does not grow fast enough, the economy can experience slowdowns and even economic depressions. So, getting the money supply growth rate right is very important. However, economists are not even sure how to accurately measure the money supply. That is, there are some big issues when it comes to monetary aggregates. Even though the money supply may not be able to be measured correctly, we do know one of the most important prices of money: interest rates. This chapter concluded by looking at how this important price of money can be used to calculate present values and FVs. In the next chapter we use these concepts to investigate the relationship between interest rates, financial markets such as the bond market, and how interest rates are determined.

IN THE NEWS. . .

Europe's Banks Are too Feeble to Spur Growth

Martin Wolf

Financial Times

October 28, 2014

Will the asset quality review and stress tests conducted by the European Central Bank and the European Banking Authority mark a turning point in the eurozone's crisis? Up to a point. They are an improvement on what has gone before. But they are not a complete fix for the banking sector, still less for the economy's wider problems. . . .

Between the first quarter of 2008 and the second quarter of this year, eurozone nominal demand rose by a mere 2.5 per cent. . . . Nominal gross domestic product grew by 5 per cent over that period. Now assume trend real growth was a mere 1 per cent and inflation 2 per cent (in line with ECB targets). In that case, nominal GDP should have been growing at 3 per cent a year. By the second quarter of 2014, nominal GDP was 13 per cent below this objective. Under Mr Issing, the ECB looked at monetary aggregates as well. In the six years to September 30[,] 2014, broad money (M3) increased by 9.6 per cent, a compound annual rate of 1.5 per cent. On both measures, the ECB has failed.

Mr. Wolf argues that while the European Central Bank is reviewing the quality of assets of the banking system, it is not doing its job in reviving the EuroZone economy. He argues that from 2008 to 2014, the money supply, as measured by M3, increased at a compound annual rate of 1.5%. This he labels a failure. Why does he do so? What is the connection between the money supply and nominal gross domestic product?

3

Bonds and Loanable Funds

3-1 Bonds Defined and Explained

Whenever the word *finance* is mentioned, people usually think of the stock market. This should not be a surprise; after all, stock prices are reported daily, if not hourly, in the press. But people who really understand finance know that it's the bond market that is the one to watch. While movements in the stock market may be dramatic—with big daily swings in the most volatile of markets—the bond market should receive the most attention, because it may send important signals about where the entire economy is headed. While reading this chapter you will begin to see why.

We discuss the bond market in much greater detail throughout the text, especially in Chapter 16, where we distinguish between short-term and long-term bonds, among other things. Our goal right now is to gain a firm understanding of what bonds are and, in general, why their prices change. To do this we will make use of a very simple supply-and-demand framework. We then will see how the bond market fits into the "larger" market for funds through the loanable funds approach. We conclude with a comparison of the loanable funds market and the bond market. There is much more to say about the pricing of individual bonds, which is included in Chapter 4.

So, though bonds may not get as much press as their financial instrument brethren (stocks), understanding the bond market will equip you with some pretty useful knowledge. Let's start off by being sure we know exactly what we mean by "bonds."

3-1a Bonds Defined

Think about what financial markets do: They bring together savers and borrowers. One way (but not the only way) savers and borrowers are brought together is through the bond market. **Bonds** are promises to repay that are issued by governments, government agencies, and corporations. Savers buy these bonds and, in most cases, get paid interest in return—called a coupon payment—usually every six months. At the end of the bond, or when the bond reaches maturity, the saver owning the bond is repaid the principal, or face value of the bond.

Bond: A written legal contract that is a promise to repay with interest; issued by a corporation, government or government agency.

For example, suppose Verizon needs to borrow money to put up new cell phone towers. Verizon is probably not going to have the cash to build the new towers lying around; thus they need to borrow money. So, Verizon will issue or sells bonds in the primary market to raise those funds. Let's suppose Verizon plans to pay back the funds in 10 years. As we discussed in Chapter 2, because of the time value of money, Verizon is going to have pay interest when it borrows these funds from savers. The rate of interest they pay to the holder of the bond is stated on the bond as the **coupon rate**.

Coupon rate: The stated rate of interest that will be paid to the holder of the bond.

The coupon rate on a bond generally doesn't change over the life of the bond, and the face value of the bond also usually does not change over time. What can and does change over time, however, is the market value of a bond.

To keep all of this terminology straight, a bit of background might be useful. In the old days corporations or governments who issued bonds would literally print a physical promise to repay—a bond. Today most bonds are electronic. But these old physical paper bonds, like the one issued by the City and County of San Francisco for the Pacific Rail Road, would have a face value (here, $1,000); a maturity date (30 years starting from May 1, 1865); an annual interest rate (7%); and a statement of who is paying—in this case the City and County of San Francisco.

Paul John Fearn / Alamy

As a side note: This bond sale was used to raise money to fund the construction of the Western Pacific Railroad between the San Francisco Bay at Alameda and the Central Pacific Railroad in Sacramento. This was part of the first Transcontinental Railroad that you may have read about in your high school history book.

Notice at the bottom of the bond are coupons, which the owner of the bond would clip off and send in each May and November and would receive in return their interest payment. The coupon rate was 7% a year, so the bondholder would receive \$35 (twice a year) each time they sent in the coupon. Also, the bond states the bondholder would be paid in "United States Gold coin dollar" since there was not one single currency in the United States at that time.

Thus, the coupon rate is the interest rate the bond issuer pays to the bondholder. Keep in mind the "**face value**" is the value of the bond stated on the "face" of the bond.

Face value (of a bond): The original amount of money borrowed by a bond issuer. This is also sometimes called the bond principal.

Today, though, most bonds are not physical printed pieces of paper with coupons that must be clipped off and mailed to the issuer. Instead, all of this is recorded electronically. For example, if we wanted to show the bond above today, we would view it on a Bloomberg screen that would look like the screen below.

On the Bloomberg screen under the "Issuer Information" section appears the name of the issuer, Pacific Railroad, which is an industrial firm, and the bond is issued in the United States. Under "Security Information" we see that it is issued in US currency; the bond matured on May 1, 1925; and pays its full face value. We also see that it has a coupon rate of 7%, which is fixed for the term. The second column shows that \$1 million worth of these bonds were issued, each at a price of \$1,000.

Thus, the Bloomberg screen offers much more information than the physical bond does. This is obviously fictitious because the bond matured well before Bloomberg ever came along. But it does demonstrate just how much information about the bond market is at the fingertips of financial market participants today.

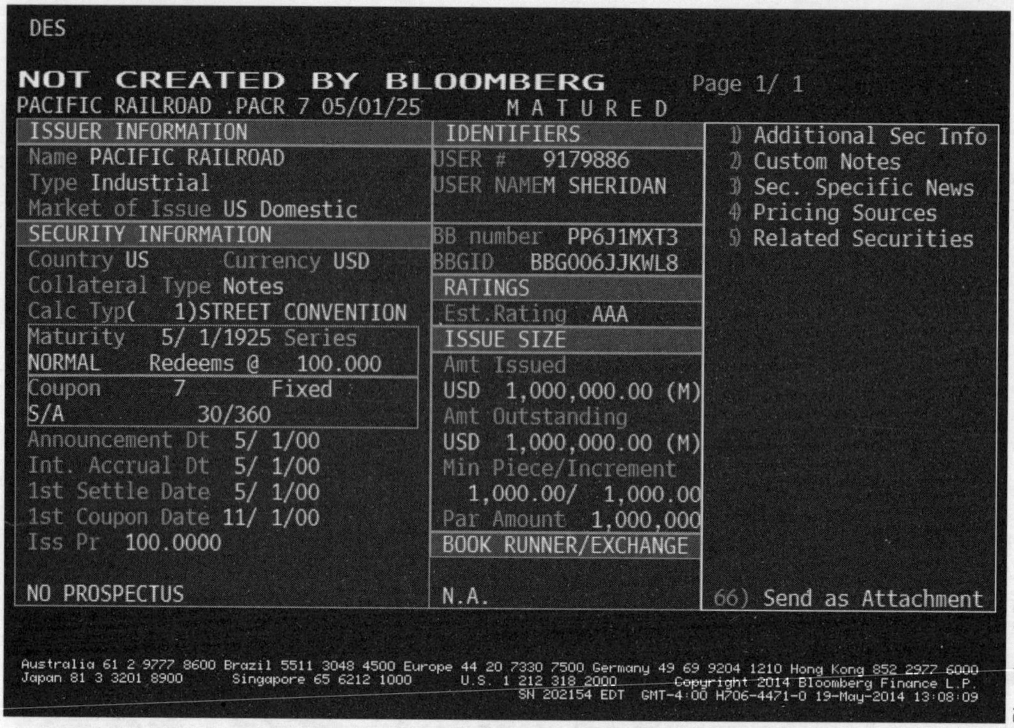

Bloomberg L.P

For a bit more realism, think about the Verizon example mentioned earlier. Suppose at the end of March 2011 Verizon issued 10-year bonds, with a 4.6% coupon rate and a $1,000 face value. If the first coupon payment would be made on October 1, 2011, and they issued $1.5 million worth of these bonds, that information would look like the screen below.

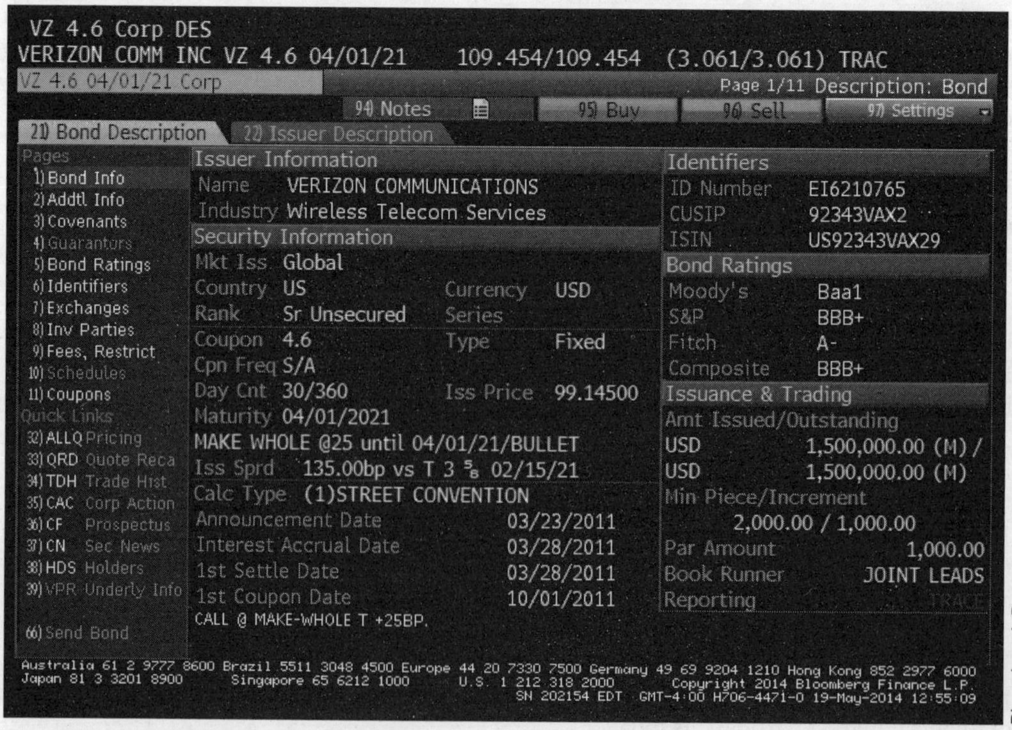

Bloomberg L.P

On this Bloomberg screen we can see under "Issuer Information" that Verizon Communications is the issuer of the bond and they are in the Wireless Telecom Services industry. Under "Security Information," notice that the bonds were issued globally, with a base in the United States, and the bonds were issued in US dollars. The coupon rate is 4.6% and is fixed—it will not change over the life of the bond. We also see that the bond matures on April 1, 2021. In the third column we see the bond rating[1] various agencies give this bond; $1.5 million worth of these bonds were issued, each with a face value of $1,000.

Now, if we go back to the middle column and look about two-thirds of the way down, we see that the issue price of the bond was 99.145. This means for every $100 of face value of the bond, the price was $99.145. This raises interesting questions: What determines the price of a bond? How are changes in the price of a bond related to the rate of return or yield the bond pays to its bondholders? To answer these questions we need to understand bond prices and yields. That is where we turn our attention to next.

SECTION REVIEW

Q1) Today, shoppers "clip coupons" before they go shopping. Explain how these modern coupons are similar *and* dissimilar to the "coupons" referred to in the bond market.

Q2) The fact that the face value of a bond does not change over the life of the bond is generally considered a benefit to the borrower. Can you explain why?

Q3) The rate of interest a bond pays is called the bond's:

a. face value.

b. coupon rate.

c. bond rating.

d. rating rate.

1 An evaluation of default risk, which we will discuss more fully later.

3-2 Bond Prices and Yields

In the previous section we learned that bonds are promises to repay, with interest, that are issued by corporations, government agencies, and governments. When bonds are initially sold in the primary market, the issuer receives the face value and promises to repay that amount at maturity. Along the way the issuer pays interest, at the coupon rate, to the holder of the bond.

But the buyer of the bond might not want to hold onto the bond until maturity. Perhaps the bondholder wants to sell it before it matures because he needs some cash. The market for "used" or previously issued bonds is called the **secondary bond market.**

Secondary bond market: The market for bonds or other debt instruments that were previously issued.

So, what price should a bondholder ask if they wish to sell the bond before it reaches maturity? Similarly, if someone is interested in buying a bond in the secondary market, how much should they be willing to pay? What type of rate of return will they earn from holding that bond? That is, how are bond prices determined and what is the relationship between bond prices and bond yields or rates of return?

It turns out there is an inverse relationship between bond prices and yields (or interest rates). Don't memorize this relationship; instead, try to understand *why* it exists. To get a grip on this concept, think about the idea of a "rate of return." A rate of return is simply the ratio of what you put in versus what you get back:

$$\textit{Rate of return} = \frac{\textit{Amount get back}}{\textit{Amount put in}}$$

Think of a simple case of placing a bet on a horse race. You make a \$10 bet and the horse finishes third, so let's suppose you get \$2 back. Thus, your rate of return would be 20% since

$$\frac{\textit{Amount get back}}{\textit{Amount put in}} = \frac{\$2}{\$10} = 0.20\text{, or }20\%$$

On a second bet you put in \$20, and again get paid \$2 back. Now your rate of return is only 10% since

$$\frac{\textit{Amount get back}}{\textit{Amount put in}} = \frac{\$2}{\$20} = 0.10\text{, or }10\%$$

Here's what happened: As the amount of money you put in went up, the rate of return went down.

It's the same idea with bonds. As the price of the bond (the amount you have to "put in" to buy the bond) increases, while the interest payments and face value (the amount you "get back") remain the same, the rate of return (or yield) declines. Thus there is an inverse relationship between bond prices and bond yields.

So why, then, do bond prices change?

3-2a Price of Bonds

The **market price of a bond** is simply the present value of the cash flow the owner of the bond can expect to receive over the life of the bond. These cash flows are the interest payments based on the coupon rate and the principal or face value of the bond at maturity.

Market price of a bond: The present value of the cash flow the owner of the bond can expect to receive over the life of the bond.

Simply put:

$$P_{BOND} = PV_{BOND} = \frac{C_1}{(1+k)^1} + \frac{C_2}{(1+k)^2} + \frac{C_3}{(1+k)^3} + \dots + \frac{C_n + Face}{(1+k)^n}$$

where C_i is the coupon payment in period i; *Face* is the face value or principal value of the bond; k is the interest rate per period; and n is the number of periods.

To see how this works, let's go back to our hypothetical Verizon example. Suppose that to raise the money needed to build cell towers, Verizon issues $1.5 million worth of 10-year bonds with a coupon rate of 4.6%. Let's also suppose it sells 150,000 of these bonds, each with a face value of $1,000. Assume that current market interest rates for a 10-year bond issued by a firm like Verizon is currently 4.6%—the same as the coupon rate. Therefore, the price of each of these bonds would be

$$P_{BOND} = PV_{BOND} = \frac{\$46}{(1+0.046)^1} + \frac{\$46}{(1+0.046)^2} + \frac{\$46}{(1+0.046)^3} + \frac{\$46}{(1+0.046)^4} + \dots + \frac{\$46 + \$1{,}000}{(1+0.046)^{10}} = \$1{,}000$$

So, when the market interest rate equals the bond's coupon rate, the market price of the bond equals the face value of the bond. If this is the case, the bond is said to be selling at **par**.

Par: Market price of a bond equals the face value of the bond.

Let's look at another example. Suppose Hewlett-Packard (H-P) is interested in building a new manufacturing plant, and they need to borrow funds to finance the project. Let's also suppose they issue 5-year bonds with a face value of $1,000 and a 4% coupon rate. Let's further assume the market interest rate is 4%. Then,

$$P_{BOND} = PV_{BOND} = \frac{\$40}{(1+0.04)^1} + \frac{\$40}{(1+0.04)^2} + \frac{\$40}{(1+0.04)^3} + \frac{\$40}{(1+0.04)^4} + \frac{\$40 + \$1{,}000}{(1+0.04)^5} = \$1{,}000$$

Again, because the market interest rate equals the coupon rate on the bond, the bond sells at par.

Most often, however, the coupon rate of a bond does not exactly equal the market interest rate because market interest rates change constantly. Let's look at what happens when market interest rates are *not* equal to the coupon rate of a bond.

Market Interest Rates Above the Coupon Rate

Suppose market interest rates for bonds similar to our H-P bond have increased to 5%. Remember, this is a 5-year bond with a 4% coupon rate and a $1,000 face value. Now, the pricing formula becomes

$$P_{BOND} = PV_{BOND} = \frac{\$40}{(1+0.05)^1} + \frac{\$40}{(1+0.05)^2} + \frac{\$40}{(1+0.05)^3} + \frac{\$40}{(1+0.05)^4} + \frac{\$40 + \$1{,}000}{(1+0.05)^5} = \$956.71$$

Look at what happened: Market interest rates went up and the price of the bond went down. This shows us the inverse between interest rates and bond prices we just discussed. Since the market price of the bond is less than the face value of the bond, the bond is said to selling at a **discount**.

Discount: When the market price is below the face value.

To understand the logic of why this happens, think about how a market for a bond would work. You are interested in selling a bond that has a coupon rate of 4%. That's a nice return when market interest rates are 2% or 2.25%. If market interest rates for that type of bond are at 5%, however, and you try to sell it for, say, $1,000, you are going to find it tough. If I am thinking about buying your bond, I am going to say, "Forget you . . . I can go out into the market and buy a bond that is going to pay me 5%, whereas your lousy bond pays only 4%! You want me to buy your bond? Lower the price."

So, if you want to sell your bond in this market—where interest rates have gone up—what are you going to do? You have to lower the price you are asking for. Therefore, higher market interest rates lead to lower bond prices. Once again, we see the inverse relationship between yields or interest rates and bond prices.

The same logic holds in reverse.

Market Interest Rates Below the Coupon Rate

Let's return to the H-P bond example. Remember, H-P is issuing a 5-year bond with a 4% coupon rate and a $1,000 face value. But let's suppose the market interest rate has fallen to 2%. Now the pricing formula becomes

$$P_{BOND} = PV_{BOND} = \frac{\$40}{(1+0.02)^1} + \frac{\$40}{(1+0.02)^2} + \frac{\$40}{(1+0.02)^3} + \frac{\$40}{(1+0.02)^4} + \frac{\$40+\$1{,}000}{(1+0.02)^5} = \$1{,}094.27$$

What happened? Market interest rates declined (they were at 4% when the bond was issued, but now they are only 2%), and the price of the bond went up. This once again shows us there is an inverse relationship between interest rates and bond prices. Because the market price for the bond is higher than the face value of the bond, the bond is said to be selling at a **premium**.

Premium: When the market price of a bond is above the face value.

Again, to understand why this happens, think about how the market for a bond would work. You are interested in selling a bond you own that has a coupon rate of 4%. That seemed like a nice rate of return when the bond was issued, but now, when interest rates on comparable funds are at only 2%, your bond that is paying 4% seems wonderful! If I am thinking about buying your bond, I am going to say, "I see you paid $1,000 for the bond, so how about I give you $1,000? That is what you paid for it." You think about this for a second and realize that my next best option is go into the market and buy a bond that pays only 2%, whereas your nice little bond pays 4%. You know I really want your bond. So will you sell it to me for only $1,000? No way! You are going to increase the price on your bond because you know I find it so desirable because of its relatively high interest rate. In this case, market interest rates went down and the price of bonds went up, again illustrating the inverse relationship between bond yields or interest rates and bond prices.

Okay, so bond prices and their yields move in opposite directions. This then raises the question, Why do bond prices change? To answer this, we make use of a simple supply-and-demand framework.

SECTION REVIEW

Q1) If you have a bond with a face value of $1,000 and a coupon rate of 2.25%, but the market interest rate for such bonds is 2.5%, will your bond sell at par, at a premium, or at a discount? Explain why.

Q2) If you have a bond with a face value of $1,000 and a coupon rate of 2.5%, but the market interest rate for such bonds is 2.25%, will your bond sell at par, at a premium, or at a discount? Explain why.

Q3) If a three-year bond with a $1,000 face value has a coupon rate of 3.5%, and the current market interest rate is 2%, what is the market price of the bond?

a. $956.75

b. $1,035.00

c. $1,043.25

d. $1,148.34

3-3 Supply and Demand for Bonds

We now know that bonds are promises to repay, with interest, that are issued by corporations, government agencies, and governments, and there is an inverse relationship between bond prices and bond yields, or interest rates. Now we need an explanation of *why* bond prices, and thus their yields, change over time. To answer this question, we can use a simple supply-and-demand framework that you most likely learned in your principles of economics courses.

In economics, supply is a price–quantity relationship from a seller's point of view. A few things to note about that definition: it is a "price–quantity" relationship; this means that the term *supply* as used in economics and finance is different from how the term *supply* is used in the military. In the military, *supply* means "stuff" used by the army. So the supply sergeant is responsible for equipping troops with helmets, boots, guns, and so on.

In economics and finance, however, *supply* means much more than just "stuff" or quantity. *Supply* is a price–quantity relationship, that is, as the price of something changes, the amount or quantity offered for sale changes as well. This is called a **change in quantity supplied**.

When illustrated graphically, a change in quantity supplied is movement along the supply curve. In general, as the price increases sellers have both the ability and incentive to offer more for sale (Figure 3-1). Thus, moving up along the supply curve as the price increases, the quantity supplied also increases. The same logic holds in reverse: If the price of the good decreases, sellers will offer less for sale, so we slide down the supply curve.

Do not confuse a change in quantity supplied with a change in supply. A **change in supply** occurs when something that impacts sellers (other than the price of the good) changes. Illustrated graphically (Figure 3-1), a change in supply is shown by a shift of the supply curve. Increases in supply shift the supply curve out, whereas decreases in supply shift the supply curve back or upward.

Change in supply versus change in quantity supplied: *Change in supply* is a change in the price and quantity relationship from a seller's perspective, whereas a *change in quantity supplied* comes about from a change in the price of the good or service.

Figure 3-1 Change in Quantity Supplied Versus Change in Supply

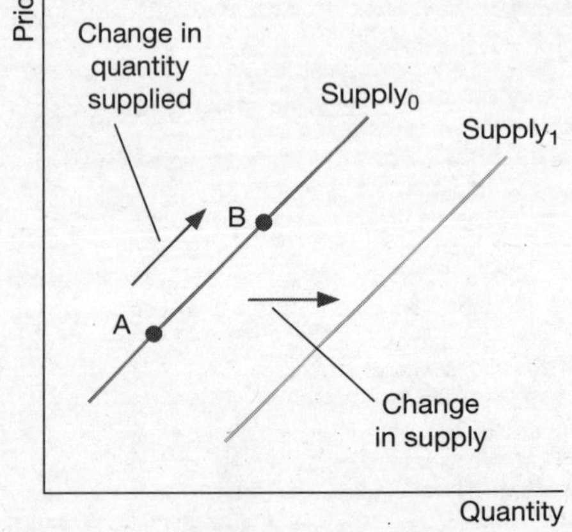

Figure 3-2 **Change in Quantity Demanded Versus Change in Demand**

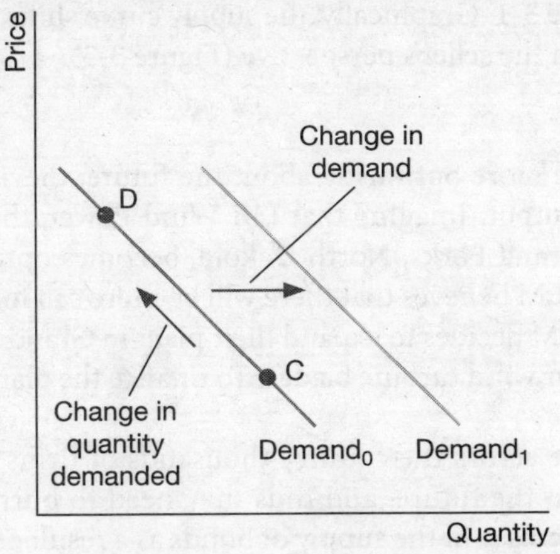

On the other hand, demand is a price–quantity relationship from a buyer's perspective. So, if the price of something increases, buyers generally buy less of the good, and thus the demand curve slopes downward. More specifically, changes in the price of a good bring about a **change in quantity demanded**; illustrated graphically this appears as movement along the demand curve (Figure 3-2).

Change in demand, on the other hand, brings about a whole new price–quantity relationship from a buyer's perspective. Thus, changes in demand are graphically shown by a shifting of the demand curve. Increases in demand shift the demand curve outward, whereas decreases in demand shift the demand curve back, or toward the origin.

Change in demand versus change in quantity demanded: *Change in demand* is a change in the price and quantity relationship from a buyer's perspective, whereas a *change in quantity demanded* comes about from a change in the price of the good or service.

With these economics concepts in mind, let's think about how they apply to the bond market.

3-3a The Supply of Bonds

On the supply side of the bond market we have the sellers of bonds. In the **primary market** bonds are being sold for the first time by the issuers: corporations, governments, and government agencies. As the price of bonds increases, or their yields decrease, these issuers will want to issue more bonds because the yield, or the interest rate the issuers have to pay to bondholders, has decreased. So, as the price of bonds increases, the borrowing costs of bond issuers decline. Thus, in the primary market, as the bond prices increase, the quantity of bonds in demand increases; that is, the supply curve of bonds slopes upward.

Primary market: The initial sale of a bond.

The same outcome occurs in the secondary bond market, or the market for used bonds. As bond prices increase, bondholders now have an incentive to sell their now more valuable bonds and pocket the capital gain. Thus, as the price of bonds increases in the secondary market, we have an increase in the quantity supplied of bonds.

Remember, however, that a supply curve holds for only one point in time. Over time things that bring about a whole new price–quantity relationship from the seller's point of view can and do change. That is, many things bring about a change in supply.

3-3b Change in the Supply of Bonds

A change in things from the seller's perspective other than the price of a bond brings about a change in supply, see Table 3-1. Graphically, the supply curve shifts, representing a new price-quantity relationship from the seller's perspective (Figure 3-3).

Business Expectations

If businesspeople become more optimistic about the future, they will want to borrow more money to expand their output. Imagine that LM Wind Power, the Danish manufacturer of wind turbine blades in Grand Forks, North Dakota, becomes optimistic about the future of the wind turbine market. LM believes that there will be more call for their blades as the overall economy expands. Thus LM decides to expand their plant in Grand Forks to meet the expected increased demand for their wind turbine blades. To finance the plant expansion, LM will issue more bonds.

Now imagine there are across the country thousands of firms just like LM: These firms expect sales to increase in the future, and thus they need to borrow more now to increase output. The result is an increase in the supply of bonds as a result of this increased confidence in business.

Table 3-1 Changes in the Supply of Bonds

Change	Change in Supply of Bonds
Improved business expectations	▲
Worsened business expectations	▼
Higher inflation expected	▲
Lower inflation expected	▼
Larger government budget deficits	▲
Smaller government budget deficits	▼
More investment tax credits	▲
Fewer investment tax credits	▼

Figure 3-3 Change in the Supply of Bonds

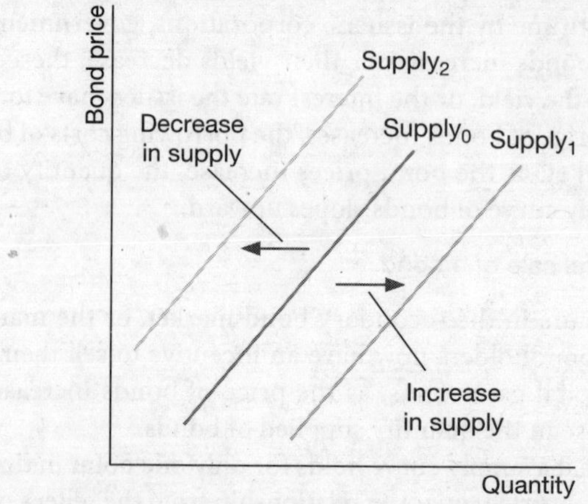

Expected Inflation

If you think there will be inflation in the future, you want to borrow more now. The logic is pretty straightforward: Inflation reduces the **real cost of debt**. To understand why, imagine you have a $100 debt and you earn $20 an hour. That means you have to work five hours to pay off that debt. Now imagine that there is inflation, so your wages go up—but the amount of your debt does not go up with inflation. So now your wage rate is $25 an hour; that means you have to work only four hours to pay off the $100 debt. Thus, the real cost of the debt has declined.

Real cost of debt: The burden of debt measured in constant terms.

If firms expect that there will be inflation in the future, they want to borrow more now because the real burden of that debt will decline with inflation. Firms borrow more by issuing more bonds, or the supply of bonds will increase, that is, more bonds will be offered at every price.

Government Deficits

Remember, firms are not the only ones who issue bonds; so too do governments and government agencies. When governments spend more than they take in or run bigger budget deficits, they have to go out and borrow the difference. Thus, as government budget deficits increase, governments issue more bonds at every price, that is, the supply of bonds increases.

Investment Tax Credits

Let's suppose the City of Irving, Texas, gives Kimberly-Clark a $5 million tax credit to expand its headquarters in the city. To get this tax credit, imagine the consumer goods producer has to spend $60 million to expand its headquarters. So, to get the $5 million tax credit, Kimberly-Clark has to spend $60 million. Where will Kimberly-Clark get that $60 million? It will most likely issue bonds. Thus an increase in the amount of investment tax credits leads to an increase in the supply of bonds in the bond market (Figure 3-4).

To determine the impact of changes in the supply of bonds, we need to investigate the other side of the bond market: the demand for bonds.

Figure 3-4 Kimberly-Clark Sells More Bonds

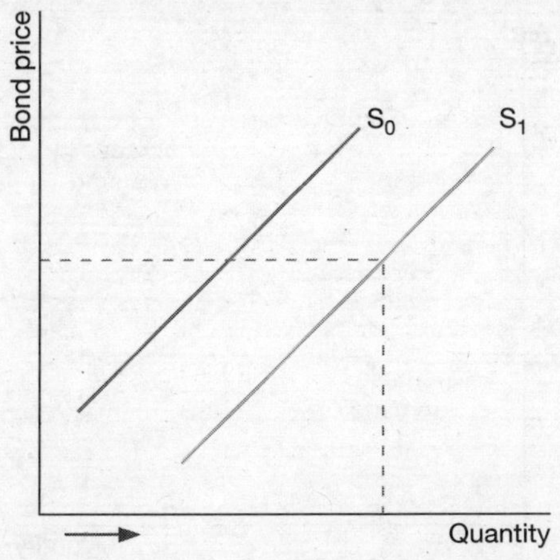

3-3c The Demand for Bonds

Remember, the demand for bonds is the price–quantity relationship from the bond buyer's perspective. The buyers of bonds are savers or surplus units—people and entities with an optimal level of expenditure in the current time period that is less than their current income. So what do these surplus units do with their excess funds? Some of those funds are used to purchase bonds.

As the price of bonds declines, bond buyers have both the incentive and ability to buy more bonds. The bond yields, or rates of return paid to savers, increases, making the bonds more desirable. Similarly, as the price of bonds decreases, savers can afford to buy more bonds with their savings. Thus as the price of bonds falls the quantity demand of bonds increases (Figure 3-5).

Figure 3-5 Demand for Bonds

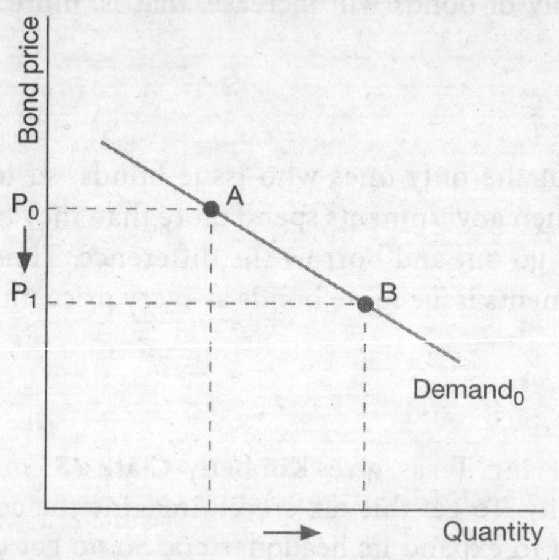

3-3d Change in the Demand for Bonds

Just as with supply, the demand curve holds for only one point in time. From a bond buyer's point of view, things that bring about a whole new price–quantity relationship can and do change over time (Figure 3-6). Let's take a look at each of these factors in turn.

Figure 3-6 Increase and Decrease in Demand for Bonds

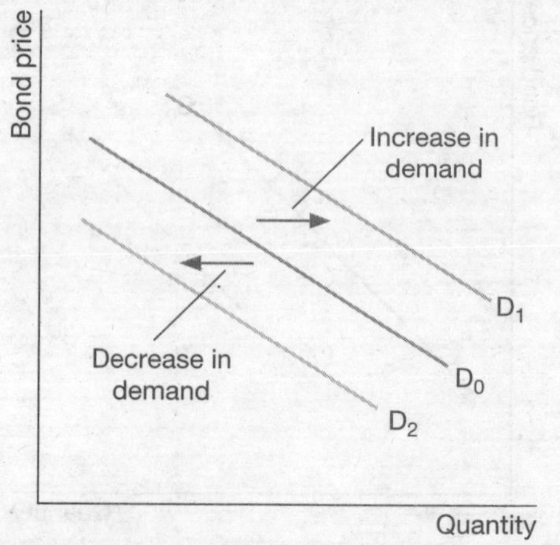

Wealth

When the wealth of a society increases, the demand for bonds also increases. To understand why this occurs, think about it in terms of households and their savings. When a household's wealth increases, it can use this wealth to increase consumption, pay taxes, and/or save. A portion of these new savings might make its way into the bond market because households now purchase more bonds at every price. Thus, as wealth increases, the demand for bonds increases.

Expected Relative Returns to Bonds

As the expected relative returns to bonds increases, the demand for bonds increases because savers desire relatively higher returns. Imagine that savers fear that that stock prices are about to fall. If—and this is a very big if—savers consider stocks and bonds as substitutes and expect stock prices to decline, they will likely sell off their stocks and buy bonds. Or, more generally, if the expected returns to bonds are higher relative to those of other investment options, the demand for bonds will increase.

Relative Riskiness of Bonds

One of the risks of buying a bond is **default risk**. Default risk—the risk that a borrower will not pay interest or principal as promised—can increase at any time. As we discuss in more detail in Chapter 4, sometimes default risk increases because of something the borrower has done, and sometimes it increases because of things outside the control of the borrower. Regardless of the reason why it occurs, investors in bonds hate it when default risk increases. If default risk increases, savers will stay away from the now more risky bonds and put their money instead into "safer" assets. So, as the default risk of bonds increases, the demand for bonds decreases.

Default risk: The risk that a borrower will not pay interest or principal as promised.

Liquidity of Bonds

Liquidity, or the ease and cost of converting an asset into cash, is very important to bond buyers. In general, liquidity is a good thing: If you have an asset, you would like to be able to turn that asset into cash relatively easily and at a low cost, holding everything else constant. So, bonds with a higher level of liquidity—those that are easier and cheaper to turn into cash—are preferred to bonds that are less liquid. Thus, as the level of liquidity of bonds increases, the demand for those bonds increases. The level of liquidity may increase because the number of buyers of those bonds increases and/or the level of development of the secondary market for bonds increases.

Liquidity: The ease and expense at which one asset can be converted into another asset.

Information Costs

When a saver wishes to buy a bond, they must go out and collect a fair amount of information. They need to understand who is selling these bonds, who the issuer of the bond is, how the issuer has lived up their promise to repay in the past, what current yields on bonds are, what the expectation of yields is in the future, among others. Collecting all of this information has costs. These costs may be explicit—that is, costs that involve the payment of money—or these costs may be implicit, which include opportunity costs such as time spent to find the information. The higher these "information costs" involved in purchasing a bond, the less likely the investor is to purchase these bonds. So, as the information costs of bonds increases, there is a decrease in the demand for bonds (Table 3-2).

So, many factors that can and do change over time can bring about a new price–quantity relationship from a bond buyer's point of view. That is, a number of factors bring about a change in demand for bonds. To understand the impact of these changes in the demand for bonds, we need to bring the demand side of the bond market together with the supply side to discern how the bond market determines bond prices and yields.

Table 3-2 Changes in the Demand for Bonds

Change	Change in Supply of Bonds
Wealth levels in society increase	▲
Wealth levels in society decrease	▼
Relative return to bond increases	▲
Relative return to bond decreases	▼
Relative riskiness of bond increases	▼
Relative riskiness of bond decreases	▲
Liquidity of bonds increases	▲
Liquidity of bonds decreases	▼
Information costs incurred by investors increase	▼
Information costs incurred by investors decrease	▲

3-3e Equilibrium in the Bond Market

If the market price of bonds is higher than the equilibrium price, the quantity of bonds supplied will be greater than the quantity of bonds demanded; that is, a surplus of bonds develops. To understand why this occurs, remember that there is an inverse relationship between bond prices and yields. So, at a very high price or a low yield or interest rate, the bond suppliers are willing to sell a great number of these bonds because the borrowing cost is low. At this high price, or low yield, however, savers are not interested in buying many of these bonds. The result is a surplus in the bond market (Figure 3-7).

The bond market works like any other market when there is a surplus: Sellers cut the asking price and offer less for sale, while this lower price encourages buyers to increase the quantity demanded. Thus we slide down the supply curve and down the demand curve until the market achieves equilibrium.

The same logic happens in reverse if the market price for bonds is less than the equilibrium price: The quantity of bonds demanded will be greater than the quantity of bonds supplied. To understand why, remember the inverse relationship between bond price and yields. Buyers of

Figure 3-7 Bond Market Surplus

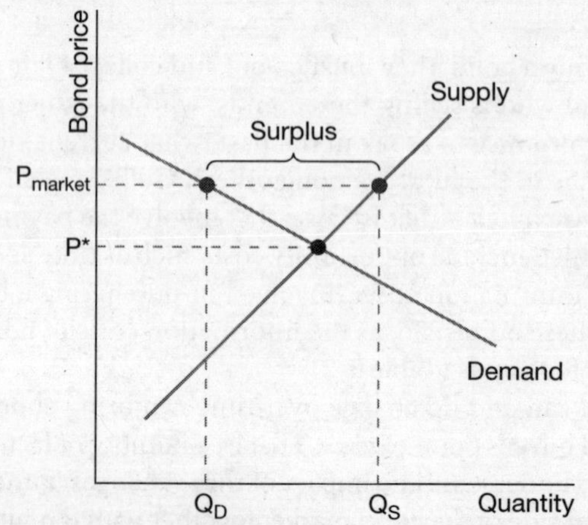

Figure 3-8 Bond Market Shortage

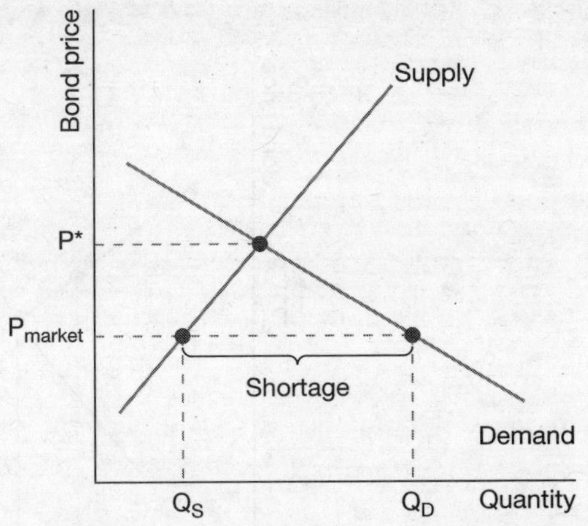

bonds love a very low price, or a very high yield. They want to buy many bonds with this nice high return, so the quantity of bonds demanded is high. On the other hand, suppliers of bonds hate this low price, or high yield or high interest rate, they have to pay to borrow. Thus, the quantity of bonds supplied is very low.

When the quantity demanded is higher than the quantity supplied, a shortage develops (Figure 3-8). This shortage is erased, however, as sellers of bonds respond by offering more bonds for sale at a high price (or lower yield). This higher price and resulting lower yield results in a reduction in the quantity of bonds demanded. Thus, we slide up the supply curve and up the demand curve until the equilibrium is reached.

3-3f New Equilibrium in the Bond Market

Remember that equilibrium in the bond market holds only if nothing else changes. As we have seen, however, many things can and do bring about changes in the supply of and/or demand for bonds. See Figure 3-9 on the next page.

But the bond market is only one way in which borrowers borrow money and savers save money. Next we take a broader view of this interaction between borrowers and savers and the determination of interest rates. We again make use of a simple supply-and-demand framework, but this time we examine the supply of and demand for loanable funds.

SECTION REVIEW

Q1) You read in the financial press that market participants expect stock prices to increase dramatically in the near future, while at the same time business confidence is increasing. Explain in words and show graphically what will happen in the bond market if the first change is larger in magnitude than the second.

Q2) Stories appear in the financial press reporting two economic developments: Wealth levels in the United States are increasing, while at the same time the relative riskiness of bonds issued by American corporations is decreasing. Explain in words and show graphically what will happen in the US bond market because of these two events.

Figure 3-9 **Change in Supply and Demand of Bonds. The Graphs Show an Increase (a) and Decrease (b) in the Supply of Bonds and an Increase (c) and Decrease (d) in the Demand for Bonds**

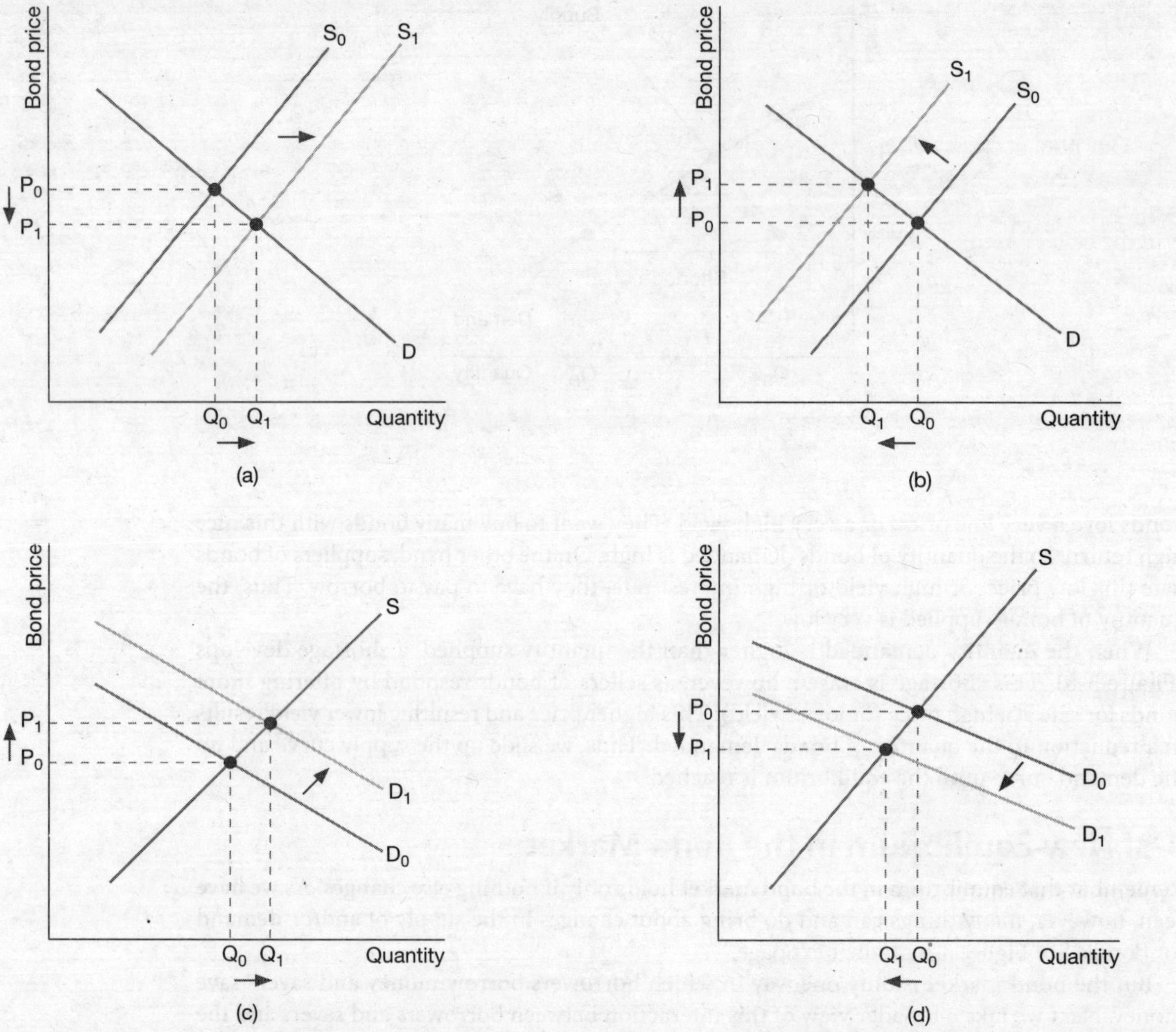

Q3) If the market price for bonds is higher than the equilibrium price, what is the result, and what will change to bring about equilibrium as price falls, ceteris paribus?

a. Shortage; quantity demanded will increase and quantity supplied will decrease.

b. Surplus; quantity demanded will increase and quantity supplied will decrease.

c. Surplus; quantity demanded will decrease and quantity supplied will increase.

d. Shortage; quantity demanded will decrease and quantity supplied will increase.

Supply and Demand for Loanable Funds

3-4

Imagine that there exists a basket full of money. Savers contribute money to the basket and borrowers take money out of the basket. This basket is called the "pool of loanable funds" (Figure 3-10). Negotiations between the savers and the borrowers determine the price of the loanable funds. This price of loanable funds is the interest rate.

Our pool of loanable funds story mentioned "the" interest rate, as if there is only one interest rate in the economy. This is a simplification because there are thousands of different interest rates in the market at one point in time. But we can make this simplification because we are interested in the general trend of interest rates; this is what our loanable funds story is going tell us.

To understand how the loanable funds market works, let's think about each side of the market in turn.

3-4a The Supply of Loanable Funds

Savers provide funds for our pool of loanable funds. These savers, or surplus units, are entities who have an optimal level of expenditure in the current period that is less than their current income. These savers or surplus units include the following.

Households

When a household's after-tax income is greater than their utility-maximizing consumption level, they bring this "surplus" income to the financial markets as savings. In terms of loanable funds, they add this surplus income, or loanable funds, to the pool of loanable funds.

Firms

When a firm has a level of income in the current period that is greater than its profit-maximizing level of expenditures, it too brings this "surplus" income to the financial markets as savings. In this case, firms also may contribute to the pool of loanable funds.

Governments

When a government runs a budget surplus it is collecting more in tax revenue than it is spending. The government entity then brings this "surplus" tax revenue to the financial markets in order to lend it to others. Governments—be they national, state, or local governments or government agencies—may also contribute to the pool of loanable funds.

Rest of the World

As our financial markets become more globally intertwined, we see people, firms, and governments from around the world bringing funds to our financial markets. Thus, the rest of the world can contribute to the pool of loanable funds.

Figure 3-10 Loanable Funds

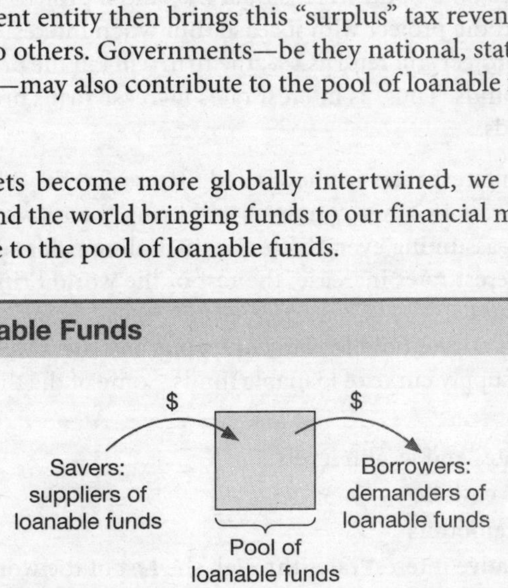

Figure 3-11 **Supply of Loanable Funds**

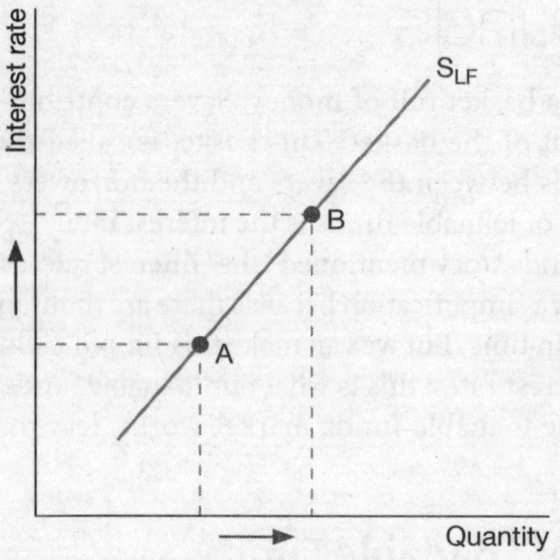

These four groups of savers, or surplus units, are represented graphically by the upward sloping curve of the supply of loanable funds. As with almost all supply curves, quantity is on the horizontal axis and price is on the vertical axis (Figure 3-11). Remember, the interest rate is the price of loanable funds.

To understand why the supply curve of loanable funds slopes upward, consider two points, A and B. As interest rates increase, we observe an increase in the quantity of loanable funds supplied; our surplus units bring more funds to the pool of loanable funds. To get an idea of why this happens, think about the different groups that make up surplus units.

Households As interest rates increase, the opportunity cost of consumption—instead of savings—increases for households. Thus as interest rates increase, households bring more of their after-tax income to the pool of loanable funds.

Firms As interest rates increase, the opportunity cost of funding projects with current cash increases. If interest rates on a bond were, say, at 2%, and a project with the same risks paid 4%, the firm would fund the project with its cash. But when interest rates or yields on bonds increase to 5% and the project still returns 4%, the firm will kill the project and bring that cash to the pool of loanable funds. Thus, as interest rates increase firms bring more of their cash to the pool of loanable funds.

Rest of the World If interest rates in the United States increase relative to interest rates in the rest of the world, savers in other countries will bring their savings to the United States, seeking higher returns—assuming everything else, including risk and inflation rates, remains unchanged. Thus, as interest rates increase, the rest of the world brings more of their savings to our pool of loanable funds.

But remember, supply curves hold for only one point in time. Over time things can and do change, giving us a new supply curve of loanable funds. Some of the things that can and change over time include:

- Household savings rates and wealth levels
- Firms' profitability or cash flows
- Government surplus amounts
- Savings levels and relative interest rates through the rest of the world
- Expected rate of inflation (future inflation worries decrease the supply of loanable funds)
- Monetary policy (expansionary policy increases the supply of loanable funds)

To determine the impact of these changes in the supply of loanable funds, we need to investigate the other side of the market, or the demand for loanable funds.

3-4b The Demand for Loanable Funds

Borrowers in financial markets take funds from our pool of loanable funds. These borrowers, or deficit units, are entities who have an optimal level of expenditure in the current period that is greater than their current income. These borrowers or deficit units include the following.

Households

When a household's utility-maximizing level of consumption is greater than their current after-tax income, they might borrow the difference from the financial market. Or, they might withdraw savings they have from previous time periods. In terms of loanable funds, they are withdrawing funds from the pool of loanable funds.

Firms

When a firm has a profit-maximizing level of expenditures that is greater than their income in the current period, they too must borrow to make up the difference. In this case, firms borrow from the pool of loanable funds.

Governments

When a government runs a budget deficit they are spending more than what they are collecting in tax revenues. To make up this difference, the government has to borrow funds in the financial markets or borrow money from the pool of loanable funds. Governments—be they national, state, or local governments or government agencies—may withdraw or borrow funds from the pool of loanable funds.

Rest of the World

As our financial markets become more globally intertwined, we see people, firms, and governments from around the world borrowing funds from our financial markets. Thus, the rest of the world can withdraw or borrow funds from the pool of loanable funds.

These four groups of borrowers, or deficit units, are represented graphically by the downward-sloping demand curve of loanable funds. As with almost all demand curves, quantity is on the horizontal axis and price is on the vertical axis. Again, remember that the interest rate is the price of loanable funds (Figure 3-12).

Figure 3-12 **Demand for Loanable Funds**

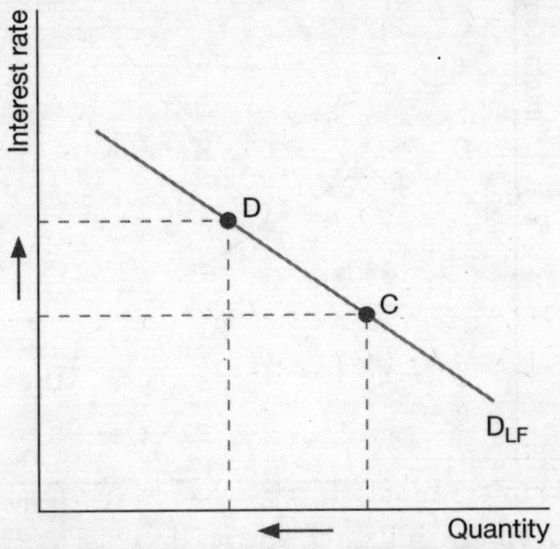

To understand why the demand curve of loanable funds slopes downward, consider two points: C and D. As interest rates increase we see a decrease in the quantity of loanable funds demanded. As interest rates increase, some deficit units that were willing to borrow at the lower interest rate now find borrowing too expensive at the higher interest rate. To get an idea of why this happens, think about the different groups that make up our deficit units.

Households Higher interest rates on loans mean higher monthly payments for households. Thus, some of those households that could afford to borrow at a lower interest rate, and thus have a lower monthly payment, now find the monthly payments too high. Thus, as interest rates increase, households borrow less.

Firms As interest rates increase, the cost of capital for firms increases. When considering which projects to fund, firms compare the expected rate of return on a project with the prevailing interest rate. When interest rates are low, firms may be willing to fund a number of projects. But as interest rates increase, more projects are no longer "worth it" and are cut or eliminated. Because firms are funding fewer projects they borrow less or take fewer funds out of the pool of loanable funds.

Rest of the World If interest rates in the United States increase relative to interest rates in the rest of the world, borrowers from the rest of the world who are borrowing in the United States may choose instead to borrow at home. Thus as US interest rates increase, we see a decrease in the quantity of loanable funds demanded.

Remember, demand curves hold for only one point in time. Over time things can and do change that give us a new demand curve of loanable funds. Some of the things that can change over time include:

- Household expected income levels
- Firms' confidence in the future
- Amounts of government deficits
- Rest of the world's borrowing needs and relative interest rates
- Expected rate of inflation (future inflation worries increase the demand for loanable funds)

To have the loanable funds model be the most useful, we need to bring together both sides of the pool of loanable funds. Again, our supply-and-demand curves become very useful (see Figure 3-13).

Figure 3-13 The Loanable Funds Market in Equilibrium

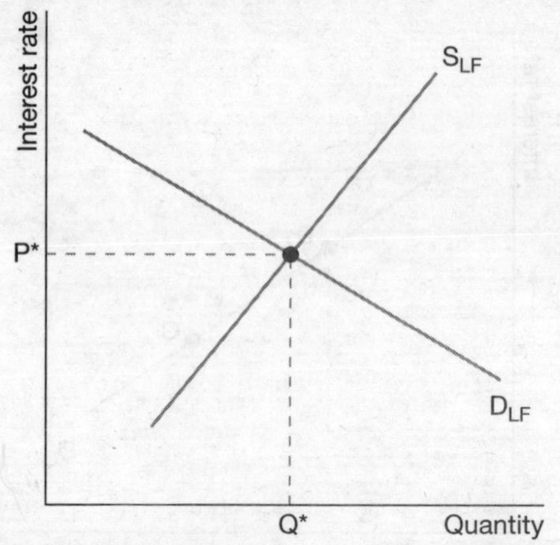

As with any other market, if the price (remember, the price of loanable funds is the interest rate) is higher than the equilibrium price, a surplus develops. In the loanable funds model, if the interest rate is higher than the equilibrium interest rate, the quantity of loanable funds supplied is greater than the quantity of loanable funds demanded—sure enough, a surplus develops. These "unborrowed" funds result in interest rates falling and few loanable funds being offered. These lower interest rates result in increases in the quantity of loanable funds demanded. Thus, we slide down both the demand and supply curves of loanable funds until we reach the equilibrium point, where the quantity supplied equals the quantity demanded, or the market-clearing interest rate.

The same logic applies if the market interest rate is less than the equilibrium interest rate. Now a shortage develops: Many deficit units want to borrow at that low interest rate, but few surplus units want to offer funds at that low interest rate. To meet that unmet need, surplus units might offer more funds, but only if they can get a higher interest rate. Those higher interest rates, however, lead to a decrease in the quantity of loanable funds demanded. Thus, we slide up both the demand and supply curves of loanable funds until we reach the equilibrium point, where there is no longer any shortage.

3-4c New Equilibrium in the Loanable Funds Market

Once again, remember equilibrium in the loanable funds market holds only if nothing else changes. But we have seen a long list of things that can and do bring about changes in the supply and/or demand for loanable funds (Table 3-3).

We have looked at two important markets: the bond market and the loanable funds market. Next we want to review how these two markets are similar and how they are very different. Along the way, you will, I hope, be convinced of just how important these two markets really are.

Table 3-3 Changes in the Loanable Funds Market

Change	Change in Supply of Bonds
Expected household income increases	D_{LF}* ▲
Business confidence increases	D_{LF} ▲
Government budget deficits increase	D_{LF} ▲
Rest of the world borrowing in the United States increases	D_{LF} ▲
Expected inflation increases	D_{LF} ▲ and S_{LF}** ▼
Number of savers increases	S_{LF} ▲
Household wealth and savings rates increase	S_{LF} ▲
Business profits and cash flows increase	S_{LF} ▲
Government budget surpluses increase	S_{LF} ▲
Rest of the world saving in the United States increases	S_{LF} ▲
Expansionary monetary policy	S_{LF} ▲
Contractionary monetary policy	S_{LF} ▼

* D_{LF}, demand for loanable funds.
**S_{LF}, supply of loanable funds.

SECTION REVIEW

Q1) During the Reagan Administration in the 1980s, the US government ran large government budget deficits, which many argued would slow down the US economy. Using the loanable funds framework, explain in words and graphically why this argument was being made.

Q2) During the Reagan Administration in the 1980s, while the US government was running large government budget deficits, the rest of the world was also bringing large amounts of their savings to the United States. Using the loanable funds framework, explain in words and graphically why this may have contributed to the economic expansion of the 1980s.

Q3) Assume the loanable funds market is in equilibrium. An increase in the demand for loanable funds will result in a ________ equilibrium interest rate as the quantity of loanable funds demanded ________ and the quantity of loanable funds supplied ________ as the market moves to a new equilibrium.

a. higher; increases; decreases

b. lower; decreases; decreases

c. higher; increases; increases

d. lower; increase; increases

The Bond Market and Loanable Funds Market Compared

3-5

Sometimes really important things are a smaller set of something just as important. Think about smartphones. The iPhone is a type of smartphone, but not all smartphones are iPhones. Think about social media. Twitter is one way that we interact using social media, but it's not the only way. Social media also includes Facebook, Instagram, flickr, Tumblr, Yelp, and so on. Therefore, Twitter is a subset of social media.

Something similar occurs with the bond market and the loanable funds market. The loanable funds market is the market in which savers and borrowers come together. One way (but not the only way) in which savers and borrowers come together is the bond market. Savers and borrowers can also come together through banks, credit unions, and other types of financial markets. Figure 3-14 illustrates another way to think about it.

What can make this more confusing is that borrowers—the demanders of loanable funds—can borrow funds by selling bonds; that is, being the suppliers of bonds. Savers can save by bringing their funds to the financial markets—being suppliers of loanable funds. One way they can do this is by buying, or being the demanders of, bonds.

Let's think about some things the bond market and the loanable funds market have in common.

3-5a The Fisher Effect

When inflationary expectations increase, financial market participants will want to borrow more. At the same time, savers want to flee financial assets and instead buy real assets and/or leave the economy for another one. So when inflationary expectations increase:

- Demand for loanable funds increases, or there is more borrowing. One way for borrowers such as corporations to borrow more is to sell more bonds, which increases the supply of bonds.
- Supply of loanable funds decreases, or there are fewer funds being offered in the market. One market surplus units are exiting is the bond market; thus, there is a decrease in the demand for bonds.

Figure 3-14 The Bond Market and the Loanable Funds Market

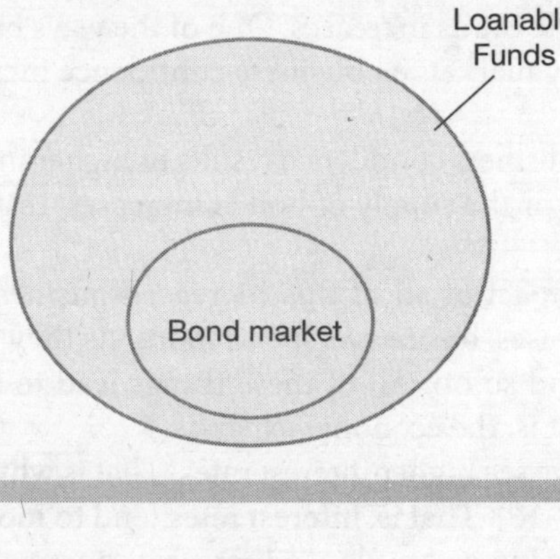

Figure 3-15 **The Fisher Effect Occurs in Both the Bond Market (a) and Loanable Funds Market (b) When Inflationary Expectations Increase**

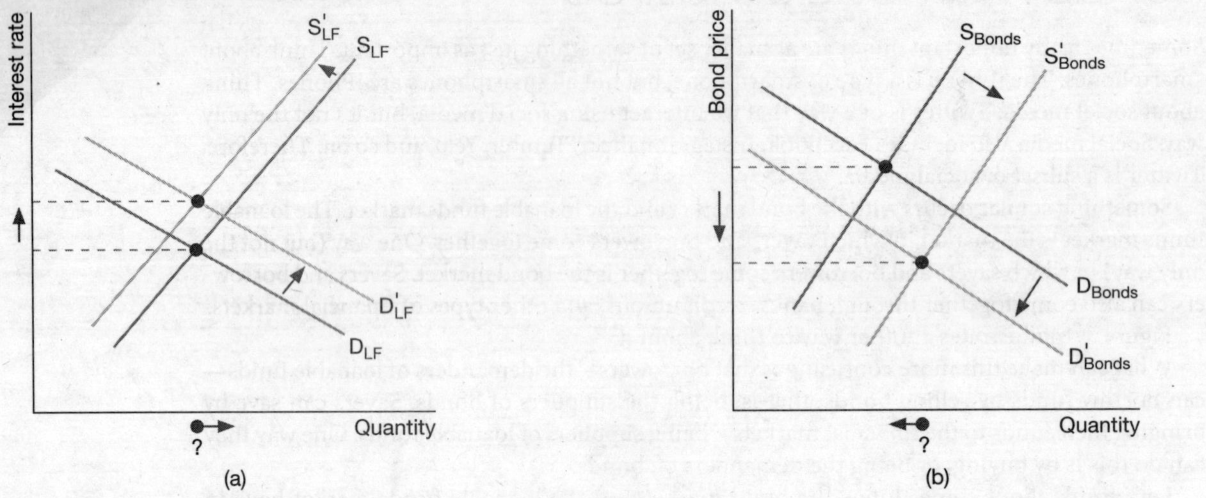

Thus, notice the outcomes (Figure 3-15):

- In the loanable funds market, the increase in demand and decrease in supply lead to a higher interest rate (Figure 3-15a). Thus, as inflationary expectations increase, (nominal) interest rates increase. That is the Fisher Effect.
- In the bond market, the increase in supply and decrease in demand lead to lower bond prices (Figure 3-15b). But remember, there is an inverse relationship between bond prices and bond yields, or interest rates. So, again, we have increasing inflationary expectations resulting in higher interest rates. That is the Fisher Effect.

Therefore, from both the loanable funds and the bond markets we get the same result!

3-5b Business Cycles and Confidence

Think about what happens when business confidence increases. When confidence in the future increases, businesses are more likely to borrow and spend more. Let's suppose businesses are more confident that sales will be higher in the future, so they are more likely to fund more projects. To fund those projects, firms have to borrow more. So, as business confidence increases, demand for loanable funds increases. One of the ways businesses can borrow more is to sell bonds in the primary market. As business confidence increases, the supply of bonds increases.

As we see, the increase in business confidence results in higher interest rates; the demand for loanable funds increases and/or the supply of bonds increases, resulting in lower bond prices or higher yields.

Think about the other impact of all of this increased business confidence. As business confidence in the future increases, businesses spend more. As they spend more they hire more workers, buy more inputs, and so on. All of these things lead to a higher level of real gross domestic product (GDP); that is, the economy expands.

As the economy expands we see higher interest rates. That is why it is often said that interest rates are procyclical (Figure 3-16). That is, interest rates tend to move along with the economy or the business cycles. As business confidence increases, borrowing and spending increase and the economy expands. But this increased borrowing leads to higher market interest rates.

Figure 3-16 Procyclical Interest Rates as the Economy Expands

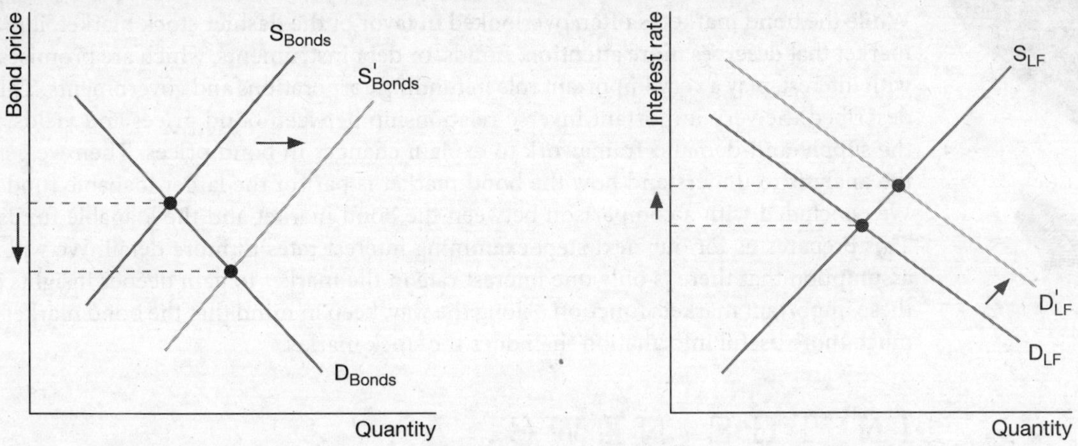

As the old saying goes, what goes up must come down. When business confidence falls, or businesses become more worried about what the future holds, they cut back on their borrowing and spending. This reduction in borrowing can lead to a lower level of total output, and real GDP falls. This declining GDP can then lead to an economic slowdown. But this reduced borrowing leads to a decrease in the demand for loanable funds. One way in which firms can borrow less is by offering fewer bonds for sale; thus, the supply of bonds decreases.

From this we can understand how the bond market and the loanable funds market work in the same way and give us the same result. This occurs because the bond market is a subsector of the loanable funds market. Changes that impact the bond market also impact the overall loanable funds market. Keep in mind, however, that things can impact the loanable funds market that do not impact the bond market.

For example, if consumers become more confident in the future, they might go out and borrow and spend more. While this increased consumer borrowing leads to an increase in the demand for loanable funds, it does not impact the supply of bonds because households cannot issue bonds.

So, not everything that impacts the loanable funds market impacts the bond market. The bond market is a subset of the loanable funds market.

SECTION REVIEW

Q1) Explain why changes in the demand for bonds change the supply of loanable funds.

Q1) Explain why a change in the demand for loanable funds may *not* change the supply of bonds.

Q3) You read in the financial press that the economy of Finland is sliding into a recession. What will happen in the bond market and the loanable funds market in Finland, ceteris paribus?

a. Bond prices will decrease and interest rates will increase.

b. Bond prices will increase and interest rates will decrease.

c. Bond prices and interest rates will decrease.

d. Bond prices and interest rates will increase.

3-6 Conclusion

While the bond market is often overlooked in favor of the flashier stock market, it is the bond market that deserves more attention. Bonds, or debt instruments, which are promises to repay with interest, play a very important role in funding corporations and governments. This chapter described the very important inverse relationship between bond prices and yields. We used the supply-and-demand framework to explain changes in bond prices. Then we generalized the analysis to understand how the bond market is part of the larger loanable funds market. We concluded with a comparison between the bond market and the loanable funds market. This prepares us for our next step: examining interest rates in more detail. We will relax the assumption that there is only one interest rate in the market to gain deeper insights into how these important markets function. Along the way, keep in mind that the bond market provides much more useful information than does the stock market.

IN THE NEWS. . .

US Companies Increasingly Borrow in Euros

Andrew Bolger
Financial Times
December 17, 2014

US companies are showing increasing willingness to issue investment grade bonds in euros for a combination of financial and strategic reasons.

This year investment-grade US companies have issued euro-denominated bonds worth $48bn, a 23 per cent increase on the previous year and almost three times the comparable figure in 2012, according to Dealogic.

"We have observed a significant increase in the number of US companies issuing in Europe and in particular in the number of inaugural issuers, which suggests a secular shift rather than a temporary increase," said Alexander Menounos, head of Morgan Stanley's Emea investment grade fixed income syndicate. . . .

Big issuers of investment grade bonds are attracted to the euro-denominated market because of its rapid recovery since the financial crisis, almost doubling between 2010 to its present level of annual issuance, running at $341bn. . . .

Another reason for Europe's popularity with issuers is the relative scarcity of new supply of investment grade paper, which has performed strongly for investors during the year.

Can you show graphically and describe in words what is happening in both the bond market and the loanable funds market in Europe? How do you think these changes will impact households and business firms in Europe?

4

Interest Rates in More Detail

4-1 Interest Rates in More Detail and Default Risk

US Navy Admiral Hyman Rickover, called the "father of the nuclear Navy," reportedly once said, "The devil is in the details, but so is salvation." This means that although digging into the details of an issue can be cumbersome, unpleasant, and frustrating, it can also bring great insights that may be missed by focusing only on the general condition. While Admiral Rickover was probably referring to national security, the same can be said for financial markets. Let us next, then, take Admiral Rickover's advice and dig into the details of financial markets.

In Chapter 3 we saw how the loanable funds model as well as the supply and demand of the bond market can be used to explain interest rate movements in general. While those two models are very useful, and we use them again here and in other chapters, they also have their limitations. To use a two-dimensional version of each model we have to assume there is only one interest rate. This assumption is fine so long as one is interested in the general movement of interest rates. But if we want to be a bit more exact to get a better understanding of how financial markets work, we need to relax that assumption. That is, we now want to investigate why different financial instruments have different yields or pay different interest rates.

4-1a Default Risk

In many ways a financial instrument, such as a bond or loan, is an agreement between two parties. Think about a bond: The buyer of the bond agrees to lend some money to the bond issuer. That part of the agreement is easy enough to enforce. The other side of the agreement is more difficult to enforce: The issuer of the bond agrees to pay over time interest payments as well as the face value of the bond. Because the bond issuer's promise is fulfilled over time, there is the potential that the borrower will not live up to that promise. This brings up the issue of default risk.

Default risk is the risk that a borrower will not live up to their promise to pay interest or principal or both as they have pledged.

Default risk: The risk that a borrower will not pay interest or principal or both as promised.

Default, or failure to repay, can occur for a wide variety of reasons. Some of these reasons are under the direct control of the borrower, and some are beyond the borrower's control. The borrower may make bad decisions—a firm may expand too quickly or a household can live beyond its means. Other causes of default the borrower may have no control over: The overall economy may enter into a recession or a natural disaster may occur, causing the borrower's economic condition to worsen and rendering them unable to repay.

Regardless of the cause of the default, the lender is negatively affected by this lack of repayment. Thus, the greater the probability of default, the greater the probability the lender will be negatively affected. That is why the greater the default risk, the more the lender is going to ask to be compensated for lending funds.

The rate at which the lender needs to be compensated for taking on more default risk is what is called the **default risk premium (DRP)**. The DRP is represented mathematically as

$$\mathbf{IR}_{\text{market},i,t} = \mathbf{IR}_{\text{risk-free},t} + \mathbf{DRP}_{i,t}$$

or

$$\mathbf{DRP}_{i,t} = \mathbf{IR}_{\text{market},i,t} - \mathbf{IR}_{\text{risk-free},t}$$

where $\text{IR}_{\text{market},i,t}$ is the market interest rate the borrower *i* pays at time *t*. This market interest rate is made up of the interest rate a borrower who has no default risk would pay at time *t*, or $\text{IR}_{\text{risk-free},t}$ plus the DRP borrower *i* must pay at time *t*.

Default risk premium: The rate at which a lender is compensated for taking on more default risk.

So, let's say that in August 2016 an interest rate of 4.5% is paid by the Rigsby Corporation, borrower *i*. Let's also suppose that, at that same time, an interest rate of 2% is paid by the US Treasury when it issues debt. The interest rate on Treasury securities is often considered the risk-free rate because the chances the US government will default on its debt is very, very small. Thus, in this case, the Rigsby Corporation must pay a DRP of 2.5%, or 4.5% minus 2%.

4-1b Calculating DRP

While the concept of the default risk premium or DRP is relatively straightforward and calculating it from existing market interest rates and government securities yields is a matter of simple arithmetic, coming up with the correct default risk premium is anything but simple or straightforward. Stated differently, calculating the DRP ex post is simple, whereas calculating the DRP ex ante is not.

To determine the DRP any one borrower should pay at any one point in time takes a great deal of effort and skill. Think about what must be done to correctly calculate the DRP: You have to be able to look into the future and determine the probability that the borrower will not repay as promised. Keep in mind that this probability will be influenced by many events—things like natural disasters and the state of the economy in the future—the outcomes of which are not currently known.

Because accurately calculating the DRP is so difficult, many look for shortcuts in doing so. One of these shortcuts is looking at the borrower's bond rating. For reasons we will discuss more in-depth in Chapter 16, it is dangerous to assume the bond rating accurately reflects the actual probability that a borrower will default. Many argue that the bond rating system is full of misaligned incentives that greatly reduce the usefulness of the bond rating as a measurement of default risk.

So, be leery of using the bond rating system as a perfect measurement of default risk. It is not a perfect measurement. So, how then does one measure default risk? Often it is best to measure changes in the DRP over time.

4-1c Comparing Default Risk of Different Financial Instruments

We can use the supply and demand of the bond market to examine changes in the default risk premium or DRP. Figure 4-1 shows the DRP paid by the Rigsby Corporation. Notice that the price of Rigsby Corporation bonds is lower than the price of US Treasury securities. Remember,

Figure 4-1 Default Risk Premium

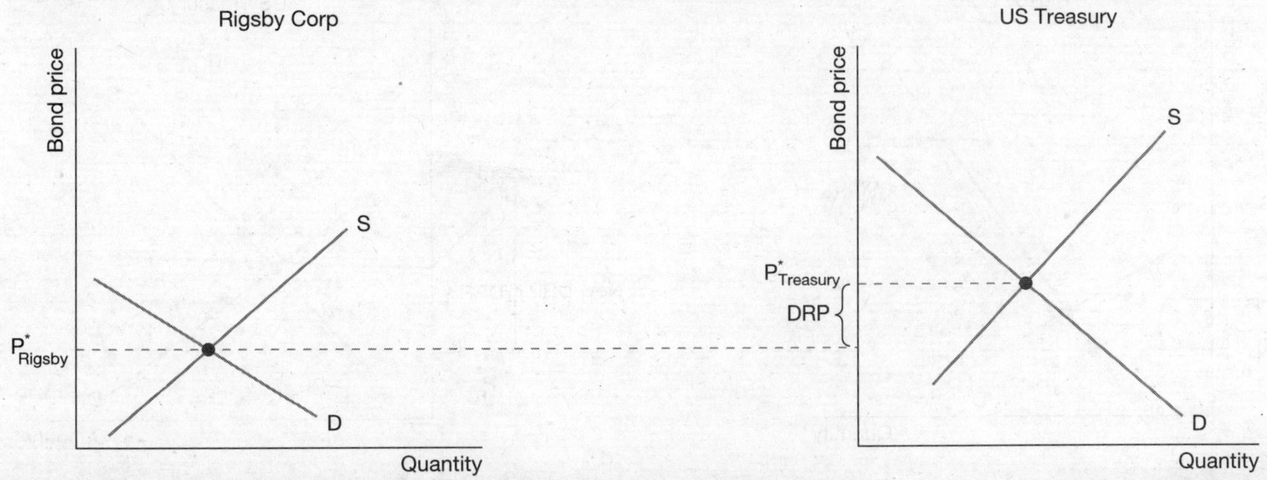

there is an inverse relationship between bond prices and yields or interest rates. So, because the Rigsby Corporation bonds are at a lower price, the corporation is paying a higher interest rate.

Keep in mind, though, that these supply-and-demand relationships hold for only one point in time. Things that bring about changes in supply and/or demand for bonds in each of these markets can and do change over time.

For example, let us suppose that market participants become worried about the future state of the economy. They worry that businesses like the Rigsby Corporation might see a decrease in their sales volume and thus might not generate enough income to make the interest payments on their bonds. Bond buyers then may be less likely to buy Rigsby Corporation bonds, that is, there may be a decrease in the demand for Rigsby Corporation bonds.

Instead, bond buyers may be more likely to buy the "sure bet" of US Treasury securities. Thus the demand for US Treasury securities increases. This selling of corporate bonds and buying of governments bonds as a result of increased uncertainty is called a "**flight to quality**" (Figure 4-2).

Flight to quality: Movement of financial resources from financial instruments with default risk to financial instruments with lower levels of default risk. Often occurs because of increased uncertainty over future economic or market conditions.

But flight to quality as a result of increased default risk can be shown in a more general way. We start off with the gap between the price of Rigsby Corporation bonds and that of US Treasury bonds. Notice the lower price of Rigsby Corporation bonds, implying a higher yield than the US Treasury bonds. This gap in bond prices is the **default risk premium spread.**

Default risk premium spread: The difference in yields between assets with different levels of default risk.

When the flight to quality occurs, the demand for Rigsby Corporation bonds decreases. Funds flow from the bond market for Rigsby Corporation bonds and into the "safer" market for US Treasury bonds. As a result, we see an increase in demand for US Treasury bonds. Notice the DRP spread also increases.

This is not just an academic exercise. There was a large flight to quality at the outbreak of the financial crisis in 2007 and 2008. The interest rate "risky" borrowers (read: from any entity other than the US government) had to pay shot up, while the yields on US Treasury

Figure 4-2 Flight to Quality

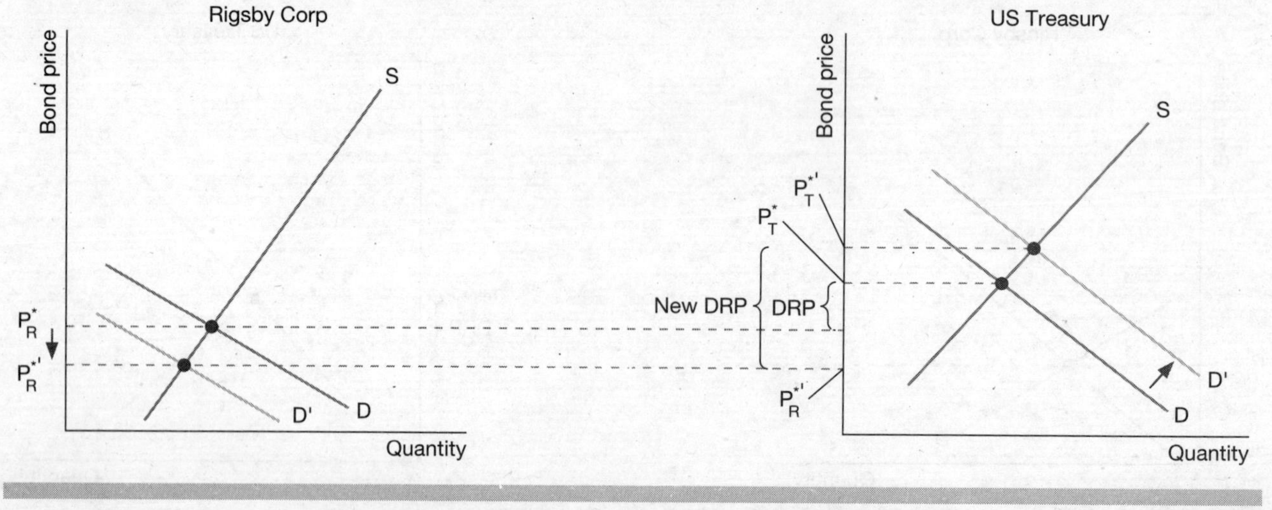

securities decreased dramatically. Keep in mind why this is important: As the cost of borrowing increases for firms, they are less likely to fund projects. Instead, they look to cut projects, lay off employees, and cut spending. Thus thousands of people in the private sector can lose their jobs when there is a flight to quality.

Default risk of different borrowers is only one reason why financial instruments pay different yields or different interest rates. Let's think more about that *t* variable: time. Why might borrowers with the same default risk have to pay different interest rates at different times? One reason is due to inflationary expectations. This is where we turn our attention to next.

SECTION REVIEW

Q1) Firms borrowing in developing countries such as Brazil often have to pay a higher default risk premium, ceteris paribus, than similar firms borrowing in the United States. Explain why this is the case.

Q2) Offer an explanation to someone with no training in economics for why the yield on US government bonds is used as a substitute for the risk-free rate.

Q3) You read in the financial press that the recent flight to quality is reversing. What will happen in the bond market?

a. Yields of US Treasury bonds will decrease relative to the yields of corporate bonds.

b. Prices of US Treasury bonds will decrease relative to the prices of corporate bonds.

c. Yields of US Treasury bonds will increase relative to the yields of corporate bonds.

d. Prices of US Treasury bonds will increase relative to the prices of corporate bonds.

4-2 Real Versus Nominal: The Role of Inflation

Inflation, or the continuous increase in the general level of prices, can be a very nasty thing. Inflation distorts the price-signaling mechanism, can lead to a redistribution of wealth upward, and, perhaps worst of all, can stagnate the economy.

4-2a Why We Worry About Inflation

To understand why inflation is so evil, imagine you run a firm. You are trying to figure out how much to produce and thus how many inputs to buy. Then, imagine that the selling price increases in the market in which your firm is selling. What do you make of this? It could be that demand for what you are producing is increasing. If this is the case, you should clearly increase the level of output and, by extension, buy more inputs.

But wait a minute. Do you really want to run out and hire more people, rent more office and production space, plus buy more raw materials? What if the price increase in your market is driven by an increase in the rate of inflation? Because increases in wages and salaries tend to lag behind the inflation rate, a higher rate of inflation today might mean your customers will buy *less* of your output in the future, not more! If that's the case, you should not buy all those additional inputs. Instead, you should reduce the amount of inputs you buy.

Not only does inflation distort the price-signaling mechanism, it also redistributes wealth in favor of the wealthy. When inflation increases, wages and salaries tend to increase, but, as mentioned, their increase lags behind that of inflation and is often less than the rate of inflation. Thus people who depend on wages and salaries for their consumption see their ability to consume falling with inflation—wages and salaries simply do not keep pace with inflation.

On the other hand, the very wealthy often don't depend on wages and salaries for income to support their consumption levels. The very wealthy depend on assets or investments to generate the income that allows them to consume. When there is inflation, the wealthy can reallocate their assets to protect them from inflation. For example, the value of real assets such as gold, silver, diamonds, and real estate tends to increase along with, and sometimes faster than, the rate of inflation. Thus the wealthy can often benefit from inflation as the value of their assets increases faster than the rate of inflation.

So, with inflation, the wealthy often benefit, whereas people who depend on wages and salaries suffer as their consumption levels change. Inflation therefore redistributes wealth toward the wealthy and away from those with lower levels of wealth who depend on wages and salaries.

In addition, inflation is so evil because it can misallocate resources and paralyze the entire economy. As inflation rates increase, businesspeople cut back on their level of economic activity because they are uncertain of what is going to happen to costs and revenues in a world with increasing prices. We also observe the impact of inflation in our financial markets.

4-2b Real Versus Nominal Interest Rates

When there is inflation, borrowers get to pay off their debts using a "cheaper" currency, or a currency that is easier to get. Think about someone who borrows \$100 and earns \$10 an hour. It would take 10 hours to earn enough income to pay off that debt. But now imagine there is inflation, and wages increase to \$15 an hour. Now the debt can be paid off in less than seven hours, so less effort is required to pay off that debt.

On the other hand, think about this from the point of view of a saver. This person works very hard and is able to save \$100. With this \$100 she could buy a cell phone, or she could lend the money to someone else who could buy a cell phone. So, this saver lends to someone else enough resources (\$100) to buy a cell phone. But now imagine there is inflation and the price of the cell phone increases to \$150. The person who borrowed the money now pays back the loan: $100. Our saver says, "Hey, wait a minute. I lent that person enough resources to buy an entire cell phone, but now I am paid back with resources that can only buy two-thirds of a cell phone." Savers suffer from inflation because they get paid back in a "cheaper" currency, or a currency that does not buy as much as it used to.

This is why inflation leads to higher interest rates: Savers want to save less and borrowers want to borrow more because of the outcomes of inflation. This is what the American economist Irving Fisher first pointed out with the Fisher Effect:

Nominal or market IR = Real IR + Rate of inflation

So if the real interest rate (IR) is 2% and the inflation rate is 3%, then the nominal or market interest rate should be 5%.

Most often, however, the real interest rate is not observed. Instead, we usually have the nominal or market interest rate and the rate of inflation. These two rates are used to solve for the real interest rate by rewriting the equation as

Real IR = Nominal IR − Inflation rate

The real interest rate, as opposed to the nominal or market interest rate, is used in making business and economic decisions.

To understand why, imagine Sami is thinking about buying a one-year bond with her excess income. One bond she is considering is issued by the energy company ConocoPhillips in Houston, Texas, and pays a nominal 6% annual percentage rate or APR. The other bond she is considering is issued by the Imperial Oil Limited Corporation in Calgary, Alberta, Canada, and pays a 5% APR. If she compares only the nominal interest rates offered by these two bonds issued by energy companies, she would pick the ConocoPhillips bond. But what about inflation?

Let's suppose Sami also believes the inflation rate in the United States will be 4% over the year she holds the bond, whereas the inflation rate in Canada will be only 2% over that same time period. Then the real interest rate on the ConocoPhillips bond will be only 2%, whereas the real interest rate on the Imperial Oil bond will be 3%. Therefore, she is better off buying the Imperial Oil bond. If Sami focuses on the nominal interest rate she makes the wrong decision! Making economic and financial decisions based on real interest rates, not just nominal interest rates, is very important.[1]

4-2c Ex Post Versus Ex Ante

There can be a difference between real and nominal interest rates, depending on whether someone is looking to the future or looking at the past. Using past inflation rates gives us the **ex post** real interest rate (IR):

Ex post real IR = Nominal IR − Actual inflation rate

Using the expected rate of inflation gives us the **ex ante** real interest rate:

Ex ante real IR = Nominal IR − Expected inflation rate

Ex post: Using the actual rate of inflation.

Ex ante: Using the expected rate of inflation.

One useful way to keep these terms—*ex post* and *ex ante*—straight is to think about the suffix of each. With ex post, the term *post* means "after." Think about a postgame interview that takes place after the end of a football game: *Postgame* means "after the game." In the same way, ex post real interest rate is the interest rate calculated using the inflation rate that has already occurred or the actual rate of inflation.

1 We are ignoring the impact of changes in exchange rates.

In terms of ex ante, think about a game of poker that you may have played or seen played on television or in the movies. Before each hand is dealt, players must "ante up," or put their chips into the pot before the cards are played. Thus the term *ante* means "before." So, an ex ante real interest rate is a real interest rate based on the expected or forecasted rate of inflation.

Differences between ex ante and ex post real interest rates tells us that the forecasted inflation rate was very different from the actual inflation rate. To understand why this is the case, and why it is important, let's review an example.

4-2d Example of Ex Ante Versus Ex Post

Imagine Sunita works for Disney World in Orlando, Florida, and is responsible for investing the excess cash Disney World generates each month. She is thinking about having Disney buy some bonds that have a 4% nominal or market interest rate. Wisely, however, she is concerned about real, not just nominal, interest rates or rate of returns. She thinks the inflation rate over the length of the bond will be 1.5%, so she calculates the ex ante real interest rate at 2.5%.

Ex ante real IR = Nominal IR − Expected inflation
Ex ante real IR = 4% − 1.5% = 2.5%

After she buys the bond and holds on to it, imagine the actual inflation rate turns out to be 3.25%! Then the ex post real interest rate is only 0.75%.

Ex post real IR = Nominal IR − Actual inflation
Ex post real IR = 4% − 3.25% = 0.75%

Sunita is going to have a lot to explain to her supervisor! Why did she anticipate a 2.5% real return and yet get only a 0.75% real return? She clearly made a mistake in predicting the rate of inflation.

This ex post real interest rate is sometimes called the **real realized rate of return**, which makes sense. Real realized means the actually realized real rate of return, not what people thought the real rate of return was going to be.

Real realized rate of return: The rate of return earned after controlling for inflation.

When making an investment decision—whether buying a bond or funding a project—using the real interest rate or rate of return, not just the nominal rates, is important. Inflation can drive a big wedge between the nominal rates and the real rates. So don't forget inflation!

Another important variable to not forget is tax rates. How interest earned is taxed can have a major impact on which financial asset you decide to purchase. It is this issue of taxes we turn to next.

SECTION REVIEW

Q1) Explain why businesspeople should use the real interest rate instead of the nominal interest rate when making economic decisions.

Q2) Explain why rapid changes in the rate of inflation, as well as inflationary expectations, make business investment decisions difficult.

Q3) If the ex ante real interest rate is less than the ex post real interest rate, which of the following happened?

a. Actual inflation rate is less than the expected inflation rate

b. Actual inflation rate is greater than the expected inflation rate

c. Actual inflation rate is equal to the expected inflation rate

d. The expected inflation rate was zero.

Taxes

4-3

As the old saying goes, the only things that are certain in life are death, taxes, and change. Let's worry about death later and instead focus on taxes and change. Specifically, let's think about how taxes and tax rates affect the interest rates paid on different financial instruments.

4-3a Before- and After-Tax Returns

Interest earned from holding a bond is considered income. Sure, it's not the same kind of income you earn when you go to work and get paid a wage or a salary. Wages and salaries are called labor income—income earned from "selling" your time, effort, and brains to an employer. "Renting" your money to a borrower is sort of the same thing: You are paid for the use of your money, just as in the labor market you are paid for the use of your time, effort, and brains.

So the interest you earn from lending money—say, from buying a bond—is going to be subject to income tax. Remember, income taxes are imposed by the federal government, most state governments, and some local governments. Keep in mind that we also have a progressive income tax, that is, the higher the level of income, the higher the marginal tax rate paid.

Investors and savers are interested in the after-tax rate of return. Or

$$i_{AT} = i_{BT}(1 - z)$$

where i_{AT} is the interest rate, or rate of return, after tax, and i_{BT} is the interest rate, or rate of return, before the tax is paid. In this case, z is the marginal tax rate paid by the saver or investor.

Let's say Lisa has a bond with a coupon rate of 7%, but she faces a 25% marginal tax rate. That means her after-tax rate of return on the bond is

$$i_{AT} = 0.07 \times (1 - 0.25) = 0.0525, \text{ or } 5.25\%$$

But if she was in the 35% marginal tax bracket, her after-tax rate of return would be

$$i_{AT} = 0.07 \times (1 - 0.35) = 0.0455, \text{ or only } 4.55\%$$

As you can see in Table 4-1, the higher the marginal tax rate, the lower the after-tax rate of return. Notice how the after-tax rate of return can be significantly lower the higher the marginal tax rate paid by the saver. That is why some savers or investors want to hold tax-free or tax-exempt financial instruments.

TABLE 4-1 Comparison of Before and After Tax Rates of Return

Tax Rate (%)	Before-Tax Rate (%)	After-Tax Rate (%)	Calculation
0	7	7	since $0.07 \times (1 - 1) = 0.07$
10	7	6.3	since $0.07 \times (1 - 0.10) = 0.063$
15	7	5.95	since $0.07 \times (1 - 0.15) = 0.0595$
25	7	5.25	since $0.07 \times (1 - 0.25) = 0.0525$
28	7	4.69	since $0.07 \times (1 - 0.28) = 0.0469$
35	7	4.55	since $0.07 \times (1 - 0.35) = 0.0455$
39.6	7	4.23	since $0.07 \times (1 - 0.396) = 0.04228$

4-3b Municipal Bonds and Taxes

Local municipalities and taxing districts provide important public goods to society. We will discuss these important entities and their debt instruments called **municipal, or "muni," bonds** in more depth in Chapter 16. For now, understand that these important state and local governments, school districts, water districts, public transportation systems, and so on need to raise capital, and they do so by issuing bonds.

Municipal (muni) bonds: Bonds or debt issued by state governments, local governments, and/or local municipalities.

To make it easier for these local government entities to sell their bonds (and to keep their financing costs low), the interest paid on these muni bonds is not currently subject to federal income tax. Think about what this means, especially to someone in one of the higher income tax brackets. Because a saver does not have to pay income tax on the interest they earn from holding a muni bond, these bonds are more desirable, ceteris paribus, than corporate bonds. The investor would be indifferent between the corporate bonds or corporate debt and the muni bonds only if the after-tax rate on the corporate debt was equal to the before-tax rate on the muni bond. Or

$$i_{BT} = \frac{i_{AT}}{(1 - z)}$$

where i_{AT} is the interest rate, or rate of return, after tax; i_{BT} is the interest rate, or rate of return, before tax is paid; and z is the marginal tax rate.

Imagine Rachel is considering two bonds, a corporate bond and a muni bond that are exactly the same except for their yields. Suppose Rachel is in the 28% tax bracket, and the muni bond she is thinking about buying pays a 6% interest rate. So the after-tax rate and the before-tax rate on the muni bond is the same at 6%.

Rachel knows if she buys the corporate bond she has to pay to the government as taxes 28% of the interest she earns on that corporate bond. How high would the yield on the corporate bond have to be to make her indifferent between the corporate bond and the muni bond?

$$i_{BT} = \frac{i_{AT}}{(1 - z)} = \frac{0.06}{(1 - 0.28)} = 0.08333$$

So the corporate bond would have to pay a before-tax interest rate of 8.33% to make her indifferent between that bond and a muni bond paying 6%.

Muni Bonds, Taxes, and the Future

Think about this example from the point of view of the municipality trying to raise capital. If the municipality did not have this "tax advantage," it would have to pay 8.33% to get Rachel to buy their bonds. Thanks to the fact that muni bond interest is not currently subject to federal income tax, the municipality can borrow money "more cheaply" and pay only 6% to Rachel.

In 2013 there was a movement to limit the size of the tax advantage of muni bonds. Suggestions to cap the tax exemption for interest on muni bonds at 28% for taxpayers in the top tax bracket were made. To understand how this works, let's suppose Thurston, who is in the top income tax bracket, earned $10,000 in interest on his muni bond holdings in a year. Under the proposal, Thurston would pay $1,160 in federal income tax on that interest income—39.6% of $10,000 is $3,960—but 28% of the $10,000, or $2,800, is exempt. So, of his tax bill of $3,960, the amount exempt is $2,800, which means Thurston has to pay the remaining $1,160 in taxes.

Some argue this is a way to "get the rich to pay more" taxes. Notice the proposal does not end the tax advantage of muni bonds for everyone; it only affects those in the highest tax bracket. As of 2013, that means it would apply to individuals making more than $406,000 or families making more than $457,000 a year. Keep in mind, too, that the proposal would not completely eliminate the tax advantage of these wealthy people because the exemption of 28% would still apply.

On the other hand, others[2] argue that even this modest reduction in the tax advantage of muni bonds would result in much higher borrowing costs for local municipalities and taxing districts. These people contend that fewer schools and hospitals would be built as a result. It would, they argue, result in funds that would have gone to building roads, bridges, and highways instead of going to fund corporations, including financial institutions that have already received taxpayer-funded bailouts. Finally, opponents of the proposal believe that it would result in higher borrowing costs for local municipalities, and who would ultimately pay this higher cost of capital for these government entities? Average taxpayers like you and me!

So what is the future of the tax advantage of muni bonds? Will these local government and taxing authorities continue to benefit from having the interest they pay being exempt from federal income taxes? Or will this "tax loophole" be closed once and for all? Remember, one of the three things in life that is for certain, in addition to death and taxes, is change.

Next, then, let's take a look at something else that is constantly changing: the yield curve.

SECTION REVIEW

Q1) Do you think the preferential tax treatment of muni bonds should be eliminated? Or, should the tax benefit of muni bonds be reduced? Why or why not?

Q2) If Tommy is in the 15% income tax bracket and is considering buying a muni bond that yields 3%, what yield would a corporate bond have to pay to make him indifferent between the two bonds, ceteris paribus?

Q3) If Kari is in the 35% income tax bracket and is thinking about buying a corporate bond that yields 2.5%, what yield must a muni bond pay to make her indifferent between the two bonds, ceteris paribus?

a. 2.15%
b. 1.79%
c. 1.625%
d. 1.055%

2 See http://www.forbes.com/sites/kellyphillipserb/2013/07/16/ending-tax-breaks-on-municipal-bonds-shifts-burden-to-the-rest-of-us/.

4-4 Yield Curves

Imagine you have some money saved and are considering buying some bonds. The bonds you are considering are exactly the same except for the length to maturity of the bonds. That is, the bonds have the same level of default risk, the interest they pay is taxed the same, and so on—every aspect of the bonds is the same, except for the amount of time until they mature. Why then would these bonds have different yields? Stated another way: Why do bonds with different lengths to maturity pay different yields?

This issue is called the "term structure of interest rates." Bonds or debt instruments that have different terms or lengths of maturity tend to have different interest rates or different yields. Why is this the case?

4-4a Yield Curve Graph

To answer this question (and it turns out there isn't just one answer) we should look at it graphically via something called the yield curve. A **yield curve** shows the yield, or interest rate, paid on bonds of different maturities at one point in time (Figure 4-3).

Yield curve: Graph of the yields of bonds or debt at one point in time.

An important thing to remember: "Term" set on the horizontal axis identifies the terms, or lengths to maturity, of the bonds we are examining at one point in time. That is, the horizontal axis is *not*, in this case, a measurement of time into the future as in what interest rates will be in the future.

4-4b Yield Curve Facts

We want to use the yield curve graph to explain the following facts about interest rates:

1. A yield curve generally slopes upward. This means that, holding everything else constant, the yield on long-term bonds tends to be higher than the yield on short-term bonds.
2. The slope of a yield curve can and does change. That is, sometimes the yield curve is flat, or there is not much difference between short-term yields and long-term yields, whereas other times the yield curve is steep, meaning there is a big difference between short-term yields and long-term yields; and sometimes the yield curve slopes downward. This downward-sloping yield curve is sometimes called an "inverted" yield curve.
3. There often are parallel shifts in a yield curve. That is, over time, short-term and long-term interest rates tend to move together. Sometimes all interest rates increase, or the

Figure 4-3 The Yield Curve

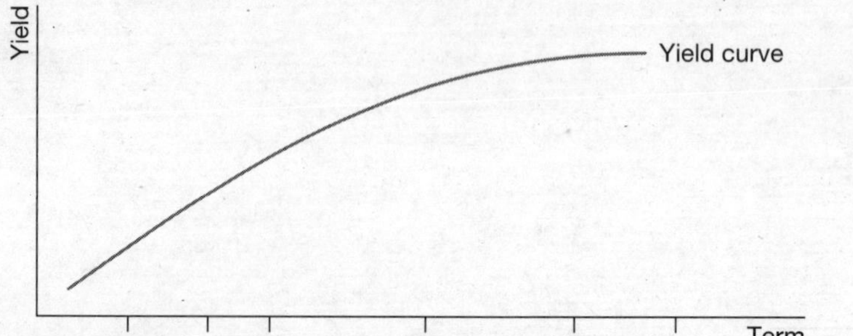

yield curve shifts upward. Other times, all interest rates decrease and there is a parallel downward shift in the yield curve.

So any theory or model that is developed to explain a yield curve should be able to explain these three facts of a yield curve. Let's take a look at the major theories or models that explain yield curves.

4-4c Pure Expectations Theory

As the name suggests, the **pure expectations theory** states that the yields on long-term bonds are made up of the market expectations of what short-term yields will be in the future.

Pure expectations theory: A framework where long-term interest rates are based on the expectations of what short-term interest rates will be in the future.

To review how this works, let's consider a simple example. Suppose you have some money saved that you will not need for two years. You can go out and buy two consecutive one-year bonds, or you can buy a two-year bond. To make things simple, let's ignore compounding for right now, and let's also assume there is no secondary bond market—that is, you cannot sell the bond after you buy it. Let's also assume everything else about the one-year bond and two-year bond are exactly the same: They have the same default risk, the same tax treatment of interest, and so on.

Let's further assume the interest rate on the one-year bond right now is 2% and the annual interest rate on the two-year bond is 4%. So you have two potential investment paths:

- Path A: Buy a one-year bond that pays 2% today and in one year buy another one-year bond.
- Path B: Buy a two-year bond today and earn 4% this year and 4% next year.

So, which do you want: path A or path B? The answer is: You don't know. With path A you do not know what the interest rate on the one-year bond will be in one year. For example, if in one year the one-year bond pays 10%, you would be much better off under path A because your average annual return would be

$$\textbf{Average annual return} = \frac{\textbf{(1-year rate today)} + \textbf{(1-year rate in 1 year)}}{\textbf{2}} = \frac{\textbf{(2\%)} + \textbf{(10\%)}}{\textbf{2}} = \textbf{6\%}$$

That 6% average annual return is much better than the 4% you would get under path B of owning a two-year bond. So under this scenario you would prefer path A.

If in one year the one-year bond pays only 3%, however, under path A you would have an average annual return of only 2.5%

$$\textbf{Average annual return} = \frac{\textbf{(1-year rate today)} + \textbf{(1-year rate in 1 year)}}{\textbf{2}} = \frac{\textbf{(2\%)} + \textbf{(3\%)}}{\textbf{2}} = \textbf{2.5\%}$$

So under this scenario you would prefer path B, with its average annual return of 4%.

Think about where you would be indifferent between path A (the two consecutive one-year bonds) and path B (one two-year bond). You would be indifferent when the two paths had the same average annual return. That is,

$$\textbf{2-year rate today} = \frac{\textbf{(1-year rate today)} + \textbf{(1-year rate in 1 year)}}{\textbf{2}}$$

But the one-year bond's rate in one year is something we currently do not know. It is something that happens in the future. Consider this, though: We can solve for it. We have one equation with three variables: the two-year bond's rate today, the one-year bond's rate today, and the one-year bond's rate in one year. However, we know only two of these variables: the two-year bond's rate today and the one-year bond's rate today. So this is a simple algebra problem: one equation with one unknown.

Let's plug in what we know and solve for what we don't know

$$\textbf{2-year rate today} = \frac{\textbf{(1-year rate today) + (1-year rate in 1 year)}}{\textbf{2}} \quad \textbf{4\%} = \frac{\textbf{(2\%)} + x}{\textbf{2}}$$

where x is the one-year bond's rate in one year. Now we just multiple both sides by 2, then subtract 2% from both sides, and we find the value of $x = 6\%$. This tells us, then, that the market thinks the one-year bond's rate in one year is going to be 6%. Remember, today the one-year bond's rate is 2%. If we visualize this graphically, it looks like Figure 4-4.

We can generalize this: According to the pure expectations theory, an upward-sloping yield curve tells us the market thinks short-term rates are going to be higher in the future than what they currently are.

Think about how amazing this is! If the pure expectations theory is correct, we now essentially have a way to look into the future and predict interest rates, or at least short-term interest rates.

Pure Expectations Theory and a Flat Yield Curve

If the yield curve is flat, the pure expectations theory suggests the market thinks interest rates in the future will be the same as they are today. To understand why, think of a simple example (again, ignore compounding and assume there is no secondary bond market).

Imagine the interest rate on a three-year bond is 4% and the yield on a six-month bond is also 4%. The graph of the yield curve for this would be perfectly flat (Figure 4-5). Think about in what instance bond buyers would be indifferent between holding a consecutive series of six-month bonds

$$\textbf{3-year rate today} = \frac{\begin{array}{c}\textbf{(6-month rate today) + (6-month rate in 6 months)} \\ \textbf{+ (6-month rate in 12 months) + (6-month rate in 18 months)} \\ \textbf{+ (6-month rate in 24 months) + (6-month rate in 30 months)}\end{array}}{\textbf{6}}$$

Figure 4-4 Graph of Yield Curve

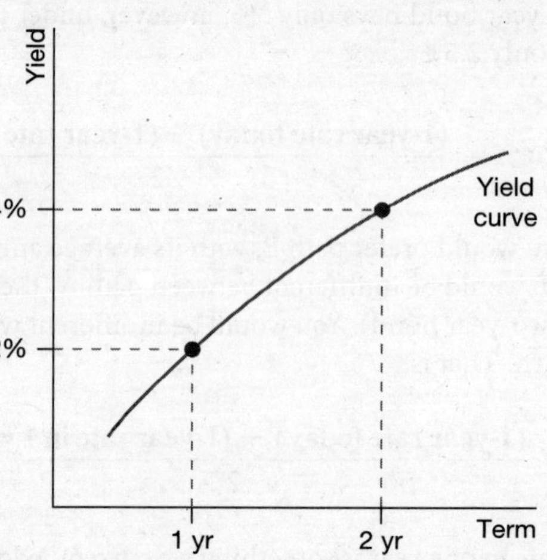

Figure 4-5 **A Yield Curve with 6 Months at 4% and 3 Years at 4%**

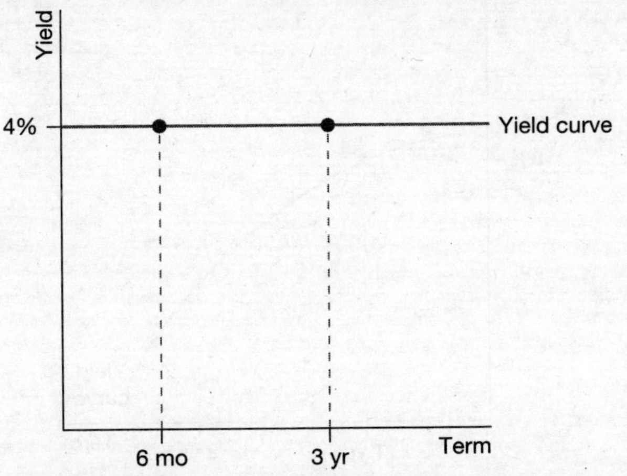

So we would have

$$4\% = \frac{4\% + ? + ? + ? + ? + ?}{6}$$

What would those "?" have to equal to get the equation to hold? Answer: They would all have to be 4%. Therefore, a flat yield curve tells us the market believes short-term rates in the future will be the same as what they are today.

Pure Expectations Theory and an Inverted Yield Curve

If a yield curve slopes downward, or is inverted, the pure expectations theory suggests the market thinks short-term interest rates in the future will be *lower* than what they are today. To understand why, let's again use a simple example where we ignore compounding and assume there is no secondary market.

For the yield curve to be inverted, or downward sloping, short-term rates have to be higher than longer-term interest rates. For example, if the one-year bond today is paying 8% but the two-year bond is paying 5%, we have a graph of the yield curve that looks like Figure 4-6.

Again, think of in what instance bond buyers would be indifferent between holding a long-term bond and a series of short-term bonds:

$$\text{2-year rate today} = \frac{\text{(1-year rate today)} + \text{(1-year rate in 1 year)}}{2}$$

which would be

$$5\% = \frac{(8\%) + x}{2}$$

So the x now equals 2%. This tells us the market thinks the one-year bond's rate in one year will be only 2%, where today the rate is 8%.

Think about what this means: The market thinks short-term rates today are "high" or will be lower in the future. High interest rates mean that borrowing costs for firms and household are high; thus firms and households are less likely to borrow and spend. But firms and households borrowing and spending less means that the economy might very well slow down. Because interest rates are procyclical, a slowing economy means lower interest rates in the future.

Figure 4-6 **An Inverted Yield Curve**

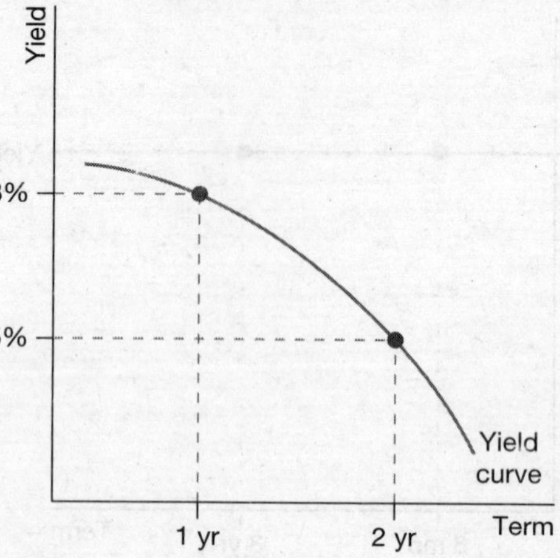

Information that the economy is about to slow down is generally seen as very bad news. That is why when the yield curve becomes inverted or downward sloping, financial market participants react negatively, and the pure expectations theory suggests they are fearing a slowdown in the economy.

Pure Expectations Theory and Reality

Be careful how much confidence you put in the pure expectations theory. It states that long-term interest rates are made up of what the market expects short-term interest rates to be in the future. And, as we saw, an upward-sloping yield curve suggests, according to the pure expectations theory, that short-term interest rates will be higher in the future.

But we also said that the yield curve tends to—that is, it most often does—slope upward. If the pure expectations theory is correct, however, that would mean that financial market participants believe that, most of the time, interest rates are going to be higher in the future than they are today. But that doesn't make sense. Why would they constantly be thinking interest rates are going to be higher in the future?

This made economists think: There has to be some explanation as to why the yield curve generally slopes upward. This led economists to the term premium theory of the yield curve.

4-4d Term Premium Theory

The **term premium theory** argues that the pure expectations theory's assumption that bond buyers are perfectly willing to substitute holding a series of short-term bonds for a long-term bond is, well, wrong.

Term premium theory: A framework where longer-term bonds have higher yields than shorter-term bonds as a way of creating an incentive for bond buyers to purchase the less desirable longer-term bonds.

Proponents of the term premium theory point out that, holding everything else constant, bondholders prefer short-term bonds to long-term bonds. They make two arguments:

1. Short-term bonds are more liquid. A bondholder can get money out of a short-term bond much quicker and easier than from a long-term bond. As a bondholder, all you have to do is hold your short-term bond to maturity and bam! You get your money back. But with a long-term bond you have to hold onto that bond for a much longer time before it matures. Or, if you hold a long-term bond you had better hope there is a well-functioning

secondary market so that you can sell that long-term bond easily if you have to. Because savers would like to have liquidity, holding everything else constant they will prefer to hold short-term bonds as opposed to long-term bonds.

2. Short-term bond prices fluctuate less than long-term bond prices. If you are an investor, you really don't want to see the market price of your investments moving around a great deal. High volatility in the market price of your investments means there is a high level of volatility in your wealth levels. In general, people don't like this. But think about bond prices and interest rates. For a given change in interest rate, the price of long-term bond fluctuates more than the price of a short-term bond. Thinking about it mathematically, the long-term bond price is going to see the numerator change more—the longer the time, the higher the exponent of the denominator—than a short-term bond. Thus long-term bond prices change more for a given change in interest rate than do short-term bond prices.

Proponents of the term premium theory argue that for these two reasons bondholders are *not* indifferent between holding a series of short-term bonds and holding a long-term bond. Instead, bond buyers *want* short-term bonds more than they want long-term bonds. So, bond issuers and sellers have to offer an incentive to get bond buyers to buy longer term, and thus less desirable, bonds.

Bond buyers offer this incentive through a higher yield. Thus, in terms of the yield curve, we have the graph seen in Figure 4-7, showing that longer-term bonds have a higher yield than shorter-term bonds.

This offers us an explanation for why the yield curve generally slopes upward, that is, because of the term premium that has to be paid to entice bond buyers to buy longer-term bonds.

Term Premium Theory and Reality

Be careful before you fully accept the term premium theory as the perfect explanation of the yield curve. Remember, sometimes the yield curve is perfectly flat. When this is the case, there would be no term premium as described by the proponents of the term premium theory. So, the question is: Where did the term premium go?

Even more troublesome to the proponents of the term premium theory is the inverted or downward-sloping yield curve. When the yield curve slopes downward, it appears that the term premium has become negative. Why would that be the case?

Figure 4-7 Graph of Term Premium

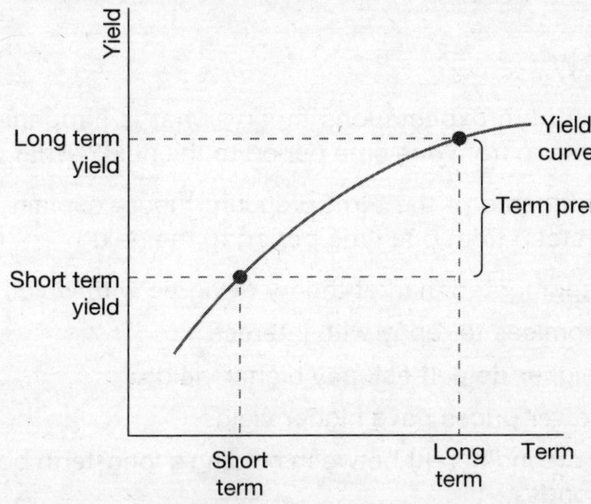

In light of this, the term premium theory does not seem to be a perfect explanation of the yield curve. This led economists to think more about the assumption of bond buyers being willing to substitute between short-term and long-term bonds.

4-4e Segmented Market Theory

Proponents of the **segmented market theory** argue that the market for short-term bonds is completely different from, or segmented from, the market for long-term bonds and that these two markets are different from the market for medium-term bonds. They point out that investors who are interested in short-term bonds want liquidity and are interested in lending money for a very short period of time. These investors are different from longer-term investors such as insurance companies, pension plans, or people saving for retirement. These long-term savers have different objectives and goals than those savers interested in buying short-term bonds.

Segmented market theory: Also called the segmented markets theory or the market segmentation theory, a framework where the short-term, medium-term, and long-term bond markets are all different or segmented markets.

Proponents of this theory also point out that the issuers of short-term bonds are different from the issuers of long-term bonds. Simply put, entities wishing to borrow money for the short term are different from borrowers who want to borrow money long term. Short-term borrowers, those in what are called "money markets," have short-term cash needs, whereas longer-term borrowers are borrowing money for long-term projects that will last years.

Think about this from a household perspective. The analysis that goes into short-term household borrowing—say, putting a purchase on a credit card—is much different from the analysis the household does for borrowing long term, for example, taking out a 30-year mortgage. Thus, the proponents of the segmented market theory argue, it makes little sense to assume that a series of short-term borrowings is the same as a long-term borrowing.

Some of these proponents go so far as to contend that the idea of a yield curve does not even make sense. Why are you playing connect the dots and drawing a line that connects different or segmented markets? If you want to understand why the slope of the yield curve changes, you should look at what is happening in the short-term debt market, the medium-term debt market, and so on, because all of these markets are different.

Be careful how far you push the segmented market theory. Remember, there often are parallel shifts in the yield curve. Thus there must be times when things impact all of these "different" or segmented markets the same way. If that is the case, one could argue that these markets (e.g., short-term debt market, medium-term debt market, long-term debt market, very-long-term debt market) may not be that different after all.

SECTION REVIEW

Q1) According to the pure expectations theory, what is happening when the yield becomes more steep from one time period to the next? What does that tell you?

Q2) How would proponents of the term premium theory explain why a yield curve becomes more steep from one time period to the next?

Q3) Proponents of segmented market theory disagree with which of the following?

a. Bonds are promises to repay with interest.

b. Bonds with higher default risk pay higher yields.

c. Bonds with lower prices have higher yields.

d. Bondholders are indifferent between holding a long-term bond and a series of short-term bonds.

Yield Curve Applications

4-5

Bond markets send signals that are of much better use than the confusing signals equity markets send. Yield curves are one good, quick way to read the signals the bond market *might* be sending. The term *might* is used because it depends on the model or framework through which you view the yield curve.

The different models that explain the yield curve should be thought of as different "tools" or "lenses" through which to view what is going on. Remember, not all tools are equally useful all of the time. A hammer is a very useful tool if you are trying to drive a nail into a two-by-four. However, a hammer is not a very useful tool if you are trying to change a light bulb. And so it is with the different models of explaining the yield curve. Some of the models sometimes work very well but work not so well other times. Let's take a look at some examples.

4-5a Inverted Yield Curve

Remember, an inverted yield curve occurs when longer-term interest rates are lower than shorter-term interest rates.

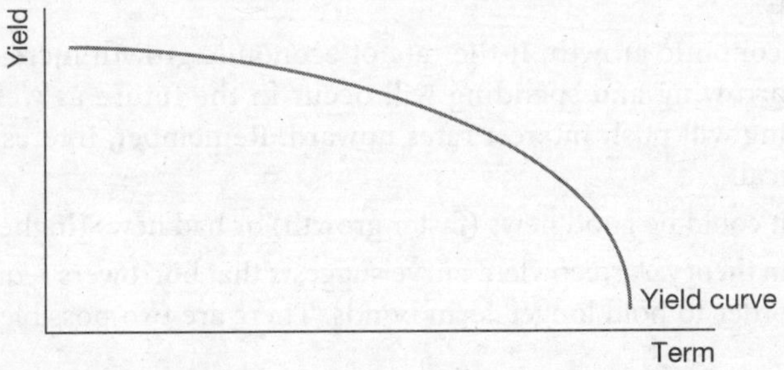

Let's look at how the different models explain this.

1. **Pure expectations theory.** An inverted yield curve suggests that short-term interest rates will be lower in the future than they are today. These relatively "high" short-term interest rates today mean there will be less borrowing, and that means less spending. This reduction in spending means the economy is going to slow down and potentially slide into an economic recession.

   Conclusion: The economy is headed for a slowdown or a recession.

2. **Segmented market theory.** An inverted yield curve comes about because the central bank, such as the Federal Reserve, is implementing a contractionary monetary policy. Monetary policy interventions usually impact only the short-term bond market. Thus a contractionary monetary policy pushes up short-term interest rates, creating an inverted yield curve. A contractionary policy is usually used to control inflation by slowing down the economy. Thus an inverted yield curve signals that the economy is going to slow down. However, if the central bank overdoes it and "tightens" too much, the economy could slide into a recession.

   Conclusion: The economy is headed for a slowdown or a recession.

4-5b Steep Yield Curve

With a steep yield curve, long-term interest rates are well above short-term interest rates.

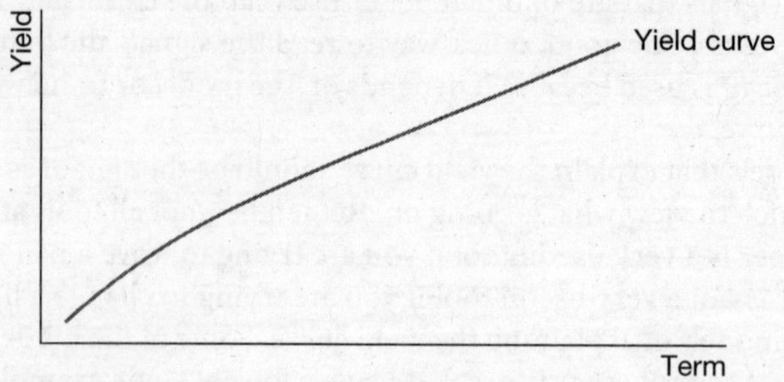

1. **Pure expectations theory.** A steep yield curve suggests that short-term interest rates will be significantly higher in the future than what they are currently. There are two main reasons why this might occur:
   (a) High inflation rates in the future. If the inflation rate is higher than interest rates in the future, even short-term interest rates will be higher than what they are today.
   (b) Faster economic growth. If the rate of economic growth increases in the future, more borrowing and spending will occur in the future as well. This increased borrowing will push interest rates upward. Remember, interest rates tend to be procyclical.

   Conclusion: It could be good news (faster growth) or bad news (higher inflation).
2. **Term premium theory.** A steep yield curve suggests that borrowers require a higher term premium in order to hold longer-term bonds. There are two possible reasons why this might occur:
   (a) Savers currently have a better use for funds. Imagine savers are considering lending money to someone else or using it themselves. If savers do not have a use for the funds they probably will lend it to someone else. On the other hand, if savers have a "good" use for the money, especially in the long term, they are going to demand a higher interest rate on their savings to get them to lend the money to someone else.
   (b) Savers worry about the future. The future is full of uncertainty. Savers could be worried about the state of the economy in the future. They might worry that if the economy weakens in the future, borrowers will not be able to repay their debts. Thus savers might require a higher interest rate to lend money well into the future. Or, savers could be worried about what the future inflation rate might be. Savers and lenders are concerned that if inflation increases they will be paid back in a currency that buys less. Thus they require a higher interest rate to lend money for the long term.

   Conclusion: It could be good news (savers have uses for funds) or bad news (savers are worried about the future).
3. **Segmented market theory.** A steep yield curve could come about because either short-term rates have decreased or longer-term interest rates have increased. These outcomes may be caused by several things:
   (a) Expansionary monetary policy. When a central bank implements monetary policy it is usually in the short-term bond market. If a central bank pursues an expansionary monetary policy, the result will be lower short-term interest rates. Then, however, one wonders why the central bank is pursuing such a policy.

(b) Mortgage interest rates increase. The long-term bond market is often affected by what happens in the home mortgage markets. Because most home mortgages in the United States are 30 years in duration, most mortgage-backed securities also are expected to have very long-term maturities. So, if home mortgage interest rates increase (maybe there has been an increase in home buying), then long-term interest rates will increase.

Conclusion: It could be good news (central banks have cut interest rates and more homes are being sold) or it could be bad news (central banks have cut interest rates because they are worried about an impending economic slowdown and there are too many homes being built and sold).

4-5c Flat Yield Curve

A flat yield curve means there is very little to no difference between short-term, medium-term, and long-term interest rates.

1. **Pure expectations theory.** A flat yield curve suggests short-term interest rates in the future will be where they are well into the future. This means that economic and financial markets conditions are not expected to change much at all over time.

   Conclusion: Things will remain the same.

2. **Term premium theory.** A flat yield curve suggests that the term premium has gone to zero. Savers are indifferent between holding short-term debt, medium-term bonds, or long-term bonds. There is not a term premium.

   Conclusion: All bonds are the same.

3. **Segmented market theory.** A flat yield suggests things are going on in many markets at the same time. An example of this could be when the Federal Reserve undertook Operation Twist in 2011. Under Operation Twist, the Federal Reserve purchased $400 billion worth of 15-year and 20-year Treasury bonds, while at the same time selling $400 billion worth of short-term securities. The Fed wanted to flatten or twist the yield curve by pushing long-term yields down and pushing short-term yields up. The Federal Reserve continued Operation Twist when in June 2012 it announced a $267 billion short-term purchase and long-term bond sale.

   Look at what is happening in short-term and long-term markets: Long-term yields fell, while short-term yields increased; thus these markets are different.

As you can see, the various yield curve theories are useful but only to a point. They tell you what additional information you need to make a definitive call on what is happening. "Reading" the yield curve is only the first step in being able to analyze what signals the bond market is sending. As the old saying goes: The devil is in the details, but so is salvation. By digging into the details of what the yield curve is signaling, you realize the signals are *not* perfectly clear, but they do give you a path to follow.

SECTION REVIEW

Q1) Offer two different explanations for why an inverted yield curve might signal an economic slowdown is on the way.

Q2) Offer an explanation of how Operation Twist may have resulted in a flat yield curve.

Q3) Under which theory might a steep yield curve suggest market participants are worried that inflation will increase in the future?

a. Pure expectations theory

b. Term premium theory

c. Segmented market theory

d. Real interest theory

Conclusion

4-6

Admiral Rickover was correct: The devil is in the details, but so is salvation. The details of the bond market and interest rates can be thorny, messy issues. How does one properly measure default risk? How does one anticipate inflation rate correctly? What is the "proper" tax rate on interest? Why did the slope of yield curve change?

In attempting to answer questions such as these, however, we see that the bond market does send us some very powerful signals: Changes in the default risk premium forces us to wonder what is going on. Changes in the slope of the yield curve can send us out to seek more information to allow us to be better informed. Thus, it is from the details of interest rates and the bond market that we gain a better insight into what the future might hold. This could be our salvation from making disastrous financial and economic mistakes.

IN THE NEWS. . .

Swiss National Bank to Adopt a Negative Interest Rate

David Jolly

The New York Times

December 18, 2014

Switzerland is introducing a negative interest rate on deposits held by lenders at its central bank, moving to hold down the value of the Swiss franc amid turmoil in global currency markets and expectations that deflation is at hand.

The Swiss National Bank said in a statement from Zurich on Thursday that it would begin charging banks 0.25 percent interest on bank deposits exceeding a certain threshold, effective Jan. 22.

The bank acted as the crisis in Russia and plummeting oil prices have caused a run on emerging market currencies. Switzerland, known for its fiscal rectitude and banking secrecy, tends to attract capital inflows as money flees chaos elsewhere. But that puts pressure on the franc, threatening to make exporters less competitive and raising the risk that very low price pressures will tip the economy into outright deflation.

"Over the past few days, a number of factors have prompted increased demand for safe investments," the central bank said. "The introduction of negative interest rates makes it less attractive to hold Swiss franc investments, and thereby supports the minimum exchange rate.". . .

Analysts were skeptical that the new policy would significantly reduce demand for Swiss assets while emerging markets were in turmoil.

"It's an external factor that has precipitated them to take this action," said Derek Halpenny, the European head of global markets research at Bank of Tokyo-Mitsubishi UFJ in London. "Is a negative interest rate going to solve their problem? I don't think so.". . .

The central bank said the new policy was meant to push its key interest rate—the three-month London interbank offered rate for Swiss franc loans between banks—below zero. Doing so would tend to make short-term Swiss assets like franc-denominated money market funds and debt securities less attractive. The policy, which is not aimed at individuals, affects only financial institutions on the portion of their deposits over 10 million francs, or $10.2 million.

Thomas J. Jordan, governor of the Swiss central bank, told a news conference in Zurich on Thursday that the effect on the rates paid on individual savers' accounts by banks was beyond the central bank's responsibility, but that the move was "no different from any other interest rate cuts by a central bank."

The interest rates paid to savers in Switzerland are already extremely low, so there is little room for lenders to cut further.

When we talk about interest rates, we usually assume the interest rate is a positive number. As this story points out, however, interest rates can be negative. Why is the Swiss National Bank pursuing this "negative interest rate policy"? How can the concept of flight to quality be used to explain what the Swiss National Bank is doing? Do you think the policy will be effective? Why or why not?

Summary of Money and Its Prices

Tying Concepts Together

Now that we have a firm understanding of what money is and one of the important prices of money—interest rates—it is time to see how money affects the overall economy. To do so we must first put financial markets into their proper historical context. In Chapter 5 we examine the historical evolution of financial markets in the United States. Next, in Chapter 6 we develop and use the aggregate supply/aggregate demand framework so that we can better understand how changes in financial markets affect the overall economy. Finally, in Chapter 7 we look at one important component of financial markets: commercial banks. We review what commercial banks do and how they help to create money. This sets up the discussion in part III, where we examine the financial markets and their impact on the overall economy in terms of monetary policy.

5

Financial Markets Through Time

5-1 US Financial Markets in the Early Twentieth Century

The examination of history can be an insightful, intriguing intellectual journey through past mistakes, failures, and grand successes. It can also be a mind-numbing, boring parade of dead people, dates, facts, and figures that makes you long for childhood naps. This chapter is much more of the former and not the latter. The investigation of financial and economic history is fascinating. We also can learn so much from the past to help us understand where we are today and where we might be headed in the future.

The past is so richly filled with information and insight that there is no way we can cover all of the important issues in just one chapter. Thus many interesting events and people must be skipped. We start with the beginning of the twentieth century and the Panic of 1907. From there we look at the early days of the Federal Reserve and the worst economic and financial collapse of the century: the Great Depression of the 1930s.

Next we examine the economic and financial issues around World War II, the postwar boom, and how things came unraveled with the stagflation of the 1970s. We then see how the Reagan/Thatcher revolution changed financial markets, including the leveraged buyout craze and the rise of the junk bond market.

Along the way we get a picture of how our financial markets have evolved—sometimes in a well-thought-out way, but more often in a helter-skelter manner of responding to a crisis. We also see the power and influence individuals have on these massive financial markets. Through the mess that is economic and financial history, we get our current financial markets. To know where we are headed, you have to know where we have been. So, let us start at the beginning of the twentieth century.

5-1a The Early Twentieth Century

The first decade of the twentieth century saw many dramatic transformations in the financial markets of the United States. Part of the change in financial markets came about as the structure of American business evolved during the decade. Leading up to this period, during the second half of the nineteenth century, the US business sector was dominated by the creation and expansion of trusts. Trusts are horizontally integrated ownership structures that dominated key industries, including railroads, oil, steel, and banking. In this structure, firms that produce similar goods are combined. This is often done within the same industry and creates what we today call monopolies. Trusts, then, was the name given to agreements that created these monopolies. Leaders of these trusts include almost mythical figures: J. Pierpont Morgan, John D. Rockefeller, Andrew Carnegie. These titans of industry amassed huge fortunes under various price-fixing regimes created by the trusts.

These "robber barons" were reviled as much as they were put on a pedestal. In the early part of the twentieth century they came under increased scrutiny from progressive reformers such as journalist Ida Tarbell, author Upton Sinclair, and President Theodore Roosevelt. The first decade of the twentieth century saw American businesses being transformed as corporations moved away from the trust-dominated markets of the late nineteenth century and toward a structure featuring professional managers and stockholders.

The movement toward professional managers was fostered in great part by the spread of Frederick Taylor's idea of "scientific management," which is sometimes simply called Taylorism. Taylor argued for the use of time and motion studies of production processes to find the one best way to produce a good. An important part of Taylorism was to make managers responsible for the organization of the firm and the production process. In doing so, managers would be required to scientifically select, train, and monitor their subordinates.

As a result of Taylorism, the level of output of US manufacturing firms increased significantly, and with it the demand for the number of workers also increased. As a result of the success of Taylorism, the size of the US economy increased significantly during the decade. Increased corporate profits and the sharing of these profits with stockholders sent the stock markets to new highs.

The increasing stock prices, however, also resulted in increased speculation in stock markets. Quick fortunes were made as speculators borrowed large sums from commercial banks, trust companies, and brokerage houses to place wild financial bets on rising stocks. However, these speculators also were sowing the seeds of the worst economic event of the decade: the Panic of 1907.

5-1b The Panic of 1907

Since the founding of the country, Americans had been leery of big banks that stretched nationwide. This fear of "big banks" continued well into the twentieth century. As a result, during the National Banking Era (1863–1913) the United States did not have a central bank or much in the way of national banking laws. Almost all of the commercial banks were "local" and regulated on a state level. Much of that changed after the Panic of 1907.

In their 2007 book titled *The Panic of 1907: Lessons Learned from the Market's Perfect Storm*, Robert Bruner and Sean Carr[1] clearly explain how the Panic of 1907, like all financial crises, was not caused by one single event. Instead, the Panic of 1907, like most financial crises, was caused by the culmination of a number of bad things happening at once. The Panic of 1907 was triggered by wild speculation in the stock market; excessively loose lending by banks and trusts (a version of a commercial bank that invested the money of wealthy families, including making loans and issuing their version of checking accounts); a need to divert cash to San Francisco for rebuilding after the 1906 earthquake; and a lack of effective oversight of financial markets. What makes the story of the Panic of 1907 even more interesting is what ended it—one man: J. Pierpont Morgan.

The People, the Money, and the Crisis

By 1907, Morgan was entering retirement and had turned the operation of his vast financial empire over to his son Jack. Six years earlier, Morgan helped to create the world's first billion-dollar company, the United States Steel Corporation, by underwriting and selling its stock. By helping to create US Steel, Morgan sought to drive Andrew Carnegie out of the steel-making business. Morgan considered Carnegie—with his constant price cutting, desire for revenge on competitors, and manipulative behavior—a disruptive force in the American economy. Morgan wanted to create a massive firm that would concentrate on professional management, research and development and the latest engineering advancements in steel making. Morgan no longer wanted the future of his fortune and that of the US economy to be dependent on the behavior of a few men.

But as the Panic of 1907 unfolded, Morgan realized that something had to be done to calm the financial markets. He understood that if *he* did not do something to stop the panic, the entire US economy would be at risk.

Heinze: How People Can Trigger Financial Collapses

By 1907, thanks to now professionally run corporations across America, the stock markets—nationwide but especially in New York—were paying handsome returns to investors. For some, however, even these high returns were not enough. They wanted to make even more money, and they would do so by any means necessary. One such person was F. Augustus Heinze.

1 See Bruner, Robert F., and Sean D. Carr. *The Panic of 1907: Lessons Learned from the Market's Perfect Storm*. Hoboken, NJ: John Wiley & Sons, 2007.

In the autumn of 1907 Heinze had spent $50 million of his own money in a scheme to corner the market of United Copper Company stock. When someone tries to "corner a market," they buy up as much of an asset needed to control the price. Once the market is "cornered," whoever controls that asset can demand extremely high prices and thus attain huge profits.

In October 1907 Heinze's attempt to corner the market of United Copper Company's stock failed horribly: The price of shares of the United Copper Company fell 76%, instead of increasing as planned, in just two days. As the story of the failure of Heinze's scheme spread, panic gripped the New York financial markets. Rumors and unanswered questions abounded: How many other stock manipulation schemes were out there? Who was involved? Were commercial banks or trust companies involved in lending money to these speculators? How would these banks be repaid? Could they make good on deposits?

On October 18, when it became known that the Knickerbocker Trust—at the time the third largest bank trust in New York—was a business associate of Heinze, there was a run on Knickerbocker. That same day the National Bank of Commerce announced it would no longer act as a clearing house for Knickerbocker. Without a clearinghouse, no one would accept checks drawn on Knickerbocker. Thus the National Bank of Commerce announcement basically sounded the death knell for the Knickerbocker Trust unless someone could step in and save them. Things got so bad for Knickerbocker that on October 22 its tellers gave out $8 million to depositors in just three hours.

There were runs on other banks, even those that had no direct dealings with Heinze. To make matters even worse, many of the banks in New York were running out of gold. Much of the gold held by banks in New York City had been shipped to California and lent to banks in San Francisco in the face of the massive earthquake that hit the region on April 18, 1906.

The San Francisco earthquake had triggered massive fires that burned down much of the city, including bank buildings. While the bank vaults in San Francisco remained intact, they were too hot to open because of the massive fires. With the inability to open the vault doors, the banks were not able to access their gold to meet depositors' needs. Thus the New York banks saw an opportunity: lend their gold to the San Francisco banks and charge them a high interest rate. That would have been fine but for the panic now taking place in New York. The New York banks had lent out all of their gold, and when depositors wanted to withdraw their gold as well as their cash, the banks were in dire straits.

Old Man Morgan: How One Person Can End a Financial Collapse

Into this financial market panic stepped J. Pierpont Morgan. On Monday, October 21, Morgan assembled a committee of four trusted bankers to audit the financial records of Knickerbocker to determine whether it should be saved. It was a long and arduous task. Not only did they have to evaluate Knickerbocker's status, they had to determine what else would need to be done to save the financial system from collapse.

Library of Congress Prints and Photographs Division [LC-USZ62-94188]

J.P. Morgan

Every night of the week of October 21 the bankers met with Morgan in his library to plan how to survive the following business day. They devised plans to feed information to the press in order to calm the public's nerves.

On Tuesday, October 22, newspapers in New York reported that Morgan was considering stepping in and saving the Knickerbocker. But on Wednesday, October 23, the news came that Morgan would not aid the Knickerbocker Trust, stating a lack of capital and poor management.

Morgan also announced The Trust Company of America would be aided. Morgan's announcement was made after Treasury Secretary George Cortelyou had traveled to New York to meet with Morgan. Cortelyou promised that the US government would deposit $25 million into the New York City banks that Morgan deemed worth saving. Morgan also was able to convince John D. Rockefeller to deposit $10 million of his own money into New York City banks.

Thanks to Morgan's announcement, The Trust Company of America was able to withstand a bank run on October 24. It quickly became apparent to Morgan and his bankers, however, that the stock market was as in much trouble as the banks and trusts. There was a lack of money available as a result of all of the bank runs. Thus, on Thursday, October 25, Morgan went to the New York Clearing House and essentially ordered them to use certificates, which were a type of temporary loan, as cash. This would free up the remaining cash to meet depositors' needs and to provide new loans. While this was enough to keep the stock market afloat, the crisis was not over.

The next week, the City of New York issued bonds worth the $30 million it needed to stay solvent. European investors were proving to be reluctant to buy the city's bonds. The mayor of New York turned to Morgan for help. Morgan pledged his support in selling the city's bonds—but only if the city agreed to appoint a committee of bankers to oversee the city's accounting practices. Thanks to Morgan's intervention the City of New York was able to sell their bonds as planned.

As the crisis seemingly came to an end, Morgan understood that more needed to be done to stabilize the trust companies. Because the trust companies were not technically commercial banks, they did not have to abide by the more strict rules to which commercial banks had to adhere. Because of this, many commercial banks were unwilling to lend money to the trust companies during their hour of need. Morgan eventually took to locking the bankers in his library until they agreed to aid the trust companies. The announcement of the banks' plan to aid the trusts was enough to stabilize the financial markets, and by early November 1907, the panic had passed.

Lessons Learned

The Need for a Central Bank

As the dust cleared from the Panic of 1907, the lessons to be learned from the experience became clear. The US banking system had become so large and so important to the rest of the economy that it needed a "lender of last resort" during a time of crisis. In addition, to avoid financial crises, the United States needed a single currency used nationwide instead of thousands of different bank notes. Simply put, the United States needed a central bank.

SECTION REVIEW

Q1) What role did Taylorism, or "scientific management," play in the expansion of financial markets in the United States?

Q2) F. Augustus Heinze tried to corner the market for shares of United Copper. What does this mean? How did it help to trigger the Panic of 1907?

Q3) The Panic of 1907 was primarily ended thanks to the actions of:

a. the Federal Reserve.
b. President Teddy Roosevelt.
c. J. Pierpont Morgan.
d. Salmon P. Chase.

5-2 Federal Reserve in the Early Days

While the lessons to be learned from the Panic of 1907 may have been easy to discern, actually undertaking the necessary changes turned out to be much more difficult. The idea of a central bank brought up old fears of a big, powerful, government-controlled, taxpayer-subsidized entity that would rule over the entire economy. To allay these fears, Congress proceeded very slowly in undertaking financial market reform and eventually passed the Federal Reserve Act of 1913.

5-2a Early Structure of the Federal Reserve

In creating the Federal Reserve, Congress wanted something that would serve as a "lender of last resort" to the banking system, but because this entity would be there for the benefit of banks, Congress did *not* want US taxpayers to pay for it. Thus, in creating the Federal Reserve, Congress created a quasi-government agency—something created by the federal government but not really part of the government. Instead of using taxpayer money to fund the Federal Reserve, Congress required that commercial banks buy the shares of the new central bank to give the Federal Reserve the capital it needed to begin operations.

The creation of the structure of the Federal Reserve was also a compromise. Many in the northeastern financial markets wanted a central bank based on the model of European central banks, which were designed to ensure adherence to the gold standard. Those in the south and Midwest, on the other hand, wanted a central bank that would alter the level of liquidity based on the needs of the local economy. As a compromise, President Wilson agreed to a system of 12 regional banks under the control of local bankers and a Federal Reserve Board in Washington, DC, that would be responsible for the system as a whole.

In the early days of the Federal Reserve, the compromise did not work very well. There was no clear division of power, and as a result the district banks often set their own interest rates and lending policies, with little concern of how they would impact the overall economy.

What a mess. Instead of drawing a definitive line in the sand and taking a clear stand on the structure of the Federal Reserve, Wilson, by trying to appease everyone, essentially created an inoperable system. Into this mess stepped Benjamin Strong, Jr.

Strong was a well-respected banker; he had worked his way up to become president of Bankers Trust Company. He was one of the few trusted bankers Morgan had called on to audit the financial records of banks during the Panic of 1907. In 1914 Strong had been appointed the first president of the Federal Reserve Bank of New York.

Of the 12 Federal Reserve banks, the New York Federal Reserve quickly established itself as the most important. When the Open Market Investment Committee was created in 1923 to centralize the making of monetary policy, it was Strong who quickly stepped forward to take control.

Strong envisioned a central bank along the lines of the Bank of England, with the American central bank headquartered in the center of the nation's financial market: New York. Strong's powerful leadership style led to directing the Federal Reserve's operations from his post in New York.

Many scholars (including Milton Friedman and Anna Schwartz), however, argue that Strong's death in October 1928 led to a return of conflict and power struggles within the Federal Reserve. Strong's successor at the New York Federal Reserve, George Harrison (not the late former member of the Beatles), was a weak leader and did not have nearly the intellectual capability of Strong. Harrison's weak leadership proved to be a huge problem for the Federal Reserve because of the events that would unfold only a year after Benjamin Strong's death.

5-2b Financial Markets During the Great Depression

The summer of 1929 was a prosperous time for many Americans. As the country prepared to celebrate the fiftieth anniversary of Edison's invention of the light bulb, new products seemed to be popping up everywhere. A new soft drink, 7-Up, was invented by Charles Leiper Grigg; the first car radio was made by Motorola; and the stock market hit an all-time high on September 3.

It seemed everyone wanted in on the rising stock market. In August the *Ladies Home Journal* ran an article by John Jakob Raskob entitled "Everybody Ought to be Rich," extolling the virtues of investing savings in the stock market. The American public seemed to take Raskob's advice to heart, and plumbers, grocers, and barbers all seemed to be benefiting from the increase in stock prices.

The Growing Financial Storm

But financial storm clouds were growing on the horizon. Roger Babson, publisher of a well-respected newsletter, warned in a speech on September 5 that "Sooner or later a crash is coming, and it may be terrific."[2] Babson's warnings proved to be fortuitous. As news of Babson's speech made its way to the trading floor, stock prices fell by 5% that same afternoon.

But people and the market clung to optimism. While stock prices weaved up and down for the rest of the month, Charles E. Mitchell, chairman of the National City Bank of New York,[3] stated on October 15 that "markets generally are now in a healthy condition." Oh, how wrong he was.

As stock prices drifted downward, a growing number of stock speculators were receiving margin calls. That is, those who had bought stocks on credit and whose market price was falling would now have to provide more cash or else face the loss of the stocks they held. Many of the speculators, however, did not have the cash necessary to meet these margin calls and thus were forced to sell their shares. As a result of this increased selling, stock prices fell lower and more speculators received margin calls.

By the end of trading on Wednesday, October 23, the markets were selling in a near panic. Things got worse the next day; panic selling had set in. A few minutes after high noon, Mitchell was seen heading into the offices of J.P. Morgan & Company, which was across the street from the New York Stock Exchange. Pierpont Morgan had come to the rescue of the stock market and ended the Panic of 1907, but the old man was now long dead. Morgan's son Jack was in Europe, so it was the firm's senior partner, Thomas Lamont, who had called Mitchell and the heads of four other leading New York banks to Morgan headquarters.

The Failed Rescue Attempt: This Isn't 1907

Lamont, Mitchell, and the other bankers had created a pool of funds that would be used to attempt to stabilize the market. At 1:30 p.m., Richard Whitney, the acting president of the stock exchange, walked across the trading floor and yelled out an order to buy 10,000 shares of US Steel at a price well above current market prices. His gimmick worked. Prices shot back up and at the end of the day the market was very close to where it had opened that morning.

While share prices remained stable that Friday and Saturday (in those days the stock market was open from 10 a.m. to noon on Saturdays, and this practice lasted until 1952), the worst was still ahead. On Monday, October 28, stock prices fell significantly. The next day, Tuesday, October 29, 1929, things got so bad that many stocks found absolutely zero buyers. White Sewing Machine Company, whose stock had sold for $48 a share a few months earlier, had seen its price fall to only $11 on Monday. But on Black Tuesday it fell to only $1 per share because a stock market messenger boy made that offer and there were no others!

---

2 Galbraith, John Kenneth. *The Great Crash 1929*. Boston: Houghton Mifflin, 1955.

3 See *Time Magazine* online for details (http://www.time.com/time/magazine/article/0,9171,965876,00.html#ixzz0Y0x2avYv).

The sell-off continued day after day. By November 13, the market had reached its low point. In September the stock market had a total value of $80 billion, but by mid-November, $30 billion of the value had been destroyed. With it were the life savings of many of those plumbers, grocers, and barbers who thought the stock market was the quick route to lasting riches. Instead, the stock market crash left many of them penniless and unemployed.

Lender of Last Resort?

Where was the Federal Reserve in all of this? Wasn't it established in 1913 in response to the Panic of 1907 to avoid just such a financial and economic meltdown? Where was the Federal Reserve as the economy slid into the economic abyss that was the Great Depression?

Allan Meltzer, in his 2003 historical analysis of the Federal Reserve,[4] argued that the Federal Reserve followed the wrong policy doctrine at the time and thus contributed to the Great Depression. Meltzer argues that the Federal Reserve followed a policy doctrine based on the real bills doctrine, which Meltzer labeled the Burgess-Riefler doctrine.

A Misapplied Doctrine

Under the Burgess-Riefler doctrine, commercial banks could borrow from the Federal Reserve only in times of need and not to earn a profit by re-lending the funds. Also under the doctrine the Federal Reserve could induce banks to borrow and repay loans by other means. Most important, according to the doctrine, the level of bank borrowing in New York and Chicago and the level of short-term nominal interest rates would indicate whether there was a shortage or an abundance of liquidity in the market. In this framework a low level of bank borrowing and low nominal interest rates were considered evidence of easy monetary policy.

But this framework led to major policy mistakes as the stock market crashed in 1929 and the US economy nosedived into the Great Depression. As uncertainty spread throughout the economy, overall spending decreased and individual firms saw their sales plummet. To stop the financial bleeding, firms slashed prices in an attempt to generate any sales they could. But all of this price slashing combined to trigger deflation as the overall price fell and continued to fall.

With growing uncertainty, falling prices, and decreasing sales volume, firms were in no mood to go to banks to borrow money in order to buy inventory or inputs! Just the opposite: As sales volumes fell, firms became more adverse to risk; they tried to cut costs by firing more workers and cutting prices even more. The economy was in a depressive death spiral.

Because firms were not borrowing money from commercial banks, the banks had very few loans that they could bring to the Federal Reserve to use as collateral for discount window loans. Thus the level of bank lending at the Federal Reserve decreased as the economy slid further into the Depression. What was really needed was an expansionary monetary policy to get the economy moving again.

According to the Burgess-Riefler doctrine, however, everything was fine. Remember, under this doctrine, which the Federal Reserve was following at the time, a low level of bank borrowing at the Federal Reserve signaled that there was an *abundant* level of liquidity in the system and, if anything, the Federal Reserve should tighten monetary policy. Furthering the "everything is fine" argument was the fact that nominal interest rates were low, so accordingly there was no need for an expansionary monetary policy.

But things were not fine: Bank borrowing at the Federal Reserve had declined because the economy was in a nosedive, and there was little to no bank lending going on because the demand for loans had fallen to about zero. In addition, nominal interest rates were low because there was deflation, not because everything was fine.

4 Meltzer, Allan H. *A History of the Federal Reserve. Volume 1: 1913–1951*. Chicago: University of Chicago Press, 2003.

Lesson Learned

It's the Real Interest Rates That Matter

Irving Fisher explained in the early twentieth century that nominal interest rates (IRs) are made up of real interest rates plus inflation. For example, with a positive inflation rate we might have

Nominal IR = Real IR + Inflation rate
3% + 2% = 5%

But now imagine the inflation rate becomes −2% as the economy suffers from deflation, as it did during the Depression.

Nominal IR = Real IR + Inflation rate
3% − 2% = 1%

Look at what happens! Nominal IRs fall, but this is not a sign of good times; it occurs because the economy is suffering from deflation. Because the Federal Reserve was following the Burgess-Riefler doctrine, they viewed the lack of bank borrowing and low nominal IRs as a sign of sufficient liquidity in the financial system and refused to purse an expansionary monetary policy.

So the question is, Why and how could the Federal Reserve have made such a tragic mistake in judgment?

Economists still disagree. Some, like Milton Friedman and Anna Schwartz, argue that if Benjamin Strong had still been alive and running the Federal Reserve during the 1929–1933 time period, the Federal Reserve never would have made such a serious intellectual gaff.

On the other hand, Allan Meltzer argues that the Burgess-Riefler doctrine was the policy the Federal Reserve followed when Strong was leading it in the 1920s and thus, arguably, it would have followed the same policies if Strong were still alive.

One wonders who is right. If Strong had lived and realized the shortcomings of the Burgess-Riefler doctrine, could the Great Depression of the 1930s have been avoided? We will never know.

Tying Concepts Together

From our discussion of the loanable funds model in Chapter 3, we know that a decrease in consumer confidence leads to a decrease in the demand for loanable funds; that is, as consumers become more worried about their future, they are less likely to go out and borrow money. The same is true for businesses. When business confidence falls, firms are less likely to borrow money for capital expenditures or to fund new projects. Thus, as business confidence falls there is a decrease in the demand for loanable funds.

A combination of a decrease in both consumer and business confidence would lead to a significant decrease in the demand for loanable funds. A large drop in the demand for loanable funds results in a lower equilibrium interest rate, ceteris paribus. This is exactly what was happening in the early days of the Great Depression. Therefore, market or nominal interest rates were falling.

SECTION REVIEW

Q1) Low interest rates may, or may not, signal that a central bank is pursuing an "expansionary" policy. Explain.

Q2) In 1907 J. Pierpont Morgan was able to help end a financial crisis in great part by restoring confidence. Why weren't a different set of banker's actions enough to stop the financial crisis in October 1929?

Q3) When an economy is suffering from deflation, the nominal or market interest rates tend to:

a. Increase

b. Decrease

c. Become negative

d. Equal zero

5-3 Financial Markets During World War II

December 7, 1941, was a date that would "live in infamy," as President Franklin Roosevelt put it. It was on this day the Japanese attacked Pearl Harbor. The next day Roosevelt asked the US Congress for a declaration of war on Japan. Three days later, Japan's allies, Germany and Italy, declared war on the United States—and thus Americans were plunged head first into World War II.

5-3a Preparing for War

While the Japanese attack on the Pearl Harbor came as a surprise, the United States had been readying itself for the war for some time. In December 1940, union organizer and future United Automobile Workers president Walter Reuther presented a plan to convert the underutilized automobile industry to produce 500 airplanes a day for the US military. Reuther's plan was to use the unused production capacity of the US auto industry to help supply the US military while preparing to join the wars in Europe and the Pacific.

In March 1941 Congress passed and President Roosevelt signed the Lend-Lease Act, which allowed the administration to provide military and economic assistance to any country the president viewed as "vital to the defense of the United States." As a result of the lend-lease programs, US exports skyrocketed. In August 1939 the United States exported $250 million worth of goods and services, but by August 1941—thanks to the Lend-Lease program—exports hit $460 million. Most of these increased exports went to Britain, France, and later to Russia.

The Allies needed America's economic and military assistance. At the start of the war in 1939, the United States, Britain, and Canada could produce only one-fourth of the military output of Germany, Italy, and Japan. Without help from the United States the Allies would be massively outgunned by the Axis powers.

For the United States to be of help to the Allies, however, it needed to significantly ramp up its military output. To do this, the federal government had to take control of the means of production and convert them for the war effort. This meant that the government had to take control both of the labor market, which it did through the military draft as well as wage and price controls, and of the capital markets to finance the war effort.

5-3b Funding the War Effort

To figure out how to finance the war effort, economists turned to John Maynard Keynes. A few years earlier in 1940, Keynes had written a short piece entitled "How to Pay for the War." In it Keynes argued that to pay for the war the government should run budget deficits funded by borrowing from the public and the financial system. To keep inflation in check, however, he argued for the rationing of necessities. Finally, to prevent increased inequality that would come about from firms benefiting from war production, Keynes argued for high progressive income taxes.

The US government followed Keynes's playbook. From 1940 to 1946 federal government spending increased sixfold, with 75% of it being for military expenditures. This represented a massive increase in government spending. Of this increase in government spending, 40% was paid through higher taxes. Even with the increase in tax rates, the level of government debt increased from $48.2 billion in 1940 to $271 billion by June 1946. To sell this much debt, the federal government had to sell a lot—a whole lot—of government bonds.

Starting in December 1942 the federal government organized several "bond drives," culminating in the Victory Drive at the end of 1945. These war bond drives often made use of Hollywood and radio stars traveling across the country and encouraging Americans to be patriotic and "buy bonds."

5-3c Controlling Inflation During the War

Not only were the **war bonds** used to fund the government's purchases, they also were key in keeping down inflation. As consumer goods became scarce because they were being diverted for the war effort, there were fears that prices would increase dramatically.

War bond: Debt issued by the federal government to fund the spending on wars. Done in the United States most recently during World War I and World War II.

Potentially compounding the inflation problem was the massive increase in employment needed for the war effort. The military draft was used to increase the size of the Armed Forces, while every able-bodied man (and an increasing number of women) were needed in the factories to produce military equipment. With all of this increased employment and earning power, there were fears that household spending would increase but because there was a limited amount of consumer goods to buy, prices would shoot out of control.

For example, during World War I, the cost of living in the United States shot up 62% because of precisely these reasons. Selling war bonds to American households could be a partial solution. If households bought war bonds instead of spending their income on goods and services, the overall level of consumption would be held down.

Another important tool in restricting consumption, and thus inflation, was **government rationing**. During the war, if you wanted to buy gasoline, or meat, or butter, or sugar, you could not—even if you had the money to pay for it—because these goods were rationed. So in addition to needing the money to buy these goods, you also needed a ration coupon issued by the government. If you didn't have the ration coupon, you couldn't buy the good. Thus, the rationing system helped to retard household spending and thus help control inflation.

Government rationing: Limitations, implemented by a government, on the amount of goods a person can purchase; in the past put in place because of wartime shortages of many goods.

Another policy used to control inflation were the **wage and price controls** put in place by the Office of Price Administration. At first the government tried to control the prices of only a few products. But as Hugh Rockoff has shown, it becomes almost impossible for governments to control only a few prices; instead they generally have to control all prices. And so it was with the United States during World War II; by 1943, President Roosevelt gave his "hold the line" order, which essentially froze all prices in the US economy.

Wage and price controls: Also called incomes policy, an economic policy where governments place legal limits on the amount of wage and price increases.

Tying Concepts Together

A simple supply-and-demand analysis can demonstrate why there was a need for rationing and wage and price controls during World War II. Assume that the market for bread is initially at equilibrium, even though workers are unemployed. Now assume the demand for bread increases because the unemployed workers now find work thanks to the increased demand for labor for the war effort.

Any increase in demand is going to lead to a higher equilibrium price, ceteris paribus. In addition to the increase in demand, there was a decrease in the supply of bread because much of the bread that was being produced was being used by the military to feed soldiers and sailors. Thus, in our market for bread during the war, there would be an increase in demand and a decrease in supply—a sure recipe for higher prices!

Thus to keep prices from rising, rationing was used to decrease demand: You could not buy bread unless you had a ration coupon. To keep future prices from rising, wage and price controls were used to keep the market price for bread as close to the original equilibrium price as possible.

The combination of selling war bonds, rationing, controlling wages/prices seemed to do the trick. Between 1940 and 1945 the cost of living for American households increased only 20%—despite the fact that in the same time period M1 more than doubled! Unlike World War I, during which the funding of the war triggered significant increases in inflation, World War II did not result in rapid increases in the rates of inflation.

Lessons Learned

Government Deficits and Inflation

Policymakers during World War II basically realized that to finance a large increase in government spending, the government can do three things: (1) raise taxes, (2) borrow money from the public by issuing bonds, or (3) print money to spend.

During the Civil War we did number 3, and it was a disaster. Issuing greenbacks to fund the Civil War led to a financial collapse as the money supply skyrocketed. Learning from that mistake in financing World War I, we did a combination of options 1 and 2. The government raised taxes and issued Liberty Bonds. Liberty Bonds were basically 30-year, tax-free bonds that appealed to people's patriotism.

But because a large amount of the bonds were financed by an expansionary monetary policy, the result was rapid inflation. The annual inflation rates were around 17% during World War I, then around 15% until a severe recession hit in 1921.

Keynes's suggestions were adopted and worked fairly well, although wage and price controls had to be expanded to almost everything. There were seven successful war bond drives during World War II; goods were rationed, consumer spending was held down, unemployment all but disappeared, and the military won the wars in Europe and in the Pacific. All of this was accomplished with almost no inflation. A job well done.

While the World War II years were a success in terms of money and the financial system, there still existed the dark shadow of the Great Depression. Was World War II only a temporary interruption of the Great Depression? After the hostilities ended, would financial markets return to their prewar fear and angst? These were the fears policymakers and financial market participants faced as they exited World War II and began the postwar era. The fears, it turns out, were unnecessary. Instead of a return to the Great Depression, the postwar period ushered in a great economic boom.

SECTION REVIEW

Q1) There are three ways to finance a war. What are they? How were they used in the past?

Q2) During World War II there was relatively little inflation in the United States. Why was this the case?

Q3) Rationing was used in the United States during World War II in part to:

a. keep interest rates low.

b. keep unemployment rate low.

c. keep inflation rate low.

d. keep the government budget deficit low.

5-4 Postwar Boom: Home Mortgages, Consumerism, and European Unification

As World War II came to end, so too came an end to wage and price controls, rationing, and the sacrifices Americans had to make during the war. Perhaps the greatest change was the return to civilian life by the 16 million men and women who served in the Armed Forces during World War II.

5-4a Financial Markets Help Fund the "American Dream"

Many GIs were returning home from overseas and wanted to settle into the American Dream of a good-paying job and a house with a white picket fence. To make this dream come true, the US financial markets greatly expanded their lending to families to buy homes. In 1940 only about 43% of Americans owned their own homes. By 1960 that figure was close to 62%. That was made possible, in great part, by the expansion of the US home mortgage market.

At the forefront of the expanding home mortgage market were the depository institutions known as the **Savings & Loans**. The Savings & Loan industry started in the eighteenth and nineteenth centuries as Building & Loan Associations—nonprofits that would lend funds to members, mostly working-class urban dwellers, to buy homes. The mortgages offered up by the Building & Loans would usually require a 50% down payment with amortized payback over the next 10 to 12 years. This was a much better deal than was offered by commercial banks of the time, but until the mid-twentieth century Building & Loans remained relatively small.

Savings & Loan: A depository institution that focuses on taking deposits of households and individuals. Most loans are consumer loans including home mortgages.

All that changed after World War II. The seeds for changing the mortgage market had been sown during the Roosevelt Administration in the 1930s. The Federal Housing Administration (FHA) was created in 1934 to insure mortgage lenders against losses that might arise from defaults. With default risk limited, Savings & Loans were more willing to lend money on mortgages. The FHA also developed the 30-year, fixed-rate mortgage loan program that allowed borrowers much lower monthly payments.

Library of Congress Prints and Photographs Division [LC-G613-T-68560-05-x]

Busy savings & loan lobby, circa 1954.

Federal Government Assists in Home Buying

The Roosevelt Administration also created Fannie Mae (formally the Federal National Mortgage Association), which would buy FHA-insured mortgages from Savings & Loans and other mortgage originators. Fannie Mae would then pool these mortgages together and sell them to institutional investors. The advent and expansion of the FHA and Fannie Mae greatly standardized mortgage lending practices. Now households could buy a house with a 20% down payment in cash and pay back the remaining 80% over 30 years at a fixed interest rate.

In 1944 the Veterans Administration (VA) was given the power to guarantee mortgage loans, just like the FHA. The difference, naturally, is that VA-guaranteed loans were mortgage loans made to veterans of the Armed Forces. The VA guarantee loan program greatly increased the demand for mortgages, especially after World War II.

In addition to all of these new homes being built, families needed to furnish them. Again, the Savings & Loans were there to provide consumers with credit for durable goods purchases, which included not just things for the home but also other consumer products such as automobiles and lawn mowers. Americans had saved their incomes during World War II and now in the booming postwar economy could use this savings and expanded access of credit to satisfy their "pent-up demand."

All of this increase in consumer spending led to the economic expansion, or economic boom, in the postwar period. As consumers spent, US firms were willing and able to produce to meet this increased desire to spend. Further encouraging US firms to produce were very low market interest rates.

Federal Reserve Helps Keep Postwar Economy Booming

To keep the economy expanding and to keep borrowing costs for the government low, the Federal Reserve used tools of monetary policy to keep market interest rates low. Until 1951 monetary policy was actually determined by the Treasury Department and carried out by the Federal Reserve. The Treasury used the Federal Reserve to keep market interest rates low, and as a result, private borrowing and spending continued at very high levels.

The combination of consumer savings during the war, along with increased access to household credit and borrowing (thanks to the Savings & Loans), coupled with low interest rates resulted in a powerful surge in consumer spending. This increased consumer spending more than made up for the decrease in government spending at the end of World War II. The result was a rapidly growing US economy in the aftermath of the war. This postwar economic boom resulted in significant increases in the standard of living of most Americans.

5-4b Push for European Economic and Financial Integration

While the US economy boomed after World War II, our European allies were hoping much the same would happen to them. Unfortunately, it took much longer for the European economies to recover after the war. Some in Europe wondered whether western Europe should try to create an economic setup similar to that of the United States.

While the United States was experiencing a postwar boom, the leaders of western Europe desired to create a "United States of Europe." There were several reasons why a "united Europe" seemed like a very good idea. First, there was the Cold War. Europe was divided roughly in half: Western Europe included democracies with more or less market-based economies, whereas Eastern Europe was under the Soviet sphere of influence, with its centrally planned economy. Naturally, the western European countries wanted to be united, both politically and economically, in the face of Soviet power in the east.

Second, mistakes were made at the end of World War I. The Treaty of Versailles that ended World War I placed huge war reparations on Germany and the losing side of World War I. As a result of these economic punishments, Germany suffered from very high rates of inflation during the 1920s. These high rates of inflation helped contribute to the economic instability that then led to the rise of the Third Reich and Adolf Hitler. So, not wanting to make the same mistakes again, instead of punishing West Germany and Italy for World War II, the other Western nations realized they should rebuild them and trade with them. Thus, both West Germany and Italy were welcomed into the new United Europe.

To make western Europe more economically united, trade barriers between the member nations were lifted. In addition, capital was allowed to flow relatively unencumbered between the western European countries. As a result of this freer and more open trade, the western European economies and financial systems prospered in the years following World War II.

Lessons Learned

Financial Markets' Effect on the Overall Economy

In the period after World War II, financial markets had a significant impact on the overall economy. If financial markets effectively turned saving into borrowing, then aggregate spending may increase and the economy could boom. But this was possible only if borrowing costs and uncertainty remained low.

But the good times would not go on forever. The desire to keep interest rates low and spending high eventually started to cause problems for the United States and its European allies. That is where we turn our attention next.

SECTION REVIEW

Q1) What roles did the US federal government and the Federal Reserve play in helping to expand the home mortgage market after World War II?

Q2) Why was there a push to economically and financially integrate western Europe after World War II?

Q3) Savings & Loan Associations were established to lend money to households so that the households could:

a. purchase houses.

b. fund their children's education.

c. afford to retire comfortably.

d. purchase automobiles.

Effects of Stagflation and the Reagan/Thatcher Revolution on Financial Markets

5-5

The United States economy continued to hum along through the 1950s and most of the 1960s. There were some economic slowdowns, but for the most part the economy continued to expand, with only moderate rates of inflation.

5-5a The Rise of Stagflation

By the late 1960s, however, a new problem started to emerge: growing unemployment, along with increasing rates of inflation. The economy was stagnating and at the same time suffering from inflation. A new term entered the American lexicon: **stagflation**.

Stagflation: A time when the economy suffers from high rates of inflation and economic stagnation, often a high and/or increasing unemployment rate.

Stagflation perplexed most economists of the time; they thought that inflation most often came about because of increasing labor costs due to falling unemployment rates. The logic was that as the economy expanded, increased competition for workers led to higher wages. These higher labor costs then were passed on to consumers in the form of higher market prices. Thus, inflation resulted because of falling unemployment rates.

But with stagflation the economy was experiencing growing inflation *and* growing unemployment at the same time (Figure 5-1). This simply was not supposed to happen.

At first, many economists thought this was a temporary problem. The unemployment rate started to increase in late 1969. The civilian unemployment rate had increased by 3.4% in August 1969, but it increased to 3.7% by October of that year. By June 1970 the unemployment rate had shot up to 4.9%, and by December 1970 it was at 6.0%. Even as the economy moved out of recession in 1971, the unemployment rate did not decline to its 1969 levels. The unemployment rate remained high as the economy expanded—this did not seem to be a temporary problem. At the same time the inflation rate picked up in 1966 and continued to increase in 1967, 1968, and 1969. It was clear that stagflation was not going away.

From Bad to Worse: The Oil Supply Shock

Things got worse with the oil supply shock after the Arab-Israeli Yom Kippur War in 1973. The United States had supported Israel in the war, and the oil-exporting Arab nations did not like this one bit. To punish the United States for assisting Israel, the Organization of Petroleum Exporting Nations (OPEC) banned together and decided to cut off oil exports to the United States, which was very dependent on this imported oil—this "oil embargo" was like a punch in the stomach to the US economy. Oil—and its most important by-product, gasoline—was suddenly in short supply. Waiting in long lines to buy gasoline was not uncommon during those days.

OPEC knew that they had a powerful economic weapon, and they used it to their advantage. They announced they would increase oil exports, but only after rapid, massive increases in the price of oil. Americans had no choice: The price they paid for gasoline would quadruple by 1974!

In terms of money and the financial system, the oil supply shock took a bad situation and made it much worse. The US stock market, which was already in a free fall in January 1973 because of growing inflationary pressures, continued its rapid downward descent. Between January 11, 1973, and December 6, 1974, the New York Stock Exchange's Dow Jones Industrial Index lost over 45% of its value.

Figure 5-1 **Stagflation Occurring as a Result of Increased Unemployment and Increased Inflation**

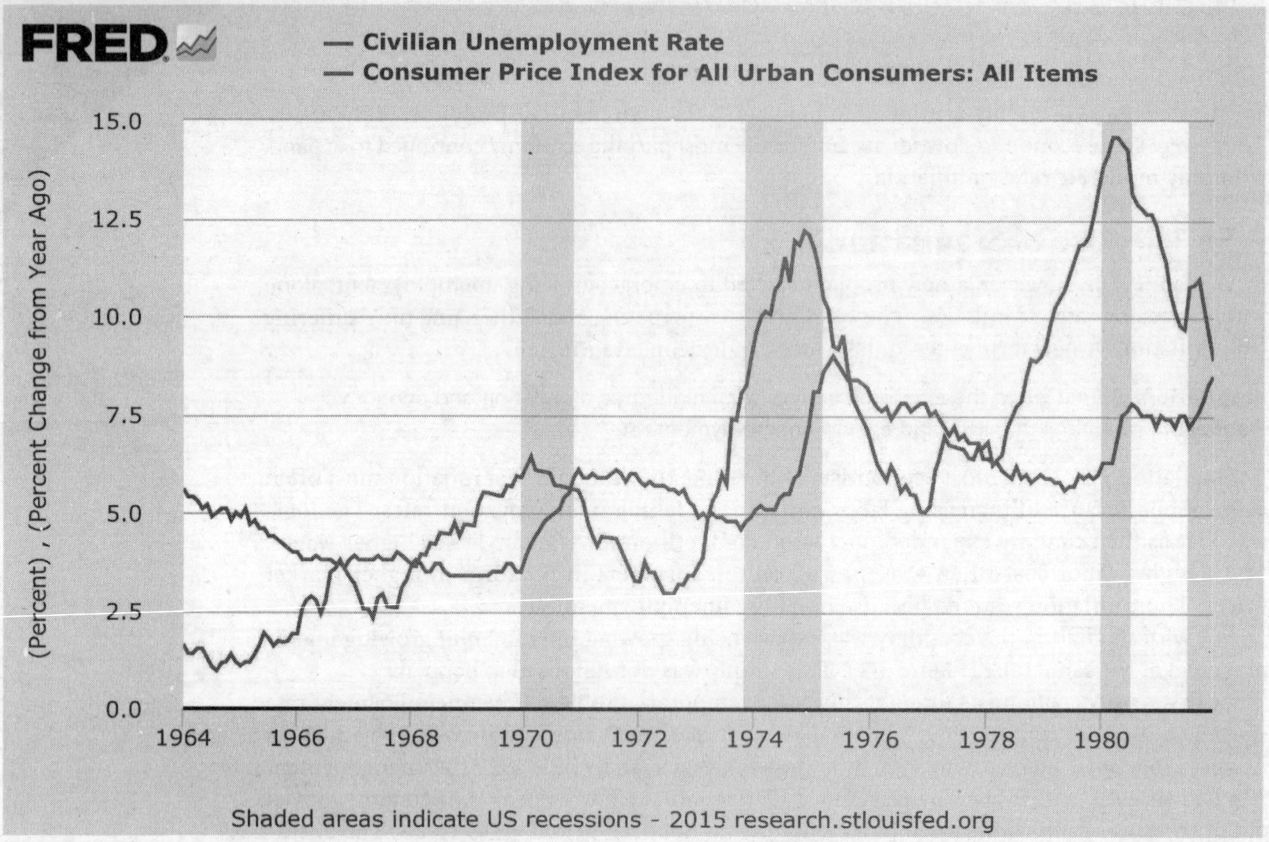

Source: Copyright 2014 by the Federal Reserve Bank of St. Louis.

Throughout the rest of the 1970s, things didn't get much better. The cost of living continued to increase, as did growing concerns over rising unemployment. The economy slipped again into a recession in 1974 and 1975. Even the US bicentennial celebration in 1976 could not end the economic gloom brought on by stagflation.

5-5b Paul Volcker

In 1979 President Jimmy Carter announced the appointment of new Federal Reserve Chairman: the 6'7"-tall, cigar-chewing Paul Volcker. Volcker had been serving as president of the Federal Reserve Bank of New York and had a long history of public service. But taming the stagflation giant that had the US economy in its grip would turn out to be his biggest challenge.

Volcker was ready for the fight. He immediately determined that to control inflation the Federal Reserve should no longer worry about keeping interest rates low; instead, it should concentrate on growth rate of the money supply. Volcker contended that the only way to wrestle inflation under control was to reduce the growth rate of the money supply. By reducing the growth rate of the money supply, however, US interest rates, which were already very high, would increase to even higher levels.

Tough Monetary Medicine to Fight Inflation

EdStock/iStockphoto.com

Paul Volcker

Higher market interest rates would be a disaster for the economy in the short run. Thus the Federal Reserve was reluctant to raise interest rates significantly to combat inflation. When Volcker took over as the Federal Reserve chair on August 6, 1979, the Federal Reserve followed a confusing monetary policy that was a combination of targeting the money supply and interest rates. In his first Federal Open Market Committee (FOMC) meeting as Federal Reserve chair on August 14, 1979, the committee voted 4–3 on a split decision to raise interest rates slightly. The press and the financial markets took the split vote as a sign the Federal Reserve was going to be timid in its approach to fighting inflation.

When Volcker returned from an International Monetary Fund meeting in early October 1979, he decided the Federal Reserve needed to take a strong stand against inflation. Volcker called a secret meeting of the FOMC on October 6, at which he proposed a switch in monetary policy to focus more completely on control of the money supply and let interest rates go where they may.

In association with the great focus on the money supply, the FOMC voted to widen the range of the federal funds rate. The range went from 11.25% to 11.75% to a range of 11.5% to 15.5%, which represented a huge increase. As a result, the federal funds rate shot up and ended the year close to 14%. By April 1980, the federal funds rate was at an astonishing 17.6%. As the interest rates in the United States increased, so did the unemployment rate: It peaked in August 1980 at 7.8% as the economy slid into a recession.

Why the recession was happening was clear: Volcker. As the economy continued to weaken, Volcker came under growing pressure to change course. There were public protests against him and the Federal Reserve. The bricklayers union sent truckloads of bricks and dumped them on the steps of the Federal Reserve, protesting the high interest rates that were killing the homebuilding industry. Farmers were so upset by the high costs of capital that they used their tractors to block the front entrance of the Federal Reserve building.

Through it all, Volcker was unfazed. He knew that his policies would be painful in the short run, but in the long run they would be worth it. Carter's loss in the presidential election in 1980 was one of the "costs" of Volcker's policies. Jimmy Carter learned that it is difficult for a political party to maintain the presidency if the economy is not doing well in an election year. Thanks in great part to Volcker's tight monetary policy to control inflation, the economy was not doing well in 1980.

5-5c Reagan and Thatcher

Ronald Reagan's victory over Jimmy Carter represented a major change in economic policy. A year earlier, in 1979, Margaret Thatcher had been elected prime minister in the United Kingdom. Reagan's and Thatcher's elections represented a movement toward a more deregulated economy, especially in financial markets, with lower taxes and lower inflation.

The economic policies of Reagan and Thatcher did not focus on short-term fluctuations in the economy; instead, they focused on longer-term issues: growing the economy, controlling inflation, and creating economic opportunities. Reagan's overall approach to economic policy meshed well with Volcker's anti-inflationary, contractionary monetary policy.

Thus, after Reagan took office in 1981, Volcker and the Federal Reserve continued to tighten monetary policy even though it would mean a long, deep recession. The recession of 1981–82 was the worst economic slowdown since the Great Depression. The unemployment rate was 10.8% in December 1982 as the economy hemorrhaged under the grip of tight monetary policy. But it was needed to wring inflation out of the economy.

Once the economy started to demonstrate that inflation had finally been brought under control, Volcker and the Federal Reserve started to ease their monetary grip on the economy. As interest rates were allowed to fall, the economy started to grow and expand without inflation. Volcker had done it: He had slayed the inflation dragon.

Reagan reappointed Volcker to another four-year term as Federal Reserve Chair in 1983. That Reagan, a republican, would keep a democrat like Volcker in such an important position as chairman of the Federal Reserve was unprecedented. But it seemed Reagan was more interested in what worked as opposed to political party affiliation.

Lessons Learned

Money Matters

Economists learned from this time period that money did matter. It wasn't just spending that was the key to economic success; the amount and growth rate of money also matter. Economists realized that an excessively expansionary monetary policy can trigger inflation, whereas an excessively contractionary monetary policy, with its increasing interest rates, can not only slow an economy but also trigger a deep recession. This time period taught economists that monetary policy is, in fact, a very powerful tool.

SECTION REVIEW

Q1) Explain why economists in the 1960s were so perplexed about why stagflation had occurred.

Q2) In the twenty-first century Paul Volcker is greatly respected, yet during the early 1980s he was one of the most disliked people in America. Why was Paul Volcker so disliked in the early 1980s? Why do you think so many people changed their opinion of him?

Q3) Which of the following explain why Ronald Reagan and Paul Volcker agreed on economic policy?

a. They were both from the same political party.

b. They both wanted to focus on long-term outcomes, not short-term issues.

c. They both believed that low interest rates would stimulate the economy.

d. They both believed that inflation was a good thing.

Savings & Loans and Junk Bonds

5-6

While the Reagan Administration's policies in the early 1980s successfully controlled inflation, some outcomes were less than perfect. One outcome of the push to reduce the amount of regulation, especially in financial markets, was the Savings & Loan crisis.

Savings & Loans played a key role in the housing boom of the post–World War II era. They took in deposits, mostly from households; paid a maximum of 5.5% APR on these deposits; and lent the funds through 30-year, fixed-rate mortgages at about 8%. Thus they had a nice 250-basis point (2.5 percentage points) interest rate spread. With this positive interest rate spread, they covered their costs, paid salaries, and usually earned a profit. Life was good.

5-6a The Savings & Loan Crisis

Then it all changed. As market interest rates increased with the rise in inflation, the Savings & Loans started to lose deposits to money market mutual funds, which could pay higher rates of interest. The interest rates the Savings & Loans could pay were capped by a law called **Regulation Q** that dated back to the 1930s. Because the Savings & Loans were losing deposits during the late 1970s, they turned to Congress for help. In 1980 Congress passed the **DIDMCA** (Depository Institution Deregulation and Monetary Control Act), which allowed the Savings & Loans to pay a market interest rate on deposits.

Regulation Q: The interest rate on bank deposit accounts ceiling in effect from 1933 to 2011.

DIDMCA: The Depository Institutions Deregulation Monetary Control Act of 1980. The act sought to increase the amount of competition in financial markets while also granting the Federal Reserve additional regulatory oversight.

The Savings & Loans could now pay competitive interest rates on deposit accounts and therefore could compete with other savings alternatives. Problem solved, right? Well, no. This only created a bigger mess. Remember, the Savings & Loans were earning interest at a rate of 8% on all of those 30-year, fixed-rate mortgages they had written over the years. That was fine when, under Regulation Q, they had to only pay 5.5% on deposits. But now, because of DIDMCA, they were paying over 10% APR on deposits and earning only 8% on their loan portfolio. The Savings & Loans now had a negative interest rate spread!

In less than two years the Savings & Loans went back to Congress to ask for even more help. This time Congress responded by passing the **Garn-St. Germain Act**, which, among other things, allowed the Savings & Loans to write a wide variety of mortgages—other than 30-year, fixed-rate mortgages they had provided in the past—and a wider variety of loans to both individuals and business.

Garn-St. Germain Act of 1982: An act designed to reduce the amount of regulation over the Savings & Loan or thrift industry.

Deregulation and Misaligned Incentives

Both DIDMCA and the Garn-St. Germain Act were considered methods of financial market "deregulation," meaning the removal of government regulation. Much regulation, however, including deposit insurance, remained in place. What DIDMCA and the Garn-St. Germain Act did was usher in an era in which depository institution managers were encouraged to take on a great deal of risk since depositors were almost fully protected from loss thanks to the expanded deposit insurance coverage.

As a result of these misaligned incentives, many Savings & Loans wrote very risky loans: commercial real estate development loans, energy loans, and others. Because these loans had a relatively high level of default risk, they carried with them a relatively high interest rate.

If these loans were successful and did not default, the Savings & Loan would be very profitable and could share this increased profit with depositors through high interest rates on deposits. If these risky loans did not pan out and fell into default, causing the Savings & Loan to fail, the depositor could simply turn to the government, who insured the deposits through the Federal Deposit Insurance Corporation, for their money. Thus it was often called "heads I win, tails the government loses."

And, oh, how the government lost: $160 billion worth of losses. Many of the Savings & Loans' risky loans did, in the end, fall into default. Because of these defaults, more than 745 Savings & Loans eventually failed. The crisis essentially all but wiped out the Savings & Loan industry. Making the situation even worse, the government was slow to respond to the crisis and did not tackle the Savings & Loan crisis in earnest until the end of the 1980s with the passage of FIRREA (Financial Institutions Reform, Recovery, and Enforcement Act) in 1989.

Lessons Learned

Need to Address Causes of Problems, Not Symptoms

One of the most important lessons learned from the Savings & Loan crisis is the importance of addressing the cause of a problem instead of the symptoms of a problem. In 1980 the loss of deposits by the Savings & Loans to other financial intermediaries was a symptom of the need for reform of the industry. The Savings & Loan industry was not well equipped to deal with the changing financial markets in the last 30 years of the twentieth century. Instead of undertaking much-needed reform of the industry, DIDMCA merely addressed the symptom of the industry losing deposits. Because Congress did not address the cause of the problem, new issues emerged by 1982.

In 1982 Congress again addressed a symptom—this time the negative interest rate spread—instead of addressing the cause of the problem: the need for structural reform of the industry. Therefore the crisis did not end with the passage of the Garn-St. Germain Act; instead the problem became bigger and bigger.

Finally, in 1989, Congress did address the cause of the problem—the structure of the industry—and closed down the failing Savings & Loans. Unfortunately, the delay in the government's response allowed the size of the problem to grow significantly. Others have argued that even FIRREA in 1989 did not address some of the deeper fundamental structural flaws in our financial markets. They argue that the economic crisis that started in 2007 is, in great part, a result of the lack of addressing these fundamental structural problems.

5-6b Leveraged Buyouts and Junk Bonds

Another of the outcomes from the push for deregulation of markets during the 1980s was the leveraged buyout (LBO) craze. A **leveraged buyout** is the acquisition of a public or private company where the buyout is financed mostly by debt (called leverage). In a typical LBO, up to 90% of the purchase price of the firm is funded by debt.

Leveraged buyout: The acquisition of a public or private company where the buyout is financed mostly by debt (leverage).

In an LBO the assets of the acquired company are used as collateral for the debt that is issued to buy the acquired company's outstanding stock. The debt interest and principal payments then are met using the cash and cash flows of the acquired company and/or by selling off the assets of the company.

LBOs had been a common takeover method for decades, but during the 1980s the number of LBOs increased significantly, in part because of the deregulation of financial markets and the relaxation of antitrust and securities laws that led to the approval of mergers that previously would have been challenged by the Justice Department.

Rise of the Junk Bond Market

The expansion of the high-yield or "junk bond" market was another thing that allowed for the rapid increase in the number of LBOs. Because LBOs generally are viewed as very risky, entities attempting to undertake an LBO often had a difficult time borrowing the money to fund the takeover. Thanks to Michael Milken and the investment firm for which he worked (Drexel Burnham Lambert), however, by the late 1970s the market for risky bonds had increased significantly.

In the late 1960s, while in graduate school, Milken was influenced by the studies of credit markets done by W. Braddock Hickman and others at the Federal Reserve Bank of Cleveland. Hickman's work showed that a portfolio of risky, or "junk," bonds offered risk-adjusted returns greater than portfolios of safe or investment-grade bonds. These studies told Milken that if one picked junk bonds correctly, one could earn a very sizeable return given the risk being undertaken.

Milken spent most of the 1970s proving that Hickman was right: Investing in junk bonds could earn investors high rates of return. By the early and mid-1980s, Milken was the "junk bond king." Investors were lining up to buy the junk bonds he was ready to sell. As a result, takeover artists who were putting together LBOs knew they could raise the money they needed for their LBOs thanks to Milken and Drexel.

Thus, Milken and the expanding junk bond market helped to feed the LBO craze of the 1980s. Despite the hundreds of millions of dollars Milken was making in commissions, however, it wasn't enough for him.

In March 1989 a federal grand jury indicted Milken on 98 counts of racketeering and securities fraud. Milken eventually pleaded no contest and was sent to prison. Drexel Burnham Lambert eventually filed for bankruptcy protection in 1990 and sued Milken for $1 billion in damages he had caused. Milken eventually served about 2 years of his 10-year sentence, was diagnosed with cancer (which he successfully beat), and has since spent most of his time as a philanthropist (he is barred for life from the securities industry) dedicated to education and medical research.

Lessons Learned

LBO Controversies Still Exist

The LBO market remains controversial to this day. Some claim that leveraged buyouts are a positive market force because the threat of a buyout forces management to improve the efficiency of their firms, eliminate waste, and reform or sell off low-performing divisions. Others argue that LBOs result in management focused excessively on the short term: They worry about the potential for a hostile takeover and thus worry only about keeping the current stock price high. Even after an LBO, so much of the cash flow of the firm has to go to servicing the debt that little is left over for long-term uses such as research and development or updating capital equipment.

SECTION REVIEW

Q1) How did DIDMCA and the Garn-St. Germain Act cause more problems for Savings & Loans than they solved?

Q2) How did the rise of the junk bond market help to increase the number of LBOs?

Q3) The term *leverage* refers to:

a. the amount of debt that is being used.

b. the price of bonds that are being sold.

c. the maximum interest rate banks can pay on deposits.

d. the default risk of a bond.

Conclusion

5-7

As we continue through the twenty-first century, will we learn from the economic and financial history of the twentieth century? As we look back on the twentieth century we see the Panic of 1907 led to the creation of the Federal Reserve. While this lender of last resort essentially failed to do its duty during the early days of the Great Depression, the Federal Reserve did have a much better track record for the rest of the century. We will spend a fair amount of time throughout the rest of the book examining in more detail what the Federal Reserve is, what it has done in the past, and how it may impact the future of money and financial markets.

We also examined the role money and financial markets played during World War II and the postwar economic boom. But we also discovered the problems that came about with the stagflation of the 1970s. We saw how financial markets were restructured during the Reagan/Thatcher revolution, including the rise of LBOs and the junk bond market.

Along the way we saw the powerful impact individuals can have on financial markets and the performance of an entire economy. People such as J.P. Morgan, Benjamin Strong, and Paul Volcker—to name only a few—had a powerful impact on our financial markets. Others, through their mistakes, caused great damage to our financial markets and economic system. In light of this, do not think of financial markets as cold, impersonal things. Remember, changes in these markets have a direct impact on your current and future well-being.

IN THE NEWS. . .

Yes, the Federal Reserve Has Enormous Power over Who Is President

Matt O'Brien

The Washington Post

January 13, 2015

The arc of the political universe is long, but it bends towards monetary policy.

That's the boring truth that nobody wants to hear. Forget about the gaffes, the horserace, and even the personalities. Elections are about the economy, stupid, and the economy is mostly controlled by monetary policy. That's why every big ideological turning point—1896, 1920, 1932, 1980, and maybe 2008—has come after a big monetary shock.

Think about it this way: Bad monetary policy means a bad economy, which gives power back to the party that didn't have it before. And so long as the monetary problem gets fixed, the economy will too, and the new government's policies will, whatever their merits, get the credit. That's how ideology changes.

In 1896, for example, Republicans completed their transformation from being the anti-slavery party to the anti-inflation one. Back then, the U.S. was on the gold standard, but there wasn't enough gold. Miners had found so little of it that overall prices were falling, which was particularly bad news for anyone who'd borrowed money. That's because wages fall if prices do, so debts that don't become harder to pay back. The result was two decades of slower-than-it-should-have-been growth where the economy was in recession more often than not. . . .

Well, at least until World War I. That's because Republicans agreed on fiscal and financial policy, but not on regulation. That split let Woodrow Wilson win a three-way race in 1912, and, despite getting reelected on the slogan that "he kept us out of war," he didn't in 1917. Now, gold had already been pouring into the U.S., fueling inflation, as people moved it out of Europe, but once we joined the Allies, we also partially suspended the gold standard by banning gold exports.

That left us with higher prices and a big pile of shiny rocks after the war ended. So, in 1920, the Fed raised rates so much that prices not only stopped rising, but actually started falling. A deep recession followed, right before the presidential election. That, together with general war weariness, was enough for an extreme mediocrity like Warren G. Harding to win the biggest popular vote victory, by percentage points, on record just on the strength of three word[s]: return to normalcy. A year later, the Fed lowered rates, the Roaring Twenties were born, and the conservative orthodoxy of low taxes and low spending once again seemed to be vindicated.

It wouldn't [last] for long. Households, you see, went on a borrowing binge in the 1920s. They borrowed money to buy cars. They borrowed money to buy homes. And, yes, they borrowed money to buy stocks. So once the market crashed, this pyramid of debt did too. Even zero interest rates weren't enough to stop the economy's free fall. This only got worse when people panicked, sometimes justifiably so, that all these bad debts would make their banks go bust. That became a self-fulfilling prophecy as people rushed to pull their money out before everyone else, and the Fed, which was more concerned about propping up the gold standard than propping up the financial system, let everything collapse.

This article argues that monetary policy helps determine election outcomes because of its impact on the economy. Yet it begins by talking about 1896, well before the Federal Reserve was established, and the United States had a monetary policy. However, the main point is changes in the financial market, especially money markets and foreign exchange markets, can have a significant impact on the economy and on elections. What role did money and financial markets play in 1896 and the "roaring" 1920s?

6

Aggregate Supply and Aggregate Demand

6-1 Introduction and Keynes's Aggregate Demand

Wouldn't it be nice to have a pair of economic omnioculars? You could slow down the economy and watch things happen more slowly. The economic omnioculars would allow you to see the moves of the economy with clear labels. (For those of you who are not familiar with the wizarding world, omnioculars were used by Harry, Ron, and Hermione to watch the Quidditch World Cup in *Harry Potter and the Goblet of Fire.*)

The aggregate supply (AS)/aggregate demand (AD) framework could be thought of as a pair of economic omnioculars. With an understanding of how the AS/AD framework functions, one can get a better understanding of why economies suffer from slowdowns and recessions. The AS/AD framework also shows us why money and financial markets are important to the function of the overall economy.

The AS/AD framework is in many ways similar to the supply-and-demand framework you used in your microeconomics coursework. Or you may have seen the AS/AD framework in your macroeconomics coursework. We want to use this framework to better understand the impact money and financial markets have on the overall economy, so this presentation may be a bit different than one you have seen before.

In this chapter we examine why John Maynard Keynes developed the ideas of aggregate supply and aggregate demand to explain the Great Depression of the 1930s. We then consider how the description of the aggregate supply curve changed over the decades, evolving into the rational expectations approach to AS/AD. Finally, we examine some of the controversies over the AS/AD framework that still exist.

6-1a Keynes's Challenge

British economist John Maynard Keynes first laid out the logic of the AS/AD framework in his 1936 book *The General Theory of Employment, Interest and Money*. Keynes faced a daunting challenge: explaining the Great Depression that had in its grips almost the entire world economy.

Karl Marx

According to the way economists understood how the economy worked at the time, the Great Depression simply should not have occurred. Classical economists believed that markets effortlessly achieved equilibrium. In equilibrium the quantity supplied equals the quantity demanded. That is, in equilibrium there are no surpluses and there are no shortages. Everyone who wants to buy a good at the market price finds the good available, and everything that is produced is bought up. According to Say's law, everything that is produced will be bought up as a market moves toward equilibrium.

But in the early 1930s markets clearly were not in equilibrium. In the market economies of the United States and Europe there were simultaneously massive surpluses and massive shortages. Across the United States there were massive shortages of food, as hundreds of people stood in line for hours at soup kitchens. There were massive surpluses in the labor market as the unemployment rate in the United States approached 25%. How could this be happening? Where was Say's law? Where was the classical economist's equilibrium? Didn't they say equilibrium would always come about?

There was a group who had an answer: the Marxists. Karl Marx, writing during the industrial revolution in the mid-nineteenth century in Germany and England, predicted that capitalism would fail under the weight of growing unemployment. Marx observed that the economies of Germany and England were becoming more and more mechanized as the industrial revolution progressed. He saw factory work replacing farming as workers migrated to urban areas. But Marx did not see this as economic progress; he saw it leading to the collapse of capitalism through growing unemployment.

Marx had predicted that capitalists, in their unending quest for higher profits, would replace workers with machines without realizing that it was the workers who buy the things the capitalists produce. Because workers have been replaced by machines, the unemployed workers no longer have the income to buy the goods produced by the capitalists. Thus the capitalists' sales and profits decrease. And because capitalists don't like falling profits, they fire more workers in an attempt to keep costs down. This simply leads to more unemployment, and the process repeats.

Pictorial Press Ltd/Alamy

Vladimir Lenin

Marx envisioned this growing unemployment continuing until there was a workers' revolution in which the workers take over the means of production and create a workers' paradise. In the workers' paradise, everyone would work as hard as they were able and get everything they need.

Marx's view of the future, however, did not come to fruition in Germany or England. Instead Marx's ideas were first put into practice in Soviet Russia. After the October 1917 Revolution in Russia, the Bolsheviks, under Vladimir Lenin, put in place their version of Marxism. Instead of waiting for growing unemployment to result in the collapse of capitalism, the Bolsheviks decided to jump to the conclusion: Outlaw capitalism and create a workers' paradise under Soviet central planning.

By the 1930s it seemed that the Soviet Union was economically surpassing the West. Thanks in part to Soviet control of the media, news of the Soviet famine of 1932–33 never made it to the West until the 1990s. Instead, to the outside world the Soviet Union seemed to experience huge economic success through the 1930s, while the West was suffering under the growing unemployment brought on by the Great Depression.

Thus many in the United States and Europe thought the Marxist-based Soviet central planners might be on to something. Marx had anticipated capitalism would fail under the weight of growing unemployment, and growing unemployment is what the United States and Europe were experiencing.

DIZ Muenchen GmbH, Sueddeutsche Zeitung Photo/Alamy

John Maynard Keynes

While economists in the West were at a loss to explain this growing unemployment, the Marxists had an answer: Soviet-style central planning. Thus during the 1930s communist central planning started to gain in popularity in Europe and the United States.

Into this intellectual battle stepped John Maynard Keynes. Keynes viewed it as his responsibility to "save capitalism" from Marxist central planning. But Keynes faced a huge problem: How could he explain the Great Depression without conceding that capitalism was a failure?

Keynes's solution was to say that traditional classical economics, with its market-clearing equilibrium with no surpluses and no shortages, does happen—but only in the long run. Keynes famously stated: "… but in the long run we are all dead." Thus, he argued, we could not wait for markets to clear themselves. Instead, because prices do not adjust as quickly as our simple microeconomic supply-and-demand curves suggest, according to Keynes something else needed to be done to push the economy out of the Great Depression.

6-1b Keynes's Aggregate Demand

To explain why the supply and demand of classical economics were no longer applicable during the Great Depression, Keynes argued that to understand the macroeconomy one needed to use aggregate supply and aggregate demand. The term *aggregate* simply means "total," so think of aggregate demand as total demand or, if you will, total spending. By the same logic, aggregate supply is the total supply, or the total amount of goods and services produced. While Keynes developed the ideas of aggregate supply and aggregate demand, he did not come up with the AS and AD curves himself; they were developed over time as an interpretation of Keynes's general theory.

Perhaps the easiest way to understand how AS and AD work both separately and together is to visualize them graphically. Keep in mind that the interaction between AS and AD determines the actual level of real output, or real gross domestic product (GDP), and the actual price level.

Remember, in supply-and-demand analysis of an individual good, the relative price is set on the vertical *y*-axis and quality is set on the horizontal *x*-axis. In AS and AD it is a little more complex. As seen in Figure 6-1, graphically we have real GDP on the horizontal *x*-axis and the price level[1] on the vertical *y*-axis.

The AD curve has a downward slope for three main reasons: Pigou's wealth or the effect of real balance, Keynes's interest rate effect, and the foreign trade effect.

Pigou Effect

A. C. Pigou, writing in 1943, was concerned about the role prices and savings might play in postwar economic recovery. Pigou argued that lower prices would increase the purchasing power of the public's savings and thus result in a higher level of spending. What happens if you have \$100 in savings and the price level is 100? You can buy a given amount of stuff with your savings. Now imagine the price of everything you want to buy is cut in half—the price level

Figure 6-1 **The Aggregate Demand Curve**

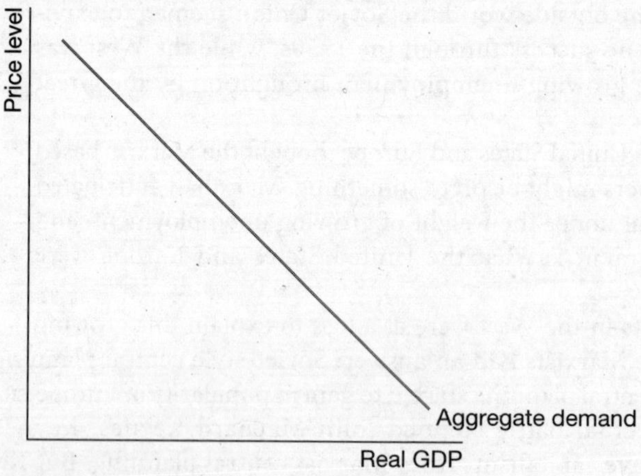

1 Some versions of AS/AD have the inflation rate on the vertical *y*-axis and real GDP on the horizontal *x*-axis. An argument can be made that this "dynamic" version of AS/AD makes more sense, so increases or decreases in the rate of inflation can be discussed, instead of increases or decreases in the price level; decreases in the price level (called deflation) are rare. We won't get into this controversy; instead, we will stick with the more conventional "price level on the vertical axis" approach. This controversy does, however, demonstrate one of the shortcomings of graphical analysis. A formal, mathematical presentation would be much more precise, and we could show many more interactions by using more math. The downside to using a more formal mathematical explanation is that it takes a longer time to develop. This is why we will stick with the less-than-great graphical explanation.

Figure 6-2 Movement Along the Aggregate Demand Curve

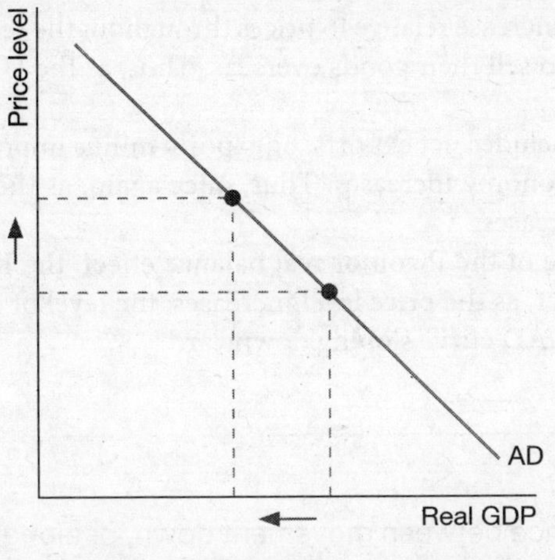

falls to 50—but you still have $100 in savings. Now your savings buys twice as much stuff! Thus Pigou's argument: If the price level falls, the purchasing power of peoples' savings increases—they can and will buy more stuff—and thus the total level of spending increases.

The Pigou effect can also work in the opposite direction when prices rise, as can be seen in Figure 6-2. That is, the real value, or purchasing power, of assets with fixed nominal values, such as bank savings accounts or bonds, decrease as prices increase. The Pigou effect is also sometimes referred to as the real balance effect because the real, or inflation-adjusted, value of the assets decreases as the price level increases. That is, as the price level increases, the real balances of savings decrease along with the total level of spending.

Keynes's Interest Rate Effect

The second reason why the AD curve slopes downward comes from John Maynard Keynes. Keynes argued that with a constant money supply, a higher price level results in an increase in the demand for money because more money is needed to purchase the same amount of goods and services. This increase in demand for money while the supply of money remains the same means that the price of money will increase. One of the most important prices of money is the interest rate. So, as the price level increases, interest rates increase.

As interest rates increase, however, the level of business spending decreases because as interest rates increase the cost of capital for firms increases. As the cost of capital increases, firms cut back on the number of projects they fund because the rate of return on these projects may not be any higher than the prevailing interest rate. So, as firms are funding few projects, the overall level of business investment spending decreases.

The higher interest rates brought on by a higher price level also lead to a decrease in consumption spending, especially spending on consumer durable goods. Higher interest rates mean higher borrowing costs for consumers who wish to borrow money to purchase consumer durable goods such as automobiles, furniture, and appliances. Thus, again, higher price levels bring on higher interest rates and thus a lower level of total spending.

Foreign Trade Effect

The third reason why the aggregate demand curve is down-sloping is the foreign trade effect. To understand how this works, consider an American consumer who can either buy goods in the United States or overseas. When US prices increase relative to prices overseas, our

American consumer will be more likely to buy goods overseas as opposed to in the United States, holding everything else constant. Thus, as US prices increase, the amount Americans import increases.

Similarly, as US prices increase relative to prices throughout the rest of the world, US exporters find it more difficult to sell their goods overseas. Thus, as the US price level increases, US exports decrease.

Because total output includes net exports, or exports minus imports, total output decreases as the price level in an economy increases. Thus, once again, as the price level increases, the level of real spending decreases.

To summarize, because of the Pigou or real balance effect, the Keynes interest rate effect, and the foreign trade effect, as the price level increases, the level of real output decreases; this appears graphically as the AD curve sloping downward.

SECTION REVIEW

Q1) Explain the difference between movement down, or along, the aggregate demand curve and a shifting out of the aggregate demand curve.

Q2) What is the Pigou effect and how does it result in a downward-sloping aggregate demand curve?

Q3) What did Karl Marx consider to be the main economic problem that would ultimately cause the collapse of capitalism?

a. High inflation

b. Growing unemployment

c. Excessive government debt

d. High interest rates

Shifts in Aggregate Demand

6-2

Just as we have different explanations of why the AD curve has the shape that it does, we also have different explanations for why the AD curve moves. Basically, the explanations all come down to the same idea: Changes in spending that come about because something other than the price level changes result in a shift of the AD curve. Slightly oversimplified, this means that increases in spending shift the AD curve out, whereas decreases in spending shift the AD curve back (Figure 6-3).

To review how this works, think about AD as total demand or total spending in terms of national income accounting or GDP. Remember, using the expenditure method, GDP is the sum of spending on final goods and services. Therefore we have

$$AD = C + I + G + (X - M)$$

Thus, changes in consumption (C), investment (I), government spending (G) and/or net exports (X − M) will bring about changes in AD. In addition, changes in the money supply also bring about changes in total spending and thus shift the AD curve.[2]

6-2a Changes in Consumption

Remember that consumption is household spending on durable goods, nondurable goods, and services. It includes things such as shoes, food, and haircuts. A household's level of consumption is based on its current, after-tax, net of savings income level, as well as what they think will happen in the future.

Taxes

If income tax rates increase, consumers have a lower level of disposable, or after-tax, income and thus a lower level of consumption. The logic is pretty straightforward: If the government takes more money away from you in the form of higher income taxes, you have less to spend on shoes, food, and haircuts. Naturally, all other things hold constant.

But this is not the end of the story. As you spend less on shoes, the shoemaker's income decreases, so she spends less and consumption is reduced again. This is the spending multiplier

Figure 6-3 Increases and Decreases in Aggregate Demand

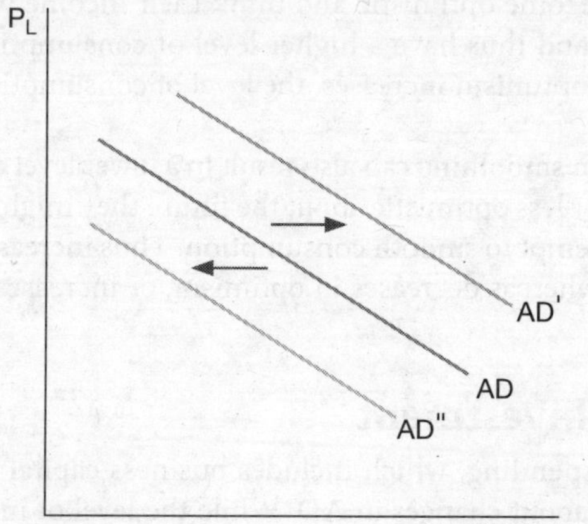

2 Net exports are exports (X) minus imports (M), or X − M.

effect, which we discuss in Section 6-2f, but the main idea is a onetime decrease in consumption—say, from higher income tax rates—sets off a chain reaction that decreases total spending, or AD, by much more than the initial decrease.

The same logic holds for a reduction in income taxes: As a household's disposable income increases, part of that increase in income makes its way into increases in spending. An increase in spending increases someone else's income, and the process repeats.

However, not all of the increase in disposable income makes its way into consumption. Some of that increase in disposable income goes into savings, another thing that can change the level of consumption and AD.

Savings

Increases in savings come at the cost of current consumption if disposable income does not increase. The question then becomes, What happens to this savings? If the savings makes its way into investment, then we have an increase in investment, which further increases AD, as we discuss in Section 6-2b.

On the other hand, what if savings does not equal investment? What if households save more than firms want to invest? Or, what if households save money, not by bringing it to the financial markets, but by sticking their savings under the mattress or in the cookie jar? In that case savings is a leakage; it is potential spending that leaks out of the economy.

In the 1930s this is arguably what Keynes saw: people saving money but not by bringing it to the financial markets because many of the banks were failing. He also saw a large amount of business investment opportunities that where not being undertaken. Thus in his version of the consumption function, savings acts as a major leakage in the economic system.

Consumer Optimism

Another thing that Keynes saw affecting financial markets and the aggregate economy was the level of consumer optimism. Think about what happens when people become optimistic about their future. Suppose—for whatever reason—people reasonably believe that things are going to be better in the future: They will earn a higher income, have a smaller chance of being unemployed, and so on. They most likely will borrow now against their future expected higher incomes. This is what economists call **consumption smoothing**.

Consumption smoothing: The idea that people do not like to have a low level of spending one period and a high level of spending the next period. Instead, they borrow and save to ensure that they have a relatively smooth level of consumption over time.

Thus, if consumers become optimistic and think their income will increase in the future, they may borrow today and thus have a higher level of consumption and repay the debt in the future. Therefore, as optimism increases, the level of consumption increases as a result of consumption smoothing.

However, consumption smoothing can also result in a lower level of current consumption. If people become worried or less optimistic about the future they might cut back on current consumption, again in an attempt to smooth consumption. Thus increases in consumer optimism shift the AD curve out, whereas decreases in optimism, or increases in consumer pessimism, shift the AD curve back.

6-2b Changes in Investment

Changes in investment spending, which includes business capital spending and new home construction, also bring about changes in AD. While the level of investment spending is significantly less than the level of consumption spending, investment spending turns out to be much more volatile than consumption. Thus a good deal of the movement in AD can come from changes in investment spending. Changes in business investment spending can occur because of changes in interest rates and/or changes in business expectations about the future.

Interest Rates

Interest rates are one of the main drivers of changes in investment spending and thus AD. This is one of the reasons why we spend so much time in this book examining interest rates.

To understand why changes in interest rates affect investment spending, think about the spending decisions of firms: **capital budgeting** decisions. Managers of firms essentially compare the rate of return on a project to the prevailing interest rate, holding everything else constant.

Capital budgeting: The process by which a firm determines whether to pursue a project. Projects include research and development of new products, continued production of an existing product, construction of a new facility, and continued operation of an existing facility, among others.

Capital Budgeting For example, suppose Nokia is thinking about launching a new smartphone. The managers at Nokia have to figure out how many phones they are going to sell and at what price, then compare this revenue to the costs of designing, producing, and marketing the new phone. Let's suppose they do all of those calculations and determine it will cost them €100 million to bring the phone to market and they expect to earn revenues of €103.5 million, both in present value terms. Should Nokia undertake the project?

The answer is: It depends on the interest rate. Let us suppose that market interest rates are very high. So, for the same amount of risk or uncertainty for the same amount of time, Nokia could take that €100 million and, instead of producing the new phone, buy a bond that would pay an 8% rate of interest. Thus they could generate €108 million from buying and holding the bond instead of the €103.5 million from funding the project. With these high interest rates, the managers of Nokia would likely kill the project, thus reducing the overall level of investment spending, and instead buy a bond.

Rate of return on project < Interest rate = Project not funded

On the other hand, if market interest rates were only 2%, Nokia management would earn a higher rate of return from funding the project as opposed to buying the bond. Thus, as interest rates decrease, more projects are funded, the level of investment increases, and the AD curve shifts out.

Rate of return on project > Interest rate = Project is funded

Changes in interest rates have the same impact on other markets, including the home building market. As interest rates decrease, more people can afford to buy homes because lower mortgage interest rates result in lower monthly payments.

Thus as interest rates decrease, people who previously could not afford the monthly mortgage payments on a new house now can afford the payments. This means that more people are likely to buy houses and the number of new housing starts increases, which means investment increases and the AD curve shifts outward.

Business Optimism

Business optimism can also play a role in capital budgeting decisions and thus the level of business investment spending. To understand how this can occur, think more about our Nokia capital budgeting decision.

When making the capital budgeting decision, our Nokia managers had to forecast the future sales of their new smartphone. If they are optimistic about the future of the economy, and thus optimistic about future sales of their new smartphone, they may forecast strong sales. These strong sales forecasts in turn make it more likely that the new smartphone project will be funded and the level of investment will be higher.

On the other hand, if the Nokia managers are pessimistic about the future, they may forecast lower expected sales, and thus the project will have a lower rate of return and be less likely to be funded. Thus if managers are less optimistic in general, they will be less likely to fund projects and the overall level of investment will be lower.

Keynes and Business Optimism Keynes described this level of business optimism as the "animal spirits" of businesspeople. For Keynes, one of the main drivers of business investment spending was the "herd mentality" of businesspeople. Keynes believed that in making their spending decisions, businesspeople look around and see what other businesspeople are doing and then do the same. Thus high levels of optimism were contagious, as were waves of gloom and doom.

Changes in investment spending can be difficult to predict and very volatile. If interest rates change rapidly, they can cause major shifts in the level of investment and thus in AD. So, if our goal is to be able to explain where the economy and financial markets are headed, explaining what is going to happen to interest rates is imperative because changes in interest rates impact investment spending—and thus the overall economy—by changing AD. This is one of the reasons why we spend so much time examining changes in interest rates.

6-2c Changes in Government Spending

The third factor that can bring about a change in AD is government spending on final goods and services. Notice we don't say "all government spending," only government spending on final goods and services. We specify because only final goods and services are included in the calculation of GDP.

Remember, when we talk about government spending on final goods and services, we are not simply talking about federal government spending in general; rather, we are talking about government spending on final goods and services at the federal, state, and local government levels.

For example, if the state of California decides to buy new desks for its public schools, this is an increase in the government spending on final goods and services. Similarly, if the US federal government decides to buy more F-15 fighter jets for the Air Force from Boeing for, say, \$35 million, that \$35 million will increase government spending and thus shift the AD curve outward.

6-2d Changes in Net Exports

The fourth factor that can shift the AD curve by changing total spending is net exports or exports minus imports. To determine why net exports are included, think about what GDP is trying to capture: the total output or total spending that occurs in an economy during a certain period of time, be it a month, a quarter, or a year. GDP does this by totaling the amount of spending that occurs in the economy during that period of time.

However, some of the spending that goes on in the economy involves buying things that are not produced within the economy. Thus for GDP to measure correctly how much the economy is actually producing, this amount of spending needs to be removed, which is why spending on imports is subtracted in the calculation of GDP.

Just as important is the production of goods and services that are not bought locally but instead are shipped overseas and bought elsewhere. If we want GDP to measure correctly how much our economy is actually producing, we have to include this spending that is not taking place within our economy, which is why exports are added to our calculation of GDP.

So, if the level of exports increases, the AD curve shifts out, whereas if the level of imports increases, the AD curve shifts back.

6-2e Changes in the Money Supply

A final reason why AD might change is a change in the money supply. An increase in the money supply allows for an increase in the number of transactions that occur in an economy. Writing in 1911, Irving Fisher first pointed this out with his quantity theory. The logic behind Fisher's idea is that if the money supply increases and the rate at which people use money, called the **velocity of money**, stays the same, then the total market value of the transactions that take place can increase. More money means more total spending.

Velocity of money: Also known as the turnover rate of money, the number of times in a time period a unit of money is used.

Fisher went on to suggest that if the economy is already at equilibrium and people have the stuff that they want, then an increase in the money supply leads to higher prices, but the level of real output remains the same. Thus, in terms of AD, an increase in the money supply leads to an increase in AD by increasing either the price level, the level of real total spending, or a combination of both. Therefore an increase in the money supply leads to an increase in AD.

The same logic holds when the money supply decreases, only in reverse. A decrease in the money supply results in a decrease in AD; that is, the demand curve shifts back or toward the origin.

6-2f Keynes's Spending Multiplier

As we have seen, changes in several things—consumption, investment, government spending, net exports, and the money supply—bring about changes in AD. Remember, however, that a onetime change in any of these does not stop there. Instead, a onetime change in spending goes through the economy several different times; that is, it causes a spending multiplier effect.

The logic behind the spending multiplier is simple: One person's spending is someone else's income. For example, assume the government spends \$100 million buying new Jeeps from the Chrysler Corporation. What is Chrysler going to do with this \$100 million? It will use part of the \$100 million to pay the wages and salaries of its employees. It will use another part of this \$100 million to pay suppliers for parts and stock- and bondholders for use of their capital, and yet another part of the \$100 million will be paid to the government as taxes. All of these entities—Chrysler employees, Chrysler suppliers, Chrysler stock- and bondholders, and the government—now have additional ability to spend because their incomes each went up.

Now the question becomes: How much of this additional income will actually be spent? To answer this question, Keynes came up with the **marginal propensity to consume (MPC)**. The MPC is the change in consumption brought about by a change in disposable income:

$$\text{MPC} = \frac{\Delta \text{ in Consumption}}{\Delta \text{ in Disposable income}} = \frac{\Delta C}{\Delta dY}$$

Marginal propensity to consume (MPC): A change in the desired level of consumption brought about by a change in the level of disposal income.

For example, if the disposable income of an economy increased by \$100 billion and, as a result, consumption increased by \$89 billion, the MPC of the country would be 0.89. This says that for every \$1 increase in disposable income, consumption spending increases by \$0.89, with the remaining \$0.11 going to savings.

The concept of MPC now allows us to construct the simple Keynesian multiplier formula. To calculate the total change in spending brought about by a onetime change in spending, we take the level of increase in spending and multiply it by 1 divided by 1 minus the MPC.

$$\Delta \text{GDP} = \Delta \text{ in initial spending} \times \frac{1}{1 - \text{MPC}}$$

For example, as seen in Figure 6-4, if the economy has an MPC of 0.80, then a onetime increase in spending of \$20 billion increases the GDP by \$100 billion. Thus, a onetime increase in spending shifts the AD curve by much more than the initial increase in spending.

Figure 6-4 **A Shift of the Aggregate Demand Curve as a Result of the Spending Multiplier Effect**

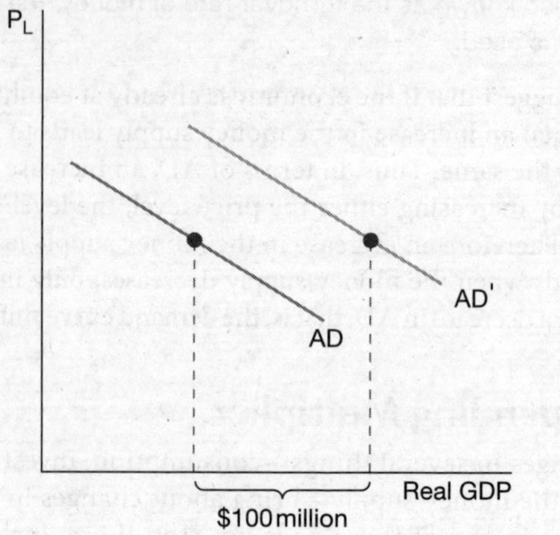

Deriving the Simple Deposit Multiplier

The Keynesian multiplier can also be explained using simple algebra. First, remember that, from a household perspective, a change in income (we will abbreviate income with Y and change with the Greek symbol Δ) gets divided up between a change in consumption (ΔC) and a change in savings (ΔS), or

$$\Delta Y = \Delta C + \Delta S \tag{1}$$

Next, we assume savings equals investment, so the equation becomes

$$\Delta Y = \Delta C + \Delta I \tag{2}$$

But the change in consumption is the MPC times the change in income

$$\Delta C = MPC \times \Delta Y \tag{3}$$

Substituting equation (3) into equation (2) gives us

$$\Delta Y = MPC \times \Delta Y + \Delta I \tag{4}$$

Rearranging the terms gives us

$$\Delta Y - (MPC \times \Delta Y) = \Delta I \tag{5}$$

or

$$\Delta Y\,(1 - MPC) = \Delta I \tag{6}$$

Dividing both sides by (1 − MPC) gives us

$$\Delta Y = \Delta I \times \frac{1}{(1 - MPC)} \tag{7}$$

Another, more general way to derive the multiplier is to start with the aggregate expenditure equation

$$Y = C + I + G$$

However, consumption is a function of income:

$$C = a + (MPC \times Y)$$

When this is substituted into the first equation, we get

$$Y = a + (MPC \times Y) + I + G$$

which reduces to

$$Y = \frac{(a + I + G)}{(1 - MPC)}$$

Changes in total spending come from changes in consumption, business investment spending, government spending, and/or net exports. These changes in total spending bring about changes in AD via the spending multiplier. To evaluate the total impact of these changes on AD, we need the other side of the aggregate economy: aggregate supply. We turn our attention next to AS and the AS curve.

SECTION REVIEW

Q1) If the MPC is 0.9 and consumption increases by $50 million, determine what will happen to total spending according to the spending multiplier.

Q2) If the MPC is 0.7 and business investment spending decreases by $10, determine what will happen to total spending according to the spending multiplier.

Q3) If savings is greater than investment, what is the implication for aggregate demand?

a. Actual spending is less than potential spending as a result of leakages.

b. Actual spending is greater than potential spending as a result of capital budgeting.

c. Actual spending is less than potential spending as a result of inflation.

d. Actual spending is greater than potential spending as a result of head mentality.

6-3 Aggregate Supply

Now that we understand AD, we need to put it together with **aggregate supply**. The AS curve shows the level of real output that is produced at different price levels. Defining AS is the easy part. Figuring out what that relationship actually looks like is the hard part. There turns out to be a fair amount of debate over what the AS curve looks like and how it moves. Let's go back and start with how Keynes originally described AS.

Aggregate supply: The relationship between the real level of output produced and the price level in a given time period.

6-3a Keynes's Original Aggregate Supply Curve

Originally, the AS curve was thought to be flat or horizontal until the economy reached **full employment**. Once the economy reached full employment, it was assumed that the AS curve became perfectly vertical.

Full employment: The level of real output at which all resources are being efficiently and effectively used.

To understand how this works, remember when Keynes was writing: during the Great Depression of the 1930s. In those days Keynes saw huge amounts of unemployment and constant prices. He rationalized that there was a level of output in the economy where all of the resources would be efficiently used. This was called the full employment level of output.

Keynes hypothesized that when the level of output is less than the level of full employment, some of the resources in the economy are being underutilized. If firms want to increase output in this setting, they can buy as many inputs as they want at the going market price.

Now extend this idea to the overall economy. Producers can increase output by hiring inputs at the going market price for these inputs. Thus as output increases, there is little upward pressure on the price level.[3] This can been seen graphically as a movement from point A to point B in Figure 6-5.

Figure 6-5 A Two Part Aggregate Supply Curve at Less Full Employment

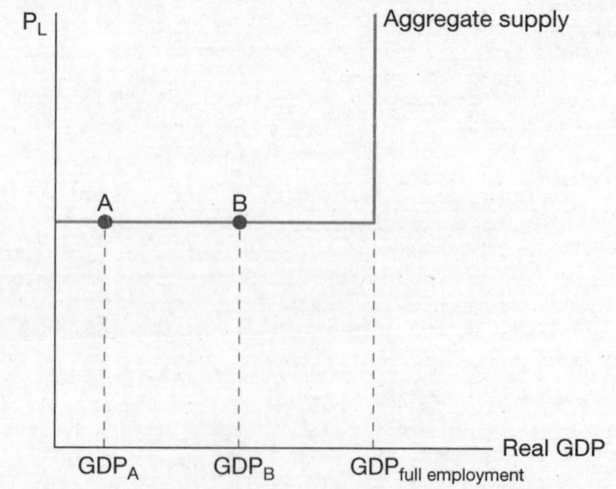

3 It was further suggested that even *if* costs were increasing, firms would have a very difficult time passing these higher costs along to consumers because so many of them had no job. Thus, if the level of output is below full employment, output can increase without an increase in the price level.

Figure 6-6 **The Economy at Full Employment**

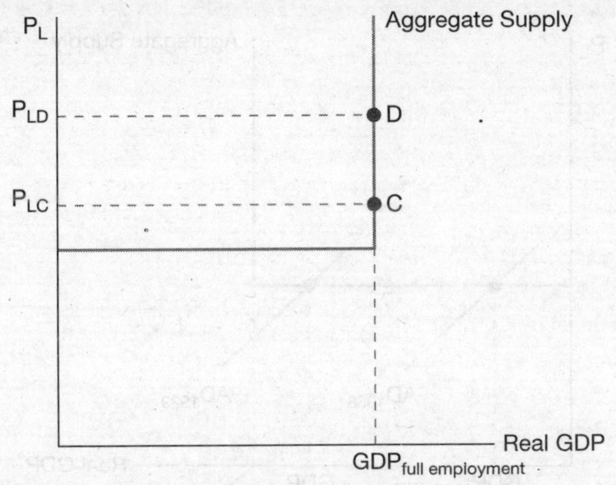

The story changes, however, once the economy reaches full employment. Now all of the inputs or resources are being used effectively. Now, to increase output, firms have to offer higher prices for the inputs they need to increase output. These higher input prices mean higher costs of production. Firms pass these higher costs along to their customers in the form of higher prices. So, at full employment, the price increases while output remains at the full employment level. This can be viewed graphically as a movement from point C to point D in Figure 6-6.

Keynes's Original Aggregate Supply and Sliding into the Depression

To review how Keynes used this framework, consider the US economy in 1929. During the 1920s, the US economy was growing and expanding. This time period was referred to as the "roaring '20s," with a high level of consumer spending on everything from automobiles to radios to household electrical appliances. Thus by 1929 the actual level of output was very close to full employment. In Figure 6-7 this is GDP_{1929}. As described in Chapter 5, however, an asset bubble was forming in US equity markets.

Suddenly, in October 1929, the stock market asset bubble burst. Panicked selling swept through equity markets. As Keynes's "animal spirits" of businesspeople turned negative, business investment spending decreased dramatically. As businesses cut spending they laid off workers, pushing the number of unemployed upward and thus depressing the level of consumption.

All this reduction in spending shifted the AD curve back and back; the level of output decreased and economy contracted. Thus a negative shock to the financial market pushed the economy into the Great Depression.

By 1933 the level of real GDP had decreased dramatically. Now the level of output was significantly less than the full employment level of output. The economy was suffering from a huge gap between the actual level of output (GDP_{1933}) and the full employment level of output (GDP_{FE}). But Keynes had a solution: government spending.

Keynes's Original Aggregate Supply and Getting out of the Depression

From Keynes's point of view, because investment spending was in the grip of negative animal spirits of businesspeople, it could not be relied on to reverse the decrease in spending. Complicating matters, Keynes argued, prices were slow to adjust, or "sticky," and thus costs were not falling, which could have induced firms to produce more and increase hiring. Because firms were not hiring, unemployment remained high, and thus consumption would not be the

Figure 6-7 **Aggregate Supply–Aggregate Demand from 1929 to 1933**

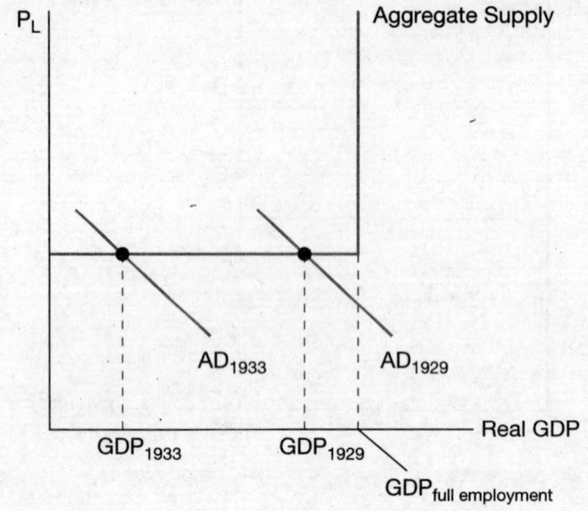

source of spending to end the Depression. International trade disputes had broken out around the world, and thus spending would not increase as a result of increased exports. Thus, Keynes determined, the only spending variable left was government spending.

Keynes indicated government spending must increase to "prime the pump" of overall spending. As government spending increased under the Roosevelt Administration, the AD curve shifted out, the level of real GDP increased, and the economy moved out of the Great Depression, as can be seen in Figure 6-8.

Keynes's Original Aggregate Supply and World War II

Then, on December 7, 1941, the Japanese attacked Pearl Harbor. The next day President Roosevelt declared war on Japan, and on Germany shortly after. Remember, as described in Chapter 5, government spending had to increase to fight the war. And as goods and services were being used for the war effort, the US economy approached full employment.

Figure 6-8 **Aggregate Supply–Aggregate Demand from 1933 to 1942**

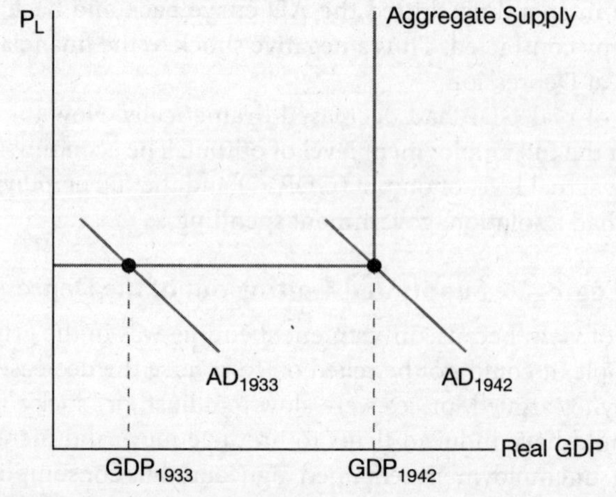

At full employment, continuous increases in government spending to fight World War II resulted in higher price levels or skyrocketing inflation rates. To control prices and input costs, the US government imposed wage and price controls and limited spending through rationing.

The combination of wage and price controls and rationing did the trick. During World War II, the United States did not suffer from high rates of inflation, despite the economy being at full employment.

6-3b Keynesian Three-Part Aggregate Supply

While the two-part Keynesian AS/AD framework worked well to explain the Depression and World War II, by the late 1940s a number of Keynes's followers began to view the two-part AS curve as too restrictive (Keynes died in 1946, so he was not around to offer his insight to this debate). Some input markets, it was argued, can start to experience shortages and higher prices even though the entire economy is not yet at full employment. To reflect this condition the postwar Keynesians proposed a three-part AS curve (Figure 6-9):

- Flat horizontal part: recessions and depressions with stable prices
- Upward sloping part: some, but not all, input markets experience shortages
- Vertical part: all input markets "clear"

The existence of the three-part Keynesian AS curve then gave rise to an interesting question: Is there a trade-off between the two major evils that face the macroeconomy, that is, inflation and unemployment? The three-part Keynesian AS curve seems to suggest the answer is yes. Notice in Figure 6-10, as spending increases, the economy moves from AD_0 to AD_1 to AD_2; the price level increases (or the rate of inflation increases) as the level of output increases or the unemployment rate decreases.

New Zealand economist A. W. Phillips set out to look for the inflation–unemployment trade-off in historical data. Sure enough, he found what did seem to be a trade-off between inflation and unemployment. He plotted the data, connected the dots, and created a curve that has ever since been named after him: the Phillips curve.

Keynesian Model Grows in Popularity

Thus, during the 1950s to the 1970s, the three-part Keynesian AS/AD model grew in popularity and use. Why not? It helped to explain why the Great Depression came about, how to get out of the Depression, how to manage the economy during World War II, and the post–World

Figure 6-9 The Three-Part Aggregate Supply Curve

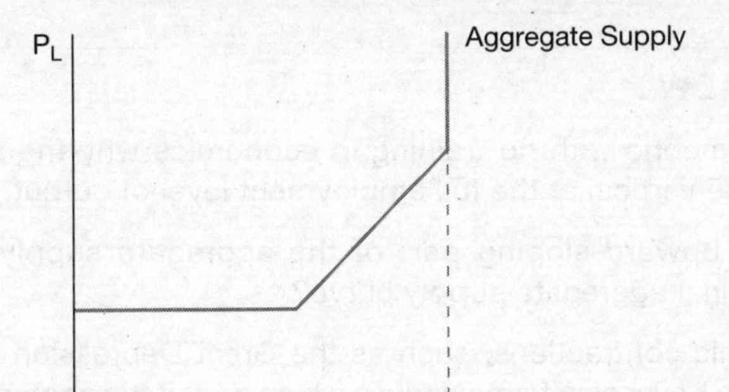

Figure 6-10 The Three-Part Aggregate Supply–Aggregate Demand with Three AD Curves

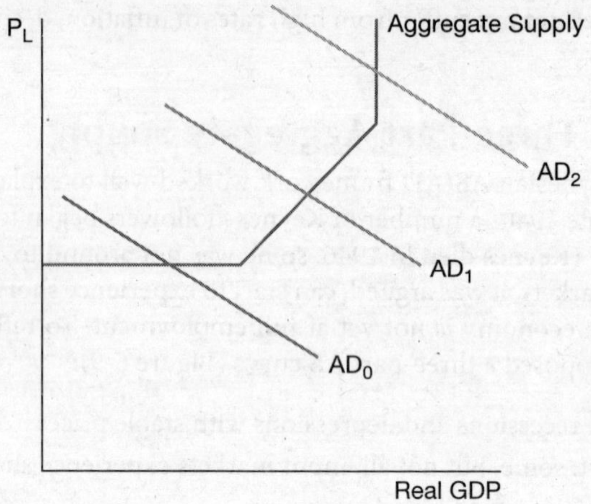

War II economic boom. It became so widely used that in 1965 *Time Magazine* named Keynes their "Man of the Year," even though he had been dead for 21 years!

The Keynesian framework placed *a lot* of emphasis on AD and the need to keep the "animal spirits" of businesspeople in check. It was the negative animal spirits in financial markets that led to the drop in AD that triggered the Great Depression. We got out of the depression only with the government priming the spending pump that was AD and the imposition of strict regulations on businesses and financial markets. The postwar boom came about because consumer and business spending was high and stayed high, thanks to low interest rates and extensive government regulation of financial markets. We discuss those things in more detail throughout the rest of the book.

But, by the late 1960s and into the early 1970s, the three-part Keynesian AS/AD model started to develop problems. The rise of stagflation led many economists to question just how useful the Keynesian approach really was. Some economists started to develop a new way of viewing the macroeconomy, building models based on sound microeconomic fundamentals. These models are often referred to as rational expectation models. Next we look at how this new approach brought changes to the AS/AD framework.

SECTION REVIEW

Q1) Explain to someone with no training in economics why the aggregate supply curve might be vertical at the full employment level of output.

Q2) Why was an upward-sloping part of the aggregate supply curve added to Keynes's original aggregate supply curve?

Q3) Deep economic contractions, such as the Great Depression of the 1930s, are depicted in the Keynesian framework as which part of the aggregate supply curve?

a. Vertical
b. Horizontal
c. Upward sloping
d. Downward sloping

The Rational Expectations Approach to AS/AD

6-4

While the three-part Keynesian AS curve was very useful in explaining how the economy worked during the first five decades of the twentieth century, by the late 1960s it was running into difficulties. The three-part Keynesian AS curve fell short of explaining the problem of **stagflation**.

Stagflation: Economic condition where the economy is suffering from a relatively high and often increasing inflation rate and stagnant economic growth often accompanied by an increasing unemployment rate.

The three-part Keynesian AS curve had difficulty in explaining stagflation: An increase in the price level was usually brought about by increasing AD on the upward or vertical portion of the AS curve. But if this were true, real output and employment would have to be increasing, not decreasing as they actually were.

6-4a Changing Assumptions

The inability to explain stagflation led economists to question some of the underlying assumptions of the Keynesian approach. One of these assumptions was that of adaptive expectations. In the Keynesian framework, if something happens you react or adapt to it. For example, if your disposable income increased, then you adapted to this new income level by spending some of it and saving the rest.

But, economists questioned, don't people plan? Don't they form expectations about the future? They may not predict the future perfectly, but don't they learn from their mistakes? Take the spending/saving example: Do people really save only because their current income changes? Don't people save because, in part, they plan for the future?

If in an attempt to explain how the economy works you allow people to plan and form expectations about the future, you get very different outcomes than the traditional Keynesian approach. One of the major things that changes is the AS curve.

In terms of AD, the rational expectations approach is just like the Keynesian approach. The AD curve slopes downward and moves as changes in consumption, investment, government spending, net exports, and the money supply changes. So the AD curve is almost exactly the same in the traditional Keynesian and rational expectations approaches. The major difference between the two approaches, in terms of the AS/AD framework, comes in relation to AS.

6-4b A Different Approach to Aggregate Supply

In the rational expectations approach people form expectations about the future using all available information, and if they make mistakes, they learn from them. As a result of this, in the rational expectations approach there are actually two AS curves: a short-run AS (SRAS) curve and a long-run AS (LRAS) curve. These two curves come about because this class of models starts from a microeconomic foundation. Remember, in microeconomics there is a big difference between the short run and the long run, but in the Keynesian approach there was no long run.

SRAS Curve

In the rational expectations approach the SRAS curve slopes upward. To understand why, think about an individual firm making a decision about how much to produce. The producer determines that at a given price level they will produce a given level of output. Now assume that their initial estimation of what the price will be is wrong! Let's say the actual price level turns

Figure 6-11 An Upward-Sloping Short-Run Aggregate Supply Curve

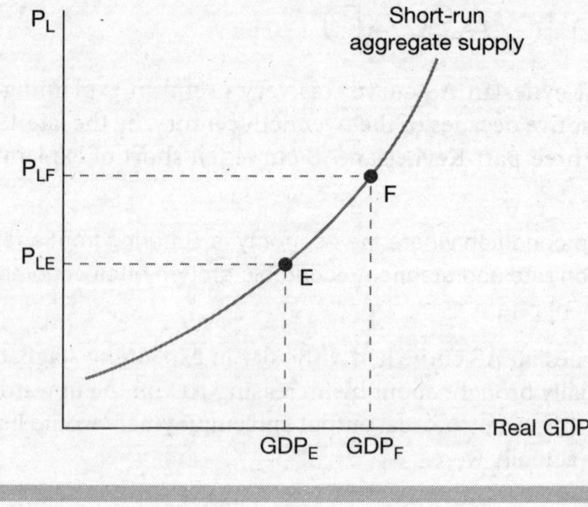

out to be higher than what they expected, holding everything else constant, including costs. The producers think, "Great! Prices have increased. Let's take advantage of this higher market price and produce more."

So, if the actual price level turns out to be higher than what they thought, they produce more. The same logic is at work, just in reverse: If the price level turns out to be lower than what they thought, they produce less. Take this same logic and aggregate it up to the entire economy: If producers expect a price level of P_{LE}, as in Figure 6-11, they will produce a level of output of GDP_E. But, if the actual price level turns out to be P_{LF}, holding everything else constant—including costs—sellers will produce at an output level of GDP_F. Thus we have an upward-sloping SRAS curve.

This SRAS curve can and does move, however. Just like the supply curve you saw in microeconomics, the SRAS curve will move if the cost of doing business changes, seller expectations change, or the number of sellers changes. Figure 6-12 graphically shows decreases (SRAS to SRAS′) and increases (SRAS to SRAS″) in short-run aggregate supply.

Figure 6-12 Increases and Decreases in the Short-Run Aggregate Supply

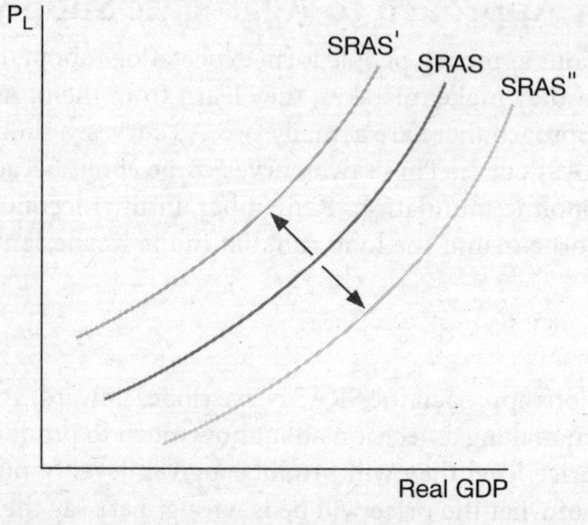

Cost of Inputs Change If the cost of inputs increases, sellers will either pass these costs along to buyers in the form of higher prices and/or reduce the amount they offer for sale. Thus, if the cost of inputs increases, the SRAS curve shifts backward.

The same logic, just in reverse, applies if the cost of inputs decreases. When the cost of inputs is reduced, producers can pass these cost savings along to their customers in the form of lower prices and/or they can use these cost savings to buy more inputs and increase the level of output. Either way, the decrease in the cost of inputs results in a shifting out of the SRAS curve.

Taxes Change For producers, taxes are an important cost of doing business. Thus, if a firm's taxes increase, the firm will either pass these higher taxes along to customers in the form of higher prices and/or reduce other costs by reducing the level of output. Either way, the increase in taxes paid by the producers results in a decrease in the SRAS; graphically, this appears as a shifting back of the SRAS curve.

Seller Expectations Change One of the worst things a businessperson can do is to miss a potential sale; missing a potential sales means that the customer is likely to go to the competition and buy their good or service. Once a firm loses a customer, it is very difficult to get that customer back. Losing a potential sale because they don't have enough product to sell is an unmitigated disaster for a business. So, if sellers reasonably expect sales to increase in the future, they will increase output today to be sure not to miss a potential sale. Thus, if sellers' expectations across the economy increase, we can expect to see an increase in SRAS; graphically, the SRAS curve shifts out.

But the future is wrought with uncertainty. Market participants hate uncertainty. So, if uncertainty increases and/or business expectations turn negative, we can expect producers to pull back and offer less for sale. Thus, if sellers' expectations fall or become negative, we can expect a decrease in the SRAS; graphically, the SRAS curve will shift back.

Number of Sellers Change An increase in the number of sellers in the market results in more output being offered at every price level; this appears graphically as the SRAS curve shifting out. One reason this might occur is because the economy opens itself up to trade with other nations. By doing so, the number of potential sellers in a market increases.

A decrease in the number of sellers in an economy has the opposite effect. Now, at every price level less is being offered for sale. Thus, if the number of sellers in an economy decreases, the SRAS curve shifts back.

Long-Run Aggregate Supply

The LRAS curve represents the "potential" level of real output of an economy. This potential level of real output is determined by the amount of resources the economy has—its land, labor, and capital—and how effectively it uses these resources, that is, the level of total factor productivity.

The LRAS curve is perfectly vertical at the natural level of output because the amount of resources and total factor productivity are, in the long run, independent of the price level (Figure 6-13). To understand why, think about the level of resources (land, labor, and capital) as well as why the amount of resources an economy has doesn't really have anything to do with the price level. Take land, for example. Does the United States sprout a new state every time prices increase? No, of course not. The amount of land in the United States is basically fixed—it certainly doesn't change with the price level. And so it is with the level of other resources as well: They are independent of the price level.

Over time, of course, the level of the resources (land, labor, and capital), as well as total factor productivity, can change. When either the level of resources and/or the level of total factor productivity increases, the potential level of output increases. As either the level of resources and/or total factor productivity increases, the LRAS curve graphically shifts out, or to the right (Figure 6-14).

Figure 6-13 The Long-Run Aggregate Supply Curve

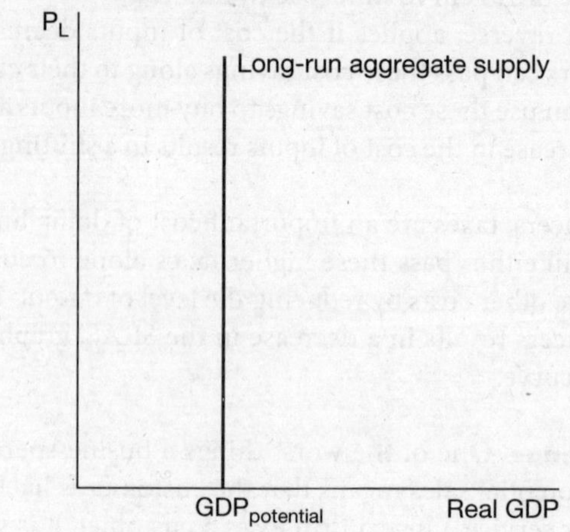

Figure 6-14 Economic Growth: The Long-Run Aggregate Supply Moved from 1935 to 2012

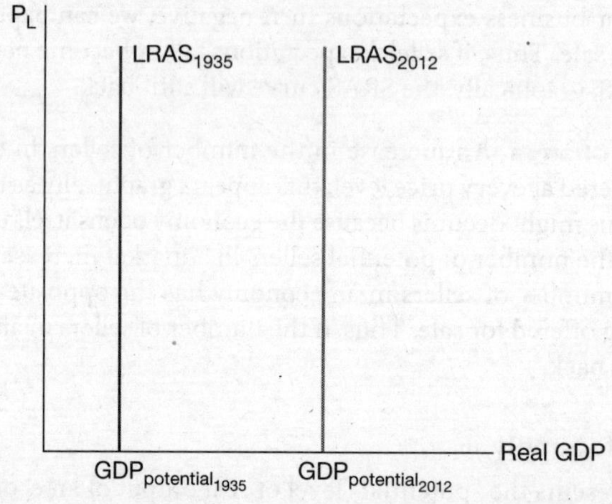

In thinking about the LRAS curve and the potential level of output, also think about how they might correspond to the actual level of output. Just like any "potential" level, the actual level might not be at its potential. Sometimes economies underperform: They don't use all of their resources or they don't use all of their resources effectively. If this happens, the actual level of output is less than the potential level of output, or there exists an "**output gap**." This output gap, where actual GDP is less than potential GDP, is also sometimes called a "recessionary gap."

Output gap: The difference between the actual level of real GDP and GDP potential.

On the other hand, an economy can sometimes be producing at a level above its long-term potential. In this situation the actual GDP is greater than the potential GDP. But this situation does not last long.

To review why actual GDP cannot stay above potential GDP for very long, think of an analogy using a car engine. You might be able to press down on your car's accelerator and rev the car engine—the tachometer might even go into the red as you continue to rev the engine at a very high rpm level. But you can't do this forever. If you continue to rev the car engine at very high revolutions per minute, eventually the engine will burn up. (Don't try this at home.)

And so it goes with an economy. An economy can have an actual level of output above its potential for a short period of time, but eventually prices will increase and the economy will "break" as it suffers from growing inflation. When this occurs, the level of output will return to, at most, the potential level of output.

SECTION REVIEW

Q1) Explain the difference between movement along the short-run aggregate supply curve and shifts of the short-run aggregate supply curve.

Q2) Why is the long-run aggregate supply curve vertical? Why might the long-run aggregate supply curve move?

Q3) If the cost of doing business for producers increases, which of the following occurs?

a. The short-run aggregate supply curve becomes flat.

b. The short-run aggregate supply curve shifts outward.

c. The short-run aggregate supply curve becomes steep.

d. The short-run aggregate supply curve shifts inward.

6-5 Business Cycles

Now that we have the three pieces of the rational expectations framework—AD, SRAS, and LRAS—let's bring them all together.

6-5a Bringing Together Aggregate Demand, SRAS, and LRAS

The actual level of output, or actual GDP, is determined by the intersection of the SRAS (output) and AD (spending). This actual level of output can and does change as the SRAS and/or AD changes.

As described above, the actual level of output can be higher than the potential level of output for a short period of time. To understand how this works graphically, let's start at the long-run equilibrium, where the SRAS curve crosses the AD curve at the long-run aggregate supply curve (Figure 6-15). The actual GDP equals the potential GDP; everything is as it should be.

Figure 6-15 Equilibrium in the Aggregate

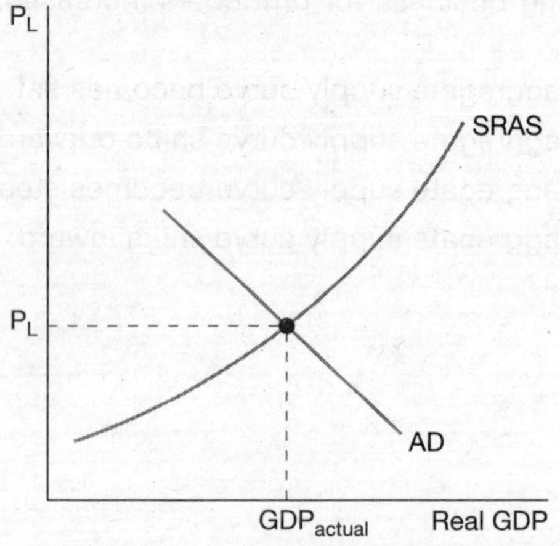

Let's suppose there is an increase in AD. Maybe consumers' credit becomes too loose. For whatever reason, suddenly the consumers can access credit and they don't use it wisely. Instead, households borrow and spend like crazy. All of this increase in consumption shifts the AD curve outward. Now, the new AD curve intersects the SRAS at a point to the right of the LRAS curve. This is movement from point A to point B in Figure 6-16. Now we see that the actual GDP is above the potential GDP. This is often described as the economy "overheating."

But the economy won't stay at point B for long. With all of this excessive spending going on, sellers are going to be scrambling to keep up with the increase in demand. Eventually there will be an increase in demand for resources from all of the sellers, who want more land, labor, and capital to keep up with the increased household spending.

We know from microeconomics, however, that if there is an increase in demand for resources, the market price of these resources are going to go up, ceteris paribus. As the market price of these resources increases, the cost of doing business for the sellers in the economy also increases.

In our discussion of the SRAS, we said that an increase in the cost of inputs faced by sellers causes a shifting back of the short SRAS curve. But as the SRAS curve shifts back, the level of output decreases and the price level increases. In Figure 6-17 we see the economy move from point B to point C.

Figure 6-16 Initial Equilibrium then Overheating

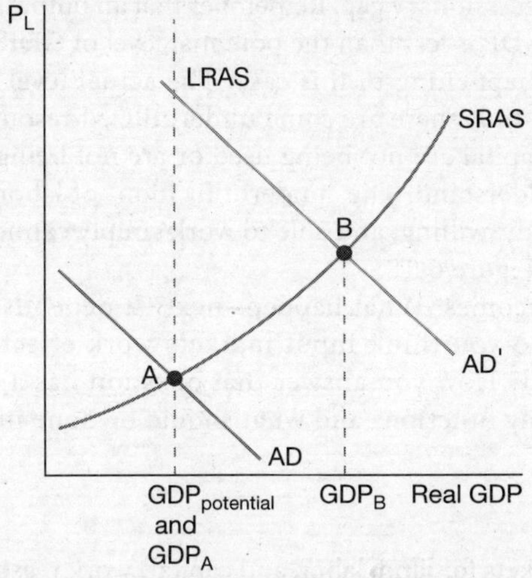

Figure 6-17 A Shifting SRAS Caused by Overheating

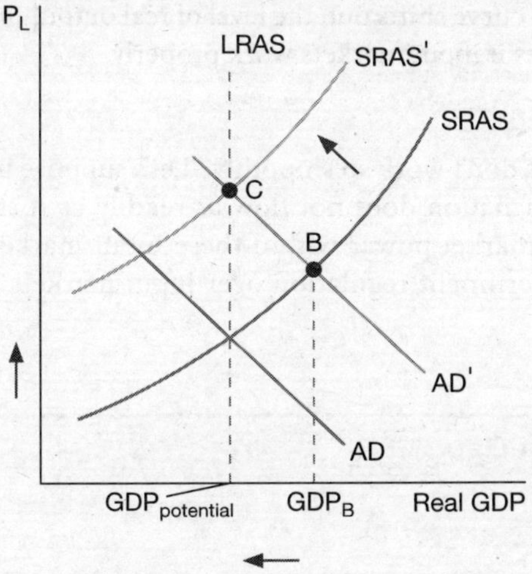

The end result of an overheating economy, where actual GDP is greater than the potential GDP, is not good; the price level increases (or inflation gets worse) and the level of output falls back to the potential (or the economy slides into a recession).

Thus, this framework shows us the danger of an overheating economy. Be careful when you see the level of real GDP increasing rapidly. You have to ask yourself, Is this economy overheating? This is a difficult question to answer. It is simple (sort of) to draw these AD/AS curves on paper, but it is difficult to determine where these levels are in real life. For example, what is the "potential" GDP of the United States right now, this very minute? How do you know for certain? Maybe reasonable people will disagree on what the potential GDP of the economy actual is. If you can't determine the potential GDP, how do you know if the economy is overheating?

6-5b Business Cycles: How Fast Do Gaps Close?

Another area of debate or controversy with regard to the short-run/long-run AS/AD curve has to do with the output or recessionary gap. Remember that an output or recessionary gap occurs when the actual level of GDP is less than the potential level of GDP.

Think about what is happening in this case: The actual level of output is less than the potential level of output; thus there are some underutilized resources. That means some of our land, labor, and/or capital are not being used or are not being used efficiently. Labor is perhaps the easiest to understand. The "underutilization" of labor means unemployment—some people who are ready, willing, and able to work simply cannot find jobs. The economy finds itself at point G in Figure 6-18.

The question then becomes: What happens next? It depends on what you have to say about input markets. Do you think input markets work effectively and efficiently? Or are they slow to respond? How you answer that question has a lot to say about how you think the overall economy functions and what should be done in terms of the structure of financial markets.

Efficient Input Markets

If input markets (the markets for land, labor, and capital) work reasonably well, then an output gap should close itself. Think about what an output gap means in terms of inputs: There is an underutilization of resources, or some inputs are going unused. If markets work correctly, the market price of these unused resources should decrease as these markets move to equilibrium. But a decrease in the market price of inputs is a reduction in the cost of doing business for firms. As we have seen, a reduction in the cost of doing businesses brings about an increase in the SRAS. Thus the SRAS curve shifts out, the level of real output increases, and the gap closes! Recessions end themselves if input markets work properly.

Imperfect Input Markets

But what if input markets don't work so smoothly? Let's suppose prices of inputs don't adjust quickly, or suppose information does not flow as readily as it should. Perhaps there is an unequal distribution of market power within these input markets. Or suppose there is an excessive amount of government regulation over input markets that do not allow them to adjust so quickly.

Figure 6-18 Output Gap

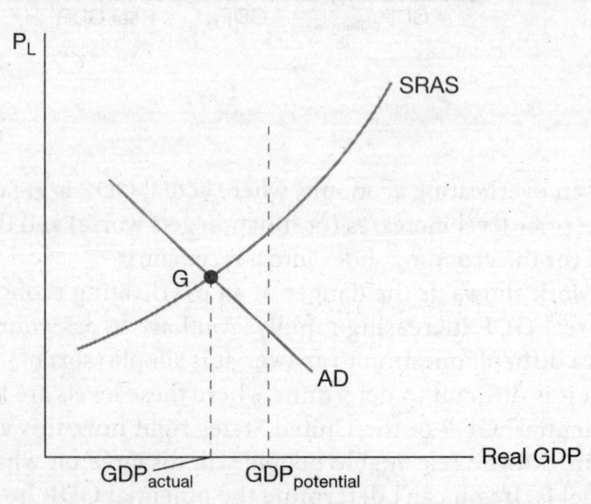

If any of these things exist, then the economy can get stuck at point G in Figure 6-18 for a long time. That is, if input markets don't work efficiently, the output gap can last a long time, or recessions will not end themselves.

It is generally agreed that input markets (especially financial markets and labor markets) do not work as efficiently as we would like. Thus recessions don't automatically end themselves; that is, recessions can last for a long period of time. The debate among economists is why input markets (especially financial markets) are imperfect. How can we make our financial markets operate in a more efficient and effective way so that they can "help" the economy to end recessions more quickly?

These are the type of questions that are going to occupy us through the rest of this book. We will delve into the issues of money, banking, and financial markets and institutions with an eye toward understanding how these different markets and institutions function and how they impact the overall global economy.

SECTION REVIEW

Q1) Bobby believes input markets, such as financial markets, are efficient. Use aggregate supply and aggregate demand to explain why this leads Bobby to believe economic slowdowns will "end themselves."

Q2) Johnny believes input markets, such as financial markets, are inefficient. Use the aggregate supply and aggregate demand to explain why this leads Johnny to argue that government policy is needed to end economic slowdowns.

Q3) If the economy is currently "overheating," this means:

a. actual GDP is higher than potential GDP.

b. there is "too much" spending in the economy.

c. inflation rates will probably increase in the future.

d. All of the above.

6-6 Conclusion

The AS/AD framework may not be the perfect economic omnioculars. While it does give us a tool with which we can examine movements of the overall economy, as we have seen it is not without its controversies. Yet the AS/AD framework was developed in the midst of a huge controversy: explaining the Great Depression. The concepts of AD and AS that John Maynard Keynes created certainly did a remarkable job of explaining why the Depression came about, how to get out of it, and what to do with the economy during World War II.

The Keynesians built on Keynes's original work to give us the three-part AS/AD framework, which did a decent job in explaining the postwar economic boom. When this model stumbled in explaining the stagflation of the 1970s, however, the rational expectations approach gave us a more microeconomics-based AS/AD framework. But even this improvement did not give us a perfect understanding of how and why business cycles work.

Through it all we have seen the importance of money and financial markets. Throughout the rest of our examination of money, banking, and financial markets and institutions we will return to the AS/AD framework to gain better insight into how changes in and across financial markets impact the entire global economy.

IN THE NEWS. . .

What Went Wrong with Economics

The Economist
July 18, 2009

Of all the economic bubbles that have been pricked, few have burst more spectacularly than the reputation of economics itself. A few years ago, the dismal science was being acclaimed as a way of explaining ever more forms of human behaviour, from drug-dealing to sumo-wrestling. Wall Street ransacked the best universities for game theorists and options modellers. And on the public stage, economists were seen as far more trustworthy than politicians. John McCain joked that Alan Greenspan, then chairman of the Federal Reserve, was so indispensable that if he died, the president should "prop him up and put a pair of dark glasses on him."

In the wake of the biggest economic calamity in 80 years that reputation has taken a beating. In the public mind an arrogant profession has been humbled. Though economists are still at the centre of the policy debate—think of Ben Bernanke or Larry Summers in America or Mervyn King in Britain—their pronouncements are viewed with more scepticism than before. The profession itself is suffering from guilt and rancour. In a recent lecture, Paul Krugman, winner of the Nobel prize in economics in 2008, argued that much of the past 30 years of macroeconomics was "spectacularly useless at best, and positively harmful at worst." Barry Eichengreen, a prominent American economic historian, says the crisis has "cast into doubt much of what we thought we knew about economics."

In its crudest form—the idea that economics as a whole is discredited—the current backlash has gone far too far. If ignorance allowed investors and politicians to exaggerate the virtues of economics, it now blinds them to its benefits. Economics is less a slavish creed than a prism through which to understand the world. It is a broad canon, stretching from theories to explain how prices are determined to how economies grow. Much of that body of knowledge has no link to the financial crisis and remains as useful as ever.

And if economics as a broad discipline deserves a robust defence, so does the free-market paradigm. Too many people, especially in Europe, equate mistakes made by economists with a failure of economic liberalism. Their logic seems to be that if economists got things wrong, then politicians will do better. That is a false—and dangerous—conclusion.

Rational fools

These important caveats, however, should not obscure the fact that two central parts of the discipline—macroeconomics and financial economics—are now, rightly, being severely re-examined. . . . There are three main critiques: that macro and financial economists helped cause the crisis, that they failed to spot it, and that they have no idea how to fix it.

The first charge is half right. Macroeconomists, especially within central banks, were too fixated on taming inflation and too cavalier about asset bubbles. Financial economists, meanwhile, formalised theories of the efficiency of markets, fuelling the notion that markets would regulate themselves and financial innovation was always beneficial. Wall Street's most esoteric instruments were built on these ideas.

But economists were hardly naive believers in market efficiency. Financial academics have spent much of the past 30 years poking holes in the "efficient market hypothesis". A recent ranking of academic economists was topped by Joseph Stiglitz and Andrei Shleifer, two prominent hole-pokers. A newly prominent field, behavioural economics, concentrates on the consequences of irrational actions.

So there were caveats aplenty. But as insights from academia arrived in the rough and tumble of Wall Street, such delicacies were put aside. And absurd assumptions were added. No economic theory suggests you should value mortgage derivatives on the basis that house prices would always rise. Finance professors are not to blame for this, but they might have shouted more loudly that their insights were being misused. Instead many cheered the party along (often from within banks). Put that together with the complacency of the macroeconomists and there were too few voices shouting stop.

Blindsided and divided

The charge that most economists failed to see the crisis coming also has merit. To be sure, some warned of trouble. The likes of Robert Shiller of Yale, Nouriel Roubini of New York University and the team at the Bank for International Settlements are now famous for their prescience. But most were blindsided. And even worrywarts who felt something was amiss had no idea of how bad the consequences would be.

That was partly to do with professional silos, which limited both the tools available and the imaginations of the practitioners. Few financial economists thought much about illiquidity or counterparty risk, for instance, because their standard models ignore it; and few worried about the effect on the overall economy of the markets for all asset classes seizing up simultaneously, since few believed that was possible.

Macroeconomists also had a blindspot: their standard models assumed that capital markets work perfectly. Their framework reflected an uneasy truce between the intellectual heirs of Keynes, who accept that economies can fall short of their potential, and purists who hold that supply must always equal demand. The models that epitomise this synthesis—the sort used in many central banks—incorporate imperfections in labour markets ("sticky" wages, for instance, which allow unemployment to rise), but make no room for such blemishes in finance. By assuming that capital markets worked perfectly, macroeconomists were largely able to ignore the economy's financial plumbing. But models that ignored finance had little chance of spotting a calamity that stemmed from it.

What about trying to fix it? Here the financial crisis has blown apart the fragile consensus between purists and Keynesians that monetary policy was the best way to smooth the business cycle. In many countries short-term interest rates are near zero and in a banking crisis monetary policy works less well. With their compromise tool useless, both sides have retreated to their roots, ignoring the other camp's ideas. Keynesians, such as Mr Krugman, have become uncritical supporters of fiscal stimulus. Purists are vocal opponents. To outsiders, the cacophony underlines the profession's uselessness.

Add these criticisms together and there is a clear case for reinvention, especially in macroeconomics. Just as the Depression spawned Keynesianism, and the 1970s stagflation fuelled a backlash, creative destruction is already under way. Central banks are busy bolting crude analyses of financial markets onto their workhorse models. Financial economists are studying the way that incentives can skew market efficiency. And today's dilemmas are prompting new research: which form of fiscal stimulus is most effective? How do you best loosen monetary policy when interest rates are at zero? And so on.

But a broader change in mindset is still needed. Economists need to reach out from their specialised silos: macroeconomists must understand finance, and finance professors need to think harder about the context within which markets work. And everybody needs to work harder on understanding asset bubbles and what happens when they burst. For in the end economists are social scientists, trying to understand the real world. And the financial crisis has changed that world.

This article raises the question of the link between macroeconomics and financial economics. The authors argue that the current crisis that began in 2008 was caused, in great part, by financial market participants often misapplying and misunderstanding both macroeconomics and financial economics. Why do you suppose so many people in financial markets got it so wrong?

The authors also are very critical of the "professional silos" that have developed between the fields of macroeconomics and financial economics. They call for a "reinvention" of macroeconomics and financial economics. What do you think this "reinvention" should entail? What do you think the future of these two fields should look like and why?

7

Banks and Money

7-1 Why Banks Exist: Asymmetric Information

If financial markets worked like the perfect competition markets that were discussed in microeconomics, life would be so much easier. Remember from microeconomics that in a perfectly competitive market there is perfect information: Everybody knows everything they need to know, there is free entry and exit—anyone can enter and/or level the market at any time, there are zero transaction costs, and output is homogenous—everybody is selling the exact same thing. In perfect competition the outcomes are perfectly efficient.

If financial markets were perfectly competitive, again, there would be perfect information: All of the lenders would know the deadbeats who won't repay the money they borrow. All of the savers would know what type of rate of return they are going to earn on their savings. Also, if financial markets were perfectly competitive, savers would easily find borrowers because each would have perfect information about the other. Finally, perfectly competitive financial markets would mean the markets are efficient and thus all savers would be able to buy financial assets in the exact maturity and amount they need to meet their needs. Life indeed would be nice if financial markets were perfectly competitive.

But in microeconomics we learned that perfect competition happens only in theory, not in reality. Unfortunately, no markets—especially financial markets—are perfectly competitive. Because of this, there is a need for and an important role to be played by depository institutions.

In this chapter we examine this need for depository institutions and the important role that they play.[1] We first address the question of why banks exist. One of the main reasons they exist is to deal with the problems of adverse selection and moral hazard. After examining these two issues in depth, we explore what banks actually do in the creation of money. We then use the concepts of the simple deposit multiplier to investigate why depository institutions are so important to the proper function of a market economy. We will see that depository institutions are so important that modern economies have created central banks, in part, to keep the banking system working properly. Central banks are the topic of the next chapter.

7-1a Asymmetric Information

Depository institutions, such as commercial banks, savings banks, credit unions, and Savings & Loans, exist because information is not perfect and market outcomes are not perfectly efficient. To understand why, think about the issue of asymmetric information.

There are many examples, not just in financial markets, of **asymmetric information**, or where information is not equal or even. Sometimes either buyers or sellers don't have the same information as the other side of the market. Think about prices, labor markets, and interviewing for a job. If you have ever interviewed for a job you may have gotten the advice, "Don't ask how much the job pays in the first interview." Did you ever consider how odd this advice really is?

Asymmetric information: Information that is not equal or even.

The person interviewing you knows how much the job pays, but you, as the interviewee, do not. Thus there is asymmetric information in this market. What if you spend a large amount of time and effort in preparing for the interview and you get offered the position, only to find out that the level of compensation for the job is ridiculously low? You would be upset because you have just wasted a precious resource: your time.

---

1 In later chapters we will examine banks in more detail, including delving into the components of bank balance sheets, the risks banks face, and how the banking system has evolved over time.

Thus, asymmetric information in markets can lead to inefficient outcomes; the scarce resources of society can be wasted or misallocated. Therefore economists are very concerned about asymmetric information. They ask questions such as, Why does asymmetric information come about? How can it be corrected?

The 2001 Nobel Prize in economics went to George A. Akerlof, A. Michael Spence, and Joseph E. Stiglitz for their analysis of markets that suffer from asymmetric information. In 1970 Akerlof published in the *Quarterly Journal of Economics* his groundbreaking paper entitled "The Market for 'Lemons': Quality Uncertainty and the Market Mechanism." Akerlof was describing the problem of **adverse selection.**

Adverse selection: A situation where undesirable results occur because the two parties in a transaction, the buyer and seller, have different amounts of information.

Adverse Selection

Akerlof brilliantly applied the example of the used car market to demonstrate the problem of adverse selection. To understand how this works, think about the used car market and assume there are two types of used cars: good, reliable used cars that will last a long time and bad, lousy used cars that are going to fall apart in a few months. The good cars are the "cream puffs" and the bad cars are the "lemons."

Your friend wants to buy a used car and he needs your help. Just like all of the buyers in the market, your friend naturally can't tell if a given used car is a cream puff or a lemon. But the seller of the car knows! The seller knows exactly how the car has been running, how it has been maintained, and how it has been driven. That is, the seller knows full well whether he is selling you a cream puff or a lemon. Let's further assume that buyers like your friend would be willing to pay $20,000 for a cream puff of a car but only $12,000 for a lemon. The sellers of the nice cream puff car may be willing to sell their reliable used car for $18,000 and the sellers of the lemons are willing to unload their clunkers at $10,000.

What happens? Because there is only one price for a given car, buyers like your friend, who do not know the quality of the car, might reasonably be willing to pay the average between the cream puff and the lemon, or $16,000. At a market price of $16,000, the sellers of cream puffs are unwilling to sell; remember, they want $18,000 for their high-quality used cars. The sellers of the lemons are more than happy to sell their lousy car at the market price of $16,000. Thus, the lemons come to dominate in the market and drive out the cream puffs.

You realize this and tell your friend that while the market is willing to pay a price based on "average" quality, only the lemons are being sold in the market. You tell your friend not to buy unless the price falls. Other buyers in the market can figure out the same thing and the problem repeats itself. Now imagine that the lemons come in two different qualities: really bad and really, really bad. Again, the one market price would be the average between the really bad and the really, really bad, thus driving the really bad out of the market so only the really, really bad remain. The process then repeats. As you can see, this can continue until the market collapses.

Solution to Adverse Selection

The solution to this adverse selection, or when only low-quality goods are offered for sale, is a better flow of information. In the used car market this is solved in part by reputable entities such as CarMax or new-car dealers selling used cars. These sellers have a reputation at stake when selling used cars and thus they have an incentive to offer only the cream puffs for sale.

CarMax, for example, points out that all of their cars go through a 125-point inspection before being offered for sale in one of their stores. If you go into a CarMax store, the sales representative will show you how they examine cars to determine that they are selling only the cream puffs. Only a fraction of the vehicles that CarMax buys ever makes it to their sales lot. Most of those that don't make the cut are sold at wholesale auction or to other dealers.

CarMax seems to be doing a pretty good job. In 2015 CarMax operated more than 140 used car superstores in more than 70 different cities. CarMax has sold more than five million vehicles since it was founded in 1993 in Richmond, Virginia. In the 2014 fiscal year CarMax had net earnings of $492 million and was one of *Fortune*'s "100 Best Companies to Work For." Clearly, finding a way to solve the adverse selection problem can be very profitable.

Adverse selection happens in many different markets, not just the used car market. Next we take a look at how adverse selection comes about in financial markets.

SECTION REVIEW

Q1) While Akerlof described adverse selection in the used car market, can you think of how adverse selection might arise in the labor market? Or even in dating?

Q2) CarMax offers a solution to the lemons problem in the used car market. What other ways might the lemons problem be resolved?

Q3) Akerlof changed the conditions of perfect competition by adding in what factor that often occurs in real life?

a. Price differences
b. Time dimension
c. Uncertainty
d. Different sellers

Adverse Selection in Financial Markets

7-2

While Akerlof demonstrated how adverse selection and the lemons problem can arise in the used car market, he and others also pointed out that adverse selection can arise in financial markets in a variety of different ways. Think about the following:

- **In bank lending: Bad borrowers know who they are, but lenders don't.** When a borrower approaches a bank and applies for a loan, the borrower may know their "quality," or their ability and willingness to repay a debt, but lenders may not. Simply put: Information is unequal—the borrower knows more about themselves than does the lender. Thus, if the lender is unsure whether the borrower is high quality or low quality, the lender may charge an interest rate that is the average between what the high-quality borrower and the low-quality borrower would pay. This "average" interest rate would be attractive to the low-quality borrow, but it would seem high to the high-quality borrower. As a result, only the low-quality borrowers would be left in the market borrowing funds, while the high-quality borrowers would refuse to pay the high interest rate required of them by the lender.
- **In the bond market: Issuers know if they can repay, bond buyers don't.** In the primary bond market the issuer of the bond, either a government or a corporation, is controlled by people who know a great deal about the ability of the bond issuer to repay the debt. For example, the people who control the government or the corporation know much more about what the future might hold for the bond issuing entity than someone on the outside. So, if bond buyers are uncertain about the ability of the bond issuer to repay, the low-quality bond issuers will dominate the market, while high-quality bond issuers will no longer offer their bonds for sale.
- **In the equity market: Directors know potential future profits, shareholders don't.** Remember that the market price of a stock reflects the discounted future profitability of the corporation. This naturally involves a great deal of uncertainty. The directors of the corporation may know a lot more about the future potential profitability of the firm than would any outside stockholder. So the outside stockholder, who cannot tell the difference between future high-valued stock and future low-valued stock, might offer only the average expected future value. Thus the equity market will be made up of future low-valued stock, while the future high-valued stock is never brought to the market.

7-2a Overcoming Adverse Selection in Financial Markets

Financial markets seek to overcome the adverse selection problem in several ways. Keep in mind, these attempts to overcome the adverse selection problem do *not* mean the problem has been completely resolved.

Information Collection

If someone is interested in buying a financial asset, say, a corporate or government bond, they will try to figure out the possibility that the issuer of the bond will not live up to their promise to repay. As we will discuss further in Chapter 16, the bond rating system has been around since the beginning of the twentieth century to assist bond buyers in determining the relative "safety" of bonds in the market. The idea behind the bond rating system is that the three main bond-rating firms—Moody's, Standard & Poor's, and Fitch—all specialize in gathering information and passing judgment on the ability of borrowers to repay. Thus, the bond-rating agencies apply a rating to the potential default risk of the borrower: AAA is the best, whereas C is the worst.

The bond ratings are thus relatively easy to understand and easy to find. While these are great advantages, they also result in one of the bond rating system's biggest faults. The bond rating system, or any collection of information, suffers from the **free-rider problem**.

Free-rider problem: A situation where some members of society benefit from the consumption of a good or service without paying for the good or service.

Here is how the free-rider problem works. Imagine you go out and spend a lot of time and energy researching a company to determine whether the firm will repay its debt and/or its future profitability. I, on the other hand, am rather lazy, but I too want to know the riskiness and potential future profit of a firm. But instead of doing my own research, I simply watch and see what you do. I know that you have done all of the hard work in researching the firm, so I follow you into the market and offer the same prices you are offering. Thus, I am free-riding: I am getting all of the benefit of your hard work and research while paying nothing for it.

The free-rider problem leads to a major problem: You might not be willing to undertake the research and analysis if you know that I am simply going to free-ride you. Thus, if there is a potential for free-riding, private entities simply may not collect information to overcome the adverse selection problem. This has led some to argue that this is a market failure and thus the government needs to step in and correct the problem.

Government-Required Disclosures

As a reaction to potential market failure in the private collection of financial market information, the Securities Act of 1933 established disclosure rules for issuers of securities in the primary markets. A year later in 1934, the Securities Exchange Act set down rules for buying and selling securities in the secondary market. The 1934 act also created the Securities and Exchange Commission (SEC), which is responsible for enforcing the two acts as well as other rules and regulations surrounding the disclosure of information to investors.

The SEC seeks to enforce the securities law by requiring public companies to submit quarterly and annual reports. In addition, company executives must submit a "Management Discussion and Analysis" that explains how the company has done over the past year. To make it easier for investors to access these reports, the SEC maintains an extensive online database called the Electronic Data Gathering Analysis and Retrieval system, or EDGAR for short.

All of this is done in an attempt to overcome the free-rider problem in the private collection of financial market information, which is needed to resolve the adverse selection problem. Banks, too, seek to overcome the adverse selection problem by gathering vast amounts of information.

Screening

Think about the information your commercial bank knows about you. If you have a checking account with the bank, they know how much money you earn each month and have a pretty good idea of where you spend your money. In addition, if you apply for a loan, the bank will ask you all sorts of information about your assets, debts, and income. With all of this private information—that is, information that is not available to anyone in the public—the bank can get a better idea of your ability to repay your debts. The same is true whenever you apply for credit. The lender will obtain all sorts of information from you to better screen you to and determine whether you have the ability to repay.

What's true for individuals is also true for firms. When a firm applies for a loan the operators of the firm have to supply the borrower with a great deal of information on how the firm has operated in the past and its future projections. This private information has to be in a format that is easily understandable to someone outside of the firm. This is one of the reasons why a well-functioning accounting system is so important to the proper function of financial markets.

Adverse selection is just one of the ways that asymmetric information can rear its ugly head. Remember, adverse selection usually occurs before a financial transaction takes place. But after the financial transaction is completed, asymmetric information can result in a moral hazard, which is the next concept we want to examine.

SECTION REVIEW

Q1) How does the existence of "free riders" help to perpetuate the adverse selection problem?

Q2) It is often stated that "we live in an information age," yet the adverse selection problem still exists. Why?

Q3) Which government regulatory agency was created, in great part, to help overcome the adverse selection problem in equity markets?

a. The Federal Reserve
b. The United States Treasury
c. The Department of Justice
d. The Securities and Exchange Commission

7-3 Moral Hazard

Adverse selection is only one of the problems that can arise from asymmetric information in markets. While adverse selection takes place *before* a market transaction occurs, another problem, **moral hazard**, can arise *after* the transaction takes place. Moral hazard exists when one party of a transaction has difficulty monitoring the behavior of the other party after the contract begins. Simply stated, the existence of a contract alters people's behavior because the incentives have changed.

Moral hazard: One entity takes on an excessive amount of risk because it knows another entity will bear the burden of those risks.

7-3a Moral Hazard in Corporate Governance

To understand why moral hazard is a problem, think about how it can arise in the management of a corporation. The owners of the corporation—the stockholders—hire managers to run the firm. The stockholders want a management team that will work hard to ensure the firm is profitable without taking on too much risk. The stockholders find a management team that seems like a bunch of honest, hardworking people, so the stockholders decide to hire these managers and pay them a nice salary.

But after the management team takes over running the firm, they realize that if the firm fails they will be out of a job and lose the nice salary they are being paid; thus the management team decides to play it safe. They do not launch new products because they view new products as being too risky. Without new products, however, the firm fails to keep up with the market and sales start to slump. The conservative management is actually destroying the wealth of the stockholders. While all of this is going on the stockholders are clueless—they can't keep an eye on what is happening in the firm day to day.

Thus, the existence of the contract between the shareholders and the management team changed the management team's behavior because of the incentives. With the employment contract, now the management team had a lot to lose if things went bad and not much to gain if things went well.

This example is not pure fiction; it is exactly what happened in corporations in the United States throughout the 1950s and 1960s. It is referred to as the **principle–agent problem** in agency theory. The principles (the stockholders) hire the agents (the management team) to run the firm. The problem is, the agents cannot diversify their human capital; that is, they can only work for one firm at a time. Thus the existence of the labor contract, through which the management is paid a salary, creates an incentive for them to be excessively conservative in their running of the firm. Thus, as has been shown, the management destroyed stockholders' value by being excessively risk adverse during this time period.

Principle–agent problem: The problem of motivating one party (the agent) who has been hired by another party (the principle) to act in the best interests of the hiring party.

7-3b Moral Hazard in Financial Markets

While the moral hazard problem is a major issue in executive compensation, it is also a major problem in financial markets. Consider the following:

- **Moral Hazard in Insurance.** Think about how you would drive your car if you had no automobile insurance. If you get into an accident, payment for the repair of any damage to your car will have to come out of your own pocket. Thus you are likely to be a very cautious driver, constantly worried that you are going to get into an accident.

Now imagine that you have automobile insurance with no deductible and a premium that never changes. You could now be a very lax driver; you might use a brick wall to help stop your car. What do you care if the car is damaged? You would simply submit a claim into your auto insurance company and have them pay for the repairs.

What happened? Your driving behavior changed (from cautious to lax) because the contract (the insurance policy) changed the incentives. This is not good for the insurance company because they cannot monitor your daily driving behavior; they are subject to a massive moral hazard problem.

- **Moral Hazard in Lending.** Suppose a bank lends money to a fine, upstanding person who has always handled their money in a prudent manner. But this person was always prudent with *their own* money. Now this person has "the bank's money," which they see as someone else's money and thus are willing to spend it wildly on gambling and elaborate entertainment! The bank cannot keep tabs on every borrower every day, so they face a moral hazard when lending money.

  This example is, unfortunately, an actual event. Several years ago I was employed by a bank and was responsible for, among other things, a portfolio of consumer loans. In one loan, the bank's customer seemed like a great person: steady job, cash on hand, and so on. But once the customer had the bank's money in the form of a loan, he became a financial Dr. Jekyll/Mr. Hyde. I had to track down the customer for payment on the loan month after month. Finally, the customer admitted that he had spent the loan proceeds foolishly because it was "the bank's money" and not their own. The customer explained that with his own money, he would be very careful, but the bank's money he used for risky bets. He reasoned that if the bets paid off he would enjoy the benefits as well as repay the bank. On the other hand, if the bets did not pay off, the bank would suffer the losses because he was unable to repay the bank loan. It was a perfect example of a moral hazard: The loan changed the bank customer's behavior because, in the customer's eyes, the incentives had changed.

- **Moral Hazard in Debt and Equity Markets.** Go back to the description of the principle–agent problem that faces stockholders of a corporation. The existence of the labor contract between the stockholders and the management of the firm changed the managers' behavior because their incentives changed. A similar thing can occur in debt and equity markets with the issuing of financial instruments.

  Think about it this way: Managers of a firm may be very particular about what projects they fund when they are using the start-up capital they themselves put into the firm to get it going. However, once the firm can obtain funds from the financial markets, either through borrowing by issuing bonds or raising capital by selling stock, the managers might act very differently. They may view the proceeds from bond and equity sales as "someone else's money" and thus be more carefree with it. Perhaps they will spend lavishly on luxury office equipment or fund risky projects they think will be "fun." It might be very difficult for bond issuers or stockholders to keep an eye on all of the managers' spending.

7-3c Overcoming the Moral Hazard Problem in Financial Markets

Given all of these potential moral hazards, it may be surprising that *any* financial contracts exist. How these contracts are structured, however—to avoid the moral hazard problem—is part of the reason why they do exist. Here are some of the ways in which financial markets attempt to overcome the moral hazard problem.

- **Deductibles and Adjustable Premiums.** Most insurance contracts include deductibles and premiums that can be adjusted based on claims. A deductible is the amount of damage that the insured must pay out of their own pocket. For example, if someone has an automobile insurance policy with a $500 deductible, when they get into an accident they will have to pay for the first $500 worth of damage. This is done in large part to control for the moral hazard problem. Once a claim for damages is submitted, the insurance company often increases the insured premium, or how much the insured must pay for the insurance. This again is done to control the behavior of the insured after the insurance contract is created.
- **Restrictive Covenants.** Covenants are legally binding promises that are made by the bond issuer to the bondholder; they are explicitly laid out in the bond contract. Restrictive covenants can be financial covenants that may, for example, limit how much debt the firm can issue or require the firm to maintain a certain amount of cash. Restrictive covenants can also be nonfinancial, such as requiring the management to provide certain information to shareholders and debt holders or requiring outside approval before the firm sells any major assets. These restrictive covenants are intended to keep management from doing things that might be harmful to the stakeholders' value.
- **Compensating Balances.** When a bank makes a loan to a person or a firm, they sometimes require that borrower to maintain at the bank a checking or savings account with a certain minimum balance. The purpose of this, in part, is to ensure that the borrower has some secondary means to make payments on the loan, just in case their primary repayment source does not work out as planned. In addition, the compensating balances can be used as a way of monitoring the financial status of the borrower.

  To understand how compensating balances perform a monitoring function, think about how much your bank knows about you when they look into your checking account. They can see how fast you spend your money and on what you are spending your money. Thus, the bank can glean a lot of information about your behavior by looking at your checking account. The bank can use this information to warn them of any potential moral hazards that may develop when you receive a loan from the bank.
- **Corporate Board of Directors.** In a corporation, the board of directors is supposed to watch over the actions of the executive branch of the corporation, in part to ensure there is no moral hazard problem. Simply put, a corporate board of directors is a group of people who are legally responsible to govern a corporation. The board of directors traditionally answers to the stockholders of the corporation. A more modern version of the board of directors is one that answers to the stakeholders of the corporation—everyone who has an interest in and/or can be affected by the corporation, including bondholders, employees, and the local community.

  In many European economies the main responsibility of the board of directors is to the employees of the firm, with stockholders taking a second position. Even in this situation, the board of directors acts to ensure a moral hazard problem does not exist with the employment contracts of the executives of the corporation. If the board of directors believes that the executives of the corporation are not acting in the best interests of the stakeholders of the corporation, they have a legal responsibility to correct the situation. This, of course, can be a very subjective decision that must be undertaken by the board of directors.

Thus the commercial banking system can play a significant role in helping to overcome the asymmetric information problem that results in the adverse selection and moral hazard problems in financial markets. But the important role of the banking system does not end there. To review why banks are so important to the proper functioning of the overall economy, next we examine more in depth what commercial banks and other depository institutions do.

While overcoming the asymmetric information problem (in the form of adverse selection and the moral hazard problem) is an important role banks play, it is not the only one. Next we look at the other important things banks do in addition to solving the asymmetric information problem.

SECTION REVIEW

Q1) What is the relationship between the principle–agent problem in corporate governance and the moral hazard problem?

Q2) Explain how compensating balances help to resolve the moral hazard problem in bank lending.

Q3) High deductibles are used in which financial market to help address the moral hazard problem?

a. Equity market

b. Bond market

c. Insurance market

d. Bank deposit market

7-4 What Banks Do

Although slightly oversimplified, depository institutions—or what we will refer to simply as "banks"—do two things: take deposits and make loans. By doing these two things, banks provide some important services to their depositors, borrowers, and investors. Banks provide liquidity, lend in large amounts, reduce transaction costs, and pay returns to investors. Let's consider why each of these things is critically important to the functioning of a market economy.

7-4a Provide Liquidity

Think about the differences between bank depositors and borrowers in terms of length of time. In general, depositors want to have access to their funds at any time. To understand why, think about checking accounts, or what we will call "demand deposits." Let's suppose someone gets paid the first of every month by having their paycheck deposited directly into their demand deposit account. During the month, this depositor withdraws funds to pay bills, buy food, and so on. Thus this demand deposit account holder wants to be able to convert their demand deposit into other assets in a quick, easy, and inexpensive way. We say that this account holder wants liquidity.

Liquidity is defined as the ease and expense at which one asset can be converted into another asset. Demand deposits are very liquid; that is, converting a demand deposit into cash is easy and inexpensive. On the other hand, an automobile is illiquid; that is, it takes a long time and a lot of hassle to sell a car or to convert the car into another asset: cash.

Liquidity: The ease and expense at which one asset can be converted into another asset.

So, in general, bank depositors such as demand deposit account holders want liquidity; they want to be able to convert their bank accounts into cash quickly, easily, and inexpensively.

Borrowers, on the other hand, want to borrow for a long time. Think about someone who borrows money to purchase a new car. This borrower is interested in paying back the amount borrowed over the next 4 to 6 years. People who borrow money to buy a house are looking to pay back the money over the next 30 years. This desire to borrow for a relatively long time also extends to businesses who want to borrow money to buy office equipment, machinery, and so on. These business borrowers are looking to pay the loans back over the next 5 to 10 years. Thus, in general, borrowers from the bank want illiquid loans; that is, they want to pay back over long periods of time.

Thus, we have a **liquidity mismatch**: Savers want liquidity and borrowers want to sign illiquid loans. If banks or other financial intermediaries did not exist, we would have a huge problem. Very few loans would be written because relatively few savers would be willing to tie up their funds for long periods of time. This is where banks provide an important service: They are providers of liquidity. That is, banks provide liquidity to depositors while writing loans that will not be paid back for a long time.

Liquidity mismatch: A situation in which there is a lack of unity between the contractual amounts and dates of cash inflows and outflows.

7-4b Reduce Transaction Costs

Even if we could solve the liquidity mismatch between savers and borrowers—maybe there would be enough long-term savers to provide funds to long-term borrowers—we would still face the problem of transaction costs. One of the biggest transaction costs in financial transactions are search costs.

Search costs in financial markets are the implicit and explicit costs involved in savers and borrowers looking for each other. To understand why search costs are important, think of what a hassle it would be if you were a saver and there were no banks. You, as a saver, would have to hunt high and low to find someone who wants to borrow your money. The same problem exists for borrowers; without banks they would have to spend a great deal of time looking for people to lend them money.

Search costs: The implicit and explicit costs involved in savers and borrowers looking for each other.

Thank goodness banks and other financial intermediaries exist. They greatly reduce transaction costs by bringing savers and borrowers together. Because banks exist, you as a saver don't have to spend long hours searching out potential borrowers. Instead, all you have to do is take your savings to a bank and they will find the borrowers.

Even if we can solve the search cost problems, there are other transactions costs, such as the implicit and explicit costs of drawing up contracts. Again, assume you are a saver and there are no banks or other financial intermediaries. Even if you could find a borrower, now you have to draw up an agreement between you and the borrower. Do you know how to write a legal contract that will ensure repayment? Do you know how to secure a lien on collateral? Do you know what interest rate to charge the borrower? Chances are the answer to these questions is NO.

Once again, thank goodness there are banks and other financial intermediaries; they greatly reduce transaction costs by specializing in writing financial contracts. Because banks write thousands of financial contracts a year, they benefit from economies of scale. Remember, **economies of scale** is the concept that as output increases, the cost per unit decreases. Thus, because banks write thousands of financial contracts, their cost per contract is low. Thus, banks greatly reduce transaction costs for both savers and borrowers.

Economies of Scale: As output increases the cost per unit of output declines.

7-4c Block Lending

Another mismatch between savers and borrowers can arise in the size of the transactions. Savers generally save small amounts, whereas borrowers generally want to borrow much larger sums. Again, banks and other financial intermediaries come to the rescue. They gather together a bunch of small savings into one big bundle to then lend out to a borrower.

Even more important than the bundling of savings, banks offer savers the ability to diversify their risks. To understand why this is important, once again think of yourself as a saver in a world that lacks banks. Even if you could resolve the liquidity and search costs by finding a borrower who wants to borrow your money for the exact amount of time you want to save, you face the problem that you are lending all of your funds to one borrower. As the old saying goes, you are "putting all of your eggs into one basket"—or you are undiversified. If something unexpected happens to that one borrower, all of your savings may be lost.

Again, thank goodness for banks and other financial intermediaries; they offer savers **diversification**. Instead of lending your savings to just one borrower, the bank spreads your savings among the thousands of borrowers to whom the bank lends. Thus, when you put your savings into a savings account at a bank, you are not "putting all your eggs into one basket" because the bank is diversifying your savings by lending it to literally thousands of different borrowers. Thus, if something unexpected does happen to one, or even more, of those borrowers, you are unaffected by it.

Diversification: A means of reducing risk by holding a variety of assets.

Thus, banks provide a wide variety of important services. Without these services, a market economy would suffer from higher costs, lower levels of borrowing and spending, and thus weaker overall economic performance. However, perhaps one of the most important functions a bank performs is its creation of money. To review how this works, let's first look at the simple deposit multiplier and what insights it offers us.

SECTION REVIEW

Q1) Explain why economies without banks suffer from high search costs.

Q2) Explain how banks offer diversification to savers even if a depositor puts all of their funds into a single bank account.

Q3) Which of the following has the highest level of liquidity?

a. The stock of a Fortune 100 corporation

b. A bond issued by the US Government

c. A bank checking account

d. A bank savings account

Simple Deposit Multiplier

7-5

As we have seen, banks do a wide variety of things. Perhaps one of the most important things they do is create money. To learn how banks create money we will go over the simple deposit multiplier[2] that you may have seen in your principles of economics courses. To review how the simple deposit multiplier works, let's assume we run the Anchor Bank in Madison, Wisconsin.

7-5a Day 1 at Anchor Bank

At 8:00 a.m. we open the doors of the Anchor Bank and in walks a woman. This woman has a briefcase in her hand, which she places on our desk and proceeds to open. In the briefcase is $10,000 in cash, and the woman informs us that she wants to open a checking or demand deposit at Anchor Bank.

We agree to open the account for her. We take her $10,000, put it in the bank's vault, and proceed to have her sign the proper forms to open the demand deposit account. After she signs all the necessary paperwork, we give the woman checks and a debit card for the account and she leaves the bank.

We wait for another customer to come into the bank. No one else shows up. It is now 4:00 p.m. and we close the bank's doors. Before we can leave for the day, however, we need to balance the bank's books.

To balance the bank's books, remember the accounting equation:

Asset = Liabilities + Net worth (or Bank capital)

The accounting equation *always* has to hold. Thus, if the left side of the equation changes, the right side of the equation must change by the exact same amount in the same direction. As will be described in more depth later, a bank's balance sheet generally looks like the one shown in Table 7-1.

Now let's think about what happened during the bank day. The woman gave the bank $10,000 cash, for which the bank gave her a demand deposit account. Thus, in terms of the bank's balance sheet, the bank's cash/reserve holding increased by $10,000. Therefore, we see under assets that the cash/reserves increase by $10,000.

© Megan Brandl

AnchorBank headquarters at 25 West Main Street in Madison, Wisconsin

Table 7-1 Bank Balance Sheet Listing Assets and Liabilities

Assets	Liabilities and Bank Capital
Cash/reserves	Demand deposits
Business loans	Savings accounts
Consumer loans	Loans from other banks
Mortgages	Other borrowings
Bonds	
Other assets	Bank capital

2 The simple deposit multiplier is called "simple" in part because it makes some simplified examples, such as banks hold no excess reserves, there is only one required reserve ratio, and the public holds no cash.

Table 7-2 Demand Deposit

Assets	Liabilities and Bank Capital
Cash/reserves + $10,000	Demand deposits + $10,000

In addition, the bank also gave that woman $10,000 in the form of a demand deposit. Demand deposits are a liability on the bank's balance sheet because they represent things the bank owes to others. Thus, as we see in Table 7-2, assets went up $10,000 and liabilities went up by $10,000, so the balance sheet balances!

But now the bank faces another problem: That woman depositor is going to want to be paid interest on her deposit. Thus our bank needs to earn some interest income by lending part of that $10,000 to other customers. This then raises an interesting question for the bank: How much of the $10,000 should the bank lend out?

The bank would like to lend out all $10,000 to earn as much interest income as possible, but it cannot because that woman could come in and want part of her $10,000 back. So, again, the question is, How much should the bank lend out and how much should it hold in reserves in order to meet the cash needs of its depositors?

This question, as it turns out, is one of the oldest questions in banking. It dates back literally centuries. Fortunately, bankers today in modern financial systems do not have to contemplate the answer to this question. Instead, banks are told by one of their regulators what portion of deposits they must hold in the form of reserves. That is, the banks are told what their required reserve ratio is.

The **required reserve ratio** is the proportion of deposits banks must hold in the form of cash or reserves. These reserves[3] may be held in the form of vault cash and/or deposits at the central bank.

Required reserve ratio: The proportion of deposits banks must hold in the form of cash or reserves.

Let us suppose that we at the Anchor Bank contact our regulator and discover that, for this type of account at our bank, the required reserve ratio is 10%. That is, we have to hold 10% of the $10,000 deposit—or $1,000—in the form of reserves. But we don't have just $1,000 in reserves, we have all $10,000 in reserves. The reserves in excess of the required reserves that a bank holds are called "excess reserves."

Total reserves = Required reserves + Excess reserves

Thus, here we have:

$10,000 = $1,000 + $9,000

It is the $9,000 in excess reserves we would like to lend out, but no one else came into the bank. Thus, we end the bank day with $9,000 of excess reserves.

7-5b Day 2 at Anchor Bank

At 8:00 a.m. we open the bank doors and into the bank walks a very nice fellow. We learn that his name is Bob, and Bob tells us that he is interested in borrowing some money because he wants to buy a car. We have Bob fill out a loan application; we run a credit check and determine he is a fine credit risk. We ask Bob how much he is interested in borrowing, and he informs us he wants to borrow $9,000. We perform the calculations and determine Bob can comfortably afford the monthly payments to repay the $9,000 plus interest.

3 The concept of reserves is actually more complicated than this, as we shall see in later chapters, but for now this definition of reserves will suffice.

Next, we ready the loan documents for Bob to sign. We tell Bob that once he signs the loan document, we will deposit the $9,000 into a checking account for him, and when he finds a car that he likes, he can write out a check to the car seller. Bob agrees, signs the loan documents, and leaves with the paperwork and his new checkbook.

We now wait for the next customer to come into the bank. We wait, but no one else comes into the bank. At 4:00 p.m. we close the bank's doors, and once again we must balance the books. On this day, we created a loan for Bob. The loan document, which is Bob's promise to repay, is an asset to the bank. The bank could, if it wanted, sell this loan in the secondary market. Thus, in writing the loan the bank created a $9,000 asset.

Just as important, when the bank created the loan for Bob it also created a $9,000 demand deposit for Bob. Remember, demand deposits are a liability to the bank, thus the bank's liabilities increased by $9,000 (Table 7-3). Thus, assets went up by $9,000 and liabilities increased by $9,000, so the balance sheet balances!

Think about the liability side of the bank's balance sheet for a minute. Remember, in Chapter 2 we described the M1 money supply as containing demand deposits. So, when the bank lends money and creates a new deposit, the bank is creating new money! This, it turns out, is how modern banking systems create money: through the banking system.

Table 7-3 Bank Lends $9,000

Assets	Liabilities and Bank Capital
Loans + $9,000	Demand deposits + $9,000

Tying Concepts Together

In Chapter 2 we defined money as "anything that is generally acceptable in exchange for goods and services and/or repayment of debt." We described how the M1 measurement of the money supply contained coins and currency in the hands of the public, demand deposits, travelers checks, and other checkable deposits. If the level of demand deposits in the system increases, there is an increase in the money supply. This is exactly what happens when a bank writes a loan and creates a new demand deposit for the loan customer.

But the money supply process is *not* going to stop there. Once Bob finds a car that he likes, he is going to write out a check to the car seller. The car seller then will deposit that check into their bank account, say at Citibank. Now Citibank has a new deposit of $9,000. As we just described, when a bank receives a deposit, it wants (and needs) to lend out the majority of that new deposit. If we assume that Citibank also has a required reserve ratio of 10%, it will hold 10% of the $9,000 (or $900) in the form of reserves and lend out the remaining $8,100. When it does so, Citibank will create $8,100 of new money.

This new $8,100 will be deposited into another bank that will again hold 10% in reserves and lend out the remaining $7,290. When it does so, this bank will create $7,290 of new money. This new money will be deposited into another bank, and the process repeats.

What we have here is a geometric series. In each step of the series, the amount being passed on to the next round is reduced. The amount of new money created is passed on to the next round, but that amount is reduced by the amount that is held in reserve. We can calculate the total impact of this. We stop when the new amount being created is just one cent, by use of the geometric series formula.

Thus, we have the simple deposit multiplier formula, which is

$$\Delta\text{Deposits} = \Delta\text{Money supply} = \text{Initial deposit} \times \left\{\frac{1}{RRR}\right\}$$

where *RRR* is the required reserve ratio.

So, in this example it would be

$$\Delta\text{Deposits} = \Delta\text{Money supply} = \$10{,}000 \times \left\{\frac{1}{0.10}\right\} = \$100{,}000$$

Tying Concepts Together

Bank Deposits and Loanable Funds

Imagine that banks see a surge in deposits. Banks want to lend these funds to earn interest income. In terms of the loanable funds framework, this would mean that there are now more funds to be lent at every interest rate—or there is an increase in the supply of loanable funds. As we described earlier, this would graphically shift the supply curve of loanable funds outward (Figure 7-1).

The result of this increase in the supply of loanable funds, ceteris paribus, is a lower equilibrium interest rate and a high equilibrium quantity. Thus, an increase in deposits in the banking system, ceteris paribus, results in lower market interest rates and a higher equilibrium quantity in the loanable funds market.

While the simple deposit multiplier is a fairly simple math problem, it offers great insight to people who understand how to apply it. Next we examine more in depth just what the simple deposit multiplier is telling us.

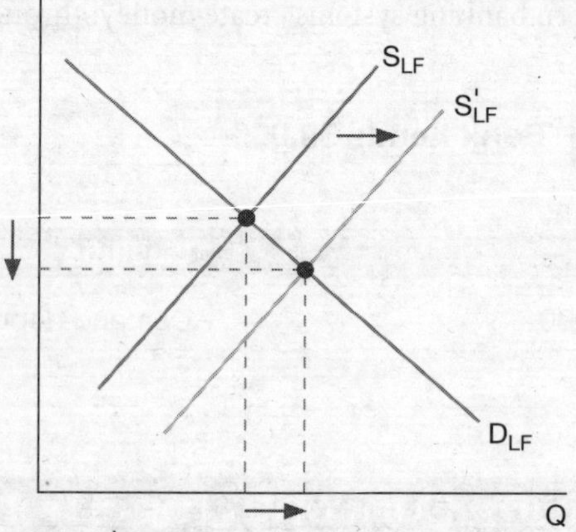

Figure 7-1

Increase in the Supply of Loanable Funds from Increased Bank Deposits

SECTION REVIEW

Q1) If $100 million is deposited into the banking system, what would happen to the money supply, according to the simple deposit multiplier, if the required reserve ratio is 4%? What if the required reserve ratio is 6%? What do you think will happen to interest rates and the overall economy if this change in the required reserve ratio took place?

Q2) If $100 million is withdrawn from the banking system, what would happen to the money supply, according to the simple deposit multiplier, if the required reserve ratio is 4%? What if the required reserve ratio is 6%? What do you think will happen to interest rates and the overall economy if this change in the required reserve ratio took place?

Q3) According to the simple deposit multiplier, what happens if there is a deposit and the required reserve ratio is zero?

a. The money supply grows forever.

b. The money supply equals zero.

c. The growth rate of the money supply is zero.

d. The economy will collapse.

What the Simple Deposit Multiplier Tells Us and Its Problems

7-6

There are a couple of key insights to draw from the simple deposit multiplier: First, banks can create as well as destroy money; second, banks are subject to bank runs; third, banks can harm the overall economy if they do not lend. Let's consider each in turn.

7-6a Banks Create and Destroy Money

Remember in Chapter 2 we examined the various money supplies. We said that one of the most important components of M1 were demand deposits. With the help of the simple deposit multiplier, we can now see how the level of demand deposits increases. When a bank receives a deposit, it lends out the majority of that new deposit by creating new money. This new money then is deposited into another bank, and the process repeats. Thus, a one-time deposit into the banking system is going to wind up increasing the money supply by much more than that initial deposit. This is what the simple deposit multiplier captures.

The process can also work in reverse. Imagine Anchor Bank holds only its level of required reserves with a required reserve ratio of 10%. Now assume a customer comes into the bank and withdraws $5,000 cash. The bank needed that $5,000 to back up $50,000 worth of deposits.

Anchor Bank no longer has the customer's $5,000 account, so we no longer need the $500 in reserves that was "backing up" that account. Anchor Bank does, however, need $4,500 to have enough reserves for the other $45,000 it has on deposit.

So Anchor Bank will have to sell $4,500 of assets—perhaps corporate bonds or government bonds that it holds—to get the $4,500 in cash or reserves it needs. As luck would have it, the next customer in line presents a check for $4,500 drawn from another bank (say, Wells Fargo), which she is going to use to repay a loan she has at our bank.

We then take that check to Wells Fargo, present it for payment, and take $4,500 in cash from Wells Fargo. Thus we have the $4,500 in cash we need to meet our reserve requirement. But, if Wells Fargo was holding only the minimum required reserves, they now face a shortfall of reserves. So the process will now repeat. Therefore the simple deposit multiplier can be used to show how money gets created as well as how the money supply decreases.

The important thing to remember is that a large portion of our money supply is created through the banking system, not through a printing press somewhere. It is when banks lend money that money is created, and it is through the banking system that the money supply is decreased.

Thus banks play an important role in the creation and reduction of the money supply. While banks are critically important, they are also very fragile, and the system may not work as smoothly as we just described.

7-6b Banks Are Subject to Bank Runs

In our example above, notice what happens if all of the depositors of a bank show at once and want their money back in cash. Think about the point where the Anchor Bank had made the loan to Bob, the loan customer. The Anchor Bank had $19,000 in demand deposit liabilities ($10,000 of the woman's, and $9,000 of Bob's), but the bank had only $10,000 in cash or reserves. If all the depositors showed up to the bank at once and wanted cash, the Anchor Bank would be in big trouble.

When all (or a large number) of the depositors of a bank want their money back at once, this is called a bank run. Fortunately, bank runs are rare today, but they do happen. During the autumn of 2008 there was a bank run at a relatively large depository institution in the United Kingdom called Northern Rock. Northern Rock suffered a bank run because depositors feared the lender was suffering huge losses because of its involvement in the US subprime mortgage market.

Commercial banks often used architecture as a subtle way to instill depositor confidence in the bank.

One of the biggest problems with bank runs is that they can be self-fulfilling prophecies. If people believe that their money is safe in the banking system, and they leave their money in the banks, then their money is safe—the system works as it is designed. If, however, people begin to question the safety and soundness of the banking system, and they respond to this uncertainty by pulling their money out of the banking system en masse, they can trigger a bank run. They can cause the banking system to become unsafe! Thus the self-fulfilling prophecy: If they believe the system is safe, it is safe. If they question its safety, they can make it unsafe.

This then raises the question, How do you make people believe the banking system is safe? In the old days it was often done with architecture.

Bank buildings were massive buildings with large cement pillars in front. Why were they designed this way? The answer to this question is, in part, to give depositors confidence that their money was "safe" behind all of the bank's bricks, mortar, and cement. It was really just a mind game to increase the level of confidence among depositors. But if it resulted in depositors having confidence in their banks, then all of the cement was worth it.

Since the 1930s the banking system has sought to instill confidence in depositors through government-sponsored deposit insurance. In the United States the Federal Deposit Insurance Corporation currently insures deposits up to $250,000 per account per institution. This insurance scheme seems to have worked well; the number of bank runs since the 1930s in the United States has fallen to essentially zero. As we will see later, however, deposit insurance is not a panacea. Critics of deposit insurance argue that the current system may cause as many problems as it resolves.

7-6c If Banks Don't Lend

The simple deposit multiplier shows us how the money supply increases in a modern market economy. This occurs when banks lend money. But the simple deposit multiplier is also useful in helping us think about the "counterexample": what happens when banks do *not* lend.

Suppose that bankers become worried about the future status of the economy. The bankers become concerned that, as the economy weakens, borrowers will have a more difficult time repaying their debts, including bank loans. Fearing increasing loan default rates in the future, banks curtail their current lending activities. In this case the bankers' fear of the future causes them to stop lending.

When private borrowers find borrowing from banks difficult, economists call this a **credit crunch**. These credit crunches can come about because banks become concerned about the future of the overall economy or because banks are already experiencing a decline in the market value of their assets. This is exactly what happened in 2007 and 2008. As the financial crisis unfolded, banks around the world started to realize that the assets they held that were tied to the US subprime mortgage market were decreasing rapidly in value. In response to these falling asset prices, bankers around the world greatly reduced their lending, triggering a global financial crisis.

Credit crunch: A reduction in the general availability of credit most often seen as an irrational increase in risk aversion.

Tying Concepts Together

Aggregate Supply/Aggregate Demand and Credit Crunch

A credit crunch—when banks stop lending—can have a disastrous effect on the overall economy. To understand why, think about short run–long run aggregate supply/aggregate demand framework. A reduction in bank lending would result in a decrease in consumption spending (households cut back on spending on consumer durable goods because they can no longer borrow funds for those purchases) and investment spending (new housing starts and business investment spending decline because of a lack of credit), causing the aggregate demand curve to shift back (Figure 7-2).

If all the talk of the credit crunch reduces sellers' expectations of the future or if entrepreneurs have to use their own, more costly, capital instead of being able to raise capital in financial markets, then the credit crunch can also cause a reduction in the short-run aggregate supply.

The combination of this reduction in aggregate demand and reduction in short-run aggregate supply results in a significant decline in real gross domestic product—that is, the economy can slide into a recession. The impact on the price level is uncertain because it depends on the size of the decrease in the in short-run aggregate supply relative to the aggregate demand.

Thus, a credit crunch, ceteris paribus, can result in a significant decline in real output and either inflation or deflationary pressures—even more uncertainty!

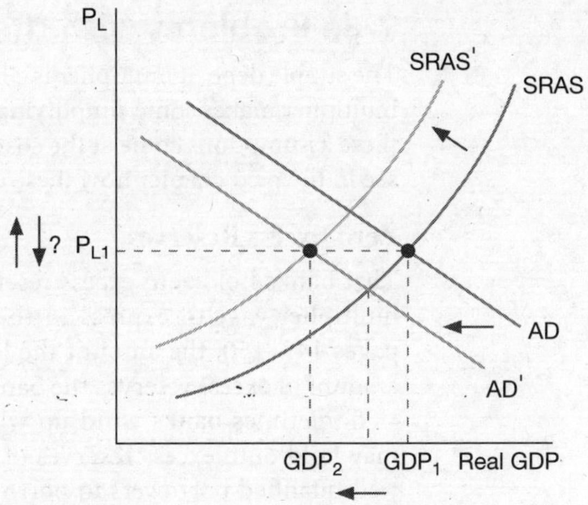

Figure 7-2
Macroeconomic Impact of a Credit Crunch

A credit crunch means that the simple deposit multiplier stops working. As banks stop lending, money stops being created. Remember why this important: As David Ricardo pointed out in the eighteenth century, if the money supply does not increase fast enough, the economy will slow down. This is precisely what happened in 2007 and 2008: The global credit crunch triggered a worldwide economic recession.

7-6d If There Is a Lack of Banks

While the simple deposit multiplier can help us to understand better why global economic meltdowns occur, it can also help us to understand why some poor neighborhoods remain poor. To understand this impact of the simple deposit multiplier we need to alter our concept of "economy." Think about an economy not as a nationwide economic system but instead in terms of a neighborhood.

Imagine our economic system is a neighborhood with houses, parks, restaurants, shops, automobile dealers, and repair shops. In a system with banks, each of the households and firms are savers and borrowers. Banks take in deposits and lend out the majority of those deposits, thus creating money and increasing the amount of economic activity.

If the economic system has no banks, however, the lending does not take place, the money supply does *not* increase, and, most important, the level of economic activity does not increase. Because of the lack of economic activity, unemployment may increase, businesses may fail; in short, the entire economic system may stagnate. Thus a lack of banks can result in economic stagnation.

This is not just an abstract example. Economists such as Ross Levine at the Haas School of Business at the University of California, Berkeley, have spent a great deal of time studying the relationship between financial market development and economic development. In numerous academic articles Levine, his coauthors, and others inspired by his work demonstrated that financial market development can play an important role in economic development. Simply put, a lack of financial market development will stifle economic development, resulting in slower economic growth, higher unemployment, and a lower standard of living for people in the economy.

While the simple deposit multiplier is a powerful tool in that it allows us to understand how money is created and it vividly demonstrates the importance of depository institutions, the simple deposit multiplier is far from perfect. Next let's take a look at some of the shortcomings of the simple deposit multiplier.

7-6e Problems with the Simple Deposit Multiplier

The simple deposit multiplier is a handy little tool, but it is just that: simple. The simple deposit multiplier makes some simplifying assumptions that make it easier to use and understand, but these assumptions come at the cost of making the simple deposit multiplier unrealistic. We will see in the next chapter how these oversimplifications can be corrected.

Zero Excess Reserves

That banks hold zero excess reserves is the first assumption that makes the simple deposit multiplier easy to express in the form of a geometric series. Notice in our example on pages 149–150, the amount the loan customer wanted to borrow was exactly equal to the amount of excess reserves the bank held. In reality, life isn't so simple.

Sometimes banks wind up with excess reserves, by choice or by circumstance. Banks may hold onto excess reserves of their own choosing; perhaps they could not find enough well-qualified borrowers to borrow all of their excess reserves. Or banks may wind up with excess reserves as a result of circumstances beyond their control, for example, perhaps the demand for loans decreases.

If banks do hold onto excess reserves, then these funds "leak out" of the banking system and reduce the size of the deposit multiplier. We will make adjustments to the simple deposit multiplier to allow for these "leakages" in the following chapters.

The issue of banks holding onto excess reserves is not just an academic exercise; this can and does happen during credit crunches. For example, during the financial crisis that started in 2007, anxiety over the growing number of subprime mortgage defaults in commercial banks around the world restricted their lending. As banks held onto excess reserves, firms could not get access to the credit they needed for daily business activities. Thus businesses contracted their spending and the global economy entered into a recession.

Nonbank Public Holding Cash

Another "leakage" can occur in the simple deposit multiplier if the nonbank public holds on to cash. The simple deposit multiplier assumes that all of the new money that a bank creates when it makes a loan is deposited into another bank. This, of course, may not happen. Households, or even firms, might convert some of the newly created demand deposits into cash and hold on to that cash. Thus, this amount of the money supply "leaks" out of the banking system and thus cannot be re-lent by another bank. So, if the nonbank public holds on to cash, the size of the deposit multiplier is reduced. We will make adjustments to the simple deposit multiplier for this type of leakage in the next chapter, as well.

The issue of the nonbank public holding on to cash instead of depositing into a bank, and thus reducing the size of the deposit multiplier, can be a major concern. Think about a developing country where the banking system may not be very well developed. In this type of setting households and firms may conduct many of the their transactions in only cash simply because banks don't exist. With a lack of banks, however, there is a lack of money creation. Remember what David Ricardo told us about a lack of money creation: If there is not enough money in the economy, the economy can slow, sliding into a recession or even a depression. This may help to explain why many poor countries remain poor: a lack of financial market development.

Many also blame an increase in the amount of cash held by the nonbank public as contributing to the Great Depression of the 1930s. As Americans began to worry about the safety and soundness of the banking system, they started to hold on to more and more cash. The problem is that this large increase in cash holdings means that the deposit multiplier is shrinking, and thus the money supply can cease to increase and may even decrease. This is exactly what happened: The money supply decreased, spending dried up, and the economy slid into the Great Depression.

These are things to keep in mind when you are thinking about the simple deposit multiplier formula. Understand that changes in this formula have a significant impact on people's lives. Thus it's not just some mathematical formula—it is so much more than that.

SECTION REVIEW

Q1) Explain how architecture may have been used to avoid bank runs.

Q2) You read a story in the press that there are growing fears of a credit crunch. What impact might this have in terms of the simple deposit multiplier?

Q3) Which of the following is not an assumption of the simple deposit multiplier?

a. Banks always earn a profit.

b. Banks hold no excess reserves.

c. Consumers hold no cash.

d. There is one required reserve ratio.

7-7 Conclusion

Because we do not live in a world of perfect information, depository institutions, or banks, have an important role to play. Banks help us resolve the adverse selection and moral hazard problems that arise out of the existence of asymmetric information. In doing so, banks provide society with liquidity, lower transaction costs, and the ability to lend in large blocks. This lending of depositors' funds also allows banks to create (as well as destroy) money through the simple deposit multiplier.

When the banking system works well, the money supply expands and contracts along with economic activity; but life isn't always so smooth. Banks can suffer from bank runs, they can refuse to lend, and/or there can be a lack of banks—all of which negatively affect the entire economy. Similarly, if banks hold on to excess reserves or the public holds on to large amounts of cash, the simple deposit multiplier loses its effectiveness in explaining how our financial system works. Thus we need to move beyond the simple deposit multiplier to understand fully how our financial system creates and destroys money. In the next chapter we look at central banks, entities created in large part to keep the banking system running smoothly. We also will see the important role modern commercial banks play in the conduct of monetary policy by making use of the banking system.

When the banking system works well, the economy can thrive and standards of living can increase. But when the system fails to work properly, innocent people can have their economic lives destroyed. Keep that in mind as you think about the role banks play in our economic system.

IN THE NEWS. . .

Bank Lending to UK Manufacturers Slows Amid Concern

The Guardian
January 27, 2015

Bank lending to Britain's factory owners slowed in December according to industry figures on Tuesday that indicate growing unease among manufacturers at the prospects for 2015.

The British Banker's Association (BBA) reported that growth in bank lending to the manufacturing sector more than halved in the last six months and declined by £624m in December, compared to a £217m expansion of credit in the previous month.

The figures also show that borrowing by companies outside the financial sector contracted by £15.7bn in 2014, compared with a decline of £11.6bn in 2013.

The BBA played down the sharp decline, saying the figures can be volatile. It said much of the contraction in lending to non-financial firms was due to a collapse in borrowing by real estate businesses and a switch by large corporations from bank lending to the bond markets as a source of finance.

It said that 2014 saw positive borrowing growth in the manufacturing, wholesale and retail sectors.

But the recent decline in manufacturing chimes with comments by the British Chambers of Commerce, which has called on the government to boost investment to overcome nervousness in the sector.

Richard Woolhouse, the BBA's chief economist, said: "Business lending has been falling as larger firms have used the bond market rather than borrowing from banks. . . ."

The article describes the decline in British bank lending to businesses. Use the tools of the simple deposit multiplier to explain what impact this might have on the UK economy in the future.

Summary of Money and the Overall Economy

Tying Concepts Together

We have learned how money and financial markets affect and have affected the overall economy. We have seen that when money flows properly and financial markets work correctly, the overall economy benefits. But things do not always work so smoothly. To ensure a stable supply and flow of money, central banks were created. In Chapter 8 we look at a variety of central banks around the world but focus mainly on the Federal Reserve. In Chapter 9 we examine the tools of monetary policy central banks have at their disposal, and in Chapter 10 we review how these tools are used in terms of the money supply multiplier. Finally, in Chapter 11 we learn that monetary policy is not without controversy when we delve into the debate over the conduct of monetary policy.

8 Central Banks

8-1 Evolution of the Fed

The Federal Reserve (sometimes referred to as "the Fed") is one of those things that people may hear a lot about—in the popular press, from the talking heads on television, and in the business press—but if you ask them to really explain what the Fed is and how it came to possess the power it has today, you usually get blank stares or even worse: misinformation. This problem became worse in the aftermath of the financial crisis of 2007–2008. As the Fed struggled to keep the financial system from completely caving in, many complained that it was "overstepping its bounds"; a member of Congress labeled the Fed "the world's counterfeiter." Strong words for an institution that most people don't really understand.

Over the next few chapters we will shed some much needed light on what the Federal Reserve and other central banks actually do and what they don't do. We start off by tracing the evolution of the Fed from its founding to its current form. This will give us a foundation for understanding the current power structure of the Fed: who does what and why. Next we delve into the functions and balance sheet of the Fed, where we will see how its balance sheet changed significantly during the current crisis, triggering much of the controversy described above. We conclude by comparing the structure of the Fed to that of other major central banks around the world, including the much older Bank of England and Bank of Japan, as well as the much younger European Central Bank and the Bank of Canada. When our journey through these chapters reaches an end, you will, I hope, have a better understanding of what central banks do and why they are important yet so misunderstood.

8-1a Evolution of the Federal Reserve

As was described in Chapter 5, the **Federal Reserve** was created in 1913 in response to the Panic of 1907. The Owen-Glass Federal Reserve Act of 1913 established what would become the central bank and monetary authority of the United States that we have today. The Federal Reserve system of today, however, bears little resemblance to the system created in 1913.

Federal Reserve: The central bank and monetary authority of the United States.

When the Federal Reserve system began operation, it was a collection of 12 independent regional banks whose purpose was to maintain the gold standard and be a "lender of last resort" to commercial banks. These regional banks would lend money to commercial banks only when the commercial banks provided "eligible paper" or "real bills" as collateral. These real bills would, in theory, include loans to entities that would use loan proceeds only to produce goods and services, not for speculation. Thus, under the **real bills doctrine**, the Fed banks would provide liquidity so that the additional money would be used only for "real" as opposed to speculative purposes.

Real bills doctrine: Central banks should lend money to commercial banks if and only if the commercial banks use those funds to support "real" (as opposed to speculative) economic activity.

Debate over Power

When the Federal Reserve system was created, there was a great deal of controversy over the size and power of the Fed's regional banks. The original act called for the creation of the Reserve Bank Organization Committee, which would determine which cities would receive Federal Reserve banks. The act specified that no fewer than 8 but no more than 12 cities would receive Federal Reserve banks and that the nation then would be divided into Federal Reserve districts. The act held that each Fed district would contain only one Federal Reserve city, the idea being these cities would be the major financial centers of the country.

There was little doubt that New York would be a Federal Reserve city, but there was a contentious question over how much larger and more powerful the New York Fed would be than the other Federal Reserve regional banks. Many of New York's powerful banks, such as J.P. Morgan, wanted an all-powerful New York Fed that would rival the size and power of the central banks of Europe.[1] The powerful New York financiers argued that the New York Fed should be given fully *half* of all of the funds being provided to the entire Federal Reserve system!

Naturally, many across the country worried that an all-powerful New York Fed would have complete domination of the entire US financial and economic system. Secretary of the Treasury William McAdoo and Secretary of Agriculture David Houston both reportedly shared the belief that the central banks of Europe should deal with the entire Federal Reserve system, not just the New York Fed.

Eventually, the New York Fed did not turn out to be all powerful, as many in the New York financial district wanted. The Reserve Bank Organization Committee eventually decided to create 12 Federal Reserve districts across the country, with New York being only one of them. So while the New York Fed did emerge to have the most influence compared with the other 11 Fed district banks, the New York Fed was not "all powerful."

Each of the 12 newly created Federal Reserve banks initially operated independently in their own respective regions. Each had its own board of directors and its own president. Commercial banks within the district would become a member of the Fed if they met certain requirements, including purchasing stock in their regional Federal Reserve bank.

Overarching this system of 12 regional Federal Reserve banks would be a board of governors in Washington, DC, initially housed in the Treasury Department. The board of governors originally provided oversight and examination of the Federal Reserve banks, but the power of the Federal Reserve system lay not with the board of governors in Washington, but with the regional banks across the country. These regional banks set their own **discount rate**—the interest rate they would charge on the loans they made to commercial banks; the board of governors played a minor role at best.

Discount rate: The interest rate the Federal Reserve charges on loans it makes to member banks. These discount loans are made at the Fed's discount window.

Structural Changes in the Fed During the Great Depression

The structure of the Fed was dramatically altered in response to the Great Depression of the 1930s. The Banking Act of 1935 brought major changes in the structural makeup of the Fed. The act consolidated the power of the Fed in the board of governors and greatly reduced the influence of the regional Fed banks. The act created the **Federal Open Market Committee (FOMC)**, which would become the most powerful policymaking committee within the Fed and perhaps within the entire country. While the regional Federal Reserve banks continued to set their own discount rates, the true power of the Fed had shifted to Washington and the board of governors.

Federal Open Market Committee (FOMC): The committee within the Federal Reserve that is responsible for setting monetary policy.

The 1935 act also made major steps in creating a politically independent central bank. It removed the secretary of the treasury and the comptroller of the currency from the Fed's board and ensured the newly named governors of the Fed would be removed from political pressure. While the Fed's monetary policy still remained under the control of the Administration, the seeds of a truly independent central bank had been planted. We examine the issue of central bank independence in greater detail in Chapter 11.

Next we look more closely at the current structure of the Fed: Who makes the decisions in this very powerful yet often misunderstood institution?

1 See "The Founding of the Fed," available from http://www.newyorkfed.org/aboutthefed/history_article.html.

SECTION REVIEW

Q1) When the Fed was created, one of its main purposes was to maintain the gold standard. What does this mean?

Q2) The Federal Reserve Bank of New York has a great deal of influence over financial markets to this very day. Yet the New York Fed is not as powerful as many wanted it to be in the early part of the twentieth century. Explain why the New York Fed is today not "all powerful."

Q3) Changes to the structure of the Fed during the Great Depression included:

a. creation of the FOMC.

b. consolidation of power in the board of governors.

c. increasing the political independence of the Fed.

d. all of the above.

Current Structure of the Fed

8-2

The structure of the Federal Reserve that was created by the Banking Act of 1935 is, basically, what we still have today. Perhaps the easiest way to understand the structure of the Fed is to examine it in terms of a power pyramid (Figure 8-1).

8-2a The Chair

Sitting atop the Fed's power pyramid is one person: the chair of the board of governors. Since February 2014 this has been Janet Yellen. How did Dr. Yellen get this job? The chair is appointed by the president of the United States and confirmed by the US Senate to a four-year renewable term. That's it. There are no other formal qualifications, no legal requirement for a background in finance or economics, merely appointment by the president and confirmation by the US Senate. Now, this is not to suggest Dr. Yellen is unqualified! She is one of the most respected economists in the world. Do note, however, that there is no legal requirement that the Fed chair have any background in economics or finance.

Notice also that the chair is confirmed not by the entire US Congress but only the Senate, which is the smaller of the two houses of Congress. The House of Representatives, traditionally thought of as the "people's part" of the legislature, gets no say in who heads the Federal Reserve. Yet the Fed chair often is referred to as the "second most powerful person in the United States"—second, that is, only to the president himself. Thus the "second most powerful person" in the country is not elected by anyone, merely appointed by the president and confirmed by the US Senate. As we will see, some have questioned whether this is how things should function in a "representative democracy" such as the United States.

J.M. Eddins, Jr/McClatchy-Tribune/Tribune Content Agency LLC/Alamy

Janet Yellen

Figure 8-1 Power Pyramid Illustrating the Structure of the Federal Reserve

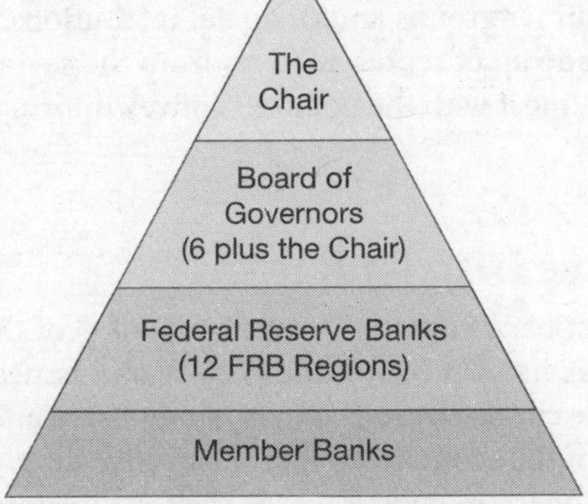

8-2b Board of Governors

Coming next in the power structure of the Fed is the board of governors. There are six governors in addition to the chair. These governors, similar to the chair, are appointed by the president and confirmed by the US Senate. One difference between the governors and the chair is their terms: The governors serve 14-year, nonrenewable terms. Thus, once they are confirmed by the Senate the governors essentially never have to answer to the public, or officials elected by the public, ever again.

The governors are important and powerful people. To ensure that too much power does not accrue to any one area of the country, only one member of the board can be from any one Fed district. While the governors are very influential, many people in financial markets do not know who these people are. A list of the biographies of the current governors can be found at http://www.federalreserve.gov/aboutthefed/default.htm.

Each of the governors plays an important role in the operation of the Fed. Their work focuses on one of three major areas: operations of the Fed, commercial bank regulation, or monetary policy.

- **Operations of the Fed.** The board of governors is responsible for monitoring the budgets and operations of the 12 Fed district banks, including setting the salaries of top executives of the district banks. The board of governors also is responsible for the efficient allocation of money and coins throughout the economy. It operates the Fedwire, which is a high-speed communications system for transferring funds and securities between banks.
- **Commercial Bank Regulation.** The Fed board of governors is responsible for approving and overseeing commercial bank mergers and acquisitions, as well as supervising financial holding companies, international banking facilities in the United States, Edge Act corporations, and the foreign activities of member banks. The board is further responsible for the implementation of many federal laws governing consumer credit and community development.
- **Monetary Policy.** One of the reasons the Fed is so powerful is because of its responsibility over monetary policy. As we will see, while this is a huge responsibility, it is also very controversial. We will examine the tools of the Fed in the conduct of monetary policy in the next chapter.

Assisting the board of governors in carrying out these important responsibilities is a large staff of over 200 economists who provide the governors with analysis and insight. The governors also gain input from a group of advisory councils. The Federal Advisory Council is made up of 12 bankers, one from each of the 12 Fed districts, who meet with the board of governors four times a year. The Consumer Advisory Council is made up of 30 members of the public representing different consumer groups and financial institutions. Finally, the Thrift Institutions Advisory Council, made up of representatives from the savings bank, credit union, and savings and loan industries, meet with the board to convey information on what is happening in their industry.

8-2c Federal Reserve District Banks

The Federal Reserve district banks are the "banks for banks" of the Federal Reserve system. Each one of these banks has its own board of directors and issues its own stock. These Fed banks are responsible for the check-clearing system, supervising and examining banks in their district, and keeping track of the economy in their respective districts.

Each Fed bank has nine board members: Three class A directors who come from member banks in the district are elected by their fellow member banks in the district; three class B directors who are business leaders also are elected by banks in the district; and three class C directors

Tying the Concepts Together

As Figure 8-2 shows, the United States is broken up in an odd way among the 12 districts. Notice that of the 12, only 3 districts lie entirely west of the Mississippi River. In part this is an accident of history. Remember, the Fed was created, and the Fed districts laid out, in the early part of the twentieth century. In 1914 the vast majority of the US population lived east of the Mississippi River, so in 1914 terms the map may make more sense.

Even taking that into consideration, however, there are still some oddities. For example, as discussed earlier, one of the goals was to have Fed cities be the major financial centers of the United States. With this in mind, having Fed cities of New York, Chicago, and San Francisco makes perfect sense. But notice that Richmond, Virginia, also is a Fed city. Richmond is a lovely city, but a financial center on par with the likes of Philadelphia and Boston? No. So how did Richmond become a Fed city? The chairman of the House Committee on Banking and Currency at the time was Congressman Carter Glass from Virginia. One can only wonder whether it is merely a coincidence that Richmond, Virginia, is a Federal Reserve bank city and the major architect of the Federal Reserve Act just happens to be from Virginia.

While the Federal Reserve districts may divide up the United States in an odd manner, it in no way diminishes their importance.

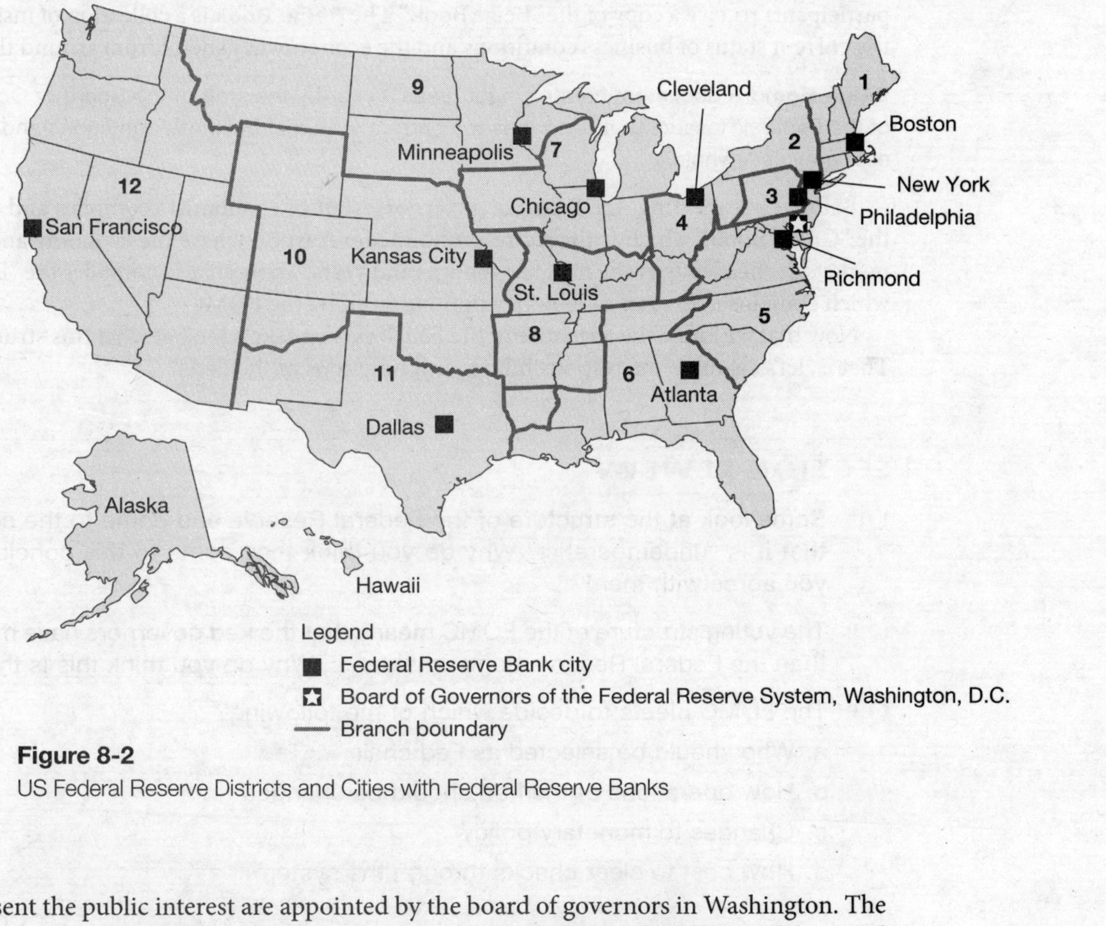

Figure 8-2
US Federal Reserve Districts and Cities with Federal Reserve Banks

who represent the public interest are appointed by the board of governors in Washington. The Fed banks have this structure to ensure that bankers do not dominate the policies of these Fed district banks. For example, the class B and C directors are not allowed to be officers, directors, or employees of any member bank. Further, class C directors are not allowed to hold stock of any member bank.

The Fed banks are run by a group of executives, called the officers of the bank, who make the day-to-day decisions. These officers are headed by the president, who is elected by the district bank's board of directors subject to the approval of the board of governors, and the vice president. The president of the Federal Reserve bank is most often the public face of the bank and makes the big strategic decisions, whereas the vice president is responsible for operational tasks: check clearing, distribution of coin and currency, building maintenance, technology issues, and so on.

8-2d Federal Open Market Committee

One area of overlap between the board of governors and the Federal Reserve district banks is the committee responsible for the conduct of monetary policy: the FOMC.

The FOMC consists of the 12 voting members: the 7 governors plus 5 of the 12 Federal Reserve bank presidents. The president of the Federal Reserve Bank of New York is a permanent voting member, whereas the other four slots rotate among the remaining 11 Fed bank presidents. All 12 Fed bank presidents attend the FOMC meeting and participate in the proceedings, although only 5 get to vote. Often the votes are unanimous or there is only one dissenting vote, so the voting power may not be as powerful as it at first seems.

The FOMC normally meets eight times a year but can, and does, meet more often when the economy is not doing well and/or if there is a financial crisis underway. Before each meeting, the participants receive a copy of the "Beige Book." The **Beige Book** is a collection of insights about the current status of business conditions and the economy in general from around the country.

Beige Book: A document created eight times a year by the staff of the Board of Governors of the Federal Reserve that describes the current status of business conditions and of the US economy as a whole.

Before each meeting, the board of governors' staff of economists compiles and distributes the "Green Book," which is the staff's economic forecast on where the economy and financial markets are headed over the next few months and years. The staff also compiles the "Blue Book," which contains a discussion of policy options faced by the FOMC.

Now that we know the structure of the Fed, let's next take a look at what this structure does. That is, let's examine the responsibilities and functions of the Fed.

SECTION REVIEW

Q1) Some look at the structure of the Federal Reserve and come to the conclusion that it is "undemocratic." Why do you think they come to this conclusion? Do you agree with them?

Q2) The voting structure of the FOMC means that the Fed governors have more votes than the Federal Reserve bank presidents. Why do you think this is the case?

Q3) The FOMC meets to decide which of the following?

a. Who should be selected as Fed chair

b. How operations of the Fed should be changed

c. Changes to monetary policy

d. How best to clear checks through the system

8-3 Responsibilities, Functions, and Balance Sheet of the Fed

While the Federal Reserve is perhaps best known for its role as a central bank conducting monetary policy, the Fed, like other central banks, has a great deal of responsibilities beyond monetary policy.

8-3a Responsibilities of the Fed

The Federal Reserve system has many responsibilities. Some of these responsibilities, such as conducting monetary policy, are well known while others are a bit more obscure. Let's examine what these various responsibilities include.

Financial Market Oversight

The Federal Reserve is responsible for supervising and regulating a number of different financial market entities. These include state-chartered banks that are members of the Federal Reserve, bank holding companies (companies that own and control commercial banks), financial holding companies (companies that own investment banks and insurance companies in addition to commercial banks), foreign branches of member banks, Edge Act and agreement corporations (limited-purpose entities that engage in foreign banking activities), and the US activities of foreign banks. We discuss the specifics of banking regulation in Chapter 15.

However, the Fed's oversight of financial markets does not stop at bank examinations and regulation. The Fed also has responsibility for reviewing bank mergers, acquisitions, and expansionary proposals. If banks want to merge or acquire another bank or expand, the Fed is responsible for assessing the potential impact this change would have on the competitiveness of financial markets.

Fiscal Agent of the Treasury

The Federal Reserve Act of 1913 states that the Federal Reserve banks are to serve as the fiscal agents and depositories of the US federal government. In general, as the government's fiscal agent, the Fed acts in place of the government in matters of revenue collection, debt issuance, and maintenance of the government's checking account. The term *depository* refers to the idea that the public will send their various federal tax payments to the Fed.

Initially, the fiscal agent function of the Fed was a very labor- and paper-intensive process. During World War I, the Fed handled the government's issuance of Liberty Loan bonds and Victory Notes. This required the Fed to send out the paper securities and collect payments from around the country. During World War II, the Federal Reserve banks were responsible for issuing, servicing, and redeeming War Savings Bonds. During the war, this became the single biggest responsibility of the banks. According to the Fed's 1942 annual report, by the summer of 1942, approximately 4,000 Federal Reserve bank employees, which was 20% of the Fed's workforce, were involved in war bond operations.

During the 1960s and 1970s the Fed's role of fiscal agent continued to expand as various government agencies and government-sponsored enterprises issued their own debt, which again was administered by the Fed. Compounding the Fed's workload was the increased issuance of treasury securities as the size of the federal government debt continued to grow during this time period. The Fed tried to keep up with the increased paperwork by creating the automated clearing house (ACH) in the 1970s. The ACH used 1970's "cutting-edge technology" such as magnetic tapes, punch cards, and room-sized computers to help process government as well as private payments.

It wasn't until the late 1990s that the fiscal agent responsibility of the Fed changed dramatically. Thanks in great part to improvements in information technology, the Fed could finally move away paper-intensive methods of managing the government's payments. Today, many of the payments to and from the government are done using the Internet, through sites such as TreasuryDirect and the Automated Standard Applications for Payments system (ASAP.gov).

Consumer Protection

The Federal Reserve board is responsible for writing and enforcing financial market regulations to implement many of the consumer protection laws passed by Congress. For example, in 1968 Congress passed the Truth in Lending Act to protect consumers by requiring lenders to state clearly key terms of the lending agreement and fully disclose all costs. The board implemented the act by creating Regulation Z, which lays out specifically what information about the terms and costs of credit as apply to mortgages, credit cards, automobile loans, and other types of consumer credit needs to be provided to consumers.

The Fed is responsible for enforcing many other consumer protection laws, including the Community Reinvestment Act, the Fair Credit Reporting Act, the Fair Credit Billing Act, and the Truth in Savings Act. The Federal Reserve also responds to consumer complaints about the policies and practices of financial institutions. It also seeks to educate the public on their rights in financial market transactions.

Fed Criticized on Consumer Protection In the wake of the financial crisis of 2007-2008, the Fed has come under increased criticism that it has not done enough to protect consumers in financial market transactions. Then-Harvard Law School professor and chair of the five-member Congressional Oversight Panel of TARP Elizabeth Warren criticized plans to house a new "Consumer Financial Protection Agency" (CFPA) within the Fed. Warren argued in a number of interviews that a CFPA within the Fed would be weak and serve the interest of banks over the interest of consumers. As Warren stated in an interview with the Huffington Post, "My first choice is a strong consumer agency. My second choice is no agency at all and plenty of blood and teeth left on the floor." Warren described the fight over the CFPA as "A dispute between families and banks."

Dissemination of Economic Information

The board of governors and the 12 Federal Reserve banks also provide a great deal of information on the current status of the economy and financial markets. Each of the 12 Fed banks produces a wide collection of reports on the economy in their regions, which can be accessed free on their websites. In addition, the staff economists at the board and Fed banks produce a wide variety of economic studies and working papers that examine topics ranging from labor market conditions to international finance. All of these publications are free to the public.

So, the Fed has a lot on its plate. It does so much more than just set and carry out monetary policy and thus influence interest rates. This became very clear during the financial crisis of 2007-2008. The Fed is responsible for keeping the financial markets functioning properly, and during a financial crisis that can be a daunting challenge. To understand how the Fed dealt with the financial crisis, it might be beneficial to take a look at the Fed's balance sheet a little more in depth. So that is where we turn next: the Fed's balance sheet and how it has changed recently.

8-3b The Fed's Balance Sheet

Examining balance sheets can be a dreadfully boring exercise. A balance sheet, with its different classes of assets and liabilities, can be a complex blur of names and numbers. If done properly, however, examining a balance sheet can provide a great deal of insight and trigger many interesting questions, such as "What on earth is going on?" and "Why did they do that?"

And so it is with the balance sheet of the Federal Reserve. We first examine the Fed's balance sheet as it stood on March 22, 2007, on the eve of the crisis that began in the summer of 2007. Then we will see how it changed radically over time in response to the crisis, arriving at its status on March 24, 2010. Examining the Fed's balance sheet is much more than a dull exercise in accounting; instead, it offers us a window through which we can watch as the biggest economic crisis since the Great Depression batters US and global financial markets.

A comparison of balance sheets of all of the Federal Reserve Banks looks like this:

Assets (in billions $)	March 22, 2007	March 26, 2008	March 25, 2009	March 25, 2010	May 8, 2013
Securities	780.8	612.3	761.3	2,018.0	3,243.2
(Treasury securities, federal agency debt, mortgage-back securities)					
Repurchase agreements	29.8	106.8	0.0	0.0	0.0
Term auction credit		80	468.6	3.4	0.0
Gold/SDR	13.2	13.2	13.2	16.2	16.2
Coin	0.9	1.3	1.8	2.1	2.0
Discount loans	0.03	37.6	136.2	82.5	0.4
Items in process of collection	2.9	0.8	0.5	0.2	0.5
Other	39.1	43.7	50.1	96.2	53.1
Holding of commerical paper funding facility			241.3	7.8	0.0
Holding of Maiden Lane I-III, TALF & Aurora			72.4	90.2	1.9
Central Bank liquidty swaps			327.8	0.0	7.3
Total assets	866.73	895.7	2,073.2	2,316.6	3,324.6
Maiden Lane I - Bear Stearns purchase by JPMorganChase Maiden Lane II and III - purchase of AIG assets http://www.newyorkfed.org/markets/maidenlane.html					
Liabilities					
Currency outstanding	770	780.6	863.1	893.0	1,142.5
Reserve repos	38.4	40.8	66.4	54.7	88.2
Depository institution deposits	11.3	21.6	822.4	1,147.7	1,869.7
Treasury deposits	4.7	4.9	256.1	150.0	133.6
Foreign & other	0.3	0.5	6.7	3.0	24.4
Deferred available cash items	3.8	2.7	2.9	2.1	1.3
Other	5.8	3.8	9.4	12.7	9.6
Total liabilities	834.3	854.9	2,027.0	2,263.2	3269.3
Capital	32.4	40.8	46.2	53.0	55.2
Total liabilities plus capital	866.7	895.7	2,073.2	2,316.2	3,324.5

Source: Federal Reserve Statistical Release H.4.1 various editions www.federalreserve.gov/releases/h41

Let's take a look at what is happening step by step. The best place to start is by examining the assets the Fed holds.

- **Securities.** The Fed's largest asset is its holdings of securities, which includes government securities such as US Treasury bills, notes, and bonds; federal agency debt; and privately issued mortgage-backed securities. The Fed uses its holdings of government securities for its open-market operations, which we discuss in more detail in Chapter 9.

  Notice from March 2007 through March 2009 the Fed's holding of securities remained relatively constant. By March 2010 though, its holdings of securities had increased dramatically and continued to increase through 2013. Initially, almost all of this increase was a result of the Fed's increased holdings of mortgage-backed securities. The Fed bought over $1 trillion worth of mortgage-backed assets in a little more than a year in an attempt to stabilize financial markets. By 2013, however, the Fed's holdings of longer-term government debt also had increased dramatically.

- **Repurchase Agreements.** In a **repurchase agreement**, or Repo, the Federal Reserve makes a temporary loan to selected primary dealers of government securities. In a Repo the primary dealer sells to the Fed a security (e.g., a Treasury bill or a mortgage-backed security) with the agreement to buy it back at a set date in the future. Thus the primary dealer is agreeing to repurchase the security from the Fed. The Repo is essentially a secured loan from the Fed to the primary dealer. Repos are most often very short-term loans, usually made overnight, are rarely longer than 14 days, and are never longer than 65 business days. They are used primarily for short-term increases in the liquidity of the financial system.

  Repurchase agreement: A financial transaction where a primary dealer sells a security to the Federal Reserve with the agreement to buy it back at a set date in the future.

  Before the crisis, the number of Repos was relatively small compared with the rest of the assets on the Fed's balance sheet. As the crisis grew in 2008, the Fed significantly increased its use of Repos, but by 2009 and into 2010 the Fed had turned to other, less traditional tools to deal with the crisis.
- **Term Auction Credit.** One of the new tools the Fed developed in an attempt to stabilize financial markets during 2008 and 2009 was term auction lending through the term auction facility, or TAF. Through TAF the Fed would essentially auction off money to qualified financial institutions. The Fed's goal was to increase the amount of liquidity in financial markets and thus keep the entire financial system from collapsing. On the Fed's balance sheet, we can see that the TAF did not exist in March 2007, but by March 2009 it had grown to $480 billion. By March 2010, however, as the crisis was easing, the TAF had fallen back to a level of just under $3.5 billion. By 2013 the TAF no longer existed. We will examine the TAF in more detail in Chapter 9.
- **Gold and Special Drawing Rights.** These assets used to be of more importance when the value of the dollar was tied to gold. Since the early 1970s, however, the dollar has not been tied to gold, yet the Fed still carries gold as an asset on its balance sheet.
- **Coin.** Notice the level of coins on the Fed balance sheet is relatively small and does not vary all that much. Notice also the coins show up as an asset of the Fed's balance sheet because they are issued by the Treasury. So, when the Fed gets coins from the Treasury, this asset increases, as do the Treasury deposits on the liability side of the Fed's balance sheet.
- **Discount Loans.** Remember, the Fed was established to be a lender of last resort to the financial system, especially during a time of crisis. Originally, a bank would need to bring its loan portfolio to the Fed to use as collateral on a loan from the Fed.

  These discount loans, which take place at the discount window, have an interest rate attached to them: the discount rate. We will see in Chapter 9 the importance of discount window lending in the Fed's operation of monetary policy.

  Notice the volume of discount loans was very tiny in March 2007: only $29 million. A year later, however, the volume of discount loans had shot up to $37 billion as member banks turned to the discount window for much-needed cash. By March 2009 the volume

Tying Concepts Together

Remember in Chapter 2 we discussed the time value of money. The main idea was that money received in the future is worth less than that same amount of money received today. Thus we have a discounted time value of money. In this situation the loans a bank brings to the Fed to pledge as collateral are simply promises to pay in the future. These future cash flows need to be discounted to arrive at what they are worth today. Thus the loans are called "discount loans" in part because the Fed is discounting the future promises to repay.

of discount loans had increased even further to $136 billion. Clearly, the level of borrowing at the discount window increased significantly as the crisis grew. By March 2010, as the crisis was abating, discount window lending tapered off to $82.5 billion, still well above the March 2008 levels and still massively higher than the precrisis levels in March 2007. By 2013 the amount of discount loans had fallen to less than $1 billion, still significantly above the precrisis levels in 2007.

- **Items in the Process of Collection.** This asset comes about as the Fed does its job in overseeing the payments system. Here's what happens: Some checks are brought to the Fed for payment by commercial banks. The Fed, in turn, takes these checks and sends them off to the bank upon which they are drawn. The Fed then is repaid the funds it provided to the first bank as it gets paid by the bank on whom the checks are drawn. Thus, as this process is taking place—it is sometimes called "float"—the Fed has checks that are in the process of making their way back to the institution upon whom they are written.
- Other assets include things like the Federal Reserve bank buildings, computer systems, and so on.

Commercial Paper Funding Facility, Maiden Lane, AIA Aurora LLC, and ALICO Holdings LLC, were all emergency lending facilities the Fed created to deal with financial crisis.

On the liability side of the Fed's balance sheet we see what the Fed owes to others:

- **Currency Outstanding.** This represents Federal Reserve notes issued by the Federal Reserve minus the amount held by Federal Reserve banks. So the figure represents the amount of Federal Reserve notes (paper currency) held by the public and the banking system.
- **Reverse Repos.** These are the reverse of repurchase agreements. That is, reserve repos occur when the Fed borrows money from primary dealers with the agreement the Fed will pay back the money. Usually, these loans last overnight, but they can last up to 65 business days. The impact of a reserve repo is to withdraw reserves from the banking system. They are usually used to make short-term adjustments to the level of liquidity within the banking system.
- **Depository Institution Deposits.** Remember, the Fed is a bank for banks; it holds the deposits or reserves of member banks. Notice how the level of depository institution deposits increase as the crisis builds. This is the much discussed "credit crunch": depository institutions were "sitting on" cash, in part by placing it on deposit at the Fed, instead of lending it out to businesses and households. Even as the crisis faded in March 2010 the level of depository institution deposits at the Fed continued to grow. This led many critics to complain in 2010 that "banks are still not lending," despite the high quarterly profits many were reporting.
- **Treasury Deposits.** Recall that the Fed is the fiscal agent of the US federal government and thus holds the Treasury's checking account. This appears on the Fed's balance sheet as a liability. As described above, this liability increases when the Fed buys coin and currency from the Treasury. From March 2008 to March 2009, this liability increased 50-fold! This was driven mostly by a new account, created in September 2008, called the "Treasury supplementary financing account." As described by the Treasury's press release dated September 17, 2008:[2]

> The Federal Reserve has announced a series of lending and liquidity initiatives during the past several quarters intended to address heightened liquidity pressures in the financial market, including enhancing its liquidity facilities this week. To manage the balance sheet impact of these efforts, the Federal Reserve has taken a number of actions, including redeeming and selling securities from the System Open Market Account portfolio.

2 See http://www.ustreas.gov/press/releases/hp1144.htm

> The Treasury Department announced today the initiation of a temporary Supplementary Financing Program at the request of the Federal Reserve. The program will consist of a series of Treasury bills, apart from Treasury's current borrowing program, which will provide cash for use in the Federal Reserve initiatives.
>
> Announcements of and participation in auctions conducted under the Supplementary Financing Program will be governed by existing Treasury auction rules. Treasury will provide as much advance notification as possible regarding the timing, size, and maturity of any bills auctioned for Supplementary Financing Program purposes.

This means that the Treasury auctioned extra Treasury bills to the public, and the receipt of these sales was placed on deposit with the Fed. Thus the Fed's liabilities (the Treasury's new deposits) increased. But if liabilities increase, in order for the balance sheet to balance, either a different liability must decrease, assets must increase, or capital must decline.

Liabilities decreasing would not be a good option; that would mean either currency in circulation would decrease or depository institution deposits at the Fed would have to decrease. Either of these actions would trigger the simple deposit multiplier in reverse, thus causing the money supply to contract and most likely pushing the economy into a deeper recession. Decreases in the Fed's capital level would also not be a good option. Therefore, that leaves only increases in the Fed's assets.

The Fed offset the supplementary Treasury auction of Treasury bills by buying private assets and thus increasing the asset side of its balance sheet. But what assets would the Fed buy? To answer this, look back at the asset side of the Fed's balance sheet. Remember the Fed's huge increase in the holding of securities such as mortgage-backed assets? Do you recall that large increase in the Fed's assets as a result of the TAF? Thus the Treasury helped fund the Fed's increase in assets without requiring the Fed to "print money" to buy them. This is the importance of the increase in the "Treasury deposits" on the Fed's balance sheet.

- **Foreign and Other Liabilities.** Foreign liabilities are foreign central bank deposits at the Federal Reserve.
- **Deferred Available Cash Items.** These are checks that have yet to be cleared though the check-clearing system.
- **Other.** This category represents, in part, the money the Fed owes to member banks for the 6% dividend the Fed pays on the 3% of net capital the member banks are required to contribute to the Fed. In return, the member banks get nonvoting stock in their regional Federal Reserve bank and access to the discount window.
- **Capital.** This represents the profits the Fed has earned, which mainly come from the assets they purchase. Excess capital is turned over to the Treasury Department and Congress, which they spend as they see fit. The Fed's profits that flow back to the government are included in the federal budget as "miscellaneous revenue."

Thus, by examining the Fed's balance sheet, we can see how the Fed responded to the financial crisis as it unfolded from 2007 to 2013. On the asset side of the Fed's balance sheet we see how the Fed stepped into the financial markets, buying huge amounts of mortgage-backed securities. We also see the Fed creating the TAF and the commercial paper fund facility to pump liquidity into the financial system and the Maiden Lanes and other limited liability corporations to deal with the financial market meltdown.

The liability side of the Fed's balance sheet indicates depository institutions holding on to large amounts of reserves as the crises worsened. These levels of reserves continued to increase as the credit crunch dragged on. The Treasury deposits at the Fed swelled in response to changes on the asset side of the Fed's balance sheet.

Thus, by examining the Fed's balance sheet, we can understand how the Fed responded to the growing financial and economic crisis. As we will see in later chapters, these moves by the Fed were controversial. We will ponder the questions, Where these the right moves to make? How should things be done differently in the future? And, perhaps most important, What can be done to prevent such a crisis from ever happening again?

In attempting to address these questions, it is important to remember that as powerful as the Fed is, it does not operate in a vacuum. Instead, the Fed functions in a truly global financial market. Thus, to fully appreciate the role of central banks in our global economy we must also understand the other major central banks around the world. In the next section we examine the Bank of Japan, the Bank of England, the European Central Bank, and the Bank of Canada.

SECTION REVIEW

Q1) What does it mean that the Federal Reserve is the "fiscal agent" of the US government?

Q2) In what ways did the Fed's balance sheet change in response to the global financial crisis?

Q3) The main purpose of term auction lending was to:

a. reduce the rate of inflation.
b. increase market interest rates.
c. reduce the amount banks borrow from the Fed.
d. increase the level of liquidity in financial markets.

8-4 Other Central Banks: Bank of Japan and Bank of England

8-4a Bank of Japan

The central bank of Japan, called the Bank of Japan, was founded in 1882 and has been in the same building in Tokyo since 1896. In 1998, with the passage of the Bank of Japan Act, the bank became an independent central bank. The act states "the Bank of Japan's autonomy regarding currency and monetary control shall be respected." While this may sound like the act created a fully independent central bank, that's not quite the complete story. The act also states the bank shall "always maintain close contact with the government and exchange views sufficiently." We examine the issue of central bank independence in more detail in Chapter 11.

Responsibilities of the Bank of Japan

Issuing Bank Notes As with all central banks, the Bank of Japan is responsible for disseminating the country's currency and coins. In doing so, the Bank of Japan also guards against the counterfeiting of its currency. If you have ever seen a Bank of Japan bank note, you may notice the great lengths the Bank of Japan has gone to in order to frustrate counterfeiters: yen notes are multicolored miniature pieces of art, complete with holograms and hidden text. To help disseminate these bank notes, the Bank of Japan has 32 branches across Japan and 7 representative offices overseas.

Financial Market Stability The Bank of Japan uses both off-site monitoring of commercial banks, in which Bank of Japan staff conduct research through interviews with financial institution officials and gather financial market data, and on-site examinations, in which Bank of Japan staff visit depository institutions and investigate their safety and soundness. In its off-site monitoring the Bank of Japan staff watches the funding and investment policies, liquidity position, and profitability of depository institutions. During its on-site audits, Bank of Japan staff evaluate depository institutions' internal control mechanisms and contingency plans: what the bank will do if something unexpected occurs, such as a natural disaster like an earthquake or typhoon or a financial disaster like a bank run and or stock market crash.

If unexpected events, such as a global financial crisis, do occur, the Bank of Japan is ready to step in as a "lender of last resort" to the Japanese banking system. During the recent financial crisis, the Bank of Japan went beyond its traditional role of lender of last resort as it purchased directly large amounts of commercial paper and corporate bonds.

Photo Japan/Alamy

Bank of Japan

Even these "unconventional" steps by the Bank of Japan to ensure financial market stability were criticized by some in Japan as not going far enough. These critics argue that the expansion of the Bank of Japan's balance sheet by buying assets was not as great as the actions of the Federal Reserve.

Governor Masaaki Shirakawa responded to these criticisms by stating, "such criticism shows a complete misunderstanding of the facts." Shirakawa argued that expansion of the Fed's balance sheet reflected the fact that US capital markets, which account for about 70% of US firm funding, had seized up to such an extent that the Fed had no choice but to purchase a wide variety and large quantities of financial assets. In Japan, by contrast, the situation was not as dire, and thus less dramatic action was required by the Bank of Japan.

Shirakawa points out that the Bank of Japan's balance sheet had already expanded significantly in response to the financial crisis in Japan that began during the late 1990s. Thus, with an already bloated balance sheet, the Bank of Japan's response to the current crisis may seem minor, but in fact it was still a significant unconventional change in policy. As the Japanese commercial paper and bond market seemed to be rebounding, the Bank of Japan ended its outright purchases of commercial paper and corporate bonds in December 2008.

Monetary Policy When not responding to global financial market meltdowns, the main responsibility of the Bank of Japan is to use monetary policy to pursue price stability. The Bank of Japan Act mandates the Bank of Japan use its monetary policy to pursue a single goal: price level stability.

The Bank of Japan's Policy Board is charged with keeping the price level stable—controlling inflation as well as guarding against deflation—through its monetary policy. At its monetary policy meetings the nine-member policy board discusses the current economic and financial situation in Japan and around the world and decides where it is going to set it targets for bank lending rates and the amount of liquidity it will provide to the financial system. The monetary policy meetings are held once or twice a month and usually last two days. At the end of the meetings the governor holds a press conference to announce and explain any changes in monetary policy.

8-4b Bank of England

The Bank of England was established over 300 years ago in 1694 to serve as the English government's banker and debt manager. When William of Orange and Queen Mary took the throne after the Glorious Revolution of 1688, England's finances were a mess: The government was heavily in debt and the money and credit system of the country had fallen apart. Scottish businessman and financier William Paterson had an idea for how to fix this financial mess. He envisioned the creation of a new bank, one that would have a monopoly over the creation of bank notes. In return for this market power, the bank would make a very generous loan of £1.2 million to the government. The new bank would be capitalized by selling the equivalent of shares to the public. Paterson's scheme turned out to be very popular with the public: All of the shares in the new bank were snapped up by eager investors in only 12 days. Thus was born the Governor and Company of the Bank of England, or what we today call simply the Bank of England.

In actuality the Bank of England is misnamed. It is actually the central bank for all of the United Kingdom, not just England; Great Britain is made up of England, Scotland, and Wales, whereas the United Kingdom adds Northern Ireland to these three.

While the Bank of England was originally a privately owned bank, it was nationalized, or taken over by the government, in 1946. In 1997 the bank received its independence from the government when it was announced that full responsibility of monetary policy was being shifted to the bank. Thus, today the Bank of England, while still completely owned by the government and accountable to Parliament, is for the most part a politically independent central bank.

Bank of England

Responsibilities of the Bank of England

The Bank of England today has two primary responsibilities: monetary stability and financial stability.

Monetary Policy According to the Bank of England monetary stability means stable prices and confidence in the British pound. The BoE uses an explicit inflation target of 2% per year in its conduct of monetary policy to bring about monetary stability. If the bank fails to achieve this goal, it must explain this failure in an open letter to the government's chancellor of the exchequer. The Bank of England's monetary policy is conducted by its monetary policy committee, or the MPC. This committee is made up of nine members: the governor of the Bank of England, who is the head of the Bank of England; two deputy governors, one responsible for monetary policy and the other for financial stability; and four outside experts, all of whom have expertise in monetary policy. The MPC meets for two days every month to decide on monetary policy. Leading up to the meeting, the members of the MPC meet for half a day with the Bank of England staff to discuss current policy options. The decisions made during the MPC meetings are based on a majority vote; the governor casts the deciding vote in case of a tie. A representative of the treasury is allowed to sit in on the MPC meeting but cannot vote.

The decisions of the MPC are announced at 12 noon on the second day of the meeting. The minutes of the meeting, including a record of the vote, are released to the public two weeks after the meeting. Each quarter the bank publishes its inflation report, which gives an analysis of the UK economy and other factors the MPC used in making its monetary policy decisions.

Financial Stability In the aftermath of the global financial crisis of 2007–2008, the British parliament undertook steps to increase the Bank of England's responsibility to ensure financial stability. The passage of the Financial Services Act of 2012 came into force on April 1, 2013, creating a new regulatory framework. The Act abolished the previous tripartite system where the Financial Services Authority (FSA), the Treasury Department, and the Bank of England shared regulation of the entire British financial system. Critics contended the tripartite system failed to anticipate the global crisis and reacted poorly once the crisis began.

The 2012 Act replaced the FSA with two entities: the Financial Conduct Authority (designed to protect consumers) and Prudent Regulatory Authority (designed to regulate financial institutions), which is part of the Bank of England. The Act also created the Financial Policy Committee (FPC) of the Bank of England, which was given the responsibility to ensure both micro and macro financial stability and can instruct the other two regulators to undertake financial market reforms. The Act makes it clear that it is now the Bank of England that is the main regulator of British financial markets.

SECTION REVIEW

Q1) In what ways are the Bank of Japan and the Bank of England similar to the Federal Reserve?

Q2) In what ways are the Bank of Japan and the Bank of England significantly different from the Federal Reserve?

Q3) Critics of the Bank of Japan argue that it played a role in the global financial crisis. What do these critics argue?

a. The Bank of Japan raised interest rates too quickly as the crisis was beginning.
b. The Bank of Japan did not expand its balance sheet as much as the Federal Reserve did in response to the crisis.
c. The Bank of Japan should have cut taxes to stimulate spending in Japan.
d. The Bank of Japan purchased far too many bonds at the beginning of the crisis.

Other Central Banks: European Central Bank and Bank of Canada

8-5

8-5a European Central Bank

The European Central Bank (ECB) was created in 1998 in preparation for the launch of the euro, which occurred January 1, 1999. The ECB, with its headquarters in Frankfurt, Germany, is one of the latest steps in European integrations that started with the Treaty of Rome in 1957. In 2014 the EuroZone was made up of 18 countries: Austria, Belgium, Cyprus, Estonia, Finland, France, Germany, Greece, Ireland, Italy, Latvia, Luxembourg, Malta, the Netherlands, Portugal, Slovakia, Slovenia, and Spain (Figure 8-3). Three countries belong to the European community and qualify to use the euro but do not: the United Kingdom, Sweden, and Denmark. Six other European communities might begin using the euro once they qualify: Bulgaria, the Czech Republic, Hungary, Lithuania, Poland, and Romania.

Figure 8-3 The Currency Status of European Union Countries

©Ioan Panaite/Shutterstock.com

European Central Bank

ECB Structure

The ECB is headed by the president and the vice president, who are elected by the governments of the countries that use the euro. In November 2011 Italian economist Mario Draghi became the third ECB president, taking over for Jean-Claude Trichet. The vice president, Vítor Constâncio, has held the post since 2010.

The ECB has three governing bodies: The governing council, the general council, and the executive board. They each have different structures and different responsibilities.

Governing Council The ECB's main and most important governing body is the governing council, which meets twice a month: once to plan monetary policy[3] and once to discuss operation of the ECB. It is made up of the executive board, which is described below, as well as all of the governors, or heads, of the central banks of the EuroZone. The governing council is responsible for deciding monetary policy, the issuance of bank notes, and the management of reserves and foreign exchange market operations. Each member of the governing council has a single vote when making decisions.[4] In the case of a tie, the president of the ECB casts the deciding vote. The ECB president also chairs the governing council meetings and is the main voice of the ECB.

©matthi/Shutterstock.com

Mario Draghi

After each of the monetary policy meetings the president and vice president of the ECB meet with the global press to discuss and defend their decisions. You can watch these press conferences live on the Internet.

General Council The general council is responsible for transitional issues of countries who wish to begin using the euro. The general council is made up of the president and vice president of the ECB and the governors of *all* of the European Union central banks, including those that do not currently use the euro. The general council meets generally once every three months and offers advice to countries who wish to use the euro. Once all the countries of the European community use the euro, the general council is designed to be dissolved.

Executive Board The executive board of the ECB meets every Tuesday and implements monetary policy decisions made by the governing council and manages the day-to-day operation of the bank. The executive committee is made up of the president, vice president, and four outside members who are monetary policy experts. Members of the executive board are appointed by the governments of the EuroZone countries.

Responsibilities of the ECB

Monetary Policy As with many modern-day central banks, the main responsibility of the ECB is monetary policy. Unlike other central banks, however, the ECB is responsible for the monetary policies of many different nations, all with their own unique set of challenges. Thus the ECB often finds itself weighing the interests of several different nation-states at the same time. As we will discover in the next chapter, maneuvering around these different political obstacles can be very challenging.

---

3 Starting in 2015 the ECB policymaking committee will meet every six weeks instead of monthly.

4 If Lithuania does join the EuroZone in 2015, the voting system in the governing council will change to a system in which national central bank governors take turns holding voting rights on the governing council.

Foreign Exchange Operations The ECB has to be sure that the value of the euro remains relatively stable in comparison with other currencies. The ECB must ensure that the value of the euro does not swing wildly day to day as a result of a lack of or a glut of euros in foreign exchange markets. In doing so, the ECB may buy and sell euros on its own—called unilateral intervention—or as part of a coordinated effort with other central banks, called concerted intervention. These interventions can be carried out directly by the ECB and/or by the national central banks that are part of the euro system.

Maintenance of the Payments System The ECB must ensure that transactions between the various commercial banks in the euro system operate smoothly every business day. The ECB does this, in part, by its operation of a real-time settlement system for large payments, called TARGET2.

Holding and Management of Official Foreign Reserves of Euro Area Countries When the Euro was introduced in January 1999, the foreign reserves of the member nations' central banks were transferred to the ECB. The ECB manages this portfolio of foreign currencies with the objective of maintaining proper levels of liquidity, security, and return on investment for the national central banks.

8-5b Bank of Canada

For decades after Canada was formed in 1867, the Canadian people did not see the need for a central bank. The Bank of Montreal acted as the government's banker, and the Canadian system of nationwide banking functioned in a stable manner. The private, large, countrywide banks had branches in rural areas as well as urban areas, with few bank failures or bank runs. Thus Canadians didn't believe their banking system needed a "lender of last resort." With the Bank of Montreal acting as the fiscal agent for the government and no need for a lender of last resort, why would Canada need a central bank?

During the late 1920s there was growing dissatisfaction with the monetary system in Canada. Several academic economists across Canada worried that, on the one hand, the existing system lacked sufficient flexibility and, on the other, could suffer from excessive lending. A major problem was that the Canadian banks were very dependent on external capital flows. As Robin Neill from Carleton University pointed out, Canadian banks of the time would expand and contract their lending with the rise and fall of global economic activity. As the global economy expanded, as it did in the 1920s, cash flowed into Canada most often to purchase Canadian agricultural exports. When the global economy contracted, however, the money spigot was shut off and Canadian banks greatly reduced their level of lending.

The Great Depression of the 1930s brought the question of a lack of central bank in Canada to the fore. Prime Minister Richard Bedford Bennett was concerned that the faltering Canadian economy desperately needed stabilization. In February 1934,[5] Bennett established a commission to study the question of a need for a Canadian Central Bank. The Royal Commission was headed by Lord Hugh Pattison Macmillan, a well-respected member of the House of Lords with an expertise in banking and finance.

Bloomberg/Getty Images
Bank of Canada

5 See "Business: Bank of Canada," *Time Magazine*, March 5, 1934 (http://www.time.com/time/magazine/article/0,9171,747141,00.html).

After two months spent examining the question, Lord Macmillan's Royal Commission recommended the creation of a central bank that would have the ability to issue bank notes and control the supply of credit. Each private commercial bank would be required at all times to maintain 5% of its deposits on deposit at the new Bank of Canada. A week after Macmillan submitted his report, the prime minister announced the central bank would be created. In March 1935 the Bank of Canada began operation, initially as a privately owned institution that sold its shares to the public. The Bank of Canada was nationalized in 1938 and today remains part of the Canadian government.

Structure of the Bank of Canada

The Bank of Canada is headed by the governor of the Bank of Canada,[6] who functions as the CEO of the bank. The governor is appointed by the prime minister to a seven-year, renewable term. The governor heads the governing council, which also includes as members the senior deputy governor and four deputy governors. The board of directors of the Bank of Canada is made up of the governor, the senior deputy governor, and 12 outside directors from across Canada. The 12 directors are appointed to three-year terms and can be reappointed. The governor is the chair of the board of directors.

Responsibilities of the Bank of Canada

Monetary Policy The governing council is responsible for the conduct of Canadian monetary policy. Late in 2000 the Bank of Canada developed a system where they would have eight preset, or "fixed," dates per year on which it would announce its "key policy rates." The key policy rates are the bank's target for the overnight rate, which is the interest rate at which financial institutions borrow and lend to each other for one day, or overnight.

Leading up to the fixed-date meeting, the governing council is briefed by the bank staff on the current state of the Canadian economy as well as current financial market situations. After this briefing, the governing council meets with the monetary policy review committee, which is made up of 12 advisors traditionally from across Canada. These meetings usually take place on the Friday before the fixed-date meeting.

The governing council meets and operates on a unanimous or consensus basis. The governing council meets on the fixed-date Monday, and by the end of the day they reach a consensus on the level of the key policy rate. Then, with the help of staff members skilled in communications, a press release that outlines the logic behind the decision is drafted. Early Tuesday morning the decision is confirmed, and at 9 a.m. the key policy rate is announced.

Four times a year, in January, April, July, and October, at 10:30 a.m. on the Thursday following a key policy rate announcement, the Bank of Canada releases its "Monetary Policy Report," a publication that details the governing council's outlook. The Monetary Policy Report is released at a press conference, where the governor and senior deputy governor field questions from the global financial press. The release of the report is followed by testimony from the governor and senior deputy governor before the Canadian Parliament and its various committees.

Most often, the governor and senior deputy governor face questions about the two major goals of Canadian monetary policy: flexible exchange rates and inflation control. In 1991 the Bank of Canada announced a formal, explicit inflation target between 1% and 3% annual inflation. Their stated goal is to keep the inflation rate at the midpoint of this range at 2%. We discuss in Chapter 11 the controversies that exist over having an explicit inflation target.

While monetary policy is one of the most important responsibilities of the Bank of Canada, it is not their only one. The bank is also responsible for making sure the Canadian financial system runs smoothly.

6 Stephen S. Polz became the ninth governor of the Bank of Canada in June 2013. Dr. Polz succeeded Mark Carney, who left the Bank of Canada before his term expired to become the governor of the Bank of England.

Maintenance of the Financial System The bank states its goal is to "actively promote [a] safe, sound and efficient financial system" both in Canada and around the world. During the financial crisis that began in 2007, the Canadian economy did much better than most advanced countries. Then-governor of the Bank of Canada Mark Carney stated in June 2010 that he believed that Canada was able to avoid much of the global economic crisis thanks in great part to Canada's strong financial system. Carney stated: "Canada entered the recession with notable advantages, including a well-functioning financial system, strong corporate balance sheets, and relatively healthy household finances. We will have to draw on these advantages during the recovery."[7]

In a 2013 study[8] the Bank of Canada concluded that Canada was able to avoid much of the global financial crisis mainly because of the "solid approach to risk management on the part of the Canadian banking system. . ."—an approach that was, the bank argued, fostered and encouraged by the Bank of Canada thanks in great part to lessons learned during housing crises in Canada during the early 1980s and again in the early 1990s.

One wonders whether the rest of the world will ever learn from crises the way that Canada did.

SECTION REVIEW

Q1) How is the structure of the ECB similar to that of the Federal Reserve? How is it different?

Q2) How is the structure of the Bank of Canada similar to that of the Federal Reserve? How is it different?

Q3) The financial and economic system in Canada functioned very differently from financial systems in other Western countries. In what way was Canada's experience different?

a. Canada entered an economic depression, whereas other countries suffered only a recession.

b. Canada suffered from very high rates of inflation, whereas other countries did not.

c. Canada avoided much of the global financial crisis mainly because of well-run banks.

d. Canada's financial system collapsed well before the crisis hit other countries.

7 Full text of the speech by Bank of Canada Governor Mark Carney is available from: http://www.reuters.com/article/idUSN1616401620100616.

8 See Arjani, Neville, and Graydon Paulin, "Lessons from the Financial Crisis: Bank Performance and Regulatory Reform." Bank of Canada Discussion Paper 2013–4. 2013.

8-6 Conclusion

Even though central banks may not be well understood by the majority of the public, these lenders of last resort, conductors of monetary policy, and stabilizers of financial markets do play a very important role in the functioning of the global economy. It wasn't always this way; as we have seen, central banks have developed over a variety of time periods and in a variety of ways.

The Federal Reserve—perhaps the most influential of the modern-day central banks—has a structure and list of responsibilities that has evolved over time. We saw how changes in the Fed's balance sheet can give us greater insight into how the Fed responded to the financial and economic crisis that began in the summer of 2007. We will examine these changes in more detail in the next chapter, where we will learn how the Fed's tools of monetary policy have changed.

We concluded by examining some of the other central banks in our global economy. We sampled their responsibilities and structures, as well as how some of them responded to the financial crisis. In the next chapter we examine the tools in monetary policy more closely.

IN THE NEWS. . .

What Is Quantitative Easing?

The Economist
January 14, 2014

America's Federal Reserve surprised markets in December by starting to "taper" (ie, gradually reduce) its programme of monthly purchases of government and mortgage bonds—a process known as "quantitative easing", or QE—from $85 billion a month to $75 billion. Some worry that scaling back QE could endanger America's recovery or create financial instability in emerging markets. Meanwhile, expectations are rising that the European Central Bank may soon launch its own QE programme to boost the euro-area economy, where high unemployment is contributing to deflation.

To carry out QE central banks create money by buying securities, such as government bonds, from banks, with electronic cash that did not exist before. The new money swells the size of bank reserves in the economy by the quantity of assets purchased—hence "quantitative" easing. Like lowering interest rates, QE is supposed to stimulate the economy by encouraging banks to make more loans. . . .

The jury is still out on QE, however. Studies suggest that it did raise economic activity a bit. But some worry that the flood of cash has encouraged reckless financial behaviour and directed a firehose of money to emerging economies that cannot manage the cash. Others fear that when central banks sell the assets they have accumulated, interest rates will soar, choking off the recovery. Last spring, when the Fed first mooted the idea of tapering, interest rates around the world jumped and markets wobbled. Still others doubt that central banks have the capacity to keep inflation in check if the money they have created begins circulating more rapidly. Central bankers have been more cautious in using QE than they would have been in cutting interest rates, which could partly explain some countries' slow recoveries. At least a few central banks are now experimenting with stimulus alternatives, such as promises to keep overnight interest-rates low for a very long time, the better to scale back their dependence on QE.

The article points out that there has yet to be a final verdict on quantitative easing (QE). Do you think these policies were effective? Should the European Central Bank follow in the Fed's footsteps and pursue their own QE? Why or why not? What else might the ECB do to stimulate the EuroZone's economy?

9

Monetary Policy Tools

9-1 Overview

Tools are wonderful things—if they are used correctly. For a handyman, a carpenter's hammer is a useful tool if she wants to drive a nail into a 2 × 4. However, if our handyman wants to change a light bulb, a hammer is not a useful tool. Thus tools are useful if and only if you know how and when to use them.

What is true of a handyman's toolbox is also true of monetary policy. Central bankers have a collection of "tools" at their disposal; however, one of the keys to successful monetary policy is in knowing which tool to use when.

Tools also change as time goes by. Once razor-sharp hedge trimmers can dull with use and soon become ineffective. So it is with monetary policy tools. Monetary policy tools that once were very effective can lose their usefulness as market conditions and the economy change and evolve.

So what are these tools of monetary policy? How and why have they changed? How are they used in light of the current economic setting? In this chapter we begin with what has arguably been in the past the Federal Reserve's (also referred to as the Fed) most powerful tool: open market operations (OMOs). We then look at one of the Fed's oldest tools: discount window lending. But, like so many tools, OMOs and discount window lending do not always have the same level of effectiveness.

During the recent economic crisis, for example, OMOs proved to be relatively ineffective, and thus the Fed has had to bring new tools into its tool kit.[1] These new tools, called emergency lending and quantitative easing, had never been used before. We examine what these tools are and why they came about. Next we look at the seldom-used required reserve ratio. Then we review three reasons why the Fed's tools may not work as well as the Fed would like them to. Finally, we examine the tools of monetary policy that the European Central Bank has at its disposal. This sets the stage for the next chapter, where we examine how the Fed and the European Central Bank have used their tools in the past in the conduct of monetary policy.

9-1a Open Market Operations as a Monetary Tool

OMOs are the most flexible, and thus the most often used, of the Fed's tools in the conduct of monetary policy. The Fed has several different ways to conduct OMOs; however, most often OMOs are undertaken by the buying and selling of government securities to influence the level of bank reserves.

One of the keys to understanding OMOs is to keep in mind that this is the buying and selling of government securities in the secondary market. This means the Fed is not buying government securities directly from the government. Instead, it is buying/selling government securities from or to a private entity.

To understand how an OMO works, imagine a highly simplistic world where there is a big room in which the buyers and sellers of government securities meet to trade. Let's further suppose the Fed is pursuing an expansionary OMO, that is, the Fed is seeking to increase the level of bank reserves and thus increase the monetary base to push market interest rates lower.

Expansionary OMO

The Fed enters the room (the market) and approaches someone who is interested in selling government bonds. Suppose in the room is Ms. Rice, who had at some point in the past purchased $10 million of government securities. Ms. Rice now would like to sell these bonds, perhaps because she needs cash.

1 Expansionary fiscal policy also was used to combat the Great Recession, but that is beyond the scope of our discussion here.

Tying Concepts Together

How an Expansionary OMO Affects the Fed Funds Market

The impact of this expansionary OMO is first felt in the Fed funds market. Remember, the Fed funds market (discussed in Chapter 7) is where banks with excess reserves lend them to banks that are lacking reserves. When the Fed buys government securities from the public, there are more banks with excess reserves, or, in terms of the Fed funds market, there is an increase in the supply of federal funds.

As can be seen in Figure 9-1, an increase in the supply of federal funds pushes the equilibrium federal funds rate downward. This is exactly what the Fed wanted: lower market interest rates.

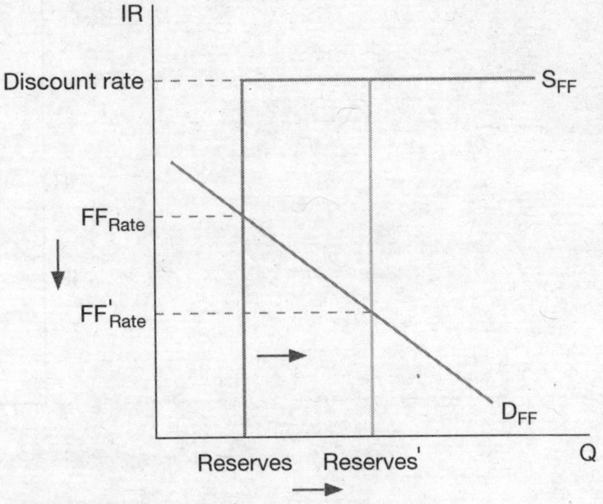

Figure 9-1
Expansionary Open Market Operation

The Fed will engage in a transaction with Ms. Rice: She will send to the Fed $10 million of government securities. Let us further assume Ms. Rice has a demand deposit account at Bank of America. To pay Ms. Rice for the securities, the Fed will deposit $10 million into Bank of America's account at the Fed and then inform Bank of American to credit Ms. Rice's account for the $10 million.

Thus the transactions are:

$10 million in government securities goes from Ms. Rice to the Fed.

The Fed puts $10 million into Bank of America's member bank reserves account at the Fed. Bank of America sees its cash/reserve account (which includes the deposits it has at the Fed) increase by $10 million.

Bank of America credits Ms. Rice's demand deposit with $10 million and thus Ms. Rice sees her demand deposit balance increase by $10 million.

In terms of balance sheets what happens is:

Fed's Balance Sheet		Bank of America		Ms. Rice	
Assets	Liabilities	Assets	Liabilities	Assets	Liabilities
Gov't Securities + $10m	Member bank Reserves + $10m	Cash/ reserves + $10 m	Demand Deposits + $10m	DDA + $10m Gov't Securities − $10m	

The most important of these is what happens to Bank of America: With this open market purchase the Federal Reserve has increased the level of bank reserves. With this increase in reserves, Bank of America can now lend out its excess reserves. By doing so, Bank of America is doing exactly what the Fed wants: increasing the money supply.

When the money supply increases, this is an increase in the supply of loanable funds. Remember from our earlier discussion, an increase in the supply of loanable funds, ceteris paribus, leads to lower market interest rates (Figure 9-2).

Figure 9-2 Increase in the Supply of Loanable Funds

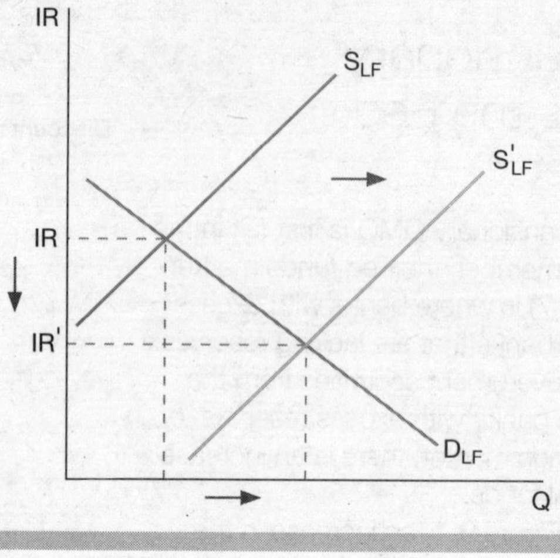

Thus, as a result of buying government securities, the Fed has increased the level of bank reserves, which in turn results in a reduction of interest rates. Again, this is exactly what the Fed wanted: an expansionary OMO.

The same logic, but in reverse, holds if the Fed wants to reduce the amount of bank reserves and thus push up interest rates. This is called a contractionary OMO.

Contractionary OMO

In a contractionary OMO, the Fed enters the room (the market) with government securities that it wants to sell. Let's suppose the Fed has $5 million worth of government securities it plans to sell. The Fed approaches Mr. Beans, who has some extra cash with which he is looking to buy some government securities.

The Fed will engage in a transaction with Mr. Beans: The Fed will send him $5 million worth of government securities. Let us further assume Mr. Beans has a demand deposit account at Citibank. To be paid for the securities, the Fed will take $5 million out of Citibank's account at the Fed and then inform Citibank to debit Mr. Beans's demand deposit account.

Thus the transactions are:

$5 million in government securities goes from the Fed to Mr. Beans.

The Fed pulls $5 million out of Citibank's member bank reserves account at the Fed. Citibank sees its cash/reserve account (which includes the deposits it has at the Fed) decrease by $5 million.

Citibank debits or reduces Mr. Beans's demand deposit by $5 million and thus Mr. Beans sees his demand deposit balance decrease by $5 million.

In terms of balance sheets what happens is:

Fed Balance Sheet		Bank of America		Ms. Beans	
Assets	Liabilities	Assets	Liabilities	Assets	Liabilities
Gov't Securities − $5m	Member bank Reserves − $5m	Cash/ reserves − $5m	Demand Deposits − $5m	DDA − $5m Gov't Securities + $5m	

Tying Concepts Together

How a Contractionary OMO Affects the Fed Funds Market

When the Fed sells government securities to the public, there are fewer banks with excess reserves, or, in terms of the Fed funds market, there is a decrease in the supply of federal funds (Figure 9-3).

The decrease in the supply of federal funds pushes the equilibrium federal funds rate upward. This is exactly what the Fed wanted: higher market interest rates.

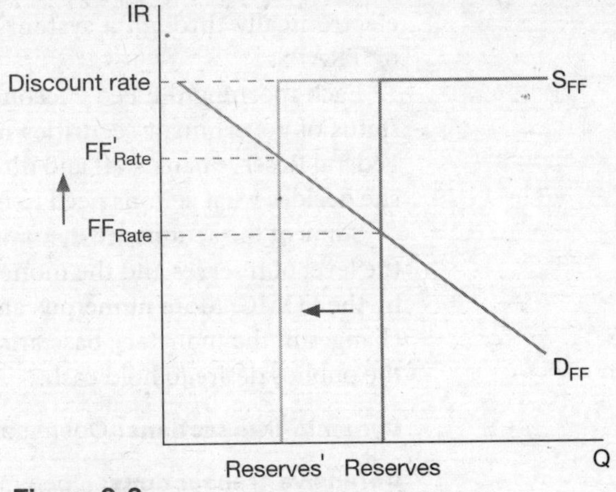

Figure 9-3

Contractionary Open Market Operation

When the money supply decreases, it is also a decrease in the supply of loanable funds. Remember from our earlier discussion, a decrease in the supply of loanable funds, ceteris paribus, leads to higher market interest rates (Figure 9-4).

Thus, as a result of selling government securities, the Fed has decreased the level of bank reserves, which in turn results in an increase in interest rates. This is exactly what the Fed wanted: a contractionary OMO.

OMOs in Reality

This simplified story is *not*, of course, how OMOs actually work. In reality OMOs are undertaken by the open market trading desk at the Federal Reserve Bank of New York. The Fed's account manager, a vice president with the Federal Reserve Bank of New York, oversees the trading desk activities.

Figure 9-4 Decrease in the Supply of Loanable Funds

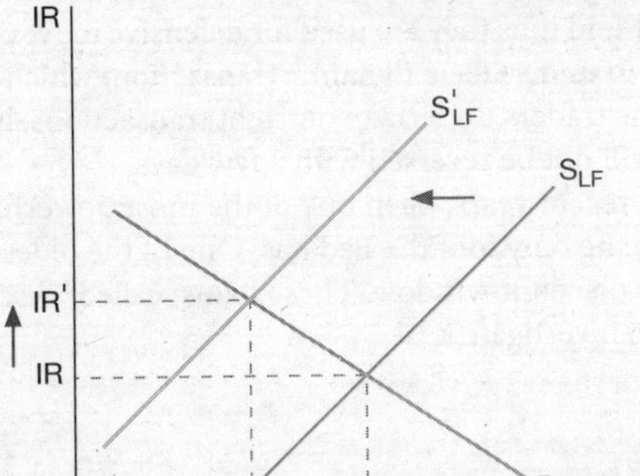

The Fed doesn't buy and sell government securities from/to the general public. Instead they use a group of about 15 "primary dealers"[2] who are private securities firms or commercial banks[3] selected by the Fed to trade in government securities. The trades are done electronically through a system called the Trading Room Automated Processing System, or TRAPS.

Each morning the Fed's account manager discusses with market participants the current status of government securities markets. From these discussions, along with data from the Federal Reserve bank staff and directives from the Federal Open Market Committee (FOMC), she decides what actions need to be taken.

Some of the actions are **dynamic transactions**. These are transactions designed to change the level of reserves and the monetary base as part of a change in monetary policy as directed by the FOMC. More numerous are **defensive transactions**. These are transactions to offset changes in the monetary base arising from changes in market conditions, such as changes in the public's desire to hold cash.

Dynamic transactions: Open market operations designed to change the level of reserves.

Defensive transactions: Open market operations designed to maintain the level of reserves.

The account manager oversees a group of analysts and traders at the trading desk who work together as a team to ensure that the market-determined federal funds rate is within the target band set by the FOMC. For defensive transactions, the traders generally undertake two types of transactions. **Repurchase agreements**, or repos, are transactions in which the Fed buys securities from a primary dealer with the agreement that the primary dealer will buy them back at some point in the future (usually 1 to 15 days). Thus, repurchase agreements add reserves to the banking system. The name "repo," that the Fed applies to these transactions, is from the counterparties' point of view, not from the Fed's point of view. The opposite of repos are **matched sale-purchases**, or reverse repos. These are transactions in which the Fed sells securities to a primary dealer with the agreement the Fed will buy them back in the near future.[4] The security is bought back at the same price for which it was sold. When the Fed sells the security it is withdrawing reserves from the financial system.

Repurchase agreement: The selling of a security with an agreement to buy in back in the future.

Matched sale-purchases: An arrangement where the Federal Reserve sells government securities to a primary dealer or the central bank of another country with the agreement to purchase the security back within a short period of time, usually 1 to 15 days.

Because the repo and reserve repo transactions are reversed within a few days, their effects on reserves are temporary and thus they are used for defensive moves. If, on the other hand, the account manager wishes to undertake a dynamic transaction, which will have a more permanent effect on reserves, the traders undertake outright transactions, buying and selling securities in transactions that will not be reversed with a few days.

While OMOs have, in recent years, been one of the most powerful and most used tools in the Fed's tool kit, it is not the only tool the Fed has. One of the oldest tools used by the Fed is the lending it does at the discount window. These loans, called "discount loans," are the next tool of the Fed we want to investigate.

---

2 For a current list of primary brokers see http://www.newyorkfed.org/markets/pridealers_current.html.

3 For more about primary dealers see the Federal Reserve Bank of New York's Current Issues at http://newyorkfed.org/research/current_issues/ci15-4.pdf.

4 For a discussion of repos in more detail see http://www.newyorkfed.org/research/current_issues/ci9-6.pdf.

SECTION REVIEW

Q1) Explain the steps the Federal Reserve goes through when conducting an expansionary open market operation. Who is affected and how?

Q2) Explain the steps the Federal Reserve goes through when conducting a contractionary open market operation. When and why might the Federal Reserve do this?

Q3) If the Federal Reserve wants to increase the level of reserves in the banking system, it will undertake:

a. a dynamic contractionary transaction.

b. a defensive expansionary transaction.

c. a dynamic expansionary transaction.

d. a defensive contractionary transaction.

9-2 Monetary Policy Tools: Discount Window and Term Auction Facility

Another important tool of monetary policy the Fed has at its disposal is the lending of funds to depository institutions at the discount window. Starting in 1980, all depository institutions that have accounts with the Fed that are subject to reserve requirements can borrow funds at the discount window. Before 1980, only commercial banks that were members of the Federal Reserve system were allowed to borrow money at the discount window.

Discount window lending actually takes place at the 12 Federal Reserve banks. Before 2003, only eligible institutions who had exhausted all of their other sources of funds could borrow money at the discount window. Since 2003, however, the Fed may extend credit, historically on an overnight basis, to financially strong institutions with ample capital. This type of lending is referred to as **primary credit**.

Primary credit: Healthy banks are allowed to borrow from the Federal Reserve for short periods of time, historically overnight.

Each Federal Reserve bank sets the eligibility requirements for primary credit, although there is a set of criteria that is standardized throughout the Federal Reserve system. The idea behind primary credit has always been to ensure there is enough liquidity within the financial system. If, on the other hand, an individual depository institution suffers from a lack of liquidity, it can borrow funds from the discount window in what is called **secondary credit**.

Secondary credit: Banks suffering from financial difficulty can borrow from the Federal Reserve, but they must pay a penalty interest rate above the discount rate.

In addition to primary and secondary credit borrowings, financial institutions that experience an unusually large change in liquidity needs during certain predictable times of the year can borrow at the discount window in what is called **seasonal credit**.

Seasonal credit: Credit given to a limited number of banks that experience unusually high swings in their levels of reserves during different seasons of the year.

Most of the lending under seasonal credit is to small and medium-sized depository institutions in primarily agricultural areas, although some are in economies that rely heavily on seasonal tourism.

Even though there is a clear difference between primary credit (safe depository institutions) and secondary credit (depository institutions that are facing financial difficultly), there is a significant "**stigma effect**" from borrowing at the Fed. That is, financial market participants often look negatively on an institution that borrows from the discount window, even if that institution is borrowing under primary credit.

Stigma effect: A situation in which commercial banks fear that borrowing from the central bank will be considered as a sign of financial weakness.

9-2a When Traditional Policies Fail

The "stigma effect" became a major problem for the Fed during the summer of 2007. As uncertainty gripped financial markets, commercial banks started to worry about their own need for reserves as well as the creditworthiness of other banks. As a result of this uncertainty, the supply in the Fed funds market decreased and the federal funds rate increased well above the Fed's target.

Fed officials faced a problem: They could use OMOs to increase the level of bank reserves, but given the current panic-stricken nature of financial markets, whether the banks would lend the increases in their reserves to their customers was uncertain.

If the banks did not relend these reserves, capital in financial markets would become scarce, and firms and households would not be able to borrow the funds they need for their desired level of spending. If spending decreased, this would slow the overall economy and potentially push it into a recession. This lack of lending is called a **credit crunch**. It seemed the US markets were on the brink of experiencing the worst credit crunch in decades.

Credit crunch: A reduction in the general availability of credit in financial markets most often seen as an irrational increase in risk aversion.

But what could the Fed do? It couldn't "force" banks to lend. All it could do was increase the amount of reserves in the banking system and hope the banks would relend these reserves. But how could the Fed increase bank reserves? OMOs were being used, but that was not enough. Because of the stigma effect of borrowing at the discount window, depository institutions were not coming to the Fed to borrow funds.

It was time for drastic measures. And that is what the Fed implemented.

In August 2007 the Fed changed the rules for borrowing at the discount window. Instead of allowing depository institutions to borrow only overnight and charging a penalty interest rate of 100 basis points (or one percentage point) above the federal funds target, the Fed allowed banks to borrow up to 30 days and renew for another 30 days, and the penalty rate was reduced to only 50 basis points (half of a percentage point) over the federal funds target.

This was a significant change in the conduct of monetary policy. And it didn't work.

The stigma effect was simply too large; banks were not willing to risk being considered "weak" by borrowing at the discount window. Clearly, more drastic action was needed.

Term Auction Facility

In December 2007 the Fed announced an entirely new way to inject liquidity into the financial system: the term auction facility, or TAF. The TAF would be a combination of OMOs and discount window lending. As the name suggests, through the TAF the Fed would anonymously "auction" short-term loans to financial institutions to get around the stigma effect.

How the TAF Worked When the Fed was going to auction funds through the TAF, it would send out a notice soliciting bids from all interested parties. The Fed would announce how much it planned to auction and a minimum interest rate bid. This minimum interest rate bid is designed to be very close to the existing market interest rates; in this way the TAF is not a "penalty interest rate," which would be seen as the bidders paying a premium above market interest rates.

The Fed also set up the TAF as a uniform price or single-price auction. That is, everyone who "wins" the auction pays the same price. This form of auction, used in Treasury auctions of its securities, helps to make banks more comfortable in bidding for funds since they no longer have to worry that they are paying a "different price" than other banks in the auction.

To ensure wide dissemination of the funds, no one bidder was allowed to capture more than 10% of the auction size. There was a three-day period between the auction and when bidders would get their funds. This characteristic of the auction signals that the TAF participants are not desperate for funds on that very day and are thus not "running" to the Fed. Then Fed Chair Ben Bernanke suggested that this structure may have greatly reduced the stigma effect of "borrowing" from the Fed.

Benefits of TAF over Discount Window Lending The Fed viewed the TAF as offering three main benefits over discount window lending and OMOs:

1. **Control.** The auctions allowed the Fed to control exactly when and exactly how much liquidity is pumped into the system. The Fed lowering the discount rate to a level low enough to overcome the stigma effect could result in a very rapid increase in the

demand for discount loans. Further complicating matters, primary discount window loans are provided on the day they are requested, and so a large increase in the demand for discount loans could lead to big swings in bank reserves and thus complicate the Fed's ability to manage the supply of bank reserves. Because the TAF proceeds are delivered with a three-day delay, it is much easier for the Fed to manage the level of bank reserves.

2. **No more stigma.** Because all of the participants in the TAF bid simultaneously and all borrow at the same interest rate, the TAF basically allows banks to approach the Fed collectively as opposed to being seen as individually approaching the Fed with "hat in hand." Since the participants "borrow as one," the stigma effect of borrowing from the Fed is greatly reduced.
3. **Wide dispersion.** Because the Fed limits the amount any one borrower can borrow to a maximum of 10% of the auction, the TAF ensures a large number of recipients of the Fed's action. With the discount window the Fed can offer up funds, but only those banks that actually come to borrow the funds receive them. With discount window lending, there is the potential for funds to be given to only a few banks that are willing to borrow. (See Table 9-1.)

While the TAF had many positive attributes, it was also an untested tool. The Fed had created the TAF out of thin air; it had never been used before 2007 because it had never existed, or even been contemplated, before then. Whether the banks would even submit bids to the TAF auctions was unclear at the time. But they did. While the size of the auctions increased and were fully subscribed, by the spring of 2008 it was becoming clear that even the TAF was *not* enough to pull financial markets out of the growing crisis. Some additional *new* monetary policy tools were needed.

Table 9-1 Term Auction Facility: Auction Results, December 17, 2007–April 21, 2008

Auction	2007		2008							
	1	2	3	4	5	6	7	8	9	10
Date	Dec. 17	Dec. 20	Jan. 14	Jan. 28	Feb. 11	Feb. 25	Mar. 10	Mar. 24	Apr. 7	Apr. 21
Amount allocated (billions of dollars)	20	20	30	30	30	30	50	50	50	50
Minimum bid (OIS) rate (%)*	4.17	4.15	3.88	3.10	2.86	2.81	2.39	2.19	2.11	2.05
Stop-out rate (%)	4.65	4.67	3.95	3.123	3.01	3.08	2.8	2.615	2.82	2.87
Spread between stop-out rate and expected discount rate (basis points)	2	1	−40	−42	−36	−25	−8	19	45	57
Total amount bid (millions of dollars)	61,553	57,664	55,526	37,452	58,400	67,958	92,595	88,869	91,569	88,288
Bid-to-cover ratio	3.08	2.88	1.85	1.25	1.95	2.27	1.85	1.78	1.83	1.77
Number of bidders	93	73	56	52	66	72	82	88	79	83

* The OIS Rate is the overnight index swap rate.

Source: Federal Reserve Bank of New York.

SECTION REVIEW

Q1) Why did the Federal Reserve feel it was necessary to create the term auction facility?

Q2) Explain why the stigma effect may be heightened during an economic slowdown.

Q3) During a credit crunch we can expect interest rates to:

a. decrease rapidly because of a significant increase in savings.

b. increase rapidly as the economy expands quickly.

c. decrease rapidly because of increased liquidity in financial markets.

d. increase rapidly because of fierce competition over the limited funds available to borrow.

9-3 Monetary Policy Tools: Emergency Lending, Quantitative Easing, and the Required Reserve Ratio

While the TAF was successful, by the spring of 2008 it was becoming clear that even the TAF was not enough to return financial markets to "normal." Thus policymakers at the Fed decided more needed to be done to increase the level of liquidity in financial markets to head off a financial meltdown.

During 2008 and 2009 the Fed created a myriad of new programs to inject liquidity into the morbid financial markets. These programs, officially known as emergency liquidation facilities, but often simply called emergency lending programs, were created to help keep the economy from sliding into another Great Depression.

While the emergency lending programs were designed to be temporary and pull the US economy away from an economic abyss, they were not enough to return the economy to solid footing. Thus, starting in 2009, with interest rates almost at zero, the Fed turned away from targeting interest rates and began focusing on ways to continue to pump more liquidity into financial markets. These new policy measures have been labeled "quantitative easing."

These new tools were needed in part because the "old tools" of monetary policy simply were not effective. One of those old tools was changes in the required reserve ratio. We will look at why this old tool is today seldom used.

9-3a Emergency Lending

By February 2008 it was becoming clear that the Fed had to do something in addition to the TAF to inject liquidity into financial markets. The Fed realized that problems in financial markets went well beyond just depository institutions. There were problems facing "systematically critical nonbank financial institutions" such as investment banks, insurance companies, and other nonbank financial institutions.

These entities, while critically important to our financial markets, did not have a "lender of last resort" nor any well-laid-out plans of how they might be liquidated without triggering a massive financial crisis. Thus the Fed had to find a way to offer them a financial lifeline.

The Fed created a collection of short-term lending facilities that were, the Fed argued, allowed under Section 13(3) of the Federal Reserve Act, which granted the Fed the ability in unusual and exigent circumstances to extend credit to individuals, partnerships, and corporations. Below is a brief description of what the Fed created.

Term Securities Lending Facility

On March 11, 2008, the Fed announced the creation of the Term Securities Lending Facility (TSLF), a program whereby the Fed would lend up to $200 billion of Treasury securities, for a term of 28 days, to primary securities dealers for a fee. Originally, the Fed accepted investment-grade secured debt,[5] such as a federal agency debt and mortgaged-backed securities, as collateral.

The TSLF was designed to increase the liquidity in the secured or collateralized debt markets that securities dealers rely on to raise cash. In these secured debt markets securities dealers pledge their secured debt as collateral and thus borrow cash to finance their market-making and risk management activities.[6] The financial press reported that the inability of Bear Stearns to access this market was an important factor in its collapse in March 2008.

---

5 As the financial crisis worsened in 2008, the Fed expanded the list of what was "accepted" as collateral to include auto loans, student loans, home equity loans, and credit card debt.

6 These markets also provide a relatively safe and low-cost way for mutual funds, depository institutions, and institutional investors to lend their surplus cash.

Tying Concepts Together

Systemic Failure: The Financial Accelerator and Short-Run Aggregate Supply/Aggregate Demand

Recall from our discussion of aggregate supply and aggregate demand in Chapter 6 that a negative shock to the economy can result in a reduction in output as the short-run aggregate supply curve shifts back. The concept of the **financial accelerator** argues that financial markets can amplify the negative impacts of these shocks.

Financial accelerator: A negative shock to the economy may be intensified by worsening financial market conditions.

Consider that a firm's ability to borrow is tied to the market value of its assets. In order to borrow funds the firm must pledge their assets as collateral on their loans. A negative supply shock can result in a decline in the market value of the firm's assets and thus make it harder for the firm to borrow. When the firm's borrowing is curtailed, the firm borrows and spends less, reducing short-run aggregate demand as business investment spending falls. Thus, any reduction in the ability of firms to borrow can exacerbate a negative shock. For example, the failure of a large financial institution can trigger a financial accelerator. The failing financial institution sells off its assets at "fire sale" prices, which in turn drives down the price of other firms' assets. In 2008 the Fed feared that the collapse of Bear Stearns, Lehman Brothers, and AIG would trigger an unexpected decrease in the market price of a variety of assets and/or a decrease in expectations, each causing the aggregate demand curve to shift back (Figure 9-5).

The aggregate demand curve shifts back even farther as higher default risks increase the costs of credit, causing investment and consumption to decrease even more. As the risks of production increase, the short-run aggregate supply curve may shift back. The total impact of these actions and reactions is a significant drop in real gross domestic product, but the change in the price level is indeterminate. This chain reaction of events is what the Fed sought to avoid by pursuing the unconventional quantitative easing policies.

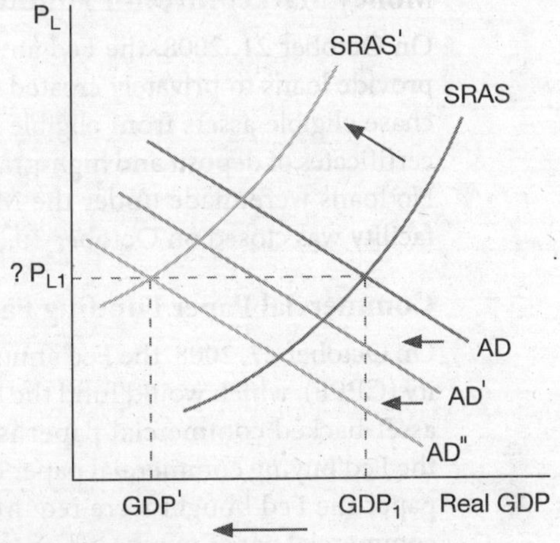

Figure 9-5
The Macroeconomic Impact of a Financial Accelerator

The TSLF offered a solution to this problem by allowing securities dealers to exchange their otherwise difficult-to-finance secured debt for much easier-to-finance Treasury securities. Treasury securities are much more easily used as collateral by securities firms and thus they can borrow the cash they need for their operations. By the end of the program in February 2010, the Fed had lent over $2.3 trillion worth of government securities to about 20 nonbank institutions.

Primary Dealer Credit Facility

Also in March 2008 the Federal Reserve established the Primary Dealer Credit Facility (PDCF), whereby the Fed lent money overnight to securities dealers who pledged acceptable collateral, which was investment-grade securities. The loans were made on the same day they were requested and had to be repaid the following business day. The interest rate the borrowing securities dealer must pay is the same primary credit rate paid by banks at the discount window. The PDCF was essentially a discount window for investment banks. When the PDCF was ended in February 2010, it had lent almost $9 trillion to only a handful of Wall Street institutions.

Asset-Backed Commercial Paper Money Market Liquidity Facility

On September 19, 2008, the Federal Reserve announced it was creating a new program that would lend money to US banks and bank-holding companies so that these entities would purchase high–quality, asset-backed commercial paper from money market mutual funds (MMMFs).

In the days leading up to the Fed's announcement some MMMFs experienced huge withdrawals from investors who worried that the MMMFs might become insolvent. Under normal circumstances, the MMMFs could have met these demands for withdrawals by selling the assets they hold. But these were not normal times. The markets for asset-backed commercial paper had dried up because of the uncertainty gripping financial markets. Thus, to meet investors' demands, the MMMFs were faced with selling their assets at "fire sale" prices—if they could sell their assets at all.

The AMLF proved to be very popular: $150 billion was borrowed in just the first 10 days of the program. By the time the AMLF was closed in February 2010, it had been used by 105 MMMFs through 11 banks and bank-holding companies.[7]

Money Market Investor Funding Facility

On October 21, 2008, the Fed announced that the Federal Reserve Bank of New York would provide loans to privately created special investment vehicles so that these entities could purchase eligible assets from eligible investors. The eligible assets would be dollar-denominated certificates of deposit and high-grade commercial paper that had maturities of 90 days or fewer. No loans were made under the Money Market Investor Funding Facility (MMIFF), and the facility was closed on October 30, 2009.

Commercial Paper Funding Facility

On October 27, 2008, the Fed announced the creation of the Commercial Paper Funding Facility (CPFF), which would fund the buying of dollar-denominated, three-month, unsecured and asset-backed commercial paper issued by US issuers. Unlike the MMIFF, this program had the Fed buying commercial paper directly. To manage risk, entities that issued the commercial paper the Fed bought were required to pay to the Fed a fee equal to 0.10% of the amount of commercial paper purchased. A total of $849 million in fees were collected by the Fed for use of the CPFF. The CPFF was closed in February 2010.

Term Asset-Backed Securities Loan Facility

On November 25, 2008, the Fed announced it was creating a facility that would lend up to $200 billion to investors, who then could purchase certain asset-backed securities. When the program began in March 2009, eligible borrowers were allowed to borrow from the Fed to finance their holdings of AAA-rated tranches of certain asset-backed securities. The Term Asset-Backed Securities Loan Facility (TALF) focuses primarily on securities backed by newly or recently issued auto loans, credit card loans, student loans, and Small Business Administration loans. Fed Chairman Bernanke stated later that the TALF may be expanded in the future to include commercial mortgages and existing securities.

Thus in the space of a few months the Fed created a dizzying array of new tools through which they hoped to inject liquidity into the starving financial market. And it worked—sort of.

7 For a detailed analysis of the AMIF, see Burcu Duygan-Bump, Patrick M. Parkinson, Eric S. Rosengren, Gustavo A. Suarez, and Paul S. Willen, "How Effective Were the Federal Reserve Emergency Liquidity Facilities? Evidence from the Asset-Backed Commercial Paper Money Market Mutual Fund Liquidity Facility." Working Paper No. QAU10-3, 2. Boston: Federal Reserve Bank of Boston, 2010.

While the emergency measures did help to stabilize financial markets, they were not enough to right the entire economy. The Fed needed to do something else, and thus quantitative easing—American style—was born.

9-3b Quantitative Easing

On November 25, 2008, in addition to its emergency lending programs already in place, the Federal Reserve announced it would purchase $100 billion of direct debt from Fannie Mae, Freddie Mac, and the Federal Home Loan Banks, along with up to $500 billion of mortgage-backed securities backed by Fannie Mae, Freddie Mac, and Ginnie Mae. The Fed was pursuing securities purchases *not* to reduce interest rates (think of a traditional expansion OMO) but to inject liquidity into markets.

Immediately following the announcement, the interest rate on a 30-year, fixed-rate mortgage decreased by almost a full percentage point. The policy move would, in the future, be referred to as **QE1**.

QE1: The first round of quantitative easing undertaken by the Federal Reserve began in November 2008 and lasted until March 2010.

Here is the time line of the Fed's other quantitative easing moves:

March 18, 2009 The Fed expands its debt purchases by announcing it will purchase an additional $100 billion in Fannie Mae and Freddie Mac debt and $750 billion in mortgage-backed securities. The Fed also announces it will buy $300 billion in longer-term Treasury bonds. The Fed announces the purchases to end by March 2010.

November 3, 2010 The Fed pledges to start a new $600 billion long-term Treasury bond buying program until June 2011. The Fed will reinvest proceeds from mortgage-related holdings to buy the Treasury debt. This has been labeled **QE2**.

QE2: The second round of quantitative easing, or extraordinary expansionary monetary policy, undertaken by the Federal Reserve from November 2010 to June 2011.

September 21, 2011 The Fed announces it will buy $400 billion of Treasury securities in a range of 6- to 30-year maturities and sell an equal amount of Treasury securities of maturities of 3 years or less. This has been labeled "Operation Twist" because it is seen as a move by the Fed to "twist" the yield curve buy pushing the yields on longer-term securities downward. The program is to end in June 2012.

June 20, 2012 Operation Twist is extended by the Fed when it announces it will purchase $267 billion of long-term Treasury securities funded by the sale of an equal amount of short-term Treasury securities.

September 13, 2013 A third round of open-ended bond purchases is announced by the Fed. This has since been labeled **QE3**. Under this program the Fed will buy $40 billion of agency mortgage-backed securities *per month*, every month, indefinitely.

QE3: The third round of quantitative easing, or extraordinary expansionary monetary policy, undertaken by the Federal Reserve from late 2013 to late 2014.

December 12, 2013 The Fed announces a new bond-buying program of $45 billion per month of long-term securities in an effort to reduce what the Fed calls an "elevated" unemployment rate. Purchase of open-ended mortgage-backed securities would increase from $40 to $85 billion per month.

May 22, 2013 Then Fed Chairman Bernanke tells Congress that the Fed will decrease its bond purchases in a few months.

June 19, 2013 Bernanke announces a "tapering" of some of the Fed's quantitative easing policies, contingent on continued and improved economic conditions.

September 18, 2013 The Fed decides it will *not* taper its quantitative easing policies.

December 19, 2013 The Fed announces it will gradually end its bond-buying programs in 2014. The Fed also announces it will immediately cut its bond purchases to $75 billion per month.

January 29, 2014 After the final meeting in which Ben Bernanke would be the Fed chair, it is announced that the Fed will reduce its bond purchases to $65 billion a month. In its statement the FOMC cites "growth underlying strength in the broader economy" as justification for this move.

March 19, 2014 After the first FOMC meeting with Janet Yellen as Fed chair, the Fed announces it will again make "a modest" reduction in its bond purchases by $10 billion per month to a level of $55 billion per month. The Fed also signaled that it plans to keep the short-term interest rate near zero after the unemployment rate falls below 6.5%.

April 30, 2014 The Fed again, as expected, announced it would reduce its purchases of Treasury and mortgage-backed securities to $45 billion a month. The FOMC stated that "Growth in economic activity has picked up recently, after having slowed sharply during the winter in part because of adverse weather conditions."

October 29, 2014 The Federal Reserve ends QE3.

9-3c Required Reserve Ratio

As we saw earlier, changes in the required reserve ratio can affect the size of the money multiplier. If the Fed increases the required reserve ratio, banks would be required to hold more reserves and thus decrease the size of the money multiplier. Conversely, if the Fed decreases the required reserve ratio, banks would be required to hold fewer reserves and thus potentially increase the size of the money multiplier.

While in theory the required reserve ratio could be a useful tool in the conduct of monetary policy, in reality it is seldom used as a monetary policy tool. One of the reasons for this is the rise of sweep accounts. With sweep accounts, a bank customer's balances above a certain amount are swept out of a checking account by the bank and put into an overnight account that pays interest. The funds are put back into the transaction account the next morning, along with the earned interest. Thus, with sweep accounts, the checking accounts have significantly lower "balances" against which deposits must be held.

The rise of ATMs is a second reason why required reserve ratios are becoming less important. As ATMs became more popular, banks found they needed more and more cash to keep the ATMs working. The cash in ATMs is counted as vault cash and thus may be counted as reserves. So as ATM use grew, the amount of reserves held by banks increased.

The impact of these changes is that the required reserve ratio has become less and less relevant. As Bennett and Peristian[8] report, about 70% of banks voluntarily have reserves that exceed their level of required reserves. Thus the required reserve ratio isn't really "binding" because banks already, on their own, hold more reserves than what are required.

In this situation raising or lowering the required reserve ratio has little effect. If banks already hold more than what is required, then cutting the required reserve ratio will not have any impact on the amount of bank lending.

Even if the required reserve ratio was binding, changes in it could cause more problems than they are worth. If the Fed significantly changes the required reserve ratio, banks would be required to change their levels of liquidity in a significant way. These changes in liquidity could then affect other financial markets, including the money market, bond market, and equity markets. Thus many unforeseen changes in financial markets could result from significant changes in the required reserve ratio.

8 See http://www.newyorkfed.org/research/epr/02v08n1/0205benn/0205benn.html.

Because of all of these issues, the Fed seldom changes the required reserve ratio in a significant way. Even though the Fed was given more leeway in setting the required reserve ratio under the Depository Institutions Deregulation and Monetary Control Act in 1980, the required reserve ratio remains a seldom-used tool in the conduct of monetary policy.

Even though the Federal Reserve does have a number of tools to use in its conduct of monetary policy, these tools do not always work as planned. Next we examine why there are problems with the monetary policy tools the Fed has at its disposal.

SECTION REVIEW

Q1) During the crisis of 2007–2008, the Federal Reserve created an alphabet soup of emergency lending programs: TSLF, PDCF, AMLF, MMIFF, CPFF, and TALF, among others. Why did the Fed feel compelled to do so?

Q2) Explain why the Federal Reserve went from emergency lending to quantitative easing.

Q3) What is the Federal Reserve trying to twist in its "Operation Twist"?

a. The shape of the yield curve

b. The size of the government's budget deficit

c. The level of profits banks earn

d. The interest rate spread between lending rates and rates paid on deposits

9-4 Problem with Tools: Money Demand

Despite all of the tools the Fed has at its disposal to manipulate the money supply, it does not have complete control over what it wants to accomplish. One of the problems the Federal Reserve faces in using its monetary policy tools is that the demand for money can be very unstable. If we think of interest rates as the price of money, then changes in either the money supply or the demand for money bring about changes in interest rates. Thus, to understand the problems the Fed faces, understanding the demand for money is important.

9-4a Irving Fisher on Money Demand

The question of what drives the demand for money has been debated by economists for a long time. One of the most influential thinkers in this debate was the American economist Irving Fisher. Writing in 1911, Fisher hypothesized that one can think about the total amount of transactions that go on in the economy in two different ways.

First, Fisher argued that one should think about the amount of money that is used in transactions and then think about how often each unit of money is used in a year. For example, if the size of the economy is $12 billion and the money supply is $3 billion, each unit of the money supply is used four times within a year. That is, the turnover rate, or velocity, of money is equal to 4. More simply:

$$\textbf{Money supply} \times \textbf{Velocity of money} = \textbf{Total output}$$

or

$$M_S \times V = GDP$$

Next, Fisher argued one can think about the total amount of transactions as the amount of goods and services bought within a year and the price of those goods and services, or the price level. That is, the price level times the amount of transactions to buy goods and services should also equal what we call today GDP.

$$P_L \times T = GDP$$

Putting these together then gives us the equation of exchange:

$$M_S \times V = P_L \times T$$

The equation of exchange tells us that if the left side increases, so too must the right side. Conversely, if one side decreases, the other must decrease as well. By itself the equation of exchange really doesn't tell us much. But Fisher thought about these components and how they might change over time. He correctly pointed out that the money supply, prices, and transactions could be measured and could then be used to solve for velocity. Thus:

$$V = \frac{P_L \times T}{M_s}$$

Velocity, or the turnover rate, of money, he then ventured, was determined by the structure of the financial markets. As technology and institutions in financial markets changed, so too would the velocity of money.

Irving Fisher

For example, if the structure of financial markets in the United States changed so that people use credit cards more and money less, but the total amount of transactions stays the same, fewer dollars would be being used for the same amount of total transactions. In the equation above, the denominator decreases, the numerator remains the same, and thus velocity increases.

Conversely, if Americans stop using credit cards and instead use cash (or some other form of money) more, but the total amount of transactions remains the same, more dollars are now being used for the same amount of total transactions. In this case, velocity decreases.

Irving Fisher believed that such changes in the technology and institutions of financial markets happened slowly and over long periods of time. Thus, he concluded, velocity could be assumed to be constant.

With velocity being constant, the equation of exchange can then be rewritten as

$$\mathbf{M_S = \frac{1}{V} \times P_L \times T}$$

Fisher went on to use the classical assumption that since wages and prices are fully flexible, the actual level of nominal output will be at the full employment level of output. Thus the level of transactions changes only slowly over time and therefore *T* can be assumed to be constant, as well. If velocity and transactions are constant over time, then changes in the price level come about from changes in the money supply.

Fisher extended this framework again and logically concluded if the money market is in equilibrium, then the supply of money is equal to the demand for money. Thus our equation of exchange results in the **quantity theory of money**.

Quantity theory of money: The concept that the quantity of money is directly proportional to the price level.

The quantity theory demand of money is simply the equation of exchange rewritten so that money supply is replaced with demand for money:

$$\mathbf{M_{Demand} = \frac{1}{V} \times P_L \times T}$$

This tells us that because velocity is constant, the demand for money is a function of nominal income. Thus, Fisher argued, people held money purely for transactions.

But Is Velocity Constant?

Fisher thought so, but back in the early part of the twentieth century the data were not available to find out for sure. Today, thanks to central banks and historical economists, we can see that velocity is, in fact, not constant. As the data show, the velocity of both M1 and M2 drops considerably during economic slowdowns (Figure 9-6). After 1982 the velocity of M1 became so unstable that the Fed dropped M1 as a target in 1987 and began to focus on M2. By the early 1990s, however, the velocity of M2 became so unstable that by July 1993 the Fed decided none of the monetary aggregates could provide a useful guide to monetary policy.

So, if velocity isn't constant and the quantity theory of money is less than perfect at explaining the demand for money, what other explanations do we have for the demand for money?

9-4b John Maynard Keynes on Money Demand

Back in 1936, even before he had solid data to back him up, John Maynard Keynes countered that velocity was not stable. Keynes attacked classicalists like Irving Fisher and their quantity theory. Keynes instead argued there were three motives for people to hold or demand money, and they all revolved around interest rates. Keynes called this theory of demand for money the liquidity preference theory because it explains why people hold liquid assets such as money.

Figure 9-6 **Velocity of M2 Money Stock**

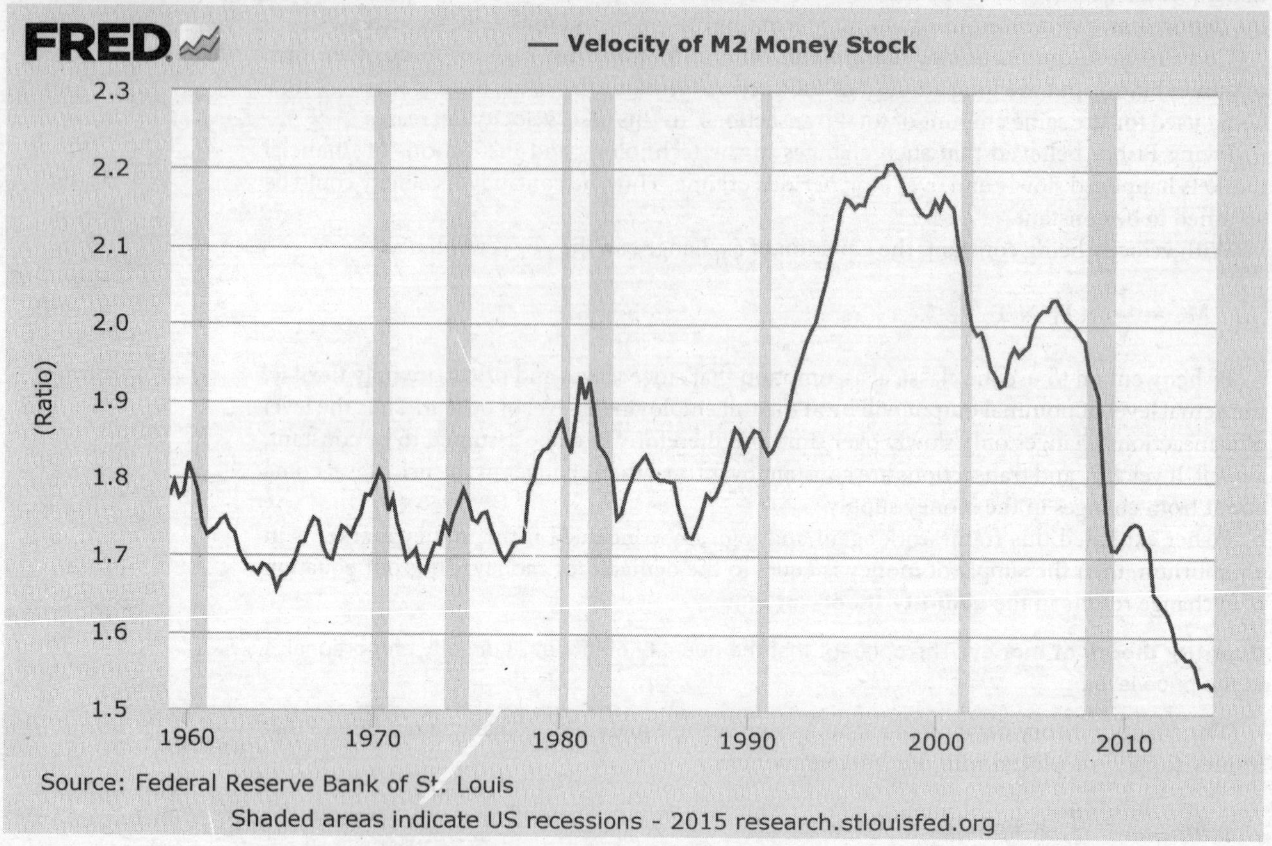

Source: Copyright 2014 by the Federal Reserve Bank of St. Louis.

Transactional Demand for Money

Keynes agreed with the classicalists that people need money for transactions or simply to purchase goods and services. Keynes went on that as people see their income increase, they want to spend a portion of this new income. Thus he concluded the demand for money increases as incomes increase because people will spend part of their additional income in transactions.

Precautionary Demand for Money

Keynes also argued that during times of uncertainty people want to hold on to money as opposed to financial assets. For example, suppose you might be interested in purchasing a new car at some point. Suddenly and unexpectedly the price of the very car you want drops, but the low price is in effect for only one day. If you don't have the money on hand, you won't be able to buy the car. So, given that there is a chance that this could happen, you want to hold on to money as opposed to some relatively illiquid financial asset.

Speculative Demand for Money

Keynes also thought about how people would hold on to to money as opposed to financial assets based on expected returns. Keynes viewed people holding their wealth as either money or bonds. Imagine you are in Keynes's world and you must decide how much of your wealth you want to hold as money and how much of your wealth you want to hold as bonds. Let's further suppose you expect interest rates to increase, or bond prices to decrease, in the future. If you are holding bonds and bond prices fall, you will suffer a capital loss, or your wealth will decrease. Thus if you think interest rates are going to rise in the future you will hold on to your money, protect the total value of your wealth, and wait for bond prices to decrease before buying them. Thus Keynes hypothesized that there is a speculative demand for money as people speculate over in what form they should hold their wealth.

Factors That Change the Demand for Money

What does this leave us with in the end? It tells us there are a variety of factors that can and do change over time that bring about changes in the demand for money. Consider the things that might bring about a change in the demand for money:

- Consumers' income and thus the amount of transactions
- The price level or the rate of inflation
- Increased uncertainty
- Change in interest rates, which affect the return on financial assets
- Transaction costs on financial assets, which affect the return on financial assets

As time went on, economists moved beyond Fisher's and Keynes's explanation of domestic money demand to consider the global factors that could affect the demand for money:

- Changes in the overseas demand for a country's goods
- Changes in the level of foreign direct investment
- Central banks' holdings of the currency

We discuss these global forces in more detail later, but as you can see the list of things that can change the demand for money is long. In addition, many of these things can change rapidly day to day or month to month. Thus, you can understand why many economists argue that the demand for money is often unstable.

Money Demand and Monetary Policy

But, if the demand for money is unstable this can cause a great deal of problems for central banks in their conduct of monetary policy. To see why, think about this question: In the conduct of monetary policy, should the central bank attempt to control the money supply or interest rates?

Controlling the Money Supply Leads to Unstable Interest Rate Assuming that the central bank can set the money supply at MS_1 and we start with an initial money demand at MD_1, the resulting equilibrium price is IR_1. If the demand for money increases to MD_2 next period, the equilibrium interest rate shoots up to IR_2. If, however, in the next period the money demand drops to MD_3, the equilibrium interest tumbles to IR_3 (Figure 9-7). The result is clear: If the central bank targets the money supply, then interest rates fluctuate greatly if money demand is unstable.

Think about why fluctuating interest rates are not good. As they are trying to decide which projects to fund, firms are going to have a difficult time making decisions if interest rates are volatile. Similarly, as they contemplate buying consumer durable goods or a house, households will change their behavior rapidly as interest rates change. Thus, if interest rates change a great deal, the amount of borrowing and spending might fluctuate along with it.

Controlling Interest Rates Requires Constantly Changing the Money Supply Because big swings in interest rates are less than desirable, central banks may choose to try to stabilize interest rates. However, this is easier said than done in a world of unstable money demand. To understand why, let's again start at MS_1 and MD_1 with equilibrium interest rate IR_1. Because of

Figure 9-7 Changes in Money Demand

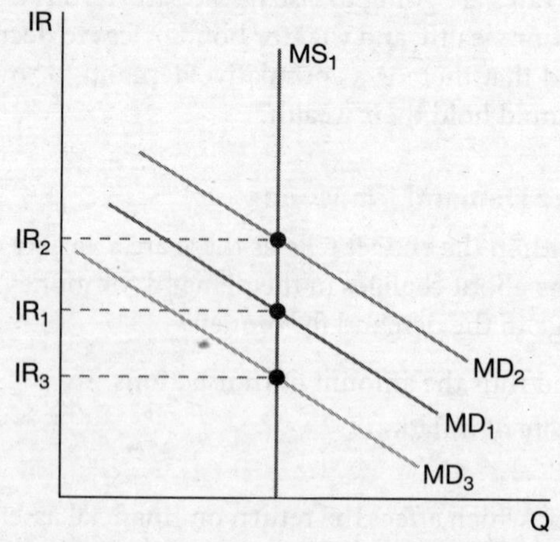

the factors listed above, suppose money demand increases to MD_2. If the central bank does not respond, market interest rates will shoot up, but since the central bank wants to keep interest rates constant at IR_1, it must increase the money supply to MS_2.

Now suppose just as the central bank has changed policy to increase the money supply, the demand for money can decrease to MD_3. To keep interest rates constant, the central bank has to backpedal and decrease the money supply to MS_3 to keep interest rates constant at MD_1 (Figure 9-8).

So, to keep interest rates constant, the central bank has to be able to nimbly control the money supply. But, as we saw, this can be wrought with problems. In drawing our graph it is easy enough to say "the money supply," but what do we mean by this exactly? Does "money supply" mean the monetary base, or M_1 or M_2, or some other measurement? You have to be able to define something before you can "control" that something. As we know, properly defining the money supply can be difficult.

Figure 9-8 Controlling Interest Rates

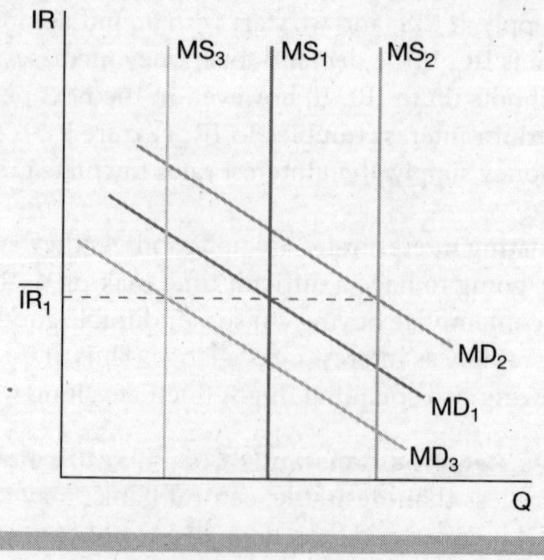

Tying Concepts Together

The Challenge of Measuring the Money Supply

Recall from our discussion in Chapter 2 of the difficulty of measuring the money supply today. Back in the early twentieth century, economists such as Irving Fisher did not have to deal with complex financial assets that have different levels of "moneyness" to them. When Fisher was writing, the money supply was pretty clear: coins in currency in the hands of the public plus demand deposits. There were no travelers' checks in those days. There were no money market deposit accounts to deal with. Thus, in Fisher's time, measuring M_S in the equation of exchange was relatively straightforward.

Is it so straightforward anymore?

Also, think about the central bank's "control" over the money supply. In drawing our diagrams we assume the central bank can easily change the money supply. But, as we learned earlier, many players—including banks and the public—can influence the growth rate of the money supply. Thus "controlling" the money supply to stabilize interest rates may not be as easy as our diagrams suggest.

An unstable money demand is not the only problem a central bank faces when using their money policy tools. Next we look at other things that get in the way of conducting monetary policy: liquidity traps and government budget deficits.

SECTION REVIEW

Q1) Irving Fisher explained the demand for money using the quantity theory of money demand. Explain this concept to someone who has no training in economics.

Q2) Explain why targeting interest rates is so difficult for central banks if the demand for money is unstable.

Q3) Fred is holding on to cash because he thinks interest rates will increase in the future and thus bond prices will decrease, making the future a good time to buy bonds. Keynes would say Fred is holding on to cash as part of which type of demand for money?

a. Precautionary

b. Speculative

c. Transactional

d. Velocity

9-5 Problems with Tools: Liquidity Traps and Budget Deficits

When the economy slows dramatically, central banks such as the Federal Reserve face another problem in using monetary policy tools: liquidity traps.

9-5a Liquidity Traps

Imagine that business leaders expect the economy to weaken significantly in the future. As they envision their sales falling, businesses will be less likely to fund projects such as launching new products. When firms refuse to undertake projects, they instead hold on to their cash.

Similarly, seeing the slowing economy, banks worry about the ability of potential borrowers to repay loans, so they scale back their lending and hold on to their cash. Fearing they may lose their jobs in the future and not be able to pay their bills, households cut back on their spending and hold on to their cash. These "fears" of a slowing economy then become a self-fulfilling prophesy: People think the economy is going to slow down, they act on these beliefs, and they actually cause the economy to slow down. Thus the economy is caught in a trap.

As a result of these actions, the amount of cash holdings, or level of liquidity, in the financial system increases dramatically. Think of the economy as swimming in cash. The economy slows not because of a lack of liquidity or a lack of cash, but because of a lack of spending. Thus the economy is said to be in a **liquidity trap**.

Liquidity trap: A situation where expansionary monetary policy fails to stimulate the overall economy because of a high level of savings and lack of borrowing in financial markets.

When the economy suffers from a liquidity trap, an expansionary monetary policy does very little to push the economy out of the slowdown. To understand why, think about what an expansionary monetary policy does: increases the amount of reserves or liquidity in the banking and financial system. In a liquidity trap, however, the financial system is already awash in cash or liquidity. Thus further increasing the level of liquidity is not all that beneficial.

Keynesians believe that liquidity traps occur quite often and thus question the usefulness of expansionary monetary policy. Their beliefs date back to Keynes's famous argument that monetary policy is like a string. That is, you can pull on a string: Contractionary monetary policy works to slow the economy. But Keynes argued you cannot "push on a string," that is, expansionary monetary policies are not effective in getting the economy out of a slowdown. According to Keynes and the Keynesians, you cannot push on a string because economic slowdowns often result in a liquidity trap.

9-5b Government Budget Deficits and Monetary Policy

While a central bank may use its tools of monetary policy to set interest rates, government fiscal policies, especially if they result in large deficits, can greatly complicate things. As we discussed in Chapter 3 and point out in the Tying Concepts Together box below, government budget

Tying Concepts Together

How Government Budget Deficits Affect the Loanable Funds Market

As we discussed in Chapter 3, when the government runs budget deficits, it is spending more than it collects in taxes and must borrow the difference. Thus, as governments run larger deficits, the demand for loanable funds increases. The government most often borrows these funds by issuing new government bonds in the primary debt market.

deficits can lead to the "crowding out" effect, which pushes market interest rates upward. If at the same time, however, the central bank is trying to pursue an expansionary monetary policy and thus lowering interest rates, fiscal policy pushes in the opposite direction.

While crowding out does make monetary policy more difficult for central banks, an even more insidious impact of government budget deficits is the **monetization of public debt**. With monetization of public debt, sometimes the government either cannot or does not want to sell its bonds in the open market. A government may not be able to sell its debt in the open market because of a high level of default risk. Perhaps the government is corrupt and does not have the support of the country's people. Bond market participants might fear that the government is about to be overthrown and a new government will take charge. The new government may then refuse to pay the debts of the former government. If this were to happen, the bondholders of the government debt would see the value of bonds they hold drop to zero. Thus, because of this fear, bond buyers may be unwilling to buy the government's debt.

Monetization of public debt: Governments require commercial banks and/or central banks to purchase government bonds.

Monetization of public debt also occurs because a government simply may not want the outside world to know how much it needs to borrow. Maybe a country's government is trying to attract foreign investors to bring capital into their country. To impress the foreign investors, the government builds fancy airports with beautiful reception areas, full of flat screen televisions and first class restaurants. Then, to impress the foreign investors outside of the airport, the government constructs wide, tree-lined highways for the would-be foreign investors to be driven down on the way to their luxurious hotels with huge rooms adorned with fine linen and thick imported towels. To pay for all of these things the government runs huge budget deficits. But if the foreign investors learn that the local government is living beyond its means, they might be less likely to invest in the country. Thus, to keep things looking nice for foreign investors without disclosing publically what a financial mess the government is in, the government monetizes public debt.

When a government monetizes public debt, it is essentially forcing the banking system to create money for the government to spend. The government forces government bonds onto the banks' balance sheets, and the banks are required to increase the size of the government's demand deposit. Thus the government debt is turned into money, and hence the name "monetization of public debt."

This creation of new money, of course, does not stop there. The newly created money will at some point be deposited into a depository institution and thus trigger a monetary expansion via the deposit multiplier. In this way monetization of public debt can lead to rapid, massive increases in the money supply. This increase in the money supply, of course, makes the job of the central bank much more difficult.

SECTION REVIEW

Q1) Explain why Keynes thought monetary policy during the Great Depression was like "pushing on a string." Was it similar during the Great Recession of 2008–2009? Why or why not?

Q2) President Abraham Lincoln funded the Union Army during the Civil War by a "monetization of public debt." What did Lincoln do?

Q3) Monetization of public debt often leads to which economic problem?

a. Inflation

b. Unemployment

c. Stock market asset bubbles

d. Falling commodity prices

9-6 Tools of the European Central Bank

The European Central Bank (ECB) conducts its monetary policy in a slightly different way than does the Federal Reserve. One of the biggest differences is that a great deal of the ECB's monetary policies are conducted by the national central banks in each of the countries that are part of the EuroZone.

The ECB has three policy tools: OMOs, standing lending facilities, and the minimum reserve requirements. Of these, the most used and thus most important are the OMOs. The term *open market operation* is used for operations that are executed on the initiative of the ECB and usually conducted in the money market, or short-term debt market.

Within OMOs, the ECB has four different tools: main refinancing operations, longer-term refinancing, fine-tuning operations, and operations that provide structural liquidity. In each of these different tools the ECB uses tenders, or a type of loan, to inject or withdraw liquidity from money markets, which allows the ECB to influence interest rates and signal in what direction it would like financial markets to move.

9-6a ECB's OMO: Tenders and Reserve Transactions

In its OMO the ECB uses both "standard tenders" and "quick tenders." These can be either fixed-rate or variable-rate tenders. Let's look at how these tenders work and the different type of tenders the ECB offers.

Here is how the ECB's tenders work: For a fixed-rate standard tender, the ECB specifies the interest rate at which it will lend funds in advance. Participating financial institutions—those that are subject to the Euro system's minimum reserve system—then bid on the amount of money they want to borrow from their national central bank at that interest rate. In a variable-rate standard tender the participating financial institutions bid the amount of money they want to borrow and the interest rates at which they want to borrow from the national central banks.

The standard tenders are usually settled in about 24 hours. That is, the time between the announcements of tender and when the depository institutions get their funds is usually about 24 hours. Quick tenders, on the other hand, are normally executed within 90 minutes of the announcement of tender, and the funding takes place immediately after the announcement of who has won the auction.

When the ECB first began OMOs in 1999, it used fixed-rate tenders, that is, the ECB stated the interest rate at which it would lend. However, it quickly discovered that there was a problem with the bidding procedure and there was huge overbidding by banks. The overbidding became such a problem that by mid-2000 the ECB switched to variable-rate tenders, but with a stated explicit minimum bid rate.

Many of ECB's OMOs are conducted in reserve transactions. In this type of reverse transaction, the central bank buys assets from financial institutions under an agreement to sell the asset back at a future date (repurchase agreement), or the central bank grants a loan against assets given as collateral. Reserve transactions are thus temporary OMOs, which provide funds for only a limited or predetermined period.

Types of the ECB's OMOs

As mentioned above, the ECB has four different types of open OMOs.

- **Main refinancing operations.** These are standard tender reserve transactions, typically repurchase agreements and collateralized loans, which are conducted once a week. The loans are reversed or paid back in one week. These operations are designed to ensure there is a proper amount of liquidity in the European financial markets. Main refinancing operations are the most important OMO the ECB has. Through main refinancing operations the ECB lends funds to financial institutions, but it always does so against some collateral the borrower must pledge. This is done to protect the ECB against potential risks in the value of assets and potential default of the borrower.

- **Longer-term refinancing operations.** These are longer-term reverse transactions conducted by the national central banks. Typically, they are done monthly, with maturities of three months. Longer-term refinancing operations also occur on an irregular basis.
- **Fine-tuning operations.** These quick tenders are conducted by national central banks on an ad hoc basis to manage liquidity and interest rates. They may also include the outright purchase of bank assets and foreign currency swaps.
- **Structural liquidity–providing operations.** These are carried out by the Euro system through reverse transactions and the issuance of debt certificates. These types of operations are rare.

ECB's Standing Facilities

Another tool the ECB has in its conduct of monetary policy are its two lending facilities or standing facilities. The standing facilities are designed to inject and absorb funds in the overnight lending market and thus help to stabilize this important bank-to-bank lending market. The ECB's marginal lending facility lends funds overnight to qualified institutions at an interest rate that is 100 basis points above the ECB's required minimum bid in open market or refinancing operations. The overnight bank-to-bank rate is usually close to the weekly refinancing rate; thus banks have an incentive to borrow in the interbank market before borrowing money from the ECB.

9-6b ECB's Deposit Facility

The ECB's deposit facility provides a floor for the interbank rate. This facility is available for institutions with excess funds; it allows them to put the funds on deposit with the ECB and earn interest. Thus, if the interbank rate is "too low," institutions with excess funds can place these funds in the deposit facility and not lend them in the interbank market. The interest rate on the deposit facility is normally 100 basis points below the ECB's required minimum bid in open market or refinancing operations.

Thus, under normal circumstances, there is a two percentage point "corridor" between the interest rate floor provided by the deposit facility and the marginal lending rate ceiling. Usually, however, the use of the marginal lending facility is limited; it supplies less than one half of 1% of the total lending within the EuroZone banking system.

9-6c ECB's Minimum Reserve Requirements

The ECB requires financial institutions to place funds on deposit, just like the Federal Reserve does in the United States. Similar to the Fed, in the EuroZone these are called "required" or "minimum" reserves. The amount of reserves each institution must hold is determined by that institution's reserve base. Institutions must hold 2% reserves against short-term deposits (those that are eligible for withdrawal in two years or less) and short-term debt securities (those with maturities up to two years) that the institution has issued. Institutions have zero reserve requirements on deposit and debt securities with maturities of more than two years and all repurchase agreements.

Similar to the Federal Reserve, the ECB can change the minimum reserve requirement as a tool of monetary policy. If the ECB wishes to pursue a contractionary monetary policy, they can increase the minimum reserve requirement, thus reducing the growth rate of the money supply. On the other hand, if the ECB is pursuing an expansionary monetary policy, it can lower the minimum reserve requirement, thus allowing banks to lend out more of their deposits. It is hoped that this increased lending stimulates the overall economy.

Thus the ECB, like the Federal Reserve, has a number of tools at its disposal in the conduct of monetary policy. In the next chapter we review how these tools are put to use as we examine the money supply process in more detail.

SECTION REVIEW

Q1) The European Central Bank uses reserve transactions in its version of open market operations. Explain to someone with no training in economics what reserve transactions are.

Q2) Explain how the European Central Bank's interest payments on the deposits commercial banks have at the ECB provides an interest rate floor for the interbank lending rate.

Q3) If the ECB is pursuing an expansionary monetary policy, it will do which of the following?

a. Lower the minimum reserve requirements

b. Lower the interest rate paid by its deposit facility

c. Purchase assets from financial institutions through open market operations

d. All of the above

Conclusion

9-7

The tools of monetary policy are wonderful things—if they work correctly. OMOs, the Fed's buying of government securities in the secondary market, works so well that it is today one of the Fed's most used tools. Discount window lending, one of the Fed's original tools, is less effective today because of the stigma effect of borrowing from the lender of last resort. Sometimes new tools, such as the term auction facility and quantitative easing, are needed, as they have been during the current financial crisis that began in 2007. Some tools, like changing the required reserve ratio, sit on the bench waiting for the appropriate time to be used.

But the tools of monetary policy can and do run into difficulty. An unstable money demand can make it very difficult for a central bank to keep interest rates in line with their monetary policy objectives. When interest rates get very low and the economy slows, financial markets can slide into a liquidity trap, and the usefulness of monetary policy tools declines rapidly. Also, when fiscal policy is not under control it too can cause problems for a central bank's monetary policy tools.

Finally, it is important to remember that the Federal Reserve is not the only central bank with monetary policy tools. The ECB has its own set of tools that it uses in monetary policy. The ECB's version of OMOs differs from the Fed's OMOs. In addition, the ECB has its standing facilities and required reserve tools in conducting monetary policy. Just as the Fed has had to change the use of its tools in the face of the global economic slowdown, so too has the ECB.

In the next chapter we will examine how central banks use their tools of monetary policy in dealing with the issues they face. We will again explore the differences between the Federal Reserve and the ECB in their approach and conduct of monetary policy. We will also contrast these two with the Bank of Japan and its conduct of monetary policy.

IN THE NEWS. . .

Easing Means Squeezing: Quantitative Easing Has Both Good and Bad Implications for Europe's Banks

The Economist
January 31, 2015

European bankers depressed by the miasma in Athens might cheer up a bit if they focused on news from Frankfurt instead. The recent unveiling by the European Central Bank (ECB) of a €1.1 trillion ($1.25 trillion) package of "quantitative easing" (QE)—the printing of money to purchase vast quantities of bonds—should be as heartwarming for them as a resurgence of the euro crisis is chilling.

Cynics might be forgiven for thinking QE is a policy designed purely to aid financiers. Banks, after all, borrow vast sums of money (from bond markets, depositors and other creditors) to acquire financial assets (corporate bonds, say, or the promise to repay a loan with interest). Even looser monetary policy helps the banks on both counts. On the one hand, it is cheaper for them to borrow money as interest rates are pushed lower. On the other, to drive bond yields down the ECB will have to drive bond prices up. Banks, which own lots of them, will be the biggest sellers. . . .

But QE is also a threat to banks' margins. The most basic measure of a lender's profitability is the gap between what it charges borrowers and the interest it has to pay depositors. But few depositors are now getting any interest at all on their savings, and it is difficult for banks to offer them negative rates. Borrowers, however, will expect cheaper loans. The result is a nasty pincer.

The assumption in the markets is that the ECB will keep interest rates low for an extended period. That undermines another lucrative trick, whereby banks borrow money repeatedly for short periods, while lending it out for long ones. Such "maturity transformation" earns a good return in normal times, when interest rates for long-term borrowing are much higher than those on short-term loans. The expectation now, however, is that interest rates will stay "lower for longer". That has dramatically reduced the difference in rates for loans of different maturities, and with it banks' opportunity to profit.

The article explains how quantitative easing has now come to Europe. But the question is, Will this policy have a net benefit or will it harm the profitability of banks? Which do you think it is? Will quantitative easing in Europe make European banks more or less profitable? Why?

10

The Money Supply Process

10-1 The Money Supply Process

In the last two chapters we discussed central banks (Chapter 8) and monetary policy (Chapter 9). Before that we talked about money and the simple deposit multiplier (Chapter 7). In this chapter we want to delve into these issues in more depth. We ended Chapter 7 by looking at some of the shortcomings of the simple deposit multiplier. In Chapter 8 we looked at the general idea of how central banks are structured and function, whereas in Chapter 9 we examined the tools used in the conduct monetary policy. Now we want to look more deeply into how central banks, in their conduct of monetary policy, affect the money supply through a multiplier process.

While we discuss monetary policy a great deal, remember, central banks do not completely control the money supply process. How fast or slow the money supply changes depends on what depositors, banks, governments, the general public, and others do. We will take a look at the effect all of these have on the money supply process.

To do this we need to introduce a new concept: the monetary base. We will then use changes in the monetary base to review how economists measure the effect of changes in monetary policy. By the end of this chapter you will have a deeper understanding of the connection between monetary policy and the money supply.

10-1a Monetary Base

To get a better understanding of the link between monetary policy and the money supply, we first need to look at the issue of the **monetary base**. The monetary base is formally defined by Anderson, Rasche, and Loesel from the Federal Reserve Bank of St. Louis as "those liabilities of the monetary authorities that households and firms use as media of exchange and that depository institutions use to satisfy statutory reserve requirements and to settle interbank debts."[1]

Monetary base: Currency in circulation + bank reserves + US Treasury currency in circulation. It is one of the narrowest measurements of the money supply.

In the United States the monetary base includes currency in circulation plus bank reserves plus US Treasury currency in circulation (primarily coins). Basically, the monetary base[2] is the foundation, or base, upon which all other measurements of the money supply are based. So, the name "monetary base" sort of makes sense—it is the "base" of "money."

The monetary base is also sometimes referred to as "high-powered money." This is because a $1 change in the monetary base results in the money supply increasing by *much more* than $1. As you can see, the monetary base, or high-powered money, plays a very important role in the money supply process and thus financial markets. To understand why the monetary base plays such an important role, let's look at each part of the monetary base.

- **Currency in Circulation.** This refers to Federal Reserve notes outside the Treasury and the Federal Reserve. Federal Reserve notes are simply the Fed's IOUs, or promises to repay—$1, $5, $10, $20, $50, and $100 bills we carry around in our pockets. Remember, this currency is money since it is a medium of exchange, unit of account, and store of value.
- **Bank Reserves.** Reserves of the banking system consist of bank deposits at the Fed plus the currency they hold in their bank vaults, called vault cash. Remember, these reserves, like Federal Reserve notes, are liabilities on the Fed's balance sheet. The level of actual bank reserves are made up of required reserves, based on the required reserve ratio, plus excess reserves—reserves held in addition to, or in excess of, required reserves.

1 See Anderson, Richard G., Robert H. Rasche, with Jeffrey Loesel, "A Reconstruction of the Federal Reserve Bank of St. Louis Adjusted Monetary Base and Reserves," 39–70. St. Louis, MO· Federal Reserve Bank of St. Louis, September/October 2003.

2 In the United Kingdom this is called "narrow money."

- **US Treasury Currency.** This mainly includes coins[3] that are produced by the US mint and other Treasury monetary liabilities. The mint is actually part of the US Treasury, which is why coins are listed as liabilities of the Treasury. Because coins are a relatively small part of the money supply, however, we will ignore them in our calculation of the monetary base.

Thus we have

$$MB = C + R$$

where MB is the monetary base, C is currency in circulation, and R is bank reserves. To understand why the monetary base is watched so closely by economists, let's examine how and why the monetary base might change.

10-1b Changes in the Monetary Base

The importance of the monetary base stems from the fact that the Federal Reserve has more control over the monetary base than it does over bank reserves. The Fed can affect the monetary base through a variety of ways including changing banks' reserve requirements, using open market operations, operating the discount window, and using other mechanisms to affect the level of bank reserves. Let's take a look at each one of these in turn.

How the Fed Affects the Monetary Base

Changes in the Reserve Requirement The reserve requirement is the amount of funds that a bank[4] must hold in reserves against specific deposit accounts. The board of governors of the Federal Reserve has the sole legal authority to set the required reserve ratio that establishes the reserve requirement for each bank. Banks must hold the reserves in the form of vault cash; if that is not enough, they must hold funds on deposit at a Federal Reserve bank.[5]

The dollar amount of a bank's reserve requirement is based on the amount of a bank's net total transaction accounts, basically, demand deposits less amounts due from other depository institutions and less cash items in the process of collection. Since 1982 the first few million dollars of net transaction accounts have been exempt from the reserve requirement. This "exemption amount" started off at $2 million in 1982 and is adjusted each year by a formula stipulated in the Garn-St. Germain Act of 1982. Effective January 1, 2014, the exemption amount was $13.2 million.

The amount of net transaction accounts subject to a 3% required reserve ratio was set at $25 million by the Depository Institutions Deregulation and Monetary Control Act of 1980. This "low-reserve tranche" level also is adjusted each year; in 2014 it was $89.0 million. Net transaction account amounts over the "low-reserve tranche" level are subject to a 10% required reserve ratio (Table 10-1).

As the level of "exemption amount" increases, the amount of the reserve requirement decreases, and thus the monetary base also decreases. As we discussed in Chapter 9 while changes in the reserve requirement could have an impact, in reality the reserve requirement is seldom changed.

Open Market Operations In Chapter 7 we discussed a slightly simplified version of the Fed's open market operation. When the Fed bought government securities in the secondary market, it increased the level of bank reserves and thus triggered the simple deposit

3 This also includes a small amount, only about $300 million, of Treasury currency that dates back to the Civil War; these are commonly referred to as "greenbacks."

4 Reserve requirements are imposed on commercial banks, savings banks, Savings & Loan associations, credit unions, US branches and agencies of foreign banks, Edge corporations, and agreement corporations. We will refer to all of these simply as "banks."

5 Banks that are members of the Federal Reserve system *must* hold funds on deposit directly with a Federal Reserve bank, whereas banks that are not members of the Federal Reserve system can hold deposits directly with a Federal Reserve bank *or* with another, usually much larger commercial bank.

Table 10-1 Required Reserve Ratios

Liability Type	Required Reserve (%)	Effective Date
Net transaction accounts		
$0–13.3 million	0	January 23, 2014
$13.3–89.0 million	3	January 23, 2014
>$89.0 million	10	January 23, 2014
Nonpersonal time deposits	0	December 27, 1990
Eurocurrency liabilities	0	December 27, 1990

multiplier. In reality, things aren't so simple. In an expansionary open market operation, when the Fed buys government securities, it writes a check drawn on the Federal Reserve Bank of New York and uses it to buy government securities either through banks or directly from the nonbank public.

If the Fed buys the government securities from a bank, the bank can redeem these checks drawn on the New York Fed for currency, or they can deposit the check with the Fed and hold the funds as reserves. Either way, the monetary base increases because either currency (C) increases or bank reserves (R) increase.

On the other hand, if the Fed buys the government securities from the nonbank public, the seller of the securities has two options: deposit the check drawn on the New York Fed into their own bank account or cash the check and hold on to the cash. If the seller of these government securities deposits the Fed's check into a bank, then the story works out just as described in Chapter 7. In this case, bank reserves (R) increase and thus the monetary base increases by the amount of the check the Fed gave to the seller.

However, if instead the entity selling the government bonds to the Fed takes the Fed's check and cashes it, the story is different: Bank reserves don't increase and thus banks don't have more funds to relend. Instead, the money supply does increase, but bank reserves don't. In this case the monetary base increases even if the buyer cashes the Fed's check because cash, or currency, is included in the monetary base.

Similarly, the Fed can reduce the monetary base with an open market sale of government securities. Whether the government securities are bought with currency or with a check, an open market sale reduces the monetary base by the amount of the sale.

To understand why this is the case, imagine the Fed sells $5 million of government securities to a bank or to the nonbank public. If the buyer pays the Fed with a check for $5 million drawn on a bank, that bank's reserves at the Fed will be reduced by $5 million when the Fed gets the check. Because bank reserves R have decreased by $5 million, the monetary base has also decreased by $5 million.

Even if the buyer of the government securities pays in cash (which is highly unlikely because most people don't have millions of dollars in cash sitting around, but if they did . . .) the same outcome would occur: The monetary base decreases by $5 million and currency in circulation C also decreases by $5 million.

Thus we see that the Fed has more direct control over the monetary base (currency and bank reserves) than it necessarily does over the level of bank reserves. This is because some of the open market operation money created by the Fed can "leak out" of the system in the form of cash holdings.

This is one of the main reasons economists who follow monetary policy like to study and watch the monetary base: It gets around the cash leakage problem of the simple deposit multiplier. But remember, open market operations are only one of the tools of monetary policy.

Discount Loans As we discussed earlier, the Fed was created to be a lender of last resort to the banking system. Recall that the Fed makes loans to commercial banks at the discount window. When the Fed makes a discount loan to a commercial bank, it credits the commercial bank's account at the Fed, thus increasing the "reserves" portion of the monetary base. Similarly, when a discount loan is repaid by a depository institution, the effect is to decrease the monetary base through the same method.

As we also discussed, starting in December 2007 the Fed also established the term auction facility. When a commercial bank enters a winning bid through the term auction facility, it borrows money from the Fed. Just as with a discount loan, the commercial bank's reserves account at the Fed increases and thus the monetary base increases.

Comparing Open Market Operations and Discount Loans

While open market operations and discount loans both have the ability to change the monetary base, the Fed has greater control over the former than it does over the latter. This is because the Fed can completely control the amount of government securities it buys or sells. If the Fed wants to sell government securities but cannot find enough buyers, it merely has to lower its asking price. By lowering the price of the government securities it is selling, the Fed is increasing the securities' yield to the buyer or decreasing interest rates. This is exactly what the Fed tries to do with open market sales: lower interest rates.

The Fed's control over discount window lending is, however, less complete. The Fed has some control over discount loans because it sets the price of the loans, that is, the discount rate. However, the Fed cannot force banks to borrow funds at the discount window.

Because of the differences between open market operations and discount loans, economists sometime divide the bank reserves (R) portion of the monetary base into "borrowed reserves" and "nonborrowed reserves." As the names imply, borrowed reserves are the reserves banks have borrowed from the Fed's discount window. Thus we have

$$\mathbf{R = R_{non} + BR}$$

where R_{non} are nonborrowed reserves and BR are borrowed reserves. The total equals R, or the level of bank reserves.

Thus commercial banks, in their willingness to borrow money from the Fed, also help to determine the size of the monetary base. Another entity that affects the monetary base is you and me: the cash-holding public.

SECTION REVIEW

Q1) Explain how the Federal Reserve's conduct of an expansionary open market operation affects the monetary base.

Q2) Explain why the Federal Reserve has more control over the monetary base when it uses open market operations than when it uses discount window lending.

Q3) Which of the following are included in the monetary base?

a. Coins in circulation
b. Currency in circulation
c. Bank reserves
d. All of the above

10-2 More Changes in the Monetary Base and the Money Supply Multiplier

We have seen that the Fed can greatly affect the monetary base; remember, however, they do not have complete control over it. Next we look at how the nonbank public and the Treasury can also affect the monetary base. Then we want to get a clearer picture of just how changes in the monetary base affect the money supply, so we will derive the money multiplier.

10-2a How the Nonbank Public Affects the Monetary Base

While central banks can have dramatic impacts on the size of the monetary base, they are not the only ones who can affect this important variable. The nonbank public can affect the monetary base in a variety of different ways.

Cash Holdings

Think about what happens when you withdraw cash from your checking account by, say, using an ATM. You have more cash, but the bank where you do your banking now has less cash or fewer bank reserves. So, in terms of the Fed's balance sheet, you just increased currency in circulation and decreased bank reserves.

In terms of the monetary base, notice the size of the monetary base has not changed but the composition of the monetary base has. This change in the composition of the monetary base is important; we discuss this in more detail later in the chapter.

Thus, as the nonbank public changes the amount of cash it holds, the amount of currency in circulation changes, and thus the makeup of the monetary base changes.

So, we have seen that the Fed and commercial banks are not the *only* ones that affect the monetary base. As the public chooses to hold more or less cash, they can and do affect the monetary base. But the list of players that affect the monetary base does not end there: The Treasury also affects the monetary base.

10-2b How the Treasury Affects the Monetary Base

The Treasury—which, remember, is part of the US federal government—can also affect the monetary base.

Foreign Exchange Intervention

The Treasury Department is responsible for foreign exchange policy in the United States. For example, suppose the Treasury and the administration decide that they want the dollar to fall against the Japanese yen. The Treasury will order the Federal Reserve Bank of New York to sell dollars and buy yen so the Treasury will have the yen necessary to buy Japanese government bonds. When the Federal Reserve Bank of New York sells the dollars, the supply of dollars in the foreign exchange market increases, and thus the value of the dollar falls against the yen, which is what the Treasury wants.

In terms of the monetary base, when the Federal Reserve Bank of New York sells dollars and buys yen, it does so through the foreign exchange department of American commercial banks. When the Fed buys the yen from a commercial bank, it deposits dollars into the bank's account at the Fed, and bank reserves increase.

Treasury Deposits at the Fed

Treasury Department activities also affect the monetary base when the federal government makes purchases or collects taxes. The Treasury has an account at the Fed called the "general account." It is out of this account that the Treasury pays for the purchases by the federal government. The Treasury also has accounts, called "tax and loan accounts," at commercial banks across the country. The Treasury transfers funds between these accounts to ensure federal government spending does not significantly affect the monetary base.

For example, suppose the US federal government is about to purchase $100 million worth of Pledge furniture polish from S.C. Johnson Company in Racine, Wisconsin. Over the past several months, as the Treasury has been collecting income tax payments from individuals and corporations, it has been depositing these payments into tax and loan accounts in commercial banks across the country.

Now that the government is ready to spend these tax payments, it will transfer $100 million from the tax and loan accounts to their general account at the Fed. When this happens, bank reserves and the monetary base decrease by $100 million. The Treasury then writes a check for $100 million to S.C. Johnson for the furniture polish. S.C. Johnson in turn deposits the check into its local bank, thus increasing bank reserves by $100 million. Thus, by using the general account and tax and loan accounts, the effect of government spending on the monetary base is very small.

Thus we see that many players can bring about changes in the monetary base: the Fed, commercial banks, the cash-holding public, and even the Treasury Department. Of these, the Fed's impact is certainly the biggest, although it is not the only effect. Remember, though, changes in the monetary base have a multiple or snowball effect on the overall money supply. To understand how, we need to examine the issue of the money multiplier.

10-2c Deriving the Money Multiplier[6]

To derive the money multiplier, let's start with a simple definition of the money supply and the monetary base

$$\textbf{Money supply } (\mathbf{M_s}) = \textbf{Currency (C)} + \textbf{Deposits (D)} \quad \textbf{(1)}$$

$$\textbf{Monetary base (MB)} = \textbf{Currency (C)} + \textbf{Reserves (R)} \quad \textbf{(2)}$$

Now, let's think about a bank when it receives a deposit. That deposit means bank reserves increase. Some of those reserves are "required" reserves (RR), whereas the rest are excess reserves (ER). So, let's show that by

$$\textbf{Reserves (R)} = \textbf{Required reserves (RR)} + \textbf{excess reserves (ER)} \quad \textbf{(3)}$$

Next, we have three variables that we must define. First is the currency ratio k, which is simply the amount of currency in circulation divided by the level of deposits. Let's assume there is only one kind of transaction deposit:

$$\textbf{Currency ratio } (k) = \frac{\textbf{Currency (C)}}{\textbf{Deposits (D)}} \quad \textbf{(4)}$$

Now we have the required reserves ratio (r_r), which is the amount of required reserves divided by, again, the amount of deposits

$$\textbf{Required reserves ratio } (r_r) = \frac{\textbf{Required reserves}}{\textbf{Deposits}} \quad \textbf{(5)}$$

Finally, we have the excess reserves ratio (r_e), which, as the name suggests, is the amount of excess reserves that banks are currently holding relative to the level of deposits

$$\textbf{Excess reserves ratio } (r_e) = \frac{\textbf{Excess reserves}}{\textbf{Deposits}} \quad \textbf{(6)}$$

6 This section maybe skipped for those who want to avoid the mathematical details.

By combining (3) and (2) we get

$$MB = C + RR + ER \tag{7}$$

We then use (4) to get

$$kD = \frac{C}{D} D = C \tag{8}$$

We then use (5) to get

$$r_r D = \frac{RR}{D} D = RR \tag{9}$$

We then use (6) to get

$$r_e D = \frac{ER}{D} D = ER \tag{10}$$

Finally, we use these last three equations ([10], [9], and [8]) combined with (7) to get

$$MB = kD + r_r D + r_e D$$

We can rewrite this equation by factoring out a D to get

$$MB = (k + r_r + r_e) D$$

We can then rewrite this equation to make it in terms of deposits:

$$D = \frac{1}{\{k + r_r + r_e\}} MB \tag{11}$$

Now, let's go back and use (1) and combine it with (4) to get

$$M_s = C + D = kD + D$$

This can be rewritten to factor out a D to get

$$M_s = (k + 1)D$$

We can rearrange those variables to give

$$M_s = (1 + k) D \tag{12}$$

Let's now combine (11), which tells us what D is equal to, with (12) to get

$$M_s = \frac{(1 + k)}{\{k + r_r + r_e\}} MB$$

This then tells us that

Money supply = MsM × Monetary base

where the money supply multiplier, or MsM, is

$$\frac{(1 + k)}{\{k + r_r + r_e\}}$$

where k is the currency ratio, r_r represents the required reserve ratio, and r_e is the excess reserve ratio.

To visualize how this works, we can plug in some numbers. For example, C = currency = \$750 billion, D = deposits = \$500 billion, R = reserves = \$51 billion, and RR = required reserves = \$50 billion (assume there is a 10% required reserve ratio). From this we know that the level of excess reserves is \$1 billion. Because the required reserves are only \$50 billion, but the banking system has \$51 billion in reserves, the remaining \$1 billion is reserves that are in excess of the required reserves, or excess reserves.

With this information we can calculate the money supply multiplier (MsM):

- The currency ratio k, which is currency/deposit, equals \$750 billion/\$500 billion, or 1.5. The required reserves ratio r_r, which is required reserves/deposit, equals \$50 billion/ \$500 billion, or 0.1.
- The excess reserves ratio r_e, which is excess reserves/deposits, equals \$1 billion/ \$500 billion, or 0.002.

Thus the money supply multiplier equals

$$\frac{(1+k)}{\{k+r_r+r_e\}} = \frac{(1+1.5)}{(1.5+0.1+0.002)} = \frac{2.5}{1.602} = 1.5605$$

Thus, with a monetary base (which is currency plus reserves) of \$801 billion, we have a money supply of

$$\$801 \text{ billion} \times 1.5605 = \$1249.96 \text{ billion, or about } \$1.25 \text{ trillion}$$

You can check this by adding the two components of the money supply: currency + deposits, or \$750 billion + \$500 billion = \$1.25 trillion. Given a required reserve ratio of 10% on deposits, and given the behavior of both the depositors, who are holding onto cash, and banks, which are holding on to excess reserves, this tells us a \$1 increase in the monetary base leads to a \$1.56 increase in the money supply as measured by M1.

But this is true only so long as the ratios we calculated do not change. As with life, however, things in financial markets are always changing. So, next, let's look at the effect of changes in some of these variables that make up the money multiplier.

SECTION REVIEW

Q1) If bank depositors hold more cash and fewer deposits, the monetary base does not change, only the composition of it does. Explain why.

Q2) Explain how changes in the Treasury's tax and loan account balance may affect the monetary base.

Q3) If US Treasury and administration officials decide they want to see the dollar rise in value against the euro, what will happen to the monetary base?

a. It will increase as bank reserves decrease.

b. It will decrease as bank reserves decrease.

c. It will increase as bank reserves increase.

d. It will decrease as bank reserves increase.

10-3 Changes in Variables of the Money Supply Multiplier and the Great Recession

We derived the money supply multiplier and shown how, given the past behavior of depositors and banks, it can be used to calculate the money supply and changes in the money supply. But what if those behaviors change? That is, how do changes in these variables affect the money multiplier formula? More importantly, how do these changes affect financial markets and people's lives?

It is the last part of this question that is most important: the impact on people's lives. Deriving formulas and plugging numbers into formulas can be an interesting intellectual challenge, but never forget that behind these numbers are people and their daily struggle to survive. The most important aspect of the formulae we use in economics and finance is how they help us to understand how people's lives are changed when the variables in our formulas change. With this in mind, let us now examine changes in the money multiplier.

10-3a Change in the Currency Ratio

The variable k is the currency ratio: the amount of currency relative to deposits that the public holds. Let us consider changes in k, the currency ratio, and how they might affect the money multiplier.

Notice that the currency ratio k appears in both the numerator and denominator of the money supply multiplier. In the numerator k is added to 1, but in the denominator k is added to r_r and r_e, the required reserves ratio and the excess reserves ratio, respectively. Because r_r and r_e generally sum to a number significantly less than 1, we can assume that in the denominator k is being added to by something less than 1.

With this simple assumption, $r_r + r_e < 1$, a change in k, the currency ratio, will change the money supply multiplier in the opposite direction because the percentage change in the numerator is less than the percentage change in the denominator. That is, an increase in k leads to a smaller money supply multiplier, whereas a decrease in k leads to a larger money supply multiplier.

The Intuition Behind a Change in the Currency Ratio

To reveal the intuition of the mathematical outcome we just described, think of currency holding as a "cash leakage" out of the banking system. That is, if the public is holding more cash relative to deposits (a higher k), more cash is making its way into the pockets of consumers and businesses, and thus banks have less cash or fewer deposits. But banks need these deposits to lend out to other customers. So, when there are more "cash leakages," the amount of bank lending is reduced and the money supply does not grow as much. Thus as k increases, the MsM declines.

The same logic applies in reverse, when k is decreasing. A lower currency ratio means that the public is holding less cash per deposit, or that more funds are staying in the banking system. This then means there is less "cash leakage" taking place, that is, banks have relatively more funds to lend. Thus we have a larger deposit multiplier, or, for every increase in the monetary base, the money supply increases more. So, a decreasing k means a larger money supply multiplier.

To understand how this works mathematically, think of two economies: one with a high k (a need for more cash) and one with a low k (a need for less cash). Assume both economies have an r_r of 0.1 and the same r_e of 0.002; the only difference is their currency ratio or k.

In country A, $k = 5$; thus the money supply multiplier is

$$\frac{(1 + k)}{\{k + r_r + r_e\}} = \frac{(1 + 5)}{(5 + 0.1 + 0.002)} = \frac{6}{5.102} = 1.176$$

Thus, in country A, a $1 change in the monetary base changes the money supply by about $1.18.

On the other hand, let us suppose country B has a $k = 2$. Then,

$$\frac{(1 + k)}{\{k + r_r + r_e\}} = \frac{(1 + 2)}{(2 + 0.1 + 0.002)} = \frac{3}{2.102} = 1.427$$

In country B a $1 change in the monetary base changes the money supply by about $1.43.

Think about what this means for a $10 million change in the monetary base. In country B, with its lower currency ratio, the money supply will change by much more. Thus, in economies with a lower currency ratio, a change in monetary policy has a much bigger impact on the money supply than in economies with a lower currency ratio and more cash leakages.

Explanations of Changes in the Currency Ratio

We just learned that changes in *k*, the currency ratio, can have a major impact on the growth of the money supply. This then begs the questions, Why might the currency ratio change? What is the ultimate impact of this change?

Level of Financial Market Development Think about an economy with a financial sector that is not very well developed. For example, consider developing countries around the world today, or perhaps the US economy 70 or 80 years ago. In these economies checking accounts may be rare. Even more rare in such economies are debt cards or consumer credit cards.

In these types of economies a large amount of transactions involving consumers take place using cash. Thus in these economies the need for cash is very high; thus the currency ratio *k* may be relatively high. As we discussed earlier, the widespread use of checking accounts by American consumers is a relatively recent phenomenon, one that increased rapidly only in the 1980s.

Therefore, in economies where the need for cash is high because of underdeveloped financial markets, the currency ratio can be very high. This means monetary policy in these economies is less effective than if the economy had better-developed financial markets—and thus less need for cash.

Tying Concepts Together

Financial Market Development and Poverty

As we saw in earlier chapters, a lack of financial market development may be a major contributor to poverty and slow economic growth. The money supply multiplier offers a more formal and complete explanation of why this is the case: A lack of financial market development, or a lack of banks, results in a higher currency ratio. At a higher currency ratio, monetary policy in turn has a relatively smaller impact on the money supply. For example, at a very high currency ratio, an expansionary monetary policy has little positive effect on the rate of growth of an economy because the expansionary policy does not result in much monetary expansion.

Public Mistrust of Banks Another reason why an economy may have a very high currency ratio is because the public does not trust the banking system. Imagine a world where people no longer believe, for whatever reason, the banking system is a safe place for their money. While these people don't trust the banks, they still need to undertake transactions to buy food, clothing, and so on. Thus when people don't trust banks they hold more cash than when they do trust the banks.

If people lose confidence in the banking system, they hold more currency and *k* increases. Think of the ramifications of this: If people don't trust banks and as a result hold on to more cash, the money supply multiplier becomes smaller and thus the money supply increases as much as it did in the past. Remember, if the money supply does not increase fast enough, there may not be enough money for the economy to continue to grow, and the economy could slide into a recession or worse—an economic depression.

This then drives home the idea of why confidence in the banking system is so important. If people begin to question the soundness of the banking system, they can actually contribute to an economic downturn, which can, in turn, make banks less stable.

We have seen that changes in the currency ratio can have a dramatic effect on the growth rate of the money supply. An increase in the currency ratio means people are holding relatively more cash, and as a result the money supply multiplier is smaller. A smaller money supply multiplier implies monetary policy will be less effective and the money supply may not grow fast enough to avoid economic slowdowns.

While k, the currency ratio, is an important variable, it is not the only variable that affects the money multiplier. Next we consider the other two variables in the money multiplier: the excess reserves ratio and the required reserves ratio.

10-3b Change in the Excess Reserves Ratio

Remember, the excess reserves ratio, or r_e, is the amount of excess reserves in the banking system relative to the amount of deposits. Because the r_e variable appears only in the denominator of the money multiplier equation, an increase in r_e results in a smaller money multiplier, whereas a decrease in r_e result in a larger money multiplier.

The logic behind this inverse relationship between r_e and the money multiplier is that if banks are holding relatively *more* excess reserves, they are lending relatively less than before. Less bank lending means less new money is being created by banks and thus a smaller money multiplier.

Perhaps it is more important to think about *why* this might be happening. Why are banks holding on to more excess reserves? There could be many reasons, but let's look at one: credit crunch.

During a credit crunch, banks and other lenders greatly reduce the amount of credit they make available to borrowers. Why credit crunches come about is still an issue debated among economists.[7] Leading up to the recent global financial crisis, some economists even doubted that credit crunches could have a significant effect on the overall economy. The crisis that started in 2007–08 left little doubt that the curtailment of credit, especially when banks hold on to large amounts of excess reserves, *can* have a large negative impact on the entire economy. Thus increases in the r_e ratio may be of concern because they could be an indication of the onset of a credit crunch.

Another important variable in the money multiplier formula to keep an eye on is the required reserves ratio.

10-3c Change in the Required Reserves Ratio

Remember, the required reserves ratio, or r_r, is the amount of required reserves banks must hold relative to the amount of deposits. Because the r_r variable, just like r_e, appears only in the denominator of the money multiplier equation, an increase in r_r results in a smaller money multiplier, whereas a decrease in r_r results in a larger money multiplier.

The logic behind this inverse relationship between r_r and the money multiplier is similar to that for r_e: If banks are holding relatively *more* reserves, they are lending out relatively less than before. Less bank lending means less new money is being created by banks and thus a smaller money multiplier.

But changes in the required reserve ratio, which in the United States is set by the Federal Reserve, does not change often. Thus in many developed countries the r_r variable does not change significantly.

---

7 See Bernanke, Ben S., Cara S. Lown, and Benjamin M. Friedman, "The Credit Crunch." *Brookings Papers on Economic Activity*, no. 2 (1991): 205–47.

In some emerging markets, however, policymakers may increase the required reserve ratio banks must meet in an attempt to "increase confidence" in the banking system and thus the economy. While this may make people believe banks are "safer," if this increase in r_r results in a slower growth rate of the money supply, and thus pushes the economy into a recession, the outcome is weaker banks, not "safer" banks. Thus when and why the r_r ratio changes bears watching.

So much for the formal modeling of the money supply process. Next let's take a look at what has actually happened to the money supply process and some of the components of the money multiplier.

10-3d Money Supply Process and Quantitative Easing

The Federal Reserve pursued quantitative easing as part of their policy to end the Great Recession. Quantitative easing began in November 2008. As we can see from Figure 10-1, quantitative easing—and the emergency lending by the Fed before quantitative easing—led to a huge increase in the monetary base.

Under quantitative easing the Fed was buying a variety of financial assets from commercial banks. Thus banks saw their level of reserves increase, but they did not significantly increase their level of lending. As a result, the level of the banks' excess reserves increased dramatically (Figure 10-2).

Because the banks were not lending the increase in reserves—instead they were holding them as excess reserves—the money supply did not grow rapidly (Figure 10-3). Thus there was very little inflation after 2008, despite the monetary base increasing rapidly (Figure 10-4). But, in terms of real GDP growth, the economy did not significantly rebound either (Figure 10-5).

Figure 10-1 **St. Louis Adjusted Monetary Base**

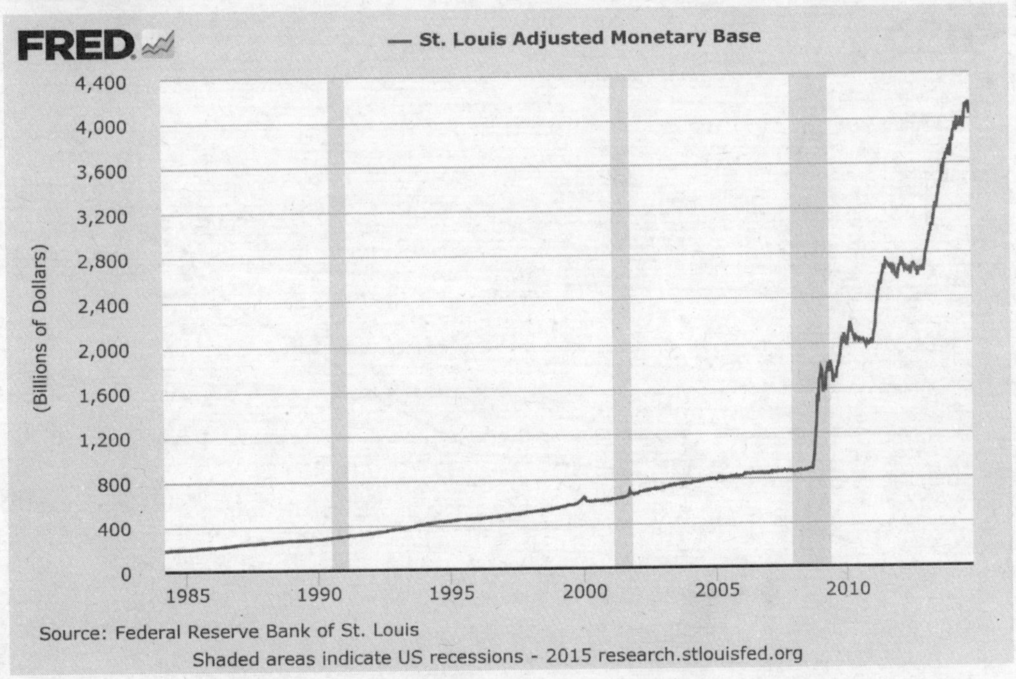

Source: Copyright 2014 by the Federal Reserve Bank of St. Louis.

Figure 10-2 Excess Reserves of Depository Institutions

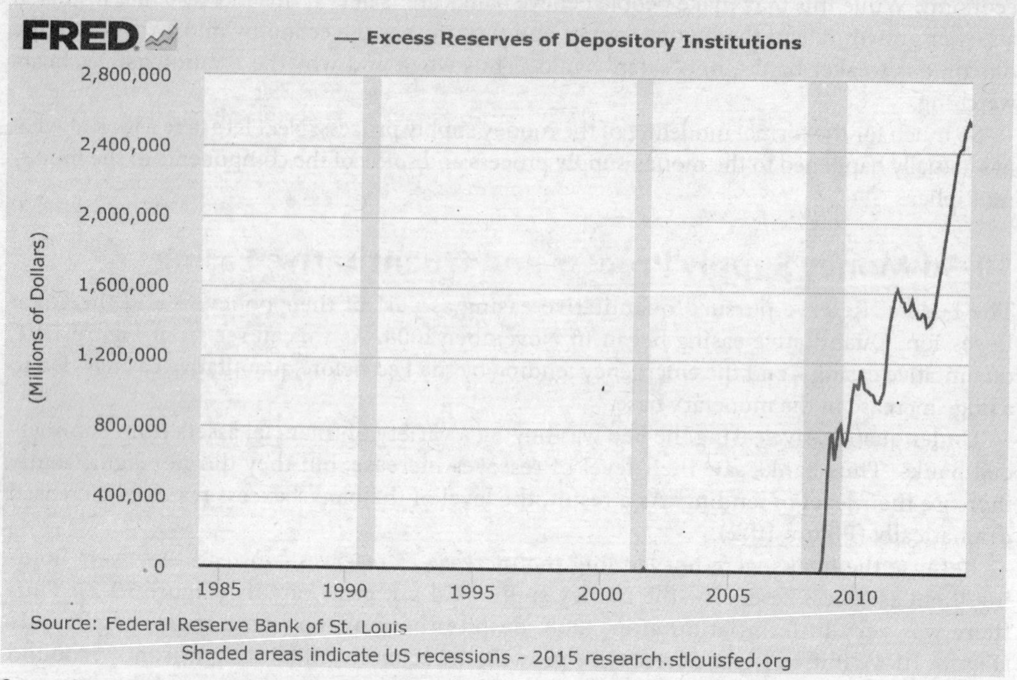

Source: Copyright 2014 by the Federal Reserve Bank of St. Louis.

Figure 10-3 M2 Money Stock

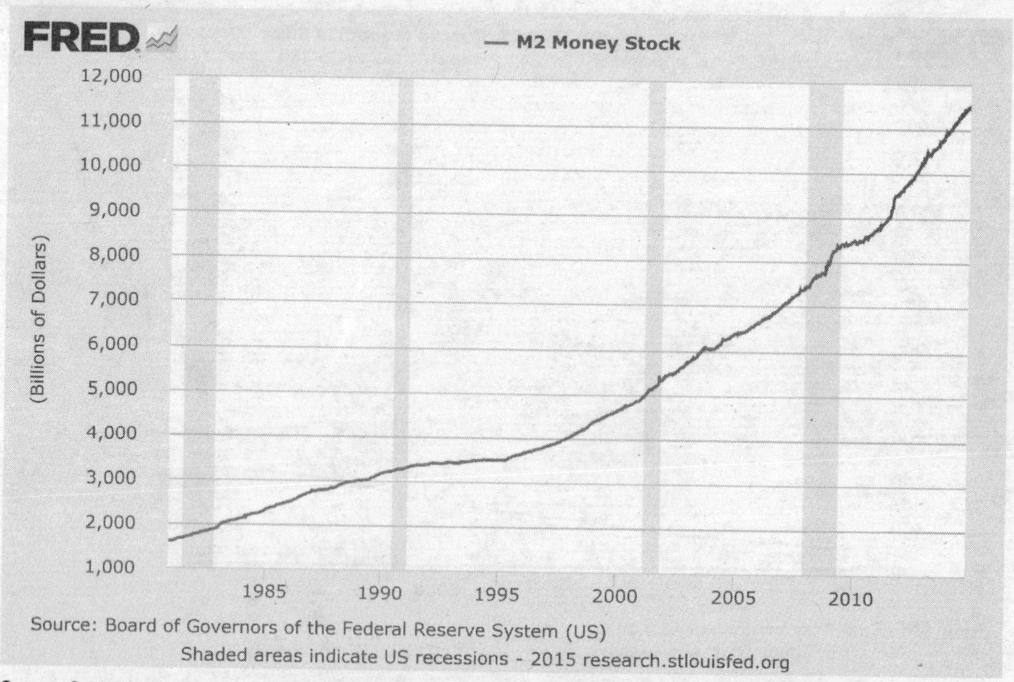

Source: Copyright 2014 by the Federal Reserve Bank of St. Louis.

Figure 10-4 **Gross Domestic Product: Implicit Price Deflator**

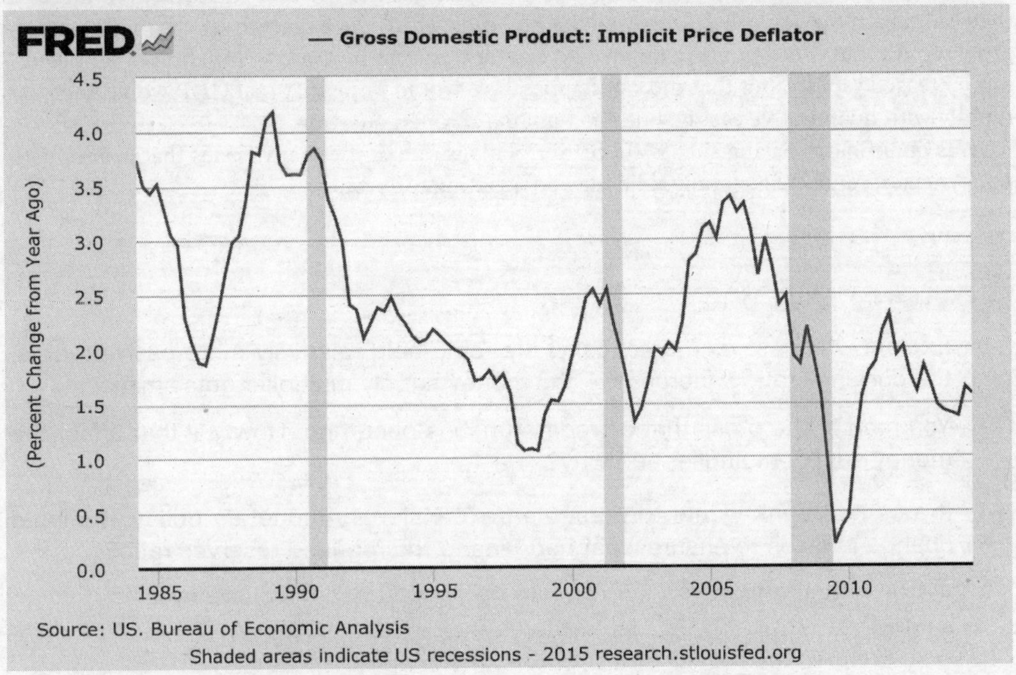

Source: Copyright 2014 by the Federal Reserve Bank of St. Louis.

Figure 10-5 **Real Gross Domestic Product, Three Decimal**

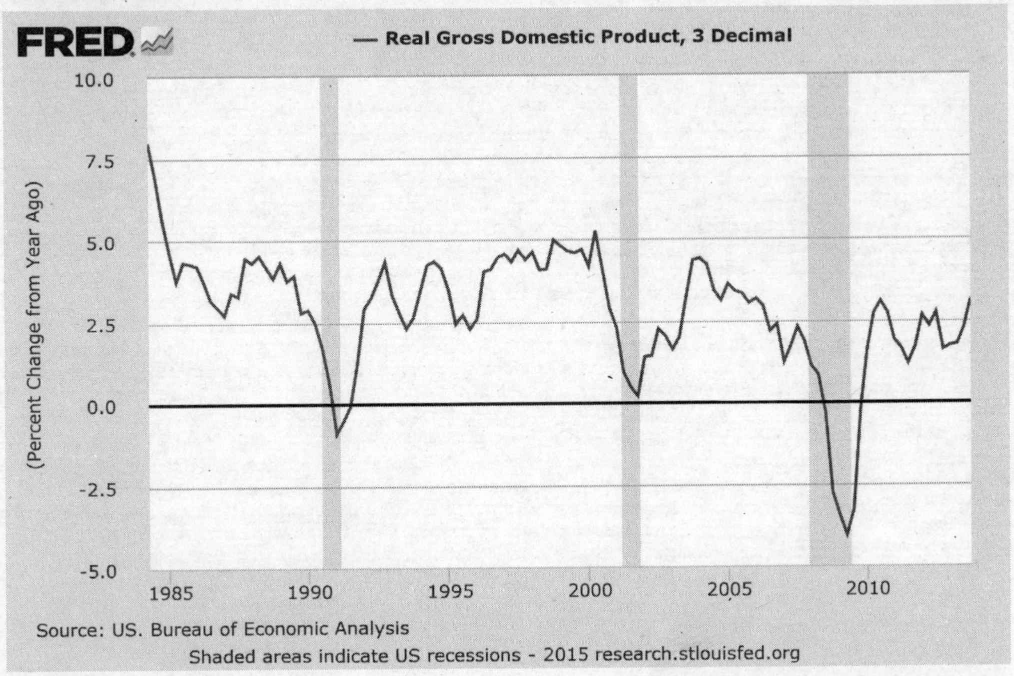

Source: Copyright 2014 by the Federal Reserve Bank of St. Louis.

So we see that with quantitative easing the monetary base did increase and thus an important goal of the policy was achieved. However, we also see that bank excess reserves also dramatically increased at the same time, suggesting banks did not use the increase in reserves to increase their lending. If the banks had increased their lending, we would expect to see the money supply grow rapidly, but it did not. We might also expect to see an increase in inflation if bank lending increased rapidly, but that did not happen. We would hope that real GDP would increase rapidly with quantitative easing, but this remains an open question.

Was quantitative easing successful or not? This is one of the many issues that economists, policymakers, and the general public may be debating for years.

SECTION REVIEW

Q1) Explain why (just mathematically) if people hold relatively more cash—that is, the currency ratio *k* increases—the money supply multiplier gets smaller.

Q2) You read in the press that a credit crunch is occurring. How will that affect the money supply multiplier and why?

Q3) If a central bank wants to pursue an expansionary monetary policy, it should change policies to ensure what happens to the required reserves ratio?

a. The required reserves ratio should be set equal to the currency ratio.

b. The required reserves ratio should be made greater than 1.

c. The required reserves ratio should be reduced.

d. None of the above.

Conclusion

10-4

The monetary base plays a very important role in the money supply process. The monetary base, basically currency and bank reserves, is what central banks like the Federal Reserve attempt to change when they conduct monetary policy. But remember, central banks are not the only ones who influence the monetary base; so too do the general public, the Treasury, and the banking system. Once the monetary base changes, a multiplier or "snowballing" usually kicks in—what we call the money supply multiplier, or the money multiplier for short.

After mathematically deriving the money multiplier we looked at changes in the variables that make it up and how changes in those variables affect people's lives. Remember, that is why the money supply process matters: It's not just a calculation; it is something that affects people in their daily lives even though they may never understand it.

The money supply process is an important and powerful one. But how the money supply process is used, especially by central banks, remains controversial. Now we need to look at how central banks use the money supply process in the conduct of monetary policy and the debates that rage over monetary policy. That is where we are headed next.

IN THE NEWS. . .

Japan's Monetary Base at Record High in June: BOJ

Kyodo News International

July 2, 2014

Japan's monetary base increased to a record 233.25 trillion yen in June, up 42.6 percent from a year earlier, the Bank of Japan said Wednesday, as the central bank attempts to boost the economy by providing huge amounts of money.

The average daily balance of liquidity that the BOJ injects, including cash in circulation and the balance of current account deposits held by financial institutions at the BOJ, grew for the 26th straight month, reaching a new record for the 16th month in a row. . . .

In its unprecedented monetary easing, started in April 2013, the BOJ aims to achieve an inflation rate of 2 percent within around two years, pledging to double the monetary base in two years and purchasing massive amounts of Japanese government bonds and other financial assets from banks.

Will the massive increase in the Japanese monetary base be enough for the Bank of Japan to hit its 2% inflation target? Do you think inflation in Japan will be above or below the 2% target? Why?

11

Monetary Policy and Debates

11-1 Monetary Policy and Debates

We lie to young people. We do this not to be mean; we do it because the truth is often too complicated for them to understand. For example, instead of explaining how the earth orbits the sun, we tell them (and sometimes sing to them) about the sun "coming up tomorrow." The sun of course really does *not* come up in the morning, but it is a nice simplification of reality so youngsters don't need to be burdened with learning astrophysics at a young age.

So it is with monetary policy. When you were younger and took your principles of economics course you (probably) were told that expansionary monetary policy is used to help end recessions and contractionary monetary policy is used to control inflation. And that is true—sort of. It certainly is not the whole story. In this chapter we take a large step toward understanding how monetary policy actually works and why it's much more controversial than what was described to you in the principles course.

So far we have looked at central banks, the tools central banks use in their conduct of monetary policy, and the money supply process. Now we want to look at how those central banks have used their tools to affect the money supply process in the conduct of monetary policy. We will see that this turns out to be rather controversial. Especially since the Great Recession, many people both inside and outside the economics profession are questioning just what exactly central banks are doing and why.

Let's start by looking at the ultimate goals and targets of monetary policy: What are central banks trying to achieve? How do they go about it? We will see that even this is controversial. Next we review how monetary policy has changed over time, paying particular attention to the role monetary policy has played in response to the Great Recession. Along the way, keep an eye on the future: How do you think monetary policy will operate in the future?

11-1a Goals of Monetary Policy

One of the things about monetary policy to keep in mind is that, traditionally, central banks were never set up to conduct monetary policy. Initially central banks, like the Bank of England, were set up to finance government spending. Central banks only discovered monetary policy—and partly by accident. As time went on the conduct of monetary policy became the main responsibility of central banks.

This then raises the question: What are central banks trying to achieve with their monetary policy and how do they go about it? Stated more succinctly, What are the goals and targets of monetary policy? The answers to these questions depend, in part, on who you ask.

Price Level Stability

Almost everyone who studies the issue seriously will agree price level stability is one of the most important goals of monetary policy. Stated more generally, the goal is to keep inflation and deflation from becoming a problem. As you no doubt learned in your economics principles course, unexpected inflation has negative effects on the economy and society because it distorts the price-signaling mechanism, it increases uncertainty, and it can lead to the misallocation of resources as people spend far too much time trying to protect their assets from inflation. Thus preventing unexpected increases in the rate of inflation can play an important role in stabilizing the economy.

Deflation can be even more destructive than inflation. Deflation is evil in part because it increases the real burden of debt. To understand why, think about a debt of $100 and an hourly wage rate of $10 an hour. That means the burden of the debt is 10 hours of work. Now assume there is deflation so that prices and wages are falling, but the level of outstanding debt remains the same. With deflation, let's assume the wage rate is reduced to $5 an hour. That means that an indebted person now must work 20 hours to repay the debt. Thus the real burden of debt has increased.

Even worse, the threat of deflation, with its increased real burden of debt, can lead to businesses and households cutting back on their borrowing and spending, thereby pushing the economy into a recession or even a depression. Thus keeping the economy from sliding into a deflationary death spiral becomes very important.

Controversies of Price Level Stability

While there is general agreement on the need for price level stability, there is a fair amount of controversy over how much and even what it means.

First, how much "price level stability" is optimal? In other words what is the "optimal" rate of inflation? Some argue that central banks, in their drive to "keep inflation low," pursue excessively contractionary monetary policy, which stifles economic growth and job creation. So, while wealthy holders of financial assets are protected under "price level stability," middle-class and working people "pay the price" in terms of higher unemployment rates.

Second, some question what "price level stability" even means. Which price level? Consumer prices? What about the difference between the headline consumer price index (CPI), which is volatile, and the core CPI, which is more stable, when excluding food and energy prices, even though it may not reflect the actual cost of living? Or should one use the personal consumption expenditure index as the measurement of inflation? Or, should the GDP deflator be used? Perhaps some combination of all of these could be used? What if inflation is mismeasured by all of them because of things like nonmarket transactions?

Third, if we can agree on the correct way to measure inflation, or the price level, and agree on the "correct" level, or inflation rate, there still is the issue of which policy the central bank should follow: **inflation targeting** or **price level targeting**. With price level targeting, the central bank uses monetary policy in an effort to achieve a particular price index over time. By contrast, with an inflation target, the central bank tries to achieve a rate of inflation, or change in the price level, over time.

Inflation targeting: A monetary policy where the central bank uses its tools to achieve a stated rate of inflation over time.

Price level targeting: A monetary policy where the central bank uses its tools to achieve a stated price index over time.

The difference can be important.[1] For example, with price level targeting, an unexpectedly high inflation rate today would be followed by a below average rate of inflation in the future. But with inflation targeting the aim is for average inflation (target) in future years, regardless of the level of prices today. So, because the central bank is obligated to offset inflationary shocks in this way, policy targeting has been labeled "history dependent" by Michael Woodford[2] of Columbia University.

As shown in Figure 11-1, assume the central bank announces an inflation target of 2%. When there is a "price shock" and the inflation rate increases to 3%, firms and households can expect future inflation to be 2% in periods 4 and 5 under inflation targeting. If it is price level targeting, however, firms and households can expect the inflation rate to be only 1% in period 5.

While many economists argue that price level targeting has significant advantages over inflation targeting, especially in fighting deflation, it is almost never used in practice. The Bank of Canada recently considered adopting a price level targeting approach to replace its explicit inflation target, but in 2011 they decided against making the switch.

1 For a more complete discussion see Michael Hatcher and Patrick Minord's explanation at http://www.voxeu.org/article/inflation-targeting-vs-price-level-targeting.

2 Woodford, Michael, *Interest and Prices: Foundations of a Theory of Monetary Policy*. Princeton, NJ: Princeton University Press, 2003.

Figure 11-1 **Inflation Targeting v. Price Level Targeting**

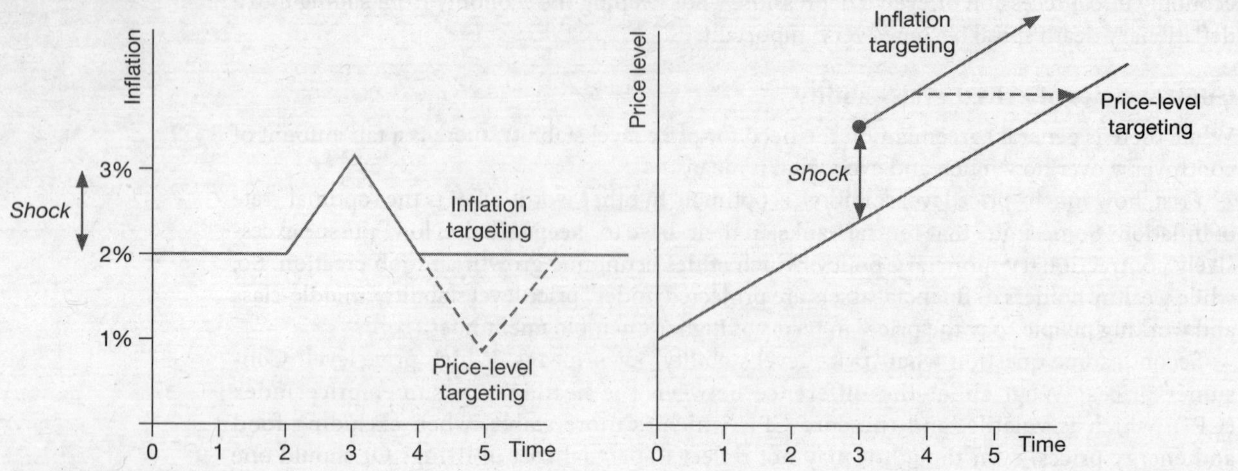

Source: Hatcher and Minord

While the debate over price level stability rages on, it is *not* the only goal of monetary policy, especially in the United States. Let's look at some of the other goals the Fed is trying to achieve with its conduct of monetary policy.

SECTION REVIEW

Q1) Explain why deflation leads to an increase in the real burden of debt.

Q2) Explain why some argue that a central bank's goal of price level stability can hurt the middle class and working people while benefiting more wealthy individuals.

Q3) Under a price level-targeting monetary policy, a sharp drop in the inflation rate today means what for the future?

a. A return to the previous rate of inflation

b. An increase in the inflation rate to the same degree as the current decrease

c. A contractionary open market operation

d. All of the above

More Goals of Monetary Policy

11-2

While price stability is one of the major goals of monetary policy, it certainly is not the only one. In fact, it is written in the laws of the United States that the government, and presumably the Federal Reserve as well, should use its economic policies to pursue full employment, economic growth, balance of trade, and balance of the government budget in addition to price stability.[3] Of these, the Fed has been most responsible for price stability and "full" or high levels of employment. But should high employment be a goal of monetary policy? What about other goals?

11-2a High Employment Goal

Not being able to find a job when you want to work is a horrible thing. Unemployment is not only costly to the unemployed worker in terms of mental stress, financial difficulty, and lack of working experience; it also negatively affects the entire economy. Unemployment in the labor market results in what economists call "underutilization of resources." That is, some of our society's resources are not being used as effectively and efficiently as they could be. Thus, with high unemployment, we are squandering some of our scarce or limited resources. Another concern is that history has shown that continuous high levels of unemployment can lead to political instability. For these and other reasons, some argue one of the goals of monetary policy should be high employment.

Controversies over a High Employment Goal

While most agree that an excessively high rate of unemployment is not a good thing, there is a fair amount of debate as to whether the Federal Reserve should have "high employment" as one of its goals for monetary policy. First, some argue that by focusing on high employment, the Fed might take its "eye off inflation." There is historical evidence to back up this claim. During the 1970s, many believe the Fed, in a desire to keep employment high, deliberately pursued an excessively expansionary monetary policy, thus triggering increases in the growth rate of the money supply and thereby pushing up the rate of inflation. Opponents to the high employment goal argue that the Fed should *not* have this "dual mandate" of fighting inflation and high unemployment; instead it should focus on only price stability.

When he was Fed Chair, Paul Volcker, in congressional testimony in 1981, went further by stating the only way to get full employment was to stabilize prices. He said:

> "I bring in price stability because we will not be successful, in my opinion, in pursuing a full employment policy unless we take care of the inflation side of the equation while we are doing it. I think that philosophy is actually embodied in the Humphrey-Hawkins Act itself."[4]

Not all economists agree however. When he was Fed Vice Chair in 1995, Alan Blinder of Princeton stated: "We have a dual objective in the Federal Reserve Act now. I think it works very well. I think the case that it is broken and needs fixing is very thin."[5]

A second argument put forward against the Fed having a "dual objective" or "dual mandate" of a stable price level *and* high employment is that there is relatively little the Fed can do about the level of employment in the first place. Think about all of the factors that go into determining the level of employment in an economy: the skill levels of the workforce, the derived demand of the output, the level of uncertainty of business, among others. Arguably, none of these things

3 This was the Full Employment and Balance Growth Act, more commonly known as the Humphrey-Hawkins Full Employment Act of 1978.

4 Federal Reserve's First Monetary Policy Report for 1981, Hearings Before the U.S. Senate Committee on Banking, Housing, and Urban Affairs, February 25 and March 4, 1981, 97th Cong. 28 (1981) (Paul Volcker, Chairman of the Federal Reserve).

5 Board of Governors of the Federal Reserve System. "Meeting of the Federal Open Market Committee." January 31-February 1, 1995.

are under the control of the Fed in its conduct of monetary policy. Why then, the argument goes, make the Fed "responsible" for something like the level of employment, when they can't even indirectly control it?

A third objective some have with the high employment goal for monetary policy is measurement. What does one mean, exactly, by "high employment"? We could agree to use the civilian unemployment rate as a quantitative measure and say we want a "low" unemployment rate. Okay, but how "low"?

Keep in mind there are several types of unemployment. There is **frictional or short-term unemployment**, where the unemployed person has decided on which job to take or has just started their job search. Can monetary policy really do anything to lower the rate of the frictionally unemployed?

Frictional or short-term unemployment: Unemployment that lasts only a few weeks or a few months as unemployed workers are searching for jobs.

Then there is **structural unemployment**. Remember, this results as some industry or sectors of the economy are contracting while others are expanding, and the people in the contracting industry may have difficulty finding jobs in the expanding industries. For example, how easy is it for an unemployed steel worker in Gary, Indiana, to fill an open position in a high-tech firm in Austin, Texas? More important, what can monetary policy do to help reduce this type of unemployment?

Structural unemployment: Unemployment that occurs as some industries or sectors of the economy are contracting while others are expanding. People in the contracting industries may have difficulty finding jobs in the expanding industries.

Finally, there is **cyclical unemployment**. This is unemployment brought about by a downturn in the business cycle. One could argue that the Fed could do something about this type of unemployment by using the tools of monetary policy to keep the economy expanding. Okay, but to what degree? That is, just how low should the civilian unemployment rate go? The unemployment rate clearly cannot be pushed to zero, but what is the "full employment" rate, or the "natural rate of unemployment"? Is it 4%? 6%? Somewhere else? If one cannot answer this question, how can and why should it be a goal of the Fed in the conduct of monetary policy?

Cyclical unemployment: Unemployment that occurs as a result of a downturn in the business cycle.

Therefore, while it is generally agreed that high rates of inflation and high rates of unemployment are the two major evils that face the macroeconomy, there is a fair amount of debate and controversy over what role the Fed should play in fighting these two macroeconomic evils. Some, on the other hand, argue the goals of monetary policy should have a more microeconomic focus. Next we look at some of the more microeconomic goals of monetary policy.

11-2b Financial Market Stability: Interest Rates and Exchange Rates

Remember, as we discussed earlier, the Fed was established in response to the Panic of 1907. From its inception the Fed has been responsible for ensuring that financial markets are stable. However, it hasn't always been successful at achieving this goal, and when it has failed the results have been a disaster.

That is why some contend the Fed should have making sure financial markets are stable as one of its primary goals—if not its only goal—of monetary policy. The Fed could do this, it is argued, by making sure that interest rates do not fluctuate wildly, that exchange rate volatility is reduced, and that financial crises do not occur.

Stable interest rates sure would make business investment decisions easier because the cost of capital for firms would fluctuate less. Stable interest rates would also increase the amount of durable goods households could purchase, because households would be able to determine how much interest they would have pay to finance the purchase of durable goods. By removing the uncertainty of rapidly changing costs of capital, some believe the level of total spending would increase.

Similarly, stable exchange rates would also make it easier to price imports and exports. With this level of uncertainty removed, the level of global trade would increase and all economies engaged in trade would experience more rapid economic growth.

Thus, by using its monetary policy tools to stabilize these individual financial markets, the Fed can help to ensure that financial crises, both global and domestic, do not occur. Some argue that by focusing too much on the macroeconomic "dual objectives" or "dual mandate" the Fed has not paid enough attention to financial market imbalances.

Controversies over Financial Market Stability Goal

While no one would seriously argue that financial market instability is a good thing, those who question this as a goal of monetary policy believe that financial market stability is a goal of the Fed *in addition* to monetary policy, not as part of monetary policy. The argument is that the Fed should be a lender of last resort to ensure there are sufficient levels of liquidity in the financial system to head off either a domestic or global financial crisis. But acting as a lender of last resort is not really part of monetary policy; rather, it falls under the "other responsibilities" of the Fed.

In addition, opponents of the financial market stability goal argue that for the Fed, or any central bank, to maintain stable interest rates in the face of an unstable demand for money would require an incredibly nimble manipulation of the money supply—something modern central banks are not capable of doing.

Finally, opponents of the financial market stability goal contend that while stable exchange rates might encourage short-term trade flows, one has to be careful about maintaining fixed exchange rates between nations that are very different. As we saw in Chapter 5, history has shown that keeping interest rates fixed for too long can lead to financial crises and even economic collapses.

So, there exist debates and controversies over the goals of monetary policy. Should the Fed be like other central banks and focus on only controlling inflation? The Fed currently operates under the "dual mandate" of both stable prices and high employment. But what should be the role of monetary policy in bringing about financial market stability? While the debates over the goals of monetary policy are sure to continue, these are not the only aspects of monetary policy that are debated. Next we turn our attention to sources of controversy other than the debate over the goal(s) of monetary policy.

SECTION REVIEW

Q1) Some argue the Federal Reserve should not have "high employment" as one of the goals of monetary policy because there are so many causes of unemployment that are beyond the Fed's control. What are these various causes of unemployment?

Q2) Opponents of the "financial market stability goal" of monetary policy believe it may be difficult for the Federal Reserve, or any central bank, to achieve this goal. Explain their argument.

Q3) The "dual goals" of current monetary policy in the United States are:

a. long-run economic growth and balanced international trade.
b. high employment and price level stability.
c. low interest rates and constant money supply growth.
d. stable financial markets and low inflation.

11-3 More Debates over Monetary Policy

While the debates over the goals of monetary policy rage, there are also debates over broader issues of monetary policy. Two of these broader issues are central bank independence and the use of targets and instruments.

11-3a Central Bank Independence

When we examined the structure of central banks we noted that most central banks today are not directly controlled by their governments. That is, central banks are generally seen as being independent of the political process: They answer only indirectly to elected officials. The question then becomes, Is this a good idea? Should central banks be independent of elected officials?

Limit Independence

On both the political right, what in the United States we call conservatives, and the political left, referred to as liberals in the United States, there are calls to limit the independence of central banks.

On the right in the United States we hear demands to "audit the Fed!," especially from libertarians, because they see the Federal Reserve as a secret organization that represents an extension of government intervention into markets and thus people's lives. When proposing legislation to "audit" the Fed and thus reduce the central bank's independence, Senator Rand Paul of Kentucky stated in 2013:

> "The Fed's operations under a cloak of secrecy have gone on too long and the American people have a right to know what the Federal Reserve is doing with our nation's money supply . . . audit the Fed has significant bipartisan support in Congress and across the country and the time to act on this is now."

In 2014 Senator Paul threatened to hold up nominees to the Federal Reserve Board of Governors unless the US Senate voted to audit the Fed. While the Federal Reserve is already audited by independent auditing firms, the reported purpose of auditing the Fed is to give Congress more say over the monetary policy decisions that the Fed makes. However, not all conservatives agree with Paul's call to audit the Fed and thus limit its independence.[6]

Another conservative complaint about the Fed, and thus the need to limit the Fed's independence, is that the Fed has gone soft on fighting inflation, accusing it of "debasing the currency." During the 2012 presidential campaign, much was made about the Republican vice presidential nominee Paul Ryan and his dislike of the Fed's dual mandate. In congressional hearings in 2011 Ryan told then Fed Chair Ben Bernanke, "There is nothing more insidious that a country can do to its citizens than debase its currency."[7]

Thus many conservatives want Congress to be more involved in setting monetary policy. This increased congressional control over monetary policy presumably will be used to increase the level of transparency of monetary policy and ensure a more contractionary monetary policy is put in place to control inflation.

It is not only those on the right, or conservatives, however, who want to limit the Fed's independence. Vermont's Independent US senator, Bernard "Bernie" Sanders, who describes himself as a democratic socialist, has long been a vocal critic of the Fed. In 2010 Sanders attached an amendment to the Dodd-Frank financial market reform bill that directed the Government Accountability Office to conduct a study—what Sanders called an "audit" of the Federal Reserve. When the report was released a year later, Sanders is reported as saying, "The Federal Reserve

---

6 See the conservative magazine *National Review* for a sample: http://www.nationalreview.com/article/312592/beware-audit-fed-noah-glyn.

7 See Sewell Chan, "In Congress, Bernanke Faces Questions About Inflation." *The New York Times*, February 9, 2011; http://www.nytimes.com/2011/02/10/business/economy/10fed.html?_r=3&.

must be reformed to serve the needs of working families, not just CEOs on Wall Street."[8] This reform presumably would include greater congressional oversight of the Fed and the ability of Congress to alter monetary policy.

Keeping Central Banks Independent

The strongest argument for keeping central banks independent is the **time-inconsistency problem** in monetary policy.

Time-inconsistency problem: The situation in which a policymaker may prefer one policy in advance, but when it comes time to implement the policy the policymaker prefers a completely different policy.

Basically, the problem is that politically controlled central banks want to pursue policies that are "good" in the short run but "bad" in the long run. The issue arises because central banks want to pursue short-term expansionary policies to encourage households and firms to borrow and spend. This increased level of spending will lead to an increase in output and an economic expansion in the short run. An expanding economy, especially right before an election, is something elected officials would, naturally, support wholeheartedly because it would greatly increase their chances of being reelected.

But the good times may not last. An excessively expansionary monetary policy could very well lead to unexpected increases in inflation. But when households and firms realize that inflation has increased, they update their inflationary expectations: Households increase wage demands, firms increase selling prices and perhaps cut back on output, potentially resulting in more inflation and lower levels of output.

In this case it would be better for the central bank not to try to fool people by pursuing an expansionary monetary policy in the first place. But remember those elected officials: If they have control over the central bank, they may push it to pursue an excessively expansionary monetary policy.

Where does that leave us? Would more political control over central banks make these powerful entities more answerable to the people and push the central bankers to do a better job controlling inflation? Or, would politically controlled central banks pursue excessively expansionary monetary policies in an attempt to keep elected officials happy? What does the empirical evidence tell us?

Academic Literature on Central Bank Independence

Michael Parkin of the University of Western Ontario points out that over the past three decades or so there has developed an extensive academic literature on the topic of central bank independence and inflation.[9] One of the more recent studies was published in 2010 by Dutch economists Klomp and de Haan,[10] who conclude that there is a negative correlation between central bank independence and inflation; that is, independent central banks do a better job of controlling inflation. But the debate is not over. For example, in 2013 Tom Cargill[11] of the University of Nevada, Reno, argued that the negative correlations may not hold up when measurement issues are corrected.

Just as academic economists do not agree completely on the relationship between central bank independence and inflation, the same occurs when discussion turns to the targets central banks should use in their conduct of monetary policy.

---

8 Tracey Greenstein, "The Fed's $16 Trillion Bailouts Under-Reported." Forbes, September 20, 2011; http://www.forbes.com/sites/traceygreenstein/2011/09/20/the-feds-16-trillion-bailouts-under-reported/.

9 For a summary see Michael Parkin, "Central Bank Laws and Monetary Policy Outcomes: A Three Decade Perspective." Presented in the session "Central Bank Independence: Reality or Myth?" organized by Thomas Cargill (University of Nevada-Reno) at the meetings of the American Economic Association, San Diego, January 4, 2013, University of Western Ontario Economic Policy Research Institute Working Paper Series, 2013-1.

10 Jeroen G. Klomp and Jakob de Haan, "Inflation and Central Bank Independence: A Meta Regression Analysis." *Journal of Economic Surveys* 24 (2012): 593–621.

11 Thomas F. Cargill. "A Critical Assessment of Measures of Central Bank Independence" *Economic Inquiry* 51, no. 1 (January 2013): 260–72.

11-3b Instruments and Targets

We discussed a number of monetary policy tools used by central banks: open market operations, discount window lending, reserve requirements, emergency lending tools, quantitative easing, and so on. We also examined the wide range of goals central banks, especially the Federal Reserve, can have. But there is also a question of how central banks, such as the Fed, should use its tools to achieve its goals.

Central banks have a major problem in the conduct of monetary policy because of lags. There are **information lags**, that is, the Fed knows where the economy is today only with a time lag. The Fed won't know for several months where, exactly, we are in terms of real GDP, inflation rate, unemployment rate, and so on. In addition, there are **impact or effectiveness lags**. That is, there is a delay between when the Fed changes policy and when that policy affects employment, output, and prices. This impact or effectiveness lag can occur anywhere from a few months to up to a year after a change in policy.

Information lag: When policymakers do not have what they need to undertake the optimal policy because of a lack of readily available information.
Impact or effectiveness lag: When a policy implemented in the present does not affect the overall economy until well into the future. As a result, when the policy's impact is achieved it may be the wrong policy for that time.

Because of these lags there is no direct tie between the Fed's tools of monetary policy and it goals. Instead, the Fed has to think about how can it use its tools to affect policy instruments—those things the Fed can directly affect—and thus hit some targets with the intent of achieving its goals.

The Good Old Days: Monetary Aggregate Targeting

Before the 1980s there was a fairly good link between M1 and M2 growth and the rate of inflation. Many economists thought, Great! The Fed or any central bank should use its tools to adjust instruments such as the level of bank reserves and target M1 and M2. These monetary targets would be easy for people to see—they would be printed in newspapers—so the general public and financial markets could keep tabs on how the central bank was doing in its conduct of monetary policy. It was well understood that if the money supply increased too quickly there would be inflation, and if the money supply did not grow fast enough the economy could slide into a recession.

So, monetary aggregate targeting was seen as the key to monetary policy: Central banks around the world would use their tools and adjust bank reserve instruments to target the growth rate of the money supply. Everything fit together nicely.

Then it all fell apart.

As we discussed earlier, financial market innovation during the 1980s resulted in rapid changes in M1 and M2, thus essentially destroying the relationship between the monetary aggregates and the rate of inflation. Even as economists came up with measurements of the money supply, none of them had a consistent, predictable relationship with the inflation rate.

Thinking More About Targets in Monetary Policy

So, if one can't really target monetary aggregates in the conduct of monetary policy, what should central banks use as target? Some have suggested having an **explicit inflation target**. That is, the central bank would state that the main, or even sole, purpose in using its tools and instruments is to hit an inflation target. The central bank would target an inflation rate of X%, and if they missed that target, they would have some explaining to do. This explicit inflation target was thought to give people confidence that inflation would be brought under control, and thus inflationary expectations would decrease. Therefore one of the advantages of explicit inflation targeting is that it reduces inflationary expectations.

Explicit inflation target: A monetary policy where the central bank states an explicit desired inflation rate and the central bank pledges to use monetary policy to achieve that inflation rate.

But, as we discussed, there are some significant problems with inflation targeting. Remember those pesky lags. Inflation targeting states that the central bank is responsible for inflation today, but with the recognition and effectiveness lags that would mean the central bank would have to have almost perfect foresight in the *past* to know what the inflation would be today in order to take corrective action in the past to stop it.

The central bank may be trying to achieve goals other than just controlling inflation, but with an explicit inflation goal the central bank is dedicating itself first and foremost to fighting inflation. Thus, many economists argue, explicit inflation targeting is too rigid: It ties the hands of the central bank and requires of it almost perfect foresight.

So, some economists suggest having an explicit inflation target is going too far. Instead, central banks should have a set of **implicit targets**. That is, central banks will make "preemptive strikes" to stop inflation before it begins. Thus central banks will not wait for inflation to show up in the data (remember those information lags); instead they will implement contractionary monetary policy before inflation begins.

Implicit target: A policy where the central bank does not state an explicit target or goal, but rather has targets that are not well defined.

The implicit targeting idea was very popular during Alan Greenspan's time as Fed Chair, from 1987 to 2006. Greenspan was held in high esteem, especially by those in financial markets, during his time in office. Greenspan would often speak in convoluted language, in part to disguise just what exactly the Fed was targeting. Greenspan's Fed made preemptive strikes to stop inflation before it began. The result, many argue, was the Great Moderation—a time of low inflation and only modest recessions. Implicit targeting was trumpeted as the way to conduct monetary policy—in the United States, at least.

And then it all came crashing down.

With the onset of the Great Recession there were many questions of "what was the Fed thinking?" and "Why didn't the Fed do something to prevent this?" Thus, since the onset of the global financial crisis there has been a call for more transparency in the Fed and its conduct of monetary policy. The days of implicit targeting may be gone forever.

Monetary Policy Instruments

That then leaves us with the questions of, What should the Fed target? What instrument should the Fed use? Should the Fed use bank reserves or interest rates as the instrument to hit its target to achieve its goals? As we have seen, the Fed can increase bank reserves, but banks will not necessarily lend those reserves. Similarly, the Fed might lower interest rates, but that is no guarantee that firms and households will borrow more and spend to help end an economic slowdown.

Thus monetary policy is full of controversies and debates. Are there ways in which to judge whether central banks are conducting monetary policy "correctly"? We turn our attention next to one potential way to answer that question: the Taylor Rule.

SECTION REVIEW

Q1) Explain how the time inconsistency problem in monetary policy is used by many to argue in favor of central bank independence.

Q2) Explain why many economists argue the explicit inflation target for monetary policy is far too rigid to be effective.

Q3) Which of the following are lags in monetary policy?

a. Information lag and impact or effectiveness lag
b. Velocity lag and turnover lag
c. Interest rate lag and unemployment lag
d. Output lag and investment expenditure lag

11-4 Taylor Rule

In 1993 Stanford University economist John Taylor set out to explain how monetary policy in the United States had operated in the previous several years.[12] In doing so he created "the Taylor Rule," which today is often used as a measure for how monetary policy should be conducted, not just how it was in the past.

11-4a Taylor Rule and Inflation

The **Taylor Rule**—not to be confused with Taylor Swift—seeks to explain what the Fed's target for the federal funds rate should be as it relates to the real, or inflation-adjusted, federal funds (FF) rate; the inflation rate; the inflation gap (the difference between the actual inflation rate and the Fed's target for the inflation rate); and the output gap (the percentage difference between actual GDP and potential GDP). The formula for the Taylor Rule is

$$\textbf{FF Target} = \textbf{Real FF rate} + \textbf{Inflation rate} + \frac{1}{2}(\textbf{Inflation gap}) + \frac{1}{2}(\textbf{Output gap})$$

Taylor assumed that the real federal funds rate, the inflation-adjusted, market determined-interest rate on bank-to-bank loans, was 2%. He further assumed that the target rate for inflation was 2%.

Taylor Rule: A rule for monetary policy that suggests how much nominal interest rates should change in response to inflation, output levels, and financial market conditions.

For the inflation rate the Taylor Rule uses the inflation rate over the past four quarters. By using this average, short-term movements in the inflation rate do not affect the rule, and thus short-term, and perhaps temporary, changes in the inflation rate do not affect monetary policy actions. However, consistent ongoing increases in the price level do affect monetary policy.

The **inflation gap**, the actual inflation rate minus the Fed's target for inflation, implies that when the actual rate of inflation goes above the Fed's inflation target rate of 2%, the Fed should pursue a contractionary monetary policy and raise its target for the federal funds rate.

Inflation gap: The difference between the actual rate of inflation and the inflation target set by the central bank or monetary authority.

For example, suppose the initial inflation rate is 2%, and assume the economy is at the full employment level of output so the output gap is zero. Using Taylor's original assumptions of a real federal funds rate of 2% and an inflation target of 2%, the federal funds target would be 4%.

$$\textbf{FF Target} = \textbf{Real FF rate} + \textbf{Inflation rate} + \frac{1}{2}(\textbf{Inflation gap}) + \frac{1}{2}(\textbf{Output gap})$$

$$\textbf{FF Target} = 2\% + 2\% + \frac{1}{2}(2 - 2) + \frac{1}{2}(0) = 4\%$$

Now let us assume, ceteris paribus, that the inflation rate jumps to 3%. According to the Taylor Rule, the target for the federal funds rate should jump to 5.5% because now

$$\textbf{FF Target} = \textbf{Real FF rate} + \textbf{Inflation rate} + \frac{1}{2}(\textbf{Inflation gap}) + \frac{1}{2}(\textbf{Output gap})$$

$$\textbf{FF Target} = 2\% + 3\% + \frac{1}{2}(3 - 2) + \frac{1}{2}(0) = 5.5\%$$

Notice what happened: The inflation rate went up by 1 percentage point, but the Taylor Rule says that the federal funds rate should go up by *more* than the rate of inflation, that is, it should go up by 1.5 percentage points.

12 See John B. Taylor, "Discretion versus Policy Rules in Practice," *Carnegie-Rochester Conference Series on Public Policy* 39 (1993): 195–214.

To understand why this is important, think about the real, inflation-adjusted interest rate, and the interest rates before and after the change in Fed policy. Remember, efficient firms and households use the real interest rate when making economic decisions, not the nominal, or market, interest rate.

Let's suppose that before the increase in the inflation rate and the Fed tightening (assuming the Fed follows the Taylor Rule), the real interest rate at which firms could borrow money was 5.75%. This would make sense since banks are lending money to each at 4% (that's what the federal funds rate is), but firms have a slightly higher default risk than banks, so firms have to pay a slightly higher interest rate to borrow than do banks.[13] With an inflation rate of 2%, the real interest rate at which firms can borrow is 3.75%. Remember, the real interest rate is the nominal or market interest rate minus the rate of inflation.

Then, all of a sudden, the inflation rate shoots up to 3%. The Fed, following the Taylor Rule, increases the federal funds target to 5.5%. That might mean that the borrowing costs for firms would shoot up to 7.25%. But remember, efficient firms use the real interest rate when making their business investment decisions, not the nominal rate. But that real interest rate also has increased. The real interest rate for firms is now 4.25%, which is the nominal rate of 7.25% minus the inflation rate of 3%, whereas it used to be only 3.75%.

Keep in mind what an increase in the real cost of capital for firms means. Some of the projects firms have undertaken in the past are no longer worthwhile. The higher cost of capital is not just a number—it represents effects on peoples' lives.

Think about Whatburger, the regional fast food restaurant chain headquartered in San Antonio, Texas. When interest rates and cost of capital were low, perhaps Whatburger was considering building several new stores across the south and perhaps expanding into the Midwest. This would result in an increase in the number of jobs required to construct the new restaurants and more jobs in staffing, managing, and marketing the restaurants. But that was when the real cost of capital was 3.75%. Now, with the cost of capital at 4.25%, maybe those restaurants will not be able to generate enough revenue to justify the borrowing costs. Thus those jobs in construction, staffing, managing, and marketing will not be created.

Remember, however, why the Fed is pursing this contractionary monetary policy. In our example the inflation rate is now higher than the Fed's inflation target. If the Fed were not to increase the real interest rate, chances are aggregate spending would not decrease and the inflationary pressures would be more difficult for the Fed to contain.

The Taylor Rule is not only about contractionary monetary policy to control inflation. It also makes some pretty clear suggestions on what to do if the economy slows.

11-4b Taylor Rule and Output Gap

The output gap is the percentage difference in the actual level of output and what the level of output would be if the economy were at full employment or the GDP at its potential.

$$\textbf{Output gap} = \left(\frac{\textbf{GDP}_{Actual} - \textbf{GDP}_{Potential}}{\textbf{GDP}_{Potential}}\right) \times \textbf{100\%}$$

If the actual GDP in the United States is, say, \$17 trillion, but economists calculate (or guess) that the economy would be at full employment (or GDP would be at its potential) at a level of \$17.5 trillion, that would give an output gap of 2.85%

$$\textbf{Output gap} = \left(\frac{\textbf{\$17 trillion} - \textbf{\$17.5 trillion}}{\textbf{\$17.5 trillion}}\right) \times \textbf{100\%} = \textbf{−2.85\%}$$

If we then assume the real federal funds rate is 2% and the inflation rate is at the Fed's target of 2%, according to the Taylor Rule the federal funds target should be 2.57%

---

13 You may recall this is the default risk premium. In this case firms are paying a default risk premium of 1.75%. Remember also that this is highly simplistic; not all firms pay the same default risk premium because not all firms have the same level of default risk on their loans.

$$\textbf{FF Target} = \textbf{Real FF rate} + \textbf{Inflation rate} + \frac{1}{2}(\textbf{Inflation gap}) + \frac{1}{2}(\textbf{Output gap})$$

$$\textbf{FF Target} = 2\% + 2\% + \frac{1}{2}(2-2) + \frac{1}{2}(-2.85\%) = 2.57\%$$

As we can see, if the output gap increases, or the actual level of GDP falls further below the potential level or further way from full employment, the Taylor Rule suggests the Fed should lower its target for the federal funds rate. From this you can also imagine cases where the Taylor Rule would imply that the target for the federal funds rate should be negative!

What if the actual level of output fell to $16 trillion while the GDP potential remained at $17.5 trillion? Let's assume everything else from our example stays the same: With a real federal funds rate of 2% and an inflation rate at the Fed's target of 2%, the output gap would be

$$\textbf{Output gap} = \left(\frac{\textbf{\$16 trillion} - \textbf{\$17.5 trillion}}{\textbf{\$17.5 trillion}}\right) \times 100\% = -8.57\%$$

Then, according to the Taylor Rule, the Fed's target for the fed funds rate would be

$$\textbf{FF Target} = \textbf{Real FF rate} + \textbf{Inflation rate} + \frac{1}{2}(\textbf{Inflation gap}) + \frac{1}{2}(\textbf{Output gap})$$

$$\textbf{FF Target} = 2\% + 2\% + \frac{1}{2}(2-2) + \frac{1}{2}(-8.57\%) = -0.285\%$$

It might be very difficult for the Fed to pay negative interest rates—that would mean *paying* banks to borrow money from the Fed instead of charging them interest. This is sometimes described as the zero lower bound of monetary policy.

However, many argued that because of the global economic downturn, this is exactly the problem the Fed faced in 2008 to 2010. Some believe this situation continued long after the Great Recession officially ended. The reason for the disagreement revolves around the level of GDP potential, or, stated differently, at what level of output the economy will achieve full employment. Is that level $17.5 trillion or $18 trillion or more? The debate rages on.

11-4c Mankiw Rule: An Alternative to the Taylor Rule

There are many points of contention with the Taylor Rule: Which measurement of inflation should be used? How does one determine the GDP level at full employment? What weights should be put on the output and inflation gaps? What should the real federal funds rates be? What is the Fed's inflation target? That is why if you go out and look for an analysis, or even a simple graph of the federal funds rate suggested by the Taylor Rule versus the actual federal funds rate, you get a mind-boggling myriad of responses.

In 2010 Andy Harless[14] suggested a more simple approach. He used research by Harvard economist Greg Mankiw[15] to create what Harless calls the "Mankiw Rule." It uses the consumer price index core inflation rate over the previous 12 months and the seasonally adjusted unemployment rate. The equation is

$$\textbf{Federal funds rate} = \textbf{8.5} + \textbf{1.4 (Core inflation} - \textbf{Unemployment)}$$

The Mankiw Rule does, in fact, do a good job of fitting the data for US monetary policy during the 1990s (Figure 11-2)—that was Mankiw's goal, after all.

14 Andy Harless, "US Monetary Policy in the 2010's: The Mankiw Rule Today," June 3, 2010. Accessed March 30, 2015. http://blog.andyharless.com/2010/06/us-monetary-policy-in-2010s-mankiw-rule.html.

15 N. Gregory Mankiw, "U.S. Monetary Policy During the 1990s," Harvard Institute of Economic Research Discussion Paper Number 1927, August 2001. Accessed March 30, 2015. http://papers.ssrn.com/sol3/papers.cfm?abstract_id=279232.

Figure 11-2 **US Monetary Policy Under Greenspan and Bernanke**

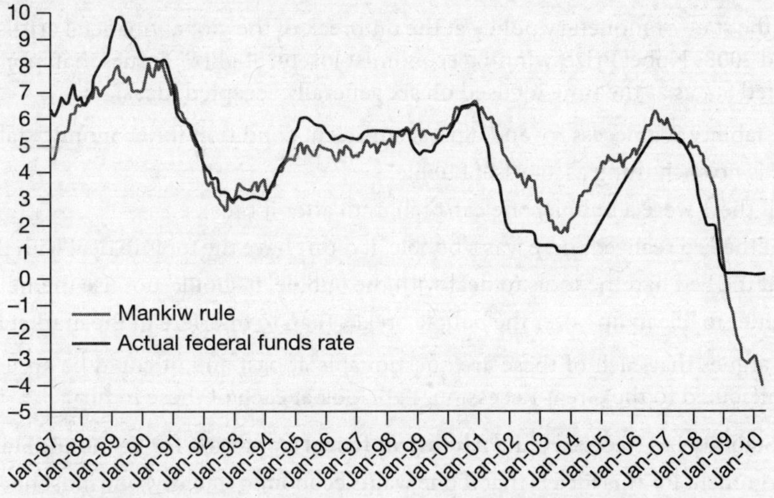

Source: Andy Harless

Starting in the first decade of the twenty-first century, however, we see a big gap open up between what the Mankiw Rule suggests and the actual federal funds rate. A similar result is seen in many applications of the Taylor Rule. Figure 11-2 suggests the actual federal funds rate was too low and remained too low until after the economy slid into the Great Recession.

This then leads to the question, What exactly was the role of monetary policy leading up to the Great Recession? We address this next.

SECTION REVIEW

Q1) Explain how the output gap and the inflation gap in the Taylor Rule are calculated.

Q2) What problems with the Taylor Rule does the Mankiw Rule attempt to address?

Q3) According to the Taylor Rule, if the real federal funds rate equals 2%, the inflation target rate is 2%, the actual inflation rate is 4%, and the economy is at the full employment level of output, what should the federal funds target be?

a. 2%

b. 3%

c. 4%

d. 7%

11-5 Monetary Policy and the Crisis

What was the state of monetary policy at the outbreak of the global financial crisis that started in 2007 and 2008? Nobel Prize-winning economist Joseph Stiglitz[16] argues that monetary policy in the United States at the time focused on six generally accepted ideas:

1. Price stability is a necessary and almost sufficient condition for economic stability.
2. There is no such thing as an asset bubble.
3. Even if there were a bubble, one can't tell until after it breaks.
4. Even if the Fed realized there was a bubble, it didn't have the tools to deal with the problem.
5. Even if the Fed had the tools to deal with the bubble, it should not use them.
6. It is better to "clean up" after the bubble breaks than to interfere in the market beforehand.

Stiglitz argues that each of these are questionable at best and, it could be argued, at worse largely contributed to the Great Recession. Let's look at each of these in turn.

1. **Price Stability Is a Necessary and Almost Sufficient Condition for Economic Stability**
   The argument for this idea is that if one wants economic stability, one must have price level stability first. No price level stability, no economic stability. Some go even further and argue that *if* you have price level stability then you *will* have economic stability. If this is how one sees the world, then monetary policy should be dedicated almost exclusively to price level stability.

   As Stiglitz argues, however, when central banks focus so intently on the economic instability brought on by inflation, or even when relative prices are out of equilibrium, they are focusing on an instability that is tiny compared with the massive disruption that comes about from a financial crisis. So, while central bankers were wringing their hands over low rates of inflation, they were completely oblivious to the growing asset bubble in the mortgage market. Why didn't monetary policymakers pay more attention to the growing mortgage asset bubble?

There was a belief that:

2. **There Is No Such Thing as an Asset Bubble**
   It was believed that asset bubbles, the irrational increase in the market price of an asset, was inconsistent with the notion of "**rational markets**," which was the dominate philosophy of the time. Under the assumption of rational markets, market participants use all available information when making prudent and logical decisions that maximize utility; if mistakes are made, they learn from those mistakes and do not repeat them. Because market participants are rational, or act as though they are rational, the irrational behavior that leads to asset bubbles must not take place. Thus asset bubbles do not take place.

   Rational market: A market where all available information is used to make correct predictions about the future and market participants learn from their mistakes. Thus, mistakes are not repeated, or they are corrected by other market participants.

   However, Stiglitz points out, this is historically incorrect. There was the "Tulipmania" in seventeenth-century Holland, the Mississippi Bubble in eighteenth-century France, the South Sea Bubble in eighteenth-century England, the stock market bubble in the United States in the 1920s, the Japanese asset bubble in the 1980s, and the dot-com asset bubble in the United States in the late 1990s. In each of these cases prices increased rapidly and irrationally, only to have the asset bubble "pop," prices plummet, and the economy dislocate.

16 This section draws on Stiglitz's speech and paper *An Agenda for Reforming Economic Theory*, prepared for the INET Conference, "What Kind of Theory to Guide Reform and Restructuring of the Financial and Non-Financial Sectors?," Cambridge University, Cambridge, UK, April 9, 2010.

Critics, however, will retort, sure, we know these were asset bubbles in hindsight, but:

3. **Even If There Were a Bubble, One Can't Tell Until After It Breaks**
The argument is that prices increase all the time and for a variety of reasons. Price might increase because of an increase in the demand for or a shortage of a good, among other reasons. When conducting monetary policy, central bankers cannot be sure that any given increase in prices represents an irrational increase in price, and thus an asset bubble, until after the bubble breaks.

Stiglitz points out, however, that this argument falsely assumes that policy decisions are done in a setting of certainty. The world is full of uncertainty and incomplete information. Monetary policy is no different. Thus monetary policymakers must use their judgment; they cannot wait to be perfectly sure of what is happening before they act. When prices increase rapidly, at historically unprecedented rates, policymakers may not be completely certain that it is an asset bubble, but they might be reasonably sure that it is. Policymakers, Stiglitz argues, need to make probability judgments.

But critics counter that:

4. **Even If the Fed Realized There Was a Bubble, It Didn't Have the Tools to Deal With the Problem**
Some believe monetary policy is set up to deal with economy-wide increases in the general level of prices. Asset bubbles, on the other hand, take place in specific markets. The Fed is not equipped to deal with individual-level market behavior.

Stiglitz points out that in 1994, more than a decade before the crisis hit, Congress gave the Fed the power to regulate the housing industry, including the power to require an increase in the loan-to-value ratio. Stiglitz admits this might not have been enough to prevent the irrational behavior in the mortgage market, but it may have mitigated the negative impact of the irrational behavior.

To this, critics might respond:

5. **Even If the Fed Had the Tools to Deal With the Bubble, It Should Not Use Them**
The Fed was reluctant to use the tools that it had, or even invent new tools to deal with new problems, out of fear that it could "disrupt" markets by changing too many of the rules and regulations of financial markets. So, the thinking goes, the damage from disrupting the markets is probably much worse than any good that can come out of preventing some prices from increasing irrationally.

Stiglitz notes that by not using the tools Congress gave it, the Fed helped to contribute to the worst economic slowdown since the Great Depression. Any negative impact on markets that resulted from them being "disruptive" would pale in comparison to the damage done from the bursting of the asset bubble.

Speaking of bursting asset bubbles, the critics would argue:

6. **It Is Better to "Clean Up" After the Bubble Breaks Than to Interfere in the Market Beforehand**
Critics believe that the Fed can be ready to pump in large amounts of liquidity once an asset bubble—if there is such a thing—bursts to ensure that the markets make a full and rapid recovery. The lack of liquidity is, it is argued, why rapidly falling asset bubbles result in economic dislocation. It is not the fault of the market that rapidly decreasing asset prices result in economic downturns; rather, the central banks do not do their job and there is a lack of liquidity in the financial markets.

Stiglitz points out that the Fed (and other central banks) massively increased the amount of liquidity in financial markets. Those actions may have kept us from entering into a downturn that would have been worse than the Great Depression of the 1930s. But the massive increase in liquidity was not enough to prevent the Great Recession. Thus, Stiglitz argues, continuing to argue that it is better for central banks to "clean up" after an asset bubble pops as opposed to doing something to prevent them borders on the absurd.

To prevent asset bubbles in financial markets, however, economists need to be able to better model financial market behavior in their macroeconomic models. Specifically, macroeconomists need to be able to model how financial market imperfections can result in asset bubbles and ultimately damage the entire economy. On this front, much has yet to be accomplished.

SECTION REVIEW

Q1) Tommy believes that markets are rational. Explain why Tommy thus would argue that asset bubbles don't exist. How would economists such as Joseph Stiglitz counter Tommy's argument?

Q2) Stiglitz argues that the Fed's focus on price stability actually contributed to the Great Recession. Explain Stiglitz's argument.

Q3) Some believe identifying an asset bubble until it breaks is impossible, and thus monetary policy should not be used to deflate asset bubbles. Stiglitz argues this argument is false because it ignores what economic concept?

a. The existence of uncertainty

b. The concept of multiple time periods

c. The idea of utility maximization

d. The difference between real and nominal income

Conclusion

11-6

The conduct of monetary policy is full of debates and controversies, but it also is complicated. When we first explain monetary policy to students who are only beginning their study of economics and financial markets, we don't tell them whole story. In principles of economics courses we often gloss over the debates about what should be the goals of monetary policy. We tend to ignore the debate over central bank independence and the confusing controversies over targets and instruments. At least things like the Taylor Rule give us a yardstick by which to potentially judge the conduct of monetary policy, but those too carry some debate. Perhaps the most important debate, however, is what monetary policymakers should have learned from the Great Recession about things such as asset bubbles and monetary policy. As we have seen, that debate continues. Now that you are no longer a beginning student in the study of these import issues, you too will, I hope, join the debate over these important, pressing issues of monetary policy.

IN THE NEWS. . .

Bank of England Silences Monetary Policy Committee Members

Philip Inman
The Guardian
March 14, 2013

The Bank of England will prevent members of its interest rate-setting committee from publishing individual opinions on the economy despite a review of its procedures calling for greater transparency.

The Bank said a "collective forecast" will remain the centrepiece of the monetary policy committee's monthly reports, effectively barring members from explaining their own views on the likely path of economic growth, inflation and unemployment.

Critics of the Bank's response to the Stockton report said the Bank's governor, Sir Mervyn King, had rejected proposals for the public to see a wider range of views because he wanted to maintain a stranglehold on the direction of policy. . . .

In response, Threadneedle Street [i.e., the Bank of England] said it agreed some procedures were opaque and there was a need for clear lines of responsibility, but said that criticisms of the MPC, which King chairs, were largely unfounded.

Explain why then-Bank of England Governor Mervyn King would want to prevent members of the Monetary Policy Committee (MPC) from stating their own views. Think about this within the context of inflationary expectations. Why then is the Bank of England "calling for greater transparency"?

Summary of Central Banks

Tying Concepts Together

Central banks do play an important role in our financial markets and in the functioning of our overall economy. When central banks around the world conduct their monetary policy, they have a variety of tools at their disposal. As we have seen, however, how they use these tools is still a matter of controversy. Ultimately, central banks need a well-functioning banking system to conduct monetary policy. It is these ever-important commercial banks to which we turn our attention next. In Chapter 12 we examine the issue of bank management by delving into banks' balance sheets and their off-balance activities. In Chapter 13 we look into a variety of risks banks face and how bank management attempts to manage these risks. Finally, in Chapter 14 we explore the issue of bank regulation, both in terms of what regulators are trying to accomplish as well as how they have in many ways failed to meet all of their expectations.

12

Bank Management

12-1 Bank Management: Balance Sheets

Many people mistakenly believe that commercial banks are, in many ways, like electricity in a house or an apartment: very useful, but mostly dull and uninteresting and thus taken for granted—that is, until it does not work properly. No electricity means your refrigerator won't work, not to mention the air conditioning or heat. Even worse, a short in the electrical system can burn your entire house or apartment building to the ground. So it is with bank management: mostly dull and uninteresting, until it does not work properly—then the result is often an economic meltdown.

We are going to take what is usually a painfully dull subject—bank management—and see that it is, in fact, a fascinating exercise of economics in action. By examining a bank's balance sheet, we will realize how managers of a bank must constantly worry about how to effectively and efficiently address changing market conditions while constantly meeting customer needs, two repeating themes in economic analysis. We then dig deeper into these issues and look at the wide variety of deposit accounts and loans banks offer. Finally we delve into the murky world of off balance sheet bank activity and see the role it played in the current financial crisis. Through it all we return to the central idea that bank management involves managing the process of asset transformation.

12-1a Asset Transformation

As we learned earlier, a commercial bank primarily does two things: It takes deposits and it makes loans. By doing so, banks provide an extremely important service, what economists call **asset transformation**. That is, banks transform the asset of savers into an asset for borrowers.

Asset transformation: The process by which a financial institution creates a new asset from existing liabilities with different characteristics. Commercial banks take their liabilities (e.g., bank deposits), which are short term and generally small in size, and transform them into large, long-term assets (e.g., bank loans).

Banks essentially turn savings into loans. But, as we shall see by examining a bank's balance sheet, this is not the only asset transformation banks perform. When conducting these asset transformations, bank management must be cognizant of the trade-offs and dilemmas they face. If bank management does this properly, the entire economy benefits from having an efficient allocation of capital. But if bank management does not do their job correctly, the result can be an economic catastrophe.

12-1b Bank Management: The Big Picture

One thing to keep in mind when you think about banks is that while they all do basically the same thing—asset transformation—not all banks are the same. There is a *huge* diversity in the size and scale of banks in the United States today. For example, compare the State Security Bank in Iron River, Wisconsin, with J.P. Morgan Chase National Association, with world headquarters in midtown Manhattan in New York City, and you will see just how different banks can be. Table 12.1 summarizes some of the major differences between these two banks as of March 31, 2013, according to the FDIC.

Small local banks like State Security Bank are usually referred to as "community banks." These community banks, as the name suggests, tend to focus on providing banking services to the local communities in which they are located. They are sometimes also called "retail banks" because they typically focus on providing services to consumers and local businesses.

Table 12-1 **Differences Between State Security Bank and J.P. Morgan Chase as of March 31, 2013**

	State Security Bank	J.P. Morgan Chase
Domestic locations	3	5,694
Employees	19	201,702
Total Assets (in million $)	81.4	1,948,150
Total Liabilities (in million $)	68.2	1,798,280
Total Equity (in million $)	13.2	149,870

These retail or community banks often are characterized as having total assets of less than $1 billion.[1]

Larger megabanks like J.P. Morgan Chase are usually referred to as money center banks because they often are located in large cities, or "money centers." These larger banks perform a wide variety of services and offer a multitude of services to their customers. The customer base of larger banks can spread across the country and typically around the world. These megabanks are so large that one of them failing could result in a collapse of the entire financial or economic system. This is referred to as "systemic risk." We will talk more about systemic risk later in Chapter 14 when we discuss bank regulation.

There are, of course, many different types of banks between the small community banks and the megabanks. It gets rather complicated, so please do not think that every bank can be neatly categorized into one definition or another. Instead, think of it as a spectrum of different bank types and sizes: On one end of the spectrum lie community banks, such as State Security Bank in Iron River; at the other end are the megabanks such as J.P. Morgan Chase, and in between are hundreds of other types of banks.

Regardless of what size and form a bank may be, they all operate under the same accounting rules and regulations. As such, we can use financial statements, especially balance sheets, as a guide when examining how banks are managed. Remember, regardless of size, banks are involved in asset transformation. To understand how banks perform asset transformation, let's first take a general look at a bank's balance sheet. Remember that the accounting equation for banks is

Assets = Liabilities + Bank capital

We described a basic bank balance sheet as looking like this:

Assets	Liabilities and Bank Captial
Cash/Reserves	Demand deposits
Business loans	Savings accounts
Consumer loans	Loans from other banks
Mortgages	Other borrowings
Bonds	
Other assets	Bank capital

1 There is actually a fair amount of debate about how exactly to define a community or retail bank. For a discussion, see "Defining the Community Bank" from the December 2012 FDIC Community Banking Study (http://www.fdic.gov/regulations/resources/cbi/report/CBSI-1.pdf).

Now we want to add more detail about what a bank's balance sheet really looks like. For example, if we were to review the entire banking system, the numbers would look like this:

Assets (Nov. 2013, in billions, seasonally adjusted, all domestic chartered)			
Cash	1,331.80		11.40%
Trading Assets	122.1		1.00%
InterBank Loans	88.6		0.70%
Securities	2,506.6		21.50%
- Treasury & Agency		1,798	
- Other		910.3	
Loans & Leases	6,684		57.30%
LESS allowances	−123.8		
- Comm & Industrial		1,592.8	
- Real Estate		3,526.6	
- Consumer Credit		1,150.1	
- Other loans & leases		1,117.1	
Other Assets	1,049.70		9.00%
Total Assets	11,659		

From this we can see that in 2013 banks were holding a large amount of cash. Banks usually hold only about 2–3% of their assets in cash, but since the beginning of the financial crisis American banks have been maintaining a larger amount of cash and a higher percentage of their assets in cash.

We also see that loans and leases make up over half of the bank's balance sheet. Thus loans are still very important to bank management. Because of this, in the next section we examine the issue of loans and loan pricing in more detail.

Switching over to the liabilities side of the balance sheet, for the US banking system as a whole it looks like this:

Liabilities (Nov. 2013, in billions, seasonally adjusted, all domestic chartered)			
Deposits	8,636.7		85.57%
- Large Time		696.1	
- Other		7,940.6	
Borrowing	933.8		9.25%
- From US banks		95.4	
- From others		838.4	
Trading	110.3		1.09%
Net Due foreign offices	55.9		0.55%
Other	355.9		3.52%
Total Liabilities	10,092.70		
Residual (Assets – Liabilities)	1,498.3		

This makes very clear how important deposits are to banks; they represent the most important source of funds for US banks. For this reason we are going to spend a fair amount of time looking at these bank deposits: What are the different types of deposits? Who uses what type of deposit account? Deposits are so important that we take up the topic next. Let's see just what bank deposits are, who uses them, and for what.

SECTION REVIEW

Q1) Hank is confused as to what banks do. He reads that banks "transform assets," but he has no idea what that means. How would you explain asset transformation to Hank?

Q2) Banks usually hold a very small percentage of their assets in the form of cash. Recently, however, banks have been holding on to larger amounts of cash. What impact does this have on the other categories of a bank's balance sheet?

Q3) Which is currently the largest liability of banks?

a. Cash
b. Loans
c. Deposits
d. Bank capital

12-2 Bank Deposits and Other Liabilities

The liabilities on a bank's balance sheet represent the way the bank *gets* funds. Remember, banks are going to be in the business of asset transformation: They transform deposits and other "borrowed" funds into loans (and other assets). So, we can see this asset transformation begin to take shape by observing banks obtaining funds, which is what banks' liabilities represent.

12-2a Transaction Deposits

Let's start our examination of bank liabilities—how banks get funds—by looking at the bank liability with which you are most likely familiar: transaction deposits, sometimes called checkable deposits. **Transaction deposit accounts** are bank accounts against which the depositor can write a check.

Transaction deposit account: A liquid bank account most often used by depositors for transferring funds to another party.

Technically, the Federal Reserve defines a "transaction account" this way:

> An account from which the depositor or accountholder is permitted to make transfers or withdrawals by negotiable or transferable instrument (e.g. a check), payment order of withdrawal, telephone transfer, or other similar device for the purpose of making payments or transfers to third persons or others or from which the depositor may make third party payments at an ATM or a remote service unit or other electronic device including a debit card. . . .

Transaction accounts come in a variety of forms. We want to concentrate on two general forms of transaction deposits: demand deposits and negotiable orders of withdrawal (NOW) accounts.

Demand Deposits and NOW Accounts

Demand deposits are traditionally accounts that are payable on demand of the depositor—thus the name. Or, they can be deposits issued with an original maturity of less than seven days or have a required notice period of less than seven days. In these cases "required notice" is the legal notice a depositor gives to a financial institution saying that the depositor plans on withdrawing some or all of his or her funds at a specific date in the future. These are almost *never* used today.

Currently, the characteristics of a demand deposit account are:

- No maturity period, or an original maturity period of less than seven days
- Payable on demand (or less than seven days' notice)
- May be interest bearing
- No limit on the number of withdrawals or transfers
- No eligibility requirements

Demand deposit accounts *used* to be checking accounts that did not pay interest, whereas NOW accounts were checking accounts that *did* pay interest. Currently, the following are characteristics of a NOW account:

- *No* maturity date
- Institution may reserve the right to request at any time written notice at least seven days before a withdrawal
- Unlimited transactions
- May be accessed by check, draft, telephone, or electronic order to pay a third party or others, or to transfer funds to another of the depositor's accounts at the same institution
- May be held by individuals, governmental units, and nonprofits

The Invention of NOW Accounts

Today there aren't many substantial differences between demand deposit accounts and NOW accounts. But it wasn't always that way. Regulation Q, which was part of the Banking Act of 1933, forbade banks to pay interest on checking accounts or demand deposits. For the three decades after World War II this wasn't that important because interest rates were very low and thus the foregone interest in holding funds in a demand deposit was not that significant.

All that changed as interest rates started to increase during the 1970s. With rising market interest rates, banks had to find a way to start paying interest on deposits in transaction accounts or would wind up losing those deposits. Regulation Q, however, forbade paying interest on demand deposits. What were depository institutions to do?

Into this fray stepped Ronald Haselton. In 1968 the Worcester Five Cent Savings Bank hired Haselton to be its new president and CEO. Haselton changed the name to the slightly more respectful "Consumers Savings Bank." But Haselton was frustrated by the amount of regulations savings banks faced compared with the commercial banking industry he just left. For example, in those days, regulations did not allow savings banks like Consumers to offer demand deposit accounts to their depositors.

The bank regulations at the time meant that a depositor at a savings bank such as Consumers would have to withdraw money from their interest-earning savings account, walk it across the street to a bank, and then deposit their money into a non-interest-bearing demand deposit just to be able to write a check to pay their bills. Haselton thought this was crazy,[2] so he devised a plan to help the consumers of Consumers.

Haselton created a "savings" account from which depositors could withdraw their funds at any time by writing a check. These negotiable orders of withdrawal, or NOW, accounts were, in fact, checking accounts that paid interest, but technically, according to Haselton, they were savings accounts.

After lengthy court battles, the NOW accounts were finally allowed. They proved to be so popular other deposit institutions started to offer them, and they spread across the country. Finally, in 1980 Congress passed legislation to allow all depository institutions to offer NOW accounts—checking accounts that pay interest.

The distinction between demand deposits and NOW accounts lasted until July 21, 2011, when the Dodd-Frank Act allowed, for the first time, depository institutions to pay interest on demand deposits. So, while the distinction between demand deposits and NOW accounts has disappeared, the importance of what Ronald Haselton did should not be underestimated. He is an example of one of the many entrepreneurial-minded bankers who brought financial innovation to the US banking system. What he started changed the structure and makeup of the American banking industry. Remember that when you look at the "transaction accounts" section of a bank's balance sheet.

Money Market Deposit Accounts

Another financial market innovation was the creation of money market deposit accounts, or MMDAs. As we discussed in Chapter 2, when we talked about monetary aggregates, MMDAs came about in response to money market mutual funds that were offered by nondepository institutions in the 1970s. As part of the wave of "deregulation" of financial markets in the 1980s, banking laws were changed to allow commercial banks in the United States to offer relatively liquid savings accounts that could pay a market rate of interest: money market deposit accounts.

You can think of an MMDA as a type of savings account: It generally pays a higher rate of interest than would a checking account because withdrawals each month are limited. It is, however, a savings account that is not as illiquid as a certificate of deposit (more about those in

2 See Joe Nocera, *A Piece of the Action: How the Middle Class Joined the Money Class*. New York: Simon & Schuster, 1994.

the next section; for now, they are completely illiquid savings accounts); as long as you don't hit the limit on the number of withdrawals each month (often it's a maximum of six withdrawals), you can think of these as being a very liquid savings account.

Because a depositor can write a check on an MMDA, they are considered a checkable or transaction account. But remember, there are limits on the number of withdrawals that can be made from these accounts, so yes, they are checkable, but it could be argued that it is a bit of a stretch to call them "transaction" accounts because the number of transactions that can be done each month are limited.

12-2b Nontransaction Accounts

While transaction accounts are liquid accounts that are useful for conducting transactions (thus the name), other bank accounts are less liquid and more useful for savings and generating interest income. These nontransaction accounts, or savings accounts, are also sometimes called "time deposits" because they must be left on deposit for a stated length of time.

Savings or Passbook Accounts

One of the oldest types of nontransaction accounts are savings accounts. In the old days depositors were given a little book, about the size of a passport, that would record the balance in the account and all transactions that occurred on that account. When the depositor went into the bank, she or he would pass the little book to the bank teller to record that day's transaction: a deposit, a withdrawal, or the payment of interest. The passbook—see, the name actually makes sense—was proof of the account that the depositor could keep.

Savings accounts still exist today but the passbook has all but disappeared. Instead, the bank produces monthly statements that show all of the transactions that went on for that account during the past month. Statements today often are made available only electronically. Many erroneously believe that savings accounts are completely liquid accounts because the depositor generally can access their funds whenever they want. Legally, however, the bank can make depositors wait, sometimes up to 10 days, before being required to give the depositors funds out of their savings account. Thus, while savings accounts might seem like completely liquid accounts, they are not. Savings accounts are nontransaction accounts.

Certificates of Deposit

Bank **certificates of deposit**, or CDs, are illiquid savings accounts for a stated length of time, or term. The depositor can pick the duration or term of the CD. They usually range from 91 days to 10 years. In general, the longer the term, the higher the annual interest rate paid. They can often be opened for as little as $1,000.

Certificates of deposit: Illiquid bank savings accounts that must be left on deposit for a stated length of time. There are usually substantial penalties for early withdrawals.

Bank CDs are a nice, virtually risk-free way to build savings. Let's suppose you have some money saved that you know you won't need for a while. It doesn't make sense to leave that money sitting in a transaction account (think checking account) where it will earn very little interest. Instead, give up that liquidity in return for a higher interest rate by putting the money into a bank CD. Let's suppose you put the money into a three-year bank CD. Each quarter the bank pays interest on the funds in the CD; you can have the interest rolled back into the CD, whereby you earn interest on the interest, or you can have the interest paid transferred to another account, such as your checking account. At the end of the three-year term you get your money back or you can roll those funds into another CD. Again, you get to pick the term of the new CD.

While you can open a CD with as little as $1,000, with over $100,000 you can open a "jumbo CD," sometimes called a "large time deposit." Jumbo CDs are a bit different from regular CDs in that the interest rate paid on them is negotiable instead of a stated rate, as for regular CDs. Jumbo CDs are also different in that there is a secondary market for them, meaning banks buy and sell the jumbo CDs among each other.

12-2c Other Liabilities

While deposits make up the vast majority of liabilities, they are not the only way banks get funds. Banks can also raise funds via other methods:

- **Federal funds purchases.** When banks that are members of the Federal Reserve system buy funds in the federal funds market, they are raising funds. These federal funds that they purchase must be paid back, with interest, and so federal funds purchased show up as a liability on a bank's balance sheet.
- **Repurchase agreements.** Banks sell financial instruments, usually Treasury securities, with the promise to buy them back in the future, often the next day. These agreements to repurchase assets sold are called "repos" and show up as a liability on a bank's balance sheet.
- **Subordinated debt.** Banks issue bonds that, in the case of liquidation, promise to pay bondholders after depositors get their funds. These bonds are thus subordinate to, or secondary to, depositors and thus called subordinated debt. When a bank sells this subordinated debt in the primary market, the bank raises funds. Since these subordinated debt issues must be repaid, they show up as liabilities on a bank's balance sheet.
- **Eurodollar accounts.** American banks issue dollar-denominated savings or time accounts outside the United States. These are called Eurodollar accounts, but don't be confused into thinking that they must be issued in Europe. They were originally created in Europe as a way for the Soviet Union to hold dollars outside of US banks. Today, Eurodollar accounts are found around the world.
- **Other borrowing and other liabilities.** Banks that are members of the Federal Reserve system can borrow from the Fed's discount window or other Fed lending facilities. Banks that are not part of the Fed can borrow from other larger banks with whom they have a correspondent banking relationship. Also included in this category are things such as liabilities from the bank's trading and income taxes that are due.

So, while deposits are the single biggest source of funds for banks, they certainly are not the only source. Next we turn our attention to the other side of a bank's balance sheet and look at assets, or the uses of bank funds.

SECTION REVIEW

Q1) Financial innovations can have dramatic effects. Explain how and why NOW accounts came about and the impact they have had on financial markets.

Q2) Not all financial assets are the right vehicle for everyone. Give an example of someone for whom a certificate of deposit would be useful. Also give an example of someone for whom a certificate of deposit would be a bad choice.

Q3) Demand deposit and NOW accounts are commonly referred to as:

a. savings accounts.

b. passbook accounts.

c. checking accounts.

d. nontransaction accounts.

12-3 Bank Loans and Other Assets

While the liabilities on a bank's balance sheet show where a bank *gets* its funds, the asset side of a bank's balance sheet shows what the bank *does* with the funds it receives. In accounting it is customary to list assets from the most liquid to the least liquid. Thus the first asset listed is the most liquid asset a bank possesses, which is, naturally, cash.

12-3a Cash

Banks can hold cash in the form of either vault cash or on deposit, usually with the Federal Reserve; if the bank is not part of the Federal Reserve system, cash is held on deposit with another, usually much larger institution. Traditionally, banks hold only a small portion of their assets in the form of cash—around 2% or 3% of assets. Starting with the financial crisis in 2008, though, banks in the United States have been holding a larger percentage of their assets in cash.

There is a fair amount of debate as to why US banks are holding so much cash. Some argue that loan demand is down—businesses just don't want to borrow money—and thus the banks "get stuck" holding cash from deposits and other sources, which no one wants to borrow. Critics of banks, on the other hand, believe that banks really don't want to lend. They point out that lending is a difficult, time-consuming, and risky activity. Thus US banks are demanding high levels of collateral and impose burdensome covenants or restrictions on borrowers' activities before they consider making a loan. The critics note that US banks have been very profitable trading financial securities and thus really don't want to lend the cash they are holding.

While cash is the most liquid of assets, it does not pay very high returns to the banks holding the cash. For example, before 2008 banks were not paid any interest on the funds they had on deposit at the Federal Reserve. In 2014 the interest rate on required and excess reserves paid to banks by the Fed was only one-quarter of 1%. Instead of holding only cash, banks naturally want to hold other assets that pay them a higher rate of return. Let's look next at what some of those other assets might be.

12-3b Securities

Banks generally want to hold a variety of financial assets to increase their return on assets. But bank management has to be careful: Higher-paying securities might also carry with them more default risk. In addition, higher-paying securities might also be less liquid, and banks need to maintain liquidity to meet the cash needs of their depositors. Thus bank management has to weigh these risks versus the rewards. Bank management generally leans toward safety (or, some might contend, they are pushed toward safety by regulations) and hold securities with low default risk and a high level of liquidity.

Of all securities, US Treasury securities have the lowest default risk. Next are securities issued by US government agencies. These two classes of assets also have a large and active secondary market and thus a high level of liquidity. Banks seek these characteristics in securities they hold, which explains why banks hold so many of them.

While US government and government agency debt are very safe and very liquid, their yields are relatively low. Thus banks need assets that give them a much higher level of return; just as important, these assets must be used by banks to determine their default risk. What is that asset? The bank's loan portfolio.

12-3c Bank Loans

Commercial banks make loans to both businesses and consumers. Different banks offer different combinations of these loans; some banks may focus on making agricultural loans to farmers and their suppliers, whereas others offer almost every type of loan made. Let's take a look at some of the different types of loans banks make.

Short-term Business Loans

- **Self-liquidating inventory loans.** In these loans the bank lends money to a firm that uses the funds to buy inventory. That inventory is then sold to the firm's customers. The firm uses that sales revenue to pay off the loan with interest.
- **Seasonal borrowing.** Some firms need to borrow large amounts of money during certain seasons and then quickly pay off the loans. Consider a summer fishing lodge in northern Wisconsin. It needs to borrow money in the spring to get their boats ready, buy tackle, and so on. Once tourists arrive in the summer, the lodge will be able to repay the loans quickly. The fishing lodge has no reason to borrow during the winter.
- **Interim construction loans.** Theses loans are made so that builders of office buildings, shopping malls, or single-family homes can purchase materials and hire the labor for construction. Once the building or home is built, a multiyear mortgage loan is written in part to pay off the interim construction loan.
- **Securities dealer financing.** Securities dealers buy and sell stocks and bonds for their clients. They must have the cash to purchase the securities that they then resell to clients. These securities dealers often borrow money from banks to do so. These short-term loans are rapidly repaid, with interest, by the securities dealer once the securities are sold.
- **Retail and equipment financing.** These include floor plan loans, which are loans made against a specific piece of collateral that a firm is going to resell, such as automobiles, trucks, boats, and RVs.

Long-term Business Loans

- **Term asset–based: fixed asset or blind-spot loans.** These are loans that are made to purchase assets, which then are pledged as collateral on the loan. The repayment schedule for such loans is usually structured to align with the revenue streams of the corporate borrower. For example, the loan can be written so that no payments are required by the borrower during seasons when the firm may not have much cash flow. This type of loan is often referred to as a "blind-spot loan."
- **Project loans.** These are for the financing of large, long-term projects such as oil refineries and power plants. With project loans, often more than one bank participates, or lends a portion of the total loan.
- **Leveraged buyouts (LBOs).** Here, an investor or a private equity fund, sometimes called a "takeover artist" or "corporate raider," borrows funds (thus the term *leveraged*) to buy all of the outstanding shares of a corporation (thus the *buyout*) in order to take the company private. Once the company is privately held, it can be improved or fixed, and the shares can then be sold at a higher price than at what they were purchased. When the shares are sold, the loan is repaid.
- **Agricultural loans.** These are loans to farmers, many of which are subsidized by the federal government, and include loans for equipment, land, feed, seed, livestock, and even things such as water and soil conservation.

While historically business loans were the main lending business of commercial banks, during the twentieth century, loans to individuals and households grew in importance. Today commercial banks are heavily involved with consumer lending, both real estate and non–real estate loans.

Short-term Consumer Loans

- **Credit cards.** These unsecured, revolving credit agreements have increased in popularity during the twentieth century. Remember, *unsecured* means the borrower does not have to pledge any assets as collateral. Revolving means the borrower can borrow any amount up to the maximum allowed, pay some or all of it off, and then borrow again up to the maximum.
- **Unsecured personal loans.** For these loans, sometimes called signature loans, the individual borrower offers no collateral, only their signature, to get the loan. Repayment terms tend to be very short term and are often for a specific purpose, such as a "bridge loan" that provides funding to the individual until a larger loan is provided.
- **Unsecured personal lines of credit.** A personal line of credit is similar to a credit card in that there is a maximum amount the borrower may borrow, but they typically do not borrow the entire amount at once. Instead, they borrow some of the funds, pay it back with interest, and then borrow more. These lines of credit are unsecured in that the borrower does not pledge any collateral on the loan.

Long-term Consumer Loans

- **Home mortgages: first mortgages.** In mortgage loans, real estate is pledged as collateral on the loan. A first mortgage is used by the borrower to obtain funds to purchase the real estate. As will be discussed in Chapter 18, first home mortgages can be amortized over 15 or 30 years and may have a fixed interest rate or an adjustable interest rate.
- **Home mortgages: second mortgages and equity lines of credit.** Over time, homeowners pay down the balance on their home mortgages. The difference between the market value of asset, such as a house, and the amount owned on the asset is called equity. Today in the United States homeowners can borrow against the equity they have in their homes. Traditionally, these home equity loans were called second mortgages and were used to make home improvements. Starting in the mid-1980s, lenders, including commercial banks, started to make a wide variety of second mortgages, based on increasing home equity levels, including home equity lines of credit. These home equity lines of credit allowed homeowners to use the loans secured by their homes for anything they wanted. However, many Americans used these home equity lines of credit to sustain a lifestyle they could not afford.
- **Automobile loans.** Consumers typically don't have the cash available to purchase an auto outright; thus they must get a loan and pledge the auto as collateral. Payback periods are usually five to seven years for new cars and three to six years for used autos.
- **Other vehicle loans.** These include motorcycle loans, boat loans, RV loans, and ATV loans, among others. Because these vehicles usually depreciate faster than automobiles and have a less well-developed secondary market, the interest rate on these vehicle loans tend to be higher than those on auto loans.

Thus a bank's balance sheet provides a great deal of information. As the recent financial crisis has shown, however, banks engage in many transactions that do not show up on their balance sheet. These "off balance sheet" transactions have proven to be very profitable for banks in recent years, but they have also caused problems for banks. We now turn our attention to these important off balance sheet transactions.

SECTION REVIEW

Q1) Explain the trade-offs banks face when they consider holding high-yield securities.

Q2) Banks offer a wide variety of business loans. Explain why banks try to seek a balance between short-term and long-term loans in their loan portfolio. What are the advantages and disadvantages of offering short-term loans versus long-term loans?

Q3) Debbie has owned her home for several years and has been paying her mortgage on time every month. She is building equity in her home, which can then be used for what type of personal loan?

a. A first mortgage

b. A second mortgage

c. RV loan

d. Unsecured loan

12-4 Off Balance Sheet Activities

Over the past several decades, commercial banks have faced a shrinking interest rate spread as competition over borrowers increased at the same time savers discovered many alternative places to save their funds. As a result, banks—especially those in the United States—turned to fees for income to replace their shrinking interest rate spread. Many of these fee-generating activities involve transactions that take place off the bank's balance sheet. In addition, banks have shifted more of their activities off balance sheet because these financial contracts do not require the bank to set aside any capital. Thus off balance sheet activities have been a way for banks to get around legal capital requirements.

12-4a Commercial Letters of Credit

Imagine that a buyer and seller of a product do not know each other. Laurie runs a wine store in Chicago and wants to purchase wine on credit to sell in her store. She wants to buy wine made in Italy by Gino. The problem is, Gino does not know Laurie, or her firm, and is not sure Laurie is going to be able to pay for the wine.

In this case Laurie goes to her bank to get a letter of credit: Her bank essentially tells Gino, "If Laurie, our customer, does not pay, we the bank will pay you." Gino agrees and sells Laurie the wine. Laurie pays Gino from the sale of the wine. The bank never lent Laurie the money, they simply made a loan commitment: a promise to lend money if necessary. Since no loan was made, there is nothing to put on the bank's balance sheet. But the bank does not extend this service to Laurie free; they charge her a fee.

12-4b Standby Letters of Credit

In a standby letter of credit, a bank promises to pay a third party if the bank's customer does not repay the third party as promised. A standby letter of credit is a much more general commitment than a commercial letter of credit because it is not tied to a specific transaction. Traditionally, standby letters of credit have been used by bank customers who issue commercial paper. If the issuer of the commercial paper cannot repay as promised, the bank steps in and pays off the holders of the commercial paper. Since the default rates on commercial paper are extremely low, banks often viewed the issuance of standby letters of credit as a relatively risk-free way to generate fee income.

12-4c Financial Derivatives: Currency and Interest Rate Forward, Futures, Options, and Swap Contracts

A financial derivative is an agreement between a customer of a bank and the bank to exchange currencies or interest payments at an agreed-upon price at some date in the future, or the right to do so. Banks also use these derivative contracts to hedge exchange risk and interest rate risk they might face. Banks sometimes use these derivatives to speculate on exchange rate and interest rate movements. Regulators generally frown on this speculative use of derivative contracts because it is difficult for outsiders to tell why, exactly, a bank engages in these derivative transactions. For example, is it for their customers, to reduce the bank's risk, or to allow the bank to be a financial market speculator?

Credit Default Swap Contracts

Credit default swap contracts (CDSs) are privately negotiated, and thus currently unregulated, contracts whereby investors are repaid if the issuer of a financial contract defaults. So, a CDS is basically an insurance policy: The bank that issues the CDS is insuring repayment to the issuer of the financial contract.

In the mortgage market, home mortgages are pooled together and sold to investors through mortgage-backed securities. The actual mortgages usually are held by a different entity called an SIV (a special investment vehicle). The SIV then issues claims on the payment streams that come from the mortgages. But if the homeowners default on their mortgages, no money flows into the SIV, and the SIV cannot make payments on the mortgage-backed securities it sold. But if the investor had purchased from a bank a CDS on the mortgage-backed security, now the bank has to pay the investor the cash flows they should have received from the bank.

To make things even more confusing, an investor can purchase a CDS even if they don't own the financial contract the CDS is insuring because a CDS is not technically insurance! This can allow investors to "bet" on mortgages not being repaid by purchasing a CDS on a pool of mortgages. Plus, keep in mind, because these are privately negotiated and thus not technically an insurance policy, banks that issue a CDS are not required to hold any amount of capital aside in case they have to make a payout.

Thus a great deal of activity in banks occurs "off balance sheet." It can be difficult for the nonbank public to understand just how safe, or risky, any given bank is since examining a bank's balance sheet provides only a partial insight into how the bank is being operated. Because it is so difficult for outsiders to judge the safety and soundness of a bank, the level of bank regulation has increased significantly over time, a topic we address in Chapter 14. One of the main focuses of bank regulation is to evaluate how effectively bank management is managing the risks the bank faces. In the next chapter we examine in more detail what are the risks banks face.

SECTION REVIEW

Q1) Commercial letters of credit and standby letters of credit tend to be very profitable for banks, yet they seldom require banks to lend money. Explain why.

Q2) Many argue that when banks started to issue credit default swaps, they started to become insurance companies. Explain this argument.

Q3) Lisa runs a commercial bank and wants to hedge her interest rate risk. Which off balance sheet transaction is Lisa going to engage in on behalf of the bank?

a. Standby letter of credit
b. Credit default swap
c. Commercial letter of credit
d. Financial derivative

12-5 Conclusion

Banks are wonderful things, when they are managed correctly. When banks are managed correctly, they transform assets and help our economy to grow. In this chapter we looked at bank management through the lens of a bank's balance sheet. We examined the bank's various deposits and other liabilities before moving on to the asset side of the bank's balance sheet. We examined the difficult nature of bank lending and balancing its asset mix. We concluded by examining what's not on a bank's balance sheet: the off balance sheet transactions.

But along the way we saw that managing a bank is a very difficult and complex undertaking. In Chapter 13 we look at the difficult trade-offs bank management must make when managing various risks.

IN THE NEWS. . .

Bloomberg

By Susanne Walker

October 6, 2014

American banks are loading up on the U.S. government debt, as sign they remain cautious on the economy even with the jobless rate at a six-year low and corporations at their healthiest in a generation.

Commercial lenders increased their holdings of Treasuries and debt from federal agencies in September by $54 billion . . . data from the Federal Reserve show. . . . Bank of America Corp. and Citigroup are among the lenders adding government bonds this year as loan growth fails to keep up with record deposits. . . .

Lenders accumulated so much cash that deposits exceeded loans by the most on record last month. That gap has widened by more than $300 billion in the past year.

Bank of America, the second-biggest U.S. bank, has more than quadrupled its available-for-sale holdings of Treasuries and federal agency debt this year to $38.7 billion as of June 30, the latest company filings complied by Bloomberg show. The Charlotte, North Carolina-based lender now holds more of the securities than at any time since 2012.

Citigroup, the New York-based lender that received a $45 billion bailout during the credit crisis, had $103.8 billion of the bonds at the end of June. That's a 19 percent increase from December and the highest since 2011, the data show. . . .

US banks are using their cash to purchase more and more Treasuries and government agency debt. What impact will this have on the yields Treasury securities pay? What broader impact might that have on financial markets and the overall US economy?

If US banks are using their cash to purchase more and more Treasuries and government agency debt, what impact does that have on the growth rate of money supply? What broader effects might this have on the US and global economies?

13

Bank Risk Management and Performance

13-1 Credit Risk

Risk is one of those concepts that everyone thinks they know what it means, but often they don't. Risk in finance is the chance that an investment will *not* pay off the expected return. But remember, there is the risk/return trade-off: In general, the higher the risk of an investment, the higher the return. Bank management wants to get as high a return as possible on the bank's assets or investments, in part to keep stockholders of the bank happy, and in part for their own benefit, since bank management compensation bonuses often are tied to stock price. So, bank management has to weigh the risk/return trade-off. What are the risks in the bank's assets or investments? Why might those investments not pay off as expected? There are many reasons why a bank's investments may not pay off as the bank management expects. We are going to look at a few of the risks banks face and how they attempt to deal with these risks.

First, we review one of the oldest risks banks face: **credit risk**. This is the risk that a borrower will not repay as promised. We consider how banks attempt to deal with credit risk when lending to consumers and lending to businesses. Then we discuss some of the other risks banks face, including interest rate risk and operational risk. We conclude with a look at how outsiders attempt to evaluate how well a bank manages their risks by considering how to evaluate bank performance.

Credit risk: The risk that a borrower will not pay interest or premium as promised.

13-1a Credit Risk in General

The future is uncertain. Predicting the future is difficult. When banks lend money, however, they must, to a certain extent, be able to predict the future. They have to determine whether a borrower will repay as promised. Sometimes banks get it wrong. Sometimes a borrower does not, or cannot, live up to their promise to repay. The risk that a borrower will not repay as promised is what we call credit risk.

Five Cs

While credit risk has been around since the first loans were made, lenders today still struggle with how to evaluate credit risk. One of the tools that has been useful is the "five Cs" of credit risk.

When a lender is sizing up a borrower to determine the amount of credit risk the lender will face, they often evaluate the borrower on five different characteristics:

Character. Simply put, can the borrower be trusted? That is, what is the "character" of the person borrowing? Have they lived up to their promises in the past? If not, why not? If a firm is borrowing, who are the people managing the firm? Can they be trusted?

Capacity. Capacity is the ability of a borrower to repay. What type of income does the borrower have? How steady is this income? Is it likely to change in the future? All of these questions go to the borrower's capacity to repay. Capacity can also entail legal capacity: For example, does the borrower have the legal capacity to borrow on behalf of a firm?

Capital. What are the borrower's assets? While capacity is a flow concept—income over a year or over a month—capital is a stock concept. What assets does the borrower have right now compared to their debts? For a firm borrowing funds, the issue of capital also deals with how much money the owners of the firm themselves have put into the firm. Small amounts of capital might suggest the owners of the firm that is seeking to borrow do not have enough "skin in the game."

Collateral. What assets can the borrower pledge so that if the loan is not repaid as promised, the lender may seize the collateral and sell it? Collateral acts as a "secondary source" or repayment of the lender. If the borrower does not repay as promised, the lender can seize and sell the collateral and use the proceeds from the sale to, at best, partially repay the loan. One must, however, be careful because not all assets can function as collateral. Lenders look at two key characteristics of any asset they might consider for collateral on a loan:

- **Valuation:** How easy is it to place a fair market value on the asset? Some assets are easy to value: Cars, trucks, and real estate top the list. Other assets, while valuable, may be difficult to place a market value on, and thus lenders are less likely to take them as collateral. For example businesses's intellectual property, things such as patents and copyrights, are difficult to value. So, while they may be valuable to the firm, they are of little use as collateral on a loan.
- **Liquidity:** How easily can the lender sell the asset if they are forced to seize it for nonpayment? It often comes down to how big of a secondary market there is for the good. Things such as motorcycles and mobile homes may be relatively easy to value, but it is often difficult to find a willing purchaser of "used" products.

Conditions. What is the overall economic climate and how does that affect the ability of the borrower to repay? While this is most likely completely outside the control of the borrower, it is something the lender has to consider. Most industries are "procyclical"; that is, as the economy expands, business improves, revenues increase, and hiring expands. But when the economy slows, business conditions worsen, revenues decrease, and layoffs begin. So, a borrower who might be doing well today may not be able to repay in a few months if the economy turns bad. It may not be the entire economy that goes bad. An industry may experience difficult times even if the overall economy is doing well. For example, for most of the 1980s and 1990s, the US economy was in an expansionary phase, yet manufacturing experienced declining conditions during these two decades.

Sometimes a sixth "C" is added to the list:

Control. Control has to do with legal conditions changing. For example, suppose an industry is going to experience significant changes because of changes in government regulations. The changes in regulations mean the companies in that industry will no longer be as profitable as they once were. That means firms in that industry might have a more difficult time repaying their loans in the future, and the employees of those firms might not have jobs in the future. Lenders need to consider these things before making loans to firms and workers in those industries.

13-1b Credit Risk with Consumers

When it comes to evaluating credit risk to consumers, the past is a good indication of the future. That is, unless there is some major intervention to change behavior, how a consumer has handled their credit in the past is a fairly good indicator of how they will handle their credit in the future.

Credit Scores and Credit Reports

Today, consumers' handling of credit in the past is reported in a standard, easy-to-compare format called a **credit report**, which is generated by credit bureaus. There are three major credit bureaus in the United States: Equifax, Experian, and TransUnion.

Credit report: Also known as "credit history," a detailed report on how an individual has attained and used credit in the past. Credit reports also often include information on the person's employment history, past residential addresses, legal action taken against the person, and number of past credit report inquiries.

When a borrower applies for a loan, or any type of credit, the potential lender can contact one of the credit bureaus and obtain the borrower's credit report. The credit report contains information on where the borrower has lived, how they have paid their debts and utilities in the past, the types of credit the borrower has currently and has had in the past, and whether the borrower has had legal action taken against them (e.g., arrests, bankruptcies, lawsuits).

To make the information in the credit reports easier for lenders to understand, the credit bureaus also provide a **credit score** for the potential borrower. This credit score is also called a FICO score (for Fair, Issac, and Company, the entity that first created these scores). The FICO score can range from a low of 300 to a high of 850. The higher the FICO score, the lower the borrower's credit risk—or so it is hoped. A FICO score over 700 is considered "good"; the majority of credit scores fall between 600 and 750.

Credit score: A numerical value that is reportedly a measurement of how an individual has used credit in the past. Often it is used as a barometer of credit risk, where a higher credit score signals lower credit risk.

Sufficient Income?

While the past is a pretty good indicator of how a consumer will handle their credit in the future, it is not the sole determinate of consumer credit risk. Lenders also consider whether the borrower has enough income to repay the new debt. This then raises the question of how much debt a consumer can afford.

Fixed Payments Approach One measurement is to examine the amount of monthly income versus the amount of monthly fixed payments. Fixed payments include rent or mortgage payments; debt payments such as student loans, car payments, and credit card payments; as well as other fixed monthly payments such as health club memberships, insurance premiums, and any other fixed rental payments such as for a storage space.

It is suggested that the maximum amount of fixed payments a consumer should have is 50% of their net income (that is, income after taxes and deductions) or 35% of their gross monthly income. If after including the payment for the new debt the borrower is under this 50% or 35% level, then the borrower does have sufficient income to handle the new debt.

Debt-to-Income Ratio Approach Another measurement uses the total monthly debt burden, excluding mortgage payments, relative to net monthly income. This debt-to-income ratio approach takes the borrower's total monthly debt payments, excluding mortgage or rent payments, and divides that amount by the net, or after-tax, monthly income.

It is suggested that the debt-to-income ratio should be no more than 0.20; that is, a borrower should have a debt-to-income ratio less than 20%. Thus, if after including the additional monthly payment for the new loan the ratio is greater than 0.20, the borrower may have problems making the monthly payments.

With either calculation the lender must also consider how the borrower's income may change in the future. If the borrower is young, well educated, and in a field that is likely to expand in the future, the lender may reasonably assume that the borrower's income will increase in the future and thus approve a loan even though the borrower currently has a high debt-to-income ratio. On the other hand, if the borrower's income is not likely to increase significantly in the future, the limits will more likely be strictly enforced.

Therefore, while the past is important in determining a consumer's credit risk, the future must also be considered. Thus evaluating consumer credit risk is not as simple as it may seem at first. However, lending to business borrowers and assessing their credit risk in doing so is even more complicated than it is for consumer lending.

13-1c Credit Risk with Business Borrowers

While the past is a very good indicator of future behavior for consumers' credit risk, assessing credit risk for business borrowers is a bit more complicated. Businesses come in so many different sizes and face so many rapidly changing challenges that simply looking at how things have gone in the past may not give an indication of how the firm will repay its debts in the future. Simply put, lending to businesses is hard. So, in addition to the five (now six) Cs relating to business, lenders attempt to minimize credit risk using the following techniques:

- **Specialized lending.** Not all business lenders lend money to every type of business. Remember, one of the things banks do is overcome the adverse selection problem by gathering information on potential borrowers. Lenders need to gather information and data on specific industries so they can learn about those industries and detect future problems. With this industry-specific knowledge they will be better equipped to judge the amount of credit risk they as lenders face.
- **Understanding cash flows.** One of the major reasons businesses fail, especially small and middle-market firms (those with annual revenues of $5 to $100 million) is because of a lack of cash flow. Thus lenders have to understand the threats to their borrowers' cash flows. Remember, cash flows can come from operations (sales less expenses), investments, and financing.
- **Secondary sources of repayment.** Banks often ask/require business borrowers to provide a secondary source of repayment other than their income from ongoing operations. These secondary sources include:
  - **collateral**, which involves pledging an asset that the lender can seize and sell if the borrower defaults;
  - **compensating balance**, whereby the borrower keeps a savings account with a specified balance amount that the lender can seize if the borrower defaults; and
  - **personal guarantees**, through which lenders sometimes require the management of a firm—especially if they are also the major shareholders or owners of the firm—to sign a personal guarantee of the business's debt. This means that if the business is unable to repay the debt, the management/owners of the firm must personally repay the business's debt. The use of personal guarantees in business lending remains very controversial.
- **Close monitoring.** After the business loan is made the lender has to keep a close eye on how market conditions are changing for that borrower. Even with the close monitoring the lender needs to be able to limit the actions of the borrower. This is often done through loan covenants. All of this is designed to limit the moral hazard problem that lenders face when they make business loans.

While credit risk is an important risk banks face, it is not the only one. When interest rates change, banks can be affected both positively and negatively. This interest rate risk is the topic we examine next.

SECTION REVIEW

Q1) Bob and Karen are both applying for a consumer loan. They both have the same current level of income and the same current level of debt. Why might Karen be more likely to get the loan if Karen is younger?

Q2) Explain why not every asset can be used as collateral on a loan.

Q3) Sunita is a loan officer at a bank. She is considering making a loan to a local business, but she is worried about the "conditions" variable of the five Cs of credit risk. What is Sunita worried about?

a. The people who are borrowing the money may not have the legal capacity to borrow in the name of the firm.

b. The firm may not have sufficient cash flow to make regular payments as required by the loan.

c. The market in which the firm is selling may experience a downturn in the near future, making it difficult for the borrower to repay the loan.

d. Laws might change and negatively affect the ability of the borrower to repay the loan.

13-2 Interest Rate Risk

In the world of commercial banking, **interest rate risk** is the risk that changes in interest rates will negatively affect the standing of the commercial bank. For decades after World War II, commercial banks in the United States did not have to worry much about interest rate risk. During this time period, the Federal Reserve used its monetary policy tools to keep overall interest rates low and stable. To discourage competition, the banking system was heavily regulated with things such as Regulation Q that kept interest rates on deposits low and stable. Thus interest rates did not change much and banks did not face much interest rate risk.

Interest rate risk: The chance that the value of an asset will change because of a change in interest rates.

Over the past few decades, however, with the Federal Reserve changing how it conducts monetary policy and allowing interest rates to fluctuate much more, combined with banking deregulation that has caused banks to face more and more competition for both deposit and loan business, times have changed dramatically. Now banks have to worry a great deal about interest rate risk. As interest rates change, both interest expense (how much banks have to pay for funds) and interest income (how much banks earn on their assets such as loans that pay interest) can change significantly.

13-2a Managing Interest Rate Risk

Thus banks need to "manage" their interest rate risk. The first step in managing risk is understanding why the risk exists and then figuring out just how much exposure a bank has. Keep in mind that changes in interest rates affect both sides of a bank's balance sheet.

When interest rates change, bank assets such as consumer loans, business loans, bonds the bank holds, federal funds sold, and other investments are affected. Similarly, changes in interest rates affect bank liabilities, such as the interest the bank must pay on demand deposits, savings accounts, and newly issued certificates of deposits (CDs).

Remember also that bank deposits tend to be short-term, whereas loans tend to be long-term. Since long-term interest rates are usually higher than short-term interest rates, banks often have a positive interest rate spread

$$\mathbf{IR}_{\text{spread}} = \mathbf{IR}_{\text{loans}} - \mathbf{IR}_{\text{deposits}}$$

Let's say a bank has a deposit customer who puts $10,000 into a 6-month CD, and the bank pays 3% on that 6-month CD. At the end of six months the depositor rolls over the funds in the CD for another six months. This rolling over continues every six months.

Let's also suppose that the bank then lends the vast majority of that $10,000 on a 5-year auto loan and charges a 5% fixed interest rate on that loan. (We will ignore required reserves for now.) So, the bank has a positive interest rate spread of 200 basis points, or two percentage points.

But there is a problem. Interest rates don't remain constant. Let's say that interest rates increase by 100 basis points. The bank now has to pay a higher interest rate on that CD when it matures, but because the loan has a fixed interest rate, the interest rate on it does not change. What has changed is the bank's interest rate spread, which has decreased by half to only 100 basis points, or one percentage point. It earns 5% but must pay 4% on the 6-month CD.

Remember why we care about this: The interest rate spread is one of the ways a bank generates earnings to pay salaries, donate to the community, and pay its shareholders. When that interest rate spread decreases, the bank's earnings also decrease, which worries stockholders. The bank might have to consider cutting expenses such as the salaries of its employees, or, if things get really bad, it might have to sell some of its assets.

13-2b Gap Analysis

As the old saying goes, an ounce of prevention is worth a pound of cure. Since interest rate risk is a major issue for banks, they want to make sure they know just how much interest risk they face. One way to measure interest rate risk exposure is by comparing the amount of interest rate–sensitive assets a bank has with the amount of interest rate–sensitive liabilities it has. This is called "gap analysis" or, sometimes more appropriately, "**interest rate gap analysis.**"

Interest rate gap analysis: The difference between the amount of assets and the amount of liabilities on which interest rates are due to reset during a specific time period.

In gap analysis bank management classifies assets as either sensitive to interest rates or not. They then do the same thing with bank liabilities: classify them as either sensitive to interest rates or not. If an asset's or liability's interest rate will change within a year or sooner it usually is labeled "interest rate sensitive."

Then the gap is simply

$$\textbf{Gap} = \textbf{Amount of IR-sensitive assets} - \textbf{Amount of IR-sensitive liabilities}$$

or

$$\textbf{Gap} = \textbf{IRSA} - \textbf{IRSL}$$

This can be done either in dollar amounts or as a percentage of total assets and percentage of total liabilities. So, if

IRSA > IRSL, the gap is positive.
IRSA < IRSL, the gap is negative.
IRSA = IRSL, the gap is zero.

Managing the Gap

If a bank thinks that interest rates will increase the future, they want a positive gap. That is, they want to hold more interest rate–sensitive assets than interest rate–sensitive liabilities because as interest rates increase, they will experience an increase in their income (more interest-sensitive assets) more than an increase in their interest expense.

But if a bank thinks that the interest rate will decline, they want a negative gap. That is, they want to hold more interest rate–sensitive liabilities than interest rate–sensitive assets. To understand why, think about what happens when interest rates fall: Banks want to take advantage of the lower interest rates by paying less on deposits and other sources of funds, such as debts it issues. However, this happens only if the bank holds a large amount of interest rate–sensitive liabilities. At the same time, when interest rates are falling, the interest income the bank earns also falls, so to offset this negative impact the bank must hold more interest rate–sensitive liabilities than interest rate–sensitive assets.

Think of it this way

$$\boldsymbol{\Delta}\textbf{Income} = \textbf{Gap} \times \boldsymbol{\Delta}\textbf{IR}$$

So, if interest rates change by 200 basis points or 2 percentage points or 0.02, and a bank has a gap of a positive \$5 million, then its income or earnings increase by \$100,000:

$$\boldsymbol{\Delta}\textbf{Income} = \textbf{\$5 million} \times \textbf{0.02} = \textbf{\$100,000}$$

Nice! Now the bank has an additional \$100,000 to pay salaries, support local community events, or pay stockholders. If instead the bank had a negative gap of \$3 million and interest rates increased by the same amount, its income would decrease by \$60,000.

While this is a nice, simple analysis that is used often, it has a problem. Remember, not all assets and liabilities have the same maturities. So banks can measure the gap at intervals by lumping assets and liabilities together based on their maturities. This gives a measurement of what the gap is over different time periods. For example, a bank may have a positive gap of $5 million over 1 year, with an incremental gap of a negative $2 million in the next 3 months, and so on.

13-2c Duration Analysis

While gap analysis is a simple and widely used tool, it misses that some assets or liabilities are more sensitive to interest rate changes than are others, even if the frequency of adjustment is the same. One way to address this is to use the concept of duration.[1]

Duration is the measurement of the life of a bond or any debt instrument. It can also be a measurement of the sensitivity of the price of a bond to a change in interest rate. Duration measures the time it takes for the bondholder or debt holder to recover the price paid for the bond or amount lent from all of the discounted future cash flows from the bond or debt instrument. The discount rate for calculating the present value of the cash flow is the bond's or debt instrument's yield. So, if the bond price and yield changes, so does its duration.

Duration of a bond: The weighted average of time until repayment of the price of a bond with a fixed cash flow; also called Maculay duration.

Duration is the weighted average of times until payment, with their weights proportionate to the present value of the payment. One way to think about it uses a two-step process. For simplicity let's assume we are looking at a bond:

1. Calculate the weight placed on each payment or cash flow from the bond. The weight (W) is simply the present value of that payment, discounted by the bond's yield; that present value then is made relative to the bond price.

$$W = \frac{\dfrac{\textit{Payment}}{(1+r)^t}}{\textit{Bond price}}$$

2. Plug those weights into the formula for each time period (1, 2, 3, etc.)

$$\textbf{Duration} = \textbf{W}_\textbf{i} + \textbf{2W}_\textbf{2} + \textbf{3W}_\textbf{3} + \textbf{4W}_\textbf{4} + \cdots + \textbf{TW}_\textbf{t}$$

More generally, the equation is

$$\textbf{Duration} = \frac{\sum_{t=1}^{n} t \times \dfrac{\textbf{Payment}_t}{(1+r)^t}}{\textbf{Bond price}} = \frac{\sum_{t=1}^{n} t \times \dfrac{\textbf{Payment}_t}{(1+r)^t}}{\sum_{t=1}^{n} \dfrac{\textbf{Payment}_t}{(1+r)^t}}$$

It is just the present values of the cash payments from holding the bond weighted by how long you have to wait (that's the *t*) as a percentage of the total payments you are going to get from holding the bond (that's the bond price). So, the longer you have to wait to get paid, or the longer the *t*, the longer the bond's duration.

Or, if interest rates increase, the duration of the bond is reduced. Remember the inverse relationship between interest rates and bond prices: If interest rates increase, bond prices decrease, and thus the fraction increases (notice *r* is in the numerator as well).

Or, by the same logic, if the interest rates decrease, the duration of the bond increases.

1 A related concept is modified duration, which is the percentage change in the price of a bond for a unit change in the yield of the bond.

Or, the higher the coupon rate, the shorter the duration because the payment variable increases. The logic is the higher the coupon rate, the more of the bond's value you get back faster, so the shorter the duration.

13-2d Banks, Duration, and Interest Rate Risk

A bank calculates the duration of each asset and liability it holds, then it calculates a duration gap as

$$\textbf{Duration gap} = \frac{\textbf{Asset duration} \times \textbf{Asset}}{\textbf{Asset}} - \frac{\textbf{Liability duration} \times \textbf{Liability}}{\textbf{Asset}}$$

So,

$$\textbf{Duration gap} = \textbf{Asset duration} - \textbf{Liability duration}\left(\frac{\textbf{Liability}}{\textbf{Asset}}\right)$$

where Asset is the market value of the asset and Liability is the market value of the liability.

The duration gap is the difference between the weighted (by the assets) duration of the bank's assets and the weighted (by the liabilities) duration of the liabilities, adjusted for the bank's asset size. If the duration gap is zero, interest rate changes affect the value of the bank's assets and liabilities equally, leaving the value of the bank unchanged.

Thus, bank management has to make a decision about the size of the duration gap it wants. By doing so, bank management is deciding how much interest rate risk they want to face. But interest rate risk is only one of the risks bank management needs to manage. Another important risk is liquidity risk. We turn our attention to this important risk next.

SECTION REVIEW

Q1) Judy runs a bank and believes interest rates will increase in the future. Explain what size interest rate gap the bank should have and why.

Q2) Explain the concept of duration to someone who has no training in economics.

Q3) You hold a portfolio of bonds. You read in the financial press that market interest rates have increased. Holding everything else constant, what has just happened to the duration of your bond portfolio?

a. Increased since bond prices have fallen
b. Decreased since bond prices have risen
c. Increased since bond prices have risen
d. Decreased since bond prices have fallen

13-3 Liquidity Risk

Liquidity risk[2] is one of the oldest risks in factional reserve banking. Remember, banks have long-term assets, such as loans and bonds, but short-term liabilities, such as demand deposits and money market deposit accounts. So, if many (or all) of the depositors show up at once and want funds from their accounts the bank is in trouble—it simply does not have enough liquid assets to meet the needs of its depositors.

Liquidity risk: The risk that a financial firm will not be able to meet its current and/or future cash needs.

A lack of liquidity, or liquidity risk, can come about as the result of an unexpected increase in withdrawals by depositors and/or by an unexpected increase in loans or payoffs of other liabilities that come due. An unexpected increase in loans could come from the bank making prior loan commitments (such as standby letters of credit) that the bank did not expect to turn into loans. The problem with these unexpected increases in borrowing is that many of these loans may quickly become problem loans because of a lack of repayment by the borrower.

To manage a liquidity risk bank, managers need to keep an eye on the sources of liquidity the bank has. If liquidity is threatened, they need to contemplate various potential solutions.

13-3a Sources of Liquidity

Primary Reserves

A bank's primary reserves include vault cash—the little scraps of Federal Reserve notes they hold in the bank vault—deposits at the Fed, and deposits at other commercial banks. Primary reserves are the most liquid assets the bank holds; the problem with them is they pay very low yields (deposits at the Fed and deposits at other banks) or zero yield (cash). So, while holding high levels of primary reserves help to ensure against a lack of liquidity, the opportunity cost of holding high levels of primary reserves can be substantial.

Secondary Reserves

Secondary reserves, as the name suggests, are the next most liquid assets the bank holds, second to primary reserves. Secondary reserves include Treasury bills, federal funds sold, federal government agency debt, commercial paper, and so on. While these secondary reserves generally have a higher return than primary reserves, they tend to be less liquid, that is, more difficult and expensive to turn into cash, than primary reserves.

Bank Loans

Commercial banks usually make loans for the interest income (and fees) they earn from them, not as a source of liquidity. But some loans, such as home mortgages and student loans, are securitizable, meaning they can be packaged and sold and thus provide liquidity to a bank. In addition, for some business loans there may exist a secondary market, again providing liquidity for a bank if necessary.

Securities

Banks usually hold longer-term securities (e.g., Treasury bonds and notes, corporate bonds) for interest income. As with bank loans, a secondary market may exist for these assets and thus provide liquidity to the bank.

---

2 The Federal Reserve Bank of San Francisco offers a definition of *liquidity risk* as the risk a financial firm "... will not be able to meet its current and future cash flow and collateral needs, both expected and unexpected, without materially affecting its daily operations or overall financial condition." See Jose A. Lopez, "What Is Liquidity Risk?" FRBSF *Economic Letter*, October 24, 2008. http://www.frbsf.org/economic-research/publications/economic-letter/2008/october/liquidity-risk/.

As you can see, there are trade-offs in managing liquidity risk: To lower liquidity risk, a bank has to accept lower returns. But those lower returns could hurt its profitability and thus its ability to continue in business. Thus a balance needs to be struck between liquidity and profitability. But what if bank management gets it wrong? If the bank suffers from a lack of liquidity, what can be done?

13-3b Solutions to Lack of Liquidity

While a bank may have several options for dealing with a lack of liquidity, none of them are perfect, and they all involve some type of trade-off. Some of the downsides to these solutions can be very costly indeed.

Borrow Federal Funds

The bank could go to the federal funds market and borrow funds from another bank with excess liquidity. Keep in mind, borrowing in the fed funds market is only a short-term or temporary solution to a lack of liquidity. Also keep in mind that if many banks are suffering a lack of liquidity, or fear that they might be short of liquidity in the near future, the federal funds market might collapse as banks refuse to lend to each other.

Borrow from the Fed

If the bank is a member of the Federal Reserve system it could go to the discount window and borrow funds from the Fed (if the bank has sufficient qualifying assets). But this might not be a perfect solution because going to the Fed carries a stigma effect. That is, banks that borrow from the Fed might be labeled as "in trouble" because they are turning to the Fed for funds. This stigma effect could result in depositors pulling more funds from the bank and thus make the lack of liquidity problem even worse.

Increase Deposits

If a bank could increase the level of deposits, it would have more cash on hand. How can a bank increase its level of deposits? Perhaps it could increase the interest rates it pays on deposits. This might, however, reduce the interest rate spread the bank enjoys and threaten the bank's level of profitability.

Sell Liquid Assets

By selling its Treasury bills, commercial paper, and other liquid assets, the bank could raise cash quickly and cheaply. If other banks are in the same position and are selling their liquid assets, however, the price these assets would fetch in the secondary market may fall rapidly. Thus selling assets at "fire sale" prices could be very costly for the bank.

Issue Commercial Paper

Commercial paper is short-term unsecured debt. Banks issue commercial paper as a way to raise cash. The problem is that if the bank is already seen as being "in trouble," finding buyers for more commercial paper that it seeks to sell may be difficult.

13-3c How Much Liquidity Is Enough?

Then comes the question: How much liquidity does a bank need? The traditional answer was to compare the level of liquid assets at a bank to those of similar banks in the same geographical region. This "benchmarking" against similar banks was fine as long as all of the other banks in the region had "sufficient" levels of liquidity. As the financial crisis that began in 2008 demonstrated, this was not a safe assumption to make!

In response to the crisis the Basel Committee on Banking Supervision laid out two measurements it believes can and should be applied to all banks of significant size. The first is called the **liquidity coverage ratio**, which compares the level of easy-to-sell liquid assets to the total cash outflows that are expected over the next 30 calendar days. The goal is a ratio equal to or greater than 1. Banks' liquidity coverage ratios began being measured in 2011, but it will not be fully in place in the United States until January 1, 2017.[3]

Liquidity coverage ratio: The ratio of a financial firm's liquid assets to its projected net cash outflows.

The second ratio in the Basel Committee's new capital requirements, called Basel III, is a more structural measurement called the **net stable funding ratio**. This requires banks to maintain a certain level of stable funding that depends on the liquidity of their assets and the extent of off-balance exposures over the next 12 months.[4] This measurement tries to ensure that if a bank suffers an increase in demand from its loan commitments, it will not suffer a shortage of liquidity. The net stable funding ratio will not be implemented until January 1, 2019.

Net stable funding ratio: The proportion of a bank's long-term assets funded by stable, long-term sources, including bank customer deposits, long-term bank borrowing, and bank capital.

While liquidity risk is one of the oldest risks banks face, we have yet to determine a perfect way to measure it, nor do we have a foolproof way of managing it. As the recent financial crisis has demonstrated, liquidity risk is an ever-present issue banks must confront.

The list of risks banks must manage is long, and we are not done with them. Next we look at other risks banks must manage.

SECTION REVIEW

Q1) Bill is confused about why liquidity risk management is such a problem for banks. He says, "It's simple. If banks are worried about liquidity risk, why don't they just hold a lot of liquid assets?" How would you answer Bill's question?

Q2) The Federal Reserve was established, in part, to be the "lender of last resort" to the banking system. Why can't we rely on the Federal Reserve to ensure there is enough liquidity in the banking system?

Q3) Which of the following is *not* a source of liquidity for banks?

a. Commercial paper
b. Real estate holdings, such as a bank building
c. Securitizing loans
d. Deposits at the Federal Reserve

3 See the Federal Reserve's press release on the implementation of the Basel Committees' suggestion on liquidity coverage ratio, available at: http://www.federalreserve.gov/newsevents/press/bcreg/20140903a.htm/.

4 According to the Basel Committee on Banking Supervision, the net stable funding ratio is designed to limit banks' "over reliance" on short-term funding and off balance sheet activities. See http://www.bis.org/bcbs/publ/d295.pdf.

Other Risks

13-4

While credit risk, interest rate risk, and liquidity risk are important risks that can threaten the very survivability of banks, they are not the only risks banks face. If not addressed properly, other risks can be just as dangerous to a bank's profitability, if not survivability. What are these "other" risks banks face?

Operational Risk

According to the Basel Committee, **operational risk** is defined as "the risk of direct or indirect loss resulting from inadequate or failed internal processes, people and systems or from external events." That's a pretty broad statement, but it means to say that losses can come about from a failure of the operation of the bank. This could include things such as theft (by either customers or employees), fraud, natural disasters, lawsuits, and terrorist attacks.

Operational risk: The risk of loss resulting from an inadequate or failed internal process or external event.

Some also add to this definition "loss of reputation" and "losses from failed strategic moves." The former can come about for a number of reasons: bad publicity, poorly chosen words by bank executives, and so on. The latter can come from a failed merger attempt or the acquisition of another bank that did not work out as planned.

Technology risk is also generally included under operational risk. Technology risk includes the losses that come about from a computer system failure or crash that result in lost earnings for the bank. The hacking of computer systems and cyber terrorism are more recently a growing part of technology and operational risks for banks. While the extent of operational risk is difficult to measure, it is still a risk bank management must attempt to manage.

Foreign Exchange and Country Risk

Banking, like so many other industries, can be affected by what goes on around the rest of the world. Changes in the value of currencies, or exchange rates, can either directly or indirectly affect a bank's profitability. Rapid swings in exchange rates can have a direct and negative effect if a bank is holding a foreign currency and the value of that currency decreases dramatically. Similarly, exchange rate swings may negatively affect the ability of a bank customer to repay their loans if that customer conducts business in a country that sees the value of its currency depreciate.

Similarly, whenever a bank's customer is affected by what happens in another country, the bank faces indirect country risk. Suppose a bank has written a number of loans to a firm that sells agricultural equipment to customers in Brazil. Suddenly there is political instability in Brazil, the Brazilian economy weakens, and the ability of Brazilian farmers to pay for their agricultural equipment plummets. Now the bank's customer is unable to repay their loans. Thus the bank faces country risk.

Bank management needs to be aware of the extent of exchange rate and country risk their bank faces. Often this risk exposure may be difficult to recognize before a crisis hits, but once a crisis in either the foreign exchange market or in another country erupts, US bank stability is threatened.

Market Risk

Market risk has to do with the potential loss a bank might suffer when the market value of its trading assets changes. This risk becomes a significant problem when market conditions change rapidly and thus the market value of a bank's trading assets decreases significantly.

Market risk: The risk of a loss occurring as a result of the decline in the market value of an asset.

Market risk proved to be a major problem during the financial crisis that began in 2008. The market value of banks' trading assets, such as mortgage-backed securities, fell dramatically. Many now view these market risks as a major threat to the stability of the banking system. As a result, in 2010 Congress passed the Wall Street Reform and Consumer Protection Act, which includes the Volcker Rule: a ban on banks holding assets for the purpose of trading and speculating for their own gain. The Volcker Rule has run into a great deal of opposition, however, especially from banks that want to continue to trade assets. These banks claim they can now manage market risk on their own and should not be prevented from trading assets for their own gain.

Risk management is an important responsibility of bank management. Investors, depositors, and policymakers all have an interest in evaluating the performance of bank management. Next we examine how bank management is doing by evaluating various measurements of bank performance.

SECTION REVIEW

Q1) Explain how a bank that makes only loans in the domestic market can still face exchange rate risk.

Q2) Explain how the Volcker Rule was designed to limit market risk banks face.

Q3) Which of the following is a type of operational risk banks face?

a. A borrower does not repay as promised.

b. The bank's computer system crashes.

c. Interest rates increase, requiring the bank to pay more for deposits.

d. All of these.

Bank Performance

13-5

One piece of evidence of how well a bank is managing its risks is the bank's performance. One can evaluate a bank's performance by looking at its income statement (a flow concept) or at a performance measure from its balance sheet (a stock concept).

One issue that that arises is what to do with these performance measurements. Some erroneously believe that simply by examining these measures one can arrive at a sound judgment on the quality of a bank's management and its risk management in particular. Life isn't that simple. The tools we are going to look at are just that: tools. They are not a crystal ball that allows one to see into the future, nor are they a precise, perfect measuring device. Instead they are just one of the many tools we should use in evaluating the quality of bank management and its ability to manage risk.

13-5a Income Statement

We can compare the different components of a bank's income statement to those of similar banks to get an idea of how a bank is performing. A bank's income statement looks at explicit revenues and expenses over a specific time period, usually a year. The different parts of an income statement are:

- **Gross interest income.** This is the income a bank generates primarily from loans, but also from investment income, federal funds sold, lending to other depository institutions, and other interest income such as that from investments. Banks usually report income from leases under gross interest income. The level of gross interest income depends on the asset makeup of a bank's balance sheet and interest rate levels. In general, as interest rates increase, interest income increases.
- **Gross interest expense.** This totals the funds the bank must pay out in terms of interest. The largest component is interest paid on deposits, but interest expense also includes interest paid on federal funds purchased, on subordinated debt, and on other borrowings by the bank. The level of interest income depends on the makeup of a bank's liabilities and interest rate levels. In general, as interest rates increase, interest expense increases.

These two major components then are used to calculate a bank's net interest income:

$$\textbf{Net interest income (NII)} = \textbf{Gross interest income} - \textbf{Gross interest expense}$$

From net interest expense we subtract the **loan loss provision**, which is the amount of income a bank adds to bank capital for this time period. Remember, this is done to set aside funds to write down nonperforming assets.

Loan loss provision: A noncash expense that banks set aside as an allowance to cover losses on loans.

Next we consider noninterest income and noninterest expenses:

- **Noninterest income.** This includes all of the fees that banks generate. These can be fees associated with a variety of financial services banks provide, including off balance sheet services, as well as fees charged on transactions accounts, ATM fees, credit card fees, trust services, and so on.
- **Noninterest expense.** This includes things such as salaries and benefits for the bank staff, office equipment, marketing expenses, payment for deposit insurance, and other operating expenses.

These then are used to calculate pretax net income

$$\textbf{Pretax net income} = \textbf{NII} + \textbf{Noninterest income} - \textbf{Noninterest expense}$$

From this, income tax paid is subtracted to arrive at the bank's net income.

13-5b Balance Sheet

We can then use the net income for a period and combine it with information from the bank's balance sheet to determine two very popular measures: return on assets (ROA) and return on equity (ROE).

Return on Assets

It is generally thought that if a bank's ROA is increasing, that is a sign that the bank is well run. This is because ROA is calculated by

$$\text{ROA} = \frac{\textbf{Net income}}{\textbf{Total assets}}$$

So, a higher ROA suggests that, holding total assets constant, the bank is generating more net income. Well, that sounds good, doesn't it? More income from the same amount of assets must mean that bank is being more efficient.

Or does it?

Think back to our discussion of bank assets. One of the largest—if not *the* largest—assets of a bank is its loan portfolio. What if a bank's loan portfolio is *not* increasing but the bank is generating more income from that loan portfolio? How might that happen? Maybe the bank is writing the same amount of loans as in the past but the current loans are much riskier! Riskier loans carry with them higher interest rates. Is that how the bank is generating higher income levels off the same amount of total assets? If so, a higher ROA does not necessarily mean the bank is being better run than it was in the past.

Return on Equity

In general, if a bank's ROE is increasing, it is a signal that the bank is being well run. That is because ROE is calculated by

$$\text{ROE} = \frac{\textbf{Net income}}{\textbf{Equity capital}}$$

So a higher ROE suggests that, holding the amount of capital constant, the bank is generating more net income. That suggests that bank management is putting stockholders' money (equity) to better use than before since the bank is now generating more net income from that equity.

But is it that simple?

Let's start with the definition of ROE and multiply it by total assets/total assets. You will agree that multiplying something by 1 does not change it. Then let's rearrange the variables a bit

$$\text{ROE} = \frac{\textbf{Net income}}{\textbf{Total assets}} \times \frac{\textbf{Total assets}}{\textbf{Equity capital}}$$

We have ROE = ROA × Equity multiplier, where the equity multiplier is simply total assets/equity capital.

So the ROE is increasing either because the ROA or the equity multiplier is also increasing. We already pointed out that an increased ROA is not necessarily a good sign. But what does a higher equity multiplier tell us?

A higher equity multiplier for a bank could mean that the bank is being better run; that is, for the same amount of equity capital, the bank is able to generate more total assets. So, bank management is putting the stockholders' money to better use than before since it is creating more assets from the same amount of equity!

Or, it could be horrible news.

Consider two banks: bank A and bank B. Each bank has $100 million in assets. Bank A has $90 million in liabilities and $10 million of equity to back up its assets. Bank B has $95 million in liabilities and only $5 million of equity to back up its assets. Clearly, bank B is a riskier bank because it holds less capital than it might need if it has written down some of its assets. In terms of the equity multiplier (EM), however, bank B looks better!

$$\text{EM}_A = \$100 \text{ million}/\$10 \text{ million} = 10$$

$$\text{EM}_B = \$100 \text{ million}/\$5 \text{ million} = 20$$

Notice in this case bank B has a higher equity multiplier. Thus, if everything else is the same, bank B will also have a higher ROE than bank A. But bank B is not a better run bank than bank A; it is actually more risky!

So what does a higher ROE or a higher ROA really tell you? Does it indicate the bank is better run if ROE or ROA are increasing? Clearly, no, not necessarily. If a given bank has a higher ROE or a higher ROA, is that bank better run than the other? Again, the answer is clearly no. Thus ROE and ROA are just tools that hopefully lead analysts to ask more questions about how a bank is actually being run.

This is why measuring bank performance is so difficult. One cannot, and should not, merely rely on financial ratios to determine how well a bank is being run or how well the bank is managing its risks. Instead, ratio analysis that uses a bank's income statement and balance sheet are only the start of a proper bank analysis.

SECTION REVIEW

Q1) Explain why an increase in a bank's ROA may or may not be a reason to purchase the bank's stock.

Q2) Why is it that an increase in a bank's ROE might be a sign that the bank is taking on more risk?

Q3) You read that a bank's net interest income has decreased. Why might this have occurred?

a. Gross interest income increased more than gross interest expense decreased.

b. Both gross interest income and gross interest expense increased by the same amount.

c. Gross interest income decreased, whereas gross interest expense increased.

d. Both gross interest income and gross interest expense decreased by the same amount.

13-6 Conclusion

Risk is one of those concepts that people often hear, but if asked what it really means, and how it applies to banks, these same people are often at a loss. Even if one can define risk, managing risks becomes even more difficult, especially for banks. In this chapter we looked at a variety of risks banks face and how they try to manage them. We reviewed the important issue of credit risk and how banks manage it differently when it comes to consumer lending verses business lending. We then discussed interest rate risk and how banks use gap analysis and duration analysis to deal with interest rate risk. We then examined liquidity risk and other risks banks face. We concluded by looking at how one might attempt to evaluate how a bank manages its risks by looking at bank performance. We saw this is anything but a clear-cut exercise; instead, using various ratios such as ROA and ROE are only the start of properly analyzing a bank.

IN THE NEWS. . .

Small Bank in Kansas Is a Financial Testing Ground

Nathaniel Popper
New York Times Deal Book
December 13, 2014

The redbrick bank in Weir, Kan., in a building cater-corner from the mortuary on Main Street, does not look much like a candidate for the bank of the future.

Inside, an Emerson boombox with a fully extended silver antenna is tuned to KJMK, Classic Hits. The huge steel vault, from the Mosler Safe Company, was used to lock up former owners of the bank overnight during an armed heist in 1959. And the storage room in the back contains an old, unlabeled bottle of brown moonshine.

Beneath these holdovers, though, the Citizens Bank of Weir—or CBW, as it was renamed—has been taken apart and rebuilt, from its fiber optic cables up, so it can offer services not available at even the nation's largest banks.

The creation of the new bank, and the maintenance of the old one, are the work of a couple who were born in India and ended up in Kansas after living in Silicon Valley and passing through jobs at Google and Lehman Brothers.

Suresh Ramamurthi, 46, and his wife, Suchitra Padmanabhan, 44, bought CBW largely with their savings in 2009, just after the financial crisis. . . .

Their work is an unusual experiment: a new kind of mom-and-pop business trying to reshape a highly regulated and innovation-resistant industry. The new services that CBW is providing, like instant payments to any bank in the United States, direct remittance transfers abroad and specialized debit cards, might seem as if they should be painless upgrades in an age of high-frequency trading and interplanetary space missions. But with most banks, it still takes longer to send money to another country or even to another state than it does to travel the same distance.

The slowness of current methods of moving money is a widely acknowledged problem in the financial industry. The Federal Reserve has been holding meetings for its initiative, called Faster Payments, which has the goal of devising safe and speedy payment methods.

But hastening the movement of money creates risk for banks, because it generally means less time to catch fraudulent transactions. Having paid fines and penalties for the outsize risks they took before the financial crisis, banks are loath to take on new risks. They have been occupied with "getting their house in order," rather than introducing products, according to Steve Kenneally, the payment systems specialist at the American Bankers Association. . . .

The most obvious problem to attack was the difficulty of making instant money transfers from one bank account to another. This is already possible in many countries, including Mexico and Britain, but in the United States the primary option that consumers have to transfer money is still the A.C.H. payment. Requests for A.C.H. transfers are collected by banks and submitted in batches, once a day, and the banks receiving the transfers also process the payments once a day, leading to long waits. Wire transfers move faster, with some being settled in hours, but they cost significantly more, and are still not instant.

Last year, big banks helped scuttle a plan that would have expedited the A.C.H. system, in part because it would have jeopardized the fees they earn from wire transfers. Large banks are experimenting with faster transfer systems, like QuickPay from JPMorgan Chase, but these are generally instant only between customers of certain banks. . . .

The article describes a trade-off in two risks banks face: liquidity risk and operational risk. By speeding up payments, banks will be able to turn deposits into cash more quickly, thus increasing liquidity, but at the risk for more potential fraud. Is it worth it? Why or why not?

The article also points out that it may not be risks the banks are really concerned with. Why do you think a change in risk management has been so slow to come about?

14

Banking Regulation

14-1 Bank Regulation

In Chapter 7 we discussed the idea of why banks exist. Hopefully from that you were convinced that banks are special or, more to the point, banks are unique. Banks are special or unique in that they face a unique set of problems and challenges, which is why banks are so heavily regulated. In this chapter we dig further into this issue of bank regulation. After a quick review of why banks are so special and unique, we look into the different types of bank regulation in the United States. We then critically examine this regulatory structure and discuss when this system failed. We then contemplate what the future of global banking regulation might look like. Along the way though, remember that banks are special.

14-1a Banks Are Special

Remember that banks exist primarily to solve the asymmetric information problem. Before financial transactions take place, banks face the adverse selection problem—essentially, low-quality borrowers want to borrow money. The key to solving the adverse selection problem in financial markets hinged on a better flow of information: better information collection, government-required disclosure, and/or bank screening of potential borrowers. For banks, the key to solving the adverse selection problem is more and better information.

More and better information is also one of the main ways banks solve the other asymmetric information problem: moral hazard. Remember, a moral hazard comes about after a financial contract has been created. A moral hazard exists when the creation of the financial contract alters behaviors by changing incentives. So, the moral hazard occurs after a financial contract, such as a bank loan, is created. Recall that the key to banks solving the moral hazard problem is monitoring borrowers or getting more and better information about what borrowers are doing after the loan is made.

So, to solve the asymmetric information problems, banks clearly need more and better information about their customers. Contemplate for a moment how much information about you your bank has. If you really think about this, it becomes a bit shocking. For example, every time you use your debit card for a purchase, your bank knows about it. Every time your employer pays you and your check is directly deposited into your account, your bank knows about it.

The same holds true for businesses. Banks know a great deal about their business customers. A bank has all sorts of information about a business's cash flow if the business has its demand deposit account at the bank. What does the bank do with all of this proprietary information? It uses this information to solve the asymmetric information problem.

Tying Concepts Together

Bank Regulation and the Overall Economy

Banks are special not only because of the information they have but also because their failure can have a dramatic impact on the entire economic system. Remember when we examined the simple deposit multiplier in Chapter 7, and when we examined the money supply multiplier in Chapter 10, we learned about the important role banks play in the creation of money. If the banking system fails to function properly, this money-creating process does not take place. Also, recall, as we reviewed in Chapter 6 with the aggregate supply/aggregate demand framework, if the money supply does not increase fast enough, total spending in the economy can decline and the real level of GDP may fall, pushing the economy into a recession or even an economic depression.

Thus, bank regulation seeks to ensure that the banking system continues to play its role in the money creation process so that the economy can continue to expand. It can be argued that no other entity in a market economy plays such an important role as do banks. Banks are indeed special.

14-1b Bank Regulation in the United States

You can see banks have a huge amount of information about individuals and about firms. Banks need this information, in part, to solve the asymmetric information problem. But this then raises a touchy issue: Because banks have so much private and proprietary information, it can be argued that society cannot allow just anyone to open a bank.

Thus, if you want to open your own bank, you cannot. You must apply to the government for permission to do so. That is, you must obtain a **bank charter**. A bank charter is a legal document that stipulates how a bank will be organized and regulated. Bank charters authorize the organization of banks and are issued either by a state banking agency or by the Office of the Comptroller of Currency, which is part of the Treasury Department. The entity that issues the charter is responsible for making sure that the bank operates in a safe and sound manner and protects the information it collects.

Bank charter: Permission issued, usually by a government or government agency, to establish and operate a depository institution.

Since bank charters can be issued on either the state level, usually by the state banking commission, or on the federal level by the comptroller of the currency, the US banking system is often referred to as a **dual banking system**.

Dual banking system: A banking system where bank charters are granted by the national government as well as state or provincial governments.

The asymmetric information problem also exists for bank depositors. While the managers of a bank know whether their bank is well run, depositors and other outsiders do not, in part because outsiders can never see the assets of any bank in detail. A bank does not disclose to outsiders to whom they have made loans and for how much. Thus, it is difficult—if not impossible—for outsiders to truly judge the quality of a bank's assets. That is why banks, in the modern era, have **government-sponsored deposit insurance**.

Government-sponsored deposit insurance: Protection offered to depositors by a government agency that protects the depositors from losses that may occur if the depository institution becomes insolvent or fails.

In the United States since 1933 the FDIC has offered deposit insurance to banks. Since the FDIC offers deposit insurance, it regularly examines banks for safety and soundness. The level of FDIC deposit insurance was increased temporarily from $100,000 per account per institution to $250,000 as part of the Emergency Economic Stabilization Act of 2008. This level was made permanent under the Financial Reform Act of 2010. Note this government-sponsored deposit insurance applies only to deposits in US banks in the United States; thus, deposits in foreign branches of US banks are not covered by FDIC insurance.

Bank Products

Bank charters and government-sponsored deposit insurance are only two types of regulations that banks face. For a long time severe limits were placed on the types of financial services or products banks in the United States could offer.

As we discussed in Chapter 5, in the early days of the Great Depression of the 1930s it was believed that commercial bank involvement in the underwriting of stocks and bonds contributed to the wave of bank failures. In response to these fears Congress passed the Banking Act, more generally known as the Glass-Steagall Act, in 1933; among other things, this act separated commercial banking, investment banking, and the insurance industry. Under the Glass-Steagall Act, banks were forbidden from underwriting almost all stocks and bonds and were banned from selling insurance.[1]

1 Under the Glass-Steagall Act, commercial banks were still allowed to underwrite newly issued US Treasury bills, notes, and bonds; municipal general obligation bonds; and limited private placement of equities and debt. But these activities were relatively small compared with the "traditional" banking business of taking deposits and making loans.

By the 1960s the Glass-Steagall separation began to be slowly chipped away. Commercial banks realized that underwriting stocks and bonds was a very profitable business, and they wanted a piece of the action. Banks complained that they should be allowed to underwrite a wider variety of municipal bonds, as well as commercial paper, and be allowed to offer discount brokerage services to their customers. After numerous lawsuits and much negotiation, bank regulators acquiesced and allowed banks into these more lucrative and more risky markets.

But as time went on, banks wanted to be allowed to do even more. By 1987 the banking industry had convinced the Federal Reserve. In April 1987 the Fed allowed bank holding companies to establish Section 20 securities subsidiaries, called Section 20 affiliates, where banks could underwrite a wide variety of commercial paper, mortgage-backed securities, and municipal bonds.

Just a decade later, in 1997, the Fed went even further, allowing commercial banks to take over directly existing investment banks. Now banks didn't need to establish Section 20 affiliates; they could own investment banks outright. As a result there was a wave of commercial bank and investment bank mergers between 1997 and 2000.

In 1999 the nail was finally driven into Glass-Steagall's coffin with the passage of the Financial Services Modernization Act, sometimes called the Gramm-Leach-Bliley Act. Among other things, this act allowed for bank holding companies to morph into "financial services holding companies," that is, holding companies that could be made up of commercial banks *and* investment banks. The bill also allowed commercial banks to own directly subsidiaries that could underwrite securities. Thus the Glass-Steagall separation between investment and commercial banking was completely gone.

Geography

The limitation on bank services is not the only example of banks finding ways around banking regulation. Another example is how banks found ways around geographical limitations. As we learned in Chapter 5, since the founding of the country, banks were regulated mostly at the state level and were forbidden from branching across state lines. The McFadden Act of 1927 forced federally chartered banks to obey state laws when it came to branching, essentially making it impossible for all banks to cross state lines.

These geographical limitations, however, placed US banks at some great disadvantages. By being tied to only one state's economy, banks' asset diversification was greatly limited. To understand why, consider a bank in Iowa that cannot take deposits or make loans outside of the state of Iowa. If farmers in Iowa have a good harvest, everything works well for the Iowa bank: Deposits increase, agricultural loans are repaid as promised, the local economy booms, and the bank thrives.

Now imagine bad weather hits Iowa and farmers' harvests fall short of expectations. (Also assume there are undeveloped derivatives markets and weak crop insurance—still a reality today in many agricultural communities.) Now depositors are pulling their funds out of the Iowa bank and agriculture-based loans are not being repaid. The Iowa banks are now illiquid and insolvent; Iowa maybe tripping into a banking crisis.

This disastrous outcome could have been avoided, it was argued, if the Iowa banks could have also made loans in other states. These "out-of-state" loans would not have been so dependent on the economy of Iowa. So, with geographical diversification, even if there are crop failures in Iowa, the bank loans made in other states are unaffected and they continue to be repaid as promised. Thus the Iowa bank does not fail just because the economy in Iowa is falling apart.

Banks believed it was in their own interest to get around the restrictive geographical limitations they faced. Banks first attempted to get around these regulations by creating bank holding companies. The idea was a bank may not be able to have branches in more than one state, but a bank holding company could own banks in several different states at one time. Thus the creation of a bank holding company was a way around the McFadden Act.

But regulators didn't let this go unchecked. In 1956 Congress passed the Bank Holding Company Act (BHCA), which, among other things, gave the Federal Reserve the power to regulate bank holding companies *and* prohibited bank holding companies headquartered in one state from acquiring a bank in another state. The BHCA, for a while, slammed the door on cross-border branching.

The banks weren't done yet in their fight for geographical diversification. The banks finally won. In 1994 Congress passed the Riegle-Neal Interstate Banking Act (officially known as the Interstate Banking and Branching Efficiency Act), which allowed banks to merge across state lines, thus enabling them to have branches in other states.

While limitations on bank products and geographical restrictions were important components of banking regulation in the past, many regulations on banks are still in place in the United States. Let's look next at what other regulations still apply to US banks and how these regulations are enforced.

SECTION REVIEW

Q1) The Glass-Steagall Act of 1933 separated commercial banks, investment banks, and insurance companies. Explain how the act was slowly chipped away at before it was finally phased out in 1999.

Q2) Ted argues that we should return to the "old days" when banks were forbidden from branching across state lines. Ted believes this will make banks safer because they will concentrate on one, narrowly defined market. Evaluate Ted's argument.

Q3) What did the Riegle-Neil Act of 1994 allow US banks to do?

a. For the first time offer deposits with FDIC insurance

b. Offer checking accounts that paid interest

c. Have branches in many different states

d. Sell newly issued government securities

14-2 Bank Balance Sheet and Bank Capital

As we have seen, over time, limits on the products banks can offer have been greatly reduced. Similarly, geographical limitations on where banks can offer services have been essentially eliminated over the past few decades. Other regulations and restrictions on banks remain in place. While some of these regulations, such as bank capital levels, are continuing to change and evolve, others have remained fairly constant. Next let's look at how regulations have been applied to banks' balance sheets and capital levels over the years.

14-2a Balance Sheet Regulations

While banks have been successful in getting around product limitations and geographical limitations, they have faced a harder time getting around balance sheet regulations.

Loan and Credit Extension Amounts

On the asset side of the balance sheet, US banks have been limited in the amount of loans they can make to any one person or entity.[2] Currently, the maximum amount a national bank is allowed to lend or extend credit to one entity is 15% of the bank's combined capital and reserves on an unsecured loan. If the loan is secured by "readily marketable collateral," however, then the limit is 25%. These limits are considered necessary to ensure banks have a well-diversified loan portfolio, and this is seen as a way to limit corruption in bank lending.

Holding of Equities

Another, more controversial asset limitation placed on US banks has to do with the holding of equities. Proponents of banning banks from holding equities argue that this makes banks safer and limits the probability of contagion of financial market failures. Proponents of the ban point out that stock market crashes are not uncommon. If banks are allowed to hold large amounts of equities and stock prices fall dramatically, it is argued, the asset side of bank's balance sheet would contract, potentially making the bank insolvent. Thus, by holding equities, banks are made less stable and thus less safe, and therefore banks should be banned from holding significant amounts of equities.

On the other hand, proponents of lifting the ban on US banks holding equities argue that the ban actually makes banks *more* risky. Here is their logic: Imagine US banks and European banks both are trying to raise capital in the global financial markets. It is well known in finance that equities generally outperform bonds in the long run. So, European banks that are allowed to hold significant amounts of equities are, ceteris paribus, going to have higher returns than will US banks that are not allowed to hold significant amounts of equities. Thus potential investors are going to view European bank stocks as more favorable than US bank stocks. What can US banks do to make their stocks just as desirable as European bank stocks? The answer: US banks need higher-performing assets. That means US banks are going to hold more risky assets, such as risky loans, because of the risk/return trade-off. Look at what happens: By not allowing banks to hold significant amounts of equities, US banks are pushed into holding riskier assets, and thus US banks are made *less safe* by the ban.

So, which is it? Does the ban on equities make US banks safer or less safe? The debate rages on.

14-2b Liabilities: Regulation Q

While the debate over whether US banks can hold significant amounts of equities on the asset side of their balance sheet still rages, there also have been debates over regulation on the other side of a bank's balance sheet. On the liabilities side, for years there was a strict amount of regulation over what banks could pay in terms of interest on deposits. This was the famous—or infamous—Regulation Q.

---

2 For a full explanation see the FDIC Law, Regulations, and Related Acts webpage at http://www.fdic.gov/regulations/laws/rules/8000-7400.html#fdic8000lending323/.

Regulation Q, or more formally Title 12, part 217 of the US Code of Financial Regulations, was in effect from 1933 to 2011. In keeping with section 11 of the Glass-Steagall Act, Regulation Q prohibited banks from paying interest on demand deposits, and until 1986 it imposed interest rate ceilings on a variety of bank deposit accounts. The idea behind Regulation Q was the belief that the bank failures during the early days of the Great Depression were caused, in great part, by banks competing for deposits. This competition, it was believed, drove down the interest rate spread between deposits and safe loans and thus pushed banks to take on more risks in a search for higher returns. Thus Regulation Q was designed largely to limit the amount of competition between banks.[3]

Even though this may have been the stated goal of Regulation Q, it sure wasn't effective in its early days. From the mid-1930s to the mid-1960s, the interest rate ceiling was above the interest rate banks paid on deposits; thus Regulation Q was an ineffective interest rate ceiling. But by the mid-1960s, market interest rates were increasing and Regulation Q became a binding interest rate ceiling. Even when it became binding, however, Regulation Q really did not reduce competition among banks; it merely shifted how that competition took place.

One way in which banks "got around" Regulation Q was by creating new financial products that were not technically demand deposits. In 1969 Morgan Guarantee Trust Company developed a program that sold participation in its loan portfolio through repurchase agreements. Banks had traditionally sold participation in their loan portfolio to other banks, so what Morgan was doing was not really new, but it came with an interesting twist. The new twist was that Morgan could buy back the loan participation at any time—either on demand or sometime in the future. In essence, Morgan had created a liquid account that would not be subject to Regulation Q.

Morgan was not the only one to create new accounts to get around Regulation Q. In 1969 Henry B. R. Brown[4] and Bruce R. Bent "invented" the money market mutual fund while working at Teachers Insurance and Annuity Association. Brown and Bent eventually went on to form the "Reserve Fund" and create the first money market mutual fund. Initially, they had difficulty finding depositors, but after an article about them and their fund ran in *The New York Times* in January 1973, depositors started to flock to the Reserve Fund. By the end of 1973, Brown and Bent had over $100 million in deposits.[5] Their success spawned a slew of competitors both inside and outside commercial banks.

Other banks were not so crafty as to create new financial products to get around Regulation Q; they merely "paid" depositors for deposits. It became relatively common for banks to offer "gifts" in exchange for deposits. Sure, the bank could not pay a depositor an interest rate higher than what was allowed under Regulation Q; instead, banks would give depositors toasters, or dinner plates, or flashlights for every deposit of more than $50 they made to a bank account. Thus the bank could advertise (and they did, constantly) that they were paying "the highest interest rate allowed by law" but in reality they were "paying" for deposits with gifts, not interest.

By the late 1970s Regulation Q had been so circumvented Congress decided to do away with the interest rate ceiling component. The passage of the Depository Institutions Deregulation and Monetary Control Act of 1980 planned to phase out the interest rate ceiling component of Regulation Q between 1981 and 1986. The only part of Regulation Q that was left was the portion of the act that prohibited the paying of interest on demand deposits. That part of the law was essentially eliminated with the passage of the Dodd-Frank Wall Street Reform and Consumer Protection Act of 2010.

While regulation over bank liabilities may have faded away over time, the regulations over bank capital have, if anything, intensified over the past few years.

---

3 Two other reasons for Regulation Q were to encourage rural banks to lend in their local communities, as opposed to placing funds on deposit at money center banks, and to allow banks to earn higher profits to pay deposit insurance premiums. See R. Alton Gilbert, "Requiem for Regulation Q: What It Did and Why It Passed Away," *Federal Reserve Bank of St. Louis Review* (February 1986): 22–37.

4 Read more about Henry B. R. Brown in a memorial in *The New York Times* from 2008, available at http://www.nytimes.com/2008/08/15/business/15brown.html/.

5 Sadly, the Reserve Fund, which evolved into the Reserve Primary Fund, collapsed during the run on mutual funds during the 2008 financial crisis. Bruce Bent eventually faced securities fraud charges brought by the Securities Exchange Commission but was acquitted on all charges in November 2012. See http://www.nytimes.com/2012/11/13/business/bruce-bent-sr-and-son-cleared-of-fraud-charges.html/.

14-2c Bank Capital

Bank capital levels serves as a cushion against a decline in a bank's asset values. To understand why, think about the accounting equation in banking:

Assets = Liabilities + Bank capital

Now imagine something goes wrong: The economy stalls and borrowers are not able to repay as promised. From a bank's perspective, that means the value of the loans it has written are declining. The bank has to "write down," or decrease, the value of the loans that are going bad. Thus the asset side of the bank's balance sheet declines.

For the accounting equation to hold when asset values are declining, something on the right side of the equal sign has to decrease. Hopefully, the bank has enough bank capital to decrease, or "offset," the decline in assets. If the bank does not have enough bank capital then the bank is insolvent, or, from a financial point of view, the bank is dead.

This is why the level of bank capital is so important: Banks must have enough bank capital to write down nonperforming assets. But what exactly is "enough" in this case? Can we leave it up to bank management to determine what is enough bank capital to hold? Probably not. To understand why, think of the incentives.

Bank Management Incentives and Bank Capital

In the modern era bank executives' compensation is most often tied to a bank's stock price. Simply put, the higher a bank's stock price, the more executives get paid. When a bank, or any corporation, earns a profit, it can pay that profit to stockholders in the form of a stock dividend, it can pay income taxes, or it can hold on to that profit in the form of retained earnings. In general, the higher the level of dividends a corporation pays, the higher the stock price, so the more dividends a bank pays to its stockholders, the higher the bank's stock price and the higher the level of compensation to bank executives.

This is what makes adding to bank capital so painful to bank executives. One way banks can add to their bank capital level is using retained earnings.[6] But remember, more retained earnings mean a lower stock price than if those earnings were paid out to stockholders as dividends. Thus bank executives have an incentive to hold the lowest possible level of bank capital because that means high levels of compensation for them.

Basel Accords

Because the incentive structure for bank executives may very well lead to undercapitalized banks, bank regulators have tried to set international standards for bank capital. These international standards are laid out in the Basel Accords.

The first Basel Accord, called **Basel I**, which was agreed to in 1988 by 12 major countries, attempted to set bank capital levels based on the riskiness of a bank's assets. Banks with riskier assets would be required to hold more bank capital compared with banks with safer assets. A weighted average approach was used: Very safe assets, such as cash, were assigned a zero weight, meaning no capital had to be set aside for those assets, whereas very risky assets were assigned a 100% weight.

Basel I: An international agreement among central banks and bank regulators that for the first time created standard definitions of bank capital and established risk-weighted bank capital level. Basel I was issued in 1988.

While this seemed like a good idea, it was difficult to put into practice. For example, how does one objectively judge the "riskiness" of a borrower? One answer was to use the borrower's

6 Banks can also add to their bank capital levels by issuing more stock, but this might be difficult if the bank is not performing well. Or the bank could sell assets to raise capital—if it can find buyers.

bond rating. This led to a second question: What if the borrower does not have a bond rating? The answer was to be conservative and assume that the borrower is one of the riskiest borrowers and assign a 100% weight. While that might be conservative, it was also overly simplistic. For example, in many developing countries there may be many safe, reliable borrowers, but they are small firms that never issued a bond and do not have a bond rating. According to the Basel I Accord, however, these borrowers are viewed as "the riskiest," and thus a bank lending to them must hold the highest level of capital possible against these loans. This made these loans very expensive for the bank, however, and thus banks started to cut back on loans to safe, reliable, but small borrowers.

It soon became clear that Basel I had major shortfalls, so in 2001 a new set of agreements, called **Basel II**, were announced. In addition to adding operational risk to credit risk, the Basel II Accord tried to improve on Basel I. Specifically, the Basel II Accord attempted to create a much better risk-sensitive measure of bank capital, and it allowed banks to use their own internal ratings-based (IRB) approach to determining capital levels. The IRB approach essentially allowed banks to determine on their own whether they were holding enough capital.

Basel II: The second of the international banking regulation accords that was issued in 2004 and was designed to be implemented in 2008. Three pillars included (1) more flexible minimum bank capital levels, (2) changed supervisory review, and (3) increased dependence on market discipline via increased bank disclosures.

With the onset of the global financial crisis, regulators realized that banks were *not* holding sufficient levels of bank capital. So, in September 2010 a revision of bank capital requirements were announced and were labeled **Basel III**. These new guidelines recommend that banks hold tier I capital (retained earnings and common stock) of at least 6% of the total risk-weighted assets, up from 4%. It also suggested no longer using the bond rating of the borrower as a measurement of riskiness. In addition, Basel III also recommended that banks maintain an extra layer of tier I capital—at least 2.5% of risk-weighted assets—by 2016. This extra layer is called a "capital conservation buffer." Finally, Basel III recommended the level of required bank capital be raised during economic good times and lowered during financial crises.

Basel III: The third and most recent international banking regulation accords, which were created in 2010 in the wake of the global financial crisis.

American banks have objected strongly to Basel III. In particular, they are upset about the requirement to hold more bank capital during the good times. Remember, holding more bank capital is costly to banks and reduces their earnings, stock price, and thus executive bonus levels. Therefore bank executives have fought back strenuously against Basel III's requirement of banks to increase their capital levels. It will be interesting to see who wins this debate: the banks or the regulators.

SECTION REVIEW

Q1) Why is it that bank executives today may not want their banks to hold sufficient levels of bank capital, even if doing so would make their banks more stable?

Q2) Explain how depository institutions successfully "got around" Regulation Q without actually breaking the law.

Q3) The Basel Accords attempted to address which of the following issues?

a. Sufficient levels of bank capital
b. Different levels of deposit insurance in different countries
c. The lack of an international lender of last resort
d. Illegal cash transfers between nations

14-3 Bank Regulation: How It's Done

Bank regulators in the United States have a lot to watch over: a bank's balance sheets, its capital levels, and where things are headed in the future. How do they keep an eye on all of these things? Well, it's not exactly how it is portrayed in the movies.

In the 1946 movie classic *It's a Wonderful Life* the Bailey brothers' Building and Loan is visited by a bank examiner, Mr. Carter, on Christmas Eve. Mr. Carter, the bespectacled bank examiner, discovers a discrepancy in the bank's financial statements—Uncle Billy Bailey misplaced an $8,000 deposit; as a result, George Bailey contemplates suicide. In the end the bank examiner is in the Bailey home to count all of the money that the people in George Bailey's life give to him to keep him from being found guilty of bank fraud. One doubts there was a more famous bank examiner than Mr. Carter.

Most bank examiners don't wind up in the movies. Instead, they read through call reports and conduct on-site examinations. **Call reports** are detailed reports of the operations and financial condition of a bank that must be filed quarterly with their main regulator. The official name is "Report of Condition and Income" for banks and "Thrift Financial Report" for thrift institutions. The call report contains financial information including the bank's balance sheet and income statement. In addition, there are standardized forms the institution must fill out. Call reports are available to the public via the FDIC website.

Call reports: Detailed quarterly reports of the operations and financial condition of a depository institution. Formally known as a "Consolidated Report of Condition and Income," commercial banks and thrifts must file them with the FDIC and credit unions must file them with the National Credit Union Association.

In addition to call reports, bank examiners can make unannounced **on-site examinations** of a bank. Examiners come into the bank and take possession of the bank's cash and marketable securities. They are trying to determine whether what is reported on the call reports actually exists. Next, the examiners go through the bank's loan portfolio. First they ensure lending rules and regulations are being adhered to. Then random samples of loans are fully analyzed to make sure they are all current or, if not, what is being done to bring them current. Finally, the examiners evaluate the overall management and structure of bank to ensure a set of checks and balances exist.

On-site examination: A periodic physical inspection of a bank's operations, including the quality of the bank's management, assets, lending policies, and compliance with banking regulations.

If a bank's operations are in violation of any of the banking rules and regulations, examiners can issue a **cease and desist order**. The Financial Institutions Regulator Act of 1978 empowered regulators to give out cease and desist orders; these can also be enforced by courts.

Cease and desist order: Legal notice given to a financial institution by one of its regulators, or by the courts, requiring the financial institution to take actions or follow proscriptions in the order to stop unlawful, unsafe, or unsound financial practices.

LIBERTY FILMS INC / RKO RADIO PICTURES / Ronald Grant Archive / Alamy

It is a wonderful life in the banking business thanks to Mr. Carter, on the far right, the bank examiner.

14-3a CAMELS Ratings

When bank examiners go into a bank for an on-site examination or read through the call reports, they need a standardized way to evaluate the bank. The traditional standard format they use is the CAMELS rating system. The acronym CAMELS stands for Capital, Assets, Management, Earnings, Liquidity, and Sensitivity. Regulators generally rate a bank on a scale of 1 to 5. In the CAMELS ratings a 1 is the best or highest rating and a 5 is the worst or the bottom of the scale. Banks rated a 5 are in significant trouble. Here is an idea of what the regulators are looking for:

- **Capital adequacy.** Bank examiners often look at the bank's capital ratio, or capital level divided by assets. In general, the higher the capital ratio, the lower the CAMEL score the bank receives. The more capital the bank holds, the better prepared it is to withstand future losses. But bank examiners don't rely solely on the capital ratio. They also look at the bank's overall financial condition. Can the bank raise additional capital if needed?
- **Asset quality.** What are the bank's lending policies? How do they determine who gets a loan and who gets rejected? How many problem loans does the bank have? How are these problem loans resolved? Has the bank set aside enough in loan loss reserves for their problem loans? Does the bank have a well-diversified investment portfolio? How does the bank determine its asset makeup?
- **Management.** Who are the board of directors and management team at the bank? Are they able to identify and manage the bank's risks? How is the bank managed? How are problems resolved? How are midlevel managers evaluated and promoted? How are the management team and bank employees compensated?
- **Earnings.** What is the level, trend, and stability of the bank's earnings or profits? How likely are these earnings levels to change in the future? What is the bank's return on assets (ROA)? How does the bank's earnings level compare with that of similar banks?
- **Liquidity.** Does the bank have enough, or too many, liquid assets? How might the demand for liquidity change over time? How stable are the bank's deposits? How often does the bank have to go outside (e.g., to the federal funds market, to the discount window) to obtain the liquidity it needs?
- **Sensitivity to market conditions.** This is designed to get the bank examiners to think about not just how the bank is doing to today but how might things change in the future. How will the bank fare if interest rates, exchange rates, or the overall economy change significantly in the near future? This sensitivity analysis, while only recently added to the CAMELS rating, is playing a larger role as time goes by. Static analysis, or looking only at how things are currently, is being replaced by more dynamic analysis in which sensitivity analysis plays a large role.

While the CAMELS rating gives examiners a standardized way to evaluate a bank, it is not, by any stretch of the imagination, a perfect system. Because there are so many banks, examiners cannot possibly conduct the same level of examination for all of them. Instead, if examiners worry that a particular bank might face problems in the future, that bank is added to the "problem list" of banks. These banks are given closer scrutiny and are subject to more detailed examinations.

14-3b Dealing with a Failed Institution

When a bank fails, it is up to the FDIC to decide what to do with the institution. The most straightforward approach is to close the institution, pay off the depositors, and sell or liquidate the bank's assets. This policy, aptly named **pay off and liquidate**, was the policy the FDIC used for decades. If liquidation of the bank's assets was not enough to pay off the depositors, the insured deposits would be paid off only to the stated maximum (currently $250,000), and the other depositors would obtain pennies on the dollar of deposits they had. Subordinated debt holders would be paid only after all of the depositors were paid in full, if possible.

Pay off and liquidate: A policy used by bank regulators to deal with failed or failing institutions whereby the depositors are paid their deposit balances from the liquidation of the institution's assets.

The pay off and liquidate approach is very costly to the FDIC and sometimes very disruptive to the community where the bank resides. To keep costs down and make things less disruptive, the FDIC started to pursue **purchase and assume** policies over the past few decades. In a purchase and assume agreement the FDIC finds a healthy bank to purchase the failed institution and assume all of the failed bank's liabilities. This means no depositor would lose any of their deposits.

Purchase and assume: A policy used by bank regulators to deal with failed or failing institutions whereby the regulator finds a solvent institution to purchase the performing assets of the failed or failing institution and the regulator assumes or takes over the nonperforming assets.

However, often the assets of the failed institution are not enough to cover the liabilities. In this case the FDIC has to offer some financial assistance to the healthy purchasing bank to get them to agree to the purchase and assume. In other cases the assets of the failed institution are so bad the FDIC has to strip out those bad assets, leaving only a "clean bank" for the healthy bank to take over. Under this type of purchase and assume, the amount of financial incentive the FDIC must offer to the healthy purchasing bank could be substantial. While the costs to the FDIC of purchase and assume policies could be substantial, they were certainly less, and less disruptive, than the pay off and liquidate policies.

14-3c Too Big to Fail

While the cost of closing a failed institution is sometimes the main concern of the FDIC, in other cases the fear of systemic risk dominates. Remember, systemic risk is the threat that the failure of one entity can lead to a failure of the entire banking, financial, or economic system. Systemic risk comes about because financial market participants are so intertwined that the failure of one leads to the failure of many. In addition, some fear that the failure of a large financial institution will cause panic in a wide variety of financial markets and trigger bank runs or bank panics.

The fear of systemic risk led regulators to label some large banks as so important that they were too big to be allowed to fail. The policy name was shorted to simply **too big to fail (TBTF)**.

Too big to fail (TBTF): A policy followed by bank regulators whereby some financial institutions are so important to the entire financial and economic system that these institutions will not be allowed to fail. That is, regulators will take action to ensure that these systemically important institutions continue in operation.

Institutions that are labeled TBTF would not be liquidated if they failed for fear this would trigger panic in financial markets. Similarly, if they are in financial trouble, TBTF banks might be candidates for a purchase and assume, if a purchaser could be found, but that often is unlikely because these institutions are so large. Instead, if a TBTF institution is insolvent or near insolvency, the FDIC, along with the Federal Reserve (who is responsible for regulating bank holding companies) and possibly the US Treasury, would find a way to inject capital into these failing institutions. These injections are called bank bailouts.

Opponents of TBTF argue that these policies actually take a bad situation and make it worse by creating a moral hazard. Remember, a moral hazard exists when a financial contract alters behavior by changing incentives. When a bank is labeled TBTF, the managers of that bank now know the bank will always survive regardless of what happens. This is because it has an implicit guarantee from regulators that it will always receive a bailout.

Thus, under TBTF, some bank managers see banking as a game of "heads we win, tails the taxpayers lose." That is, if a bank is labeled TBTF, its managers can take on high-paying risky assets. If those risky assets pay off as planned, the bank is very profitable and the bank executives receive large bonuses. On the other hand, if the risky assets do not pay off and thus fall into default, and the bank becomes insolvent, then the bank turns to the government for a bailout. The executives of the bank never suffer the downside of their risky behavior.

Many critics complain that the TBTF policies that date back to the 1980s are one of the fundamental causes of the global financial crisis that started in 2008. They argue that banks have learned that "heads we win, tails the taxpayers lose" has resulted in banks being able to "pocket the return" while "dumping" the risk on the taxpayers. This is sometimes referred to as "privatizing the return and publicizing the risk." This misalignment of incentives could be argued as what triggered the many financial crises in the 1980s and 1990s and led to the Great Recession.

The debate over TBTF policies rages on: Do they reduce systemic risk or do they exacerbate a moral hazard that led to the worst economic slowdown since the Great Depression? Have the modern-day Mr. Carters of *It's a Wonderful Life* helped to cause a worldwide economic crisis?

SECTION REVIEW

Q1) Robert is confused about why regulators created the too big to fail policies. What would you tell Robert?

Q2) Explain how regulators use the CAMEL rating in the regulation process.

Q3) In a "pay off and liquidate" approach, what is being liquidated?

a. The cash a bank holds

b. The insolvent institution that is being closed

c. All of the depositors' accounts at the institution in question

d. The healthy bank that is purchasing the failing institution

14-4 Consumer Protection and Failures

Banking regulation was primarily designed to keep banks safe and sound. But there was another worry: making sure banks did not take advantage of their customers. In part, there was an asymmetric information problem: Bankers knew much more about finance and banking than did their customers. This was especially true when the bank customers were individual or families.

Thus, to protect individuals and families, a number of consumer protection regulations on banks have been instituted. Some have been more successful than others. Here is just a brief sample of some of the consumer protection laws that have been enacted and the controversies that have followed.

14-4a Truth in Lending Act of 1968

Officially part of the Consumer Credit Protection Act of 1968, but more commonly known as the Truth in Lending Act, this piece of banking regulation was designed to ensure that every borrower understands what they are getting themselves into when they agree to borrow money. The act requires full disclosure of the terms and costs involved in the loan. The act applies to any entity, not just banks, that lends money to consumers or farmers.

Some of the most important components of the Truth in Lending Act is that lenders are mandated to state the annual percentage rate (APR) being charged on the loan, with an explanation of how much interest will be paid on the loan. The act applies to credit cards, home equity lines of credit, and motor vehicle loans.

The regulation that implements the act was originally Regulation Z, set by the Federal Reserve. With the passage of the Dodd-Frank Act of 2010, rule-making authority was transferred to the Consumer Financial Protection Bureau.

Some controversies have arisen over what "0% APR" loans offered by auto manufacturers really mean. Imagine an automaker, through its captive finance company, offers a consumer a 0% APR loan or a $2,000 cash rebate. If the customer chooses the 0% APR loan, they forfeit the $2,000 cash rebate; that is, they are paying $2,000 more for the car to get the loan. But doesn't that mean the auto purchaser in this case is "paying" $2,000 to finance the auto? Not according to the Truth in Lending Act. Thus, many consumer advocates argue, the Truth in Lending Act really does not produce truth in lending in many cases.

14-4b The Community Reinvestment Act of 1977

One of the most controversial banking practices in the past (some say it still exists) was the bank policy of **redlining**. With redlining, bankers would lay out a map of a city or a state and draw red lines around areas and neighborhoods into which they would not lend. These redlined areas and neighborhoods often were populated by ethnic minorities, working people, Catholics, Jewish people, and others whom bankers deemed "unworthy." Some in the banking community claim that redlining is little more than an urban myth and does not exist today, nor did it ever exist.

Redlining: The act of denying financial services to people living in a particular area.

In reaction to claims of redlining by banks, however, Congress passed and President Carter signed into law the Community Reinvestment Act (CRA) in 1977.[7] The CRA requires banks who want to merge, expand their branches, or seek to undertake any action that requires

7 The principle author of the CRA, Wisconsin Senator William Proxmire, stated, "The main purpose of the CRA is to eliminate the practice of redlining by lending institutions." See Akm Rezaul Hossain, "The Past, Present and Future of the Community Reinvestment Act: A Historical Perspective." Mansfield: University of Connecticut, Department of Economics, 2004.

regulatory approval to seek "CRA certification." To obtain CRA certification, banks must demonstrate that they are lending and providing financial services to people across their geographical area.

Banks often claim that CRA certification documentation is burdensome and expensive. They often argue that regulators should instead ask local "community leaders" whether the bank in question is providing financial services. The downside to this approach is that the bank in question often makes substantial "contributions" to the "community leader" who is to testify on the bank's behalf.

Critics of the CRA claim that despite the act's existence, and despite attempts to strengthen the regulations in 1991 and 1994, the bank practice of redlining still exists. As evidence they point to urban and minority areas where access to credit is limited to pay-day loans and other nonbank lending forms. This type of credit is expensive and short term, thus negatively affecting the ability of these areas to develop economically.

So, has the CRA legislation created excess burden on banks? Or is it an act that, while well intentioned, resulted in de facto bribing while the people in these geographical areas still cannot get access to bank loans?

14-4c Fair Credit Reporting Act of 1970

The Fair Credit Reporting Act (FCA) is enforced by the US Federal Trade Commission and is designed to regulate the collections and use of consumer credit information. The FCA was designed to ensure that credit bureaus that issue credit reports on individuals are reporting only accurate information and to create a way for people to know what is in their credit report and correct errors. The act requires creditors to provide complete and accurate information to credit bureaus or face penalties. Consumers also are granted the right to know what is in their credit report, and consumer credit reporting agencies must correct inaccurate information in credit reports usually within 30 days.

While credit reports were initially designed to be used by firms when granting credit, over the past several years they have been used by firms in the employment process. A would-be employer can run a credit check on a job applicant and use that credit information in deciding whether they want to hire the person. Employers defend this use of credit reports by claiming that how a person handles their personal finances tells a lot about how the person will handle the firm's assets.

Critics argue the FCA should ban the use of credit reports in the employment process. People who lose their job, through no fault of their own, may run into financial difficultly while searching for another job. This financial difficulty then lowers their credit rating and makes it nearly impossible for them to find work in the future. Thus, they argue, the FCA is far too weak and should regulate who uses credit reports, not just what is in them.

14-4d Dodd-Frank Wall Street Reform and Consumer Protection Act of 2010

In response to the worst economic crisis since the Great Depression, in 2010 Congress passed and President Obama signed the Dodd-Frank Act. Consumer advocates argue a major contributor to the Great Recession was how many consumers and families were taken advantage of by lenders, including banks. In the wake of the crisis there were many calls to increase the amount of consumer protection in financial markets. The Dodd-Frank Act was the result.

Among other things, the Dodd-Frank Act created a Bureau of Consumer Financial Protection (BCFP). The BCFP claims that it will, among other things, limit unfair or abusive lending practices, enforce federal consumer protection laws, and enforce laws that outlaw discrimination and other unfair treatment in consumer finance.

Many in the banking industry have claimed the BCFP is an example of government overreach and that it will result in burdensome regulation if it goes unchecked. In 2011 US Senator

Richard Shelby of Alabama wrote that by having one single person lead the BCFP, the act created a "consumer protection czar" who was not accountable to the American people.[8] Some even want the Dodd-Frank Act amended to completely eliminate the BCFP.

Critics counter that instead of creating an unruly regulatory monster, the BCFP is actually a useless bureaucracy with no real power that was created to make the American public feel like something was being done to protect them. These critics argue that the BCFP has no legal ability to actually change anything that happens in financial markets and, by being placed inside the bank-friendly Federal Reserve, any suggested changes the BCFP makes will never see the light of day.

So, is the BCFP excessive government regulation at its worst, or is it nothing more than an attempt to pull the wool over American consumers' eyes while they are taken advantage of in the financial market place?

14-4e Why Has the US Bank Regulatory System Failed?

When critics look at the banking regulatory system in the United States in the wake of the Great Recession, they all tend to agree that the system is broken. It is our financial system, after all, that was the main cause of the worst economic slowdown since the Great Depression. But where the disagreement lies is *why* this regulatory system failed to prevent the global financial crisis that started in 2008. Some of the issues are described in this section.

In many countries around the world there is a single financial market regulator, but not in the United States. The regulatory system in the United States is complicated and complex. If we limit our scope to just commercial banks, we can recognize how complicated the system is. Banks get their charters from either the state banking authority or the comptroller of the currency, each of which has their own rules, regulations, and bank examiners. Then, if the bank has FDIC deposit insurance, as almost all banks do, they are subject to the rules, regulations, and bank examiners of the FDIC. If the bank belongs to the Federal Reserve system, then it is subject to bank examiners from the Fed, as well as the rules and regulations the Fed creates for banks. On top of this, there are banking regulations from the Federal Trade Commission, the US Treasury, the US Justice Department, and other branches of the US federal government.

With all of these rules and regulations, one might think a great safety net is in place to make sure any problems that might develop are caught and resolved quickly. However, critics contend just the opposite happens: Instead of catching a problem, this web of regulators results in regulator shopping, regulatory capture, and finger pointing.

The Office of the Comptroller of the Currency and state banking authorities have been embroiled in a battle over who should be granting bank charters, leading to banks engaging in **regulator shopping**. In 2004 the comptroller of the currency issued regulations basically saying that state banking authorities could not regulate the activities of nationally chartered banks located in their state. The debate was over predatory lending practices by banks and a variety of consumer protection laws the state legislatures were passing. The comptroller, the states argued, was trying to lure banks to drop their state charters in favor of federal charters issued by the comptroller. By having a federal charter, the bank would face less hostile rules and regulations.

Regulator shopping: When banks and other financial institutions are allowed to choose their regulator, they may pit the regulators against each other and then choose the regulator that offers the most favorable regulations.

Needless to say, the state banking authorities did not take this lying down. They sued the Office of the Comptroller of the Currency and the battle was on. Some believe banks can now "regulator shop" in that they can threaten to switch their bank charter to whichever

8 See Richard Shelby, "The Danger of an Unaccountable 'Consumer Czar.'" *The Wall Street Journal*, July 21, 2011.

charter-granting entity gives them the most lenient level of regulation. The result has been weakened regulation and the willingness of regulators to turn a blind eye to many of the risky activities banks engage in.

Banks also were able to engage in excessively risky activities because bank regulators suffered from what Simon Johnson of MIT describes as **intellectual capture**. According to Johnson, intellectual capture goes beyond the traditional concept of regulatory capture—where bankers control the regulatory agency, such as the Fed—to a situation where all of society, including the regulators, believes what is good for banks is good for all. Johnson argues that over the past few decades banks have so been able to convince regulators that anything they do that increases bank profits is "good for America."

intellectual capture: The widely held belief that whatever benefits the financial industry must also be beneficial to all of society.

Johnson is not the only one raising this issue of intellectual capture. As economist John Kay explains it,[9] "regulators come to see the industry through the eyes of market participants rather than the end users they exist to serve." Thus, in banking, the bank regulators look in awe on the institutions they are to regulate instead of keeping watch over them.

On the other hand, Beatrice Weder di Mauro, a member of the German Council of Economic Experts, believes that we don't suffer from intellectual capture; rather, it is all about incentives.[10] She argues that regulators suffer from a time inconsistency policy whereby they announce a "no bail out" policy while times are good, but when a crisis hits the optimal action is to offer bailouts. She also concludes that regulators are underpaid, and offering higher pay to regulators will help to realign incentives.

While regulators might all agree they are underpaid, they certainly do not agree on which regulator did not do their job leading up to the crisis. The web of regulators has allowed each to point a finger at one of the many others as being the chief regulator that was asleep at the wheel. Critics argue that this endless finger pointing and attempting to shift blame have resulted in a lack of meaningful reform of our financial regulatory system in general and the regulation of our banks in particular.

SECTION REVIEW

Q1) The Community Reinvestment Act was created in response to the issue of redlining. What is/was redlining and how did the act attempt to address it?

Q2) Explain the controversies that exist over the Bureau of Consumer Financial Protection. How can some critics claim it has too much power, whereas other claim it has no meaningful use at all?

Q3) Scott suffers from what Simon Johnson calls "intellectual capture." What does that mean?

a. Scott believes that only highly educated people should manage financial institutions.

b. Anything that is beneficial to the financial sector Scott sees as benefiting society as a whole.

c. Scott considers the compensation paid to financial institution executives as being excessive because these executives are not the most highly educated members of society.

d. In Scott's view bank regulators are the most highly trained professionals in financial markets.

9 See John Kay, "Finance Needs Stewards, Not Toll Collectors." *Financial Times*, July 22, 2102.

10 See Beatrice Weder di Mauro, "The Dog That Didn't Bark." *The Economist*, October 1, 2009.

14-5 Conclusion

Banks are special—I hope you agree. This "special" nature has led many to argue that banks thus need regulation and oversight unlike that used for any other entity in a market-based economy. We have learned that this bank regulatory structure in the United States is complex and controversial. We reviewed how banking regulation has changed, starting with bank products and geography limitations. We then examined how bank balance sheets are regulated and the controversy over bank capital levels. Next we looked at how bank regulation actually takes place and the rise of TBTF policies. Finally, we discussed controversies around consumer protection in the banking industry and pondered the question of why this bank regulatory system failed to prevent the global financial crisis that started in 2008. Along the way we raised more questions than we answered, but that, in large part, is what makes this topic so very interesting.

IN THE NEWS . . .

Bank Financing to Drop With Tougher Rules, Poloz Says

Greg Quinn
Bloomberg News
December 11, 2014

Global banks will reduce the financing they offer to companies as tougher regulations take hold, which may slow economic growth if new competitors don't emerge, Bank of Canada Governor Stephen Poloz said.

New rules are "absolutely essential" to prevent another crisis like the one that began in 2008, Poloz said in a speech to the Economic Club of New York. The rules have led global banks to sell $700 billion of assets and operations since 2007, implying that "gaps" in financing will appear, he said.

"These areas of retreat by banks could look like good opportunities for other financial intermediaries," Poloz said. "But it would be surprising if the net effect were not to reduce the availability of credit."

New and small businesses are most likely to suffer from reduced credit, along with trade finance and infrastructure projects, Poloz said. Innovation may help offset the impact, with new funding coming from increased corporate bond sales, securitization markets and public-private partnerships, Poloz said.

Regulators must also ensure new rules don't stifle financial innovation, Poloz said, adding "Thankfully, the balance between regulation and innovation is dynamic, not static—competitive forces ensure this."

Bank of Canada Governor Poloz states that "absolutely essential" new banking regulations will result in "reduced credit" and presumably hurt the global economy. Do you agree with him? Would changes in regulations result in a net negative impact on the economy? Or, might they have a net positive impact on the economy? Why?

Summary of the Banking System

Tying Concepts Together

Bank management and regulation is a difficult job. Bank management must keep an eye on the bank's financial statements to ensure that the risks the bank faces are being correctly managed. If the bank's risks are not properly managed, bank performance may suffer. Keeping a watchful eye on bank management are various bank regulators. While these regulators have a less than spotless track record, their job will surely become more difficult as the complexity of the global banking system increases. As the financial crisis that started in 2008 demonstrates, financial institutions other than banks can also contribute to financial crises. It is these other financial institutions that we turn our attention to next. In Chapter 15 we examine the very important short-term debt market, or the money markets. In Chapter 16 we look at the longer-term debt market, or the bond market. Our focus switches to the equity markets in Chapter 17, and we conclude with a critical examination of the mortgage market in Chapter 18. Each of these markets played an important role in the recent financial crisis and continues to play an important role in our global financial markets.

15

Money Markets

15-1 Money Market Characteristics and Purpose

On August 9, 2007, the heavy rains that had pounded New York City the day before finally subsided. The sun poked through the clouds and the city was beginning to dry. Across the Atlantic, Londoners were enjoying a warm summer day. The summer of 2007 was drawing to a close, and summer vacationers were returning to the city. That Thursday could have been like any other day, except for what was occurring in the money markets in New York and London. The shock waves that started that day in money markets would set in motion an economic and financial tsunami that, in turn, would lead to the worst economic slowdown since the Great Depression.

James Carville, a political strategist and advisor to President Bill Clinton, once remarked, "I used to think if there was reincarnation, I wanted to come back as the President or the Pope or a .400 baseball hitter, but now I want to come back as the bond market. You can intimidate everybody."[1] Swings in the bond market can bankrupt corporations, alter government budgets, create massive unemployment, and contribute to financial meltdowns. Bond markets can also help to educate the population, build much needed roads, help finance household purchases, and help build hospitals.

What are these "money markets" and "bond markets"? How and why can they have such a dramatic impact on the lives of millions of people around the world? In this chapter and the next we explore the size and influence of these important financial markets. We examine the players in the money and bond markets and learn how these players determine prices of financial assets. Finally, we investigate the impact of these important financial markets in the current financial crisis.

15-1a Money Market Defined

"Money markets" are in many ways misnamed. They are not markets for currency or money (those are called foreign exchange markets); instead, they are markets for financial assets that are close substitutes for money. The financial assets bought and sold in money markets are short-term promises to repay (usually less than one year in duration), have a high level of liquidity, and have a very low level of default risk. In many ways these money market instruments are a lot like money.

Even the use of the term *market* can be confusing. Usually, when one thinks of a market, one thinks of a physical place where buyers and sellers meet, like a farmers' market. A money market, on the other hand, does not take place in one physical place. Instead it takes place during telephone calls and on blinking computer screens, through which more than a trillion dollars trade hands every business day. While many of these traders and brokers are in the financial districts of New York, London, Tokyo, and Frankfurt, they hardly ever come face to face with each other.

Thus, a formal definition of a **money market** would be "a wholesale market of short-term debt instruments that have a high level of liquidity and a low level of default risk."

Money market: A segment of a financial market where short-term debt instruments with high levels of liquidity and low default risk are traded.

Let's look at each part of this definition:

- "Wholesale market" means that the transactions that take place in the money markets are large in volume. While some smaller transactions do take place, most of the transactions are for \$1 million to \$10 million or more. Single trades of \$50 million to \$100 million

1 See Louis Uchitelle, "Ideas & Trends: The Bondholders Are Winning; Why America Won't Boom." *The New York Times*, June 12, 1994.

are not uncommon. Thus it is all but impossible for individuals to be directly involved in these markets. Instead, these markets are dominated by a network of brokers, dealers, investment banks, and commercial banks. Individuals usually access the market through a variety of brokers and dealers.

- "Short-term debt instruments" refers to the fact that this is a market for promises to repay with interest and that the repayment will take place very quickly. This is not the market for equities or currencies; instead, this is a market of IOUs. These IOUs mostly mature within a year and often in fewer than 30 days. Thus money market instruments are very short-term or short-lived financial assets.
- In part because of their short term to maturity, money market instruments have a high level of liquidity. The money market has both a primary market, where a given IOU is issued for the first time, and a much larger secondary market. In these markets over a trillion dollars is traded every working day. As described in the next two sections, the market is made up of thousands of traders each looking to buy and sell these short-term IOUs. Since there is so much volume in these markets, buying and selling these securities is relatively easy; that is, the market has a great deal of liquidity.
- In addition, because money market instruments are issued by only the biggest and safest borrowers, these IOUs have a "low level of default risk." Buyers of these securities can be relatively sure that the issuers will make good on their promises to repay. This is important because many money market instruments are unsecured IOUs; there is no collateral to back up this borrowing. But, because most of the borrowers in the money market do not have problems paying their debts, this lack of collateral is usually not a problem. This is true most of the time; however, this was no longer the case during the 2007–2009 financial crisis.

Because of these characteristics of high liquidity and low default risk, the yields on these securities are relatively low compared with the yields of other debt instruments. So, if the yield on money market instruments is relatively low, why would anyone want to buy them?

15-1b Why Are There Money Markets?

To understand why money markets exist, it is important to understand the *purpose* of money markets. Like any other market, the money market is made up of suppliers and demanders. The demanders of money market instruments are those surplus units, or savers, who have excess cash at the moment but need a safe place to park those funds for the short term.

For example, think about a business firm. Firms often have very uneven cash flow. That is, they may receive a large payment from a customer one week, but they won't need those funds to pay payroll or pay suppliers for several weeks into the future. Thus the firm needs somewhere to "park" those funds until they require them. The firm is a demander of money market financial assets. That is, the firm wants to buy the IOUs being sold in the money market.

Another example of demanders in the money market is institutional investors. Pension funds, insurance companies, endowments, and so on all may have inflows of cash that they are not yet ready to tie up for a long period of time. Thus institutional investors want to "park" their funds temporarily by purchasing money market instruments. Also, individuals who have short-term savings may buy money market instruments indirectly through a broker or a mutual fund.

Investment banks, brokers, and dealers also buy money market instruments to resell them, plus fees, to their customers. Even commercial banks buy some money market instruments, usually Treasury bills (or T-bills), so they can generate interest income. The interest income banks earn from holding money market securities either goes to improve the bank's profitability or might be paid out to depositors, such as holders of a bank's money market deposit.

Speaking of banks, all of the demanders of money market financial assets (business firms, institutional investors, and others) could simply leave their funds on deposit at a commercial bank instead of buying money market instruments. But a bank, or any depository institution, is a financial middleman that comes between the borrower and the saver. That means the bank drives a wedge, or interest rate spread, between what the borrower pays and what the savers earn. In the money market, however, the borrower and saver meet directly;[2] therefore they can split between them the wedge the depository institution would have taken. Thus the advantage for the demanders in the money market is that they earn a higher yield, all things being equal, than what they would earn by keeping the funds in the bank.

15-1c Money Market Participants

Not just anyone can issue money market instruments. Only those with good credit histories and a proven ability to repay can issue securities in the money markets. On one side of the money market are the suppliers of financial instruments, which in the primary market include the following:

- Governments, especially the federal government, which issues Treasury bills to fund its spending
- Large corporations that issue commercial paper to finance their short-term needs for capital
- Commercial banks that issue repurchase agreements and bankers' acceptance

Tying Concepts Together

Money Market and Loanable Funds When Short Term Government Borrowing Increases

Since money market instruments are short-term debt obligations, we can use the supply-and-demand framework we developed in Chapter 3 and used in Chapter 4 to examine price movements in the money market.

Let's suppose the economy slows unexpectedly. As a result, more people turn to the government for assistance, while at the same time government tax revenues decrease. The result of these two changes is that the borrowing needs of the government increase. To fund their borrowing needs, the government issues more Treasury bills. This would increase the market supply from $S_{T\text{-Bills}}$ to $S_{T\text{-Bills}}'$ in Figure 15-1A.

Because the government is now borrowing more at every interest rate, there is an increase in the demand for loanable funds. Therefore in Figure 15-1B we see the demand for loanable funds increase from DLF to DLF′. Thus the prices of T-bills fall and their yields increase, and/or market interest rates increase, as the government's borrowing needs increase.

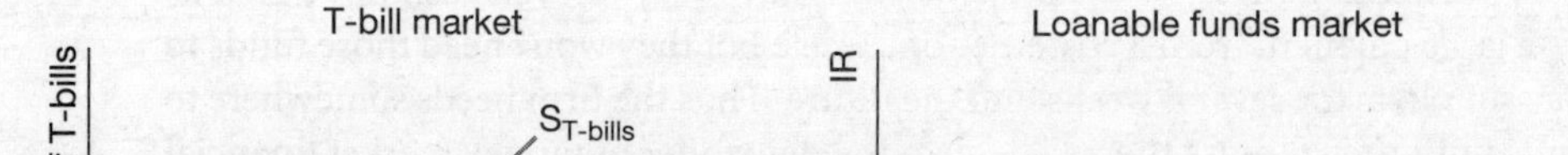

Figure 15-1
Government issues T-bills to fund deficit (left). Government borrows more to fund deficit (right).

2 Of course they don't literally meet directly. In addition, there may be brokers and dealers between the saver and borrower in the money market, but they take much less of a cut than would a depository institution in the same situation.

Suppliers in the secondary market for money market instruments include:

- The Federal Reserve, which injects reserves and thus influences the level of bank reserves; and
- Previous purchasers of money market instruments who now need cash: business firms, institutional investors, brokers/mutual funds, investment banks, and commercial banks.

To better understand how the supply side of the market works, let's look at each of the money market financial instruments, who issues them, and how they work.

SECTION REVIEW

Q1) Explain why the money market is really not "a market for money."

Q2) Johanna is an institutional investor who is looking to "park" some of her investment funds for a short time. How would you explain to Johanna why money market instruments might be useful for her?

Q3) Which of the following is *not* a characteristic of money market instruments?

a. They pay a relatively high rate of return.

b. They have a low level of default risk.

c. They have a high level of liquidity.

d. They comprise a significant secondary market.

15-2 Money Market Instruments: Treasury Bills

Remember that money market instruments are promises to repay, with interest, that are highly liquid and have a low level of default risk. Also remember that, in addition to the primary market, there is a large secondary market for money market instruments. Some of the most important money market instruments are Treasury bills.

15-2a Treasury Bills in Detail

The US federal government is just like you and me[3]—when they spend more than they take in, they have to borrow the difference. So, when the federal government runs a budget deficit, or they are spending more than they are bringing in through taxes, they must borrow the difference. One way the US federal government borrows to fund its deficit is buy selling Treasury bills in the money market.

The Treasury Department auctions T-bills weekly to raise the funds the federal government needs for its spending. These T-bills have maturities of 28, 91, and 182 days. From time to time, as its funding needs change, the Treasury Department also auctions T-bills with different maturity dates.

In 1998 the government lowered the minimum denomination of T-bills to only $1,000 to allow individuals to purchase T-bills along with institutional investors. Individuals can purchase T-bills over the Internet directly from the government, or they can buy them indirectly from brokers and through mutual funds.

In addition to government auctioning of T-bills, there is a huge secondary market for T-bills. Perhaps someone who purchased a 1-year T-bill now doesn't want to wait the entire year to get their cash back. In this case they can enter the secondary market for T-bills and sell their T-bill to someone else. In 2015 there were about $1.4 trillion in T-bills outstanding. There are about 25 financial institutions that "make a market" in T-bills by buying and selling them for their customers, including depository institutions, insurance companies, pension funds, and money market mutual funds.

The government doesn't actually pay interest on T-bills; instead, they are sold at a discount. This means T-bills are issued at a price below their face value, and once they reach maturity the government pays the holder the face value. Let's look at how T-bills are priced.

Treasury Bill Pricing

As we mentioned, Treasury bills, like a lot of money market instruments, do not have interest coupon payments as traditional bonds do. Instead, they are sold at a discount from their stated or face value. Once the maturity date is reached, the holder of the T-bill is paid the face value.

There are two ways of calculating the yields on Treasury bills: the older, traditional way that was used mostly before calculators, called the discount rate yield; and the more accurate (but more complicated to calculate) investment rate yield.

The **discount rate yield** (DRY) is simply

$$\text{DRY} = \frac{F - P}{F} \times \frac{360}{n}$$

where F is the face price of the T-bill, P is the market price of the T-bill, and n is the number of days to maturity. To understand how this works, let's look at a simple example.

Discount rate yield: A simple measure of a bond's return, using a 360-day year, that is calculated relative to the face value of the bond.

---

3 Keep in mind though that in many ways the federal government is *not* like you and me. One of the most important ways we are different is default risk.

Example 1: Suppose you buy a 60-day T-bill with a face value of $1,000 at a price of $990. Thus the DRY would be

$$\text{DRY} = \frac{\$1{,}000 - \$990}{\$1000} \times \frac{360}{60}$$

Since the dollar signs cancel out in the first part and we can simplify the second part, we get

$$\text{DRY} = \frac{10}{1{,}000} \times 6 = 0.06, \text{ or } 6.0\%$$

Example 2: Suppose you buy a 60-day T-bill with a face value of $1,000 but at a price of $995. Now the DRY would be

$$\text{DRY} = \frac{\$1{,}000 - \$995}{1000} \times \frac{360}{60}$$

Since the dollar signs cancel out in the first part and we can simplify the second part, we get

$$\text{DRY} = \frac{5}{1{,}000} \times 6 = 0.03, \text{ or } 3.0\%$$

But the DRY, or discount rate yield, has some odd components. In the first part of the equation we are calculating the return one gets from holding the T-bill relative to the face value rather than the price paid. Think of it from the point of view of someone buying these T-bills. Wouldn't they be more interested in knowing the rate of return they are earning relative to the amount they are paying? If so, it would make more sense to divide the difference between the face value and price by the price instead of the face value.

The second odd component is the use of 360 instead of 365—the actual number of days in a year (or 366 in leap years). Since T-bills by definition mature in less than a year, we need to calculate the rate of return for the portion of the year the T-bill is held. There are 365 days in a year, but the DRY uses 360.

These two oddities can be corrected for using the **investment return yield**, or IRY. The IRY is calculated this way:

$$\text{IRY} = \frac{F - P}{P} \times \frac{365}{n}$$

investment return yield: A measurement of a bond's return, using a 365-day year, that is calculated relative to the price paid for the bond by the bondholder.

In terms of our examples above we would now have the following:

Example 1a: The 60-day T-bill with a face value of $1,000 at a price of $990 would have an IRY of

$$\text{IRY} = \frac{\$1{,}000 - \$990}{\$990} \times \frac{365}{60}$$

Or, simplifying, we get

$$\text{IRY} = \frac{10}{990} \times 6.0833 = 6.1448\%$$

Example 2a: The 60-day T-bill with a face value of $1,000 but now at a price of $995 would have an IRY of

$$\text{IRY} = \frac{\$1{,}000 - \$995}{\$995} \times \frac{365}{60}$$

Or, simplifying,

$$\text{IRY} = \frac{5}{995} \times 6.0833 = 3.057\%$$

You might be tempted to ask, "Who cares? The difference between the DRY and IRY is pretty small, so why bother with the more complicated IRY?"

To understand why the difference between the two can be important, consider the second example: The difference between the results in Example 2 and Example 2a is 5.7 basis points, or 0.057%. It may not seem like much, but consider the following hypothetical example. You work for the treasury department of a large corporation. Your supervisor tells you that your firm has $2 million that they don't need for the next 60 days. She wants you to calculate how much they can earn from different investments. The impact of 5.7 basis points on $2 million for 60 days is $187.23. Do you have $187 that you would like to give to the firm to make up the difference?

Now that we have seen a simple example, let's take a look at how this works in reality. You can review the prices of T-bills paid on the Treasury's web page at http://www.treasurydirect.gov/instit/annceresult/annceresult.htm (Table 15-1).

CUSIP	Term	Auction Date	Maturity Date	Price per $100
912796DS5	4 weeks	08/05/2014	09/04/2014	99.998444

Let's suppose on August 5, 2014, you purchased a four-week T-bill that matured on September 4, 2014. The market price for that T-bill was $99.99844 for every $100. Thus, if you purchased that four-week T-bill that had a face value of $1,000, you would have paid $999.98 for it. Remember, the discount rate yield is calculated by

$$\text{DRY} = \frac{F - P}{F} \times \frac{360}{n}$$

where F is the face value of the bond, P is the purchase price of the bond, and n is the number of days to maturity. So, in this example the DRY would be

$$\text{DRY} = \frac{\$1{,}000 - \$999.9844}{\$1{,}000} \times \frac{360}{28} = 0.000015600 \times 12.857142 = 0.0200\%$$

Table 15-1 Treasury Bill Yields and Prices

Security Term	CUSIP	CMB	Issue Date	Maturity Date	High Rate	Investment Rate
4-Week	912796DS5	No	08/07/2014	09/04/2014	0.020%	0.020%
13-Week	912796ED7	No	08/07/2014	11/06/2014	0.025%	0.025%
26-Week	912796DG1	No	08/07/2014	02/05/2015	0.050%	0.051%
4-Week	912796DR7	No	07/31/2014	08/28/2014	0.030%	0.030%
13-Week	912796EB1	No	07/31/2014	10/30/2014	0.030%	0.030%
26-Week	912796ER6	No	07/31/2014	01/29/2015	0.055%	0.056%
4-Week	912796BX6	No	07/24/2014	08/21/2014	0.025%	0.025%
52-Week	912796EN5	No	07/24/2014	07/23/2015	0.110%	0.112%

whereas the investment rate yield is calculated this way:

$$\text{IRY} = \frac{F - P}{P} \times \frac{365}{n}$$

where again F is the face value of the bond, P is the market price of the bond, and n is days to maturity. In this example the investment rate yield is

$$\text{IRY} = \frac{\$1{,}000 - \$999.9844}{\$999.9844} \times \frac{365}{28} = 0.00001560024 \times 13.035714 = 0.0203\%$$

So, in August 2014, a 28-day, or 4-week, T-bill would pay you an annualized interest rate of about 2/100 of 1%. By historical standards this is very, very low. We can see this in Figure 15-2.

T-Bill Auctions

Each Thursday the Treasury announces how many and what types of T-bills it will sell via auction on the following Monday. Bidders then can submit either competitive bids or noncompetitive bids. In a competitive bid the Treasury ranks all bids from the highest to the lowest price offered. It then accepts the highest bid first, and then the next highest bid, and so on until the amount determined by the Treasury is sold. No one bidder is allowed to purchase more than

Figure 15-2 Secondary Market Rate for 3-Month Treasury Bills

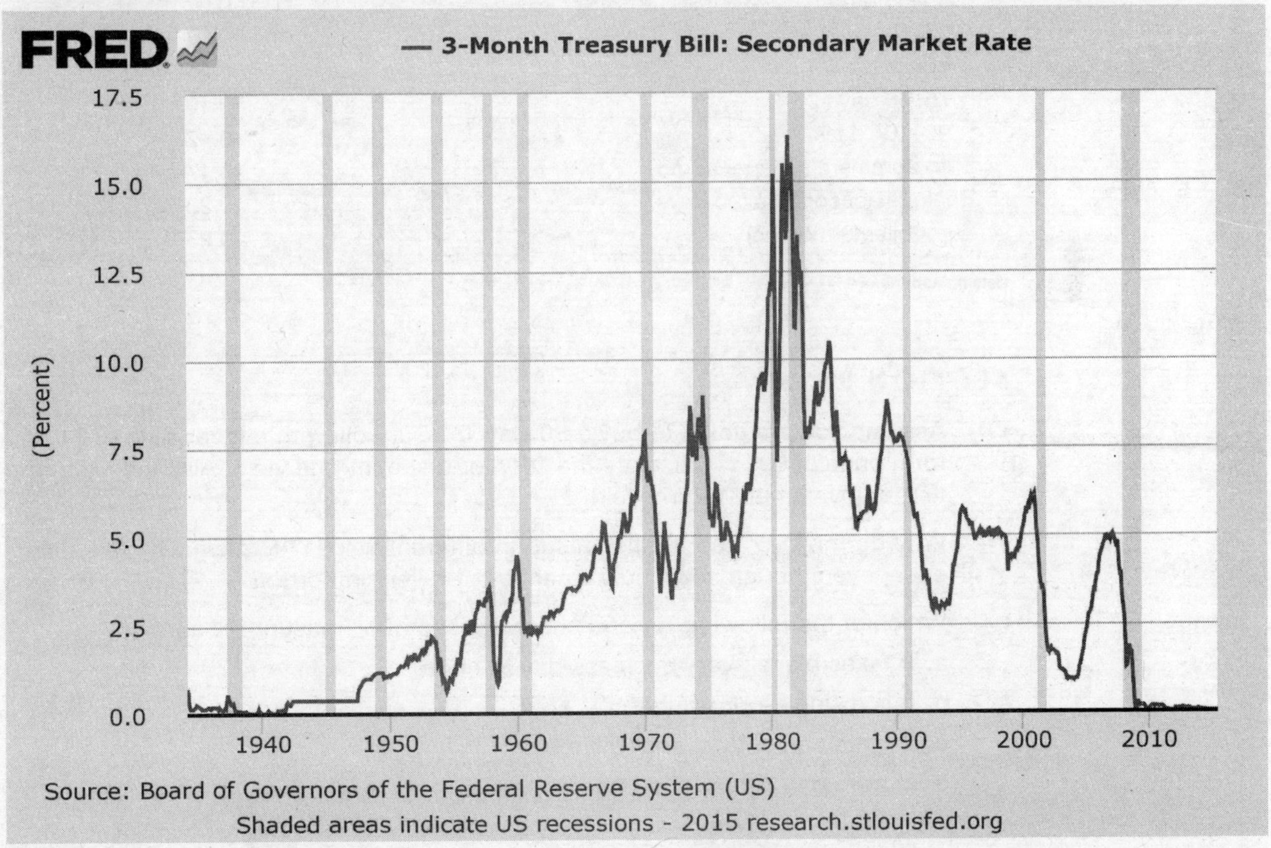

Source: Copyright 2014 by the Federal Reserve Bank of St. Louis.

35% of any one issue. The bidder of each accepted bid then pays the lowest bid accepted. That is, everyone whose bid was accepted pays the same price. This is done to avoid the "winner's curse."[4]

In the noncompetitive bidding process bidders include in their bid only the amount of Treasury bills they wish to buy. The Treasury accepts all noncompetitive bids it receives, again with the stipulation that no one bidder is allowed to purchase more than 35% of any one issue. The price for noncompetitive bids is set as the lowest price of any accepted bid.

As Table 15-2 shows, Treasury bills, while an important part of the money market, are not the only money market instrument. Next we examine some of the other financial assets that make up this important short-term and very liquid market.

TABLE 15-2 Sample of Money Market Rates on August 7, 2014

Instrument	Interest Rate (%)
T-bill	
1 month	0.025
3 month	0.030
6 month	0.051
Prime rate	3.25
Federal funds	0–0.25
Commercial paper	
30–44 days	0.06
45–55 days	0.07
57–59 days	0.07
60–74 days	0.08
75–88 days	0.10
90–104 days	0.12
Euro commercial paper (4 mo)	0.17
Bankers acceptance (90 days)	0.23
Eurodollar (3 months)	0.23

Data from: http://online.wsj.com.

SECTION REVIEW

Q1) Assume you are going to buy a 90-day Treasury bill with a face value of $1,000 for a price of $944. Calculate the DRY, or discount rate yield. Also calculate the IRY, or investment return yield.

Q2) Why do the DRY and the IRY result in different values? Explain why this difference, even though seemingly small, can be very important.

Q3) Which of the following is *not* a characteristic of a Treasury Bill auction?

a. It takes place every business day at noon.

b. It is a single-price auction.

c. Buyers can enter competitive bids.

d. Buyers can enter noncompetitive bids.

4 In an auction the "winner's curse" comes about when there is uncertainty over the value of what is being auctioned. For example, suppose you are going to bid at an auction of a rare painting. You are not certain, but there is a chance the painting is a forgery. Now assume you win the bidding! That means you were willing to pay more for the painting than everyone else. What if everyone else knows the painting is a forgery. Oh, no . . . you won the auction. You have suffered the "winner's curse."

Money Market Instruments Other Than Treasury Bills

15-3

While Treasury Bills play a very important role in the money market, they are not the only money market instruments. Some of the other short-term, unsecured debt instruments that make up the money market include federal funds, commercial paper, repurchase agreements, negotiable certificates of deposit, banker's acceptance, and Eurodollars. Let's take a look at each of these in turn.

15-3a Federal Funds

Just as the term *money market* is a bit off, so too is the term *federal funds.* People often think federal funds are borrowed by the federal government. Or perhaps they think the Federal Reserve sets the federal funds rate. Neither is true.

The term *federal funds* comes from the idea of what the market originally was: a short-term market, usually overnight, where banks would lend to each other. For example, a bank might have excess reserves and thus a large amount of funds on deposit at the Fed. A second bank might not have enough reserves or lacks enough cash to meet the needs of its customers for the next business day. In this case the second bank, the one lacking reserves, approaches the first bank—the one with excess reserves—and says, "Hello, fellow banker. Would you be willing to lend me some of those funds you have on deposit at the Fed?" The first bank responds, "Sure, I will lend you the funds I have on deposit at the Fed, but I will charge you an interest rate on those funds." Thus the interest rate became known as the federal funds rate and the market became known as the federal funds market.

Today, things have gotten more complicated. Many borrowers and lenders in the federal funds market do not actually have reserves on deposit at the Fed. These include larger banks that are not part of the Fed, smaller banks that borrow money from money center banks instead of the Fed, and nonbanks such as thrifts, US branches of foreign banks, and government securities dealers. They really don't have funds on deposit at the Fed, but they still lend funds to each other through the federal funds market.

But some things from the old days remain the same. Federal funds transactions are still almost always overnight loans, they are unsecured, and they use funds that are immediately available. The terminology also remains the same: The institution that is borrowing the funds creates a liability called "federal funds purchased," whereas the institution lending the funds creates an asset called "federal funds sold."

Federal Funds Floor

One thing that changed on October 9, 2008, is that the Fed started paying interest on the bank deposits it holds. The Fed now pays the average of the targeted federal funds rate minus 10 basis points on required reserves and the lowest targeted federal funds rate minus 75 basis points on excess reserves. The goal is to establish a price floor in the federal funds market. To understand how this establishes a price floor, think about a bank that has excess reserves. If the lowest targeted federal funds rate is 1.25%, that means they could get 0.50% by simply leaving the funds on deposit at the Fed. This also means the lowest interest rate they would be willing to accept in the federal funds market is slightly above 1.25% since the federal funds market has some credit risk associated with it. So, by paying interest on reserves, the Fed has essentially created a price floor in the federal funds market. By establishing a price floor, the Fed is trying to guarantee that interest rates do not fall so low as to create deflation. Deflation, or falling prices, can be very destructive, especially for business firms.

15-3b Commercial Paper

Commercial paper is one of those terms in the money market that actually makes sense. Commercial paper is essentially unsecured IOUs issued by large, well-known, and trusted corporations. Thus, if you think about unsecured IOUs as being paper, then commercial paper is IOUs issued by trusted corporations or commercial operations.

Commercial paper: Short-term, unsecured debt issued most often by well-established corporations. Maturity is typically less than 270 days.

Commercial paper is issued by corporations who need to raise funds for a short period of time. For example, suppose Harley-Davidson, Inc., the Milwaukee-based manufacturer of motorcycles, needs cash to meet its payroll at the beginning of each month. The problem is that motorcycles don't sell very well during the winter, so in January, February, and March Harley-Davidson has what is known as a cash flow problem: Cash flows out to pay employees but there is not enough cash coming in because of slow sales.

In this case Harley-Davidson would go to the commercial paper market, sell its commercial paper, and thus borrow the funds it needs to pay its payroll. The commercial paper would have a short maturity because, naturally, when spring and summer arrive, Harley-Davidson will be selling a lot of motorcycles and have cash in excess of its needs. Thus it can pay off its commercial paper borrowing in a short time frame.

Harley-Davidson may issue commercial paper for reasons other than raising cash to pay its payroll. For example, Harley-Davidson also has a financing division called Harley-Davidson Financial Service, or HDFS, that provides financing to customers who purchase Harley-Davidson motorcycles. To raise funds to lend to their customers, Harley-Davidson sells commercial paper in the money market. Since Harley-Davidson traditionally has a much lower default risk than an individual, the company can borrow funds at a much lower interest rate than its consumers. For example, suppose Harley-Davidson can borrow funds in the commercial paper market at 2% and then relend the money to its customers to buy Harleys at 10%; then Harley-Davidson has a nice 800–basis point interest rate spread. This interest rate spread adds to the company's profitability. This source of profit became so important to Harley-Davidson that by 2007, fully 55% of all the motorcycles it sold were financed by HDFS. In 1999 only 22% of the motorcycles Harley-Davidson sold were financed by HDFS. As a result of the success of HDFS, Harley was making more money by financing motorcycles then they were by producing and selling them. But, as we will see, the good times did not last forever.

15-3c Repurchase Agreements

A repurchase agreement, or repo, is a financial arrangement whereby one party sells an asset (usually a Treasury bill) with the agreement to buy the asset back, or repurchase it, at a specific date in the future, often at a higher price. Repos are usually very short term, often overnight or lasting only a few days.

In the past government securities dealers such as Bear Stearns and Merrill Lynch sold T-bills to banks with a promise to buy them back the next day. Securities dealers then used the cash from the repo to buy other securities (stock and bonds) that they resold to "make a market" for these securities. Thus securities firms came to depend heavily on the repo market to fund their daily operations.

As we saw in Chapter 11, the Federal Reserve also relies on repos in its conduct of monetary policy. The same is true for the European Central Bank. Thus repurchase agreements play an important role in the operation of the overall money market.

15-3d Negotiable Certificates of Deposit

A certificate of deposit (CD) is basically an illiquid bank account. That is, deposits cannot be made to the account, nor can funds be withdrawn from the account, until it reaches its maturity date. Negotiable certificate of deposits can be thought of as large CDs; in fact, they are sometimes called "jumbo CDs," which are larger than the amount of deposit insurance. There is also a secondary market for negotiable CDs; thus they are called "bearer instruments" in that whoever holds the CD at maturity receives the principal plus any interest that is due.

To open a negotiable CD, savers must have large amounts of savings, usually at least $100,000; most often they are sold in lots of $1 million each. The interest rates paid on negotiable CDs are determined by negotiations between banks and their depositors, but the rates paid are usually close to the rates paid on Treasury bills.

Negotiable CDs were first invented in 1961 by National City Bank[5] (now CitiGroup) as a way to raise funds. Even though the banking industry has changed a great deal since 1961, negotiable CDs are still used by banks as a way of purchasing funds and managing their liabilities.

15-3e Banker's Acceptances

Banker's acceptances are used in international trade when two parties don't know each other well. Imagine a producer of wood floors in Finland has agreed to send their floors to M&M Flooring in Austin, Texas. The Finnish wood producers are not sure that M&M will be able to pay for the wood flooring materials it ships. To entice the Finnish wood producers to ship the flooring, M&M gets a letter of credit from its bank. The letter of credit basically says that if M&M cannot pay for the floors, the bank will.

Banker's acceptances: A common way to facilitate trade; a promise by one party to pay another party in the future, which is accepted or guaranteed by a bank.

When the Finnish company receives the letter of credit, it then ships the goods to M&M in Texas. To get paid, the Finnish company presents the letter of credit, along with proof it shipped the goods, to its bank in Finland. The Finnish bank then creates a time draft for the Finnish wood floor producer and sends it, along with proof of shipment, to M&M's bank in Texas. When M&M's bank gets the time draft, it stamps it "Accepted" and sends the banker's acceptance back to the Finnish bank so that the Finnish bank can sell it on the secondary market.

15-3f Eurodollar Accounts

Eurodollar accounts are another one of those things in finance where the name isn't exactly correct. Eurodollar accounts are dollar-denominated deposits outside of the United States, but not necessarily always in Europe.

Eurodollar account: A bank account that is denominated in a currency other than the currency of the country in which the depository institution resides.

Eurodollar accounts came about as the level of world trade increased in the twentieth century. Some firms overseas receive payments for their goods in US dollars. Because these firms may need to make payments in dollars in the future, they don't convert these dollars into their local currencies. Instead, they deposit these dollars at their local bank and thus create Eurodollar accounts.

The bank that received these dollar deposits may in turn lend the funds to another entity that needs to borrow in dollars. Thus there is a Eurodollar market in which these account balances are borrowed and lent. These Eurodollar transactions are typically for $1 million or more; thus the Eurodollar market is dominated by governments and large corporations.

While the money market is the market for short-term IOUs, there is another market for longer-term borrowing: the bond market. In the next chapter we turn our attention to this longer-term borrowing and lending market, the ever important bond market.

---

5 See "The Negotiable CD: National Bank Innovation in the 1960s," available at http://www.occ.gov/about/what-we-do/history/150th-negotiable-cd-article.html.

SECTION REVIEW

Q1) Explain how the Federal Reserve paying interest on deposits created a floor in the federal funds market.

Q2) How might a firm use the issuance of commercial paper as a way to deal with its seasonal fluctuations in sales?

Q3) A money market transaction in which one party sells a financial asset with the agreement to buy it back in the future is called:

a. a commercial paper transaction.

b. a standby letter of agreement.

c. a repurchase agreement.

d. a negotiable certificate of deposit.

Conclusion

15-4

Money markets, while arguably misnamed, are important financial markets. These markets—where short-term, unsecured financial instruments are traded—are an important tool in providing funding for governments and corporations, as well as an important investment vehicle for savers. The money market consists of the well-known and often discussed Treasury bill market as well as the federal funds market. Also included in this important market are less well-known but still important financial markets such as the commercial paper market, the repo market, and the markets for negotiable CDs, banker's acceptance, and Eurodollars.

Far too often the money markets are overshadowed by the long-term debt market: the bond market. In the next chapter we examine the bond market in more detail, and we discuss how both of these markets suffered badly during the recent financial crisis. Thus, if one wants to fully understand why the financial crisis came about, one needs to understand how these important financial markets function and why they did not function during the crisis.

IN THE NEWS. . .

Fed Explores Overhaul of Key Rate

Robin Harding

Financial Times

July 10, 2014

The US Federal Reserve is exploring an overhaul of the Federal funds rate—a benchmark that underlies almost every financial transaction in the world—as it prepares for an eventual rise in interest rates.

The Fed funds rate is the main measure of overnight US interest rates and is based on the actual rates reported by brokers for overnight loans between US banks.

According to people familiar with the discussion, the Fed could redefine its main target rate so that it takes into account a wider range of loans between banks, making it more stable and reliable. . . .

In particular, the Fed is looking at redefining the funds rate to include Eurodollar transactions—dollar loans between banks outside the US markets—as well as traditional onshore loans between US banks.

Other closely related rates that it could include are those on transactions for bank commercial paper and wholesale (negotiable) certificates of deposit between banks. . . .

In recent months, the Fed has started collecting detailed short-term borrowing data from banks on a form called FR2420.

That data could form the basis of a redefined Federal funds rate. . . .

Ira Jersey, director of interest rate strategy at Credit Suisse in New York, said Eurodollars were a very close substitute for Fed funds. . . .

Mr. Jersey said he thought including Eurodollars would be unlikely to change the Fed funds rate much right now but the effect when interest rates were higher was hard to judge.

The article discusses how financial data surrounding money markets might change in the future, specifically, how what we call today the "federal funds rate" may change to include other money market instruments. How might this change be beneficial to financial markets? How might this change be disruptive to financial markets?

16

Bond Markets

16-1 The Bond Market

In the previous chapter we looked at the borrowing and lending of funds in the short-term market, or the money market. In this chapter we turn our attention to the longer-term borrowing and lending of funds in the bond market.

In Chapter 3 we explained that a bond is a promise to repay with interest over time. That is, a bond is nothing more than a long-term IOU. Remember we also said that issuers of bonds consisted of government entities and corporations.

The bond market is huge. According to the Securities Industry and Financial Markets Association, in 2014 the total amount of bonds outstanding in the US bond market was about \$35 trillion,[1] with the money market adding an additional \$3.9 trillion. By comparison, according to the World Bank, the size of the US stock market, based on domestic companies, was \$18.8 trillion in 2012.[2] So, in the United States the debt market is more than twice the size of the equity market. The bond market makes up 90% of the debt market. Therefore, the bond market is important just based on its size. As we shall see, however, the bond market is not only large, but it is also very important for other reasons as well. Let's take a closer look at who issues bonds and why, as well as some of the controversial issues that surround the bond market.

16-1a Government and Agency Bonds

As we discussed previously, governments often fund their spending by issuing debt. If current government spending is greater than current tax revenues, the government can issue bonds to make up the shortfall. Or, governments or government agencies can issue bonds today that will be repaid with future tax revenue to allow for current spending on various government projects. Essentially, governments issue bonds to allow for current spending, and this current spending is funded by future tax revenues.

The bonds issued by the US federal government that mature between 1 and 10 years are called Treasury notes. The US federal government bonds that mature in more than 10 years are referred to as Treasury bonds.

Since Treasury notes and Treasury bonds are issued by the US federal government, the probability of default is extremely small. Think about this: To repay its debt, the US government simply has to collect enough taxes from firms and households. That is relatively simple compared with what a corporation has to do to repay its debt: buy inputs, produce a good, sell the good, collect payment from its customers, and so on. There are a great many things that can go wrong for a firm in that chain of events. For the government, however, it is relatively easy and straightforward: levy and collect taxes. Even if the government has trouble doing that, it could simply print money to repay its debt.[3]

Because of the very low level of default risk, government debt—including Treasury notes and Treasury bonds—pay relatively low interest rates compared with other bonds in the market. But this is not to say these government bonds are risk free. Because of their longer maturity dates, when interest rates change, Treasury notes and bonds have bigger swings in their market prices than do Treasury bills or other shorter-term debt. Thus government bonds have price risk, even if their default risk is almost zero.

Treasury Inflation-Protected Securities (TIPS)

Another risk with government bonds is the threat to returns when there is inflation. As rates of inflation increase, the real rate of return on government bonds decreases. To address this issue, in 1997 the US Treasury started offering TIPS, or Treasury inflation-protected securities.

1 See http://www.sifma.org/research/statistics.aspx

2 See http://data.worldbank.org/indicator/CM.MKT.LCAP.CD

3 In the modern era a government would force the central bank, or the banking system, to create the money for the government to spend.

TIPS are inflation-indexed bonds whereby the bondholder is protected from increases in the rate of inflation. With TIPS the interest rate on a bond does not change, but the principal amount used to calculate the interest payment does change as the consumer price index changes. So, when the bond reaches maturity, it is redeemed at either its inflation-adjusted principal or at par, whichever is greater.

Separate Trading of Registered Interest and Principal (STRIPS)

In 1985 the Treasury began offering investors the ability to separate interest payments from principal repayment on Treasury bonds. STRIPS, or separate trading of registered interest and principal securities, are traditional Treasury bonds except that the principal has been separated (or stripped) from the interest or coupon payments. Investors can choose to purchase either the future principal repayment or the future interest payments of the bond.

STRIPS are offered in a zero-coupon bond form. That is, STRIPS do not make periodic interest payments; instead, they are sold at a discount from their face value. Upon maturity of the STRIPS, the holder is paid the face value. This means the purchaser knows exactly how much they will be paid at maturity.

For example, suppose a 20-year Treasury bond has a face value of $20,000 and a coupon rate of 5%. The principal repayment can be stripped from the 40 semiannual interest payments to thus create 41 STRIPS. The zero-coupon STRIPS then are discounted to the present value using prevailing interest rates and term to maturity.

If the principal repayment of $20,000 was discounted by 5% for 20 years, it would sell for $7,538 before commission and fees. Thus an investor could buy the STRIPS today for $7,538 (plus commission and fees) and know that in 20 years they will receive a payment of $20,000. There is also a secondary market for STRIPS, so the investor wouldn't necessarily have to hold on to the security for the full 20 years if she didn't want to.

Popularity of STRIPS STRIPS have been popular in great part because investors know exactly how much they are going to be paid and when. Also, since STRIPS are offered by the US Treasury, they are very safe, with virtually no default risk, and are very liquid thanks to the secondary market. Another advantage of STRIPS is the relatively small amount of money it takes to purchase one. While an investor can purchase a Treasury security for a minimum of $10,000, STRIPS sell at a fraction of that price because they are a zero-coupon security. The zero-coupon characteristic of STRIPS also means there is no reinvestment risk compared with traditional periodic interest-paying bonds.

Before the Treasury offered STRIPS, a number of private securities dealers created their own zero-coupon securities by stripping Treasury notes and bonds. These securities were given interesting feline names, such as TIGRs (treasury investment growth funds), often pronounced "tigers," which were created by Merrill Lynch; CATS (certificates of accrual on treasury securities) from Salomon Brothers; LIONS (Lehman investment opportunity notes); and COUGRs (certificates of government receipts). Strange names, but true.

Government Agency Bonds

Over the years the US Congress has authorized several governmental agencies to issue their own debt. For example, Ginnie Mae, or Government National Mortgage Association (GNMA); Fannie Mae, or Federal National Mortgage Association (FNMA); and Freddie Mac, or Federal Home Loan Mortgage Corporation (FHLMC) were established initially to help provide liquidity to the mortgage market.

These agencies would sell bonds in the market and use the proceeds to buy mortgages from the financial institutions that wrote them. The agencies then would pool these mortgages together and sell slices of the pooled mortgages to a wide variety of investors.

Since investors believed these government agencies had the full backing of the US government, the agencies could borrow funds in the market at a relatively low interest rate. Even though these rates were generally higher than Treasury bill rates, the agency bonds were often viewed as almost perfectly default risk-free. During the years leading up to the mortgage crisis that started in 2008, these agency bonds were relatively safe from default. Because default rates on home mortgages were so low, the agencies kept very low levels of capital against potential defaults.

As we will see, these once "safe" government agency bonds turned out to be not so safe after all. The near collapse of Fannie Mae and Freddie Mac caused such shock waves through financial markets in 2007 and 2008 that they nearly led to a collapse of the entire global financial system.

Municipal Bonds

While the US federal government issues Treasury bills, notes, and bonds to fund their spending, state and local governments also need to issue bonds to borrow money to fund their expenditures. The bonds issued by state and local governments are called municipal, or "muni," bonds.

For example, Houston, Texas, is one of the fastest growing cities in the United States. Its warm climate, low cost of living, and welcoming attitude toward outsiders has resulted in steady increases in the population. But along with economic and population growth comes a strain on public goods such as roads.

Much of the highway system around Houston was designed and built in the 1960s, a time when the city was only a fraction of its current size. By the 1980s, Houston's highways were bursting at the seams. However, Harris County, where most of Houston lies, simply did not have millions of dollars lying around to build new highways.

Realizing the problem, in 1983 voters in Houston authorized the issuance of up to $900 million in bonds to build and operate a system of toll roads around the Houston area. Shortly after the vote, the Harris County Toll Road Authority (HCTRA) was created to borrow, build, and manage toll roads around Houston.

There are two types of municipal bonds: general obligation bonds and revenue bonds. As the name suggests, the proceeds from **general obligation bonds** are used by the issuing government for general expenses and are not targeted for a specific project. Most general obligation bonds must be approved by taxpayers because future taxes will be used to repay the debt plus interest.

General obligation bond: A bond issued and backed by a state or local municipality to raise funds that will be used for a variety of public works projects.

For example, the HCTRA issued general obligation bonds for some of the design and construction costs of the toll roads it built. In 2004 the HCTRA issued $250 million in general obligation bonds for the construction of the Katy Toll Road that connected the western suburb of Katy, Texas, to the heart of Houston. However, none of the revenues generated from the Katy Toll Road were used to pay interest or principal on the general obligation bonds.

Revenue bonds, on the other hand, are repaid in part using the cash flow from a particular cash-generating project. For example, in 2000 the citizens of Fort Bend County, Texas, which lies adjacent to Harris County, approved a $140 million revenue bond issue to create the Fort Bend County Toll Road Authority (FBCTRA). In 2004 the new Fort Bend Tollway was opened; this connected to existing tollways managed by the Harris Country Toll Road Authority. The tolls collected on the Fort Bend Tollway go to pay the interest and principle of the revenue bonds issued by the FBCTRA.

Revenue bond: A bond issued and backed by a state or local municipality to raise funds that will be used for a specific income-generating project.

Federal Income Tax Exemption of Muni Bonds The interest paid to holders of municipal bonds is exempt from federal income taxes. This feature makes muni bonds very attractive to savers in high tax brackets; it also means that municipalities can borrow money at a lower interest rate than they would if the interest they paid was fully taxable.

To understand why this is the case, consider the following:

Equivalent tax-free rate = Taxable intereste rate × (1 − Marginal tax rate)

Suppose we have a corporate bond with a 7% interest rate and a saver who faces a marginal tax rate of 28%. Also suppose a tax-free municipal bond has a rate of 5.25%. Which should our saver choose?

For the corporate bond, the equivalent tax-free rate is

Equivalent tax-free rate = 0.07 × (1 − 0.28) = 0.0504 = 5.04%

Since the muni bond pays a higher rate (5.25%) than the equivalent tax-free rate (5.04%), the saver will choose the muni bond, ceteris paribus.

Thus, when comparing bonds with taxable interest payments with tax-free bonds such as muni bonds, investors cannot simply compare rates of return. Instead, investors must be certain that they are comparing equivalent tax-free rates of return; otherwise they may be making inefficient use of their resources.

Default Risks with Muni Bonds Although muni bonds are issued by state and local governments, they are not risk-free promises to repay. General obligation bonds are usually viewed as having a lower default risk than revenue bonds. This is because revenue bonds depend on a specific source of revenue for repayment. If that specific source or project does not perform as planned, then repayment of the bond can become doubtful.

A 2003 study by Fitch Reporting also found that there is a moderate correlation between economic downturns and muni bond default rates. That is, as the economy slows, the level of defaults in municipal bonds increases. As the economy slowed in 2008 and 2009, there were growing concerns that the amount of muni bond defaults would escalate significantly. We discuss later in the chapter how this market was affected by the larger financial crisis.

SECTION REVIEW

Q1) Explain how TIPS, or Treasury inflation-protected securities, actually protect investors from inflation.

Q2) Shoma is thinking about buying a municipal bond. She notices some are revenue bonds, whereas others are general obligation bonds, but she does not understand what these are. How would you explain this to Shoma?

Q3) Sunita wants to earn the highest possible after-tax return on her savings. She has two options: a corporate bond and a tax-free government bond. The corporate bond yields 5%, and Sunita is in the 25% marginal tax bracket. What equivalent tax-free rate would a government bond need to have to make her indifferent between the corporate bond and the government bond?

a. 5.25%

b. 4.00%

c. 3.75%

d. 2.75%

16-2 Corporate Bond Market

As we discussed earlier, corporations often have very uneven cash flows. In some periods their income is greater than then their current expenses, whereas other times their optimal level of expenditures is much greater than their current income. For example, in March 2008 candy maker Mars announced that it was going to purchase chewing gum maker Wm. Wrigley Jr. Company of Chicago for about $23 billion. But to purchase Wrigley the Mars Corporation faced a problem: It didn't have enough cash lying around to buy the outstanding Wrigley stock. To solve this problem, Mars announced that it was going to issue bonds to finance the purchase of Wrigley stock. Thus, by issuing bonds, Mars was able to purchase Wrigley and greatly expand their product line.

But not all bonds are the same. In addition to the term and coupon rates, bonds have a wide variety of different characteristics. Each of these unique characteristics can affect the bond price and thus its yield to investors.

16-2a Characteristics of Corporate Bonds

Remember that while bonds are a corporation's promise to repay with interest, stocks represent ownership of a corporation. Since stockholders have the power to hire and fire the executives of a corporation, those executives may pay more attention to the interests of stockholders than they do those of bondholders. To more closely align the interests of bondholders and executives, many bonds carry with them **bond covenants**, which either tell management what to do or place restrictions on what management can do.

Bond covenants: A portion of a bond agreement that specifies what the borrower (the bond issuer) may or may not do during the life of the bond.

Most often bond covenants are "financial covenants" that specify, for example, that management must maintain a stated leverage ratio, or a debt-to-equity ratio, within a given range. These types of ratios are designed to make sure that management does not overload the corporation with debt. Covenants can also be "nonfinancial," such as requiring management to provide financial information to bondholders, placing restrictions on the selling of assets, and/or making sure the assets of the company have adequate levels of insurance. In general, bonds with covenants have lower interest rates because the restrictions on what management can and cannot do makes the firm more stable and the bonds less risky.

When a corporation issues a long-term bond, it may wish to pay off all or part of the bond early, before it reaches its maturity date. To allow the issuer of a bond to pay off its bond early or recall it, the bond must have a **call provision**. The call provision of a bond stipulates under what conditions the issuer can buy back the bond or pay it off early. Bonds with call provisions usually have multiple call dates and stated prices of the buyback.

Call provision: A clause in a bond contract that allows the issuer of the bond the right to buy back all or part of the bond issued before the bond's maturity date.

The call provision of a bond might state that a bond due June 1, 2030, is callable on June 1, 2017, at a price of 105% of par. The **indenture**, or bond contract, usually includes a table of call dates and prices. The call price is normally higher than the face value of the bond, but it decreases the closer the bond comes to its maturity date. For example, the issuer may offer 105% of the face value if it calls the bond after 4 years, but it may offer only 102% if it calls the bond in 10 years because it is closer to the bond's maturity date.

Indenture: A legal contract between the bond issuer and the bond holder or purchaser. The contract lays out the legal requirements of the borrower or bond issuer.

Sometimes the early buyback of bonds is required under the terms of a **sinking fund**. A sinking fund is a pool of money a corporation sets aside to help repay a bond issue. Sinking funds are often created to help ensure the bond issuer can repay the face value of the bonds they issue.

Sinking fund: A pool of money set aside for the repayment of a bond.

For example, suppose Fred's Beer Company sells a 10-year bond with a $10,000 face value and a coupon rate of 5%. The issuer has to pay bondholders $250 twice a year for the next 10 years, which may not be much of a financial strain for Fred's. But at the end of 10 years Fred's has to repay the $10,000 face value, which might cause some cash flow problems for Fred's, especially if the company is in a poor financial condition when the bond matures. The company may be in fine shape today, but how many beers will they be selling 10 years from now?

To reduce the risk of being short on cash 10 years from now, the company may create a sinking fund for repurchasing a portion of the existing bonds, say, every year. By repaying a portion of its debt each year, the company will face a much smaller payout when the bonds mature. Sinking fund provisions usually allow an issuer to repurchase their bonds periodically and at a specific price, usually at par or the prevailing market price.

A sinking fund might sound a lot like a call provision, but they are different. Sinking funds usually limit how many of the bonds the issuer can buy back early, whereas call provisions often allow the issuer to pay off all the bonds it issues. Also, sinking fund buyback prices are usually lower than call provision buyback prices, so the holder of a bond from a company with a sinking fund actually stands to lose more money should a sinking fund provision result in the early payoff of their bond.

Some bonds can be converted into shares of common stock at some point in the future at an agreed-upon price. Although **convertible bonds** generally have a lower yield than nonconvertible bonds with the same characteristics, convertible bonds allow a bondholder to share in the success of the economic growth of the firm. From an issuer's point of view, convertible bonds are beneficial because they require lower interest payments than nonconvertible bonds. The downside to the issuer is, if the firm is successful in the future, this success will have to be shared with bondholders as they convert their bonds to common stock.

Convertible bonds: A bond where the bondholder can convert the bond into a specified number of shares of stock of the firm that issued the bond.

While bonds have many different characteristics, one of the most important distinguishing features of a bond is the potential for default. Bond buyers are very concerned about default risk. Yet properly evaluating default risk is a difficult thing to do. Next we examine one of the most controversial methods used to evaluate default risk: the bond rating system.

SECTION REVIEAW

Q1) Jenny is considering purchasing a bond, but she notices that the bond has many covenants. She is unsure what they mean. How would you explain these covenants to Jenny?

Q2) Why do bonds have sinking funds? How are they different from a call provision?

Q3) A convertible bond allows for a bond to be converted into what at a future date?

a. Cash

b. Stock

c. Dividend

d. Interest payment

16-3 Bond Rating Debate

When an investor is interested in buying a bond in either the primary or secondary market, one of the biggest worries is default risk. That is, what are the chances the issuer of the bond will not pay interest and/or repay the principal as promised? To help alleviate that fear, entities called bond-rating agencies offer their opinion on the level of default risk of various issuers of bonds.

16-3a Evolution of Bond Ratings

The first to start offering bond ratings on the potential of default was John Moody in 1909. He assigned letter grades to the bonds issued by railroads, making it easier for investors to evaluate the default risk of various railroad companies' debt. Bond purchasers loved Moody's new system because instead of having to dig through mountains of data to determine default risk, all they had to do with Moody's bond-rating system was look at the letter grade and compare it with that of similar bonds. Moody's rating system was simple, straightforward, and easy to use. It was a huge success.

As is often the case, success breeds imitation, and so it was in the bond-rating business in the early twentieth century. In 1916 Poor's Publishing Company, which eventually became Standard & Poor (S&P for short), began offering its own bond ratings to investors. Fitch Publishing Company, which was founded by John Knowles Fitch in 1913, began offering its own letter-grading system of bonds in 1924. Each of them found their own slice of the market, and each thrived as the financial markets expanded through the 1920s.

Even as the economy collapsed in the face of the Great Depression, the three bond-rating agencies thrived. These rating agencies grew in influence during the Great Depression of the 1930s as newly empowered government bank regulators used the bond-rating system to evaluate the soundness of bank assets.

After World War II, however, the influence of the three bond raters started to wane as the amount of bond defaults steadily declined. As the postwar economic expansion resulted in fewer bond defaults, financial market participants began to wonder: If the probability of defaults are so low, who needs a bond rating anymore?

As the economic and financial system became more turbulent with the stagflation of the 1970s, the stature of the bond-rating agencies grew once again. By 1975, bond-rating agencies had become so important that the Securities and Exchange Commission (SEC) stepped in and deemed the three agencies as nationally recognized statistical rating organizations (NRSROs). With this recognition, the SEC gave a de facto "stamp of approval" to the three bond-rating agencies: Moody's, S&P, and Fitch. To this day these three remain the main bond-rating agencies.

16-3b Bond-Rating System Today

Each of the three bond-rating agencies have a slightly different way of evaluating bond issuers. Each bond that is rated is given a letter rating. The scales are shown in Table 16-1.

In addition to rating the bond issuer, the bond-rating agencies also sound an alarm if an issuer is about to be downgraded. For Moody's, this system is called "Under Review," for Standard & Poor it is called "Credit Watch," and for Fitch it is called "Rating Watch." A downgrade in a bond rating can cost an issuer millions of dollars because issuers with a lower bond rating have to offer a higher interest rate to borrowers to offset the increased default risk.

Conflicts of Interest?

Initially, the bond-rating agencies earned their income by selling manuals full of financial data, as well as financial advisory services, to the purchasers of bonds. Slowly, over time, as the bond-rating agencies started to offer ratings on a wider variety of financial

TABLE 16-1 Letter Ratings of Default Risk Assigned by the Three Main Bond-Rating Agencies

Credit Risk	Moody's	Standard & Poor's	Fitch
Investment grade			
Highest quality	Aaa	AAA	AAA
High quality	Aa	AA	AA
Upper medium	A	A	A
Medium	Baa	BBB	BBB
Not investment grade			
Lower medium	Ba	BB	BB
Lower grade	B	B	B
Poor grade	Caa	CCC	CCC
Speculative	Ca	CC	CC
No payments/bankruptcy	C	D	C
In default	C	D	D

assets—including commercial paper, preferred stock, syndicated bank loans, collateralized debt obligations, and other financial instruments—their business model began to change.

Instead of charging the buyers of bonds for the bond ratings, the agencies started to charge fees to the issuers of these instruments. For example, assume the Wisconsin Teachers Retirement Fund is considering buying bonds issued by CSX Railroad, but Wisconsin Teachers Retirement Fund wants to be able to evaluate the default risk of the CSX bonds. Initially, the bond-rating agencies would charge Wisconsin Teachers Retirement Fund for the bond rating. Under the current "issuer pays" method, however, CSX would pay the bond-rating agencies to provide the bond rating.

This issuer pays model created a potential conflict of interest. When the issuer pays for the bond rating, the bond-rating agency now has a stake in how well the bonds sell. If the bonds sell well, the issuer is more likely to sell more bonds in the future and thus generate more income for the bond-rating agency in the future. If the bond does not sell well, however, perhaps because of a low bond rating, the issuer is less likely to issue more bonds in the future, much to the detriment of the bond-rating agency. Thus, under the issuer pays model, the bond-rating agency has an incentive to rate the bonds higher than what they actually deserve.

The counterargument to this conflict of interest is the issue of reputation. The argument goes something like this: The bond-rating agencies are only as "good" as their reputation. So, if a bond-rating agency is deliberately rating bonds higher than they should be, that agency's reputation will suffer, few people in the market will believe their ratings, and eventually the agency will be driven out of business. Assuming backward deduction, a rational manager of a bond-rating agency works to protect its reputation, and long-term survivability, and thus will not rate bonds higher than what they actually deserve.

So the question becomes, How much does reputation matter to the bond-rating agencies? Clearly, the bond-rating agencies do not have a perfect record. The big three bond-rating agencies were all giving high bond ratings to the debt issued by Enron and WorldCom right up until the two giants imploded into bankruptcy in the early 2000s. Only after the defaults started to occur did the bond-rating agencies lower the bond ratings.

Despite their failure to sound a warning about Enron and WorldCom, the three big bond-rating agencies were not forced out of business by market forces. In fact, they became more profitable as the housing bubble grew from 2003 to 2007. The bond-rating agencies were later blamed by many for contributing to the housing asset bubble by giving high ratings to securities backed by subprime mortgages. When defaults on the risky subprime mortgages increased and the highly rated securities fell into default, again the bond-rating agencies were not forced out of business.

In the wake of the most recent financial crisis there have been more calls to reform and regulate the bond-rating agency. The Dodd-Frank Act of 2011 created the Office of Credit Ratings (OCR) within the SEC. The OCR, which began operation in 2012, oversees the rating agencies, including S&P, Moody's, and Fitch, as well as other smaller rating agencies. While the OCR produces reports of industry activity and monitors rating agencies to make sure they comply with existing rules, it has no direct enforcement power over the rating agencies.

There are many unresolved questions raised by the current financial crisis. What role will the bond-rating agencies play in the future of our financial markets? Have their reputations been permanently negatively affected, or will they come through this crisis unscathed as they did after Enron and WorldCom blew up? Will more regulations be placed on these rating agencies? Might they even be forced to break up to create more competition within the bond-rating business?

SECTION REVIEW

Q1) Initially, bond ratings were paid for by the bond purchaser. Today bonding ratings are under an "issuer pays" model. Explain how the two forms are different.

Q2) Explain why some argue the "issuer pays" model creates a conflict of interest.

Q3) Which of the following correctly describes the role of the bond-rating agencies in the subprime mortgage asset bubble?

a. The bond-rating agencies warned early on that subprime mortgages were going to have a high level of default.

b. The bond-rating agencies gave high ratings to assets backed by subprime mortgages, thus encouraging the growth of the asset bubble.

c. The bond-rating agencies informed government regulators, but not the general public, of the high level of default risk of subprime mortgages.

d. All of these.

Debt Market During the Crisis

16-4

In the autumn of 2008 the debt markets were in the midst of a panic. The broader US economy was contracting at an alarming rate, unemployment was increasing, bank lending was decreasing, the stock market was dropping, and consumer confidence was sinking.

By September 2008 the Dow Jones Industrial Average had lost more than 500 points, more than 4% of its value, in just one week. Lehman Brothers, an investment bank that dated back to before the Civil War, filed for bankruptcy. Merrill Lynch, one of the stalwarts of Wall Street, had been forced to sell itself to Bank of America. AIG, the insurance giant, was on the verge of collapse. The financial markets were truly in a stunned state of confusion.

When confusion, uncertainty, and panic dominate life, it is human nature to seek out order, certainty, and calm. In this way financial markets are just like the rest of life: When the markets are in grip of uncertainty, there is a desire by investors to seek out certainty and stability. It is what we referred to in Chapter 4 as a flight to quality.

Within a debt market, a flight to quality occurs as investors pull their money out of markets with various levels of uncertainty and put it into "safe" markets such as Treasury securities. This is exactly what happened in the autumn of 2008.

16-4a Flight to Quality

In early September 2008 the difference in yield between a 20-year Treasury bond and a Moody's Baa-rated, 20-year corporate bond was less than 270 basis points. By early October 2008, that difference had increased to over 390 basis points. The 20-year Treasury bond was yielding 4.39% on September 2, 2008, whereas Baa-rated bonds were yielding 7.07%. But by October 7, 2008, the Baa bond yield had shot up to 8.05%, whereas the 20-year Treasury yield had fallen to 4.15%.

As we discussed in Chapter 4, when funds flow out of markets with higher default risk and into the markets of securities with lower default risk, economists call this a flight to quality. As fear and uncertainty gripped the markets, investors started to sell off the Baa-rated corporate bonds and flee into the Treasury market. As a result, there was an increase in supply in the secondary market for Baa bonds as holders of these bonds rushed to sell them. Many of these funds then flowed into the Treasury bill (T-bill) market, resulting in an increase in demand for Treasury bonds.

We can see this graphically using the loanable funds framework in Figure 16-1. Here we have the loanable funds market for T-bills and the loanable funds market for Baa-rated bonds. Note that, initially, the difference between the interest rate in the T-bill market and the interest rate in the Baa market is the default risk premium spread. That is, it is the additional return investors require, over the T-bill or risk-free rate, to get them to hold Baa-rated bonds.

But, as the flight to quality takes place, there is a decrease in the supply of loanable funds in the Baa market as investors panic and sell their Baa-rated bonds. These funds then flow into the "safe" market of T-bills. Thus the T-bill market sees an increase in the supply of loanable funds. As a result of this flight to quality, the interest rate in the Baa market shoots up, while the interest rate in the T-bill market falls. Consequently, the default risk premium spread gets larger, or the spread between T-bill yields and Baa-rated bond yields increases.

Flight to Quality and the Commercial Paper Market

The flight to quality and thus the increasing default risk premium spread hit many companies hard. Harley-Davidson, for example, which could issue 30-day commercial paper in 2004 and pay around 1% in annual interest, saw its borrowing costs for 30-day commercial paper jump past 6% in October 2008.

Figure 16-1 **Loanable funds market for Treasury bills (T-bills; left) and Baa-rated bonds (right)**

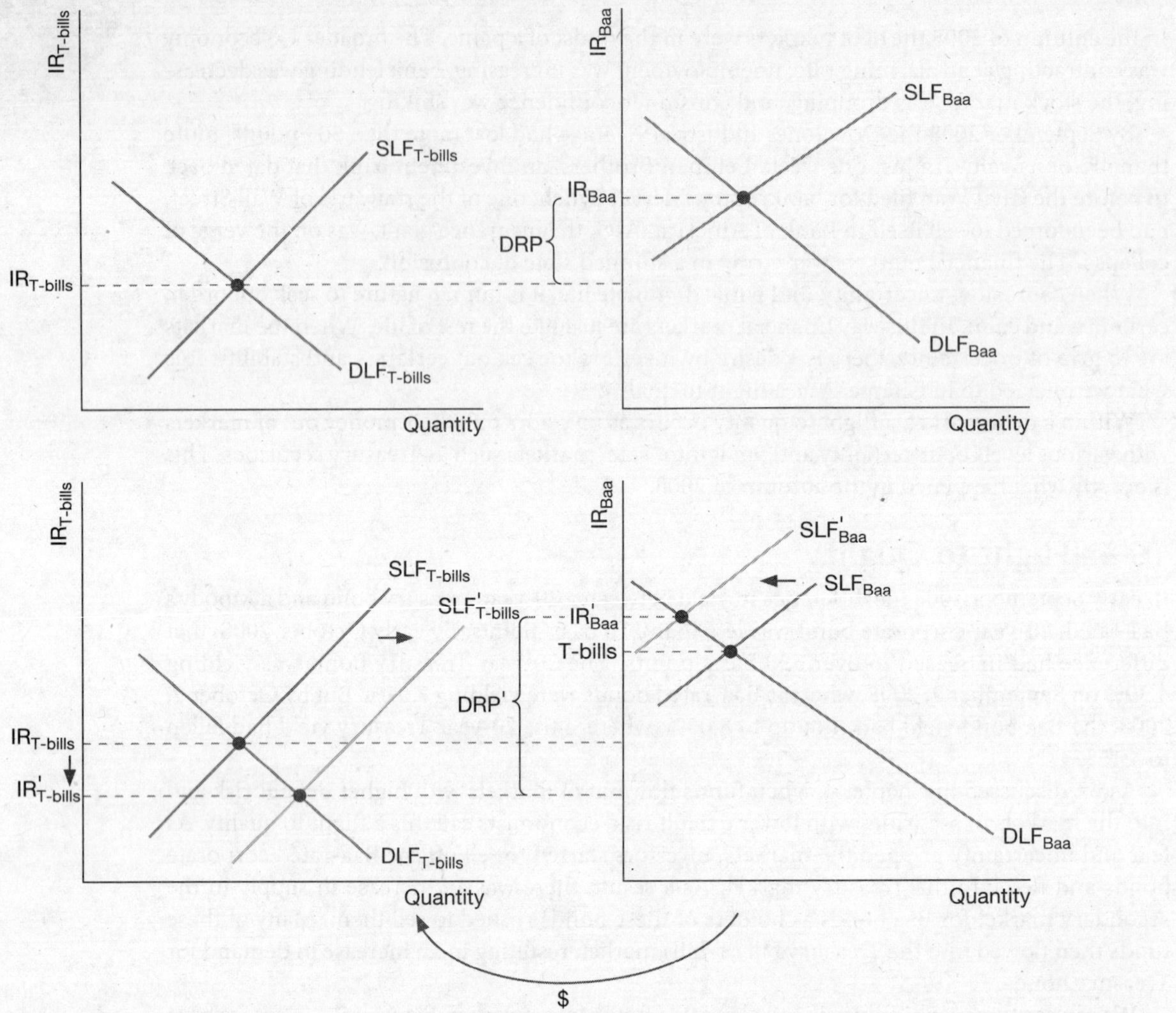

To make matters worse for Harley-Davidson, not only were its borrowing costs increasing, its sales of motorcycles were falling rapidly as the economy contracted. In the first quarter of 2009 Harley-Davidson's profits fell 39% from the year before. In the second quarter of 2009 Harley-Davidson reported its profits fell a whopping 91% from the year before. As a result, Harley-Davidson announced 2,400 of its employees would lose their jobs, and they were looking to close their production facility in York, Pennsylvania.

Flight to Quality and the Municipal Bond Market

Private borrowers such as Harley-Davidson were not the only ones negatively affected by the flight to quality. Issuers of municipal bonds also were hard hit by the flight to quality in 2008. Atlantic Health, which operates hospitals in New Jersey and New York, saw its borrowing costs skyrocket in February 2008. Where previously Atlantic Health could borrow funds in the short-term municipal bond market at 3%, when the flight to quality hit, their short-term interest rate shot up to 12%.[4]

4 See Liz Wolgemuth, "The Credit Crunch Squeezes Municipal Bonds." *U.S. News & World Report*, February 28, 2008.

Compounding the problem for municipal bonds in 2008 was the financial trouble of many municipal bond insurers. These bond insurers promised to make good on the municipal bond issuers' promises to repay if the issuers themselves could not do so. Thus these bond insurers helped to reduce the default risk of municipal bonds. The problem was that many of these municipal bond insurers also had offered insurance on financial assets backed up by subprime mortgages. As the number of subprime mortgage defaults increased, the assets based on these mortgages started to fail, and bond insurers were left with huge liabilities to pay. With these increasing debts, buyers of municipal bonds began to question the value of the "promises to pay" issued by these bond insurers. Once the bond insurance was of questionable value, there was a massive flight to quality out of the municipal bond market.

Global Flight to Quality

While there was a flight to quality with the US financial markets in the autumn of 2008, there was also a global flight to quality. "What you are seeing is a straight panic reaction," said Phillip Lang, investment director at Standard Life Investments in Edinburgh, Scotland, reported Bloomberg. Around the world, investors were busy pulling funds out of riskier debt markets and into safer markets, such as US Treasury securities.

We can see this graphically if we consider the loanable funds market for the rest of the world compared with the loanable funds market for U.S. Treasury securities (Fig. 16-2). As the flight to quality grips the markets, funds flow out of the rest of the world's market, or the supply of loanable funds decreases, and make their way into the US Treasury market, pushing the interest rates for treasuries down. Thus the global flight to quality pushed up the borrowing costs for the rest of the world, while the interest rate on Treasury securities fell.

One of the uncertainties that gripped the debt markets in the autumn of 2008 was the uncertainty over liquidity. Investors worried that as financial markets were bogged down in a morass of uncertainty, the ability to convert financial instruments into cash would become a major concern. As a result of the concern over liquidity, financial market participants fled less

Figure 16-2 Global flight to quality. ROW, rest of world

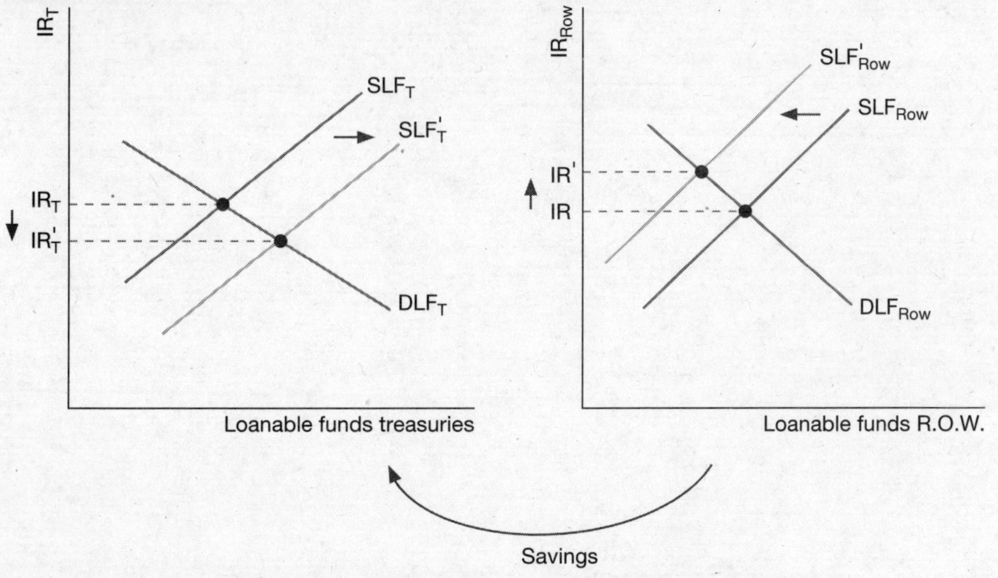

liquid markets and into markets that offered more liquidity, ceteris paribus. The movement out of less liquid markets and into more liquid markets is what economists call a **flight to liquidity**.

Flight to liquidity: A situation in financial markets where investors move funds from less liquid financial assets into financial assets that offer a higher level of liquidity.

This flight of liquidity can be seen in the interest rate spread between 3-month Treasury bills and 20-year Treasury bonds. The 3-month T-bill is a much more liquid financial instrument than the 20-year Treasury bond. Even though they have the same level of default risk and the same tax treatment of dividends, the 3-month T-bill reaches maturity sooner and has a larger secondary market than do 20-year Treasury bonds.

The interest rate spread between a 3-month Treasury bill and a 20-year Treasury bond was 99 basis points on September 2, 2008. The 3-month T-bill yielded 1.68%, versus 2.69% for the 20-year T-bond. But, as the flight for liquidity ensued, investors rushed out of the 20-year T-bond market, pushing its yield up to 4.41% by September 10. The rush into T-bills pushed their yields down to 0.24% by the same date. Thus, by September 10, the spread between the 3-month T-bill and 20-year T-bond had increased to a whopping 410 basis points!

SECTION REVIEW

Q1) Explain, in words and graphically, how private borrowers such as Harley-Davidson are negatively affected by a flight to quality.

Q2) Explain, in words and graphically, how the financial crisis that started in the United States led to a worldwide flight to quality.

Q3) During times of crises, funds can flow from long-term debt markets to shorter-term debt markets. This is often referred to as a:

a. flight to yield.

b. flight to liquidity.

c. flight to shortness.

d. flight to level.

Conclusion

16-5

As the current financial crisis demonstrates, bond markets can have a far-reaching impact on the lives of people around the globe. During good times, the bond market provides capital for longer-term government borrowing on the federal, agency, state, and local levels, as well as provides to firms longer-term capital in a variety of customizable formats.

As we have seen, however, these markets can also help to transmit problems from one financial market to another. Flights to quality and flights to liquidity can cause the problems in one bond market to spread quickly to other bond markets around the world. Even in good times, the bond markets are not without their controversies. The bond rating debate will go on well after the current crisis passes.

In the next chapter we examine the ever more controversial equity markets. Among other things, we will review the debates that rage over explaining and predicting movements in these important financial markets.

IN THE NEWS. . .

SEC Is Gearing Up to Focus on Ratings Firms

Timothy W. Martin

The Wall Street Journal

June 25, 2014

The government's top credit-rating watchdog has kept a low profile since taking the job two years ago to help prevent another financial crisis. That may be about to change.

Thomas J. Butler, head of the Securities and Exchange Commission's Office of Credit Ratings, said he has referred multiple cases to the agency's enforcement division and is helping to complete several industry regulations to address quality and transparency of how big debt deals are rated.

Those moves signal a potential flurry of regulatory activities involving ratings firms, which have been largely untouched as government oversight has increased in most other financial sectors in recent years. . . .

Some critics have questioned whether the office has moved quickly enough to bring substantive changes to an industry widely blamed for helping trigger the financial crisis, largely by giving top ratings to mortgage bonds that later soured and left investors with billions in losses.

They point out the three biggest firms—S&P, Moody's and Fitch Ratings—still dominate the industry, despite lawmakers saying they hope to attract new entrants. Momentum to adopt major revisions, such as changing the business model or standardizing ratings across asset classes, also has petered out.

"While we've made some progress, I'm frustrated that key reforms still aren't fully implemented," said Sen. Al Franken (D-Minn.) . . . issuers of bond deals pay ratings firms to grade their deals, a model that Sen. Franken and others have said gives firms an incentive to comprise their criteria in order to win business.

The article discusses the difficultly of reforming the bond-rating agencies in the face of the recent financial crisis. The article points out the potential conflict of interest the bond-rating agencies have, yet many see the recent moves as not enough "reform" of the current system. How might the bond-rating system be reformed to help ensure a more efficient bond market?

17

The Stock Market and Efficiency

17-1 The Stock Market: Buying and Selling

It is hard to avoid news about things taking place in the stock market. From stories in the business press about what is happening to share prices of individual firms to two-minute news updates on network television telling us what the Dow closed at today, we are inundated with news about the stock market. Yet, when push comes to shove, many people's understanding of the stock or equity market is rather limited. Many people, for example, don't know the difference between common and preferred shares, or what exactly this Dow thing is everyone keeps referring to. By the end of this chapter you will hopefully have a much better understanding of this important financial market.

17-1a The Stock or Equity Market

Let's start by making sure we understand what stocks are. Simply put, stocks, or shares, represent part ownership of a corporation. This is why stocks or shares are sometimes referred to as equity, as in equity analyst; the term *equity* can mean ownership. The stock market, then, is the market for the buying and selling of stocks or shares, or—as it is sometimes called—the equity market.

Buyers of stocks or shares of a corporation are interested in owning part of the corporation that issues the shares so that the investor can get a share of the corporation's future profits, called dividends. In a worse case, if a corporation is liquidated, the shareholders get what is left over after taxes and the corporation's debts are repaid. This is called a **residual claim**. On the other hand, from a corporation's point of view, selling their shares in the stock market allows them to raise funds they need to finance their operations or expansions.

Residual claim: The amount that stockholders are paid at the liquidation of a corporation after taxes, debts, and other claims have been satisfied.

The stock market thus allows savers to easily buy shares of a corporation and thereby share in the corporation's future profits, and it allows corporations to raise the capital that they need. Let's take a look at each side of this market in turn.

Corporations Issuing Stock

If a corporation wants to raise capital, it might go out and borrow funds or it might issue stock—sell ownership shares of the corporation. If the corporation borrows money, it has to pay back those funds with interest. However, there is no required payback when a corporation raises funds by issuing shares of stock. A corporation that sells its shares to investors doesn't have to buy back the shares from its stockholders. It might choose to do so—called a **share buyback**—but it is not under any obligation to do so.

Share buyback: When a corporation buys back shares it previously sold to investors; also called share repurchase.

Not only do corporations not have to "repay" the stockholders, the corporation doesn't have to pay *any* of its profits to the shareholders in the form of dividends if it doesn't want to. Remember, dividends, the distributions of cash, shares, or other property the corporation pays to stockholders, are usually paid out of current earnings or profits. Some well-established corporations pay out 80% or 90% of their earnings or profits, whereas many startups and technology companies may not pay any dividends at all.

Savers Buying Stock

One of the main reasons why savers, or surplus units, wish to buy stock is because they want to share in a corporation's future profits. But remember, this paying out of dividends is not guaranteed, so there is risk in purchasing stock. The buyer of the stock faces the uncertainty that the corporation my not pay dividends in the future or that the dividends they do pay are lower than what is anticipated. The dividends a corporation pays could be paid in the form of cash, additional stock, or whatever form the board of directors of the corporation chooses. It is, however, most often in the form of a cash dividend.

In addition to getting a claim on future profits of the corporation, stocks also come with voting rights. For example, common stockholders are the ones who elect the corporation's board of directors, authorize the issuance of new shares of stock, approve amendments to the corporate charter, and adopt or amend the corporate bylaws. Stockholders get to cast their votes at the corporation's annual meeting or they can assign a proxy. A proxy is a legal form whereby a shareholder transfers their voting rights to someone else, usually another shareholder.

So, would you like a slice of a corporation's future profits? Would you like to have the power to vote on who is going to be on the corporation's board of directors? If so, then you are interested in buying the corporation's stock. But what type of stock do you want to buy?

Types of Stock: Common versus Preferred

There are two general types of stock: common stock and preferred stock. **Common stock** is the most popular form of stock. Startup firms issue common stock to raise much-needed capital to cover costs and pay for expansion of their businesses, whereas existing firms often issue common stock to finance ongoing operations or expansion.

Common stock: Shares of a corporation that entitle the holder to a claim on the corporation's assets at liquidation and where holders are paid a portion of the corporation's profits through dividends decided by the corporation's board of directors. Holders of common stock elect the board of directors and vote on corporate policy.

Holders of common stock get to vote at the annual meeting, get paid dividends (if there are any), and hope that the value of the shares they own increases over time.

Unlike holders of common stock, those who own **preferred stock** usually do not get voting rights at the annual corporate meeting. But the major advantage to preferred stocks is that stockholders are paid dividends before those who hold common stock are paid. The amount of the dividend paid to those who own preferred stock is fixed and never changes. So, in some ways preferred stock is like a combination of a bond—fixed payment is due each period—and common stock: A holder of preferred stock is part owner of the corporation and thus has a claim, ahead of people owning common stock, on the assets of the corporation.

Preferred stock: Shares of a corporation that entitle holders to a claim on the corporation's assets at liquidation senior to common stock holders. Holders are entitled to a fixed dividend payment that is paid before common stock dividends.

So, you have decided what type of stock you want to buy. The next decision you have to make is from what market do you want to the buy the stock? Do you want to buy shares that have never been owned by someone else, or do you want to buy already outstanding shares?

Primary versus Secondary Market for Equities

When stocks are sold by a corporation to members of the public, this is called a primary market transaction. In the primary market the corporation has an investment bank sell its shares to the public. An initial public offering, or IPO, is when the corporation sells its shares in the primary market to the public for the first time. We discuss investment banks and the IPO process in Chapter 24.

Most stock market transactions, however, are not IPOs or another type of primary market transaction. Instead, most stock market transactions are in the secondary market—someone who had previously purchased the stock is now selling it to someone else. Who are these "someones" buying and selling stock in the secondary market?

Buyers and sellers in the secondary equity market can be either institutional investors or individual investors. Institutional investors include insurance companies looking to invest premium payments, pension funds, endowments looking for long-term investments, securities firms buying and selling for customers and their own account, and some financial institutions buying and selling for customers.

Exchanges and Over the Counter

These secondary market transactions take place through a securities exchange where brokers who represent investors buy and sell the securities. Or, the transactions take place over the counter (OTC), where a network of dealers buy and sell stocks not listed on one of the exchanges. Many OTC trades are done by the National Association of Security Dealers Automatic Quotation (NASDAQ) electronic quoting system.

In the old days the difference between exchanges and OTC were pretty clear: Exchanges had a trading floor where brokers would buy shares from and sell shares to each other, and only well-established stocks would be listed on exchanges. The OTC market did not have a physical trading floor; instead, the brokers would communicate with each other—initially by phone—to buy and sell lesser-traded shares of generally smaller, less well-known companies.

Today, thanks in large part to technology, the differences are becoming more blurred. While the New York Stock Exchange (NYSE) still has its trading floor, the majority of trades on the NYSE—over 80% (in 2007 it was only 60%)—are done by the NYSE Super Display Book System, which is an electronic trading platform that matches buyers and sellers. Both the NYSE and NASDAQ offer extended trading sessions, both before and after the "regular" trading day. While the trading in these "premarket" and "after-hours" sessions is still relatively light, it is yet another way that the differences between exchanges and OTC are fading away.

Who Lists Where?

Perhaps the biggest difference to disappear is what company's shares are traded where. Again, it used to be that big, well-established companies traded on exchanges like the NYSE, whereas small, less well-known companies had their shares traded OTC, like NASDAQ. This was primarily because to have its shares listed (and thus traded) on an exchange, a company had to fill out a lengthy application and meet certain restrictions (such as the number of shares outstanding, earnings level over the past three years, and market value).

Then in the 1990s some successful information technology (IT) and tech startup firms changed whose shares traded where. As the IT startups grew and became very profitable—so big and profitable that they became eligible to be listed on the exchanges—they continued to list their shares on NASDAQ. That is why you might hear NASDAQ referred to as the "technology heavy" NASDAQ when reported in the press. For a couple of decades NASDAQ was dominated by shares of technology companies.

But even this has started to change. In 2014 NASDAQ OMX Group reported that IT stocks now made up only 38% of NASDAQ's listings (based on market capitalization, or the market value of the shares) compared with 57% of listings in 1999. Telecommunications companies, biotechnology firms, and retailers such as Whole Foods and Staples now list on NASDAQ, along with technology companies such as Apple, Facebook, Intel, and Microsoft.

Whether it is primary versus secondary markets or the exchanges versus OTC, we are talking about buyers and sellers of shares or equities or stocks agreeing on a price at which to exchange their shares. But how exactly do economists explain how these stock prices are determined? How are they reported? And—perhaps most controversial—are these prices rationally determined? These are the issues to which we now turn.

SECTION REVIEW

Q1) Austin has some money saved and is thinking about buying some corporate stock. He can't decide whether he should buy common stock or preferred stock. What things should affect his decision?

Q2) Crusty is an old-time investor who has not kept up with the changing structure of financial markets. How would you explain to Crusty how the differences between over the counter and stock exchanges have changed over the past 40 years?

Q3) IPOs take place in which of the following equity markets?

a. Buybacks

b. Secondary

c. Primary

d. Proxy

17-2 Pricing Common Stock

The price of a share of common stock is to many people a complete mystery. They hear reports that the "Dow closed higher today on active trading" and might know this means stock prices have increased, but they have no idea how or why. As it turns out, the pricing of shares isn't really a big mystery; the various methods are usually just applications of the time value of money concept. What makes the pricing of common stock so difficult, though, is not the calculation; it is what numbers to put into the simple algebraic formula. Another issue is which method of equity price is the "best" one to use? Let's take a look at some of the different ways to calculate stock prices.

Dividend Discount Model: Single Period

Remember back in Chapter 2 we looked at the issue of the time value of money—the idea that a dollar in the future is worth less than that same dollar today. We said that because of the time value of money, cash you get in the future has to be discounted to calculate its current or present value.

Think about the time value of money in terms of stock or equity prices. Remember, stocks or equity shares give you a claim on the future profits or earnings of a corporation, plus the **liquidation or salvage value.**

Liquidation or salvage value: The total value of a company's fixed assets when the company ceases to operate. The company's intangible assets such as reputation and good will are excluded.

Think about the idea that you buy a share of a corporation today, and the corporation will pay you a dividend (or a slice of their profits) in one year and then immediately close up shop. When the business closes, its assets are sold, debts are paid, and whatever is left over is given to the shareholders. Thus, as a stock or equity holder, you get the liquidation, or salvage, in one year.

The present value in time t of those cash payments that occur in time period $t + 1$ is calculated as

$$PV_t = \frac{DIV_{t+1}}{(1+r)^1} + \frac{LIQ_{t+1}}{(1+r)^1}$$

where DIV_{t+1} is the dividend you receive in $t + 1$ and LIQ_{t+1} is the liquidation or salvage value you receive in $t + 1$. Assume that the dividend in time $t + 1$ is \$10, the termination value of the share is \$2, and the rate of time preference (r) is 5%. Then the present value of the \$12 cash flow in one year would be \$11.42:

$$PV_t = \frac{DIV_{t+1}}{(1+r)^1} + \frac{LIQ_{t+1}}{(1+r)^1} = \frac{\$10}{(1.05)^1} + \frac{\$2}{(1.05)^1} = \$9.52 + \$1.90 = \$11.42$$

Since the present value of the cash stream of holding the stock is \$11.42, someone (with the same information set) would be willing to pay no more than \$11.42 for that cash stream; that is, the price of the share would be \$11.42.

So, the market price of the share of stock—which is the claim on these cash flows—is \$11.42. Thus you can see the market price of a share of stock is simply the discounted cash flows the share of stock provides.

Dividend Discount Model: Multiperiod

In the example above we assumed the corporation issuing the shares would be around for only the next period. This, of course, is pretty unrealistic; most corporations are expected to be around for a long while. In fact, they are expected to be around so long that their liquidation or salvage values are viewed as being so far into the future that they can be ignored.

For instance, notice in our example that if the liquidation or salvage value is expected to be \$2 per share, and the corporation is expected to go out of business in 75 years, with a discount rate of 5%, that liquidation or salvage value is worth only \$0.02. That is why, in the multiperiod case, the liquidation or salvage value often is ignored.

Instead, the value of a share is assumed to be the discounted dividends that share is going to pay the shareholder. Mathematically this is

$$Price_t = PV_t = \sum_{t=1}^{\infty} \frac{DIV_t}{(1+r)^t}$$

While this is a bit more realistic than our previous formulation because it allows for multiple periods, it is also still a bit unrealistic for many corporations because dividends are not expected to remain constant forever. In the 1950s Myron Gordon,[1] along with Eli Shapiro,[2] came up with a simple pricing formula that allowed for growth in dividends at a constant rate. This is sometimes referred to as the Gordon growth model. In this framework the price of a share in time period *t* is

$$Price_t = PV_t = \frac{DIV_t}{(r-g)}$$

where *g* is the rate at which the dividend is expected to grow. In their model Gordon and Shapiro assumed that the dividend growth rate *g* would never be higher than the required rate of return or rate of time preference (*r*), and these are all in real terms.

So the Gordon growth model did give us a more realistic way to calculate the price of a share, but it wasn't completely realistic. For example, it requires the analyst to accurately predict what the corporation's dividend payments are going to be, plus it requires perfect knowledge of what the dividend growth rate is going to be over time.

What about firms that keep some or even all of their earnings in the form of retained earnings and perhaps don't pay out any dividends at all? The Gordon growth model suggests the stock price should be zero. Yet may technology companies (such as Apple) and new startup firms do not pay any dividends to shareholders. Instead of paying dividends, many startup firms plow all of their profits back into the firm. Clearly, the price of these firms' stock is not zero! So, we have a bit of a problem if we think the Gordon growth model is the perfect way to calculate stock price.

PE Ratio

Another way to calculate the price of stock that does not depend on predicting dividends in the future is the PE ratio. The PE ratio simply means the price, or current price of the share, relative to the earnings per share the corporation is expected to generate (EEPS). Earnings per share are simply a corporation's net income divided by the number of shares outstanding. Mathematically, the PE ratio is

$$PE\ ratio = \frac{Price\ per\ share}{Expected\ earnings\ per\ share}$$

1 See Myron J. Gordon, "Dividends, Earnings and Stock Prices." *Review of Economics and Statistics* 41, no. 2 (1959): 99–105.

2 See Myron J. Gordon and Eli Shapiro, "Capital Equipment Analysis: The Required Rate of Profit." *Management Science* 3, no. 1 (1956): 102–10.

So, if you multiply the PE ratio by the earnings per share, you get the stock price

$$PE\ ratio = \frac{Price\ per\ share}{EEPS} \times EEPS = Price,$$

The PE ratio is often easy to get; it is published on websites such as Yahoo! Finance, WSJ.com, FT.com, CNNMoney, and many others. What does the PE ratio tell you? As it turns out, this can be a complicated question to answer.

If the PE ratio for a given share is *higher* than the PE ratio of "similar" firms, then you might think these shares are expensive and may not want to buy them. On the other hand, a high PE ratio might mean the market thinks this firm's earnings are going to increase in the future. That would mean purchasing this stock now would be a good idea. Or it might mean that the market sees this firm as stable and reliable, and thus you have to pay a premium to buy the shares. Is that a positive or a negative? It depends on whether you want stability and are willing to pay for it. So, is a high PE ratio a good thing or not? It's not that simple!

On the other hand, if the PE ratio of a given firm is *lower* than the PE ratio of "similar" firms, then you might think its shares are cheap or a bargain. Or, a low PE ratio might mean the market thinks this firm's earnings are going to decrease in the future. A low PE ratio might also mean that the market sees this firm as unstable or unreliable, and thus people are dumping the shares at low price. So, is a low PE ratio a good thing or not?

The PE ratio shows us the importance of other stocks in helping to determine whether any given stock price is a "good deal." Next we turn our attention to the stock market overall, looking at the prices of all of the stocks in the market at once.

SECTION REVIEW

Q1) Explain in words how the time value of money is related to the price of stocks.

Q2) Steven is very excited. He just found out that the stock he is about to buy has the lowest PE ratio of the stocks of similar firms. Why is he happy? How would you explain to him why he might not want to be so happy?

Q3) According to the Gordon growth model, a stock with an expected dividend payment of $10 next year and an expected growth rate of dividends of 4% should sell at what price if the investor's discount rate or required rate of return is 6%?

a. $500

b. $100

c. $10

d. $5

Stock Market Overall: Performance, Indexes, and Regulation

17-3

While the prices of individual stocks can move around a great deal as investors' expectations of dividends change and as expected rates of return change, changes in the overall equity market can also bring about changes in individual stock prices. Thus it is important to understand the factors that drive the overall stock market, how to measure changes in the overall market, and the rules and regulations that guide the equity market.

17.3a Overall Performance

It is important to keep in mind that the stock market does not operate in a bubble. What happens in the "outside world" can and does affect the equity market. So, if you really want to understand where the equity market is and might be headed, you have to keep an eye on economic conditions and what is happening in other financial markets.

Business Cycles

History tells us that stock prices tend to be procyclical. That is, the stock market tends to move in the same direction as the overall economy: As the economy expands, stock prices tend to increase, whereas as the economy slows or even contracts, stock prices tend to decrease.

As the economy expands and employment increases, households' disposable income usually increases. This increase in the level of disposable income leads to more consumption, the spending multiplier kicks in, and the economy expands. To meet this increased consumer demand, firms increase output, sales increase, and thus corporate earnings and profits increase. Because stock prices are, for the most part, a reflection of expected future corporate earnings, stock prices increase.

But of course the economy isn't always expanding. When the economy weakens, corporate sales decrease and firms try to cut back on output. But firms still have fixed costs they need to pay, so reduced sales revenues mean lower corporate earnings or profits. These lower earnings expectations, then, naturally lead to lower stock prices.

Thus the stock market is said to be procyclical, increasing when the economy expands and decreasing when the economy slows or—even worse—slides into a recession.

As Figure 17-1 shows, while there is not a perfect correlation between the stock market (here measured by the Wilshire 5000 Index) and the business cycle, you can see that the stock market declines during economic recessions (the areas in gray). During the times when the economy is expanding, the stock market generally rises.

This helps to explain why stock market participants watch the macroeconomy so closely. But, as we have described, being able to predict where the overall economy is going to be in the future is anything but certain. See the Tying the Concepts Together box for more details.

Interest Rates

If determining the path of the overall economy is difficult, so, too, is determining where interest rates are headed. As we have seen through the use of the loanable funds model, there are a myriad of factors that can and do change over time and bring about changes in interest rates. For our purposes here we will also learn that changes in interest rates bring about changes in stock prices.

Think about the dividend discount model of stock prices described earlier in the chapter. In the denominator of that equation is the return investors require, or the investor's rate of time preference. So, if market interest rates increase, that rate of time preference goes up. Thought of another way, with increasing interest rates, investors demand a higher return on equities. Thus, as interest rates increase, stock prices decrease.

Figure 17-1 Equity Prices and the Business Cycle

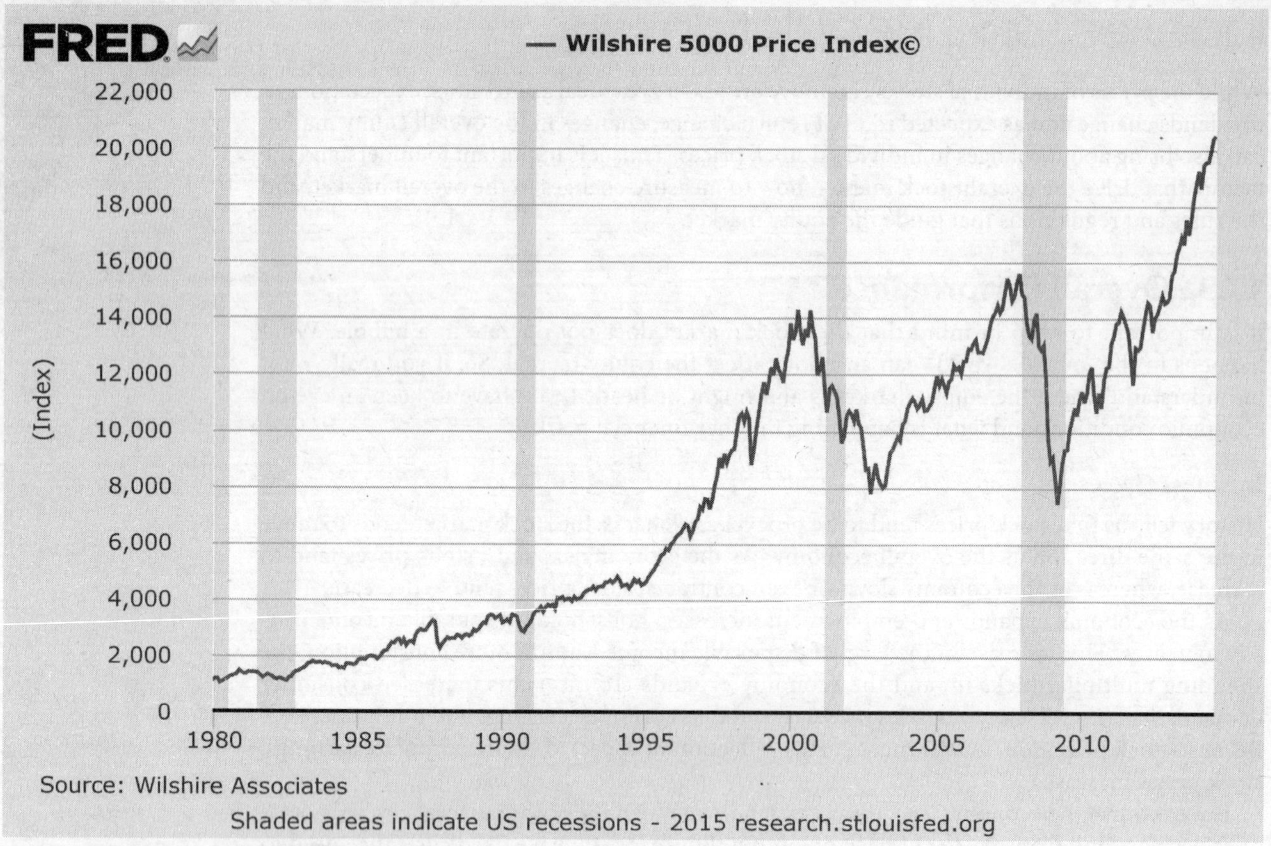

Source: Copyright 2014 by the Federal Reserve Bank of St. Louis.

Tying Concepts Together

Remember back in Chapter 5 we discussed how financial markets have changed through time. We looked into how US financial markets changed throughout the twentieth century: from the early days of the Fed, through the roaring '20s, to the Great Depression of the 1930s, World War II, the postwar boom, the stagflation of the 1970s, and then the difficulties with S&Ls and the creation of junk bonds in the 1980s, up to the current crisis. Then in Chapter 6, when we examined the aggregate supply/aggregate demand framework, we discussed in a more formal sense why business cycle fluctuations occur.

Through it all the stock market has reflected both of these changes: booms and busts in financial markets and changes in the business cycle. As Figure 17-2, the US stock market, as measured by the Dow Jones Industrial Average (or simply the Dow), follows roughly what was happening in financial markets and the overall economy.

The grey vertical bars represent economic recessions. In almost every one of the economic recessions the Dow decreases. This makes sense, since as the economy slows, the expected current and future profitability of corporations decreases and thus the price of their shares falls. But during the boom times—the 1920s, the late 1940s through the mid-1960s, and the 1980s and 1990s—we see the Dow increasing.

Notice, however, there is not a perfect correlation between the business cycle and stock market performance. Some times the Dow falls but the economy is not in a recession. In addition, there are times when the economy is in a recession and the Dow rises. If one understands how equities are priced, they can better understand why there is not a perfect correlation between stock prices and the overall economy.

Figure 17-2 Equity Market and Business Cycles

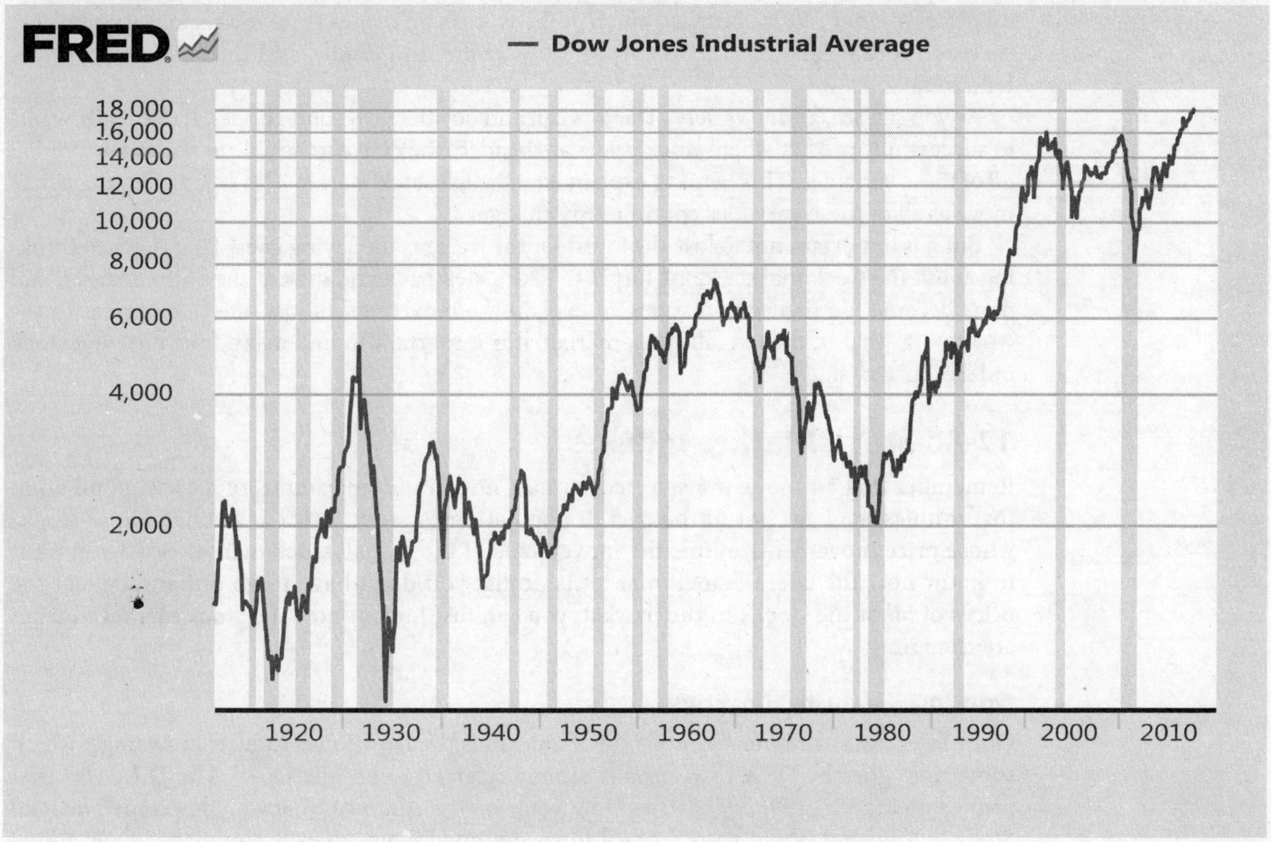

Source: Copyright 2014 by the Federal Reserve Bank of St. Louis.

The same logic holds in reverse: If interest rates decrease, holding everything else constant, stock prices go up. Mathematically, this occurs because the interest rate *r* appears in the denominator of the dividend discount formula as well as the Gordon growth model formula. The logic is as interest rates fall, the rate of time preference of investors declines, or investors become more patient. Think of it from an investment opportunity cost perspective: If interest rates, and thus the rate of return on bonds, are falling, stocks seem like a better alternative. Therefore, as the return on bonds decreases, the demand for stocks increase and thus stock prices increase.

Global Setting

We live in a global financial world. What happens on the other side of the world can and does affect what happens in the equity markets in the United States. As Chan, Karolyi, and Stulz pointed out back in the early 1990s,[3] changes in global financial markets impact US equity markets. This impact can be either positive or negative. As the economies around the world expand, sales of US-made goods overseas might increase, thus increasing the earnings of US corporations and leading to higher US stock prices. On the other hand, weaker economic performance overseas might result in fewer US exports and lower earnings and thus depress American stock prices.

3 See K. C. Chan, G. Andrew Karolyi, and Rene M. Stulz, "Global Financial Markets and the Risk Premium on U.S. Equity." *Journal of Financial Economics* 32, no. 2 (1992): 137–68.

But the impact of the rest of the world on US equity prices need not be limited to just global economic conditions. Political unrest or even uncertain political futures overseas can affect the US equity markets. For example, when tensions in the Middle East increase, world oil prices might increase because much of the world's oil comes from the region. As oil prices increase, future earnings of US corporations come into doubt, and thus US equity prices tend to fall.

As you can see, a wide variety of factors can and do affect US equity prices. If one really wants to successfully predict where stock prices are headed, they have to be able to accurately predict *all* of these variables. This helps to explain why the US stock market is so volatile: Equity prices move as all of these variables continuously change.

But it is important not to lose the forest for the trees, as the saying goes. That is, when thinking about the stock market, don't forget to take a step back and look at the entire market, and don't become too focused on trying to explain the movement of just one stock price. To see "the forest," that is, the overall stock market, it is important to understand the different stock indexes that exist.

17-3b Stock Market Indexes

Remember that an index is a selected sample, not a random sample, of a given population that mimics the behavior of the overall population. A stock index is a collection of stocks whose price movements mimic the movements of the overall stock market. So, if you want to know how the overall stock market is doing, you don't have to go out and collect the prices of *all* of the stocks in the market; you can just look at how the stock market indexes are changing.

Dow Jones Industrial Average

One of the oldest and most famous stock indexes is the Dow Jones Industrial Average, which sometimes goes by DJIA or is usually simply referred to as "the Dow." The DJIA was first printed on May 26, 1896, by Charles Dow, who was the editor of what would become *The Wall Street Journal* and, along with Edward Jones, founded Dow, Jones & Company.[4] Dow added up the prices of the 12 stocks that he thought best represented the overall market. He then divided that number by 12. Thus was born the DJIA. The Dow is what is called a "price-weighted index" (PWI):

$$PWI = \frac{\sum_{i=1}^{n} P_{i,t}}{Divisor}$$

where i is the number of stocks in the stock market index and t is time. $P_{i,t}$ is the price of stock i at time t. The Divisor can be chosen to ensure that the PWI equals a certain value. Originally, in 1896, Dow picked 12 for the Divisor. In 1916 the index was expanded by adding 8 more stocks, so the Divisor became 20. In those days the DJIA was calculated with paper and pencil as soon as the stock prices were known.

In 1923 Dow turned over the crunching of the numbers to Arthur "Pop" Harris, who had been hired by the firm at the age of 22 in 1908. Pop Harris's job became a bit more complicated when in 1928 the keepers of the DJIA decided to increase the number of stocks in the index to 30. For the better part of the next four decades, Pop Harris[5] calculated the DJIA every hour on the hour for the Dow Jones News Services, the publisher of *The Wall Street Journal*.

---

4 The first average Dow reportedly calculated was on July 3, 1884, which was made up of 11 "representative" stocks: 9 railroad stocks and 2 industrial stocks. This was published in the Customer's Afternoon Letter, a four-page newsletter put out daily by Dow, Jones & Company. Some claim that the real beginning of the DJIA did not occur until October 7, 1896, the day on which continuous daily publication of *The Wall Street Journal* began.

5 Arthur "Pop" Harris died in 1964. He retired from Dow Jones in 1963 after working for the firm for 55 years.

The year 1928 was also important because that is when it was decided that the Divisor needed to be changed to keep the DJIA historically accurate. The Divisor has changed many times over the years since then because of stock splits,[6] stock dividends, and changes in the makeup of the index. Over time the Divisor for the DJIA has been adjusted many times. It was most recently changed in September 2013 to 0.1557159051117, which means that every $1 change in the price of a stock in the DJIA results in a 6.42-point change in the Dow.

The stocks that make up the Dow also have changed over the years. After the close of trading on September 20, 2013, the index removed Alcoa, Bank of America, and Hewlett-Packard (Alcoa had been part of the Dow for 54 years) and replaced them with Goldman Sachs, Nike, and Visa. The change in the makeup of the 30 stocks that compose the Dow resulted in a change in the Divisor.

Is the Dow Still Useful?

Some suggest that the Dow has outlived its usefulness; after all, it is made up of only 30 stocks, and most of them are still "old line" companies. You can understand why limiting the number of stocks in the index made sense in the early days, before computers: It took a long time to gather all those numbers, add them up by hand, double-check the calculations, and then finally report the number. With computer technology, however, all of this can be done in seconds for hundreds of stocks. Plus there is the issue of what stocks to include; the Dow is made up of "blue chip" stocks, well-established companies that have been around for a long time. But this then means that a lot of growth stocks are excluded. But if it is the smaller, growing companies that are pushing the stock market ahead, might the DJIA be mismeasuring what is actually happening in the overall stock market?

S&P 500

It is because of these types of questions other stock indexes were created. One of the most popular alternatives to the DJIA is the S&P 500 index. Standard & Poor's (at that time called Poor's Publishing) put out its first stock market index in 1923 and covered 233 companies. Because of its large size, the index was published only weekly. The S&P 500 index as we know it today was first introduced in 1957.

The S&P 500 is a market value–weighted index. That is, each stock in the index is weighted by its market capitalization, or the current market price per share multiplied by the number of outstanding shares.[7] The market capitalization values for each stock are then added to obtain the total market cap of the index, which is divided by a divisor, called the index divisor, relative to a base year. The S&P 500 base period is 1941–1943, when the index was set to equal 10. You often see this noted as $1941 - 43 = 10$.

$$\textit{Market value–weighted index} = \frac{\sum_{i=1}^{n} (P_{i,t} \times Q_{i,t})}{\textit{Index Divisor}}$$

The stocks that make up the S&P 500 are picked by a committee,[8] so the companies represented are not necessarily the 500 biggest corporations. The committee picks companies to be included in the index so they are a good representation of the entire US economy.

6 To understand why a stock split might be a problem, consider a simple example of a three-stock index. Able Corp. stock sells at $15, Baker Corp. stock sells at $20, and Charlie Corp. stock sells at $25. So, the average of these three is $20. But if the Baker Corporation decides to do a two-for-one stock split (meaning people who own one share of Baker Corp. stock will now own two shares), the price of Baker Corp. stock will become $10, with twice as many shares outstanding. The average of the three shares now is $16.66, even though nothing has really changed. So, the divisor would have to be adjusted to keep the average at $20 so that it accurately reflects what is happening in the market.

7 In 2005 the actual calculation of the index was changed a bit so that the index weighting was based on the number of shares available for public trading. This is called "float" weighting. Only a small number of companies that make up the index have a public float less than their total capitalization.

8 See "S&P Indices: S&P U.S. Indices Methodology," Standard & Poor's, June 2012.

Wilshire 5000

The Wilshire 5000 stock index was first published in 1971 and includes more than 3,500 common stocks. It consists of all of the US stocks for which there is readily available data. To be a part of the Wilshire 5000, the stock must be issued by a corporation with headquarters in the United States, the stock must be actively traded on a US-based stock market, and there has to be widely available information on the stock price. As with the S&P 500 index, the Wilshire 5000 is a market value-weighted index.

17-3c Regulation

The stock market is ultimately a market: a place where buyers and sellers meet. For any market to work effectively and efficiently, market participants must have confidence in the structure of the market. That is, buyers and sellers have to trust that they are being dealt with in an honest manner.

After the stock market crash of 1929, many people both inside and outside the market lost confidence in the US equity market. In those days regulation of the stock market was almost nonexistent. Fraud, deception, and scandal were regular occurrences. With the 1929 crash it became clear that confidence in the US equity market had reached an all-time low.

In response to the evaporation of confidence in equity markets, Congress passed the Securities Act of 1933 and the Securities Exchange Act of 1934. The former required companies selling stock to file a registration statement and to provide a prospectus that offers details on the company when it issued new stock. The 1934 act established the Securities and Exchange Commission (SEC) to regulate stock markets and enforce the 1933 act.

As the SEC states on its web page, it's mission ". . . is to protect investors, maintain fair, orderly, and efficient markets, and facilitate capital formation."[9] That is, the SEC is responsible for ensuring there is full and fair disclosure of information on securities to investors. Thus the SEC focuses on reducing the asymmetric information problems that may exist in the US equity market. But keep in mind that the job of the SEC is *not* to keep investors from making bad investment decisions. Instead, the SEC is there to try to ensure that investors have complete and accurate information.

What investors do with that information is an entirely different issue. Do investors use the information they have in an efficient manner? Or are they more driven by psychological factors? It is this question to which we now turn.

SECTION REVIEW

Q1) Harry is an old-time investor. He tells you, "When I was young I was told the Dow Jones Industrial Average tells you everything you need to know about how the stock market is doing. Is that still true?" How would you answer Harry's question?

Q2) Why do stock market analysts need to be able to "predict" macroeconomic changes?

Q3) The S&P 500 Index is different from the Dow Jones Industrial Average in that:

a. The S&P 500 is a market value–weighted index, whereas the DJIA is a price-weighted index.

b. The S&P 500 is a broader index because it is composed of the prices of more stocks than the DJIA.

c. The S&P 500 has a wider variety of stocks than does the DJIA.

d. All of the above.

---

9 See "The Investor's Advocate: How the SEC Protects Investors, Maintains Market Integrity, and Facilitates Capital Formation," available at http://www.sec.gov/about/whatwedo.shtml#.U-j7hvldV8E.

The Stock Market: Efficient or Not?

17-4

It is generally agreed that information drives markets. But to what extent is this statement true for the stock market? Initially, economists debated over just what information stock market prices reflect. This was the debate over the level of stock market efficiency: weak, semistrong, or strong. More recently, however, economists have posed a much deeper question: Are stock market participants really rational at all? If the answer is no, what, then, does drive stock market prices? Let's take a look at each of these issues.

17-4a Efficient Market Hypothesis

The debate over the question of stock market efficiency—that is, do shares' market prices always accurately incorporate and reflect all relevant information—goes all the way back to the mid-nineteenth century. The French statistician Louis Bachelier was the first to address the issue that eventually became the question of stock market efficiency. In his 1900 PhD dissertation at the Sorbonne entitled "Théorie de la Spéculation" ("Theory of Speculation"), Bachelier modeled the random process that became known as Brownian motion and applied it to stock prices. But Bachelier was ahead of his time, and his work was ignored for 50 years until it was pointed out by the famous economist Paul Samuelson.[10] In the early 1960s Eugene Fama at the University of Chicago Booth School of Business built on Samuelson's work and created the **efficient market hypothesis**, which argued stock markets were efficient. That is, the stock market did reflect all available information.

Efficient market hypothesis: The idea that it is impossible for any one investor to earn a return above the average market return because the market is efficient in that market prices reflect all relevant information.

It was argued that securities markets, and the stock market specifically, seemed to be a good approximation of the theoretical "perfectly competitive" market economists had developed. In a perfectly competitive market there are no economic profits, or abnormal profits, in the long run. This is because with perfect information and free entry into the market, the existence of an economic or abnormal profit would draw new entrants into the market. Thus in the stock market traders could not earn an economic or abnormal profit if the stock market was efficient, that is, if market participants used all available information. Fama summarized this by saying:

> An efficient capital market is a market that is efficient in processing information. The prices of securities observed at any time are based on "correct" evaluations of all information available at that time. In an efficient market, prices "fully reflect" available information.[11]

The efficient market hypothesis can be broken down into three levels of efficiency.

Weak Form of Efficiency

The weak form of efficiency assumes that stock market prices reflect all market-related information, including historical price movements and volume. If the weak form of efficiency holds, then investors cannot earn an abnormally high profit by using historical price movements.

Evidence: Probably holds. Research shows that successive stock price movements are random, and the correlation between one day's prices and the next are, for all practical purposes, zero.

---

10 For the story of Samuelson's "discovery" and more background on Bachelier, see Jeremy Bernstein, "Paul Samuelson and the Obscure Origins of the Financial Crisis." *New York Review of Books*, NYR Blog, January 11, 2010. http://www.nybooks.com/blogs/nyrblog/2010/jan/11/paul-samuelson-and-the-obscure-origins-of-the-fina/.

11 See Eugene Fama, "Efficient Capital Markets: A Review of Theory and Empirical Work." *Journal of Finance* 25 (1970): 383–417. See Eugene Fama, "Efficient Capital Markets: A Review of Theory and Empirical Work." *Journal of Finance* 25 (1970): 383–417.

Semistrong Form of Efficiency

The semistrong form of efficiency assumes that stock prices reflect all public information, including announcements by firms, economic news and developments, as well as political news and developments. Market-related information is a subset of all public information, so if semistrong efficiency holds, the weak form also has to hold. But the weak form can hold without semistrong efficiency holding. If semistrong efficiency holds, then investors cannot make an abnormal profit by trading on public news releases because that information will be reflected in prices. That is, investors cannot benefit over and above the market return by trading on new information.

Evidence: Probably does hold. The empirical evidence suggests financial markets generally do incorporate news information, so if investors are trading based on public information, they are probably too late because the market prices already reflect that information. A large academic literature has been generated around "event studies" using stock market data to test how market prices react to various "events."

Strong Form of Efficiency

The strong form of efficiency assumes stock market prices reflect all information, including private or inside information. So, if the strong form holds, there is *no* set of information that allows investors to make an abnormal profit, or a return greater than the market return.

Evidence: Hard to say, but probably does not hold. Because private information is difficult to ascertain and measurement issues abound, it is difficult to test the strong form of efficiency. There have been several cases where people with inside information have illegally traded on that information and earned returns significantly greater than those from the overall market. This suggests that stock prices do not, in fact, contain private or inside information.

For several decades academic financial economists debated over just "how" efficient financial markets are; only a small group dared to question the efficient market hypothesis. With the financial crisis that started in 2008, however, more and more economists, journalists, policymakers, and market participants began to question it.

17-4b Behavioral Finance

Those in the field of behavioral finance argue that many financial market outcomes, including much stock market behavior, can be understood using economic models in which some people are not fully rational. Behavioral finance seeks to combine the findings from behavioral and cognitive psychology to explain market behavior and outcomes.

While the general approach is very old, Adam Smith discussed psychology as a part of market behavior in the eighteenth century. It was the work of Daniel Kahnemen and Amos Tversky in the early 1970s that kicked off the field of behavioral economics, using psychology to explain economic behavior. Kahnemen and Tversky's findings were revolutionary; they argued that instead of being rational, many people used mental shortcuts to make market decisions.

It really wasn't until a 1985 article by Werner F. M. DeBondt, then at the University of Wisconsin—Madison, and Richard Thaler, at the time at Cornell University, did the field of behavioral finance finally emerge.[12] DeBondt and Thaler discovered that people overreact to

---

12 See Werner F. M. De Bondt and Richard Thaler, "Does the Stock Market Overreact?" *The Journal of Finance* 40, no. 3 (July 1985): 793–805. Available from: http://faculty.chicagobooth.edu/Richard.Thaler/research/pdf/DoesStockMarketOverreact.pdf.

unexpected and dramatic new events. This overreaction then might explain why the weak form of efficiency holds, but it does not mean that stock market participants are rational. In fact, quite the opposite.

Up to this point, financial economists were aware that there were "anomalies" to the efficient market hypothesis, but these were considered minor. There was the January effect, where for some reason stock prices were higher during the month of January. And there was the day-of-the-week effect: Holding everything else constant, stock prices were higher on Fridays. While proponents of the efficient market hypothesis brushed off these "anomalies" as outliers, to others they implied that stock prices change for no fundamental reason at all. A different explanation suggested that stock prices are driven more by psychology than by facts. This is why DeBondt and Thaler's finding was so shocking; there was evidence that people in the stock market were consistently overreacting.

During the 1980s and 1990s, the field of behavioral finance grew and expanded. Some of the topics the field now covers include:

- **Overconfidence.** It is reported that 80% of drivers consider themselves to be above-average drivers. This same overconfidence can lead stock market participants to assume their forecasts of future corporate earnings are more accurate than they really are.
- **Confirmation bias.** Studies show that many stock market participants place more weight on information that agrees with their preexisting opinion. Also, people are more likely to deem unreliable research that contradicts their opinions.
- **Framing matters.** How a question is framed might affect the answer a person gives and how they act. For example, the disposition effect has been well documented: People hang on to losing stocks that they already own for far too long. This violates the well-known "sunk costs don't matter" principle from marginal analysis. The other side of the disposition effect is that individuals tend to sell winners too soon in an attempt to "pocket the money" quickly, even though there is no rational reason to believe the price will fall in the future. There is also the house money effect: People are more likely to risk money that they have already "won" compared with money they "earned."
- **Heuristics.** Instead of using all relevant information, people rely on rules of thumb, standard practices, or mental shortcuts to make decisions.

Some, however, argue that even if some market participants are irrational, that does not mean market outcomes are irrational. Instead, they believe the irrational behavior creates a market opportunity or an arbitrage opportunity. Rational traders can earn a profit by "taking advantage" of the irrational traders.

Proponents of behavioral finance counter that there are significant limits to arbitrage, and thus the market may not "correct" these irrational behaviors. Limits to arbitrage include:

- **Noise trader risk.** The noisy traders, the irrational ones, keep pushing the market price away from the rational price.
- **Implementation costs.** The transaction costs of having to buy and then sell shares from irrational traders might be more than the potential arbitrage gain.

Still others believe that while individual investors may be irrational from time to time and the market may not correct all of the irrational behavior at once, that does not mean the overall market is irrational. Thus the efficient market hypothesis holds, and it is still the best way to analyze stock market movements.

The financial crisis that started in 2008, however, pointed out that the irrational behavior of financial market participants can result in massive swings in the market's overall performance and directly affect the rest of the economy. But the most recent crisis was not the first financial market asset bubble to pop. The stock market also crashed in 1929, 1987, and 1990. And these asset bubbles and crashes, as we discussed earlier, are not limited to the United States.

So there exists an open question: Is rationality a safe assumption to make when analyzing stock market behavior? If, as the behavioral finance literature suggests, market participants are driven by psychology and often are irrational, what does that mean about how we explain stock price movements? It is a debate that will most likely rage on for years.

SECTION REVIEW

Q1) Joel is confused about what "efficient stock market" means. How would you explain this concept to Joel?

Q2) Some people argue that the rise of behavioral finance raises questions about the level of efficiency in the stock market. Explain this argument.

Q3) The assumption that the stock market reflects all information, both public and private, is referred to as:

a. Strong form of efficiency
b. Mildly strong form of efficiency
c. Semistrong form of efficiency
d. Weak form of efficiency

Conclusion

17-5

While the stock market is reported on constantly in the business and popular press, accurately analyzing this important financial market is rather complicated and full of debate. After examining what stocks are, the differences between common and preferred stocks, and who buys and sells them and how, we tackled the difficult issue of pricing common stocks. While the discounted cash flow framework is a useful tool, it has its limitations. We also examined the difficulty in forecasting and even measuring total stock market performance. Perhaps the most controversial issue we examined is the efficient market hypothesis. In the end our analysis of the stock market may have raised as many questions as it answered. The most difficult question may be the one everyone wants to have answered: Where is the stock market headed next? The best answer may be, "it depends."

IN THE NEWS. . .

The Trend Is Your Friend Till It Isn't

Noah Smith
BloombergView
August 5, 2014

One time a very smart guy told me that the only stock he was really willing to make big bets on was Apple Inc. When I asked him why, he chuckled and said "It goes up!" That was in September 2012. The idea that a stock "goes up," like some law of nature, is an example of a very important behavioral bias: trend-following.

Trend-following, which has always been a puzzling phenomenon, has received some attention in the finance literature lately. Robin Greenwood and Andrei Shleifer looked at a large number of surveys of investors, and found that people's expectations of future returns are often just extrapolations of the recent past. Of course, those expectations usually turn out to be wrong, but people apparently believe them enough to bet on them—when stocks go up and expectations soar along with them, money usually flows into equity mutual funds, only to lose out when stocks return to the long-term average, rather than the recent average. . . .

Trend-following is related to a phenomenon that psychologists have called the hot-hand fallacy, after the supposedly mistaken notion that basketball players have streaks of good shooting. There's just one problem with this theory: As it turns out, hot hands probably do exist! The "fallacy" isn't always a fallacy.

Sometimes the underlying structure of the world changes rapidly, and sometimes it changes slowly. If we assume it changes rapidly, then we think that every run of good returns signals an underlying change for the better, and every bad run means that something fundamental is going wrong. But it seems like when it comes to finance, that sort of assumption is more often wrong than right—with disastrous consequences for trend-following investors. . . .

The article discusses an issue behavioral finance economists have found among stock market participants: trend-following, which is related to the hot-hand fallacy. Have you ever suffered from this? When? What were the results? Do you see others suffering from this? How do you think this might affect things like the S&P 500?

18

The Mortgage Market

18-1 Mortgages and the Bigger Picture

Home ownership—it's one of those things that is looked upon as being as "American" as baseball, apple pie, and the Fourth of July. Images of the "American Dream" often center on a smiling family standing in front of their new house with a white picket fence. Hollywood movies have contributed to this view because they seem to suggest every American family owns their own home.

But, as is often the case, Hollywood doesn't get the story quite right. In 2009, while about 68% of American families did own the home in which they lived, in the District of Columbia less than 45% did. In the state of New York only 54% of families owned their homes, and in California only 57% did. Of those who did own the house in which they lived, very few owned the house outright; instead, almost all had their home mortgaged.

Home mortgages, once considered a wonderful conduit for "average" Americans to own their own home, have now become a growing source of anxiety and angst for many Americans. These same mortgages are at the center of the recent financial crisis, the worst since the Great Depression of the 1930s. How can it be that home ownership and mortgages, once viewed so positively, have come to cause American families and the global economy such misery? That is the question we seek to address in this chapter.

Home mortgages: A loan for which residential real estate is used as collateral. The lender may take possession of the property if the borrower fails to repay the money.

To understand how home mortgages came to play such a pivotal role in the current crisis, we need to understand the "language" of the mortgage market. Thus, after examining the impact the mortgage market has on the larger US economy, we delve into the basic concepts of the mortgage market. From there we discuss how mortgage payments work and why many American families get into trouble. Then we consider the new types of mortgages that have come about within the past few decades and examine the secondary mortgage market. Finally, we explore the role the mortgage market played in the recent crisis.

18-1a The Broad Mortgage Market

In the early days of the twentieth century, home ownership rates in the United States were relatively low. As Table 18-1 shows, before the end of World War II the rate of home ownership in the United States remained fairly constant, within the range of about 43% to 48%. During these years, financing a home purchase was very difficult for a typical family. Home mortgages required the buyer to have at least half of the purchase price in cash, and only if they were a solid credit risk could they then borrow the other half of the purchase price. Saving up half the purchase price of a house could take an average family several decades.

Even if a family could save enough for the hefty down payment, the family borrower would face another problem: potential foreclosure in just a few years. Repayment of mortgages in this era often was not spread out over 15 or 30 years as they are today; instead they were five-year balloon payments. Every five years the borrower had to pay the entire mortgage balance in full, usually by getting another five-year balloon payment loan. If the lender chose not to issue another of these loans, however, the family would be forced to sell the house to repay the loan or face foreclosure.

During the Great Depression of the 1930s, the default rates on home mortgages soared as household incomes fell. At the start of 1934 it was estimated that approximately half of all urban homes with mortgages were in default. In response to the mortgage crisis federal, state, and local governments stepped in to provide relief. At the state level, 28 states imposed moratoria on home foreclosures. As Figure 18-1 shows, a variety of government agencies were created at the federal level to deal with the growing mortgage crisis.

Things started to change in the US mortgage market after World War II. Thanks in great part to the reforms put in to effect during the Great Depression and the pent-up demand resulting from rationing during the war, after World War II the level of home ownership in the United States increased significantly.

TABLE 18-1 Homeownership Rates* in the United States, 1890–1965

Year	Rate
1890	47.8%
1900	46.7%
1910	45.9%
1920	45.6%
1930	47.8%
1940	43.6%
1945	53.2%
1950	55.0%
1956	60.4%
1960	61.9%
1970	63.3%

*These rates exclude Hawaii and Alaska.

Source: U.S. Bureau of the Census, Historical Statistics: Colonial Times to 1970, 1989.

Figure 18-1 Federal Agencies Created During the Great Depression in Response to the Mortgage Crisis

Federal Home Loan Bank System (FHLB)
- Authorized under Federal Home Loan Bank Act of 1932
- Established 12 regional Federal Home Loan Banks
- Created to provide a stable source of funds to member firms for residential-mortgage and economic-development loans

Home Owners' Loan Corporation (HOLC)
- Established by the Home Owners' Loan Corporation Act of 1933
- Purchased and refinanced distressed mortgages on 1- to 4-family homes, subject to income and loan qualifications
- Issued over one million loans between August 1933 and June 1936
- Liquidated in 1951

Federal Housing Administration (FHA)
- Established by the National Housing Act of 1934
- Offers home mortgage insurance on 1-to 4-family homes
- Intended to stabilize mortgage market and improve housing standards and conditions

Federal Savings and Loan Insurance Corporation (FSLIC)
- Established by the National Housing Act of 1934, administered by FHLB
- Provided deposit insurance for savings and loan associations
- Abolished under Financial Instituions Reform, Recovery and Enforcement Act of 1989

Federal National Mortgage Association (FNMA)
- Established in 1938 by the Reconstruction Finance Corporation at the resquest of President Roosevelt
- Created to establish a secondary mortgage market by purchasing FHA-insured loans at par and accrued interest
- 1984 National Housing Act amendment gave FNMA a federal charter to become independent of the RFC; FNMA given authority to purchage FHA and Veterans Administration (VA)–insured loans
- 1968 Chartered by Congress as a government-sponsored private corporation

Source: David C. Wheelock, "The Federal Response to Home Mortgage Distress: Lessons from the Great Depression." *Federal Reserve Bank of St. Louis Review* 90, no. 3 (May/June 2008): 133-48.

Home ownership rates continued to increase in the United States through the 1970s, driven in part by low, and often negative, real interest rates. As the US economy grew and expanded, the wages and salaries of American workers increased, putting home ownership within the reach of more and more Americans.

Today the housing industry has a huge impact on the overall economy in the United States. According to the National Association of Home Builders, residential investment spending[1] has averaged about 4% of GDP, whereas housing services[2] average between 12% and 13% of GDP each year. Thus, the housing sector accounts for about 16% to 17% of the entire US economy. This large sector of the economy played a major role in the 2007–2009 financial crisis, so it is important to understand how this large financial market functions.

Tying Concepts Together

Mortgage Market and Monetary Policy

Imagine that the central bank is worried about future inflation. As we discussed in Chapters 8 through 11, if a central bank pursues a contractionary monetary policy to stop inflation, market interest rates most often increase. This often means that interest rates in the mortgage market increase as well.

But higher mortgage interest rates mean higher monthly payments for households, and thus many families may not be able to purchase homes. This decrease in spending on housing and housing services has a major impact on GDP since the housing sector makes up 16% to 17% of GDP.

Thus, when mortgage rates increase, total spending in the economy can be negatively affected and can slow the entire economy. So, changes in monetary policy affect the entire economy, in part through how these changes in monetary policy affect the mortgage market.

Let's start with basic mortgage market terminology and concepts. From there we will examine mortgage payments, and then delve into how these markets have evolved.

SECTION REVIEW

Q1) Kevin thinks home ownership is part of "the American dream" and has been achieved by most Americans. Why is Kevin incorrect?

Q2) Home ownership rates in the United States started to increase after World War II. Why did this occur?

Q3) Which of the following is *not* a federal government agency designed to assist families getting a home mortgage?

a. Federal Housing Administration (FHA)

b. Federal National Mortgage Association (FNMA, or Fannie Mae)

c. Federal Home Loan Bank

d. Sallie Mae

1 *Residential investment spending* is defined as the construction of new single-family and multifamily structures, in addition to residential remodeling, production of manufactured homes, and broker fees.

2 Consumption spending on housing services includes gross rent (including utilities) paid by renters, owner-imputed rent (and the estimate of how much it would cost a homeowner to rent the house in which they live), and utilities.

Basic Mortgage Concepts

18-2

When a person or a family finds a house or a condominium they want to buy, and their written offer to buy the property has been agreed to by the seller, the buyer typically needs to get a mortgage to finance the purchase. In today's market there is a wide variety of mortgage originators: commercial banks, Savings & Loans, mutual savings banks, mortgage brokers, among others. Let's take a look at some of the decisions a borrower has to make in terms of what size and type of mortgage they are going to get.

18-2a Down Payment

A borrower first has to decide how much of a **down payment** they are going to make. The down payment has to be nonborrowed cash that the borrower has out of their own resources. Today, borrowers generally have to have at least 20% of the purchase price as a down payment and can get a mortgage for the remaining 80%.

Down payment: The amount of the purchase price a buyer must provide out of their own financial resources.

To put this in perspective, according to the National Association of Realtors, in 2013 the median house price in the United States was around $197,000. That means a 20% down payment would require the purchaser of a median home to have $39,400 in cash.

The 20% down payment requirement becomes even more daunting if you live in the Northeast United States. In the Northeast a median house is priced at $248,900 and requires $49,780 in cash to make a 20% down payment. Still worse is the West, where the median house price was just over $276,000; that requires $55,200 in cash to make a 20% down payment.

For a young person, say someone right out of college, these 20% down payment amounts are a great deal of cash. This down payment money *cannot* be borrowed, nor typically can it be a gift from a parent or a relative. The funds must come from the individual financial resources of the borrower. If the borrower does not have the 20% down payment in cash they may have to seek private mortgage insurance (PMI).

18-2b Private Mortgage Insurance

If the borrower does not have the 20% down payment in cash and has, say, only 10% of the purchase price in cash, then the borrower needs to purchase **private mortgage insurance**.[3]

Private mortgage insurance: An insurance policy that pays the lender of the mortgage in the case of default by the borrower. The policy typically pays the lender a percentage of the outstanding loan principal, accrued interest, and expenses. State laws usually state this percentage may be no more than about 25% to 30% of the claimed amount.

Usually, the lender buys the insurance and charges the borrower for the insurance premiums. With PMI, in the event of a default by the borrower the lender is paid a percentage—usually 25% to 30%—of the outstanding loan balance and costs associated with the property foreclosure. Thus PMI insures the lender against a major loss in the case of default by the borrower.

18-2c Fixed-Rate or Adjustable-Rate Mortgages

Let us assume, through skimping and saving, a homebuyer has 20% of the purchase price in cash for the down payment. The next decision the borrower has to make is what type of mortgage they want: a **fixed-rate mortgage** or an **adjustable-rate mortgage (ARM)**.

3 For an extended explanation of PMI see "The Role of Private Mortgage Insurance in the U.S. Housing Finance System," available at http://www.usmi.org/wp-content/uploads/2014/11/Promontory-study-I-Role-of-PMI.pdf.

Fixed-rate mortgage: A loan where real estate is used as collateral and the interest rate paid by the borrower does not change over the life of the loan.

Adjustable-rate mortgage (ARM): A loan where real estate is used as collateral and the interest rate paid by the borrower may be changed by the lender under terms stated in the loan.

As the name suggests, with a fixed-rate mortgage, the interest rate charged on the mortgage does *not* change during the life of the mortgage. From a borrower's perspective this is a nice advantage because the borrower will have a good idea of what their monthly mortgage payment will be well into the future. (How to calculate monthly payments is explained later in the chapter.)

With an ARM, the lender has the ability to change the interest rate charged on the mortgage at certain intervals, as market interest rates change. The interest rate adjustments on ARMs usually are based on a published index, such as the yield on one-year Treasury bills, the London Interbank Offer Rate (LIBOR), or the Cost of Funds Index (COFI).

ARMs are usually structured so that the initial interest rate on the mortgage loan remains constant for a set period, anywhere from one to five years or even longer. After the initial period ends, the interest rate can be adjusted based on terms laid out in the mortgage agreement. For example, a 4/1 ARM means that the interest rate is held constant during the first four years and can be adjusted each year after that.

ARMs and Risk

ARMs shift the interest rate risk from the lender to the borrower. To compensate borrowers for this increased risk, ARMs usually have lower initial interest rates than do fixed-rate mortgages. So, people who are interested in lower interest rates—and thus lower monthly payments—can find ARMs very enticing.

But ARMs can be risky for borrowers. If interest rates increase dramatically, borrowers with ARMs can see their monthly mortgage payments increase rapidly. To minimize these risks, ARMs may also have interest rate or payment caps, that is, maximum interest rates or upper limits of monthly payment. These caps shift some of the interest rate risk back onto the lender, however, so ARMs with caps have slightly higher initial interest rates than ARMs without caps.

18-2d Insured Mortgages

Another way a borrower might be able to set a lower interest rate on their mortgage is if the mortgage is federally insured. Mortgages whose repayment is guaranteed by the Federal Housing Administration (FHA) are called, naturally, FHA mortgages, whereas those guaranteed by the federal government's Veteran's Administration (VA) are called VA loans.

To qualify for an FHA or a VA loan, a borrower must meet certain restrictions: FHA loans require the borrower to meet certain debt ratios, have a fairly good credit and work history, as well as a steady income stream to be able to afford the mortgage payment. There are also upper limits on the purchase price of the house. However, FHA loans require as little as a 3% down payment.

VA loans are designed for current or former members of the armed forces and their surviving spouses and families. VA loans also require the borrower to have a fairly good credit history, meet certain debt ratios, and have appropriate income levels.

18-2e Discount Points

Yet another way for a borrower to lower the interest rate on a mortgage is by paying discount points, or, more simply, "paying points." Discount points are interest payments made at the beginning of the mortgage. In exchange for paying the points the lender lowers the interest rate on the mortgage.

A mortgage loan on which the buyer pays one point means the borrower pays 1% of the loan amount at the *loan closing*, the meeting where the borrower signs all of the loan paperwork and gets the keys to their new house. If the purchase price of the house is $170,000, a borrower who is paying one point would have to bring $1,700 to the closing, in addition to their down payment and other closing costs.

18-2f Mortgage Payments

In a mortgage loan the borrower agrees to pay a monthly amount of principal plus interest that will pay off the loan in full by its maturity. If the payments pay off the loan in full by the end of the loan, the loan is said to be "fully amortized."

To understand how this works, remember from Chapter 3 on interest rates we saw that:

$$\textbf{Loan Amount or PV} = \frac{Payment}{(1+i)} + \frac{Payment}{(1+i)^2} + \frac{Payment}{(1+i)^3} + \cdots + \frac{Payment}{(1+i)^n}$$

where *Payment* is the fixed monthly payment, i is the interest rate on the loan, and n is the term of the loan or the last payment.

Another way to write this is:

$$\textbf{Loan amount} = \textbf{Payment}\ (\textbf{PVIFA}_{i,n}),$$

where PVIFA is the present value of an interest factor with an interest rate of i and a period of n. The thing to remember is to convert the interest rate into a monthly interest rate if you are doing this calculation on a financial calculator.

For example, if a homebuyer wants to purchase a house with a market price of $170,000 and they have a 20% down payment, then their loan amount will be $130,000. Let's assume they get a 30-year fixed-rate mortgage at 6%. Then their monthly interest and principal payment will be $815.39.

$$\begin{aligned} &\$136{,}000 = \text{Payment}\ (\text{PVIFA}_{0.5,360}) \\ or\quad &\$136{,}000 = \text{Payment}\ (166.7914) \\ or\quad &\text{Payment} = \$136{,}000/166.7914 \\ or\quad &\text{Payment} = \$815.39 \end{aligned}$$

Remember, to determine this using a financial calculator, use

$$N = 30(12) = 360$$
$$PV = -136{,}000$$
$$I = 6/12 = 0.5$$
$$FV = 0$$

Then hit the payment button to get CPT PMT = 815.39.

To understand how this works out, consider Table 18-2, which shows how slowly a loan balance decreases. In the early years of the mortgage the vast majority of payments go to interest.

In this example the loan starts on July 2, 2016, with the first payment due August 1, 2016. Notice that of the first payment of $815.39, only $135.39 goes to reduce the principal, while a whopping $680 goes to interest. Thus, the next month the balance has barely decreased.

Even by the end of the first year, of the twelfth payment only $143 goes to whittle down the principal, while $672 of the payment goes to interest. So, by the end of the first year, the borrower has made almost $9,800 in mortgage payments and over $8,100 has gone to interest.

TABLE 18-2 **Payments on a $136,000, 30-Year Fixed-Rate Mortgage with a 6% Annual Interest Rate**

Number	Date	Balance ($)	Payment ($)	Applied to Principal ($)	Applied to Interest ($)	Cumulative Interest ($)
1	8/1/2016	136,000.00	815.39	135.39	680.00	680.00
2	9/1/2016	135,864.61	815.39	136.07	679.32	1,359.32
3	10/1/2016	135,728.55	815.39	136.75	678.64	2,037.97
12	7/1/2017	134,472.93	815.39	143.02	672.36	8,114.57
48	7/1/2020	128,846.92	815.39	171.15	644.23	31,814.42
354	1/1/2046	5,595.26	815.39	787.41	27.98	157,455.45
355	2/1/2046	4,807.85	815.39	791.35	24.04	157,479.49
360	7/1/2046		811.33	807.28	4.06	157,539.94

Homeowner Moves After Four Years

Let's suppose that after living in the house for four years the homebuyer wants to move to a new house. The homeowner has made over $39,000 in mortgage payments but they still owe almost $129,000 on the mortgage!

Remember, they started out four years ago owing $136,000, so the mortgage balance has barely decreased in four years. If they plan on selling the house, they had better hope the market value of the house has increased significantly (they will have to pay the realtor 6% of the sales price in commission), or else they will owe more on the mortgage than what they will get from selling the house!

Homeowner Stays in the House

Maybe instead of selling the house after four years, the homebuyer decides to stay in the house and continue to make the monthly mortgage payments. Thirty years later, the mortgage will finally be paid off.

Notice in Table 18-2 that the January 1, 2046, payment (think of how old you will be in 2046) of $815.39 has $787 going to principal and only $27.98 going to interest. Finally, the last payment on July 1, 2046, $807 goes to principal and only $4.06 goes to interest. Note that by the end of the mortgage the homebuyer has paid over $157,000 in interest—but they borrowed only $136,000.

18-2g A 15-Year Versus a 30-Year Mortgage

To understand how things can change, consider the same mortgage but now with a 15-year amortization (Table 18-3). Notice the monthly payment increases from $815 for a 30-year mortgage to $1,147.65 for a 15-year mortgage. This higher monthly payment may be shocking to the homebuyer, but also notice how much is saved in terms of interest paid.

By the end of the loan, the borrower pays a total of $70,576 in interest compared with $157,539 on the 30-year mortgage. Also consider how much faster the principal is paid down under the 15-year mortgage compared with the 30-year mortgage.

Again, assume our homebuyer decides to sell the house after four years. With the 15-year mortgage, the outstanding mortgage balance is a little more than $111,000; thus, even after

TABLE 18-3 **Payments on a $136,000, 15-Year Fixed-Rate Mortgage with a 6% Annual Interest Rate**

Number	Date	Balance ($)	Payment ($)	Applied to Principal ($)	Applied to Interest ($)	Cumulative Interest ($)
1	8/1/2016	136,000.00	1,147.65	467.65	680.00	680.00
2	9/1/2016	135,532.35	1,147.65	469.98	677.66	1,357.66
3	10/1/2016	135,062.37	1,147.65	472.33	675.31	2,032.97
12	7/1/2017	130,725.35	1,147.65	494.02	653.63	8,003.08
48	7/1/2020	111,292.59	1,147.65	591.18	556.46	29,788.38
180	7/1/2031		1,141.94	1,136.23	5.71	70,576.15

paying the realtor's 6% commission, there is a very good chance our homebuyer will make a profit in selling their house. This assumes, of course, that home prices have not decreased dramatically over those four years.

Lower Interest Rate

Now let's suppose everything remains the same—a 30-year fixed-rate mortgage for $136,000—but now let's assume the interest rate is only 4%. In Table 18-4 we can see that the lower interest rate results in a lower monthly payment: $815 for the 6% interest rate 30-year mortgage compared with $649 for the 4% interest rate 30-year mortgage.

Notice, however, a big difference comes in later years. By the forty-eighth payment, just under $21,000 cumulative interest is paid on the 4% interest rate loan compared with $31,800 paid on the 6% interest rate loan. At the end of the loan, the 4% loan means the borrower pays a total of slightly less than $97,750 compared with $157,500 on the 6% mortgage.

TABLE 18-4 **Payments on a $136,000, 30-Year Fixed-Rate Mortgage with a 4% Annual Interest Rate**

Number	Date	Balance ($)	Payment ($)	Applied to Principal ($)	Applied to Interest ($)	Cumulative Interest ($)
1	8/1/2016	136,000.00	649.28	195.05	453.33	453.33
2	9/1/2016	135,804.55	649.28	196.60	452.68	906.01
3	10/1/2016	135,607.44	649.28	197.26	452.02	1,358.04
12	7/1/2017	133,808.25	649.28	203.26	446.03	5,396.41
48	7/1/2020	128,846.92	649.28	229.13	420.16	20,984.11
354	1/1/2046	4,484.99	649.28	636.45	12.84	97,710.32
355	2/1/2046	3,850.66	649.28	638.57	10.71	97,721.03
360	7/1/2046		647.13	644.97	2.16	97,742.53

You can perform a similar "sensitivity analysis"—that is, you can see how the outcomes change when you alter some of the assumptions: loan amount, annual interest rate, number of payments per year, any additional payments, and so on—by downloading a loan amortization template that can be used in Microsoft Excel.[4]

18-2h Taxes and Insurance

Keep in mind that the above calculations are *only* for interest and principal on the mortgage loan; they do not represent the entire monthly payment. In addition to interest and principal, most people "escrow," or save for property taxes and homeowner's insurance each month.

Annual property taxes can be a fairly large one-time payment for most people. Property taxes are the main source of revenue for many local government entities including cities, counties, and school districts. Property tax is usually calculated as a percentage of the assessed market value of the property.

According to the American Community Survey from the US Census Bureau, in 2008 the national median real estate property tax was 0.96% of the home's assessed market value. That may seem like a small number, but consider: The median house price is $197,400; thus a 0.96% property tax rate would come to $1,895 a year. This is why many people choose to escrow for property taxes each month. To escrow enough for property taxes, the median homebuyer would have their monthly house payment increase by $158 a month.

Homeowner's insurance must also be paid each year. The lender requires the borrower to insure the collateral against unforeseen accidents; this insurance is sometimes called hazard insurance. The insurance will pay to have damages repaired resulting from fire, wind, vandalism, or other causes that would result in a decrease in the market value of the house. Note that damage from flooding is usually excluded, and flood insurance maybe required if the house is in a location where flooding may occur.

The Federal Reserve estimates that homeowner's insurance averages about $3.00 per $1,000 of the home's purchase price. Thus, for a median home with a purchase price of $197,400, this would be another $592 a year, or about $49.35 a month. Thus, property taxes and homeowner's insurance add another $208 to the monthly payment for a median home.

Coming up with enough money every month to make the monthly "house payment" can become quite a challenge. During the past 20 years, this has become even more challenging for many Americans because nonmortgage debt loads have also increased. As a result, there was growing pressure to make mortgages "more affordable" to cash-strapped, heavily indebted American households. Thus "new" types of mortgages began to appear.

SECTION REVIEW

Q1) Adjustable-rate mortgages offer lower interest rates than fixed-rate mortgages, yet ARMs are often viewed as "more risky" than fixed-rate mortgages. Why is this the case?

Q2) Other than getting an adjustable-rate mortgage, what can a home purchaser do to get a mortgage with a lower monthly payment?

Q3) If a homeowner decides to save money each month to pay property taxes and insurance on their home, this is referred to as:

a. escrow.

b. amortization.

c. discretionary savings.

d. forward savings.

---

4 Download a template at https://templates.office.com/en-us/Mortgage-Loan-Calculator-TM10000110.

New Types of Mortgages

18-3

During the first decade of the twenty-first century, the home mortgage market in the United States underwent some major transformations. As house prices rose and American savings rates dropped, it became more difficult for homebuyers to come up with the 20% cash down payment traditionally required to purchase a house. As we discussed above, private mortgage insurance was available for homebuyers who had a down payment of less than 20%, but since Americans were taking on more and more credit card debt and saving literally almost nothing, many homebuyers had zero savings to use as a down payment.

18-3a Zero-Down Home Mortgages

In response to the lack of funds for a home mortgage down payment, some mortgage lenders started to offer "zero-down" mortgages. As the name suggests, with these mortgages, the lender provides 100% of the purchase price of the house. While these new zero-down mortgages resulted in more people being able to get mortgages, they also carried with them hidden risks.

One of the main reasons lenders had always required borrowers to have a down payment in cash was that down payments were a way of aligning the incentives of the lender and borrower. That is, the lender wanted to make sure that the borrower did not have an incentive to default on the mortgage and simply walk away from the house they had purchased. By requiring a down payment, the borrower now had "some skin in the game," or they had their own assets wrapped up in the house. If the borrower defaulted on the mortgage and walked away from the house, they would lose all of their down payment plus any home equity they had built up.

Thus, a borrower with "skin in the game" was much less likely to default on a mortgage than a borrower with no personal financial stake in the house. Market data showed that this idea was correct: When borrowers had a traditional down payment of 20% or more, the default rate on mortgage was very low, only about 2%.[5] But with the zero-down mortgages, while more people could now qualify for a mortgage, the incentives between borrower and lender were no longer aligned.

18-3b Teaser-Rate ARMs

As we described above, adjustable-rate mortgages traditionally have lower initial interest rates than do fixed-rate mortgages. This is because with an ARM, the risk that interest rates may increase in the future is borne by the borrower. These ARMs may make perfect sense for a buyer who plans on living in the house they are buying for only a few years. Maybe the buyer plans to move to another city or buy a different size house in a few years. In these cases an ARM is a desirable alternative to a traditional fixed-rate mortgage.

In the first decade of the twentieth century, however, many homebuyers were enticed solely by the low interest rate of ARMs relative to fixed-rate mortgages, perhaps ignoring or not understanding the inherent interest rate risk that was involved. Further complicating matters, several mortgage lenders started offering ARMs with extremely low initial interest rates—and thus lower initial monthly payments—but these initial low interest rates would increase dramatically in a few years. These mortgages were often called "teaser-rate ARMs."

Teaser-rate ARMs might start with a very low interest rate of, say, 1% for the first few years of the mortgage. Then, after the teaser-rate period expires, the interest rate on the mortgage

5 See Gene Amromin and Anna L. Paulson, "Default Rates on Prime and Subprime Mortgages: Differences and Similarities," *Profitwise News and Views*, Federal Reserve Bank of Chicago, September 2010, 2–10.

would be calculated using one of the market indexes (one-year Treasury rate, LIBOR, or COFI) plus a "margin," or an additional interest rate charged by the lender to either recoup the interest lost during the teaser-rate period and/or to compensate the lender for the additional risk of these teaser-rate ARMs.

For example, suppose the initial teaser rate is 1%, but at the end of the teaser period the mortgage interest rate resets to 10%:

Index:	6%
Margin:	4%
Fully Indexed Rate:	**10%**

Thus, this borrower would see the interest rate on their mortgage jump from 1% to 10%! On a $170,000 mortgage, this would mean the monthly principal and interest payment would go from $547 to $1,492. If the borrower was just able to afford the old monthly payment, they might find it impossible to make a new higher monthly payment.

Many borrowers, however, didn't understand what a "fully indexed rate" meant when they signed the mortgage papers at the closing. All they noticed was the low initial monthly payment they thought they could afford. Still others may have known what the "fully indexed rate" implied, but they believed they could sell the house quickly at a higher price than what they were paying at closing. This concept, called "flipping," became very popular in "hot" real estate markets in California, Florida, and Nevada in the early 2000s.

18-3c Negative Amortization Home Mortgages

Further driving many of these "hot" real estate markets in the first decade of the twenty-first century was negative amortization mortgages, or NegAms. With NegAms, the monthly mortgage payment paid by the borrower is less than the interest charged over the month, so at the end of the month the mortgage balance increases. Most negative amortization mortgages allowed the negative amortization to go on only for the first few years of the mortgage. It was assumed that at the end of these first few years, the borrower's ability to pay a higher mortgage payment that covers both interest and principal would increase, or the mortgage would be refinanced.

As housing prices increased rapidly in many markets across the country during the first decade of the twenty-first century, the option of a NegAm mortgage became more enticing. A borrower could purchase a house for, say, $400,000, make negatively amortized mortgage payments of a few thousand dollars a month, and have the mortgage balance increase to say $450,000 in two years. Let's assume that by the end of the two years, if the market price of the house had increased to, say, $600,000, the borrower then had $150,000 in equity. Thus the homeowner has a $150,000 profit from having a NegAm mortgage.

18-3d No Documentation Home Mortgages

Perhaps the riskiest of the "new" mortgages were those that did not require any verification of income or assets of the borrowers. These mortgages were called no documentation, or "no doc," mortgages. In a booming, highly competitive real estate market lenders want to write mortgages as fast as they can; each mortgage represented a commission they would earn. But, undertaking "due diligence" to verify a borrower's income, assets, credit history, and so on took time and slowed down how quickly the mortgage originator received their commission.

As you can imagine, the potential for deception and fraud was overwhelming. Sometimes the deception was on the part of the borrower, who would misrepresent their income and financial status. Other times it was the loan originator who would falsely report the borrower's financial status to ensure that the mortgage application would be approved by others in the mortgage industry.

We may never know exactly how much fraud was perpetrated with these no doc mortgages. Here is one example from *The San Francisco Chronicle*:[6]

> One Oakland woman, who asked not to be identified, explained how she exaggerated her income—with encouragement from her mortgage broker—when she refinanced her home.
>
> "He didn't say anything illegal out loud," she said. "He didn't say 'lie,' he just made a strong suggestion. He said, 'If you made $60,000, we could get you into the lowest interest level of this loan; did you make that much?' I said, 'Um, yes, about that much.' He went clickety clack on his computer and said, 'Are you sure you don't remember any more income, like alimony or consultancies, because if you made $80,000, we could get you into a better loan with a lower interest rate and no prepayment penalty.' It was such a big differential that I felt like I had to lie, I'm lying already so what the heck. I said, 'Come to think of it, you're right, I did have another job that I forgot about.' "

Stories such as this one were repeated thousands of times across the country. However, it was not just those with first mortgages, where the mortgage loan proceeds are used to purchase a house, who found themselves in difficulty during the mortgages crisis. The second mortgage market also experienced increased default rates. We turn our attention next to the market for second mortgages.

SECTION REVIEW

Q1) Why might zero-down home mortgages have a higher default rate than traditional home mortgages?

Q2) Explain why adjustable-rate mortgages, while beneficial for some, often turned out to be very harmful to others, especially the teaser-rate variation of the ARM.

Q3) A home mortgage where the monthly payment is not enough to pay the monthly principal payment is called a:

a. teaser mortgage.

b. NegAm mortgage.

c. upside-down mortgage.

d. default mortgage.

6 See http://www.sfgate.com/cgi-bin/article.cgi?f=/c/a/2008/02/03/BU9OUP1M8.DTL.

18-4 The Secondary Mortgage Market and MBAs

One reason for the advent of so many "new" types of mortgages was the proliferation of different holders or purchasers of mortgages. As we discussed in more detail in Chapter 5, the Savings & Loan industry was fortified by legislation passed during the Great Depression of the 1930s to lend money to families for home mortgages. For decades, the main provider and holder of home mortgages was the Savings & Loan industry.

When interest rates were low, the Savings & Loan industry worked reasonably well: S&Ls took in deposits, paid 3% on those deposits, and lent the money out on 30-year fixed-rate mortgages at 6% interest. But this structure also created a problem: The Savings & Loans, and other mortgage lenders, would have long-term assets (the 30-year fixed-rate mortgages) and short-term liabilities (savings and checking accounts). This could become problematic if the depositors wanted access to the majority of their funds. The mortgage lenders were simply too liquid.

What was needed was a way for the mortgage lenders to sell off some of their mortgages, thus turning an illiquid asset into a liquid asset and allowing depository institutions to meet the cash needs of their depositors. That is, the mortgage market needed a secondary market for mortgages.

18-4a Problems in Developing a Secondary Market for Mortgages

A problem in developing a secondary market for mortgages was that mortgages were usually too small for institutional investors to purchase. Institutional investors are interested in investing tens or hundreds of millions of dollars at once; their smallest investments are usually \$5 million. However, the average mortgage loan is usually about \$200,000, and many institutional investors don't want to deal with such small financial instruments.

Another problem with mortgages is that they were not standardized. Mortgages mature at different times, have different interest rates and different terms. No two mortgages are exactly the same; this is different from corporate or government bonds, which are all very standardized.

Third, mortgages are difficult for an institutional investor to analyze. For example, it would be difficult for an institutional investor to examine the default risk of every single mortgage borrower.

Fannie Mae to the Rescue

During the Great Depression of the 1930s, the federal government established the Federal National Mortgage Association (Fannie Mae) to buy FHA-qualified mortgages from the Savings & Loans and other thrift institutions. The goal of Fannie Mae was to buy FHA mortgages so that mortgage lenders would have cash to meet depositors' needs and thus could write even more mortgages to the public. Fannie Mae would then resell these mortgages to institutional investors such as pension funds, endowments, and insurance companies. In doing so the federal government helped to create a secondary market for FHA mortgages.

Fannie Mae addressed each of the three problems that had plagued the secondary mortgage market. When Fannie Mae purchased the mortgages from the mortgage originators, it would pool these mortgages together and sell portions of the mortgage pool to institutional investors by creating a new financial instrument: a **mortgage pass-through**. Fannie Mae would then service the mortgage, that is, take the payments from the household and pass these payments through to the institutional investors who owned "parts" of the mortgages. This solved the "size issue" because these pools of mortgages were now large enough for institutional investors.

Mortgage pass-through: A financial instrument created when mortgages are pooled together and shares or participation certificates in the pool are sold to investors. The shares or participation certificates pay to the holder the payments of principal, interest, and prepayments from the underlying mortgages. Thus the payments from the mortgages are passed through to the share or participation certificate holders.

The "standardization issue" also was addressed by these pass-through mortgage securities. Because Fannie Mae was functioning as the loan servicer, it collected the mortgage principal and interest payments from the various mortgages (different sizes and terms) and created a nice, even, steady stream of payments to the institutional investors. Thus, Fannie Mae smoothed out and standardized payments to the institutional investors.

Finally, the "difficult-to-evaluate issue" also was addressed because Fannie Mae required loan originators to make sure only FHA, VA, or other government-qualified mortgages were included in the pools. So, as long as the institutional investors had confidence in Fannie Mae's ability to ensure that the mortgages being pooled together all had a government guarantee of repayment, they didn't need to evaluate each individual mortgage.

Throughout the post–World War II period, the secondary market created by Fannie Mae worked relatively well. The Savings & Loan industry expanded, American suburbs were built, and institutional investors had new, long-term securities in which to invest their funds.

Ginnie Mae and Freddie Mac Join In

By the late 1960s, Fannie Mae had gotten so big that the Johnson Administration, facing a huge government budget deficit because of the Vietnam War, decided to sell off, or privatize, Fannie Mae. After being sold, Fannie Mae would continue to buy FHA mortgages, but the newly created Government National Mortgage Association (Ginnie Mae) would provide the guarantees for timely repayment of principal and interest on FHA loans. In 1970 Congress created the Federal Home Loan Mortgage Corporation (Freddie Mac), whose initial purpose was to buy conventional mortgages (those that couldn't be included in Ginnie Mae pools) and create a secondary market for these mortgages. At the same time, Fannie Mae was allowed to buy private mortgages as well. By 1976 Fannie Mae was purchasing more conventional mortgages than it was government-guaranteed mortgages.

18-4b Mortgage-Backed Assets

Today there are a variety of mortgage-backed assets in addition to the original mortgage pass-throughs. The two most common are the modern pass-throughs and collateralized mortgage obligations (CMOs) or collateralized debt obligations (CDOs).

Modern Pass-Throughs

Pass-through mortgage securities, as described above, are sometimes also called participation certificates. They are the oldest and most basic form of mortgage-backed assets. Most of them are issued or guaranteed by Ginnie Mae, Fannie Mae, and Freddie Mac. While these financial instruments were useful in creating the secondary market for mortgages, they were not without their problems. One of the biggest problems they faced was **curtailment or prepayment risk**. Curtailment risk is the risk that a borrower will make additional principal payments on the loan and thus reduce the total amount of interest paid. Prepayment risk is that a borrower will repay the loan in its entirety before maturity and thus limit the amount of interest paid.

Curtailment or prepayment risk: The risk that a borrower will repay a loan early or before the loan's final payment date.

To address these two types of early repayment risks (both of which reduce the interest paid), collateralized mortgage obligations (CMOs) were created.

CMOs and Collateralized Debt Obligations

A collateralized mortgage obligation works in many ways like a mortgage pass-through: Lenders pool mortgages together, but now the pool is cut up into different slices. The French word for slice is *tranche*, and the slices of these mortgage pools are called *tranches*. Each tranche is then its own CMO.

Later on the same structure would be used for nonmortgage loans. Loans would be pooled together and then sliced into tranches. These slices or tranches of nonmortgage loans are called collateralized debt obligations, or CDOs.

(To make things even more confusing, there is no general agreement on terminology: A mortgage-backed security with tranches, what is often called a CMO, is sometimes also called a CDO. But a CDO backed by mortgages is sometimes called a mortgage-backed asset. A CDO, for example, can be made of nonmortgage loans such as credit card loans, automobile loans, student loans, and so on, bundled together.)

Each tranche offers its own risks and returns to investors. For example, the first loans that are repaid early (or default) are placed into the lowest-rated tranche, whereas the loans that are the last to be repaid early (or those with the lowest likelihood of default) are placed in the highest or senior tranche. Since each tranche has different risks, they have different prices or yields.

The bottom tranche pays the highest interest rate but is the first one to lose money. The top tranche pays the lowest interest rate but is the last one to lose money as a result of default or early repayment. Since each tranche has its own risk/return payoff structure, the CMO or CDO creator has the ability to sell to multiple investors, each of which has their own risk preferences.

In a traditional pass-through security, if 5% of the borrowers do not repay their loans, every one of the holders of the pass-through loses 5% of their money. But with a CMO or CDO with, say, three tranches, each with 33% of the pool, only the holders of the bottom tranche would lose their money if 5% of the borrowers do not repay, not the holders of the top two tranches.

In reality, though, many CMOs and CDOs have multiple tranches. A CMO or CDO might have a tranche for every bond rating, as Figure 18-2 lays out.

Figure 18-2 Structure of the CMO Market

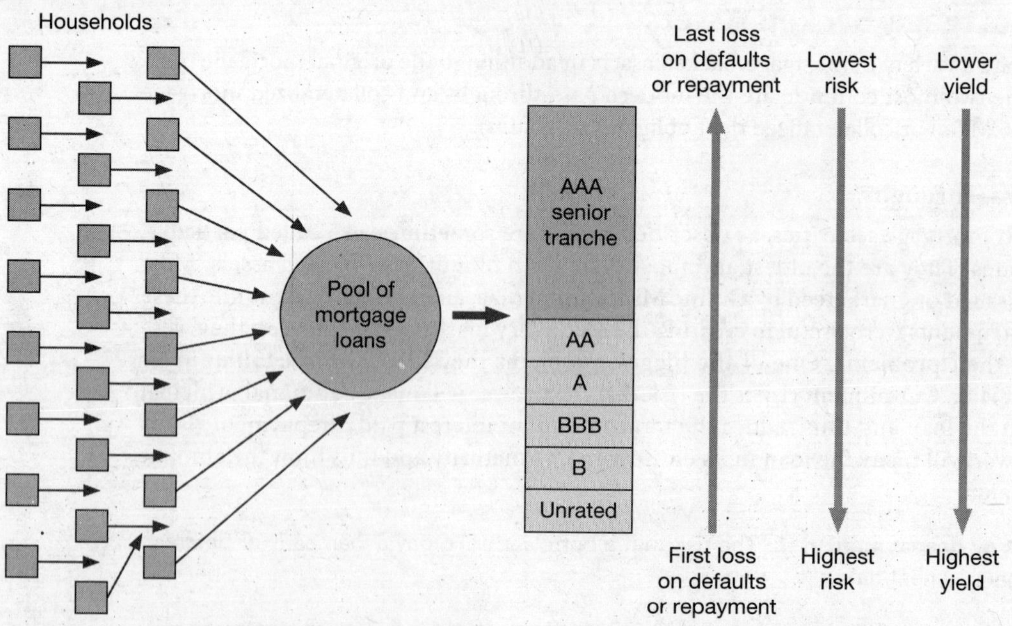

18-4c Growth of the CMO and CDO Market

While CMOs and CDOs had many advantages to both buyers and sellers, there was a significant problem: How should a CMO or CDO be priced?

Markets had the ability to price bonds for a long time, but CMOs and CDOs were different: There was default risk, just like bonds, and there was interest rate risk, also just like bonds. CMOs and CDOs also had prepayment risk, and because mortgages were not standardized, it became difficult to compare different mortgages to gauge correctly the different risks that existed.

A major breakthough came in 2000 when an article by David X. Li appeared in the *Journal of Fixed Income*.[7] Li offered an elaborate mathematical model that could be used to price collateralized debt obligations, or CDOs, of which CMOs are but one type.

Li's model, called the Gaussian copula model, provided a simple way to measure correlation, or the degree to which one variable moves with another, and thus a simple way to price CDOs, including CMOs.

Correlations are important because savers want to diversify their risks. In the 1990s, as the global markets expanded, large amounts of savings from Japanese, Chinese, and US institutional investors needed to be invested. At the same time, American corporations wanted to borrow more and American households were racking up huge amounts of credit card debt and automobile loan debt. And of course there were home mortgages: Americans were borrowing more to fund their home-buying.

But the problem that faced the investors was correlation: What if all of these asset prices, corporate bonds, collateralized credit card debt, collateralized auto loans, and collateralized mortgages moved together? During the good times this would be fine: The values of all these assets would rise together. But during the bad times, the prices of all of these would fall together, and that would not be good—the institutional and foreign investors could get wiped out at once.

This why Li's Gaussian copula model was so useful: It boiled all of these complex relationships between different assets into one simple number! It made it so easy; all a bond trader would have to do was put numbers into the "quantitative black box" and out would pop a value—they would know instantly how to price the CDOs.

Copulas

The idea of a copula in statistics starts with a set of random variables that are narrowed down to a smaller selected number of random variables. The variables that are retained are called "marginal variables" because they use sums of random variables that were, in the old days, hand-written in the margin of spreadsheets. These marginal values have a probability distribution that is called the "marginal distribution." These marginal distributions can be transformed into a uniform distribution, which then allows for a recombination of the marginal variables. There is a theorem in statistics, called Sklar's theorem, that basically says if you do these transformations, you can couple the probability of the variables into one number. It allows you to take the marginal distributions and band them together into a single distribution.

This concept of copulas (Latin for "coupling," which is what is being done) was used by Li to transform the probability of default of different assets (for example, two different bonds) into a single distribution, thus enabling pricing of the CDO that results from the single distribution. The problem Li ran into was that bonds really don't default that often, especially if you are looking at, say, US government bonds. So, instead of actual probabilities of defaults, Li used credit default swap prices. A credit default swap is basically an insurance policy someone can take out against the potential default of a bond.

---

7 David X. Li, "On Default Correlation: A Copula Function Approach." *The Journal of Fixed Income* 9, no. 4 (2000): 43–54. http://www.iijournals.com/doi/abs/10.3905/jfi.2000.319253.

Li used an increase in the price of a credit default swap on a bond to be the same as an increase in the probability of default on that bond. This, it turns out, is a questionable thing to do. It assumes that the credit default swap market always prices risk absolutely correctly. Another problem is the credit default swap market is very young—it basically didn't exist 20 years ago. Thus, there is a very limited amount of data that can be used in constructing the copula and thus pricing CDOs and CMOs.

Yet another problem with Li's approach is that there is a multitude of ways to model dependence. The particular choice of the Gaussian copulas did not capture well the conditional correlations between defaults, especially in the case of a large downward shock, which happens infrequently and thus may be thrown out, although when they occur the result can be disastrous.

The Gaussian copula assumes that the default rates *all* have a normal distribution. Thus, defaults, or the tails of the distribution, are highly unlikely. But if defaults occur more often than the average, the Gaussian copula would be invalid! That means there would be no way to price CDOs. Many people believe this triggered the financial crisis when many of the mortgages started to default at the same time, or were correlated. The Gaussian copula could not account for this and thus could not provide a price for the CDOs! When this happened, all that traders saw on their trading screens were "error" messages instead of a price. Panic quickly set in.

There is an ongoing debate about how much "blame" should be placed on the Gaussian copulas and the creation of CDOs for the financial crisis that stared in 2008. As we shall see, attempting to blame one single thing or one financial product for the crisis is to misunderstand why the crisis came about. To understand why, let's take a closer look at what happened during the financial crisis that centered on the home mortgage market.

SECTION REVIEW

Q1) What is Fannie Mae? What was it originally established to do?

Q2) Explain what a CMO is. How do tranches work?

Q3) In a collateralized debt obligation (CDO) such as a collateralized mortgage obligation (CMO), the senior tranche:

a. comprises the oldest mortgages.

b. has the lowest risk of all the tranches.

c. pays the highest return of the all the tranches.

d. is the only tranche that does not have government insurance.

18-5 The Mortgage Market, Government Policies, and the Global Financial Crisis

Certainly one of the major causes of the current crisis was the financial markets misuse of Gaussian copulas. It seems many in the financial markets either forgot, or never learned, the risks of using copulas. With Li's relatively simple formulation, it became "easy" for traders to price CDOs.

According to the Securities Industry and Financial Markets Association, the total CDO issuance in 2004 was $157 billion, in 2005 it was $272 billion, in 2006 it was $552 billion, and in 2007—even as the crisis was beginning—it was $503 billion. These represent massive increases in the size of a market in a very short period of time. The consulting firm Celent estimated the size of the global CDO market to be close to $2 trillion by the end of 2006. Li himself warned of the misuse of his models. In a 2005 interview with the *Wall Street Journal* Li stated, "Very few people understand the essence of the model." But many on Wall Street ignored his warnings as the CDO market, and the CMO market in particular, continued to expand rapidly.

Another thing driving the expansion of the CMO market was the rapid relaxation of underwriting standards in the mortgage market. **Subprime mortgage loans** are loans that are made to borrowers who do not have a high enough credit rating, income, or collateral to qualify for a traditional mortgage. Changes in banking laws in the early 1980s allowed for the creation of subprime mortgages, but until the early 2000s they composed a relatively small portion of the mortgage market.[8] In 1993 fewer than 25,000 subprime mortgages were used to purchase homes and 80,000 subprime mortgages used to refinance an existing mortgage. For comparison, in 1993 2.2 million prime home mortgages were used to finance the purchase of a home and 5.2 million prime refinance mortgages.

Subprime mortgage loan: A home mortgage where the borrower has substandard qualifications.

As Simon Johnson and James Kwak describe in their 2010 book *13 Bankers*,[9] in the 1990s and 2000s there was an explosion of all types of mortgage lending, although the subprime market expanded drastically. These subprime mortgages were packed into mortgage-backed assets and sliced and diced into CMO and CDOs. These CDOs then were sold to institutional investors around the world. The mortgage originators no longer were concerned with default risk because they packed the subprime mortgages together into CDOs, which then were sold worldwide. The institutional investors didn't worry about defaults because the Gaussian copulas were being twisted into telling them there was little default risk to worry about.

Adding fuel to this housing asset bubble were policymakers in Washington. Both the Clinton and George W. Bush Administrations pushed increased home ownership as one of their important economic policy objectives. In 1995 the Clinton Administration set a rate of home ownership goal of 67.5%, even though the current rate was only 65%. (The home ownership rate reached a peak at 69% at the height of the housing asset bubble.) To achieve this goal, the Department of Housing and Urban Development mandated that Fannie Mae and Freddie Mac use 42% of their funds to fund mortgages for low- and moderate-income households. The requirements were raised to 50% in 2000 and 56% by the Bush Administration and Congress in 2004.[10]

8 For more details of the evolution of the subprime mortgage market, see Souphala Chomsisengphet and Anthony Pennington, "The Evolution of the Subprime Mortgage Market," *Review*, Federal Reserve Bank of St. Louis 88, no. 1 (January/February 2006): 31–56. https://research.stlouisfed.org/publications/review/06/01/ChomPennCross.pdf.

9 For more details see Simon Johnson and James Kwak, *13 Bankers: The Wall Street Takeover and the Next Financial Meltdown* (New York: Pantheon Books, 2010).

10 See Wayne Barrett, "Andrew Cuomo and Fannie and Freddie." *The Village Voice*, August 5, 2008. http://www.villagevoice.com/2008-08-05/news/how-andrew-cuomo-gave-birth-to-the-crisis-at-fannie-mae-and-freddie-mac/.

In 2002 the Bush Administration's Blueprint for the American Dream sought to increase the number of minority homeowners by 5.5 million in 10 years. The plan stated:

> Ensuring that a steady supply of capital is available to fuel home ownership growth is an essential responsibility of Blueprint Partners who play a role in the primary mortgage market, which deals directly with consumers, and the secondary market, whose role is to ensure a steady supply of capital to lenders. The commitments of these organizations include increasing the amount of funds available to primary lenders—effectively increasing the number of mortgage loans primary lenders can originate.[11]

The result of the increased pressure from Washington to create more mortgages, combined with the wave of "new" mortgages with lax underwriting standards, the misalignment of incentives with the originate-to-securitize structure of the markets, and, finally, the misuse of financial models, resulted in the housing asset bubble. It all came crashing down starting in the summer of 2007. The result has been the worst economic slowdown since the Great Depression of the 1930s. At the heart of this meltdown was the subject of this chapter: the home mortgage market in the United States.

SECTION REVIEW

Q1) Explain how the economic policies of both the Clinton and George W. Bush Administrations toward home ownership helped to contribute to the financial crisis.

Q2) Explain how an increase in defaults of home mortgages in the United States could affect savers on the other side of the world via CMOs.

Q3) In subprime home mortgages the term *subprime* refers to:

a. the fact that the interest rates on these mortgages were below the prime rate.

b. the idea that these mortgages were offered to young borrowers who had their prime earning years ahead of them.

c. the fact that the borrowers had a credit history that was not as good as a typical or prime borrower.

d. the idea that these borrowers had a much higher savings rate than a typical borrower.

11 See http://archives.hud.gov/initiatives/blueprint/blueprint.pdf.

Conclusion

18-6

The mortgage market was once thought of as an important, if relatively dull, portion of the American financial markets. Mortgage markets were important because they allowed families to take part of the "American Dream" of home ownership by borrowing money at a fixed interest rate and paying it back over 30 years. But the mortgage market also had its own terminology, acronyms, and abbreviations. Studying these markets could seem like a blur of confusing calculations and long payback periods.

But as we have learned, by understanding the payment structure of mortgages, one can begin to understand why the recent financial crisis took place. As "new" mortgage structures came about and risk was mispriced because of misapplications of financial models and government prodding, the result was the housing asset bubble.

The bursting asset bubble affected not just households and lenders in the United States; its impact was felt around the world. In the next two chapters we delve into how this was possible by examining exchange rates and the structure of our global financial architecture.

IN THE NEWS. . .

Bank of America Set to Settle Mortgages Case for $16bn-plus

Kara Scannell and Camilla Hall
The Financial Times
August 6, 2014

Bank of America has reached an agreement in principle to pay more than $16bn in cash and consumer relief to US authorities to resolve allegations of misselling mortgage-backed securities, people familiar with the matter said.

The bank will pay around $9bn in cash and provide $7bn in consumer relief, such as modifying home loans and refinancing mortgages, as part of the deal, these people say.

If finalised, it will be the Department of Justice's largest settlement with a single entity, exceeding the $13bn pack that JPMorgan Chase agreed last year. . . .

BofA, which has already paid $9.5bn to resolve a similar lawsuit by the Federal Housing Finance Agency, last week was ordered by a US judge to pay $1.3bn more to US authorities.

The judgment followed a trial which found BoA's Countrywide unit liable of defrauding Fannie Mae and Freddie Mac, the government-backed mortgage groups, by fast-tracking mortgages through a programme called "Hustle" without checking the borrowers' ability to repay the debt. . . .

BoA has built its litigation reserves this year ahead of a potential deal with the DoJ. The bank took a $4bn legal charge in the second quarter and reported its first quarterly loss in almost three years in the first quarter after a $6bn legal charge. . . .

The article points out another mortgage market practice—called "hustle"—that has come to light recently. Clearly, this practice harmed consumers and thus resulted in litigation. When judges and juries impose financial penalties on guilty parties in lawsuits, some of the damages are "compensatory damages," meant to compensate those who were damaged, whereas other financial penalties imposed are "punitive damages," intended to deter the guilty party and others from engaging in similar behavior. For punitive damages to be effective, they must be significant enough to be a deterrent. How much of this settlement was compensatory and how much punitive? Do you think the amount of the fine was "enough" to be an effective deterrent in the future? Why or why not?

Summary of Financial Markets

Tying Concepts Together

Financial markets extend well beyond our large, money-center commercial banks. As we have learned, the money markets, bond markets, equity markets, and mortgage markets play an important role in allocating capital. When these markets work well, they help to allocate capital efficiently and help the global economy to expand. But when these markets falter, as they did during the financial crisis that began in 2008, the results can be disastrous. The crisis that started in 2008 showed clearly just how intertwined our global financial markets and economies are. In the next section we examine this intertwining more closely. In Chapter 19 we explore the second price of money: exchange rates. In Chapter 20 we look at the structures and controversies that make up the current global financial architecture. We will see that the pace of reform has been very controversial.

19

Foreign Exchange Markets

19-1 Foreign Exchange Market Basics

You have probably heard it hundreds of times: We live in a globalized world. It's passé, but it is true. As the recent financial crisis demonstrates, our global economy is much more intertwined than it was a generation ago. This is not your parents' global economy.

As economies around the globe become more intertwined, the need to exchange currencies naturally grows. For example, suppose Hans in Stuttgart, Germany, wants to buy an American-made Dell computer. To buy the computer, Hans has to exchange his euros for US dollars. The same holds true for Stan in Milwaukee, Wisconsin, who wants to buy a bond issued by the British mobile phone service provider Vodafone. Stan has exchanged his dollars for British pounds to buy the Vodafone bond. As goods markets and financial markets around the world become more intertwined, the need to buy and sell currencies grows.

The Bank for International Settlements recently reported that the average daily turnover in the foreign exchange market was an eye-popping \$5.3 trillion during April 2013. To put this into perspective, the daily amount of transactions only three years earlier was \$4.0 trillion, and it was \$3.3 trillion in 2007. So, from 2007 to 2013, the amount of daily transactions in foreign exchange markets increased by 61%. Clearly, these markets are huge, and understanding them is important to understanding how financial markets function.

In this chapter we examine the very important foreign exchange market. We begin with the basics of the exchange rate market, using the tools of supply and demand. As we will see, *many* things can and do change over time that put pressure on the exchange rate to change. But we will see that changes in the exchange rate are ultimately disruptive to an economic system. Thus in the last section we review past attempts to stabilize the exchange rate through different exchange rate regimes. We examine why these old regimes collapsed, which will set the stage for our further discussion of exchange rate regimes and controversies in the next chapter.

19-1a Exchange Rate Basics

Exchange rates are simply another price of money, similar to interest rates. It is sometimes difficult to think of money as having a price, but that is what exchanges are: the price of one currency in terms of another currency.

For example, we can talk about dollars in terms of euros or euros in terms of dollars. Let's say the current exchange rate is

\$1 = €0.69, or \$1.44 = €1

So, \$1 will get you €0.69, or you need to give up \$1.44 to get €1. The convention is to quote exchange rates in four to six decimal places, such as

\$1 = €0.693963, or €1 = \$1.440099

This type of notation can seem like a lot of numbers to digest for those of us used to prices with only two decimal places. The exception to these long numbers is when exchange rate values are greater than 20; then it is custom to quote in only two decimal places, such as

\$1 = ¥95.33 or ¥0.0104

Exchange rates have their biggest impact when these market prices for currencies change. We discuss later why exchange rates might change, but first let's look at what happens when this occurs.

Currency Appreciation

To understand the impact of a **currency appreciation**, let's look at a simple example of the US dollar versus another currency, the peso. Let's suppose that the following are the dollar-to-peso exchange rates:

Yesterday: $1 = 20 pesos, or 1 peso = $0.05
Today: $1 = 50 pesos, or 1 peso = $0.02

Currency appreciation: An increase in the market value of a currency.

So, between yesterday and today the dollar has appreciated against the peso. Notice that yesterday, $1 would get you 20 pesos. But today, with the appreciation of the dollar, that same $1 now gets you 50 pesos.

Impact of Currency Appreciation To understand the impact currency appreciation has on various markets, think about an American producer of pens who wants to sell his pens in a country that uses the peso. Further assume that, to stay in the pen-making business, the American pen producer calculates he needs to get $1 per pen. Yesterday, his $1 pens sold for 20 pesos in the country that uses pesos. Today, however, with the appreciation of the dollar (holding everything else constant), his $1 pens sell for 50 pesos in the country that uses pesos.

On the other hand, assume a producer makes gumballs in the country that uses the peso. Further assume that the gumball maker determines that to stay in business she needs to get 1 peso per gumball. Let us also assume that she sells many of these gumballs in the United States.

Yesterday these 1-peso gumballs sold for $0.05 in the United States. With the appreciation in the market value of the dollar, however, Americans have to give up fewer dollars to buy the same amount of imports. Today, holding everything else constant, the 1-peso gumballs sell for only $0.02 in the United States.

Thus, as the dollar appreciates, US-made goods selling overseas become more expensive, whereas imports to the United States become less expensive, holding everything else constant. This, naturally, can be generalized to other currencies: As a currency appreciates, exports get more expensive and imports get less expensive, ceteris paribus.

This then begs the question: Is an appreciating or "strong" currency a good thing? The answer depends on who you are.

Winners and Losers from Currency Appreciation If you are an exporter or you work for a firm that greatly depends on sales in foreign markets, the last thing you want to hear is that your home currency has "gained strength" in the foreign exchange market. The reason is clear: As your home currency appreciates or strengthens, your exports are going to be more expensive for foreigners to buy. That is, you will be at a price disadvantage in those foreign markets.

If you like imports, however, you *want* to see your home currency appreciate or gain in strength. As our gumball example demonstrates, when a currency appreciates imports become less expensive because now less of the home currency has to be given up to buy the same amount of imports, ceteris paribus. So, if you work for a company that buys a great deal of inputs from overseas, a stronger currency means your firm's cost of doing business may have just declined!

On the other hand, if you work for a firm that faces a lot of foreign competition in the local market, you do not want the home currency to appreciate or gain in strength. A stronger currency means that your foreign competitors can now lower their prices in the local market. This is not good news for your firm.

Notice that a "strong" currency is not necessarily a good thing. Some people and some firms suffer as a currency appreciates or strengthens. Thus, even though a "strong currency" might seem desirable, remember that appreciating currencies, especially if they appreciate greatly in a short period of time, can be very destructive.

But, as the saying goes, what goes up can come down—and so it is with currencies.

Currency Depreciation

To analyze a **currency depreciation**, let's return to our simple dollar/peso example. Suppose the dollar-to-peso exchange rates are:

Yesterday: $1 = 20 pesos, or 1 peso = $0.05

Today: $1 = 10 pesos, or 1 peso = $0.10

Currency depreciation: A decrease in the market value of a currency.

So, between yesterday and today the dollar has depreciated, or lost value, against the peso. The dollar that fetched 20 pesos yesterday gets only 10 pesos today. Thus, the dollar has fallen—or weakened, or lost value—against the peso.

Impact of Currency Depreciation To understand the impact of the dollar's depreciation, recall our American pen producer selling his $1 pens in an economy that uses the peso. Yesterday those $1 pens sold for 20 pesos in the country that uses the peso. Today, however, with the depreciation of the dollar, the American-made $1 pens sell for only 10 pesos in the country that uses the peso. Thus, as the dollar weakens, holding everything else constant, US exports are less expensive overseas.

On the other hand, recall those 1-peso gumballs selling in the United States. Yesterday Americans had to hand over $0.05 to get 1 peso to buy the gumballs. Today, however, with the weakening dollar, Americans have to give up $0.10 to buy those same 1-peso gumballs. Thus, as the dollar depreciates, imports in the United States become more expensive.

This again raises the question: Is a "weak" or depreciating currency a good thing? Just as before, the answer depends on who you are.

Winners and Losers from a Currency Depreciation If you work for a firm that exports a great deal of output, you want to see your currency weaken or lose value in the foreign exchange market. On the other hand, if you like to buy imports or if you work for a firm that buys a great deal of its inputs overseas, then you do not want your home currency to depreciate.[1]

If, on the other hand, you run a firm that faces a great deal of foreign competition within your local market, then a weaker currency is beneficial for you because it forces the price of those imports up, holding everything else constant.

So, a weak or depreciating currency is also not necessarily a good thing. This is especially true if the currency loses a great deal of value in the foreign exchange market in a relatively short period of time. For example, during the Asian financial crisis of 1997–1998, the Indonesian rupiah went from around 2,000 rupiah to the dollar up to 18,000 rupiah to the dollar. As a result, the price of food—much of which is imported in Indonesia—skyrocketed, triggering food riots across the country. More than 500 people were killed in the riots, and the Indonesian economy lost 13.5% of its GDP. Clearly, rapid depreciations of a currency are not good.

If both rapid appreciations and rapid depreciations are not good things, the question is: Why do they occur? To answer this question, we turn to a simple supply-and-demand analysis of the foreign exchange market.

---

1 It seems straightforward that as a currency weakens, just as the dollar did in the example above, the trade surplus (imports > exports) corrects itself as exports increase. This, however, does not always happen; in fact, Stephen Magee of the University of Texas at Austin has shown that the trade imbalance gets worse for a few months. This outcome is called the J curve. It was first described by Magee, who explained that import and export orders are taken several months in advance. Thus, immediately after a currency's value drops, the volume of imports remains the same, but the price—in terms of the domestic currency—rises. The value of exports, however, remains the same, so the measured size of the trade imbalance gets larger. (See Stephen P. Magee. "Currency Contracts, Pass-Through, and Devaluation." *Brookings Papers on Economic Activity* 1 (1973): 303–25.)

SECTION REVIEW

Q1) Julie runs an export business in Austin, Texas, and sells a large amount in Mexico. What would she like to see happen to the US dollar in terms of the Mexican peso? Why?

Q2) Kari runs a firm in Los Angeles, California, that buys a lot of its inputs from a supplier in Australia. What would she like to see happen to the US dollar in terms of the Australian dollar? Why?

Q3) If the value of the Indian rupee decreases, which of the following will occur?

a. The price of Swiss-made watches in India will decrease.

b. The price of Indian-made computers will increase in Canada.

c. The price of German-made cheese in India will increase.

d. The price of Indian-made spices in India will decrease.

19-2 Foreign Exchange Supply and Demand

Remember, the foreign exchange market is just that: a market. Just as in any other market, the foreign exchange market includes buyers and sellers who meet, and their interactions determine market prices.

19-2a Foreign Exchange Market Participants

There are four types of market participants: banks, brokers, customers, and central banks.

- **Banks** and other financial institutions are the biggest participants. They earn profits by buying and selling currencies from and to each other. Roughly two-thirds of all foreign exchange transactions involve banks dealing directly with each other.
- **Brokers** act as intermediaries between banks. Dealers call them to find out where they can get the best price for currencies. Such arrangements are beneficial because they provide anonymity to the buyer/seller. Brokers earn profits by charging a commission on the transactions they arrange.
- **Customers**, mainly large companies, require foreign currency in the course of doing business or making investments. Some with large requirements even have their own trading desks. Another type of customer is individuals who buy foreign exchange to travel abroad or make purchases in foreign countries.
- **Central banks**, which act on behalf of their governments, sometimes participate in the foreign exchange market to influence the value of their currencies.

With more than $1.2 trillion changing hands every day, the activity of these participants affects the value of every dollar, pound, yen, or euro.

Participants in the foreign exchange market trade for a variety of reasons:

- To earn short-term profits from fluctuations in exchange rates
- To protect themselves from loss resulting from changes in exchange rates
- To acquire the foreign currency necessary to buy goods and services from other countries

To understand how these market participants interact in the foreign exchange markets, let's look at each side in turn.

19-2b Demand in the Foreign Exchange Market

The foreign exchange market is a market for currencies. So, if we think about the foreign exchange markets for the US dollar, the demand side of this market includes people and entities who hold some other currency but want to buy dollars. We can, of course, generalize this concept as people and entities who want to buy a particular currency.

Some of the demanders of dollars in the foreign exchange market include the following.

Foreign Consumers

Consider our friend Hans in Stuttgart, whom we described earlier. Hans wants to buy an American-made Dell computer. To buy this computer he needs US dollars. Thus, Hans is a demander of dollars.

Most often, of course, consumers themselves don't actually exchange their currencies to purchase foreign-made goods. Someone—an importing firm—does this for them, but the logic remains the same: If foreign consumers want to buy more locally made goods, there is more demand for the local currency.

Foreign Investors

Toyota decided a few years ago to build its new pickup truck manufacturing plant outside of San Antonio, Texas. Because Texans buy so many pickup trucks, it made sense for Toyota to build its trucks in Texas. To build its truck plant, however, Toyota needed to buy land in Texas. To purchase that land, Toyota, a primarily Japanese company, needed to sell its yen in the foreign exchange market and buy dollars. Thus Toyota was a demander of dollars.

Similarly, any foreign firm that wants to make an investment in another country is a demander of that country's currency. The investment might take the form of foreign direct investment, such as Toyota's purchase of Texas land, or it might be a purely financial investment, such as Americans buying bonds issued by a Canadian firm. In this case the Americans are demanders of Canadian dollars.

Local Firms with Foreign-Earned Profits

S. C. Johnson & Son is a large manufacturer of consumer goods such as Ziploc storage bags and Edge shaving cream. While S. C. Johnson's headquarters are in Racine, Wisconsin, it sells its products around the world. Suppose S. C. Johnson earned in 2015 a €20 million profit from the sale of its products in Germany. While the euro profit is wonderful, S. C. Johnson has to pay its shareholders' dividends in dollars. The firm must pay its US taxes in dollars. Thus the company needs to repatriate its profits, or get them in dollars. To do this, S. C. Johnson must go to the foreign exchange market to buy dollars.

Similarly, any domestic firm that generates profits overseas eventually has to repatriate those profits. In doing so, they become demanders of their own country's currency in the foreign exchange market.

Foreign Tourists

According to the UN World Tourism Organization, each year about 51 million foreign tourists come to the United States. When these tourists arrive from Japan, England, or India, for example, they must exchange their yen, pounds, or rupees for American dollars to spend during their stay in the United States. Thus they become demanders of dollars in the foreign exchange market.

Tourists might directly exchange their domestic currency for dollars at commercial banks, hotel lobbies, or exchange rate booths at international airports. Or they might have someone else do this exchange for them, perhaps a credit card company or travel agent. Thus, not all transactions are actually done by the foreign tourists, but the impact on the foreign exchange market is still the same: As the level of foreign tourism increases, there is an increase in demand for a currency in the foreign exchange market.

Central Banks

A central bank often buys its country's own currency in the foreign exchange market to increase the currency's market price. This is called an "unsterilized intervention" in the foreign exchange market. One of the issues resulting from unsterilized interventions is that they can affect the domestic money supply and thus monetary policy.

For example, suppose a central bank wants to increase the value of its country's currency in the foreign exchange market. It buys its domestic currency in the foreign exchange market by selling a foreign currency. If through this action the central bank takes domestic currency out of circulation, the monetary base and thus the money supply contract. Thus, by intervening in the foreign exchange market, the central bank affects one of the most important variables involved in domestic monetary policy: the monetary base.

To offset this impact on the monetary base, the central bank may undertake a "sterilized intervention"; in this case it would buy government securities to increase the monetary base back to the level it was before the foreign exchange market intervention. In this way the impact of the foreign exchange intervention on the money supply is "sterilized."

Speculators

A small number of buyers of currencies are speculators who believe that the value of a given currency will appreciate in the near future. As described in detail in Chapter 23, some hedge funds have a trading strategy based on picking which currencies they believe will change in value in a significant way in a short period of time.

We can show the demand side of the exchange rate market graphically. On the vertical axis we put the value of the currency: A move up the vertical axis represents currency appreciation, whereas movement down the vertical axis represents a depreciation.

Think about what happens if the value of a currency falls, ceteris paribus. As the currency depreciates, domestic goods are less expensive overseas. We know from microeconomics, holding everything else constant, consumers will substitute more expensive goods in favor of less expensive goods. That means as domestic goods become less expensive overseas, those foreign customers will want to buy more of them. To buy more of those domestic goods, they need more of our domestic currency. Thus, as the currency depreciates, the quantity of the currency demanded increases. Graphically, we move from point A to point B in Figure 19-1. Similarly, if a currency depreciates, the price of domestic assets falls for foreign investors.

Figure 19-1 Increase in Quantity Demanded in the Foreign Exchange Market

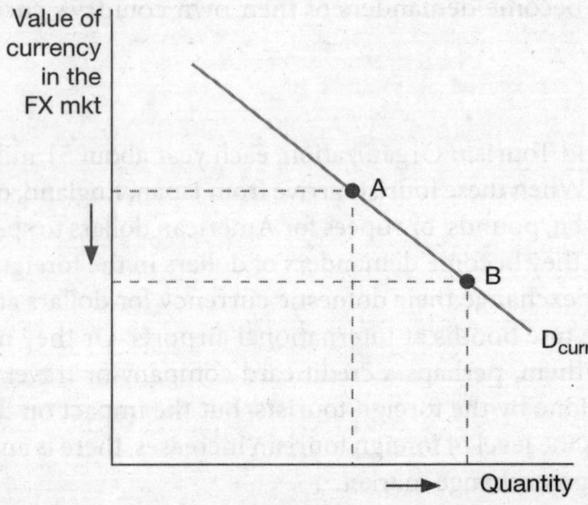

19-2c Supply in the Foreign Exchange Market

The supply side of the foreign exchange markets includes people or entities who have a currency and are interested in exchanging that currency for another. In terms of the US dollar, this means someone who currently holds dollars wants to sell those dollars and thus obtain another currency. These sellers of a particular currency include the following:

- **Domestic consumers**. Suppose that Ron in Minneapolis wants to buy a new BMW automobile that is made in Germany. To buy the BMW, Ron needs euros. Thus Ron sells his dollars to get the euros he needs to buy the BMW. Ron is therefore a seller of dollars in the foreign exchange market. Naturally, Ron doesn't do this himself; instead, someone else—in this case the importer—does it for him. But the logic is still the same: If domestic consumers want to buy more foreign-made goods, there will be more of the domestic currency offered for sale in the foreign exchange market.

- **Domestic investors that want to make foreign investments.** Suppose that Eli Lilly, a pharmaceutical producer in Indianapolis, decides it wants to sell and distribute its insulin analog drug in Mexico to help diabetics in Mexico live better lives. To set up distribution channels in Mexico, Eli Lilly has to hire Mexican employees, rent warehouse space in Mexico, and incur other expenses in that country. To pay for these expenses in Mexico, Eli Lilly needs Mexican pesos, and to buy these Mexican pesos, Eli Lilly sells dollars in the foreign exchange market. Thus Eli Lilly is a supplier of dollars in the foreign exchange market.
- **Foreign firms selling locally.** Nokia, the giant telecommunications company, is headquartered in Espoo, Finland, just outside of Helsinki. Each year Nokia generates millions of dollars in sales of its phones in the United States, but Nokia needs euros to pay its shareholders and creditors in Finland. Therefore Nokia must take the dollars it earned in the United States and sell them for euros in the foreign exchange market. By doing so, Nokia becomes a supplier of dollars in the foreign exchange market.
- **Domestic tourists headed abroad.** John in Columbus, Ohio, is planning a trip to visit his relatives in Germany. John knows that he is going to need euros to pay for his hotel room, pay for dinners in restaurants, and buy train tickets. Thus John sells his dollars in the foreign exchange market and buy euros for his trip. John thereby becomes a seller of dollars in the foreign exchange market.
- **Central banks.** Central banks might sell their currency in the foreign exchange market if they believe it has appreciated too much. Remember, an appreciating or strengthening currency makes it more difficult for exporters in that country to sell their goods overseas. Thus, to help stabilize markets, central banks might sell their currency in the foreign exchange market, putting downward pressure on the currency as the supply of the currency increases in the foreign exchange market.

We can show the supply side of the foreign exchange market graphically. Think about what happens when a currency appreciates: Holders of the currency now have to give up fewer units of the currency to buy things in foreign markets. That is, as a currency appreciates, imports become less expensive compared with domestic goods, ceteris paribus. Buyers now substitute in favor of the less expensive imports by selling more domestic currency in the foreign exchange market; thus the quantity supplied of the currency increases as the currency appreciates. This can be seen moving from point C to D in Figure 19-2.

Figure 19-2 Increases in Quantity Supplied in the Foreign Exchange Market

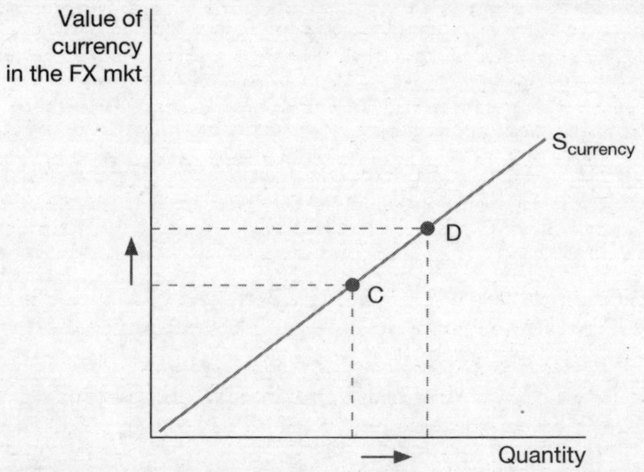

Next we want to bring these two sides together and examine equilibrium in the foreign exchange market. But, perhaps more importantly, we also want to shock this system—bring about changes other than those in the exchange rate—and examine what happens when there is a change that brings about changes in supply, demand, or both in this important market. By doing so, we will learn why forecasting exchange rate movements in the future is a very difficult task.

SECTION REVIEW

Q1) Explain why the demand curve in the foreign exchange market slopes downward. Who causes it to have this shape and how?

Q2) Explain why the supply curve in the foreign exchange market slopes upward. Who causes it to have this shape and how?

Q3) When a central bank seeks to offset the impact of its attempt to influence the exchange rate of its currency on the monetary base, this action is referred to as:

a. sterilization.

b. counter-setting policy.

c. liberalization.

d. decontamination.

Foreign Exchange Equilibrium

19-3

Bringing together these two sides of the foreign exchange market results in an equilibrium, or a market-clearing, price. As with any market equilibrium, if the market price is above the equilibrium price there is a surplus and thus downward pressure on the price. Conversely, if the market price is below the equilibrium price there is a shortage and upward pressure on the price.

19-3a Movement to New Equilibrium

We are more interested in how changes in supply and/or demand in the foreign exchange market bring about changes in the equilibrium price. That is, we are more interested in why appreciations and depreciations occur. First, assume that the exchange rate is determined solely by market forces. Things that can and do change over time and put pressure on the exchange rate include consumer preferences for imports, productivity, relative interest rates, inflationary expectations, price level difference, and foreign investment flows. Let's take a look at each one.

Consumer Preference for Imports

Let's suppose, for whatever reason, Americans suddenly want more imports. For example, assume that Americans really like Bordeaux wine from France or Ferragamo shoes from Italy. To buy these goods, Americans have to sell dollars and buy euros, which means there is an increase in the supply of dollars in the foreign exchange market. As a result of this increase in supply, there is downward pressure on the dollar, or the dollar depreciates. This can be seen graphically in Figure 19-3.

To make this more useful, let's dig a little deeper and ask ourselves: Why might this occur? That is, why do Americans want to buy more imports?

It could be that there was a successful marketing campaign. Maybe the wineries in Bordeaux undertook a successful marketing campaign and increased Americans' awareness of just how good wines from Bordeaux actually are. Or, perhaps a famous Hollywood celebrity was seen wearing Ferragamo shoes in a magazine advertisement and now everyone wants to wear Ferragamo shoes. A successful marketing campaign certainly could be the cause of this increased desire for imports.

Figure 19-3 Increase in Supply in the Foreign Exchange Market

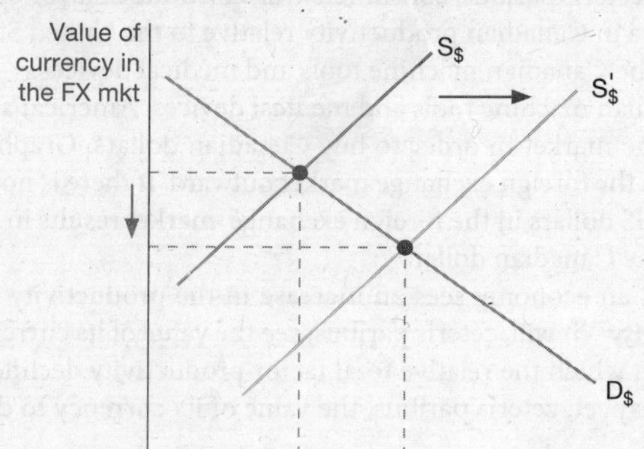

Maybe there is another explanation: consumer income. Recall that when we discussed the marginal propensity to consume, we stated that when household incomes increase, consumers tend to use part of this increase to buy more goods and services. What if incomes increase and consumers buy more goods that are not made domestically?

Economists, in the Keynesian tradition, actually try to measure this **marginal propensity to import**: the change in imports brought about by a change in disposable income.

$$\text{MPM} = \frac{\Delta \textit{Imports}}{\Delta \textit{Disposble income}}$$

Almost always it is calculated to be positive; that is, an increase in income leads to an increase in imports. A relatively large effect can mean that an increase in income can trigger a depreciating currency.

Marginal propensity to import: A change in the purchase of imports brought about by a change in the amount of disposable income

From this it is important to see that a depreciating currency is not *always* a sign of weak economy. In fact, it can be just the opposite: As the economy expands, incomes and spending increase. Some of this increase is spent on imports, thus increasing the supply of currency in the foreign exchange market and triggering currency depreciation.

This is precisely what many argue happened to the Indian rupee during the 1990s. In 1991, India suffered a major financial crisis. As a result, many reforms of the Indian economy were undertaken, and—for the most part—they worked. During the 1990s the Indian economy expanded and incomes increased, especially for the Indian middle class.

As incomes increased for the Indian middle class, these people bought many things that were not made in India. They bought electronics made in Japan, they bought movies made in the United States, and they bought biscuits made in England. How did the Indian middle-class consumers buy all of these things? They sold Indian rupees in the foreign exchange market. As a result, during the 1990s, as the Indian economy was growing and expanding, the Indian rupee continuously lost value in the foreign exchange market.

Thus, consumers' preferences for imports are one thing that can and does change over time and puts pressure on a currency exchange rate.

Productivity Differences

Suppose that Canadians find a better, quicker cheaper way of making machine tools and medical devices than producers in the United States. The Canadians can pass some of these gains in productivity on to their American customers in the form of lower market prices. We know from microeconomics that, ceteris paribus, consumers will substitute in favor of lower-priced goods. Thus, with the increase in Canadian productivity relative to the United States, Americans will substitute in favor of the Canadian machine tools and medical devices.

To buy more Canadian machine tools and medical devices, Americans sell more US dollars in the foreign exchange market in order to buy Canadian dollars. Graphically, this shifts the supply of US dollars in the foreign exchange market outward. If there is nothing to offset it, this increase in supply of US dollars in the foreign exchange market results in a depreciation of the US dollar relative to the Canadian dollar.

Thus, in general, if an economy sees an increase in the productivity of its inputs—called **total factor productivity**—it will, ceteris paribus, see the value of its currency appreciate. Conversely, an economy in which the relative total factor productivity declines compared with its trading partners can expect, ceteris paribus, the value of its currency to decline in the foreign exchange market.

Total factor productivity: A measurement of how efficiently and intensely inputs are used in the production of goods and services.

While changes in consumer preferences for imports and/or productivity changes can take several months or quarters to affect the exchange rate, the next variable can have an impact almost instantly.

Real, Risk-Adjusted Interest Rates

Imagine you work for the trust department of a corporation. Your supervisor informs you that the firm has $10 million that it does not need for the next six months. It is your job to get the highest possible rate of return on these funds, without exposing the firm to too much risk. What do you do?

One of the first lessons of asset management is diversification: You don't want to put all of your eggs in one basket, as the old saying goes. So, you would take a portion of the $10 million, convert it into yen, and buy bonds in the Japanese bond market. You would take another portion of the $10 million, convert it into pounds, and buy bonds in the British bond market. You might also want to convert a portion of the $10 million into euros and put it into a bank in Germany to take advantage of interest rates in Europe.

Then, all of a sudden, US interest rates increase relative to the rest of the world. It is those relatively higher US interest rates of which you want to take advantage. But to do so, you need dollars to buy US government bonds or to put into a US bank. So, to buy those dollars you need to pull your money out of the German bank, sell euros, and buy dollars. Similarly, you sell your bonds in the Japanese and British bond markets and convert the yen and pounds into dollars. All of this dollar buying is represented by an increase in demand for the dollar in the foreign exchange market, as shown in Figure 19-4.

So, in general, when an economy sees higher real, risk-adjusted interest rates, it will experience an increase in demand for the its currency in the foreign exchange market. Thus, if market interest rates increase, ceteris paribus, the value of the currency appreciates.

Expected Rates of Inflation

As we have learned, inflation is an evil thing: It can distort the price-signaling mechanism, result in a misallocation of resources, have very negative social impacts, and increase the overall level of uncertainty. Simply put, unchecked inflation can cause significant damage to an economy.

Figure 19-4 Increase in Demand in the Foreign Exchange Market

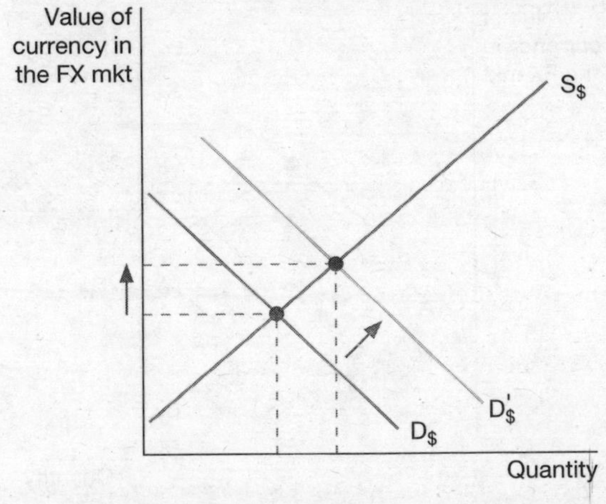

Tying Concepts Together

Changes in Monetary Policy Change Interest Rates and Thus Affect Exchange Rates

Sometimes changes in monetary policy are made solely to affect the foreign exchange market. During the Asian financial crisis in 1998, there was a huge sell-off of currencies in Southeast Asia. The one quick way to stop the sell-off and thus end the panic-driven crisis was to increase the interest rates in Southeast Asia relative to similar interest rates around the world.

But raising interest rates in the middle of crisis is a dangerous, if not impossible, thing to do. Higher interest rates would choke off any business investment spending that was still occurring and worsen the crisis. Similarly, higher interest rates in Southeast Asia would mean higher borrowing costs for households—the same households suffering from growing unemployment while paying more for imports.

So, what to do? The answer came from the US Federal Reserve. If the Fed cut interest rates in the United States, that would make the interest rates in Southeast Asia relatively higher. That is what the Fed did: It cut its target for the federal funds rate three times, all to make interest rates in Southeast Asia relatively higher. The third round of interest rate cuts worked, and the Asian financial crisis ended as the demand for the Southeast Asian currencies increased.

Because of these negative effects of inflation, if global investors fear inflation is about to take hold of an economy, they either avoid or flee that country's currency. In terms of our supply-and-demand analysis, the demand for a currency decreases because potential investors in a country are no longer interested in investing in an economy that is about to suffer from inflation. At the same time, investors who hold the country's currency rush to sell the currency as inflation fears grow. Graphically this causes the supply curve to shift out, as seen in Figure 19-5.

The total impact of this decrease in demand and increase in supply is a significant reduction in the value of the currency in the foreign exchange market. What is even worse is that these increased worries about growing inflation can be a self-fulfilling prophesy. For example, suppose a country imports a fair amount of oil and food and does not use the US dollar as its currency. An increase in inflationary fears and a significant decrease in the market value of the currency—especially against the dollar—causes the price of oil in the economy to increase significantly, since oil is priced in dollars.

Figure 19-5 Increase in Inflationary Expectations in the Foreign Exchange Market

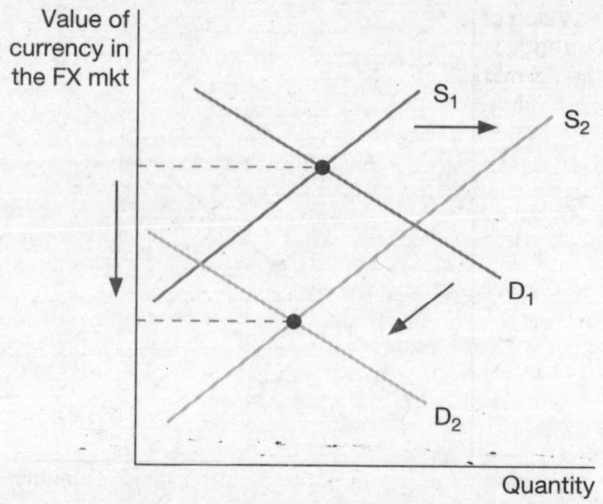

Tying Concepts Together

Central Banks' Goal of Controlling Inflationary Expectations and the Exchange Rate

Recall in our analysis of monetary policy we discussed how central banks today often focus on controlling inflationary expectations. Here we see yet another example of why controlling those inflationary expectations are so important. If market participants begin to fear that inflation is going to grip an economy, they can cause a depreciation of a currency.

What makes this so dangerous is that a depreciating currency can actually fuel the inflationary fire and thus results in an almost self-fulfilling prophesy. If people believe that there is going to be inflation, and if they trigger a sell-off of the currency, the currency depreciates, the cost of imports increases (especially the cost of oil if the country does not use the US dollar), and thus prices may increase. People fear inflation they can help trigger via the exchange rate market.

The impact of this is that firms that use oil and oil products such as gasoline, diesel fuel, and kerosene see their costs increase. The decline in the value of the currency also causes the price of other imports such as food to increase, ceteris paribus. With the cost of living increasing, workers might naturally demand higher wages, thus increasing the cost of labor for firms. With producers facing higher energy costs and higher labor costs, they may have no choice but to raise prices. A continuous increase in the general level of prices is the definition of inflation. But that is exactly what triggered all of this: the fear of future inflation.

Actual Price Differences

Another thing that can and does change over time and puts pressure on the exchange rate is actual price differences. Economies experiencing higher prices see the value of their currency depreciate to ensure there is equal purchasing power among currencies. This concept is called **purchasing power parity**, or PPP. To understand how PPP works, let's consider a highly simplified example.

Purchasing power parity: The exchange rate between currencies that equalizes the purchasing power of each currency by eliminating the differences in price levels in each economy.

Suppose a good is exactly the same in the United Kingdom as it is in the United States. Imagine that this good sells for £1 in the United Kingdom and $2 in the United States. Let's assume there are zero transaction costs and the prices of currencies change more often than the price of goods. Further assume the current exchange rate is £1 = $1. If this is the case, there is an arbitrage opportunity: The opportunity to earn a profit simply by buying a good in one market and selling the exact same good in another market at a higher price.

Here is how the arbitrage works: Assume you are an American and you have $1. According to the current exchange rate, you can exchange that $1 for one British pound. Remember, we are assuming there are no transaction costs when buying and selling currencies; we could add these costs and, while it would make the math more complicated, it would *not* change the underlying logic.

$1 → £1; buy the good in the United Kingdom; sell the good in the United States → $2

Now that you have the one British pound, you buy the good in the United Kingdom with it. Then you sell the good in the United States (remember, we are assuming zero transportation costs). The good sells in the United States for $2, so now you have $2. Look at what you just did: You converted $1 into $2 simply by buying the good in one market and selling the exact same good in another market.

Arbitrage opportunities do not last long. As we will see in Chapter 23, hedge funds have highly sophisticated computer programs that are constantly searching for such mispricing. When market participants discover these arbitrage opportunities, they attempt to undertake the above-described transaction thousands of times. Thus, there is *extensive* selling of dollars and buying of pounds.

This massive selling of dollars and buying of pounds pushes down the value of the dollar and pushes up the value of the pound. Eventually, a new exchange rate equilibrium will be reached at a new exchange rate of $2 = £1. At this new exchange rate, an American would have to give up $2 to get one British pound, and then buy the good in the United Kingdom, sell the good in the United States, and thus get $2 back.

$2 → £1; buy the good in the United Kingdom; sell the good in the United States → $2

At this new exchange rate, there is no longer an arbitrage opportunity: The American gives up $2 to get $2 at the end. What happened? Given the old exchange rates, the United States had higher prices than the United Kingdom, or the dollar was overvalued and the pound was undervalued. Thus, differences in actual price levels can and do put pressure on exchange rates to ensure equal purchasing power of each currency: This is purchasing power parity.

PPP is the idea that exchange rates adjust so that each currency has the same domestic purchasing power. *The Economist* magazine came up with an ingenious use of PPP to calculate which currencies might be overvalued and which may be undervalued. *The Economist* staff compares the price of the McDonald's Big Mac sandwich in various countries with the value of that country's currency in the foreign exchange market. It can thus determine which currencies are overvalued and thus likely to depreciate, and which currencies are undervalued and most likely to appreciate. *The Economist* refers to this as the "Big Mac Index." The Big Mac Index turns out to be fairly useful! As this index illustrates, actual price level differences are one of the things that can and do put pressure on exchange rates.

Foreign Investment Flows

Yet another thing that can and does put pressure on an exchange rate is its level of foreign investment "attractiveness." This can be difficult to quantify, but many economies in the past have become "sexy" places for investment. For example, throughout the 1990s many articles about economies in Southeast Asia appeared in the US business press. These economies were experiencing rapid economic growth driven in part by large amounts of capital flowing in from the West. The "Asian Tiger" economies, as they were known, were all the rage in the US business community. It seemed everyone wanted to make investments in one of these "Tiger" economies.

As the Tiger economies grew in popularity, American businesses bought large amounts of Southeast Asian countries' currencies in the foreign exchange market. Thus, as the value of these currencies increased, those foreigners who made initial investments in Southeast Asia saw the value of these investments increase rapidly in terms of their home currencies. These high returns fueled even more stories about these economies.

But alas, much of it was an asset bubble—the irrational increase in the market price of an asset. Asset bubbles are great for investors while they are growing, but asset bubbles pop. And so it was with the Asian Tigers; by 1999, the Asian Tiger economies had imploded in the so-called Asian financial crisis. When the bubble popped, foreign investors sold off their Southeast Asian currencies even faster than they had bought them. Thus, when foreign investment flows become negative, currencies can depreciate rapidly and even trigger financial crises.

We have a long list of things that can and do change over time and put pressure on the value of a currency. Many of these can change simultaneously, making it difficult for businesspeople to price imports and exports and make investment decisions.

Think of how nice it would be for businesspeople, as well as consumers, if exchange rates did not change so quickly. If the values of currencies remained stable, it would make global business so much easier to conduct and it would make it easier for consumers to decide what is expensive and what is cheap. We used to have a world where exchanges rates were constant. In the next section we examine different exchange rate regimes where the goal is a nice, stable exchange rate.

SECTION REVIEW

Q1) Explain in words and show graphically why decreases in inflationary expectations can lead to currency appreciation.

Q2) Gary does not understand how purchasing power parity affects exchange rates. How would you explain this to him?

Q3) You read in the business press that real, risk-adjusted interest rates in Switzerland have decreased relative to interest rates in the United Kingdom. What will happen in the foreign exchange market and thus in the goods market?

a. The Swiss franc will appreciate relative to the pound and the British will have to pay more pounds to buy Swiss watches.

b. The British pound will depreciate and thus British tourists will have to pay more pounds for their hotel stays in Switzerland.

c. Both a and b are correct.

d. None of the above.

19-4 Foreign Exchange Regimes

One of the oldest exchange rates systems was the gold standard. Put simply, each government stated the value of their currency in terms of gold. For example, in 1717 the United Kingdom fixed the value of the pound at a rate of £1 = 113 grains (or 7.32 g) of fine gold.

19-4a The Gold Standard

The gold standard began as a system designed to give local merchants and households confidence in the value of the government-issued currency. By 1880, the majority of countries, led by Great Britain, had switched from bimetallism (basing the value of currency on two metals: gold and silver), silver monometallic, and purely paper currency to using gold as the basis of their currencies.

By maintaining a fixed price of their currencies in terms of gold, these countries ensured fixed exchange rates. Barry Eichengreen showed that exchange rates throughout the 1880–1914 time period were very rigid because countries adhered to the gold standard.[2] According to Bordo and Kydland, the gold standard was maintained because the three major economic powers—the United Kingdom, the United States, and France—used their monetary policy to maintain the gold standard.[3] That is, they allowed interest rates to change in response to flows of gold. The exception to this was during major wars.

End of the Gold Standard: World War I

It was World War I that brought an end to the gold standard. During the war, governments across Europe had to raise taxes greatly to buy the resources needed to finance the war effort, but this wasn't enough. In England, despite significantly increasing taxes, the British national government debt increased 10-fold between 1914 and 1918. The story was much the same in France. During the same time period, French national debt increased from 28 billion to 151 billion francs as the French government bought much-needed war supplies.

The borrowing needs of governments became so intense that in England in 1914 the British Treasury, not the Bank of England, issued new 1 pound and 10 shilling notes. At the same time, Scottish and Irish banknotes were made legal tenders. With so much currency being produced, and neither the government nor the central bank having enough gold to fully back up all of the currency they created, England was violating the gold standard rules. Thus England slowly allowed the gold standard to die as the world slid into World War I.

Attempting to Return to the Gold Standard: The Interwar Period

The Treaty of Versailles, which ended World War I, placed huge war reparations on the defeated Germans. The countries that sided with Germany in the war also were required to pay war reparations through other treaties. By the early 1920s, it was becoming apparent that Germany, Hungary, Bulgaria, and Austria could not pay the reparations, which were denominated in gold. Most of these countries, especially Germany, also were running increasing governmental budget deficits to fund domestic programs. To pay for all of these expenses, these countries turned to printing money—the result being hyperinflation.

In 1925 England, which had suffered greatly during and after the war, attempted to return to the gold standard at the prewar rate. John Maynard Keynes warned that this was a mistake and would bring economic ruin to England, but he argued to no avail.

---

2 Barry Eichengreen, *Golden Fetters: The Gold Standard and the Great Depression, 1919–1939*. NBER Series on Long-term Factors in Economic Development (New York: Oxford University Press, 1992).

3 Michael D. Bordo and Finn Kydland, "The Gold Standard as a Rule: An Essay in Exploration." *Explorations in Economic History* 32, no. 4 (October 1995): 423–64.

With an overvalued pound, exports from the United Kingdom were too expensive for foreign buyers; as a result, the UK manufacturing sector could not find foreign buyers for their output. With a lack of sales, UK employers sought to cut their employees' wages in a desperate attempt to stay in business. In 1926 there was a general strike across the United Kingdom as workers protested the cut in wages in an attempt to make UK exports more competitive. Not just unskilled laborers took part in the 1926 General Strike. There were fights in the streets between police and strikers in London, Glasgow, and Edinburgh. Things got so bad that British Army troops were ordered into the streets of London. All of this political unrest was brought on by an attempt to return to the gold standard.

The return to the gold standard also caused problems—albeit in the opposite direction—in the United States. While the British pound was overvalued in the 1920s, the US dollar was undervalued because it maintained the gold standard at prewar levels. The United States came out of World War I in much better economic condition than its major trading partners in Europe. With the weak dollar, US exports to Europe skyrocketed, and the US economy expanded greatly during the 1920s.

In 1927 the New York Federal Reserve Bank cut its most important interest rate from 4% to 3.5% in part to help Britain stay on the gold standard. The New York Fed's goal was to make the dollar "less attractive" and thereby cause the pound to appreciate against the dollar. The now lower borrowing costs in the United States, however, combined with very loose lending standards, fueled an already growing stock market bubble.

When the US stock market bubble burst in October 1929, panic replaced euphoria across the US economy. The stock market crash, combined with a now contractionary monetary policy, the collapse of the international trading system, and massive crop failures, all helped propel the United States and much of the world into the Great Depression. In response to the collapse of the global economy, the United Kingdom went off the gold standard in 1931. The newly elected US president Franklin Roosevelt essentially took the United States off the gold standard in 1933. As the German economy suffered through hyperinflation, the Nazis seized power and the world teetered on the brink of yet another world war.

19-4b Bretton Woods

In July 1944, with war raging in Europe and the Pacific, the leaders of 44 countries met at the Mount Washington Hotel in Bretton Woods, New Hampshire. The meeting was officially titled the United Nations Monetary and Financial Crisis, but it is most often simply referred to as the "Bretton Woods Conference." At Bretton Woods, the leaders faced a daunting question: Was World War II only a temporary interruption of the Great Depression?

Many feared that once the fighting ended the global economy would slide right back into the dismal days of the depression. To avoid a rerun of the depression, the finance ministers who met at Bretton Woods correctly realized that one of the major contributors to the Great Depression was the collapse of the international trading system. They also recognized that one of the reasons for the collapse of global trade was the policies followed during the interwar period as nations struggled to return to the gold standard.

The delegates realized that gold was important; knowing that a currency could be exchanged for gold gave people confidence in it. However, maintaining the gold standard presented many daunting problems. As a result of these issues, what came out of the Bretton Woods conference was a "gold exchange system," or what is most commonly referred to as the Bretton Woods System.

The Bretton Woods System

At the center of the Bretton Woods System was gold and an anchor currency. The anchor currency was fully convertible into gold at a fixed price, while the other currencies in the system had a stable exchange rate with the anchor currency. The anchor currency in the system was the US dollar.

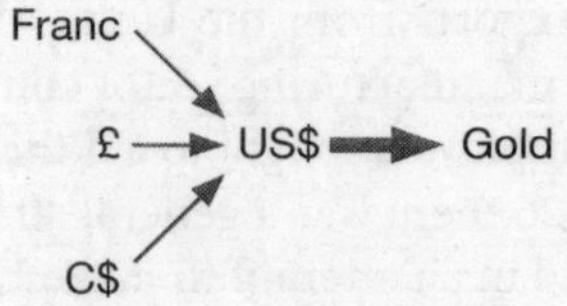

As the anchor currency, the dollar would be exchangeable for gold at a rate of $35 per ounce. The other currencies in the system would have a fixed exchange rate with the dollar, unless economic conditions warranted a change.

To oversee this system and help countries maintain their peg to the US dollar, the International Monetary Fund (IMF) was established. If a country wanted to change the value of its currency by more than 1%, IMF approval was necessary. John Maynard Keynes wanted the IMF to be a world central bank, issuing a global currency that he called the bancor. The American contingent, led by Harry Dexter White, on the other hand, wanted the IMF to ensure stable price levels around the world and rely on funds of currency and gold coming from member nations. The American version won out and the IMF, which would not issue its own currency, instead was charged with overseeing the Bretton Woods System of gold exchange.

Things went relatively well for the Bretton Woods System until the early 1970s. Stable exchange rates changed relatively little between 1946 and 1971, and the level of international trade increased significantly during the period. The high levels of international trade, in both physical goods and capital, helped to rebuild Western Europe and the Pacific after the war. With growing exports the US economy continued to thrive and expand during the postwar era. However, problems were brewing.

By the late 1960s, both a growing current account deficit and increasing inflation rates in the United States resulted in the rest of the world wanting to exchange the dollars they were holding for the gold that backed the dollars up. Things got so bad that in August 1971 President Nixon closed the gold window, essentially driving a stake through the heart of the Bretton Woods System. The countries in the system attempted to maintain their pegs to the dollar, but by 1973 the system collapsed as countries around the world ended their link to the dollar.

Thus the death of the Bretton Woods System is usually dated to 1973. Since 1973 the world has searched for another stable and yet flexible exchange rate system. In the next chapter we examine various regimes that have been attempted, and we look into the controversial policy of fixed exchange rates.

SECTION REVIEW

Q1. Why did the attempt to return to the gold standard after World War I not work out so well?

Q2. Andy is completely confused about the Bretton Woods System. He does not understand how it functioned. What would you tell Andy?

Q3. During what time period was the Bretton Woods System in place?

a. From 1812 until World War I

b. Between World War I and World War II

c. From the Great Depression until the end of World War II

d. From the end of World War II until the 1970s

Conclusion

19-5

The foreign exchange market is a huge, dynamic market. Large swings in this market can destroy governments, create political instability, and ruin the daily lives of individual families. But when these markets work well they can also help to rebuild economies after devastating wars and encourage economic growth by efficiently allocating resources around the world.

As we have seen, there is a long list of things that can and do change over time that put pressure on the exchange rate: consumer preferences for imports, productivity differences, real/risk-adjusted interest rates, inflationary expectations, actual price differences, and foreign direct investment flows. Swings in exchange rates were dampened, for a while, under the gold standard and the Bretton Woods gold exchange system. Yet both of these systems were fatally flawed.

In the next chapter we pick up this discussion by examining exchange rate regimes since the death of the Bretton Woods System. We also examine the debate over fixed exchange rates and ask the question: Does each country really need its own currency?

IN THE NEWS. . .

Growth Forecast Cuts Hit Australian Dollar

The Financial Times
August 8, 2014

There were further losses for the Australian dollar on Friday after the country's central bank cut its domestic economic growth forecasts for the year.

The Reserve Bank of Australia reduced its forecast for GDP expansion in 2014 to a range between 2 percent and 3 percent, down from a range of 2.25 percent and 3.25 percent in its regular quarterly statement on monetary policy.

The cut reflects the impact of lower metals prices, which make up the bulk of Australia's exports, and the slowdown in investment in the mining sector in line with the fall in prices. . . .

The currency—which fell sharply on Thursday after the unemployment rate reached a 12-year peak—fell as much as 0.4 percent to $0.9236 on Friday, its lowest level since the beginning of June. It took its losses over the week to 0.8 percent, the worst performance among currencies from the G10 group of economically developed nations.

Annette Beacher, head of Asia-Pacific research at TD Securities, looked at the RBA's language on monetary policy and concluded: "To us, [the RBA's statement that] 'the most prudent course is likely to be a period of stability in interest rates' is far less emphatic than May's 'current accommodative monetary policy setting is likely to be appropriate for some time yet'".

This article touches on a number of things that can affect the value of a currency in the foreign exchange market: economic growth performance, international trade levels, labor market behavior, and monetary policy. The author of the article implies that of these, monetary policy changes are the most important. Do you agree? Would your view be different if this was for the United States instead of Australia? Why or why not?

20

Global Financial Architecture

20-1 Modern Exchange Rate Regimes

In the last chapter we learned that the Bretton Woods System of relatively fixed exchange rates worked fairly well for an extended period of time. Starting at the end of World War II, this "gold exchange system" (in which the US dollar was the anchor currency) helped to create a postwar economic boom in the United States and helped rebuild the Pacific and Western Europe. But, as they say, all good things must come to an end. Since the demise of the Bretton Woods System, the world has been searching for a stable yet flexible exchange rate system that will result in global economic growth and no financial crises. In this chapter we examine what has been created since the Bretton Woods System. We review the various exchange rate regimes that have been created, including the euro. We also look at the two sister institutions that were developed at the Bretton Woods Conference in 1944: the International Monetary Fund and the World Bank. We conclude with a look at what the future of our global financial architecture might hold.

20-1a Foreign Exchange Market Intervention

Since the end of the Bretton Woods System, governments and/or central banks have intervened in the foreign exchange market to a wide degree, sometimes very little, sometimes extensively. A **foreign exchange intervention** is when central banks and/or national governments engage in actions in order to influence the exchange rate of their or other country's currency. Let's take a look at how this would work, assuming that it is a country's central bank doing the foreign exchange intervention.

Foreign exchange intervention: An economic policy tool used by central banks and national governments to influence the exchange rate of a nation's currency.

Remember that central banks hold foreign currency reserves, also known as international reserves, which are nothing more than another country's currency. The central banks buy or sell their own currency, thus changing their level of foreign currency reserves in order to influence exchange rates.

Fed Wants the Dollar to Appreciate

If the Fed wants the dollar to appreciate, it buys up, say, $10 billion in the foreign exchange market while selling some other currency, let's say the euro. By buying up dollars, the demand for dollars increases and thus the dollar appreciates, ceteris paribus. On the Fed's balance sheet we would see:

Assets	Liabilities
Foreign reserves ↓ $10 billion	Currency in circulation ↓ $10 billion

Currency in circulation is decreasing because the Fed is buying up those dollars so they are no longer in circulation.

If you think about it, this is just like the Fed pursuing a contractionary open market operation. Instead of selling government bonds, the Fed is selling euros. The result is the same: The monetary base contracts.

Fed Wants the Dollar to Depreciate

The same logic holds in reverse if the Fed wants the dollar to decrease in value in the foreign exchange market. Let's suppose the Fed now sells $15 billion and buys euros. This increase in the supply of dollars in the foreign exchange pushes the value of the dollar down. On the Fed's balance sheet we would see:

Assets	Liabilities
Foreign reserves ↑ $15 billion	Currency in circulation ↑ $15 billion

Currency in circulation is increasing because the Fed is selling dollars, or increasing the amount of dollars, in order to buy euros.

Once again, this is just like the Fed pursuing an expansionary open market operation. Instead of buying bonds, here the Fed is buying euros. The result is the same: The monetary base expands.

To Sterilize or Not?

Think more about how a foreign exchange intervention changes the monetary base. If the central bank is okay with the monetary base changing, the foreign exchange intervention to push up the value of the currency has a contractionary impact on the domestic economy, whereas a foreign exchange intervention to push down the value of the currency has an expansionary impact on the domestic economy; the central bank will take no offsetting measures. This is called an **unsterilized intervention**. The central bank's action in the foreign exchange market affects (or infects, if you will) the domestic economy.

Unsterilized foreign exchange intervention: A foreign exchange intervention where the central bank or government have *not* insulated their domestic money supply or financial markets from the foreign exchange intervention. There is no offsetting policy action.

But maybe the central bank doesn't want this infection or impact to occur. The central bank wants to affect only the exchange rate and international trade; it does *not* want to change domestic monetary policy by changing the monetary base. In this case the central bank has to undertake an offsetting action. This is called a **sterilized intervention**.

Sterilized foreign exchange intervention: A foreign exchange intervention where the central bank or government undertakes an offsetting policy to insulate their domestic money supply or financial markets from the foreign exchange intervention.

Let's go back to the example where the Fed wants the dollar to depreciate. The Fed has sold dollars and bought euros. This means the monetary base has increased. To offset or sterilize this foreign exchange intervention, the Fed has to sell a similar amount of government securities, which would then reduce the monetary base.

Assets	Liabilities
Foreign reserves ↑ \$15 billion	Currency in circulation ↑ \$15 billion
Government bonds ↓ \$15 billion	Bank reserves \$15 ↓ billion

Now let's return to the example where the Fed wants the dollar to appreciate. In this case, remember, the Fed has bought dollars, sold euros, and thus decreased the monetary base. To sterilize this foreign exchange intervention, the Fed would have to buy a similar amount of government securities, which would then replenish the monetary base.

Assets	Liabilities
Foreign reserves ↓ \$10 billion	Currency in circulation ↓ \$10 billion
Government bonds ↑ \$10 billion	Bank reserves ↑ \$10 billion

In either case, sterilized or unsterilized, the Fed—or any central bank or government that is undertaking the foreign exchange intervention—is attempting to manipulate the exchange rate. Now that we understand sterilized and unsterilized foreign exchange market interventions, let's look next at *why* governments or central banks attempt these interventions.

Remember that fluctuations in exchange rates cause disruptions in the domestic economy. Therefore central banks desire stable exchange rates. However, we also learned that there is a long list of things that can, and do, put pressure on exchange rates. So, central banks want to create a system of stable yet flexible exchange rates. The world thought it had accomplished this with the Bretton Woods System, but, as we saw, that system turned out to be too rigid.

20-1b Crawling Peg

In an attempt to establish a stable yet flexible exchange rate regime, some countries adopted a **crawling peg exchange rate system** (Figure 20-1). Under this system, the exchange rate is held constant day to day, but changes are made to the exchange rate when economic conditions warrant them.

Crawling peg exchange rate system: An exchange rate system where the stated official exchange rate remains unchanged day to day, but the official exchange is changed by the government or central bank when economic conditions warrant a change.

Thus, in a crawling peg system there is stability (the exchange rate does not change day to day) as well as flexibility. Central banks undertook a foreign exchange intervention when economic conditions changed and an adjustment was needed. It seemed like a perfectly good regime, and it was based on how the Bretton Woods System was supposed to work. But it had only one flaw: In general, it did not work. There are two main reasons why the crawling peg/managed fix did not work: bureaucracy and politics.

The idea behind the crawling peg/managed fix was that the central bank or government would intervene and change the exchange rate "when economic conditions warranted a change." But the question is: When exactly is that? As we have seen, there is a myriad of things that can and do change that put pressure on an exchange rate. This regime requires the bureaucracy of a central bank or government to stay atop all of these changes, be able to calculate with good precision the net effect of all of these changes, decide on a plan of action, and then act nimbly enough to intervene in the market to manipulate the exchange rate in time to offset any of the changes. Bureaucracies are good at doing many things, but acting nimbly is not one of them.

Thus, in a crawling peg/managed fix system, often the "official exchange rate" does not change as often as it should because the bureaucracy simply doesn't react fast enough. Even if the bureaucracy can react quickly, political pressures often keep it from doing so. There may be political pressures put on central banks to *not* devalue a currency. A "weakening currency" is often considered—wrongly, as we know—a sign of a country's "economic weakness." Thus, elected officials, not wanting to be seen as presiding over a "weakening" economy, often put pressure on central banks not to depreciate a currency even though economic conditions warrant it.

Think about why this is important. Let's say an American businessperson is thinking about undertaking an investment in Bolivia because of the large natural gas reserves there. Assume Bolivia has a crawling peg exchange rate against the US dollar. The American businessperson

Figure 20-1 The Crawling Peg Exchange Rate System

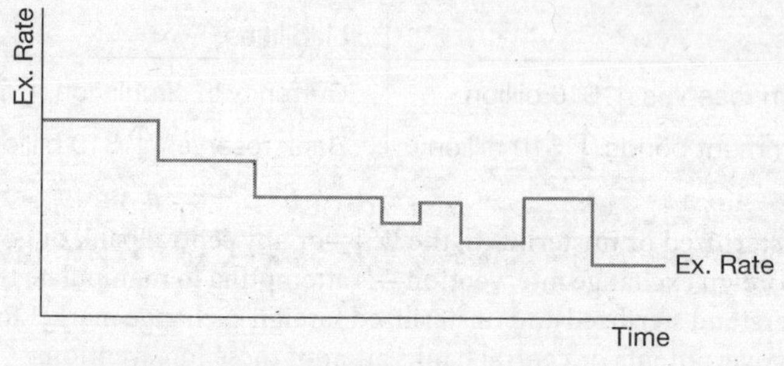

thinks, "Great, there is no exchange rate risk for me if I invest in Bolivia because they have a crawling peg against the dollar." But maybe the Bolivian currency, the boliviano, should be devalued against the dollar, perhaps because US productivity has increased faster than Bolivian productivity.

The American businessperson misunderstands the risk and undertakes the investment in Bolivia. The American generates income in bolivianos from the project. Naturally, the American wants to repatriate those profits, or bring them back to the United States in terms of dollars. The American goes to a bank in Bolivia to exchange his bolivianos at the "official" exchange rate. But the American is told the person who can do that is not at the bank today and the American must come back tomorrow. This happens day after day after day. Eventually the American realizes he is not going to be able to exchange the bolivianos for dollars at the "official" controlled exchange rate. Instead they need to be exchanged on the illegal or black market. The value of bolivianos in the black market is significantly lower than the "official" controlled exchange rate.

Thus, the American businessperson *did*, in fact, face exchange rate risk. The value of his investment in Bolivia, in terms of dollars, was falling and he did not even realize it. He did not recognize the risk he was facing because he did not understand that the crawling peg exchange rate regime, while it seems to create a stable exchange rate, in reality often does not.

But the crawling peg is only one of the exchange rate regimes that were created in the wake of collapse of the Bretton Woods System. Next we look at some of the other exchange rate regimes that were developed in an attempt to create a stable yet flexible exchange rate system.

SECTION REVIEW

Q1) Why might a central bank want to "sterilize" its exchange rate intervention?

Q2) Why does the crawling peg exchange rate regime often not work as planned?

Q3) In an unsterilized exchange rate intervention, if a central bank wants to push down the value of its currency in the foreign exchange market, it ________ its own currency, causing the monetary base in its country to ________.

a. buys; contract

b. sells; expand

c. sells; contract

d. buys; expand

20-2 More Modern Exchange Rate Regimes

The Bretton Woods gold exchange system of relatively fixed exchange rates worked very well from the end of World War II until the early 1970s. But by the mid-1970s, the Bretton Woods System had collapsed and central banks and governments around the world searched for another exchange rate regime that would give them stable yet flexible exchange rates. The crawling peg system proved to be not up to the task because it, like Bretton Woods, turned out to be too rigid. To deal with this excessive rigidity, the target zone exchange rate regime was created.

20-2a Target Zone

Under a **target zone regime**, the global market sets the exchange rate for a currency day to day, but a central bank intervenes if the currency appreciates or depreciates too much. Thus, in a target zone regime the central bank sets an upper and lower bound for the value of a currency, and it intervenes when the market value approaches one of these bounds.

Target zone regime: An exchange rate system where the central bank or government sets official upper and lower bounds for the market value of the country's currency. The market determines the exchange rate day to day, and the central bank or government pledges to undertake an intervention if the market rate approaches either the upper or lower bound.

So, target zones sounded like an ideal combination of stability and flexibility. The system would allow flexibility—the market determines the exchange rate day to day—but there is stability: no need to worry about massive appreciations or depreciations of currencies because the central bank steps in if they occur. These are sometimes called "snakes in a tunnel" because that is what the graph of one looks like (Figure 20-2).

As the daily exchange rate approaches the upper bound, the central bank steps into the foreign exchange market and sells its currency. This increase in supply in the foreign exchange market pushes down the value of the currency. The central bank continues to do this until the exchange rate moves away from the upper bound and closer to the middle of the zone. Similarly, if the daily, market-determined exchange rate approaches the lower bound, the central bank steps into the foreign exchange market and buys up its currency. This increase in demand in the foreign exchange market pushes up the value of the currency. The central bank continues to do this until the exchange rate moves away from the lower bound and closer to the middle of the zone.

Thus the target zone promised stability and flexibility. It had only one problem: It often did not work.

Figure 20-2 The Target Zone Exchange Rate System

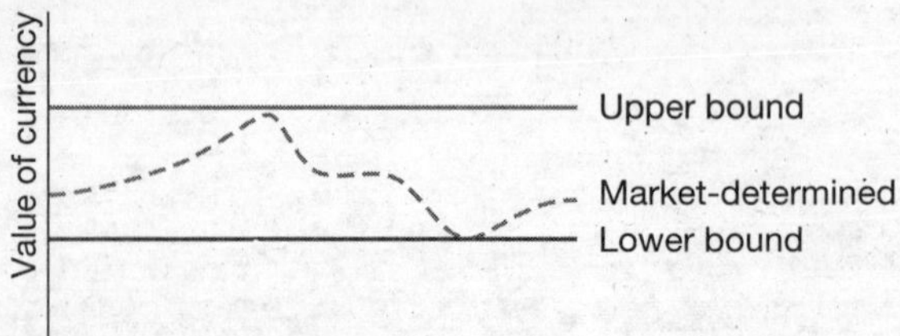

To understand why the target zone did not work as planned, think about what happens as an exchange rate approaches the lower bound. The central bank is supposed to enter the foreign exchange market and buy up its own currency. To do this, the central bank has to have significant amounts of foreign currency reserves or international reserves to do so. But do they?

In 1992 the British pound had a target zone exchange rate, along with the rest of Western Europe, called the exchange rate mechanism, or the ERM. The problem is that when the United Kingdom joined the ERM, the pound was overvalued. The United Kingdom's inflation rate was much higher than Germany's (the German mark was the main currency in the ERM), and British interest rates were far too low. George Soros, the head of the hedge fund Quantum Fund, recognized this problem, and he believed that Bank of England simply did not have the resources to defend the pound.

Starting in August 1992, Soros and the Quantum Fund started to short the pound, essentially selling the pound one day and agreeing to buy it in the future, so if the price falls between the day you sell it and in the future when you buy it, you make a profit: You sold at a high price and bought at a low price. By September 15, 1992, the pound was losing value in the foreign exchange market and was at the bottom of the target zone. Soros decided to "go for the jugular" and sold more and more and pounds.[1]

The Bank of England was running into a huge problem: They simply could not continue to buy up all of the pounds Soros was selling. Finally, on September 16, 1992—"Black Wednesday," as it is called—the Bank of England and the United Kingdom had to leave the ERM, allowing the pound to fall through the lower bound. Soros cashed in on the now lower-valued pound. It is estimated Soros profited over $1 billion on that one day.

The story of Soros and the Quantum Fund "breaking the Bank of England" is the most dramatic example of the target zone failing. Most often it fails because, as with the British pound, central banks do not have enough foreign currency reserves to withstand a speculative attack against their currency. Financial market participants lose confidence in the central bank's ability to maintain the value of its currency, and speculative attacks are the result.

This then led economists to ponder a question: How was this done in the past? That is, in the past how did financial market participants develop confidence in currencies? That got some economists to start looking back in history at colonies. How were colonies able to establish confidence in the currencies they created? The answer is currency boards.

20-2b Currency Boards

In a **currency board** the local government fixes the value of its currency to an "anchor currency" and pledges, by law, that it will convert its local currency to the anchor currency at any time. The local government's pledge is credible only if the local central bank holds enough foreign currency reserves of the anchor currency to back up the domestic currency.

Currency board: A foreign exchange regime where a central bank or national government pledges to convert or exchange its local currency to another anchor currency at any time at a stated fixed price.

During the days of European colonial power, the local currency was the currency issued by the colonial government, and the "anchor currency" was the currency of the colonial power, or the "mother country." Currency boards were very popular during the days of the British Empire, especially in the eighteenth and nineteenth centuries. But, with the scaling back of the empire, the interest in currency boards also faded.

Currency boards became popular again during the late twentieth century. Part of this popularity was due to the success the British colony Hong Kong had with its currency board.

1 See "Go for the Jugular" (http://www.theatlantic.com/business/archive/2010/06/go-for-the-jugular/57696/?single_page=true), which offers an excerpt from the book *More Money than God*, by Sebastian Mallaby.

Interestingly, though, the Hong Kong currency board was not tied to the British pound, but the US dollar. As many developing countries suffered from a loss of confidence in their currencies—and thus destructive rapid devaluations—many turned to a currency board regime as a way to instill confidence in their currency.

But, alas, the currency board regime did not prove to be a perfect solution. A currency board strips a central bank of its ability to use monetary policy to address local, country-specific problems. Manipulation of the money supply can no longer be used to control inflation or stimulate a stagnant economy; instead, changes in the money supply are used solely to maintain the currency board. This can be a very steep price for a country to pay, especially one that is subject to large external shocks.

Perhaps the most difficult problem with the currency board is that there is no way to enforce it. In a currency board the central bank pledges to issue local currency if and only if it is fully backed up by a unit of anchor currency. But how is this enforced? What "penalty" is there if the central bank does not comply? What if the government puts pressure on the central bank to stimulate the economy and thus violates the agreement made under the currency board?

Sometimes the central bank makes a commitment to the currency board that it cannot keep for reasons outside of its control. For example, Argentina had a currency board with the US dollar in the late 1990s. But the provisional governments—not the national government—forced banks in their provinces to create essentially local currency to buy the provisional government's bonds. Thus the amount of local currency increased faster than the central bank could collect dollars. Eventually, the currency board collapsed and Argentina entered a severe financial and economic crisis.

20-2c Managed Float

Currency boards were a form of a fixed exchange rate. At the other extreme are **free-floating exchange rates**. In a free floating exchange rate, the price of one country's currency in terms of another is determined purely through market forces. While a free-floating exchange rate often is discussed in a theoretical framework, it almost never happens in practice. In reality, the closest we can get to a free-floating exchange rate is a managed float.

Free-floating exchange rates: A foreign exchange regime where the exchange rate of currencies are determined purely by market forces.

In a **managed float exchange rate** regime, the government or central bank "steps into" the foreign exchange market when they see fit. Often there is no predetermined trigger as to when or why or by how much the central bank or government will intervene, but the potential for intervention is always there.

Managed float exchange rate: A foreign exchange rate regime where a central bank or national government undertakes an exchange rate intervention but generally does not announce the intervention ahead of time nor lay out specific conditions under which an intervention will take place.

One justification for a government or central bank intervening and creating a managed float regime is exchange rate overshooting. The idea of exchange rate overshooting was first put forward by Rudi Dornbusch in 1976. Dornbusch argued that because the prices of goods were "sticky" while exchange rates changed more rapidly, exchange rates were more volatile and would overshoot their "true" equilibrium value. To understand how this could happen, imagine a central bank has an unanticipated permanent increase in its money supply. This causes the currency to depreciate, so the price of goods should increase, ceteris paribus. In the goods market, however, prices adjust more slowly; there are long-term contracts where prices are set, and it is costly, both implicitly and explicitly, to change prices. Because of the price stickiness, prices of goods increase with a delay. Thus the exchange rate overshoots, or in the short run depreciates beyond, the long-term equilibrium value.

So, if one believes there is "overshooting" of exchange rates, it means that nominal or market exchange rates often are not at their "correct" long-run equilibrium values. Thus, intervention into the foreign exchange market by governments and/or central banks can help to "move" the market in the correct direction. From this perspective, a managed float exchange rate regime is more stable—or at least less volatile—than a pure free-floating exchange rate.

Today most exchange rates are some form of a managed float. Governments and/or central banks intervene in the foreign exchange market when they consider the market to be out of equilibrium. But there generally is no set time when this occurs.

To understand why this is important, think about this from the point of view of a businessperson who needs to figure out where markets are headed. To make her managerial decisions, she needs to have some idea of where exchange rates are going to be in the future. But, as we have seen, there is a long list of things than can and do put pressure on an exchange rate. This makes the businessperson's job very difficult and increases the level of uncertainty. Added to this uncertainty about where the foreign exchange markets are headed, as we have just learned, governments and/or central banks intervene into these markets unannounced and have a significant impact on various exchange rates. You can see that forecasting exchange rate movements is a difficult task indeed, but one all businesspeople must do.

Wouldn't it be nice if businesspeople didn't have to worry about this uncertainty over exchange rates? If exchange rates never changed, the pricing of exports and imports would be so much easier, and uncertainty would be reduced. That is why so many, especially businesspeople, push for fixed exchange rates. But are fixed exchange rates possible? That question is where we turn next.

SECTION REVIEW

Q1) The target zone exchange rate regime held promise because it was designed to be flexible yet stable. Why did the target zone regime not work as well as planned?

Q2) The currency board exchange rate regime worked well for Hong Kong. Why did currency boards not work so well for other countries?

Q3) Which of the following explain why exchange rates may "overshoot"?

a. Incomes change more slowly than exchange rates.

b. Exchange rates change more slowly than market prices of goods and services.

c. Interest rates change more slowly than exchange rates.

d. Market prices of goods and services change more slowly than exchange rates.

20-3 The Fixed Exchange Rate Dance

Market participants hate uncertainty. Uncertainty leads businesspeople to pull back; if there is a great deal of uncertainty about what the rate of return on a project or investment is going to be, they will pull back and not fund the project or undertake the investment. Exchange rate volatility leads to uncertainty. If exchange rates fluctuate widely, it becomes difficult, if not impossible, to forecast correctly the price of exports and imports or rates of return on foreign investments in terms of domestic currency. To reduce this uncertainty, businesspeople (and others) often push for a fixed exchange rate.

20-3a The Stability Advantage

Not only do fixed exchange rates make foreign trade and foreign investment much easier by reducing pricing uncertainties, they can enhance stability in other ways. For example, think about financial crises and central banks' credibility.

Helping to End Financial Crises

When a country experiences a financial crisis, it tends to see a rapid sell-off of its currency in a "flight to quality." This rapid depreciation of the currency pushes the prices of imports higher, which can result in a negative supply shock if the country is dependent on imports (as many countries are dependent on imported oil).

Tying Concepts Together

Flight to Quality in Loanable Funds and the Foreign Exchange Market

Remember, in a flight to quality, capital flows from the "risky" market to the "safe" market. We talked about this in terms of the loanable funds model in Chapter 3, but the same type of behavior can take place in the foreign exchange market. During a financial crisis there can be a flight to quality as market participants sell off the currency in the "risky" market and buy the currency of the "safe" market (Figure 20-3). Thus, the economy suffering a financial crisis tends to see their currency become devalued, as in the "risky" market.

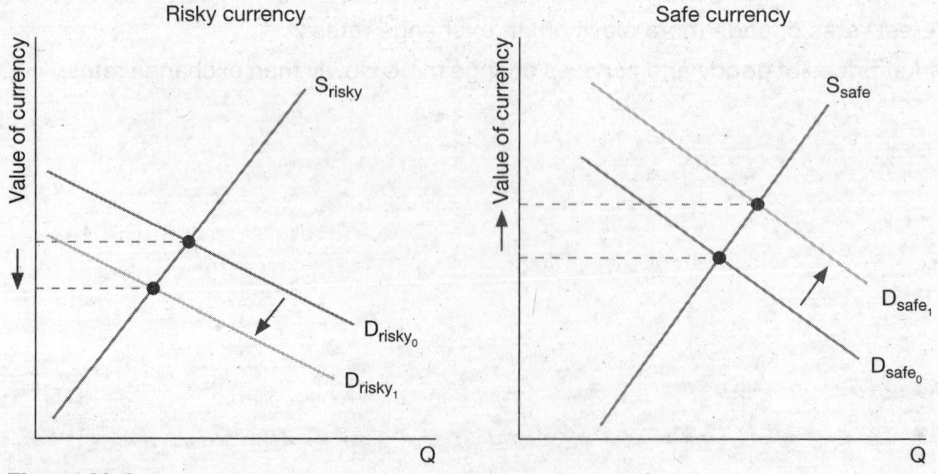

Figure 20-3
Flight to quality in the foreign exchange market. The graphs show the value of the currency in the risky (left) and safe (right) markets.

To avoid all of the negative outcomes of a rapid currency depreciation during a financial crisis, a government or central bank may seek to soothe the flight to quality by establishing a fixed exchange rate. To maintain the fixed exchange rate, the government or central bank pledges to buy its currency at a set price against some other currency. If effective, this policy essentially creates a price floor for the currency. Financial market participants then can be confident that the value of the currency will not decrease further, thus ending the panicked selling. Under this scenario the fixed exchange rate is temporary, lasting only until the panicked selling and flight to quality subside.

Establish a New Central Bank's Credibility

Another temporary use of a fixed exchange rate is to help establish the credibility of a new central bank. Imagine a new central bank is created and issues a new currency. Because this central bank is new, it has no track record of its ability to control the money supply. Thus market participants might doubt the ability of the central bank to conduct monetary policy. To establish credibility, the central bank may pledge to maintain a fixed exchange rate. To do this, the central bank must control the growth of the domestic money supply. If the central bank can do this, it will demonstrate that it has the tools and ability to control money supply growth.

With its credibility to control money supply growth established, the central bank can then move to a more market-determined exchange rate and use its tools to conduct monetary policy. Freed from the need to use monetary policy to maintain a fixed exchange rate, the central bank can now use its tools to address economic and financial problems that are particular to its economy.

20-3b Toward Monetary Integration

In both attempting to establish the credibility of a new central bank and helping to end a financial crisis, the use of a fixed exchange rate was considered temporary. In addition, the use of a fixed exchange rate could also be regarded as the first step in a more permanent change in the structure of an economy—a move toward monetary integration.

If economies seek to become more integrated, they may begin by reducing trade barriers. This is, for example, what has occurred with European integration. It started with a reduction in trade barriers after World War II, but this has only limited effects on economic integration. It can be argued that the next step in economic integration, after trade barrier reduction, is to achieve monetary integration. That is, the different economies use the same currency and have one integrated financial system and one central bank.

Often, however, as was the case with Europe, countries seeking to achieve monetary integration face a problem: They all issue their own currencies. How does one move from a situation where each economy is issuing its own currency to an outcome where all of the economies are using one currency? One solution is for all of the economies to have fixed exchange rates with each other. These fixed exchange rates eventually will be fixed to the new currency, which can then be used to replace all of the individual currencies, bringing the economies a step closer to full monetary integration.

This is what the countries of Europe did in establishing the euro. After reducing trade barriers, they moved toward monetary integration by entering into the exchange rate mechanism (ERM). The ERM was a target zone with essentially fixed exchange rates. After a bit of difficulty, this resulted in the launch of the euro in 1999.

20-3c Mundell's Optimal Currency Area

This raises an interesting question: Which economies would benefit the most from having a monetary union? Or, stated slightly differently, under what conditions would a group of economies benefit the most from having a single currency? Robert Mundell offered an answer to this in 1961 when he described what he formulated as the requirements for an optimal or optimum currency area.[2] Mundell showed that in order for economies to benefit most from having one currency, they need to have the following:

1. **Labor mobility.** People have to be able to move freely between the economies and be able to find work, housing, services, and so on when they move.
2. **Capital mobility.** Capital has to flow from where it is abundant to where it is scarce. Thus the different countries must have capital markets that are integrated in terms of rules, regulations, and structures.
3. **Wage and price flexibility.** Since each economy will no longer have the ability to use an independent monetary policy, wage and price flexibility is important so that each economy can adjust to shocks that might hit it.
4. **Coordinated fiscal policies.** This is needed so that one economy is not running a significantly larger budget deficit that would attract capital and/or require different interest rates than other countries in the currency area.

Optimal or optimum currency area: The situation where economies could join together in a currency union and the result would be a maximization of economic efficiency.

Mundell's optimal currency area can be applied to the United States. Think about the United States not as one economy, but rather as 50 different state-level economies that want to use one currency. Will these 50 different economies benefit fully from having a single currency? Let's apply Mundell's optimal currency area criteria.

1. **Is labor mobile in the United States?** Yes, very much so. It is easy for workers in one state to move to another state and find work, find a place to live, and become part of the community. In fact, the tax code actually encourages this since moving costs may be deductible from federal income taxes.
2. **Is capital mobile in the United States?** Yes, very much so. Since the late 1980s and the advent of nationwide banking, it is easy for households to move financial assets from one state to another. It has always been relatively easy for businesses to move capital from one state to another, and thanks to technology, it is even easier to do so today than it was in the past.
3. **Are wages and prices flexible in the United States?** Yes, relatively. There are still long-term wage and salary contracts, so wages and labor costs are not completely flexible. The issue arises with prices; there are "menu costs" to changing prices, so they are not perfectly flexible. However, few prices are subject to any kind of governmental control or setting.
4. **Are fiscal policies coordinated in the United States?** Yes, relatively. Many state governments in the United States are not allowed by their constitutions to run budget deficits. That means they must balance their budgets every year. So, state governments generally do not cause much disruption to financial markets by having to borrow massive sums to fund their spending.

From this simple application of Mundell's criteria, one could argue that the United States is very close to being an optimal currency area. It is important to remember that this should be thought of as a spectrum and not an absolute. That is, groups of countries can be closer to or farther away from being an optimal currency area; thinking of them as strictly an optimal currency area or *not* an optimal currency area should be avoided.

With this in mind, there has been much debate about the EuroZone. We can ask the question: Is the EuroZone an optimal currency area? When the euro launched in 1999, it was agreed that the answer was *no*. European countries were simply not integrated enough to be considered

2 Robert A. Mundell, "A Theory of Optimum Currency Areas." *American Economic Review* 51, no. 4 (1961): 657–65 .

close to being an optimal currency area. Proponents of the euro argued that even though the EuroZone was not integrated "enough," the common currency would "bring them closer together," and thus they would become an optimal currency area. The debate over whether this "European experiment" is going to work still rages.

One of the main driving forces behind European integration and the launch of the euro was the desire to stabilize exchange rates in order to encourage long-term economic growth, as well as to avoid financial crises in the short term. This relationship between exchange rates, economic growth, and financial crisis is the next issue we want to examine more in depth. To do so, we are going to focus on two "sister institutions": the International Monetary Fund and the World Bank.

SECTION REVIEW

Q1) How can a fixed exchange rate regime be used to build the credibility of a central bank?

Q2) Would you consider the United States to be an optimal currency area? Why or why not?

Q3) Which of the following is *not* a condition for countries to be considered an optimal currency area?

a. They speak the same language.
b. They allow workers to move between countries.
c. They allow capital to move between countries.
d. They allow wages and prices to adjust.

20-4 Creation of the Sister Institutions

Imagine the setting: It is the summer of 1944. World War II is far from over, but in the Washington Hotel in Bretton Woods, New Hampshire, 730 delegates from 44 Allied countries meet to plan out the postwar global economy. The delegates at that conference are worried about two main issues: a return to the Great Depression after the war ends and the potential of entering into yet another world war.

The delegates at the conference correctly realize that one of the contributors to the Great Depression of the 1930s, as well as to the political tensions that helped trigger World War II, was a collapse of the international trading system. It also is evident to them that a factor contributing to World War II was the Treaty of Versailles, which ended World War I. The delegates are committed to avoiding making the same mistakes again. To do so they create two institutions: the International Monetary Fund, usually referred to as the IMF, and the International Bank for Reconstruction and Development, which evolved into the World Bank Group, or, simply, the World Bank. The IMF would be responsible for stabilizing global financial markets and currencies, whereas the World Bank would be responsible for rebuilding and economic development.

20-4a Development and Role of the World Bank

The Treaty of Versailles, which placed huge war reparations on the losing side of World War I, was clearly, in hindsight, a huge mistake. Germany, faced with paying to the winning nations huge debts it could not afford, turned to printing money instead. The result was hyperinflation, economic stagnation, humiliation, and the rise of Adolf Hitler and the Third Reich. The lesson to be learned from the experience at the end of World War I was clear: The winning side in a war should not seek to punish the losers; rather, the winning side should rebuild the losers. It was for this rebuilding that the Bank of Reconstruction was created.

The Early Days of the World Bank

The World Bank made its first loan for $250 million[3] in 1947 to France for postwar construction.[4] Under the Monnet Plan, France would use the funds to purchase coal and oil products as well as ships, freight cars, trucks, coal-mining equipment, and raw materials including copper, tin, and chemicals. Even though this loan was not strictly for "reconstruction or development," as stipulated in the World Bank's Articles of Agreement, it was allowed under the "special circumstances" of the bank's charter. Further loans were made to the Netherlands, Denmark, and Luxembourg. The World Bank's loans were desperately needed; by the winter of 1947, many western European countries were about to run out of food for their people, fuel to heat homes, and raw materials for their firms. The World Bank loans helped to fend off starvation until the European Recovery Program, or the Marshall Plan, could be put into place.

Eventually the World Bank changed it focus away from rebuilding western Europe and the Pacific after World War II and toward helping underdeveloped countries grow. The World Bank made its first development loan in 1948 to Chile for an electrical power and irrigation project. As decades went on the amount of World Bank lending continued to increase.

---

3 That would be about $2.7 billion in 2014 dollars.

4 See "The World Bank's First Loan May 9, 1947." http://go.worldbank.org/VPEQ6VS0W0.

World Bank Structure

As the focus of the World Bank changed from rebuilding Europe to helping underdeveloped nations, the structure of the World Bank grew. Four additional organizations were created and today make up the World Bank Group. Today the five agencies are:

- **International Bank for Reconstruction and Development (IBRD).** Established in 1945, the IBRD still provides debt financing on the basis of recipient country government guarantee.
- **International Development Association (IDA).** Established in 1960, the IDA provides interest-free loans and/or grants for economic development and health care programs, usually on the basis of recipient government guarantee.
- **International Finance Corporation (IFC).** Established in 1956, the IFC provides loans primarily to the private sector without government guarantees.
- **Multilateral Investment Guarantee Agency (MIGA).** Established in 1988, the MIGA provides a wide range of insurance against various forms of risk, including political risk, most often to private sector entities.
- **International Center for Settlement of Investment Disputes (ICSID).** Established in 1960, the ICSID provides interest-free loans and/or grants, usually with recipient government guarantees.

The IBRD and the IDA focus primarily on assisting developing countries with monetary policy and provide a variety of low-interest loans, no-interest loans, and grants to recipient governments for economic development and health care services projects. The other three institutions of the World Bank Group focus primarily on assisting in private market transactions. They provide funding and offer various types of insurance, as well as dispute resolution, for entities involved in development projects.

The term *World Bank* usually refers to the IBRD and IDA; the more general term *World Bank Group* refers to all five of the institutions together. Not all countries belong to all five institutions. The IBRD contains 188 nations as members, whereas the other agencies have between 140 and 176 members.

World Bank Governance and Funding

The World Bank today is controlled by its 188 member countries, each of whom appoints two representatives to the board of governors. These representatives are usually the country's finance minister, the head of its central bank, or some other high-ranking government official. The board of governors meets once a year with the board of governors of the IMF. Voting rights are determined by each country's agreed-upon contribution, or "quota." The quotas, roughly based on the country's size and importance in the global economy, are reviewed every five years. The United States has the largest quota of 16.4%; Japan has 7.9%; Germany, 4.5%; the United Kingdom, 4.3%; and France, 4.3%. Most votes require an 85% supermajority; thus the United States has de facto veto power.

In addition to the funds the World Bank gets from its member nations, it is a major borrower in the global financial markets. The World Bank issues a wide range of debt instruments aimed at different investor groups (Figure 20-4). Bonds with many maturities, risks, and currencies are issued (Figure 20-5). With its AAA bond rating, the World Bank usually has no difficultly raising the funds that it needs.

These funds are put to use in the day-to-day operation of the World Bank. These day-to-day operations are overseen by the 24 executive directors, who include five permanent members: the United States, Japan, Great Britain, Germany, and France. The remaining 19 directors are elected by all member nations.

Figure 20-4 **The World Bank issues a wide range of debt instruments. These instruments range from large, liquid global bonds to plain vanilla retail-targeted or local currency bonds to structured notes in maturities all along the yield curve.**

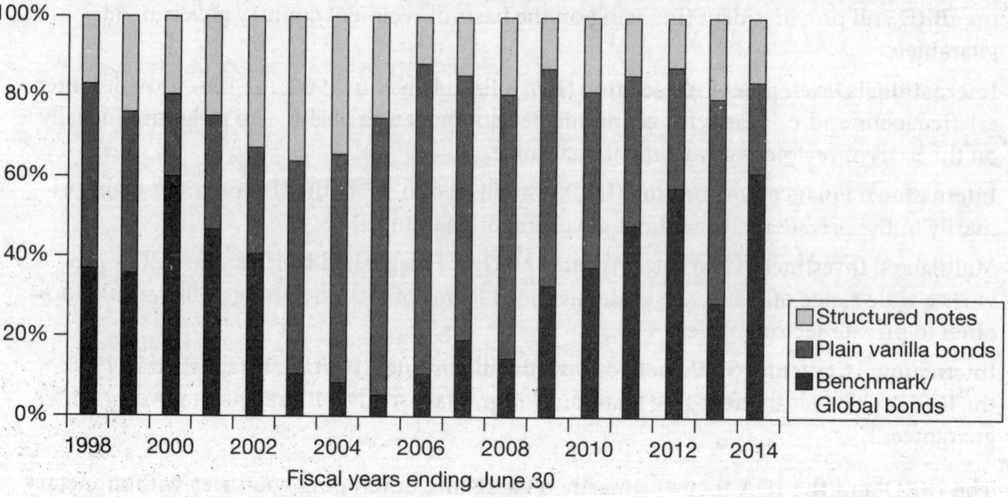

Figure 20-5 **The World Bank has issued bonds in 57 currencies. In fiscal year 2014, issues were denominated in 22 currencies.**

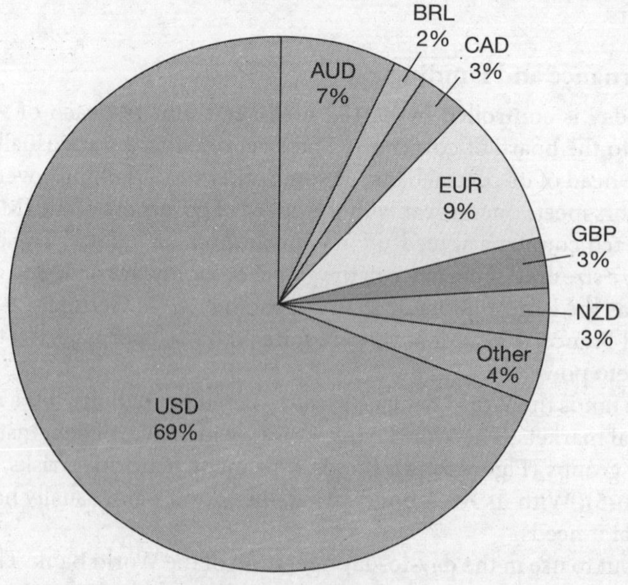

*Other includes CNY, GHS, INR, JPY, KRW, MXN, NGN, PEN, PLN, RUB, SEK, TRY, UGX, ZAR, and ZMW

Explosive Growth Under McNamara

In 1968 Robert McNamara, the new World Bank president, set a goal to double the amount of World Bank lending in five years compared with that in the previous five-year period. By 1973 that goal was attained. This meant that the World Bank would lend in one five-year period (1969–73) almost as much as it had loaned out since its founding.

Robert McNamara was used to seeing entities under his control grow massively in size, often with questionable results. Before coming to the World Bank, McNamara had served as secretary of defense under both presidents Kennedy and Johnson. As one of the most influential and powerful defense secretaries, it was McNamara who greatly increased US involvement in the war in Vietnam. In 1964 Senator Wayne Morse of Oregon called the war in Vietnam "McNamara's War."

During his tenure as secretary of defense, more than 16,000 Americans were killed in Vietnam. Just as he would do with the World Bank, McNamara oversaw a massive increase in the size of the Department of Defense. When McNamara came into office in 1962, the Department of Defense budget was $48.4 million. By 1968 it was $74.9 billion.[5] Yet the results were American humiliation and defeat in Vietnam.

Many also question the outcome of McNamara's massive buildup of the World Bank. Some have questioned how the bank made lending decisions. While the World Bank has always been led by an American, the lending decisions were not supposed to be based on political considerations. Yet many argued that the World Bank was used indirectly by the US Department of Defense and the US State Department as a way to buy political favors with leaders around the world.

The World Bank has continued to grow and currently has over 10,000 employees spread among 100 offices around the world, in addition to its headquarters in Washington, DC. The World Bank's total administrative budget for fiscal year 2014 was just over $2.5 billion. In 2012 the World Bank provided about $30 billion in loans and assistance to developing nations.

While the growth and expansion of the World Bank remains controversial, so, too, does the World Bank's sister institution, the International Monetary Fund, or IMF. Next we look into the question of why the IMF is so controversial and the role it plays in our global financial architecture.

SECTION REVIEW

Q1) Greg is a bit confused about the creation of the World Bank. Explain to Greg how and why the World Bank was created.

Q2) Why was Robert McNamara's tenure at the World Bank so controversial?

Q3) How does the World Bank get its funds?

a. It creates its own currency.

b. It borrows money from the world's central banks.

c. It is funded by national governments and borrows in the global financial markets.

d. It depends on contributions from private parties.

---

5 In 2014 dollars that would be about $515 billion.

20-5 Sister Institutions: IMF

At the Bretton Woods Conference in 1944, the Bank of Reconstruction, what we call today the World Bank, was created to rebuild after World War II and help developing nations grow. At the same conference the IMF was established to stabilize global financial markets. As the British economist and conference participant John Maynard Keynes pointed out, the names are actually reversed: the World Bank is actually a development fund, whereas the IMF is actually a bank. To understand why Keynes made this distinction, let's take a closer look at the World Bank's sister institution, the IMF.

20-5a The Development and Role of the IMF

The delegates to the Bretton Woods Conference correctly identified that one of the major causes of the Great Depression was the collapse of the global financial system. They also realized that one of the major causes of this collapse was the instability of the value of currencies.

During the interwar period, many countries struggled to return to the gold standard at pre–World War I rates. Making things worse, many countries pursued mercantilist-inspired policies designed to promote domestic economic growth at an economic cost of their trading partners. These "beggar-thy-neighbor" policies included currency devaluations created to encourage exports and discourage imports.

Ending Beggar-Thy-Neighbor

From game theory we understand how these "beggar-thy-neighbor" policies can lead to a "tit-for-tat" strategy whereby each player in a game seeks to retaliate against another. During the interwar period, one country would devalue its currency in an attempt to increase exports and block imports; that is, it shifted its economic problems onto its trading partner. The country's trading partner then would devalue its currency in retaliation. This leads to another round of currency devaluation, and the process repeats. The system eventually collapses in a race to the bottom.

To avoid these destructive beggar-thy-neighbor currency manipulations, the delegates at the Bretton Woods Conference agreed to create a gold exchange system, or the Bretton Woods exchange rate system. In this system the US dollar had its value stated in gold and was fully exchangeable at that price. Other countries would then peg their currency to the US dollar. To oversee this system, the IMF was established.

Countries that joined the IMF in the years before 1971 agreed to keep the value of their currency pegged to the US dollar. These exchange rates could be changed if a "fundamental disequilibrium" developed, but any changes in these exchange rates would have to be made through the IMF. This system was officially called the par value system, but most often it is simply referred to as the Bretton Woods System.

The number of countries that belonged to the IMF and the Bretton Woods System expanded in the late 1950s and early 1960s as many sub-Saharan African nations received their political independence from their European colonial rulers. Wanting to engage in global trade, these newly independent nations applied for membership in the IMF. The Cold War between the West and the Soviet bloc of nations limited significant expansion of IMF membership during this time period.

Problems Develop

While the Bretton Woods System was designed to be flexible, in reality it turned out to be far too rigid. Starting in the late 1960s, the United States began suffering from increased rates of inflation. With this increasing inflation, the dollar should have been devalued against the other currencies in the system. For mainly political reasons, however, this did not occur.

As the inflation rate in the United States continued to increase, the rest of the world initially absorbed the additional dollars that were being created. By the early 1970s, however, the rest of the world had had enough and started to exchange their US dollars for gold. In August 1971, with the US gold reserves decreasing, President Nixon announced that the dollar would "temporarily" no longer be exchanged for gold.

Nixon's "closing of the gold window" essentially drove a stake through the heart of the Bretton Woods System. Other countries tried to maintain their currency's peg to the US dollar, but by 1973 things had gotten so bad for the dollar that all of the countries in the system broke their peg to the dollar.

20-5b IMF Changes Focus

By 1973, with the collapse of the Bretton Woods System, the IMF now faced an identity crisis. It had been established, after all, to oversee the Bretton Woods System, but now that system was gone. What was the IMF to do?

At the same time, the world began experiencing a series of oil supply shocks. As the price of oil skyrocketed, many countries around the world faced a balance of payments crisis. They simply could not afford to pay for all of their imports, especially the now very expensive imported oil.

The IMF saw an opportunity: It could lend money to nations who were having balance of payments problems. That was, after all, part of what the IMF was supposed to do under the Bretton Woods System. To help these oil-importing nations, the IMF adapted its lending practices so that it could make loans to countries that were now suffering from the oil supply shocks.

From the mid-1970s onward, the IMF continued to focus on lending to countries with balance of payment problems or any other type of financial crises. The IMF especially increased the amount of lending to developing countries.

New Problems for the IMF

As the IMF continued to lend more and more to developing countries, many of these countries eventually had problems repaying the IMF. This problem exploded in the late 1970s and early 1980s when global interest rates increased. These higher interest rates helped push the US economy into a deep recession. This was problematic for developing countries because many of them sold their exports to the United States. With declining export revenues and increased interest expenses, many developing nations defaulted on their loans.

The problem reached a crisis stage in Mexico in 1982. The IMF stepped in to lend even more money to the Mexican government, but it also required the Mexican government to pursue what the IMF considered to be sound long-term economic policies to help ensure another crisis would never develop.

IMF Expansion

The IMF also was on hand to offer its collection of sound long-term economic policies and financial assistance to the countries of eastern Europe after the fall of the Berlin Wall in 1989. In three short years IMF membership went from 152 nations to 172—the biggest increase since the early 1960s, when many African nations joined. The staff of the IMF increased 30% in six years. The IMF, while still headquartered in Washington, DC, now had a reach that stretched around the world.

With this expanded role, many began to wonder whether the IMF was suffering from "mission creep." The IMF was established to oversee the Bretton Woods gold exchange system, but that system was long dead. Now the IMF had somehow morphed into a global credit union; its structure and funding is similar to that of the World Bank, but the IMF depends mainly on quotas and not as much on issuing bonds, as does the World Bank. In addition to lending, however, the IMF also was seen as giving policy advice—some say dictating economic terms—to many nations. This, it was argued, went well beyond the original scope of what the IMF was established to do.

Thus, the two sister institutions—the World Bank and the IMF—both were created at the Bretton Woods Conference in 1944, and both have evolved beyond their original intended purpose. These two institutions today are arguably two of the most hated financial institutions in the world. Why? The controversies over these two sister institutions is where we turn next.

SECTION REVIEW

Q1) How and why did the International Monetary Fund attempt to end "beggar-thy-neighbor" policies?

Q2) How did the "closing of the gold window" in 1971 affect how the IMF operates?

Q3) Why did the IMF suffer from "mission creep"?

a. As members left the IMF, it changed on whom it focused.

b. The collapse of the Bretton Woods System led the IMF to become a lending institution.

c. The rise of global financial markets resulted in the IMF no longer being necessary.

d. Rising inflation rates caused market interest rates to increase.

Controversies over the Sisters

20-6

The World Bank and the IMF have certainly had their successes. The World Bank was able to rebuild western Europe after World War II. This was a major achievement considering the technology that was available in the late 1940s. The IMF was also successful in helping to create that post–World War II economic boom. The stable exchange rates that the IMF oversaw helped pave the way for rapid economic growth in both North America and western Europe. Despite these successes, the World Bank and IMF are two of the most distrusted financial institutions in the world. Arguably, they are most distrusted by people in the countries that are receiving assistance from the sister institutions. But why is that?

20-6a Problems with the World Bank

Today the World Bank focuses on providing development loans, grants, and insurance in developing countries. Yet many argue the World Bank's record of success is limited. Some of the issues people have with the World Bank revolve around the results of the development policies the World Bank has pursued, whereas others criticize the World Bank for how it makes decisions.

Import Substitution Policies

For a long period of time the World Bank argued that the way to economic development for poorer countries was to block the importation of finished goods from developed countries. Instead of importing finished goods such as consumer goods, autos, and auto parts, the poor country would develop a finished goods sector itself. Thus the name "import substitution," where imported finished goods are substituted with domestically made finished goods.

The problem is, developing countries did not have a finished goods sector. That is where the World Bank came in: It would provide financing and technical assistance to create a finished goods sector in the developing country.

While important substitution policies seemed promising, their rate of success was disappointing. Many problems developed; political corruption resulted as local parties fought over who would be given World Bank funds to develop these new "infant industries." Even if somehow these new infant industries were created, they often became dependent on local government subsidies.

Thus, instead of economic development, import substitution policies often resulted in corrupt local governments that became highly indebted as they borrowed more and more from the World Bank. Sadly, the finished goods never did get produced. So the people in these countries could not buy imported finished goods, and the local finished goods producers were so inefficient that they could not produce enough to meet local demand. Thus the economies did not develop.

World Bank "Consultants"

While people in the countries receiving World Bank assistance were, arguably, not better off, one group that did undoubtedly benefit from the expanded role of the World Bank was private consulting firms hired by the bank. Before a project would be funded by the World Bank, it often required "outside" consultants to verify that the project was "needed." It is contended that these consultants did little more than fly into the developing country, spend a few days in lavish hotels, then fly back to the developed country where they lived, file a report, and collect a hefty "consultant fee."

Critics of the World Bank argue that a great deal of the funds that were supposed to go toward building roads, bridges, and schools in developing countries instead went to pay for high-priced consultants from developed countries. Thus, in the poor countries the roads, bridges, or schools were never built; instead, the people only got the bill for borrowing from the World Bank.

20-6b Problems with the IMF

While the success record of the World Bank is questionable, the success record of its sister institution, the IMF, is perhaps just as poor. Over the past four decades the IMF has focused on providing financial assistance and financial advice to countries experiencing balance of payment problems or more general financial crises.

The Reactionary IMF

While the IMF often likes to depict itself as riding to the rescue in a financial crisis and offering sound long-term economic advice, critics of the IMF contend the IMF should do more when times are good. Critics argue that the IMF may give sound long-term advice (e.g., reduce government budget deficits, collect more in tax revenue, move toward floating currencies, allow foreign ownership of banks), but these are often the wrong policies to follow during a crisis.

Critics believe that instead of focusing only on a crisis, the IMF should focus on having countries prequalify for IMF assistance during the good times.[6] Encouraging sound long-term policies during the goods times could reduce the chances of financial crises in the future.

IMF and Long-Term Lending

While the IMF today likes to say it temporarily lends money for countries to get through their balance of payments problems, records indicate that many countries continue to borrow from the IMF for decades. Thus, from the critics' perspective, the IMF has become less of a short-term lender and much more of a long-term crutch. As the lending goes on year after year or decade after decade, the interest bill that these countries have to pay continuously increases.

20-6c Problems the Sisters Share

Both the World Bank and IMF share the same basic structure that dates back to 1944. This structure has voting rights based on the quota of each country. The structure also requires a supermajority of 85% for most significant changes in policy. The United States has 16.5% of the quota and thus the same percentage of votes, meaning nothing can get done by the World Bank or IMF without the United States' approval.

In addition, both the IMF and World Bank often run into funding constraints. This is especially true after major global financial crises, which deplete the resources of both organizations as many countries seek assistance at the same time.

To address these issues, in 2010 reforms to the structure and funding of the IMF were agreed to. These changes would double the IMF quota and shift more of the quotas to emerging nations. For these changes to be implemented, ratification by each of the member nations is required. As of 2015, all countries except the United States have ratified the changes.

Some say the IMF and the World Bank have become too big and too complex, and answer to no one, so expanding their size and reach is not justified. Others contend these sister institutions are little more than a ploy to spread the reach of the US government and its corporations to the far corners of the world. These sister institutions are criticized by those on the political right and on the political left.

It will be interesting to see what role these sister institutions play in the future of our global financial markets. Will they be around in another 60 years? If so, what will they be doing?

---

6 See Allan H. Meltzer, "Report of the International Financial Institution Advisory Commission: Comments on the Critics." Pittsburgh, PA: Carnegie Mellon University, Tepper School of Business; 2000. http://repository.cmu.edu/cgi/viewcontent.cgi?article=1029&context=tepper.

SECTION REVIEW

Q1) Few argue with the idea that the policies the IMF suggests are sound long-term policies. Yet critics believe these sound long-term policies are the wrong policies for the IMF to be suggesting. Explain the critics' argument.

Q2) The IMF and World Bank often are described as "sister organizations." One could say they are "sisters" in that they are very similar yet also very different. Explain this argument.

Q3) In an "import substitutions" policy, what is being substituted for imports?

a. Cash transfers

b. Domestically made goods and services

c. Interest payments received in the future

d. Bonds that can be converted into equities

20-7 Conclusion

We examined how the global financial architecture has evolved over the past several decades. We learned how, after the collapse of the Bretton Woods System, the world struggled to find an exchange rate regime that was both stable and flexible. Each of the regimes resulted in some level of foreign exchange market intervention, be they sterilized or unsterilized interventions. Sadly, the results of these regimes have been less than unqualified successes, each with their own set of problems. The crawling peg, target zone, currency board, managed float, and especially fixed exchange rate regimes all have their problems. Robert Mundell's optimal currency area gave us a structure to use to evaluate whether one currency was good for a group of economies.

We then looked at two sister institutions that have a great deal of influence over the global financial architecture. The World Bank and International Monetary Fund, created during the summer of 1944, have undergone a great deal of change and controversy over the past seven decades. They seem to be positioned to continue to influence our global financial architecture well into the future.

IN THE NEWS. . .

G20 Gives US Ultimatum over IMF Reforms

The Financial Times
April 11, 2014

The G20 has given an ultimatum to the US to pass reforms to the International Monetary Fund or risk being left out of new changes.

Finance ministers in Washington for the spring meetings of the IMF and World Bank said they were "deeply disappointed" by failure to implement changes agreed in 2010, and gave the US until the end of the year to do so. . . .

The US is the sole roadblock to completing the IMF reforms. . . .

Despite the ultimatum, it is not clear what next steps the G20 could take, since the US has a blocking minority of votes at the fund—which is the reason its inaction has delayed the reforms in the first place.

Emerging markets have grown more and more frustrated, as their current quota does not represent their growth weight in the world and economy, and they believe the IFM was too ready to offer loans to eurozone countries on terms that would not have been extended to poorer nations. . . .

The article mentions the United States has a "blocking minority of votes" at the IMF. What is that exactly? Why does it exist? Should it change? That is, should emerging markets be given more say in the IMF? Why or why not?

Summary of Global Financial Markets

Tying Concepts Together

As our global economies become more and more intertwined, so do our global financial markets. As we have learned, trying to fix exchange rates does not bring about much-desired stability in global financial markets, and it may cause more problems than it seeks to correct. So, while we continue to seek out an exchange rate regime that is at once flexible yet stable, the sister institutions of the IMF and World Bank struggle to find their footing in the global financial markets of the twenty-first century. These sister institutions must learn how to deal with global financial markets that are much different than the world of over 70 years ago when they were created. Gone are the days when financial markets were dominated by commercial banks. Instead, the rise of other financial institutions has dramatically changed the financial markets landscape. These other financial institutions are the topics of the next and last section. In Chapter 21 we look at thrifts and finance companies that sought to fill the gaps left by large commercial banks. In Chapter 22 we examine the structure and roles of insurance companies and pension funds. The rise of mutual funds is discussed in Chapter 23, along with controversies that surround this expanding financial market. Finally, in Chapter 24 we review controversial investment banks and private equity firms to understand why these financial institutions are so much in the news and what role they may play in the future of our financial markets.

21

Thrifts and Finance Companies

21-1 Thrifts

In a speech on March 3, 2010, then Harvard Law professor Elizabeth Warren characterized the current landscape of the US financial system as one that pits "families versus banks." Warren was arguing for the need for a consumer financial protection agency to protect families against the deceptive practices of the banking industry.[1]

Warren's plea is only the latest round of families, or "the little people," trying to get access to financial services. Throughout the eighteenth and nineteenth centuries, commercial banks were just that—banks that focused on "commercial" or business customers. Commercial banks during that time were not that interested in offering accounts to individuals or households, especially if those households were headed by members of the working class.

The first financial institutions to focus on serving families, especially working-class families, were the thrifts: savings banks and Savings & Loans. In this chapter we examine the evolution and current status of thrifts as well as credit unions. We examine these depository institutions in their attempt to provide financial services to families, or "the little people." We will see that in doing so, these small depository institutions have created a fair amount of controversy. We also scrutinize one of the most controversial entities that strives to provide financial services to those outside the commercial banking system: finance companies. We look into the products provided by finance companies in order to gain a better understanding of the controversies that surround them.

21-1a Savings Banks

What are known today as savings banks were earlier called mutual savings banks or simply mutual savings associations. The "mutual" in the name represents the fact that these depository institutions were mutual associations; that is, they were owned and controlled by the depositors. The original intent of savings banks was to promote savings among society's poor.

The first savings bank is believed to have been formed in Hamburg, Germany, in 1778.[2] Although the Hamburg institution took deposits and "spare cash of domestic servants and handicraftsman," they issued annuities instead of offering deposit accounts.[3] A few years later, in 1798, a "Friendly Society for the benefit of women and children" was established in Tottenham, a district of north London in England. The society also issued annuities to members, almost all of whom were poor orphans and widows, but the society also provided payments during times of illness, or a single larger payment for "burial in case of death." Two other objectives of the society were to fund loans and create "a bank for savings" for the poor of Tottenham. In 1804 this "bank for savings" was formally organized and began operations.

Some believe the first savings bank was created in 1799 by Reverend Joseph Smith of Wendover in southeast England. Reverend Smith circulated in his parish a proposal to take deposits from his working-class parishioners during the summer months and return these deposits plus one third at Christmas. Reverend Smith's entity supposedly began operation shortly thereafter, making its start date 1800.

Savings Banks Come to the United States

While the debate over which of these European institutions can claim to be "the first" savings bank in the world goes on, it is clear that they each had a similar goal: provide a way for the poor in society to save. They both sought a way to bring some type of financial services to the least fortunate in society.

---

1 To view Warren's entire speech, go to http://www.vimeo.com/9952891/.

2 For an excellent review of the early history of savings banks, see Emerson W. Keyes, "A History of Savings Banks in the United States from Their Inception in 1816 down to 1874." New York: Bradford Rhodes, 1876. Keyes was the deputy superintendent for the banking department of the State of New York for a number of years and wrote this enriching history of the savings bank industry.

3 See William Lewins, *History of Banks for Savings in Great Britain and Ireland*. London: Sampson, Low, Son and Marston; 1866.

In the United States there is much less debate over who was the "first" to form a savings bank with a goal of increasing savings among the poor and working class. In 1816 the Massachusetts state government sanctioned the creation of a savings bank. The plans for the savings bank were put forward by the Honorable James Savage of Boston earlier that year. The first public announcement of Savage's idea appeared in a small religious monthly publication in December 1816, in which he espoused the importance of helping the poor and working class to help themselves through savings. Savage's Provident Institution for Savings was approved by the Massachusetts legislature on December 13, 1816.

Provident began operation the following spring, promising to pay depositors a 1% return quarterly—more if the institution could afford it. The first 1% dividend was declared and paid in July 1817. Thereafter, a 1.25% quarterly dividend, or a 5% annual percentage rate, was paid until 1822. This represented the first time the poor and working class in the United States had a depository institution that focused specifically on their needs. Provident continued in operation for 176 years, until 1992, when it was purchased by Fleet National Bank of Massachusetts.

Today savings banks still are found mostly in the northeast United States, and they seek to serve a wider range of households, not only the working poor. Over the preceding decades savings banks have continuously evolved and expanded. Today savings banks look much like other thrifts: Their deposits are insured by either the FDIC or a state-regulated deposit insurance scheme, and they provide financial services to a wide variety of customers. Because they focus in particular on serving their consumer depositors, most savings banks today are relatively small, with assets of less than $1 billion. By way of comparison, JP Morgan Chase had a little over $2.5 trillion in assets in 2014.

21-1b Savings & Loans

Similar to savings banks, Savings & Loans were created to offer financial services to working-class families, although they focused on one primary area: home financing. Many Savings & Loans began in the late nineteenth century as Building & Loan associations; a group of people would pool their money together for the purpose of building homes. The Building & Loan would take deposits of families and choose, usually by lottery, which family would have a house built for them by the Building & Loan. Once the house was built, the family would repay the Building & Loan over the next 30 years for the cost of the house plus some interest. Once the Building & Loan had enough funds to construct another house, the process would be repeated. In some cases the Building & Loan would cease to exist once all of the families that composed the Building & Loan had homes built. Other Building & Loans would seek new families to join in, and the association would continue in operation for decades.

Many Building & Loans were organized along ethnic lines. New immigrants from Poland, Sweden, and Italy faced discrimination when they attempted to borrow money from commercial banks for home mortgages. These families then created their own Building & Loans to build their savings as well as build a house of their own. In addition to facing discrimination from commercial banks, many new immigrants did not trust big commercial banks and instead preferred to save their money in institutions that lent money to people who were like them.

21-1c Evolution of Recent Thrifts

Both savings banks and Savings & Loans were gravely affected by the Great Depression of the 1930s. As the United States skidded into the Depression, unemployment blanketed the economy. Those who were lucky enough to hold their jobs often suffered from shorter work weeks and reduced wages. As a result, affected families could not repay the funds they had borrowed from the thrifts. To compound matters, as uncertainty spread through the economy, the thrifts, along with the larger commercial banks, experienced bank runs as depositors pulled their money out en masse.

In response to these problems, on July 22, 1932, President Hoover signed the Federal Home Loan Bank Act, which created the **Federal Home Loan (FHL) Bank System**. The goal of the act was to create a government-sponsored lender to thrifts that made consumer mortgage loans. In addition to the thrifts (savings banks and Building & Loan associations), insurance companies that wrote mortgages could also apply for membership in the FHL bank system. The act created, at the time, five FHL banks across the country and gave supervision of member institutions to the FHL bank board. With a government-sponsored lender of last resort, the remaining thrifts were able to survive the rest of the Great Depression.

Federal Home Loan (FHL) Bank System: A system of US government–sponsored banks designed to increase the amount of low-cost funds available to financial institutions for home mortgage loans, small-business loans, agricultural loans, and rural economic development loans.

While the Great Depression reduced the number of thrifts, the post-World War II economic boom saw the thrifts thrive. As Americans wanted and needed more houses, the thrifts were there to help with financing. With low market interest rates, thrifts lived by the "3-6-3 rule" of banking: pay 3% on deposits, lend money at 6%, and hit the golf course by 3 p.m.

The Thrifts as "Special"

During the postwar boom, commercial banks were subject to Regulation Q, which imposed interest rate ceilings that capped what they could pay on deposits. For the thrifts, though, there were no explicit nationwide regulations on the interest rates and dividends they could pay until 1966. Despite this lack of formal regulation of interest rate differences, the thrifts often paid higher interest rates on deposits than did commercial banks.

For example, in 1961 Savings & Loans were paying a nationwide average of about 3.92% on savings accounts, whereas commercial banks were paying only 2.91% on similar accounts. As Charlotte Rubling of the St. Louis Federal Reserve described it, during this time the thrifts were viewed as special because "these institutions enhanced the availability of credit for housing" and thus "they should be given an advantage in the competition from consumer-type savings."[4]

By the mid-1960s, however, questions were being raised as to whether the policies that treated the thrifts as "special" were really resulting in an efficient allocation of capital. There was much discussion among policymakers about the need to move toward a more competitive banking system.

In 1962, as the interest rate ceiling on deposits that commercial banks faced was raised, the rate banks paid jumped 50 basis points, whereas the rate paid by Savings & Loans rose by only 15 basis points. Proponents of a more competitive banking system argued that the reduction in interest rate controls increased the amount of competition in the banking industry by closing the gap between the interest rate paid by thrifts and interest rates paid by commercial banks. This increased competition, they contended, would benefit consumers and result in a more efficient allocation of capital. The days of the thrifts being viewed as "special" were numbered.

Thrifts' Problems Mount

As time went by, the troubles facing the thrifts mounted. Throughout the 1960s, growing inflationary pressures pushed up market interest rates that were not subject to government interest rate ceilings. The thrifts, with their portfolio of 30-year mortgages that were paying only a 6% rate of interest, were limited on how much they could pay on deposits. Thus the thrifts were experiencing increased competition for their customers' deposits. In 1966 the thrifts lost their "special" standing among regulators as the Interstate Rate Regulation Act extended Regulation Q, the interest rate ceiling, to include the thrifts. Just as the thrifts were facing more competition for deposits, they now were limited in how much they could pay for those deposits.

4 See Charlotte E. Rubling, "The Administration of Regulation Q," *Review*, Federal Reserve Bank of St. Louis (February 1970): 29–40.

With market interest rates (again, those not subject to Regulation Q) increasing, the thrifts were struggling to attract deposits.[5] From May to November 1966, deposits at Savings & Loans grew at only a 2.3% annualized rate compared with an 11% annual growth rate over the previous 4½ years. Clearly, being subject to the interest rate ceiling was hurting the thrifts' ability to attract deposits.

As the 1960s went on and inflationary pressures continued to push market interest rate upward, the thrifts found themselves in even more dire straits. By 1969, with consumer prices increasing at an annual rate of 5.46%, market interest rates on commercial paper and Treasury bills were going higher and higher. But the same was not true for the interest rates paid by the thrifts, which were subject to regulation Q. As a result, in the second half of 1969 deposits at Savings & Loans increased at a meager annual rate of 1.6% compared with 5.4% the previous year.

As the 1960s merged into the 1970s, things only got worse for the thrifts. With the economy stagnating and inflation rates pushing market interest rates higher, the thrifts again had a difficult time attracting deposits. Finally, by the late 1970s, the thrifts had enough, and they turned to Washington for help.

SECTION REVIEW

Q1) Initially, thrifts were depository institutions that often were considered "special." Why were they viewed this way?

Q2) Explain how savings banks and Savings & Loans were similar but also very different.

Q3) When market interest rates increased during the 1960s, thrifts found it difficult to attract deposits because of which Depression-era policy?

a. FDIC deposit insurance

b. SEC bond registration requirements

c. The Federal Reserve's discount loan policy

d. Regulation Q

5 For example, money market mutual funds, which began in the late 1960s, offered consumers liquid accounts, similar to thrift savings accounts, but the money market mutual funds could pay the higher market interest rates.

21-2 Savings & Loan Crisis and Today

By the late 1970s, the thrift industry was in deep trouble. These once "special" depository institutions now found themselves struggling to survive. Many argued that excessive regulation was causing the problems for the thrift industry. Thus, the industry turned to lobbying the US Congress for help.

21-2a DIDMCA and the Rise of NOW Accounts

After years of lobbying by the thrift industry, Congress passed in 1980 the Depository Institution Deregulation and Monetary Control Act (DIDMCA), which phased out Regulation Q and allowed credit unions and thrifts to offer for the first time negotiable orders of withdrawal, or NOW, accounts. These were basically checking accounts that paid interest. While DIDMCA allowed the thrifts to compete for deposits with, for example, money market mutual funds, the act actually created bigger problems for the thrifts.

After DIDMCA, thrifts could pay "market rates of interest" on some deposit accounts, but their main source of revenue was the 30-year mortgages with fixed interest rates that they had written in the past. These mortgages, which paid, say, a 6% rate of interest, were a fine source of revenue when the thrifts were paying 3% or less on deposits.

But by 1981, when a six-month certificate of deposit was paying over 15%, the pool of 30-year, fixed-rate mortgages simply were not generating enough interest income to cover the thrifts' interest expenses. Basically, with every deposit the thrifts were losing money—they simply did not have enough interest income to cover the high interest rates they were paying on deposits.

21-2b DIDMCA Is Not Enough

By 1982 the thrift industry was back in Washington, DC, asking for more relief. The result was the Garn-St. Germain Depository Institutions Act of 1982, named after its two main sponsors, Congressman Fernand St. Germain, Democrat, from Rhode Island, and Senator Jake Garn, Republican, from Utah. The act allowed Savings & Loans to make commercial, corporate, business, or agricultural loans up to 10% of the institution's assets after January 1, 1984. The act also allowed Savings & Loans to increase their consumer lending—from 20% to 30% of assets—and to expand lending to auto dealers.

Thus, the act allowed the Savings & Loans to write a wide variety of loans—lending in which they had very little experience. As a result, the Savings & Loans, desperate for loans with high interest rates, wrote many risky loans that, in hindsight, had little chance of ever being fully repaid.

21-2c Misaligned Incentives

Making things worse, many financial speculators considered the Savings & Loan industry to be a great way to place very risky bets with little downside risk. The change in banking laws also made it easier for these speculators to purchase Savings & Loans. With a reduction in regulatory oversight of the Savings & Loans, new owners of thrifts could make risky loans with corresponding high interest rates. If these risky loans paid off, great. The thrift would profit and everyone would benefit. If these new risky loans did not pay off, there was still deposit insurance. The depositors could turn to the government to be repaid.

Thus the amount of risky loans and high-risk bonds held by the Savings & Loans increased dramatically during the 1980s. Even worse, some Savings & Loan owners were viewed as little more than financial criminals. They deceived depositors and regulators and used the Savings & Loans as their own personal piggy banks. With lax regulation, these unscrupulous financiers could internalize returns while pushing risks onto the public. An often repeated phrase was that the operators of Savings & Loans saw it simply as a game of "heads I win, tails the government loses."

The Zombie Institutions

As often happens with risky assets, the value of the thrifts' assets started to decrease as the level of uncertainty about their ability to pay off both loans and bonds increased. The risky borrowers could not—or would not—repay the funds they had borrowed from the thrifts. These decreasing asset values resulted in many thrifts becoming insolvent.

Making things worse was the rise of **zombie institutions**. When a thrift became insolvent, the Federal Home Loan Bank Board traditionally would close the institution. But during the 1980s, instead of immediately closing insolvent thrifts, the Federal Home Loan Bank Board regulators often ignored the problem, allowing the failed institutions to continue operating.

Zombie institutions: Financial institutions that are insolvent but are allowed by bank regulators to continue operating.

These "financially dead" institutions were labeled "zombie institutions" because they were dead from an accounting perspective but continued to lend as if they were still alive.

As a result, the zombie institutions made it difficult for well-run institutions to survive. The zombie institutions offered loans at low interest rates to well-qualified lenders, forcing healthy institutions to do the same. Desperate for deposits, the zombie institutions offered high interest rates to savers, again forcing well-run institutions to do the same thing. Thus, the zombie institutions essentially "infected" the healthy institutions, causing problems in the industry to spread.

21-2d Attempting Reforms

By 1989, over half of the Savings & Loans across the country were insolvent. Clearly something had to be done. In 1989 Congress passed and President George H. W. Bush signed the Financial Institutions Reform, Recovery and Enforcement Act (FIRREA), which abolished the Federal Home Loan Bank Board and created the new Office of Thrift Supervision (OTS) in the Treasury Department. FIRREA provided $50 billion of taxpayer money to close down the zombie institutions. To do this job, the act created a new entity: the **Resolution Trust Corporation** (RTC).

Resolution Trust Corporation: A government agency in operation from 1989 to 1996 that was in charge of liquidating insolvent thrift institutions and selling off the assets of the failed institutions. It also arranged mergers and bailouts for bankruptcy by still operating thrifts.

The RTC was responsible for closing the failed thrifts, selling off their assets, and using the proceeds from those sales to pay off depositors. In doing so the owners of the thrifts would essentially be wiped out and the management of the thrifts would be fired. By 1999, the total cost of the crisis was estimated to be $153 billion; American taxpayers paid $124 billion and the Savings & Loan industry paid the rest.

The Savings & Loan crisis of the 1980s shook the thrift industry to its core; it would never be the same again. Instead of being depository institutions that took many risks, the thrifts had to return to their base: consumer lending.

21-2e Thrifts Today

Today, as a result of the Savings & Loan crisis of the 1980s, the thrifts that exist focus primarily on providing financial services to consumers. As Table 21-1 demonstrates, almost half of the thrifts' assets are in real estate loans. By way of comparison, for commercial banks the percentage is closer to 33%. Commercial loans, on the other hand, are only about 5% of the thrifts' assets, compared with about 12% for commercial banks.

TABLE 21-1 **Thrifts' Assets as of June 30, 2015**

Real Estate Loans	42.77%
Consumer Loans	11.31%
U.S. Government Securities	20.33%
Other Securities	6.04%
Cash & due from other DI	7.11%
Commercial Loans	5.62%
"Goodwill" & other intangibles	0.93%
Other assets	5.53%

From: https://www5.FDIC.gov/SDI

While this might represent a return to the "traditional" role of thrifts, it does not mean they are not without their own set of unique problems. The case of Washington Mutual, the nation's largest thrift until it failed in 2008, demonstrates that this sector can still be very tenuous.

Washington Mutual Bankruptcy[6]

In 1990 Washington Mutual, then a medium-sized thrift in Seattle, hired a new CEO, a 40-year-old named Kerry Killinger. Killinger's goal was to create a huge financial institution that would be ". . . more retail than banking." In 2003 he stated, "we hope to do to this industry what Wal-Mart did to theirs, Starbucks did to theirs, Costco did theirs and Lowes'-Home Depot did to their industry. And I think if we've done our job, in five years you're not going to call us a bank."[7] He wanted to revolutionize the thrift industry by providing a wide range of debt instruments—mortgages, consumer loans, credit cards, and so on—to people who traditionally did not qualify for such credit.

During the go-go years of the first decade of the twenty-first century, things went well for Killinger and Washington Mutual. By 2008, Washington Mutual had over 2,200 branches stretching from coast to coast. As Washington Mutual expanded and was profitable, Killinger also personally profited. Killinger took in over $100 million in compensation between 2003 and 2008. In 2006 alone Killinger was paid $24 million in compensation.[8] Things looked great for the once medium-sized thrift, but just as before in the thrift industry, the good times would not last forever.

In the 2008–2009 time period, as the subprime mortgage crisis was exploding, it became clear that Washington Mutual was heavily involved in the now dreaded subprime mortgage market. Financial market participants lost confidence in Washington Mutual's ability to make good on its promises to pay its debts. Even Washington Mutual depositors lost confidence in the once-mighty thrift, and they withdrew more than $16 billion in deposits in less than 10 days.

With its reputation in tatters and depositors fleeing, Washington Mutual was in desperate shape. Eventually, Washington Mutual filed for bankruptcy protection. It was the nation's second largest bankruptcy ever. Regulators sold off Washington Mutual's assets to JPMorgan Chase, thus wiping out Washington Mutual's shareholders and many of its bondholders.

6 This section may be skipped by instructors who do not wish to go into this much detail.

7 See Peter S. Goodman and Gretchen Morgenson, "Saying Yes, WaMu Built Empire on Shaky Loans." *New York Times*, December 27, 2008. http://www.nytimes.com/2008/12/28/business/28wamu.html?_r=0.

8 See Roger Lowenstein, "Kerry Killinger, the Man Who Destroyed WaMu." *Los Angeles Times*, April 16, 2010. http://articles.latimes.com/2010/apr/16/opinion/la-oe-lowenstein16-2010apr16/ (accessed May 13, 2015).

However, the real damage Washington Mutual may have caused may not be fully felt for years,[9] as the people and families to whom Washington Mutual extended credit slowly, financially bleed to death under the debts they cannot afford to repay.

AP Images/Cliff Owen

Kerry Killinger

Critics claim Washington Mutual grew too fast, extending credit en masse to those who really could not afford it. Washington Mutual was doomed to fail, according to these critics, because its credit policies simply were not sustainable. Washington Mutual's credit policies were profitable during the good times, the critics argue, but they were sure to lead to failure once the economy slowed and the ability of overextended households to repay their debts declined.

In April 2010 Killinger fired back at critics and his former regulators, saying the government takeover of Washington Mutual was "unfair" and done only to benefit "big banks."[10] In a congressional hearing, Killinger portrayed Washington Mutual as the protector of small savers and borrowers. This was despite Washington Mutual's well-documented record of charging high overdraft fees to customers and earning high profits from subprime mortgage lending. The debate over Washington Mutual may rage on for years to come.

SECTION REVIEW

Q1) Explain why the phasing out of Regulation Q by DIDMCA did not end the problems faced by the thrifts.

Q2) Explain how zombie institutions are in one sense "dead" but in another sense are still "alive."

Q3) Which government agency was created to close and liquidate the failed thrifts?

a. FDIC
b. SEC
c. RTC
d. DEA

9 Colin Barr, "WaMu: The Forgotten Bank Failure." *Fortune*, September 10, 2009. http://archive.fortune.com/2009/09/08/news/economy/wamu.fallout.fortune/index.htm

10 Colin Barr, "WaMu's Killinger: The Forgotten Goat." *Fortune*, April 13, 2010. http://archive.fortune.com/2010/04/13/news/killinger.senate.fortune/index.htm.

21-3 Credit Unions

While credit unions are similar to thrifts in that they both focus primarily on servicing households, credit unions are different from modern-day thrifts in several ways. Credit unions are nonprofit institutions, whereas thrifts today generally are for-profit entities. Also, credit unions have a different ownership structure than do modern-day thrifts. These differences at first might seem slight and irrelevant, but as it turns out, they result in credit unions acting much differently from thrifts. To understand why, let's look more closely at the differences between credit unions and thrifts.

First, and perhaps most important, credit unions are **nonprofit financial institutions**. That means they don't have to pay any corporate income taxes, either at the state or federal level, on any profits they generate. Instead, credit unions are free to hold on to their profits or, more likely, to pay these profits to their owners: the depositors of the credit union.

Nonprofit financial institutions: Financial institutions that are designed to serve their customers and do not have a profit motive.

This leads to the second way credit unions differ from thrifts: their ownership structure of a common bond. Credit unions are owned by their members, or depositors. This often means that credit unions cater to the needs of individual depositors more than larger commercial banks do. But credit unions are limited in who can be members/depositors. Credit union members must have a common bond in either occupation (e.g., a teachers' credit union, a firefighters' credit union); association (e.g., a university credit union, a union-based credit union); or geographic area (e.g., a community credit union). Some credit unions have multiple groups, such as teachers and union members. But for someone to be a member of a credit union, they must demonstrate that common bond.

These two characteristics of credit unions—nonprofit status and common bonds—result in credit unions often paying higher interest rates on deposits and charging lower interest rates on loans than their for-profit, stockholder-owned competitors, thrifts and commercial banks.

21-3a Credit Union History[11]

The evolution of today's credit unions began in the mid-nineteenth century when Herman Schulze-Delitzsch, a lawyer in Germany, grew frustrated with how loan sharks were charging extremely high interest rates on loans made to local shopkeepers and urban workers. He set out to create a credit society where merchants and the working class could borrow money from each other at affordable interest rates.

At about the same time, Friedrich Wihelm Raiffeisen was founding a similar credit society in Flammersfeld, Germany, to help local farmers. Years earlier Raiffeisen had established a society to provide loans to middle- and lower-class rural borrowers; however, the society depended extensively on wealthy supporters to subsidize it. By 1864, Raiffeisen had created a credit society that was free from subsidies from the wealthy and more recognizable as a modern-day credit union.

Credit Unions in North America

The credit unions' first venture over the Atlantic did not begin in the United States, but in Canada. In 1900 a journalist/public servant/political activist named Alphonse Desjardins organized the first credit union in North America in Levis, Quebec, Canada.[12] Desjardins recognized that, just as in Germany, high interest rates paid by the working class and small merchants on their loans had a devastating effect.

11 For a nice summary see "The History of Credit Unions" from the Credit Union National Association. http://www.ncua.gov/about/history/Pages/History.aspx.

12 Of course in Quebec French is spoken, and thus credit unions often are called a "*caisse populaire*."

Alphonse Desjardins

Desjardins was the eighth of 15 children born to an alcoholic day-laborer father and a mother who had to do housework for neighbors to feed her family. Most likely because of limited financial resources, Desjardins was not able to finish college. Instead, after he completed his military service, he set out to be a journalist and a political activist within the Conservative Party in Canada.

On April 6, 1897, a House of Commons conservative party member, Michael Joseph Francis Quinn, cited the case of a Montreal man who was sentenced to pay interest of over $5,000 on an initial loan of $150. Desjardins was reportedly so upset by this report that he set out to determine how prevalent such cases were. What he found amazed and appalled him. Desjardins discovered that small borrowers had almost no access to ordinary commercial bank lending in Canada. The working class and small merchants had no choice but to turn to loan sharks when they needed funds.

Seeking a better way, Desjardins learned of the work of Englishman Henry William Wolff. Wolff had written extensively on the use of credit cooperatives in extending credit to the rural poor, as was being done in Germany. Desjardins worked diligently to develop a plan to bring the German credit union model to North America. On December 6, 1900, in a meeting attended by about 100 people, including some of the leading figures in Levis, Desjardins launched the first credit union in North America, the Caisse d'épargne Desjardins.

The Caisse d'épargne Desjardins began operation on January 23, 1901, and by the end of November that year, it had 721 members who held nearly 2,000 shares at $5 per share. The Caisse d'épargne Desjardins was eventually renamed the Caisses Populaires Desjardins, or simply CP. While the CP started small, the idea spread quickly across French-speaking Canada.

Credit Unions Come to the United States

Alphonse Desjardins was quickly recognized as an expert in creating and managing credit unions. In 1909 he helped to establish the first credit union in the United States in New Hampshire, the La Caisse Populaire, Ste-Marie.[13] Desjardins was invited to the United States on several occasions and in 1912 met with President William Howard Taft to discuss rural credit cooperatives.

Desjardins's passion for credit unions was picked up on by Americans Pierre Jay, a banker and bank regulator, and Edward Filene, a Boston retailer. From 1906 to 1909, Pierre Jay served as the banking commissioner for the Commonwealth of Massachusetts. In that role Jay became intrigued with groups of employees who were forming their own credit cooperatives. Jay learned of Desjardins's work in Canada and contacted him on several occasions to learn how credit unions operated there. Jay's interest culminated in a 1908 conference on credit unions and passage of the Massachusetts Credit Union Act a year later.

Attending the 1908 conference with Jay and Desjardins was Boston merchant Edward Filene. Credit unions were only one of many social entrepreneurial ventures by Filene. One of five children, Filene dropped out of Harvard in 1890 to take over running the family's store when his father became seriously ill. In running Filene's Department Store, Edward was consistently interested in how to improve the quality of work and life of his employees. He instituted employee profit sharing, a minimum wage for women, a 40-hour work week, paid vacations, and health clinics for his employees. Filene also engaged in collective bargaining with his employees—all in an attempt to improve the lives of the people who worked for him. Although Filene never created a credit union himself, he spent the rest of his life speaking in favor of expansion of these nonprofit financial cooperatives.

The growth of credit unions in the United States was hampered by a need to pass state laws to allow credit unions to be created. All that changed in 1934 when Congress passed and President

13 The La Caisse Populaire, Ste-Marie that Desjardins help to found is still in operation today. The name has been simplified to St. Mary's Bank. For a reenactment of Desjardins's visit, see http://www.stmarysbank.com/about-st-marys-bank/our-history.asp.

Franklin Roosevelt signed the Federal Credit Union Act. The act allowed credit unions to be organized anywhere in the country. The law allowed credit unions to be incorporated under either federal or state laws. With the passage of the act, the number of credit unions increased significantly. At a meeting held in Estes Park, Colorado, in August 1934, the Credit Union National Association (CUNA) was formed to serve as a trade association for credit unions and leagues across the country.

Credit Unions and Businesses

While credit unions traditionally have offered financial services predominately to households and individuals, in recent years credit unions also have competed with thrifts and commercial banks for business customers. In 1998 Congress passed legislation that made it easier for credit unions to expand in a variety of ways, including business lending, but regulations limited business lending to a maximum of 12.25% of a credit union's assets. That limit was largely symbolic; most credit unions never got close to the 12.25% maximum.

Things began to change in 2003, however, when the Small Business Administration expanded its lending programs to include credit unions. This meant that credit unions could now offer federal government-subsidized Small Business Administration loans to small businesses that qualified.

Another significant change in credit unions' interest in lending to businesses occurred in October 2003, when the National Credit Union Association (NCUA), one of the main regulators of credit unions, allowed well-capitalized credit unions to make unsecured business loans.

As a result of these regulatory changes, credit union lending to small business, which was less than $10 billion at the end of 2003, increased to over $35 billion by the autumn of 2009. While this may seem like a lot of lending, small commercial banks (those with less than $1 billion in assets) made $224 billion in small business loans in 2006. Thus, the relative amount of credit union lending to businesses is very small, but that does not mean it hasn't been without controversy.

Loans by credit unions grew by $6.44 billion during 2009 (Table 21-2), but the stronger share or deposit growth resulted in the loan-to-share ratio falling from 83.1% to 76.05%—the lowest since 2004. Loan growth was driven by an increase in the amount of mortgage real estate lending. During 2009, as commercial banks were restricting their mortgage lending, the amount of fixed-rate first mortgages written by credit unions increased by $8.65 billion, or 7.05%.

Table 21-2 Credit Union Loan Distribution June 2015

Loan Type	Distribution
First Mortgage	41.0.8%
Other Real Estate	9.69%
New Vehicle	12.46%
Used Vehicle	20.52%
Unsecured Credit Card	6.15%
Other Unsecured	4.40%
Non Federal Guarantee student loan	0.44%
Leases	0.14%
Other	5.10%

Source: Call reports from NCUA.gov

Table 21-3 **Credit Union Share Distribution June 2015**

Account Type	Distribution
Share Draft	13.91%
Regular Shares	34.89%
Money Market Shares	22.87%
Share Certificates	19.12%
IRA/KEOGH accounts	7.77%
All other shares	0.88%
Non-member deposits	0.56%

Source: Call reports from NUCA.gov

Total shares grew by 10.5%, or $71.54 billion, in 2009 (Table 21-3). The strong growth in shares or deposits outpaced loan demand and thus increased funds available for investment.

21-3b Credit Union Controversies

Commercial banks and thrifts claim that, by not paying corporate income taxes, credit unions receive an "unfair subsidy" from the government. These complaints come most fervently from small, community commercial banks that compete with credit unions for smaller depositors. This debate became most heated in the wake of the financial crisis that began in 2007.

As the economy skidded into a severe recession, commercial banks greatly scaled back their lending, especially to small businesses. In the first nine months of 2009, as the economy was beginning to move out of the recession, commercial banks pulled back on their lending by 15.1%, according to Bob Arnould, Senior Vice President of Government Affairs for the California Credit Union League.[14] Credit unions, on the other hand, increased their small lending by 11% during this same period, according to Arnould.

Thus, Arnould and other proponents of credit unions argue that credit unions should be allowed to dedicate more of their assets to small-business loans. In 2010 two different bills were introduced in Congress that would allow credit unions to increase to 25% their assets dedicated to small-business loans.

Naturally, commercial banks have not been happy about credit unions trying to expand into commercial banks' traditional market: lending to businesses. Commercial banks counter that credit unions receive tax-exempt status because they are supposed to serve people and households at the lower end of the economic ladder, not businesses. The American Bankers Association (ABA) argues that if credit unions really want to make more business loans and act like banks, then the credit unions should give up their tax-exempt status. The ABA explains the lack in small-business lending after the recession as the result of weak demand for business loans and increased pressure from bank regulators to reduce risky spending and increase bank capital levels. Thus the ABA contends credit unions are not needed to fill any void in business lending.

The debate over the future role of credit unions is likely to continue: Are these nonprofit institutions that focus on the local economy the wave of the future? Or, do they represent yet another distortion in the financial markets brought about by outdated regulations and subsidies? While credit unions and their "proper" role in financial markets can lead to heated debates, these debates are mild compared with the controversies that surround finance companies.

14 See Mike Freeman, "Credit Unions Push for New Loan Rules." *San Diego Union-Tribune*, February 13, 2010. http://www.signonsandiego.com/news/2010/feb/13/credit-unions-push-for-new-loan-rules/.

SECTION REVIEW

Q1) Credit unions are similar to commercial banks in that they are both depository institutions. Explain how credit unions are also very different from commercial banks.

Q2) When it comes to lending to businesses, credit unions often argue they should be allowed to write more business loans, whereas critics contend credit unions' business lending should be restricted. Explain each side's argument.

Q3) The first credit unions, or credit cooperatives, in North America were started where and when?

a. Quebec, Ontario, Canada, in 1901

b. Boston, Massachusetts, in 1909

c. Chicago, Illinois, in 1910

d. Cleveland, Ohio, in 1912

Finance Companies

21-4

Finance companies are sometimes described as "nonbank banks." By way of comparison, commercial banks provide two main services to their customers: They take deposits, and they make loans. Nonbank banks, on the other hand, do only one of the two: They either take deposits *or* they make loans, not both. Finance companies, one type of nonbank bank, only make loans; they generally do not take deposits.

Finance companies, just like thrifts and credit unions, have been around for a long time. The first finance companies were created in the nineteenth century as retailers extended credit to individuals and families to purchase consumer goods. The consumer finance industry in the United States significantly expanded during the early decades of the twentieth century as consumer spending on things such as automobiles, radios, and household appliances increased. Today finance companies provide loans to businesses as well as households.

Finance companies differ in their customer base, either consumers or businesses, and how they are structured, either owned by another financial firm or by a nonfinancial firm.

21-4a Types of Finance Companies: Consumer Finance Companies

Finance companies that lend to individuals and families are called consumer finance companies. Most often they lend money to people who do not have access to traditional banking services because of a lack of credit, poor credit history, low income, or uneven employment. Studies also suggest that minorities and young adults make up a disproportionate percentage of consumer finance companies' customers. Finance companies provide various types of consumer loans, including those described below.

Auto Loans

Consumer finance companies offer automobile loans, most often through car dealers. If you have ever financed a car purchase through an auto dealer, you have come into indirect contact with a finance company. Sometimes the person who is handling the financing of the purchase at the car dealership works on commission or rebate basis with the finance company.

Home Mortgages

During the housing boom leading up to the crash in 2008, a growing number of finance companies offered home mortgages, especially second mortgages. Remember, a mortgage is a loan that uses real estate as collateral. A first mortgage is usually used to purchase the house or condominium. With a second mortgage, a homeowner borrows the equity built up in the house—that is, the difference between the market value and the mortgage balance—and, as with a first mortgage, uses the house as collateral.

Consumer Durables

People who do not have access to traditional banking services such as credit cards turn to finance companies to borrow money to purchase things like furniture, washers and dryers, refrigerators, and flat-screen TVs.

21-4b Types of Finance Companies: Business Finance Companies

Finance companies that lend money to businesses are sometimes called "business credit institutions." Because there is, generally, less regulation over business lending than consumer lending, many finance companies have expanded their lending to businesses. Finance companies provide a variety of loans and services to businesses, including those described below.

Floor-Plan or Inventory Financing

Imagine a retailer needs inventory to sell but does not have enough cash on hand to purchase it. The retailer can have a finance company pay the manufacturer of the goods and have the goods delivered to the retailer to sell; the finance company maintains a lien on the goods until they are repaid. The retailer sells the goods and repays the finance company for the goods, plus interest. These floor-plan loans are used in retail stores, in small grocery stores, and by auto dealers.

Leasing

Instead of buying assets such as trucks, heavy equipment, and machinery, a firm may find it advantageous to lease the equipment instead. A lease is basically a long-term rental. Some smaller firms do not have cash available to purchase these expensive items and find leasing to be a much better option.

Accounts Receivable Financing

A firm may have accounts receivable, or people and firms that owe them money, but they may need cash immediately, not promises to pay in the future. In this case a firm either can borrow against their accounts receivables or can enter into a factoring agreement. When a firm borrows against their accounts receivables, they are using the accounts receivables as collateral on a loan from a finance company. In a factoring agreement the firms actually sell their accounts receivables to the finance company at a discount. In either case the firm is turning a relatively illiquid asset, their accounts receivable, into a liquid asset, cash. Keep in mind that this is not a costless transaction for the firm.

21-4c Types of Finance Companies: Ownership

Finance companies differ in their ownership structure, which determines who they have as customers and what type of services they provide.

Captive Sales Finance Companies

These are some of the oldest type of finance companies. They are owned by a parent company and were established to help finance purchases of the goods sold by the parent company. Examples include Ford Motor Credit, GM Financial, Toyota Motor Credit, American Honda Finance, and Harley-Davidson Credit.

Sales Finance Companies

These finance companies may have originally started out as captive sales finance companies, but now they finance the purchase of goods made by other companies. GE Capital is an example.

Bank Subsidiaries

Some finance companies sit within a bank holding company. They offer services to bank customers, both individuals and businesses that may not qualify for the bank's traditional loans. Or, these bank subsidiaries may offer services to nonbank customers. Examples include HBSC Finance.

Independent Finance Companies

There are many local finance companies, some of which are stand-alone firms and others that are franchises of larger regional or nationwide finance companies. Many of these offer pay-day loans, which are very short-term loans that can, for a fee, be extended or rolled over.

21-4d Financing the Finance Companies

We have learned that finance companies use their funds to make consumer loans, business loans, and even real estate loans. But from where do they get their funds? Remember, finance companies are *not* depository institutions; thus they cannot fund their lending through deposits. Instead, finance companies are highly leveraged entities: They borrow in order to lend. Finance companies tend to have extremely low levels of net worth, especially compared to the relative value of their assets.

Small, independent finance companies often rely on bank loans for their funds. Sometimes they borrow short term to finance their lending through lines of credit, but other times, especially to finance mortgages, they may borrow over longer terms from commercial banks. Larger, more well-established finance companies can also issue commercial paper. Recall that commercial paper is short-term, unsecured debt issued primarily by well-established firms. Some finance companies have recently accessed secured commercial paper markets, where issuers of the commercial paper pledge assets as collateral that can be seized upon nonrepayment. Still other finance companies try to sell their commercial paper through commercial paper dealers, who seek out investors that are looking to purchase slightly more risky commercial paper.

Some finance companies secure longer-term funding by issuing bonds. Depending on the structure of the finance company's balance sheet, and the expectations of interest rate movements in the future, issuing longer-term bonds might make sense for some finance companies. Captive finance companies can also receive funding from their parent company through transfer credit. Still other finance companies are now being allowed, in certain states, to offer deposit accounts—the line between finance companies and thrifts is starting to blur.

21-4e Finance Company Controversies

Finance companies came under harsh attack during the financial crisis that began in 2008. In the mortgage market, many finance companies were accused of misrepresenting the risks of adjustable-rate mortgages. Other finance companies allegedly recklessly offered second mortgages at 150% or 200% of the home's equity. In other words, some finance companies were accused of lending people more than what their homes were worth.

In 2014 American Express, along with Young Turks, funded the creation of a video, almost 40 minutes long, that follows the story of four American families using finance company services, including pay-day loans and car title loans.[15] The video documents how some 70 million Americans are "shut out" of the traditional financial services market. The *New York Times* called the video a "docu-ad," saying that the video was little more than an ad for American Express's new prepaid card, despite the product not being mentioned in the video.[16]

SECTION REVIEW

Q1) Bobby is interested in borrowing money, but he cannot get a loan from a depository institution. He turns to a consumer finance company. In what ways are the loans Bobby might get from a finance company different from the loans he would get from a depository institution?

Q2) Finance companies are not depository institutions, but they still lend money. If finance companies do not take deposits, where do they get the funds they lend to their customers?

Q3) If John Deere Financial provides loans to John Deere customers and is owned by Deere & Company, then John Deere Financial is known as what type of finance company?

a. Captive sales finance company

b. Internal sales finance company

c. Customer sales finance company

d. Consumer sales finance company

---

15 See "Spent: Looking for Change." https://www.youtube.com/watch?v=YAxL4TB6pmQ.

16 See Stuart Elliot, "A 'Docu-Ad' Looks at Hardship of Those Without Bank Access." *New York Times*, June 3, 2014. http://www.nytimes.com/2014/06/04/business/media/a-docu-ad-looks-at-hardship-of-those-without-bank-access.html?_r=0.

21-5 Conclusion

The struggle to provide financial services to the "little people" has been a long one. Thrifts, which date back to the eighteenth century in Europe and came to the Americas in the early nineteenth century, attempted to provide financial services to working-class people and the working poor, with limited success. Savings & Loans helped many working-class Americans achieve part of the "American Dream" of home ownership in the early twentieth century, but they came crashing down in the Saving & Loan crisis of the 1980s. Credit unions, which are nonprofit mutual associations, also have a long history of attempting to provide financial services to their members, often the working class and the working poor. But critics contend these entities have "unfair" advantages over their for-profit competition and should be limited in size and scope. The recent rise of finance companies has been seen as a way to provide financial services to those left out of financial markets. Finance companies provide loans, without taking deposits, to both households and businesses. While finance companies come in a wide variety of structures and styles, many of them have been controversial. Through it all, the "little people"—working-class Americans and the working poor—still seem to struggle to get access to the basic financial services they need.

IN THE NEWS. . .

Consumer Protection Agency Seeks Limits on Payday Lenders

Jessica Silver-Greenberg
The New York Times
February 8, 2015

In the world of consumer finance, they are chameleons: payday lenders that alter their practices and shift their products so slightly to work around state laws aimed at stamping out short-term loans that come with interest rates exceeding 300 percent.

Such maneuvers by the roughly $46 billion payday loan industry, state regulators say, have frustrated their efforts to protect consumers.

Now, for the first time, a federal regulator is entering the fray, drafting regulations that could sharply reduce the number of unaffordable loans that lenders can make.

The Consumer Financial Protection Bureau, created after the 2008 financial crisis, will soon release the first draft of federal regulations to govern a wide range of short-term loans.

The rules are expected to address expensive credit backed by car titles and some installment loans that stretch longer than the traditional two-week payday loan . . . Certain installment loans, for example, with interest rates that exceed 36 percent, the people said, will most likely be covered by the rules.

Behind that decision, the people said, is a stark acknowledgment of just how successfully lenders have adapted to keep offering high-cost products despite state laws meant to rein in the loans.

The federal regulations taking shape will most likely set off a new round of lobbying from payday lenders.

For now, with the prospect of federal rules on the horizon, some payday lenders have begun aggressively lobbying a number of states, including [sic], Kentucky, Washington and New Mexico, tapping a former governor as a lobbyist in one battle, to weaken state laws restricting expensive loans or to quash new caps before they gain ground. . . .

Among the most hotly debated parts of the rules, the people briefed on the discussions said, are just what kinds of loans fall under the guidelines. Some lenders, they said, have pushed to keep the definition narrow, arguing that car title loans and installment loans should escape the crackdown.

The decision to include those forms of credit, the people said, could represent a significant defeat for the payday industry, especially because some lenders, responding to shifts in the regulatory landscape, have shifted to offer those loans. Shortly after Arizona effectively banned payday loans, for example, ACE Cash Express began registering its storefronts as car-title lenders.

Still, the fight is hardly over. Payday lenders have renewed their efforts to win exemptions from laws restricting the loans, according to state records. In Washington State, which prevents borrowers from taking out more than eight loans in a 12-month period, lawmakers backed by payday lenders have introduced two bills. One, for example, would double the number of loans allowed in a year.

The push has incited new concerns among consumer advocates and state regulators that payday lenders will seize on the federal rules to undermine tougher state restrictions like those in New York, which caps rates at 16 percent.

Still, for the millions of people in the 35 states that have no such limits, new federal rules may provide some protections. . . .

Do pay-day loans serve the needs of an underserved population? Or, do they take advantage of people who do not have access to traditional banking services? Why have pay-day loans come about? Why did they not exist in greater numbers in the past?

22

Insurance and Pensions

22-1 Insurance and Pensions

Risk is everywhere. When we discuss risk we are not talking about the board game you may have played; instead we are referring to the potential occurrence of a loss of something of value. Risk can take on many forms: loss of or damage to property, premature death, illness, being found legally responsible for others' loss, or outliving one's financial resources. In this chapter we examine various ways of shifting risk onto other entities. It is important to remember that risk can never be eliminated, it can only be transferred. We review how risk is shifted to another entity via the market for insurance, and we look at how people seek to reduce financial risk in retirement through pensions.

22-1a The Idea of Insurance

To understand the idea of insurance, it is first important to understand the different kinds of risk that exist. With **pure or insurable risk** there are two potential outcomes: a loss or no loss. For example, you get into an accident with your automobile, your car is damaged, and you incur a loss; or, you drive your car accident free and there is no loss. On the other hand, with **speculative risk** there are three potential outcomes: a gain, a loss, or no loss. Speculative risk is a concept discussed in asset management or investments; here instead we focus on pure or insurable risk.

Pure or insurable risk: Category or type of risk where the only possible outcomes are a loss or no loss.

Speculative risk: Category or type of risk where the possible outcomes are loss, no loss, or a gain.

Insurance involves the shifting of pure or insurable risk from the insured party to the issuer of the insurance policy, usually an insurance company. The insured party compensates the insurer through payment of a **policy premium**. The pooling of insured parties means that losses suffered by a few can be spread out over the entire group of insured.

Insurance policy premium: Fees paid by the insured to the insurer to compensate the insurer for bearing the risk of specific events that would negatively affect the insured.

Insurance and Asymmetric Information

Insurance, however, faces the asymmetric information problems that other financial institutions face: adverse selection and moral hazard. Recall that adverse selection, which happens before a financial contract is created, occurs when the people most likely to benefit from a transaction are the ones who seek it out. Moral hazard, which happens after a financial contract is created, occurs when a financial contract alters behaviors by changing incentives.

In insurance, the people most likely to suffer a loss are the ones most likely to seek out insurance, whereas the creation of the insurance policy can change people's behavior by changing incentives.

Insurance and Adverse Selection

Insurance companies address the issue of adverse selection in two main ways: successful marketing and government-mandated insurance. To see successful insurance marketing at work, consider the market for life insurance. If you think about it, life insurance really isn't life insurance; it is insurance against death, so it could be called death insurance. We don't call it death insurance in part because it would be rather difficult to get young people—those who are least likely to put in a claim on life insurance—to think about spending their money on their own death. Instead we call it "life" insurance. In addition, life insurance advertisements often feature pictures of babies and young families. Why? In part this is so those young people, who are the least likely to buy life insurance, can identify with people in the ad and be more likely to buy the product.

If successful advertising isn't enough to get those least likely to buy the insurance to purchase a policy, sometimes the insurance needs to be mandated by the government. Consider automobile insurance. Automobile liability insurance is mandatory in 49 states[1] and the District of Columbia. This ensures a large pool of people purchasing automobile insurance, not just those most likely to put in a claim.

Insurance and Moral Hazard

Insurance companies address the issue of moral hazard by requiring deductibles, changing premiums, and monitoring. If you have automobile insurance and cause an accident that requires $2,500 in repairs, the insurance company does not pay you $2,500. Instead, most insurance policies have a **deductible**, an amount of the claim or damage the insured must pay. If your policy has a $500 deductible, then you have to pay the first $500 and the insurance company pays the remaining $2,000. In this way you, the insured, have to pay for damages that come about because of "changes in behavior." Or, it is a way for the insurance company to limit moral hazard.

Insurance deductible: The amount of a loss that the insured must pay out of their own resources before an insurer pays for expenses related to the covered loss.

Also, when you submit a claim after an accident, your car insurance premium almost assuredly increases. This is another way insurance companies try to limit moral hazard: making the insured pay for their change in behavior. In an attempt to be proactive, insurance companies have taken steps to identify changes in behavior after a policy has been put in place by monitoring the insured's behavior. So, if you get a speeding ticket, your auto insurance premium is likely to increase. This occurs because the insurance company is trying to control for the moral hazard problem.

22-1b Structure of Insurance Companies

Insurance policies are sold by insurance brokers and agents. **Independent agents** may sell insurance products for a number of different insurance companies. These agents can compare policies and prices from a number of different insurance companies and pick the one that best suits the needs of their client or pays the agent the largest commission. **Exclusive agents** sell the insurance products for only one insurance company. Some larger insurance companies offer their products only through exclusive agents.

Independent insurance agent: An insurance sales agent who sells insurance products from a variety of different insurance companies.

Exclusive insurance agent: An insurance sales agent who sells insurance products from only one insurance company.

When an agent has a client who would like to purchase an insurance policy, the client's application is passed on to an **insurance underwriter**. An insurance underwriter is someone who determines the terms of coverage of the insurance policy, including the premium to be paid. In determining the premium to be paid, the underwriter consults with insurance company **actuaries**.

Insurance underwriter: A person within an insurance company who decides whether insurance is issued and under what terms.

---

1 New Hampshire is the only state that does not require auto liability insurance. It does, however, require drivers to show that they are able to take financial responsibility if they are at fault in an accident.

Actuary: An applied statistician within an insurance company who calculates risks and premiums.

Actuaries compile and analyze statistics to determine the probability of events occurring that result in a claim being submitted. After the underwriter is finished, the terms are sent to the agent and then are presented to the client. If the client agrees to the terms of the policy, the coverage begins—usually as soon as a premium payment is made.

Insurance companies collect the premiums and hope that bad events do not happen so that claims are not submitted. Insurance companies invest the premiums that are paid in so they have (hopefully) sufficient amounts of reserves to pay claims should they be submitted. Often it can be several years between when premium payments are made and when claims are submitted. Thus, insurance companies must wisely invest their excess funds, making sure they have the correct balance of liquidity, return, and risk.

If a negative event occurs that results in a claim being submitted under a policy, the claim is turned over to an **insurance claims adjuster**. The claims adjuster assesses the situation and determines the amount of compensation that should be paid to the person submitting the claim.

Insurance claims adjuster: A person within an insurance company who assesses claims on insurance policies submitted by parties who have incurred covered losses.

22-1c Insurance Regulation

The insurance industry in the United States is regulated primarily at the state level. The McCarrran-Ferguson Act of 1945 conferred to the states power to regulate insurance companies, so federal laws apply only where state laws do not. The state agency in charge of regulating insurance is often called the insurance commission. The state insurance commission is responsible for granting insurance charters and examining insurance companies, in keeping with guidelines agreed to by the National Association of Insurance Commissioners.

During the financial crisis of 2008–2009, many questions about the effectiveness of the states' regulation of the insurance industry were raised. As a result, in July 2010 the Wall Street Reform and Consumer Protection Act created the **Federal Insurance Office** (FIO).[2] While the FIO currently has no regulatory authority over the insurance industry, it is charged with monitoring the health of the insurance industry, identifying regulatory gaps and systemic risk, and monitoring to what extent underserved populations have access to insurance. The FIO reports to Congress and to the president on the status and health of the insurance industry and provides recommendations for changes in insurance regulations.

Federal Insurance Office: A federal office, housed within the US Department of Treasury, designed to monitor the insurance industry and coordinate policies that pertain to the insurance industry.

In addition to chartering and supervising insurance companies, the states' insurance commissions also are responsible for dealing with failed insurance companies. If an insurance company becomes insolvent, the state insurance commission takes control of the insurance company with the goal of stabilizing it and getting it back on its feet. If the insurance company cannot be saved, it is liquidated, and proceeds are used to pay claims. States have an **insurance guarantee fund** that is used if the proceeds from the liquidation are not sufficient to pay all of the outstanding claims.[3]

Insurance guarantee fund: A fund established and administered by state governments in the United States to protect insurance policyholders and beneficiaries in the event that an insurance company becomes insolvent or defaults on paying benefits.

---

2 For more information see http://www.treasury.gov/initiatives/fio.

3 All states have guarantee funds for property and liability insurance companies, and some states have guarantee funds for life and health insurance companies.

Insurance premiums, policy terms, sales practices, commission rates, company capital levels, and claims practices all are regulated by the state insurance commissions. All states also require the licensing of agents and brokers; agents are required to pass an exam before selling insurance.

SECTION REVIEW

Q1) Andrew is a bit confused about risk. In his investments class he learned about risk when purchasing a financial asset, and he thinks that is the same as risk when buying automobile insurance. How would you explain to Andrew the differences between different types of risks?

Q2) Today much of the regulation of depository institutions occurs at the federal level. How is the insurance industry different?

Q3) Many automobile insurance policies require a deductible to be paid by the insured. A deductible is a tool to help control for which problem?

a. Adverse selection

b. Underwriting

c. Moral hazard

d. Claims adjustment

22-2 Life Insurance

There are many different types of insurance. Not every insurance product is the right product for everyone. Because people are different and have different needs, a wide variety of different types of insurance products have been developed. In this section we look at just some of the different types of insurance that exist.

22-2a Basics of Life Insurance

One of the oldest insurance products is life insurance. As we discussed earlier, life insurance could easily be called "death insurance" because it is the occurrence of death upon which the policy pays. When a life insurance policy is first issued, premiums are based on the life expectancy of the insured. Thus, the young and the healthy pay the lowest life insurance premiums, whereas older people and those who are unhealthy (e.g., smokers, those who drink excessively, and those with past health problems) pay higher life insurance premiums.

Life insurance policies were originally designed to provide funds for widows and orphans who were left behind when a man died unexpectedly. In the nineteenth and early twentieth centuries, for example, workplace accidents resulting in death were not uncommon. Life insurance policies came about as a way to make sure the widows and orphans "left behind" would be taken care of financially. Today, life insurance has evolved into a wide variety of financial products that serve to meet the financial needs of a diverse population. Life insurance policies today are not your grandparents' life insurance.

Whole Life Insurance

In a whole life policy, the insured makes regular, level, periodic premium payments, either monthly, quarterly, or yearly. The beneficiaries receive a payment, called the **policy's face value**, at the time of the insured's death. In addition to the death benefit, a whole life insurance policy builds up a cash value over time.

Life insurance policy face value: The amount of life insurance coverage or the amount paid to beneficiaries upon the death of the insured.

Essentially, the insured overpays for the death benefit in the first years of the policy and underpays for the death benefit in the later years. The overpayments build up and are made available to the policyholder in the form of the **cash value**. The insurance company usually promises a minimum interest rate at which the cash value grows.

Life insurance policy cash value: The investment portion of some life insurance policies that accumulates over the term of the policy. The policyholder may be able to withdraw or borrow against the cash value of the policy.

When the insured dies, the beneficiary receives the death benefit or face value *and* the available cash value built up in the policy. For example, at age 22, a person could take out a $100,000 whole life insurance policy and make regular premium payments until they die at age 82. The payout to their beneficiaries could be over $500,000. Another option is that the insured can borrow the cash value while they are still alive. The annual interest rate on loans of this type is generally around 4% to 8%, depending on market interest rates and they type of policy restrictions. If the insured does not repay the loan, or repays only part of it, the balance is deducted from the death benefit when the insured dies.

Whole life insurance policies can be a simple way for people to build up long-term savings. The downside to whole life insurance, however, is that premiums are relatively high, and it can take several years for the cash value to build to a significant level.

Term Life Insurance

Term life insurance, as the name suggests, provides temporary insurance for only a specific length of time. Thus, someone could take out a term life insurance policy for 10, 15, or even 25 years. At the end of the term, the insurance coverage terminates. Term life insurance builds up no cash value; it is strictly a death benefit policy. The premiums on term life insurance are generally much lower than those for a whole life policy.

Term life insurance may be useful to someone who needs inexpensive life insurance over a short period of time. For example, a young person who just graduated from college with a high level of student loan debt might want to take out a term life insurance policy with a death benefit large enough to pay off their outstanding debts should they die unexpectedly. Or, young parents who would like an inexpensive life insurance policy might find term life insurance a good option.

Universal Life Insurance

Universal life insurance is sort of a combination of whole life and term life insurance. Universal life policies build up cash value, just as whole life policies do, but usually at a much faster rate. Basically, universal life policies have two parts: one that provides term life insurance coverage, and one that rapidly builds up a cash value.

A universal life policy consists of a flexible premium, whereby policyholders decide when and what amount of premiums they want to pay. The insurance company uses some of the premium payments to pay for the term life insurance and invests the rest of the funds in a bond portfolio, with the goal of mimicking some observable interest rate benchmark. When the value of the portfolio increases rapidly, then the cash value of the policy can increase rapidly, as well. The interest credited to the cash value is not subject to income tax so long as the cash value is not greater than the death benefit.

Universal life policies are popular with people who like the low cost of term insurance but also desire a buildup of cash value in keeping with market interest rates. The downside to universal life insurance is that if interest rates decline and stay low, the growth rate of the cash value of universal life policies may lag behind the rates paid on whole life policies.

Variable Life Insurance

Variable life insurance is a life insurance policy with a fixed premium that allows policyholders to decide where the cash value is to be invested. The insurance company generally offers the policyholder a choice of mutual funds in which to invest the cash value. Variable life has a fixed minimum death benefit, but that benefit can be significantly higher if the mutual fund performs well. There is, however, no guarantee on how the mutual fund will perform.

Some insurance companies combine the flexible payment feature of universal life insurance with the investment options of variable life insurance to create variable–universal or universal–variable life insurance policies.

Annuities

While life insurance is really death insurance, annuities could be considered "actual" life insurance, in that annuities insure against outliving one's financial resources. The purchaser of an annuity pays out a fixed amount and in return receives payments as long as the beneficiary lives.

Annuities are generally offered in a variety of forms. They can be purchased via installment premiums or with a single lump sum payment. The benefit payments can begin immediately or at some date in the future. An annuity can be structured with a "for certain" clause, such as the "annuity will provide life income with 15 years for certain." This means that the annuity will pay out to the annuitant until that person dies; if the annuitant dies before 15 years have passed, the remaining payments will go to a designated beneficiary.

Annuities are popular with people close to retirement age or those who are receiving another lump sum payment such as an inheritance, insurance payment, or lottery winnings. Both of these groups are interested in payouts over the rest of their lives.

22-2b Life Insurance Companies

According to the American Council of Life Insurers' 2014 *Life Insurance Factbook*, in 2012 there were 868 life insurance companies in business in the United States. The number reached a peak in 1988 and has been falling ever since, mainly because of corporate mergers. Most life insurance companies are structured as either stock or mutual companies. Mutual companies are owned by their policyholders and do not issue stock. Other life insurance companies are fraternal organizations and companies that underwrite life insurance policies.

In 2012 life insurance companies in the United States held a total of around $5.8 trillion of assets (Figure 22-1). Bonds made up 50%, or $2.9 trillion of the total assets of life insurers, whereas equities made up about 30% and mortgages 6%. Clearly, life insurance companies are a major institutional investor, especially in the debt market.

Liabilities of US life insurance companies comprise primarily reserves that are held to meet the claims submitted by policyholders and beneficiaries (Figure 22-2). Policy and asset fluctuation reserves are two examples. At the end of 2012, policy reserves of US life insurance companies totaled $4.4 trillion. As the insurance market has changed, so too have life insurance reserves. Annuity contract reserves now account for the largest portion of total reserves, whereas whole life reserves have declined. Asset fluctuation reserves, also known as asset valuation reserves, totaled $45 billion in 2012.

Deposit-type contracts are another major liability for life insurance companies. Financial contracts that do not incorporate mortality risks are considered deposit-type contracts. These include annuity certains (annuities with "for certain" clauses), premium and other deposit funds, dividend and interest accumulations, and structured settlements. In 2012 these reserves totaled $431 billion.

Figure 22-1 **Assets of Life Insurance Companies in 2012**

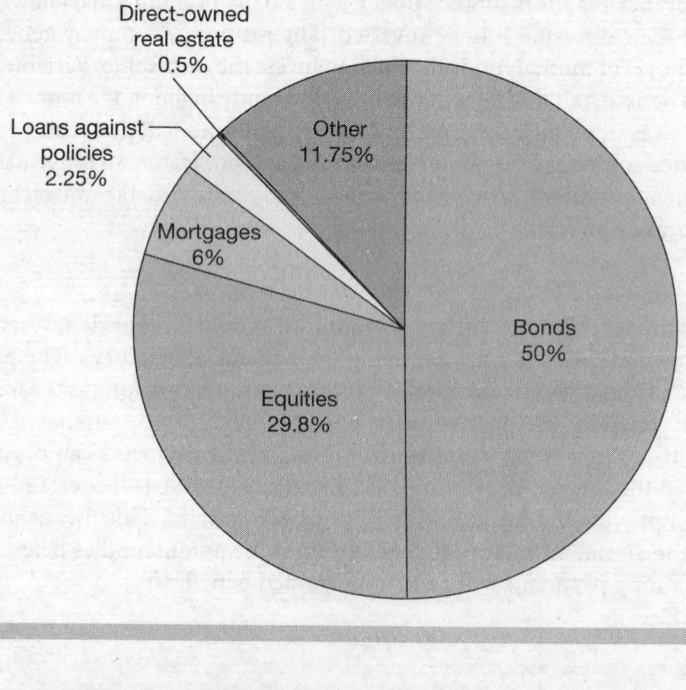

Figure 22-2 Liabilities of Life Insurance Companies Comprise Mainly Reserves

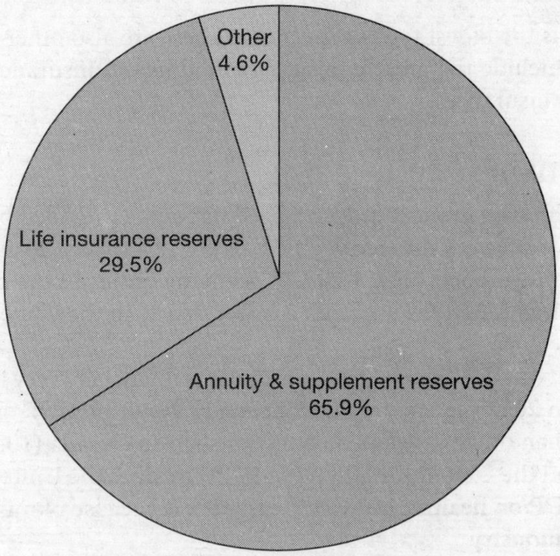

While the life insurance industry is one of the oldest and most important segments of the insurance industry, life insurance is not the only type of insurance. As times and markets have changed, so too have the insurance needs of families and businesses. Next we review the other types of insurance policies and insurance firms that exist and the important roles they play in our financial markets.

SECTION REVIEW

Q1) Sarah and David are interested in purchasing life insurance policies. Why might they may wind up paying very different life insurance premiums?

Q2) How is the makeup of assets and liabilities of life insurance companies different from those of depository institutions? Why?

Q3) Elise is a recent college graduate with student loans on which her parents have cosigned. If Elise is looking to purchase low-cost life insurance to ensure her parents will not have to repay her student loans if she dies unexpectedly, arguably the best life insurance policy for Elise is a:

a. whole life insurance policy.

b. term life insurance policy.

c. cash value life insurance policy.

d. variable annuity life insurance policy.

22-3 Other Insurance

While life insurance is the oldest type of insurance, there are also other very important types of insurance. These include the greatly misunderstood health insurance industry, as well as property and liability insurance.

22-3a Health Insurance

The provision of health care in most industrialized nations is provided by the government. In the United States it is done very differently; most of our health care costs are covered through employer-paid health insurance. How well—or, as many critics of the current system argue, how poorly—this system functions has been a major debate in the United States over the past several decades.

What is clear about our health care system is that it is financially very important. According to the World Bank, in 2012 the United States spent 17.9% of its GDP on health care. This is significantly higher than other developed countries such as Canada (10.9%), France (11.7%), Germany (11.3%), and the United Kingdom (9.4%). Why does the United States spend such a high portion of its GDP on health care? Critics argue it is because of misaligned incentives in the health insurance industry.

Health insurance in the United States is much more a payment system than it is a shifting of risk. According to the US Census Bureau, in 2011 over half of the US population (59.5%)[4] had employer-based health insurance coverage. Of the employed population aged 18 to 64 years, more than 2 of 3, or 68.2%, had health insurance through an employer.

Under an employer-based health insurance plan, the insured employee pays a portion of the insurance premium every month and also pays a **co-pay**, or a fixed charge, with each visit to a physician, specialist, or urgent care center. A co-pay is also required when filling a prescription.

Co-pay: The amount of out-of-pocket expense an insured person must pay either per visit to a health care provider or per prescription purchased.

Critics of the current system argue that under this system the employee/patient does not "see" or experience the true cost of their health care. The health insurance premium is most often deducted from the employee's pay each month, and thus can be easy to ignore or forget about. Even more troubling, the co-pay is relatively small compared with the total cost of services provided. For a routine visit to a doctor's office, the co-pay may range from $15 to $25, but the actual cost paid by insurance can easily be several hundred dollars. A visit to a specialist may have a co-pay of $30 to $50, whereas the actual cost borne by the insurance company can quickly approach a thousand dollars. Since employees/patients do not pay anywhere near the true cost of the service being provided, they are insensitive to price.

Physicians, on the other hand, often are compensated based on the number of patients they see and the number of procedures they perform. Thus, physicians have incentive to see as many patients as possible and prescribe as many procedures as they possibly can. Naturally, physicians take the Hippocratic oath or some type of professional oath that is a pledge to treat patients in an ethical manner and to do no harm. Work by people like John E. Wennberg, MD,[5] of the Geisel School of Medicine at Dartmouth College, however, demonstrates how poorly allocated health care services are in the United States.

---

4 According to the Robert Wood Johnson Foundation, this figure was even higher in 2000 at 69.7%. The Great Recession has led many companies to cut employee benefits, including employer-based health insurance.

5 See John E. Wennber and Peggy Y. Thompson, "Time to Tackle Unwarranted Variations in Practice." *BMJ* 342 (2011): d1513. http://www.bmj.com/content/342/bmj.d1513

22-3b Property and Casualty Insurance

Property and casualty insurance shifts the risk of perils—causes of loss—that could occur to property and finances because of negligence. The distinction between the two is becoming more murky, however; insurers often provide policies that offer coverage of both property and casualty insurance under one policy.

Strictly speaking, property insurance policies can be structured as **named-peril policies** or **open-peril policies**, which also are called "all-risk policies." Named-peril policies shift the risk for only those perils listed in the policy, such as fire, wind, earthquakes, or floods.

Named-peril insurance policy: An insurance policy that pays for damages incurred by the insured stemming from specific events.

Open-peril insurance policy: Also known as an all-risk policy, an insurance policy that pays for all damages incurred by the insured except for those due to specific events or circumstances.

Open-peril policies offer coverage of all losses except those that are specifically excluded. In both types of polices some indirect losses also are compensated. For example, if a retail store has a fire that requires it to be closed for repairs, not only are the cost of repairs covered by property insurance, so too are the profits the store would have generated if it had remained open. Homeowners also buy property insurance and often are required to do so if they have a mortgage on the home.

Casualty or liability insurance shifts the risk of the peril of legal liability due to negligence. Liability insurance is bought by manufacturers who might be sued for negligently producing products that cause harm or injury to people. Liability insurance also is purchased by physicians, lawyers, electricians, plumbers, and building contractors.

Casualty or liability insurance: Insurance that provides payment for losses occurring due to negligent acts or actions that cause injury or damage to others.

Most of us come into contact with liability insurance when we purchase automobile liability insurance, which provides coverage against losses resulting from legal liability through the ownership or use of a vehicle. The auto insurance policy we purchase might also have a property insurance component that covers the theft of or damage to the vehicle. In this case the auto insurance policy is both a property and casualty or liability insurance policy.

22-3c Credit Default Swaps

We mentioned credit default swaps (CDSs) before, but it is important to examine them in a discussion of insurance because that is, essentially, what they are. Remember, a CDS is the shifting of default risk of a financial instrument. Under a CDS, a bondholder, for example, can pay an entity that sells CDS to assume the risk that the issuer of the bond will not pay the interest or face value (or both) as promised. When the probability of default by the bond issuer is low, then the price of the CDS, essentially the premium on the insurance policy, is low.

From the mid-1990s to 2008, the size of the CDS market grew significantly as the market for mortgage-backed securities expanded. Mortgage-backed securities were essentially bonds that used the payments on home mortgages to make interest payments. Insurance companies such as AIG saw the sale of CDSs on mortgage-backed securities as a way to generate a very large amount of premium income without being exposed to much risk since home mortgages historically have a very low default rate.

By June 2008, the Bank for International Settlements estimated there were $57 trillion of CDSs outstanding.[6] But when subprime mortgages started to default and the mortgage-backed

6 See Rene M. Stulz, "Credit Default Swaps and the Credit Crisis," *Journal of Economic Perspectives* 24, no. 1 (2010): 73–92.

securities did not have the revenue stream to pay back as promised, the issuers of the CDSs had a problem. The issuers of CDSs (insurance regulations allow only insurance companies whose sole product they offer is financial insurance[7] to issue CDSs) faced the reality that they did not have enough reserves to pay the claims that were being submitted. As a result, a government bailout of the insurance industry needed to be arranged.

SECTION REVIEW

Q1) Ben, who has health insurance provided through his employer, has an appointment with his physician for an annual exam. Ben pays a $25 co-pay at the doctor's office. Ben tells Sheila it cost him $25 for the appointment. Sheila responds, "Oh no, Ben, you paid a lot more than $25 for that visit." What does Sheila mean?

Q2) Credit default swaps often were issued by banks, yet many argue they were actually an insurance product and thus should have been issued only by regulated insurance companies. Explain this argument.

Q3) Carolyn has just purchased a homeowners' insurance policy that will pay for damages to her house that occur only if flooding in her area takes place. What type of insurance did Carolyn purchase?

a. Closed-end insurance
b. Named-peril insurance
c. Open-peril insurance
d. Specific claim insurance

7 Insurance companies such as MBIA, Ambac, and a division of AIG had for many years offered insurance that guaranteed the timely repayment of bond principal and interest when debt issuers defaulted, but this was mainly for the municipal bond market.

Pensions

22-4

Few people want to work until the day they die. Instead, most people want a retirement. They want to be able to live out their "golden years" in comfort: playing golf, traveling, and perhaps enjoying time with their grandchildren. For many Americans, a comfortable retirement is part of the American dream. Many retired Americans today have realized this dream. However, many fear that the current generation of retired Americans will be the last to live so comfortably in retirement. The reason for this fear is simple: the changing pension system in America.

A pension is the collection of funds during a person's working years that results in regular payments made during that person's retirement. In previous centuries people relied on their children to provide for them when they got old. But with financial market innovations, increased labor productivity, and thus increased worker wages, as well as a more mobile labor force that resulted in children not living in the same cities as their elderly parents, pensions are now how most people in industrialized countries fund their retirement.

22-4a Defined Benefit Plans

One of the oldest employer-provided pension plans is the defined benefit plan. As the name suggests, the pension pays out a defined benefit during the person's retirement years. Once the employee is eligible to retire (usually based on a combination of their age plus the number of years with the employer), a formula is used to determine that amount of the benefit that will be paid. For example:

Annual payment = 2% × average of 3 highest years' income × years with firm

Imagine Janet has worked for a firm for 35 years, and the average of her 3 highest years of income with the firm works out to be $60,000. Her annual payment would be:

0.02 × ($60,000) × (35/5) = $42,000

Therefore, Janet would receive a monthly check for $3,500 during her retirement. Organized labor groups (unions) often negotiate for defined benefit pensions for their members. According to the Bureau of Labor Statistics, in 2010, 78% of union members had a defined benefit pension plan, compared with only 19% of nonunionized workers.

The defined benefits plan puts the burden of collecting and managing funds on the employer. Under a defined benefits plan, the employer needs to be certain that it is setting aside enough funds during the employee's working years and that these funds are being invested wisely to make certain the plan can pay out as promised. If things work correctly and the pension fund is **fully funded**, it will be able to meet all of its future obligations.

Fully funded pension: A retirement system that has sufficient assets to meet current and future liabilities.

In recent years, however, many defined benefit pension plans are **underfunded**. That is, the pension plans simply will not have enough funds to make good on all of the promises they made to employees. Either the employer did not set enough money aside, the funds did not grow in value fast enough, the actual outflows were more than expected, or some combination of these are reasons why pensions are underfunded. No laws make it illegal for an employer to underfund a pension.

Underfunded pension: A retirement system that has more liabilities than it does assets.

22-4b Defined Contribution Plans

Largely because of the problem of underfunded defined benefit pensions, more employers now offer only defined contribution plans. As the name suggests, these pensions are based on the amount of funds contributed during a worker's tenure. The most common types of defined contribution plans are the 401(k) used by for-profit firms, the 403(b) for public schools or universities, and the 457(b) for state and local governments.

Contributions and Investment

In these pension plans each month the employee puts a portion of their monthly compensation into the fund. The employer sometimes matches that contribution. Both Fidelity and The Vanguard Group suggest that employers contribute, on average, about 4% of an employee's wage to the employee's 401(k). That comes to a little over $3,500 a year. Many companies offer no match at all. A 2013 study from the consulting firm Aon Hewitt found the most common type of match, offered by 19% of employers, is a dollar-for-dollar match up to 6% of annual pay. Another 15% of employers in the study offer $0.50 for every $1.00 the employee contributes, up to 6% of the employee's annual pay.[8]

Another major difference between defined benefits and defined contribution plans has to do with investment decisions. In a defined benefits plan the employer makes the investment decisions. In a defined contributions plan the employee is usually offered a collection of mutual funds from the plan's administrator. The employee must then pick to which funds the contributions will be allocated. Critics of these plans argue that employees often are ill-informed about their investment choices and wind up paying high mutual fund fees.

Vested Plans and Rollovers

One major benefit of a defined contribution plan to an employee is that the funds are portable. After an initial period (usually one year of employment), the employee is **fully vested** in the plan. This means that when the employee leaves the employer, the employee can take the balance in their defined contribution plan with them. To avoid tax implications, the funds must be rolled over into another retirement plan. If the employee leaves the employer before being fully vested, she or he is allowed to take their own contributions and earnings but must forfeit the employer's contributions.

Fully vested: The ability of an employee to take all of the employer's retirement contribution with them when the employee leaves the employment of the employer.

Proponents of the defined contribution retirement plans argue that replacing defined benefits plans with defined contribution plans has greatly reduced the costs to and responsibilities of employers. The burden is now shifted to employees. Yet critics of defined contribution plans contend many employees do not understand the importance of fully contributing to their defined contribution plans, make poor decisions about where to invest their funds, and withdraw their funds well before retirement as a result of worsening personal financial situations. A 2014 survey by Bankrate.com found that a third of Americans aged 30 to 49 years have zero retirement savings.[9]

Perhaps some of the people who are not saving for their own retirement think that the American public pension system, usually referred to as Social Security, will provide for them during their retirement years. If that is the case, they may be in for a jolt.

---

8 See Andrea Coombes, "Bigger 401(k) Match Trumps Bigger Salary." MarketWatch, August 12, 2014. http://www.marketwatch.com/story/bigger-401k-match-trumps-bigger-salary-2014-08-12?page=2

9 See Bruce Kennedy, "Shocking Number of Americans Have No Retirement Savings," CBS Money Watch, August 18, 2014. http://www.cbsnews.com/news/shocking-number-of-americans-have-no-retirement-savings/

22-4c Public Pensions

Public pensions are pension plans provided by a government body. The largest and best known is formally known as the Federal Old Age and Disability Insurance Program, but most people refer to it as Social Security. The Social Security system began in 1935 and was originally planned to be a traditional defined benefits plan: People pay into the system, along with an employer match, and that money would be set aside for them for retirement.

The problem is that when the system was created in 1935 there were a number of elderly people who were destitute because of the Great Depression. These people had not paid into the system because the system had not existed until then. So, a decision was made to start Social Security as a "pay-as-you-go" system, whereby money paid in would be immediately paid out to those currently retired.

It was thought that a pay-as-you-go system would be used only to get the system going. But by the late 1940s, when all of the people who had not initially paid into the system had left it, policymakers decided to keep the pay-as-you-go-system in place. They were motivated in part by the large "baby boom" that was occurring. Following World War II there was a dramatic increase in the birth rate in the United States. Since these babies would grow up and become workers, it was assumed there would always be a large population of workers and a much smaller number of retired people. In this setting it would be easy to simply take some money from the people who are currently working and give it to the people who are currently retired. Thus, the pay-as-you-go-system stayed in place.

That is the system that remains in place to this day. In 2014 an employee's share of a Social Security contribution is 6.2% of wages, up to a cap of $117,000. Employers contribute the same amount to Social Security. Employees also pay 1.45% of wages, with no limit, to Medicare, the federal government's old age health insurance plan. Again, employers pay into Medicare the same amount as employees.

The pay-as-you-go system worked fine for a while. Then, starting in 1964, the baby boom ended as birth rates in the United States started to fall. Birth rates decreased even further in 1969 with the wide dissemination of birth control. Now, as the baby-boom generation ages and starts to retire, the generations that come after them—Generation X (born 1965–1976), Generation Y or Millennials (born 1977–1994), and Generation Z or iGen (born 1995–2012)—will be much smaller. With a smaller number of workers compared with retirees, the pay-as-you-go-system is in trouble.

A number of ideas to save Social Security have been proposed. One suggestion is to raise or completely eliminate the Social Security cap. That is, make more income, or even all income, subject to Social Security and Medicare taxes. Another suggestion is to raise the age at which people can receive benefits. The age was increased gradually in 1984 so that those born after 1960 cannot start receiving full benefits until they hit age 67. Some argue the age should be raised to 70 or 72. A more radical proposal is to "needs test" Social Security. Under this proposal, everyone would continue to contribute to Social Security, but only those in the middle or on the lower end of the socioeconomic ladder would receive benefits at retirement. The argument is that those with high incomes have the ability to save for their retirement while they are working, so they don't need Social Security. Instead, Social Security should return to what it was originally designed to do: keep the elderly out of poverty.

While the debate about what to do with America's public pension rages on, little is being done to address the challenges that face this very important pension system.

SECTION REVIEW

Q1) Stan has worked for the same firm for over 30 years and has a defined benefits pension. However, he is worried the pension fund where he works is under-funded. Explain to someone with no training in economics why Stan is worried.

Q2) Charlotte is fully vested in her defined contribution pension plan where she works. What will happen if Charlotte decides to quit her job and go work for a different employer?

Q3) Which of the following has resulted in questions being raised about the future of the Social Security public pension system?

a. Demographic changes in the US population

b. Decreasing market interest rates

c. The recent rise of defined benefits pensions

d. The increased number of self-employed Americans

Conclusion

22-5

Risk is something people most often seek to shift to others. This shifting of risk comes at a price, however. As we learned in this chapter, sometimes this risk is shifted onto insurance companies through formal contracts such as insurance policies. After examining the asymmetric information problems in the insurance industry, we investigated one of the oldest forms of insurance: life insurance. We examined some of the different types of life insurance and how life insurance companies are structured. We also reviewed other ways of shifting risk, including the very controversial health insurance industry in the United States, as well as the property and causality insurance industry and credit default swaps. We also realized that people face the risk of financial uncertainty during retirement. To deal with this, risk pensions have developed. But we also learned how the pension system in the United States has changed and evolved, including the public pension system called Social Security. In all of our discussions of insurance and pensions, it is important to remember that this financial market can only seek to shift risk. Remember, risk cannot be eliminated.

IN THE NEWS. . .

Healthcare: The Race to Cure Rising Drug Costs

David Crow and Andrew Ward

The Financial Times

February 10, 2015

Since contracting hepatitis C 25 years ago, Lucinda Porter's biggest fear has been that she would infect someone else with the deadly virus. "Whenever I cut myself and saw the smeared blood, I would panic," she says. . . .

She tried two courses of treatment, both of which failed. By 2003, she had to face up to the possibility that she would die from hepatitis C, which can lead to cirrhosis and liver cancer. . . .

Ten years later, she took part in a clinical trial for a new drug called Harvoni. Within days she knew the treatment was working and after three months doctors declared her effectively cured.

Ms. Porter is one of 140,000 American that have been treated by one of Gilead Science's hepatitis C drugs since they were launched two years ago. Harvoni and Sovalidi, an older version of the pill, are seen as "miracle drugs," offering cure rates of over 94 per cent.

But Gilead has become the symbol of out-of-control drug prices in the U.S. A 12-week treatment costs $94,500 or $1,125 a pill, attracting unwanted attention from politicians and doctors, who identify the group as one of the most hated companies in pharmaceuticals.

Peter Bach, a doctor and director at the Memorial Sloan-Kettering Cancer Center in New York, reflects the views of many in his profession when he accuses it of "corrupting behavior.". . .

After less than a year on the market, Gilead has faced a concerted push to lower the price of Harvoni. Seizing an opportunity created by the approval in December of a rival hepatitis C treatment from AbbVie, another US drugs group, the insurers and employers who fund US healthcare have forced deep discounts from both companies in return for access to patients.

Such aggressive tactics had not been commonplace in the US, where patient choice has reigned supreme. . .

Direct federal government intervention in drug prices is barred under US law—testament, critics say, to big pharma's lobbying power on Capitol Hill. But President Barack Obama's health reform—the Affordable Care Act—has created incentives to control costs, while consolidation among healthcare providers has also shifted bargaining power from drug companies to their customers.

The combination of these forces could result in the US applying the break to rising healthcare costs which, at 18 percent of gross domestic product, far exceeds those of any other nation. . . .

Ms. Porter never paid the full price for her medication—her insurance company did. The article states that health insurance companies' attempts to get lower prices for medications have "not been commonplace in the US, where patient choice has reigned supreme." How does this help to explain that the United States spends 18% of GDP on health care costs? Does the government have a role to play in the health insurance industry as it pertains to drug prices? Why or why not?

23

Mutual Funds

23-1 Mutual Funds Overview

The old saying goes, "There is power in numbers." The song "Solidarity Forever," written by Ralph Chaplin back in 1915, asks the question, "What force on earth is weaker than the feeble strength of one?" While Chaplin's song was about organized labor, the same question can be posed in financial markets: Will an individual saver investing relatively small amounts ever be able to have a well-diversified portfolio? The answer is, probably not.

Mutual funds, on the other hand, allow these savers, often individuals or families, the opportunity to diversify their savings relatively easily. A mutual fund is an investment company, as defined by the Investment Company Act of 1940, that sells shares in its various funds and uses those monies to buy a variety of investment assets.

In this chapter we examine the growing mutual fund industry. We start off by documenting how this industry has grown in the United States, especially in the past three decades. We then spend a fair amount of time looking into the wide variety of mutual funds that currently exist in our financial markets. We will learn that not all mutual funds are the same, especially when it comes to risks and the fees investment companies charge. We finish by reviewing other types of mutual funds, including exchange-traded funds, hedge funds, and real estate investment trusts. Along the way we investigate some of the controversies that exist in these rapidly expanding financial markets.

Essentially all of these different types of mutual funds are the pooling together of the small amounts of funds from individual savers by an investment company. The investment company turns the funds over to a mutual fund manager, who in turn buys a portfolio of securities. Each of the savers then owns a portion of this portfolio. What type of securities the portfolio manager purchases depends on the goals and structure of the mutual fund.

23-1a Mutual Fund Growth

Today, mutual funds and other products offered by investment companies are very popular. According to the 2014 *Investment Company Fact Book*, US investment companies have total net assets of over $17 trillion, and mutual fund assets make up $15 trillion of that total. Over 46% of American households own mutual funds; the median mutual fund assets of households owning them is $100,000.

Mutual fund ownership is, however, a relatively recent phenomenon. The mutual fund market started to increase in size ever so slightly in the late 1970s and then increased significantly during the 1980s and 1990s. The growth of mutual funds is moderated during the years of economic recessions. This makes sense, since during economic slowdowns household incomes tend to decrease, meaning they have fewer funds to save. In addition, during economic slowdowns financial assets can and often do lose value.

From Table 23-1 we can see the dramatic impact of the Great Recession. Notice how the size of mutual fund assets were increasing during the first decade of the twenty-first century until 2007, is reduced dramatically during the Great Recession, but then recovers quickly.

The financial crisis that gripped much of the economy in 2008 led to a significant decline in the size of mutual fund industry assets. The asset level of the mutual fund industry increased in 2009 but did not increase much in value again until 2012 and 2013.

This tells us that while mutual funds have increased in popularity with the American public, it is important to remember that there are risks involved in holding mutual funds. Individual investors need to keep in mind that mutual funds are not the same as federally insured deposits they may have at a depository institution.

Table 23-1 Mutual Fund Total Net Assets

Year	Mutual Funds at Year End ($billion)
1995	2,811
1996	3,526
1997	4,468
1998	5,526
1999	6,846
2000	6,965
2005	8,905
2006	10,397
2007	12,000
2008	9,603
2009	11,113
2010	11,831
2011	11,626
2012	13,044
2013	15,018
2014	15,852

Source: Investment Company Institute, *Investment Company Fact Book*, various years

23-1b Mutual Fund Regulation

To help ensure that Americans fully understand the risks involved with mutual fund investment, the industry faces a myriad of regulation. At the national level, investment companies and the mutual funds they offer are regulated by the Securities and Exchange Commission (SEC), which is responsible for regulating the structure and operations of mutual funds, including how they advertise and how they inform investors. State governments can prosecute investment companies for fraud and deceptive sales practices.

The regulations require mutual funds to provide potential investors with a **prospectus**. A prospectus is a legal document that discloses how the funds will be invested, the past performance of the fund, the risks involved, fees that will be charged to the investor, and who the fund managers are and their backgrounds.

Prospectus: A legal document containing information about the issuer of stocks and bonds. This is required by the Securities and Exchange Commission from corporations and governments that want to sell their stocks and bonds to the public. A prospectus must include information that is designed to ensure investors have the information they need to make an informed investment decision.

In terms of taxes, if a mutual fund distributes to its shareholders at least 90% of all of the taxable income it generates, then the mutual fund is exempt from income and capital gains taxes. The mutual fund's shareholders, however, *are* subject to paying income and capital gains taxes each year.

23-1c Open-End Mutual Funds

Many of the most popular mutual funds are **open-end mutual funds**. This means that the investment company can sell shares to investors at any time. The investment company can also buy back shares or allow investors to redeem their shares at any time.

Open-end mutual fund: A fund operated by an investment company that does not limit the amount of shares the fund will issue.

The price per share of an open-end mutual fund is the net value of the total assets held by the fund, divided by the number of shares outstanding. Here, *net* refers to the current market value of the assets held minus expenses incurred plus interest and dividends received.

For example, suppose a mutual fund holds the stocks of three corporations. It has different amounts of each of these stocks, and each stock has a different price. Further, assume the fund has incurred expenses in running the fund and that the stocks that it holds have generated some dividend income. Then the net asset value, or NAV, can be calculated as shown in Table 23-2.

In this case the mutual funds would be ready to buy or sell shares in the fund at a price of $7.94 per share. The NAV is calculated daily. When a mutual fund sells shares, it issues new shares at the NAV and uses those funds to buy more securities. When a shareholder in a mutual fund redeems their shares, the mutual fund can sell some of its securities to raise the cash that it needs to pay the shareholder. As a result, the number of outstanding shares decreases.

Because some shareholders might want to redeem their shares each day, mutual funds generally hold a portion of their portfolio in cash. Traditionally, mutual funds hold from 4% to 6% of their total assets in very liquid assets such as bank certificates of deposit. Some analysts suggest that the amount of cash held by open-end mutual funds is a fairly accurate predictor of future market movement.

Based on this way of thinking, if mutual funds are holding large amounts of cash, they will be buying securities in the future, and thus the stock market will advance in the near future. On the other hand, if mutual funds are holding very little cash, mutual fund managers may have to sell stocks in the future to meet the redemptions of investors, and thus stock prices will fall in the future.

Mutual funds do not need to hold only stocks and cash as they do in our simple example. Next we review the wide variety of mutual funds that exist, including the different types of assets in which they invest.

Table 23-2 Net Asset Value (NVA) Example

Stock	Shares (n)	Share Price	Value
Corporation A	100	$10	$1,000
Corporation B	50	$12	$ 600
Corporation C	80	$5	$ 400
Total stock portfolio value			$2,000
Less Management Expenses of Fund			($ 20)
Plus Interest & Dividends			$ 5
Total Market Value of Fund			$1,985
Divided by 250 outstanding shares given and NAV = $7.94			

SECTION REVIEW

Q1) If the total market value of an open-end mutual fund is $2,500 and there are 100 shares outstanding at the end of trading on Monday, what would the NAV of the fund be? What would the NAV of the fund be on Tuesday if the total market value of the mutual fund is $2,550 and there are now 110 shares outstanding?

Q2) Bob is confused about how the pricing of the open-end mutual fund he owns is actually calculated. Bob sees that stock prices have increased, yet the market value of his mutual fund, as determined by the NAV, has declined. Bob thinks that this should not happen. How would you explain this to Bob?

Q3) You read a story in the *Financial Times* reporting that mutual funds that invest primarily in equities are currently holding a high level of cash. Based on this, where do many analysts think stock prices are headed and why?

a. Stock prices are expected to increase as mutual fund managers use cash to buy stocks.

b. Stock prices are expected to decrease because mutual fund managers are holding cash instead of buying stocks.

c. Stock prices are expected to increase as mutual fund managers use cash to buy more bonds.

d. Stock prices are expected to decrease because mutual fund managers are holding cash instead of buying bonds.

23-2 Types of Mutual Funds

Mutual funds can be classified into general groups based on the types of financial securities the fund holds: equity funds, bond funds, hybrid funds, and money market funds. As of the end of 2014, the breakdown of the total net assets of the US mutual fund industry was:

Equity Funds	Bond Funds	Hybrid Funds	Money Market Funds
52%	22%	9%	17%

As we can see, equity funds accounted for the largest portion, composing over one half of the mutual fund industry based on net asset size. Let's take a look at each of these different types of mutual funds.

23-2a Equity Funds

Equity mutual funds are generally best suited for investors who have a long-term investment horizon (generally 10 years or more). While stocks tend to outperform bonds in the long run, equity prices can be volatile, and thus equity funds can suffer significant losses in the short run. There are a wide variety of equity mutual funds. Here is just a sample.

Growth Funds

The main objective of these funds is capital appreciation. The fund manager looks for stocks that have above-average growth potential. This usually includes stocks with high P-to-E ratios, which infers that investors expect strong earnings growth in the future.

Aggressive Growth Funds

These are considered speculative funds. The fund manager looks for small firms with very high and rapid growth potential. These smaller and (it is hoped) rapidly growing firms have shares with very high P-to-E ratios and, in general, high price volatility.

Growth and Income Funds

Fund managers in these equity mutual funds seek a balance between capital gains and dividend payments. This most often includes the stocks of well-established firms with consistent dividend payments but also potential for growth.

Income Funds

As the name suggests, the main objective of these mutual funds is to provide a steady source of income to fund investors through regular and consistent dividend payments. Fund managers look for equities yielding high dividends—most often stocks of older companies with slow or no growth.

International or Global Equity Funds

The home bias in investor's portfolios was first described by French and Poterba[1] in 1991 and documented by Tesar and Werner[2] in 1995. That is, despite gains from international diversification, investors generally tend to have portfolios that are overly weighted toward assets from

1 See Kenneth R. French and James M. Poterba, "Investor Diversification and Internal Equity Markets." *American Economic Review* 81 (1991): 222–6.

2 See Linda Tesar and Ingrid Werner, "Home Bias and High Turnover." *Journal of International Money and Finance* 14, no. 4 (1995): 467–92.

their home country. One way to easily correct for this is to use international and global equity mutual funds. With a global fund, the fund manager invests in equities around the world, whereas international funds tend tc invest in equities outside of the United States.

Index Funds

These funds are designed to match the return to a stock market index such as the S&P 500 or the Wilshire 5000. These funds are "passively" managed; that is, the fund manager purchases the stocks that make up the index and does not actively buy and sell shares to outperform the index. The popularity of index funds among investors has grown significantly in recent years because of their low fees and ease of diversification.

23-2b Bond Funds

Bond mutual funds are best suited for investors who want to protect the market value of their savings and those who are interested in dividend income. Thus, bond mutual funds apply to risk-averse savers as well as those near or close to retirement age.

Corporate or Investment-Grade Bond Funds

Fund managers seek out bonds with very low default risk, relatively high levels of liquidity, and stable prices. These funds often are made up of bonds and other debt instruments issued by well-established corporations.

Treasury Bond Funds

As the name suggests, these funds are made of debt instruments issued by the US Treasury. The interest earned on these bonds—and thus by these mutual funds—are not subject to state and local income taxes. Since Treasury debt is viewed as free of default risk, these mutual funds are considered a very "safe" investment vehicle.

High-Yield or "Junk" Bond Funds

Bonds that are below investment grade in terms of default risk tend to have much higher interest rates than their investment-grade counterparts. Thus high-yield or junk bond funds often pay a higher rate of return than other bond funds, but they also have a much higher level of default risk.

International and Global Bond Funds

As with their equity fund counterparts, these bond funds hold bonds issued by corporations and governments outside of the United States (international funds) or from around the world, including the United States (global funds). In the aftermath of the global financial crisis that started in 2008, the global bond market experienced one sovereign debt crisis after another as country governments had problems meeting their debt obligations. As a result, many international and global bond funds performed very poorly during this period.

Mortgage Bond Funds

Home mortgages in the United States have traditionally been considered to be a safe asset in which to invest, with a default rate of only about 2% a year. Mortgage bond funds purchase and hold home mortgages and/or mortgage-backed securities.

"Muni" or Municipal Bond Funds

Bonds issued by local governments or local authorities (e.g., school districts, water districts, transportation authorities) are called municipal or "muni" bonds. To keep borrowing costs low for these local authorities, the interest the bonds generate is generally exempt from federal income taxes. Thus, muni bond funds are well suited for savers in high tax brackets who are looking for federal income tax–free interest income.

Multisector Bond Funds

As the name suggests, in these funds the fund manager is allowed to purchase a wide variety of different types of bonds and debt instruments.

23-2c Hybrid Funds

Investment companies have recently begun to offer mutual funds that invest in different combinations of equities and debt, both foreign and domestic, both short-term and long-term, and both public and private. The proportionality of the fund can remain fixed over time or can change over time to meet the needs of the saver. In an "actively managed" fund the fund manager changes the asset allocation in response to changing market conditions. In a "passively managed" fund the asset allocation changes over the lifetime of the saver.

- **Target date funds.** In these funds asset allocation is very aggressive when the target date is far away and grows more conservative as the date draws near.
- **Target market allocation funds.** Managers of these funds continuously change the asset mix of the portfolio to ensure a constant allocation between stocks and bonds, foreign and domestic instruments, and so on.
- **Real return funds.** The goal of these funds is to ensure a real rate of return that is stable. That is, they seek a return that is protected from inflation as well as changes in the value of the dollar versus other currencies.
- **World allocation funds.** In these funds the fund manager changes the asset mix of the portfolio to ensure a constant asset value ratio between different regions of the world.

While hybrid funds attempt to achieve a certain type of return, the fact that they are "actively managed" means that there are many expenses associated with these types of accounts. For example, managers need to be compensated for their time used in constantly monitoring the fund. In addition, by constantly buying and selling shares that make up the fund, there are trading expenses that must be paid. As we examine in the next section, these fees can negatively affect the return on these actively managed hybrid funds.

23-2d Money Market Mutual Funds

As was discussed in Chapter 15, money market mutual funds invest in short-term debt securities such as Treasury Bills, commercial paper, and negotiable certificates of deposits—all of which have very low default risk. Because of this asset mix, money market funds are very liquid accounts that often offer investors the ability to write checks to access their funds at any time.

Thus, money market mutual funds are a useful investment vehicle for short-term savings. Investors may wish to have interest or dividend payments earned in other mutual funds transferred to their money market fund for easy access. Or, savers may "park" some of their funds in a money market account until they are ready to purchase some other financial asset such as a bond or equity mutual fund.

While commercial banks, thrifts, and credit unions offer their own version of money market accounts, it is important to remember that these depository institutions often offer deposit insurance, whereas money market mutual funds do not. Thus, with money market mutual funds, it is possible for investors to lose a portion of their savings. This happened in 2008 when several money market mutual funds "broke the buck" and could not fully redeem the shares investors had bought.

SECTION REVIEW

Q1) Trudy, who lives in New York, is concerned that her investment portfolio suffers from the "home country bias." Explain what Trudy is worried about and how might she use mutual funds to address her concern.

Q2) Bob lives in Texas, is 64 years old, and is close to retirement. What type of mutual funds might be best for Bob? Why?

Q3) Grace is disappointed with the relatively low rate of return she is earning on her government bond mutual fund. She sees another bond fund that invests in corporate securities offered by firms that are in financial distress and/or do not have much experience in offering bonds to the general public. She notices the return on these bond mutual funds are much higher than what she is currently invested in. Grace has just discovered what type of mutual bond fund?

a. Alternative bond funds
b. High-yield or junk bond funds
c. Municipal bond funds
d. Initial bond funds

23-3 Mutual Fund Fees

As we have learned, there is a wide variety of mutual funds, each suited to different types of savers or investors. Therefore, investors should carefully research mutual funds before investing so that they put their savings into a fund that is best suited to their needs. Investors should also understand the different fees and characteristics of the mutual funds so that, once again, they put their savings only into funds that suit their purposes.

23-3a Types of Mutual Fund Fees & Controversies

One of the most controversial issues with mutual funds is the fees they charge. Here we describe some of the fees involved with mutual funds.

Loads

Mutual fund loads are basically sales charges. They are commissions paid to brokers or financial advisors who "sell" the funds to their clients. A **front-end load** is a fee charged to the investor when they purchase the mutual fund shares. These front-end loads can be as high as 8.5%, meaning an investor who has $10,000 to invest will purchase only $915 worth of shares; the other $85 goes to the broker or financial advisor.

Front-end load: A sales charge for purchasing mutual fund shares that is charged to the investor when they make a purchase.

Back-end loads—which sometimes are also called "contingent deferred sales charges," "redemption fees," or "rear load fees"—are sales charges imposed when an investor redeems their shares. These fees are subtracted from the net asset value of shares when the investor redeems the shares. Thus, an investor may think she is redeeming mutual fund shares worth $10,000, but after the 5% back-end load is subtracted she receives only $9,500.

Back-end load: A sales charge incurred when an investor sells mutual fund shares back to an investment company.

As with the front-end load, the back-end load is most often paid to the broker or financial advisor who initially sold the fund. Depending on the mutual fund, back-end loads may decline over time. That is, the back-end fee may be 5% if the shares are redeemed within the first two years of it being purchased, but then it declines by one percentage point a year until no back-end load is charged if the shares are redeemed during or after the seventh year.

While no-load funds do not explicitly charge a sales load, that does not mean the broker or financial advisor does not earn a sales commission for selling the mutual fund shares. Instead, the sales commission is paid through a 12b-1 fee.

Annual Fees

The name *12b-1 fee* refers to the SEC statute that allows these annual fees to be charged. Rule 12b-1 allows mutual funds to charge a fee to pay more "marketing and distribution expenses," including commissions to sales people (Figure 23-1). The rules allow no-load mutual funds to call themselves "no-load" so long as the 12b-1 fees plus other fees charged to shareholders are no more than 0.25% of the fund's net asset value.

The 12b-1 fees are not the largest annual fees that mutual fund shareholders typically pay. Instead, the most expensive annual fees paid by shareholders are the **annual management fee or advisory fees**. These fees are paid to the investment company that manages the mutual fund's portfolio.

Mutual fund annual management fee or advisory fee: The annual fee investment companies charge mutual fund investors for managing the mutual fund.

Figure 23-1 Use (Percentages) of 12b-1 Fees

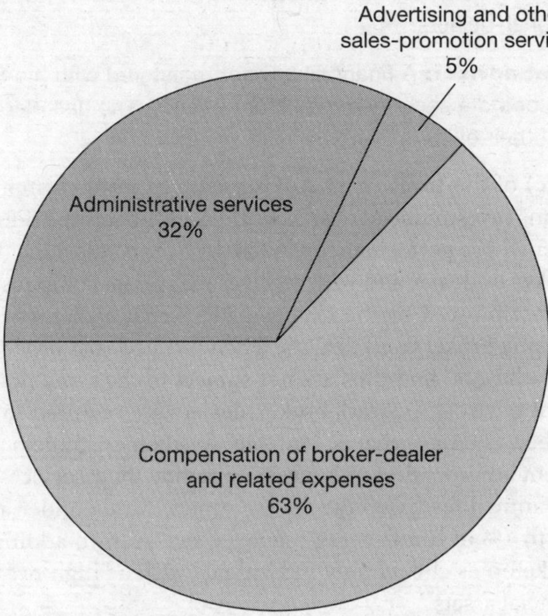

Source: Investment Company Institute, "Background Information About 12b-1 Fees." http://www.ici.org/policy/regulation/fees/ref_12b1_fees

While the amount of mutual fund fees may seem small, the average fee is about 1.3%; some companies charge 2%, whereas others charge as much as 5%. Jack Bogle, the former head of Vanguard mutual funds, has been critical of mutual fund management fees. He points out that if you earn 7% a year on a mutual fund but are charged a 2% fee, over 50 years you will lose over 63% of your gains![3]

Fee Controversies

When financial markets were booming, many mutual fund investors basically ignored the fees they were being charged. But when the global financial crisis hit and many people lost money in their mutual funds, more attention was drawn to the fees mutual funds charged.

For over 40 years, Bogle, founder and retired CEO of The Vanguard Group, one of the largest investment companies, has been an outspoken critic of many of the fees the mutual fund industry charges. Bogle has argued that individual investors could avoid a great deal of mutual fund fees by owning index funds. Since these funds are not "actively managed," the fees on them are much lower. Industry insiders argue that actively managed funds, with their significantly higher fees, do have a role to play in a saver's portfolio. The data, however, show that actively managed mutual funds do not outperform the overall market performance. This holds true over different time periods and under different market conditions.

Many critics of the industry argue that mutual funds are mostly about advertising. They contend that much of the industry is based on seeking to convince uninformed and confused savers to buy shares in mutual funds using slick advertising campaigns. These critics often believe that those selling mutual funds are more interested in making a commission than helping the savers find a sound place to invest.

3 See the PBS Frontline documentary "The Retirement Gamble." http://www.pbs.org/wgbh/pages/frontline/retirement-gamble/.

A **registered investment advisor** is legally obligated with a fiduciary responsibility to their clients. Basically, a fiduciary is someone who pledges to put the investors' interests ahead of their own. However, most brokers and financial advisors are not fiduciary representatives; they are considered broker-dealers.

Registered investment advisor: A financial advisor registered with the Securities and Exchange Commission or state securities regulatory agency who has pledged to put their clients' interests ahead of their own.

Section 202(a)(11)(c) of the Investment Advisers Act of 1940 exempts brokers or dealers from the definition of an "investment adviser" and thus eliminates the fiduciary responsibility[4] for "any broker or dealer whose performance of such services is solely incidental to the conduct of his business as a broker or dealer and who receives no special compensation therefor."

This distinction was reinforced by the US Securities Self-Regulatory Organization, which has authority in overseeing brokers and dealers, when it stated that broker-dealers are "not to be deemed investment advisors" and thus are not subject to the same fiduciary responsibility as registered investment advisors. Instead, broker-dealers are required to meet a much lower threshold, often described as doing what is "suitable" for their customers.

Registered investment advisors do not, however, provide their services free. They typically charge their clients an annual fee based on the amount of funds under advisement. This fee can range from 0.25% to 1% of funds being managed per year. In addition, many registered investment advisors take on as clients only individuals with a "high net worth"—those with over $1 million in financial assets.

Thus, for many investors who do not have a high net worth, finding a registered investment advisor who will take them on as a client can be difficult. These smaller savers are essentially left to their own means to determine where and when to invest their funds and what fees they will have to pay.

Mutual funds are not the only way to pool savers together. Next we look at other investment vehicles that pool savers together and the controversies that surround these different financial tools.

SECTION REVIEW

Q1) Jason is thinking about purchasing some mutual fund shares, but he is confused by the terminology. How would you explain to Jason the difference between a mutual fund with loads and a no-load mutual fund?

Q2) Adrienne is a registered financial advisor. What role do mutual funds and mutual fund fees play in Adrienne's career?

Q3) Doug sees that his mutual fund is charging him a 12b-1 fee. He has no idea what this is. Which of the following would correctly summarize for Doug what he is being charged?

a. A fee to purchase his mutual fund shares
b. A tax levied on mutual funds by the US federal government
c. An annual fee charged by the investment company to manage the mutual fund
d. A fee charged by a registered financial advisor to audit his mutual fund

4 The SEC attempted to further clarify the issue in 2005. See "Certain Broker-Dealers Deemed Not To Be Investment Advisors," https://www.sec.gov/rules/final/34-51523.pdf.

Other Types of Funds

23-4

Over the past several years, other ways of pooling savers together have become popular. Some of these are a variation of open-end mutual funds, whereas others—such as hedge funds and real estate investment trusts—are classified as "alternative assets" because they carry much more risk than traditional mutual funds.

23-4a Close-Ended Funds

Close-ended funds, sometimes called closed-ended funds, are mutual funds that usually only issue shares once when the fund is first created and sold through an initial public offering.[5] After that the fund is closed, with no new shares ever issued and no redemptions allowed. (See! The name "close-ended fund" actually makes sense.). Notice that close-ended funds differ from open-ended funds in that in close-ended funds the funds do *not* redeem shares, nor do they issue new shares. That is, the number of shares outstanding is always the same. The NAV of the fund can and does change as the assets in the fund's portfolio change in value. To purchase the shares of a close-ended fund, however, you have to find someone who is willing to sell their shares. Similarly, if you own shares in a close-ended fund and you want to get out of your investment, you have to find someone else to buy your shares, either on an exchange or via the over-the-counter market.

Close-Ended Pricing

Another interesting component of close-ended funds is the pricing of shares. You might think that the pricing of close-ended funds should be like open-ended funds, that is, based on the net asset value. It turns out that close-ended funds often sell at a price above their NAV—at a premium—or sometimes at a price below their NAV, or at a discount.

Some analysts argue that close-ended funds may sell at a premium because the fund holds stocks of corporations in countries that have investment restrictions. For example, in some countries investment funds are allowed to invest in equities, but individuals are not. So, the only way individuals who want to invest in that country can do so is through funds. Another reason why a close-ended fund may sell at a premium is because investors believe the fund manager has superior talent for picking assets and the fund will experience very high returns in the future.

On the other hand, close-ended funds may sell at a discount because investors do not hold the fund manager in very high regard and worry this poor-quality manager cannot be replaced easily. Another reason why close-ended funds may trade at a discount is because they are allowed to use a lot more debt than open-ended funds can, and thus they may be viewed as having more risk than open-ended funds.

It is unclear exactly why close-ended funds even exist. Do these restricted funds allow investment opportunities that are not available through open-ended funds? Are these close-ended funds poorly run and more risky than open-ended funds? Whatever the reason, close-ended funds remain with us. In 2013 close-ended funds had total net assets of $279 billion. While that number pales in comparison to the $15 trillion in open-ended mutual funds, the market for close-ended funds remains significant.

5 Close-ended funds can sometimes have additional issuance of common shares through secondary or follow-on offerings, dividend reinvestment, or at-the-market offerings. Close-ended funds are also allowed to issue preferred shares. These preferred shares are paid dividends, but unlike common shares they do not share in gains and losses of the fund.

23-4b Exchange-Traded Funds

Exchange-traded funds, or ETFs, have grown in popularity with both institutional and individual investors over the past decade: According to the Investment Company Institute, from 2003 to 2013 more than $1.2 trillion of net new ETF shares were issued. An ETF is basically an investment company that issues shares that are traded daily on stock exchanges at a market-determined price. Investors buy and sell ETF shares through a broker, just like they would any other equity shares. Most ETFs in the United States are structured similar to an open-ended mutual fund,[6] but other structures do exist, including ETFs investing in commodities, currencies, and futures contracts.

Exchange-traded fund: An investment fund that is traded on a stock exchange throughout the trading day and holds securities that trade at a price close to their net asset value.

The first ETFs introduced in 1993 were designed to track the S&P 500 index. ETFs that track an index come in two different forms: replicate index-based and sample-based. A replicate index-based ETF holds the securities that make up the index, whereas a sample-based ETF does not hold every security in the index; instead, the fund manager chooses securities that are a representative sample of the index. The sample-based ETF structure often is used when the index to be tracked comprises a huge number of securities, such as the Wilshire 5000.

In 2008 the Securities and Exchange Commission allowed several funds to offer fully transparent, actively managed ETFs. The SEC requires these ETFs to state each business day on the ETF's public website which assets and how much of each the ETF is holding. These actively managed ETFs do not seek to track a particular index; rather, they are actively managed like a mutual fund, with a stated investment objective.

Structure and Pricing of ETFs

ETFs most often do not sell at much of a discount or premium relative to their NAV. This is because of the way ETFs are structured. An ETF is created by a sponsor—an investment company or financial institution that determines the investment objective and structure of the ETF. The ETF is required by the SEC to publish daily information about the ETF's portfolio holdings. This "creation basket" lists the names and quantities of the securities and assets the ETF holds. The assets that make up the creation basket are held by an "authorized participant," usually a large institutional investor. The authorized participant can exchange the ETF shares for the assets that make up the creation basket, or it can exchange the assets in the basket for ETF shares.

This allows the authorized participant to keep the ETF share price very close to the fund's NAV. If the ETF is selling a discount (a price below the NAV of the underlying assets), the authorized participant buys shares of the ETF and sells the underlying assets, thus driving the ETF share price upward. On the other hand, if the ETF is selling at a premium (a price above the NAV of the underlying assets), the authorized participant sells the shares of the ETF and buys the underlying assets, thus pushing the ETF share price downward.

Popularity of ETFs

Some of the more popular ETFs include Spiders, or SPDRs, which stands for Standard & Poor's depository receipts. Spiders track the S&P 500 index, so investors who believe the overall direction of the equity market is upward may be interested in purchasing a Spider. PowerShares QQQ or Cubes also are very popular. These ETFs track the technology-heavy NASDAQ-100 index.

All of these ETFs have grown in popularity largely because of their low expense ratio. Often, ETFs have expense ratios of less than one-tenth of 1%. This is a much lower expense ratio than a typical mutual fund has. EFTs are also popular because, unlike mutual funds, ETFs can be

6 Keep in mind that mutual funds, however, are not traded on exchanges.

purchased any time during the day. Mutual funds, on the other hand, can be redeemed or issued only at the end of the trading day. Finally, ETFs are popular because they can be sold short. Thus, if an investor believes the price of natural gas is going to fall in the future, she should sell short the US Natural Gas Fund issued by the US Commodity Fund's ETF. If she is correct, when the price of natural gas falls, so will the US Natural Gas Fund shares, which allows her to profit when she buys back at a lower price the shares she borrowed.

23-4c Hedge Funds

Hedge funds are a type of mutual fund in that they pool the money of savers together. Unlike mutual funds, though, investors in hedge funds are not small investors; rather, they must be individuals with a high net worth because hedge funds are categorized as "alternative assets." Only those with a high net worth (and institutional investors) are allowed to invest in alternative assets because of the high level of risk in this asset class.

Thus most hedge funds tend to have a minimum investment between $1 million and $20 million. Many hedge funds are not investment companies but limited partnerships, so investors in hedge funds are not buying shares of a fund but are instead investing funds with the partnership.

SEC regulations stipulate that a hedge fund can have no more than 99 investors if the investors have a minimum annual income of $200,000 over the past two years and expect it to be at least that level in the current year *or* have a net worth of at least $1 million, either alone or with a spouse, excluding the value of the person's main residence. A hedge fund can have up to 499 investors if the investors have a net worth of at least $5 million or institutions with a net worth of at least $25 million.

Hedge funds tend to seek to remove market risk, or be market-neutral and instead place bets on relative performance. For example, a hedge fund manager bets on the relative performance of two stocks or two bonds by buying one and selling short the other. The hedge fund manager would buy or go long on the asset that had a low price or is expected to have a high return and would sell short the asset that had a high price or she believed would have a lower return. By doing so she would not care what happened to the actual market price of each stock or bond, only their relative returns. In this way a hedge fund reduces market risk and takes on more firm-specific risk in terms of relative performance.[7]

If hedge funds are correct and their bets pay off, they share their gains with their investors in a 20/80 split. That is, 20% of the profits go to the hedge funds and 80% of the profits are paid to the investors. In addition, hedge funds generally charge a 2% management fee each year. Thus, in addition to the money they invest in the fund, investors have to pay an additional 2% to the mutual fund as a management fee.

A hedge fund investment is *not* a short-term or liquid investment. Hedge funds often require investors to commit their funds for several years. Even after that time period has passed hedge funds often require investors to give 30 or 60 days' notice before they are allowed access to their funds.

In addition to investing the funds of their investors, hedge funds also use a great deal of debt or leverage. Imagine a hedge fund sees an opportunity where it can enter into a transaction for $100 and it will earn $102, which would be a 2% return. Now imagine the hedge fund can do that same transaction 20 more times. If the hedge fund borrows $2,000 and gets a return of $2,040, now it has made a profit of $42 on its $100. Ignoring borrowing and trading costs, that is a return of 42%! So, the use of leverage can greatly increase the returns hedge funds earn.

---

7 There are many different hedge fund strategies. The long/short strategy explained above is only one example. See Lee Jackson, "Ten Strategies Hedge Funds Use to make Huge Returns, and You Can Too." Yahoo! Finance, September 9, 2013. http://finance.yahoo.com/news/ten-strategies-hedge-funds-huge-123021171.html.

In the past hedge funds benefited from having little government regulation. But after the collapse of the Long Term Capital Management hedge fund in 1998 threatened the stability of the entire financial system, hedge funds came under more scrutiny. In 2008 hedge funds were accused of making the financial crisis worse by shorting the stock of many financial institutions involved in the subprime mortgage market. The SEC imposed temporary restrictions on short-selling. As a result, the Dodd-Frank Act of 2010 requires hedge funds that manage more than $100 million to register with the SEC as investment advisors. The act also limits commercial banks from investing no more than 3% of their capital in hedge funds or other alternative assets.

23-4d Real Estate Investment Trusts

A real estate investment trust (REIT) is similar to a close-ended fund that invests in real estate and/or mortgages. REITs may buy and manage income-generating real estate, such as apartment buildings, office buildings, and warehouses (equity REIT), as well as mortgages and other types of real-estate financing (mortgage REIT). REITs can be sold on stock exchanges, usually with low minimum purchase amounts. They generate returns to investors through the management of properties, mortgage revenues, and capital gains by selling properties that have increased in price.

REITs are exempt from federal income taxes as long as they derive 75% of their income from operations related to real estate and they pass through at least 90% of their net income to shareholders. REITs tend to be highly liquid assets and allow investors to diversify their portfolio into real estate without actually buying, managing, and selling any real estate.

The return on REITs is greatly affected by changes in interest rates and local real estate prices. As interest rates increase, the demand for real estate generally is reduced, and REIT returns can suffer. During the 2008–2009 financial crisis, real estate prices in general decreased dramatically, and REITs suffered significant losses, especially those that were heavily invested in subprime mortgages.

SECTION REVIEW

Q1) Explain why ETFs seldom trade at a premium or discount relative to their NAV.

Q2) Explain how close-ended mutual funds are, at the same time, in some ways very similar to but in other ways very different from open-ended mutual funds.

Q3) Which of the following are characteristics that make hedge funds different from open-ended mutual funds?

a. Investors in hedge funds are limited to individuals with a high net worth and institutional investors.

b. Hedge funds most often are limited partnerships as opposed to investment companies.

c. Hedge funds are very illiquid investments, whereas open-ended mutual funds are relatively liquid.

d. All of the above.

Conclusion

23-5

Over the past several decades, investors have been drawn to financial instruments that allow savers to pool their funds together. This has occurred in part because investors can easily and inexpensively diversify their savings. Thus, we have seen the rise of mutual funds that allow savers this much-desired asset diversification. But, as we learned, the mutual fund industry is anything but simple. There are a wide variety of mutual funds with a wide variety of investment strategies and fees. This industry is not without its controversies, especially when it comes to fees.

But mutual funds are not the only way savers are being brought together. We also examined exchange-traded funds, hedge funds, and real estate investment trusts. While these are currently offered only to individuals with a high net worth and to institutional investors, they have grown rapidly in recent years. These different ways of pooling savers together have resulted in increased competition for depository institutions, but they also have opened investors, and our entire financial system, to a new set of risks.

IN THE NEWS. . .

Influence of Money Market Funds Ended Overhaul

James B. Stewart
The New York Times
September 7, 2012

Four years after the fall of Lehman Brothers, and with a presidential campaign in full swing, everyone can surely agree on one thing: we shouldn't risk another financial crisis.

But after four years of studies, hearings and round tables, the Securities and Exchange Commission late last month abandoned efforts to impose new regulations on money market funds intended to prevent another panic like the one that occurred in 2008 and eliminate the need for a taxpayer bailout of the multitrillion-dollar funds.

The S.E.C.'s proposed changes had the backing of the White House, Treasury officials, the Federal Reserve, the Bank of England, a council of academic experts, The Wall Street Journal's conservative editorial page, the former Fed Chairman Paul Volcker, the former Treasury Secretary Henry J. Paulson, Jr. — just about every disinterested party who weighed in on the issue. . . .

So what accounts for the collapse?

Though Republicans in Congress have generally sided with the mutual fund industry, and the reforms emerged from a Democratic administration, several people I spoke to said it was a mistake to view the outcome through a prism of partisan politics. "It's not Republicans versus Democrats," a person involved in formulating the proposals told me. "It's the mutual fund industry and its allies versus the American taxpayer."

For many in the mutual fund industry, 2008 seems both a distant memory and the equivalent of a 100-year flood, something unlikely to be repeated. But just four years ago, on Sept. 16, 2008, shortly after Lehman Brothers collapsed, the Reserve Fund, the nation's oldest money market fund, "broke the buck" and set off a run on the global money [mutual] fund industry. . . .

To prevent this, the S.E.C. proposed two major reforms. The first was to report money market fund values the way every other fund does, which is the actual net asset value or N.A.V., not something rounded to $1. The idea is that investors would become accustomed to and comfortable with slight changes in values. The net asset values of many short-term bond funds fluctuate modestly, and there aren't any panics or runs just because their value declines a penny or two.

The second was to require fund sponsors, if they wanted to maintain the stable $1 value, to start holding cash reserves.

The mutual fund industry rallied against the proposals and lobbied fiercely to defeat them. The industry's self-interest is obvious: the proposals impose costs and additional regulations. More fundamentally, why wouldn't the industry and money market fund customers love the status quo? They get all the benefits of an implied government guarantee while taxpayers assume all the risk. . . .

But is it only naked self-interest that explains the industry's opposition? I spoke with John S. Woerth, a spokesman for Vanguard, which is the largest mutual fund company. . . .

"We believe the proposals, if implemented, would end money market funds," Mr. Woerth told me. "Out clients want a stable N.A.V. They write checks, pay their bills from these accounts. Would every one of these now be a taxable transaction based on gains and losses? That's untenable." As for the capital requirement, "It would be onerous and raise costs, which would have to be passed onto our clients." He noted that Vanguard's Prim money market fund this week was yielding just 0.04 percent and additional costs would bring it close to zero. . . .

In 2008, when the money market mutual fund industry was about to collapse, the US Treasury and Federal Reserve stated that money market funds would be backed by the full faith and credit of the US government. That stopped the run on the money market funds. It also made US taxpayers liable for over $3 trillion—the size of the total assets in money market mutual funds.

Would the SEC regulations destroy the money market mutual fund industry or would they make it more stable? Should money market funds report their actual NAV each day and adjust balances accordingly? Are there any other types of reforms the SEC could or should have put in place for this very important industry?

24

Investment Banks and Private Equity

24-1 Investment Banks and Private Equity Overview

Matt Taibbi, writing in *Rolling Stone* magazine, famously described the investment bank Goldman Sachs as a "great vampire squid wrapped around the face of humanity, relentlessly jamming its blood funnel into anything that smells like money."[1] Conservative pundits have described Goldman Sachs as "the world's most evil corporation,"[2] whereas those of a more liberal mind-set explain that ". . . unethical is their [Goldman Sachs's] business model."[3] How did this institution, along with so many Wall Street investment banks, become so hated?

The private equity industry also has received scathing criticism. When former private equity executive Bruce Rauner ran for governor of Illinois and when Mitt Romney ran for president, the private equity industry was described as "vulture capitalism" and the people who run it as "corporate raiders who destroy jobs." How did these limited partnerships come to draw such scorn?

24-1a Investment Banks

Investment banking isn't really banking. Investment banks do not take deposits and they seldom, if ever, lend funds. Instead, investment banks primarily assist corporations and governments in selling their financial instruments. In addition, investment banks buy and sell securities for their clients as well as on their own behalf. They also offer financial advice to their clients, both corporations and government entities.

Investment banks in the United States began in the 1800s as an offshoot of commercial banks. As the US economy was going through industrialization, many growing firms found that they could not raise enough funds through American banks. They needed investors who would buy their stocks and bonds, and these investors often were outside of the United States. For example, J. S. Morgan & Company, founded by Junius Spencer Morgan, J. Pierpont Morgan's father, which today we would call an investment bank, had offices in both London and New York. Much of the funding for the building of railroads in the United States came from European sources.

For many years investment banks were small, private partnerships. The partners put their own money into the firm and closely watched over the funds. Investment banks were seen as very conservative entities and played the role of financial market gatekeepers: They would "allow" only safe and stable companies to offer their financial instruments for sale in the market.

This structure lasted until the mid-1980s. With significant reductions in the level of government regulation of financial markets, the size and power of investment banks grew rapidly. Many investment banks switched from a partnership structure to become publically held companies, allowing them to raise more funds, hire more staff, and expand their scope and scale of operations. With another wave of deregulation in the 1990s, investment banks saw their size and power increase again. With mergers in the industry, the largest

1 Matt Taibbi, "The Great American Bubble Machine." *Rolling Stone*, April 5, 2010. http://www.rollingstone.com/politics/news/the-great-american-bubble-machine-20100405/.

2 David Hodges, "The World's Most Evil Corporation Issues a Dire Warning." The Common Sense Show, September 19, 2013. http://www.thecommonsenseshow.com/2013/09/19/the-worlds-most-evil-corporation-issues-a-dire-warning/.

3 gjohnsit, "The Latest Evil from Goldman Sachs." Daily KOS, November 21, 2014. http://www.dailykos.com/story/2014/11/21/1346544/-The-latest-evil-from-Goldman-Sachs/.

investment banks became so important to the functioning of the entire financial system they were labeled as "too big to fail," meaning they were too big to be allowed to fail, as described in Chapter 14. At the height of the financial crisis in September 2008, the largest investment banks converted into bank holding companies. Thus, if these mammoth investment banks ever ran into financial trouble, they could turn to the US taxpayers and demand to be bailed out.

24-1b What Investment Banks Do

So what do investment banks do that make them so important to the function of the entire US and global economies?

Bring New Securities to the Market

When a government or a corporation wants to issue stocks or bonds, it cannot do so by itself. Instead, it needs someone with expertise and experience in marketing, selling, and distributing financial securities. This is a service investment banks provide.

The issuance of new securities is called a **primary offering**. If a company has never offered shares for sale to the public, it is called an **initial public offering**, or an IPO. If the firm has already offered similar securities for sale, then the primary offering is called a **seasoned offering**. The new securities can be sold to anyone who is interested in buying them in a public offering, or all of the new securities can be sold to just one buyer or a small number of buyers in a **private placement**.[4]

Primary offering: The initial sale of a stock or bond by a corporation or a government or government agency.

Initial public offering: Often referred to as an IPO, the first time a corporation offers its shares for sale to the public.

Seasoned offering: The sale of stocks or bonds by a corporation, government, or government agency who has issued similar stocks or bonds in the past.

Private placement: The sale of newly issued stocks or bonds that are not offered for sale to the general public. Most often the new stocks or bonds are sold to a single buyer or a limited number of buyers.

Public offerings—regardless of whether they are an IPO or a seasoned offering—must be registered with the Securities and Exchange Commission. This can be a complicated and complex process requiring a team of lawyers, accountants, and analysts. Part of the registration process is to complete a **prospectus**. The *primary prospectus* is a legal document that describes, among other things, the financial condition of the firm, the management of the firm, and the risks of the firm's securities. Some of the printing on the front page of the primary prospectus must be in red ink, which is why they often are called "red herrings." After approval by the SEC, a *final prospectus* must be drawn up. The final prospectus must provide enough information to investors so that they can make an intelligent decision about purchasing the security and the risks involved. A prospectus is most often prepared by an investment bank, usually using the investment bank's legal staff.

Prospectus: A legal document containing information about the issuer of stocks and bonds. This is required by the Securities and Exchange Commission from corporations

4 The SEC warns investors about private placements. See "Investor Bulletin: Private Placements Under Regulation D," September 24, 2014. http://www.sec.gov/oiea/investor-alerts-bulletins/ib_privateplacements.html#.VM5l1mjF8h8.

and governments that want to sell their stocks and bonds to the public. A prospectus must include information that is designed to ensure investors have the information they need to make an informed investment decision.

An investment bank also has to determine what price to ask for shares or what coupon rate to put on bonds that are being offered for sale. To do this, the investment bank must perform due diligence. This includes obtaining a bond rating (if it is selling a bond) as well as analyzing the corporation that is issuing the stock or bond so that both investors and the investment bank can properly judge the risks involved.

To gauge market interest in the offering, the investment bank stages what is referred to as a **roadshow**. In a roadshow, representatives from the investment bank, along with representatives of the corporation or government issuing the stock or bond, go "on the road" to visit with potential investors and analysts. These potential investors are usually institutional investors such as pension funds, insurance companies, endowments, and asset managers who have large amounts of funds to invest. The analysts are the financial market analysts who will follow the stock or bond and give, buy, or sell recommendations.

Investment bank roadshow: The management of a company that is issuing securities travels around the country, often with investment bank employees, to give presentations to potential investors and analysts in order to receive feedback on the offering.

Underwriting

Once the price and terms have been determined, the investment bank often puts together an **underwriting syndicate** to sell the securities. Underwriting is the process whereby an investment bank buys all of the securities from the issuer and then resells those securities to investors. In doing so the investment bank opens itself to price risk. Thus, to assist in the sale of the securities to investors, the initial investment bank (called the lead bookrunner[5]) compiles a group, or syndicate, of other investment banks to help sell the issue.[6]

Underwriting syndicate: A group of investment banks that collectively work together to sell a stock or bond being issued.

The syndicate buys the shares from the issuer at a discount and sells them to investors. The difference between the purchase price and the sale price is called the **underwriting gross spread**. This is the fee the investment bank earns for their underwriting.

Underwriting gross spread: The difference between the price of a stock or bond the investment bank pays to the issuer and the price the investment bank charges its clients to buy the same stock or bond.

Before the syndicate purchases securities, it has to agree to the method of sale. Under a **firm commitment**, all of the securities that are not sold to investors are purchased by the investment bank. The other route is a **best effort**, whereby the syndicate puts forth its best effort to sell the securities at the sale price, but whatever do not sell are returned to the issuer. In both cases the investment bank bears the risk that the investor agreeing to purchase the securities will not live up to their end of the agreement. This is called **settlement risk**.

5 More than one investment bank can function as a lead bookrunner. Sometimes one investment bank is the dominate lead bookrunner; in other cases the bookrunners operate on an equal basis.

6 Bookrunners are responsible for determining the marketing plan, pricing, and so on, and thus receive a larger share of the issuance, thereby earning higher fees. The other members of the syndicate, called co-managers, earn lower fees. There are generally between one and seven co-managers.

Firm commitment: An agreement between an underwriter of a security and the issuing entity whereby the underwriter agrees to purchase all of the securities directly from the issuer for sale to the public at a specific price.

Best effort: An agreement between an underwriter of a security and the issuing entity whereby the underwriter promises to make a full-hearted attempt to sell as much of the security offering as possible to the public.

Settlement risk: In a securities transaction, the risk that the other side of the trade will not deliver the cash or the securities as promised.

Market-Making

Once securities have been sold to the public, the creation of a secondary market becomes important. Investment banks often are involved in making a market for securities. In market-making, an investment bank stands willing, at any time, to quote a client a price at which the bank will purchase the security, buy it from the customer at that price, or sell to the customer a security at a quoted price. The difference between the price at which the bank is willing to buy (called the bid price) and the price at which it is willing to sell (called the ask or offer price) is called the bid-ask spread. Investment banks make a profit in market-making by capturing the bid-ask spread.

Client-Related Trading

Along with making markets, investment banks' trading business is made up of traders (the people actually buying and selling securities), sales professionals (those who advise clients about what securities to buy and sell), and research analysts. Traders involved in client-related trading buy and sell securities for a profit for the bank, but they also have the objective of helping the bank's client earn a profit. Thus, sometimes traders might decide to take a lower spread or margin to assist clients or to increase trade volume.

Equity traders buy and sell common stock, stock derivatives, equity indexes, and other equity-related financial instruments. Each of these areas requires traders to have a great deal of specialized knowledge. They buy and sell equities to generate a profit, assist in underwriting, and/or assist in market-making. Prime brokers, who are typically housed in the trading division of an investment bank, focus on trading (as well as lending) equities for institutional investors, including hedge funds. Hedge funds are often the largest source of client-related revenue for the trading division of many large investment banks.

Equity trader: An investor in financial markets who buys and sells equities or stocks; often works as part of an investment bank.

Other client-related trading includes fixed income, credit products, and commodities. Traders in these three areas have historically been some of the most profitable within investment banks. These are, however, the areas that experienced major losses during the financial crisis of 2008. **Fixed-income** trading traditionally has included government and corporate bonds, commercial paper, government and agency bonds and notes, as well as interest rate derivatives. **Credit products** include mortgage-backed securities, structured credit (such as collateralized debt obligations and collateralized student loans), credit default swaps, and bank loans. **Commodities trading** includes agriculture (e.g., corn, soybeans); energy (e.g., crude oil, natural gas, electricity); and metals.

Fixed-income trading: The buying and selling of debt instruments; often a division or part of an investment bank.

Credit products: The buying and selling of debt instruments including mortgage backed securities and bank loans.

Commodities trading: The buying and selling of financial instruments tied to commodities such as agricultural products and mineral resources; often a division or part of an investment bank.

Proprietary Trading

In proprietary, or prop, trading, traders do not trade on behalf of clients; instead, they buy and sell solely for the benefit of their firm. Thus, in prop trading, traders have no responsibility to balance their interests with the bank's customers' interests. In fact, the bank's customers are often the prop trader's competition.

Prop traders do their own research but also rely on research done by others. They attempt to predict where markets are headed and place bets on those beliefs. At Goldman Sachs, prop trading was considered to be an extremely profitable business within its Trading and Principal Investment Division between 2002 and 2007. Some estimate that prop trading generated more revenue and earnings for Goldman Sachs than what the world's largest hedge fund generated during that time period.

Until the recent financial crisis hit, prop trading at many large investment banks was *the* place to be. Prop traders were often the highest-paid employees in the entire bank. In many cases prop traders used leverage to push their returns to dizzying levels, especially when markets were volatile. But with leverage comes risk. Leverage can be used to amplify gains, but it also multiplies the size of losses. When the credit crisis hit in 2008, prop traders found themselves on the losing side time and time again, causing their firms to suffer huge losses. These prop trades led to a reduction in market confidence in investment banks and caused a near meltdown of the entire industry.

Mergers and Acquisitions

While prop trading generated huge profits for investment banks, so too did their mergers and acquisitions (M&A) departments. At the heart of M&A is the buying and selling of corporate assets to assist a corporation in achieving a strategic objective.[7] Starting in the 1980s with the rise of leveraged buyouts and hostile takeovers, the M&A departments of investment banks grew from a sleepy area of the bank to one of the most exciting. Even Hollywood got into the act. Movies such as *Working Girl* and *Wall Street* featured less-than-likeable M&A experts.

In real life, M&A departments assist corporations in identifying potential merger or acquisition targets, developing pricing strategies for the merger or acquisition, and then helping to negotiate and even finance the deal. Of course, the bigger the deal the higher the fee the investment bank charges. This has led some critics to say there is an incentive mismatch in M&A: Investment banks are interested in only "doing deals" to pocket fees and have little to no interest in the long-term impact of the deal on any of the parties involved.

But why, then, are investment banks in the United States, including Goldman Sachs, so disliked by so many people? That is the next issue we turn to: the controversies around investment banks.

7 See David P. Stowell, "Mergers and Acquisitions," in *An Introduction to Investment Banks, Hedge Funds, and Private Equity: The New Paradigm*, 63–96 (London: Academic Press, 2010).

SECTION REVIEW

Q1) David is a bit confused as to what investment banks do. For example, he has heard of insurance underwriters, but David can't seem to understand what underwriting has to do with investment banks. How would you explain investment banking underwriting to David?

Q2) Explain how proprietary, or prop, trading, when done by investment banks, can result in the bank's customers becoming the bank's competition.

Q3) Your friend Cynthia works at an investment bank and tells you she is going on a "roadshow." What will Cynthia be doing?

a. Going to the government and asking for a taxpayer bailout of the investment bank.

b. Lobbying the government to reduce the amount of regulations over the investment bank.

c. Helping the investment bank sell shares of its mutual fund to the general public.

d. Assisting either a corporation or government in explaining to potential investors or analysts who is issuing a security what the security promises.

24-2 Investment Bank Controversies

The old saying is, "everybody loves a winner." If this is true, why don't more people love investment banks? If profits are a measure of "winning," then investment banks certainly are winners. So, where did things go wrong?

In its early days, investment banking was known as a "white shoe" industry. The field was full of overly conservative, risk-adverse, well-dressed, but not exorbitantly paid bankers[8] who dealt with only well-established firms and high-ranking government officials. But all of that started to change in the 1980s.

Deregulation and Going Public

As described in Chapter 5, the 1980s saw a wave of deregulation hit the financial industry. Investment banks took advantage of the rollback in regulation and easing of antitrust challenges by the Justice Department to greatly expand their M&A activity. The use of leveraged buyouts by corporate raiders allowed investment banks to earn large commissions on big blockbuster deals.

Investment banks were no longer "gatekeepers" who would conservatively decide which respected corporations would be "allowed" to issue stock or debt. Instead, with deregulation, the only question on investment bankers' minds was how much money could be made quickly.

Many critics contend the big change in the behavior of investment banks came in the late 1990s. During this time, many big investment banks changed from being private, closely held partnerships into publically traded companies. By becoming publically traded firms, the investment banks could access much more money than they could when they had to rely on the firm's partners to contribute their private funds. Going public also made it much easier for investment banks to buy other investment banks.

As a result, by the first decade of the twenty-first century, the investment banking industry was dominated by five large, New York City-based investment banks: Goldman Sachs, Morgan Stanley, Merrill Lynch, Lehman Brothers, and the smallest, Bear Stearns.

The Rise of Trading and Changing Culture

It could be argued that what changed among the big five investment banks was their culture in the first decade of the twenty-first century. Greg Smith, in his 2012 book *Why I Left Goldman Sachs*, notes that when he joined Goldman as an intern in 2000, the firm earned most its revenue from underwriting and M&A, but by 2007 the income Goldman earned from trading had increased by a factor of five in just five years. Smith argues that this focus on trading resulted in a change in culture at Goldman Sachs and other investment banks. From a culture of protecting the institution's reputation and serving clients, Smith argues, investment banks became a place where "ripping off" unsuspecting institutional clients was "the gold standard."

Critics counter that Smith left because he did not get a promotion and that his book lacks specific details about transactions in which clients were actually negatively affected. Goldman Sachs claims to have investigated Smith's allegations and but for one email can find no evidence of where traders looked negatively upon uninformed institutional investors.

Goldman Sachs and the Abacus 2007-ACI case

In April 2010 the Securities and Exchange Commission filed a civil lawsuit against Goldman Sachs for securities fraud. The SEC accused Goldman Sachs of creating and selling a synthetic collateralized debt obligation (CDO) that it secretly intended to fail. The focus of the lawsuit was Abacus 2007-ACI, one of 25 such synthetic CDOs Goldman Sachs created to bet against the housing industry.

---

8 They also tended to be predominately white, male, educated at Ivy League and preparatory schools, and from old, wealthy families.

As the Abacus portfolio declined in value, John A. Paulson, a hedge fund manager at whose request Goldman Sachs created Abacus, made money by betting against mortgage assets in the CDO. Goldman Sachs told investors that the fund was designed to gain value. Investors lost about $1 billion in the deal, while Goldman reportedly was paid $15 million in fees related to Abacus. Only three months later, in July 2010, Goldman Sachs reached an out-of-court settlement with the SEC, agreeing to pay a $550 million fine without admitting any wrongdoing.

In 2013 Fabrice Tourre, the Goldman Sachs trader who was responsible for creating and selling Abacus, was found guilty of defrauding investors. Tourre paid the SEC $825,000 in fines despite making millions of dollars during his time with Goldman Sachs. The judge in the case stated, "He has shown no remorse or contrition."[9] Tourre left Goldman Sachs in December 2012, and as of 2014 he was pursuing a PhD in economics at the University of Chicago.

Critics complained the SEC's actions were weak at best. Dennis Kelleher, head of the nonprofit organization Better Markets, a watchdog group, said the fine should not detract from the government's "indefensible" failure to bring criminal charges against more senior Wall Street executives. Kelleher said, "Wall Street recklessness, fraud and criminality were at the core of the crash and the crisis. History will judge prosecutors and regulators harshly for abdicating their duty to enforce the law way without fear or favor on Wall Street as they do on Main Street."[10]

The case did raise the question of why the SEC, the Justice Department, and the rest of the US federal government was seemingly reluctant to hold any of the large investment banks responsible for their contributions to the financial crisis and the Great Recession. Some suggest the answer lies in the "revolving door" between Wall Street investment banks and the US federal government.

The Revolving Door

In October 2008 the *New York Times* ran an article entitled "The Guys from 'Government Sachs.'" The article described how so many of the top regulators of the financial industry came from the investment bank Goldman Sachs. While many at the investment bank saw this as a way of "giving back" to society, others wondered about potential conflicts of interest.

But Goldman Sachs was not the only investment bank to send people to Washington, DC. Nor did the door swing only one way. Many people involved with regulating the financial markets quickly found lucrative positions with investment banks when their regulating days were over.

Robert K. Steel, a former vice president at Goldman Sachs, came to Washington, DC., to repair Fannie Mae and Freddie Mac, but he then left the Treasury to become chief executive of Wachovia, a full financial services firm. Wachovia was acquired by Wells Fargo in 2008 in a government-forced sale to avoid a failure of Wachovia.

Robert Rubin, who joined Goldman Sachs in 1966 and was co-chairman from 1990 to 1992, held the cabinet position of secretary of the Treasury from 1995 to July 1999. During his tenure he oversaw the dismantling of financial market regulation that dated back to the 1930s. One piece of legislation he reportedly helped to draft and lobby for in Congress was the Gramm-Leach-Bliley Act of 1999. The act was designed in large part to assist Citigroup in getting around existing government regulations. Soon after the bill was signed into law, Rubin stepped down as Treasury secretary and was appointed as an advisor to Citigroup; he was paid more than $126 million for his service to the firm when he resigned in January 2009.

Then there is the revolving door between the Federal Reserve and Wall Street investment banks. William C. Dudley, currently the president of the Federal Reserve Bank of New York, was the chief economist at Goldman Sachs for 10 years before joining the Federal Reserve.

---

9 See Nate Raymond and Jonathan Stempel, "Big Fine Imposed on Ex-Goldman Trader Tourre in SEC Case." Reuters, March 12, 2014. http://www.reuters.com/article/2014/03/12/us-goldmansachs-sec-tourre-idUSBREA2B11220140312/.

10 See Nate Raymond and Jonathan Stemple, "UPDATE 2-Big Fine Imposed on Ex-Goldman Trader Tourre in SEC Case." Reuters, March 12, 2014. http://www.reuters.com/article/2014/03/12/goldmansachs-sec-tourre-idUSL2N0M911G20140312.

The revolving door between the Federal Reserve and Goldman Sachs also seems to open in the other direction. For example, E. Gerald Corrigan was president of the Federal Reserve Bank of Minneapolis from 1980 to 1984, then president of the Federal Reserve Bank of New York from January 1, 1985, to July 19, 1993. In 1994 Corrigan joined Goldman Sachs and in 1996 was named managing director.

Many critics wonder whether too many of the rules and regulations applied by the government and Federal Reserve while overseeing financial markets—especially for investment banks—are written in the investment banking industry's favor. US Senator Sherrod Brown, who chaired the Senate Subcommittee on Financial Institutions and Consumer Protection, stated in 2014 that "It is bad enough when (investment) banks can capture the agencies that regulate them or the Congress that oversees those agencies." He continued: "But it is worse when they don't even have to, because the agencies handcuff themselves, or public servants attempt to curry favor with the companies that they supervise."[11]

While investment banks have faced a growing amount of criticism because of their power and influence, so too has another important financial market entity: private equity partnerships. We turn our attention next to this often misunderstood segment of financial markets.

SECTION REVIEW

Q1) Rodney does not understand how investment banks work. In the Abacus case, Rodney assumes Goldman Sachs would lose money since the value of assets in Abacus declined drastically. How would you explain to Rodney how Goldman Sachs actually made money on Abacus?

Q2) Explain why so many people see a "revolving door" between the investment banking industry and the entities designed to regulate and oversee it.

Q3) During what time periods did the size of investment banks change?

a. In the 1920s, as US consumer spending increased, investment banks grew in size to provide credit to American consumers.

b. Shortly after World War II, the size of investment banks grew thanks to the postwar economic boom.

c. During the inflationary times of the 1970s, investment banks grew as investors sought investments that kept pace with inflation.

d. Deregulation in the 1980s and changes in corporate structures in the 1990s resulted in growth in the size of investment banks.

11 See Sabrina Eaton, "Sen. Sherrod Brown Grills Federal Reserve Bank on Its Oversight Practices." cleveland.com, November 21, 2014. http://www.cleveland.com/open/index.ssf/2014/11/sen_sherrod_brown_grills_feder.html.

Private Equity

24-3

While investment banking has received a great deal of criticism, in part for playing such a large role in public policy, private equity market participants have done their best to shun the spotlight. But when one of their own (Mitt Romney) decided to run for president of the United States in 2012, the industry found itself in the spotlight—and often not a favorable one. The spotlight again shone on the industry in 2014 when another head of a private equity fund decided to run for a high-level public office: Bruce Rauner in Illinois. So, what is private equity? Why have market participants avoided the spotlight for so long?

24-3a It's Private, Not Public

The term *private equity* is one of those where the name actually fits. Private equity simply means that the shares of a corporation (or equity) are not publicly traded on an exchange, such as the New York Stock Exchange, nor sold to the public "over the counter." Rather, the shares are held "privately," usually by a private equity partnership.

The private equity industry has two main categories: buyouts and venture capital. The buyout side of private equity most often deals with taking publicly traded companies private, or "buying out" the stockholders. This is done to "fix" or "repair" or "improve" the company and shield it from the ebb and flow of the overall stock market. It is hoped that these improvements add value to the corporation, thus allowing the equity shares to be sold at a higher price.

The venture capital side of private equity involves investing in small or start-up firms by buying their shares and helping them to grow and improve. It is hoped that these small firms blossom so that their share prices increase and can be sold at a much higher price than what the private equity firm initially paid for them.

24-3b Private Equity Is Long-Term and Risky

Both buyouts and venture capital are long-term endeavors. It may take several years for a firm that is in trouble to be "turned around" by its private equity investors. Similarly, in venture capital, small firms do not blossom overnight. It may take several years for a small firm to become profitable, much less for their stock price to increase significantly.

The long-term success of private equity investments is very uncertain. Many of the troubled institutions in buyouts are never able to be turned around. Less than 10% of start-ups survive past their first few years. For this reason, private equity is considered to be an "alternative asset." That is, private equity is an alternative to safer, more liquid investment vehicles such as public equity, bonds, or bank deposit accounts.

Because of the uncertainty of returns and the lack of liquidity, investors in private equity funds are limited to "qualified investors." To be classified as a qualified investor, a person or a firm must meet significant minimum income and wealth levels. Basically, qualified investors must be able to demonstrate that they can afford to lose the money they are about to invest before they are allowed to do so. In addition to individual qualified investors, the main participant in private equity funds are large institutional investors such as insurance companies, pension plans, endowments, and trusts.

24-3c Private Equity Structure

The investors in a typical private equity fund are called limited partners (LPs) because their involvement in the fund is limited to the funds they invest in a private equity partnership. The LPs do not make investment decisions, nor are they involved with the firms in which the

Figure 24-1 **Structure of a Private Equity Partnership**

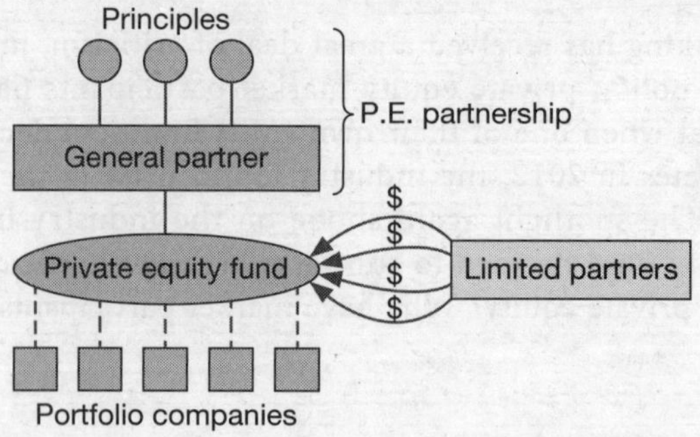

partnership invests. The private equity partnership is managed by the general partners (GPs) of the partnership. It is the GPs who decide with which companies the private equity fund will invest. The companies in which the private equity fund invests are called portfolio firms (Figure 24-1).

Private equity funds traditionally last 10 years. In the first years of the fund the GPs raise funds from the LPs and invest in portfolio firms. In addition to buying the portfolio firms, the GPs work with experts to grow and improve them. In doing so, they hope the value of the portfolio firms will increase during this time period.

In the second half of the fund's lifespan, the GPs "harvest" their investments. That is, they sell their shares of the portfolio firms. They may sell these shares to the public via an IPO, to another firm (called a strategic buyer), or perhaps to another private equity fund.

Private equity funds often have more than one fund going at a time. As Figure 24-2 shows, the private equity firm or partnership is constantly raising funds from LPs, investing in portfolio firms, and harvesting their investments. Thus, private equity firms are constantly in need of people to do these different tasks.

24-3d Private Equity Payment Streams

A limited partner does not invest all of their funds in a private equity fund all at once. Instead, an LP makes a **commitment** to the fund, and portions of this commitment are **drawn down** as the general partners need them to purchase portfolio firms. In addition, the LPs pay to the

Figure 24-2 **Private Equity Funds Often Have More than One Fund Going Simultaneously**

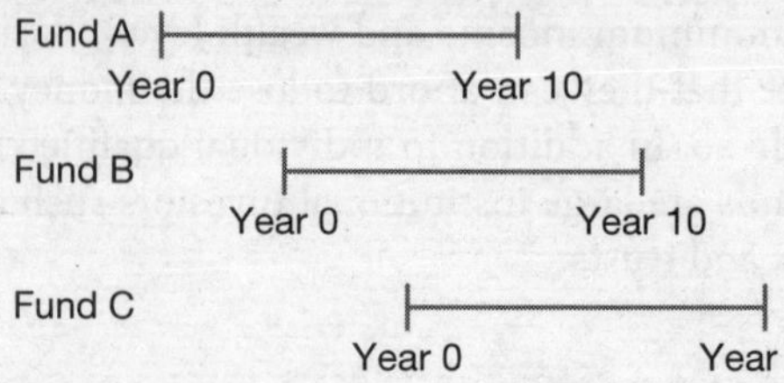

GPs a **management fee**, generally 2% of the drawn-down committed funds. This management fee goes toward the daily costs of running the fund. The GPs also put in 2% to 10% of the total fund from their own personal funds.

Private equity commitment: The size of an investment an investor pledges to a private equity fund.

Drawn down: When the general partners of a private equity fund request some of the funds an investor has pledged to invest in the fund.

Private equity management fee: The annual fee for managing the fund the general partners of a private equity fund charge to the investors in the fund.

Once the harvest phase begins and the portfolio companies are being sold, it is time for the **waterfall**, or repayment of the LPs' investment. In general, the LPs' drawn-down capital is repaid. Next there is usually a predetermined "hurdle rate," or rate of return on the funds that are paid to the LPs. Whatever is left over is then split between the LPs and the GPs on an 80/20 basis: 80% of the funds go to the LPs and 20% go to the GPs. The 20% that is paid to the GPs is called **carried interest**.

Waterfall: The structure of repayments made to the investors of a private equity fund.

Carried interest: The portion of the profits from the liquidation of a private equity fund that is paid to the general partners of the fund.

The waterfall is structured this way so that the GPs do not get a share of the profits until the LPs are paid back their funds, plus the hurdle rate. Depending on the negotiations, the GPs may also have to pay back the management fee before they get their 20%.

There is also the issue of the timing of the waterfall. Often the "payback" or waterfall takes place as each portfolio firm is sold. That, however, can create an interesting problem if the most successful firms are sold first.

To understand why an issue may arise, imagine a private equity fund is made up of three portfolio firms, and the fund spent $100 million on each to buy up existing shares. To keep it simple, let's assume there is no hurdle rate and no management fee to be repaid. The LPs put up the $300 million to buy the three firms' shares.

Let's assume the first portfolio firm's shares are sold for $200 million. The LPs are repaid the $100 million that was used to buy the shares, and the remaining $100 million is split, with $80 million going to the LPs and $20 million going to the GPs.

So far, everything is going well. But now let's assume the second portfolio firm fails and the shares are worth nothing. Let's assume the third portfolio firm also fails and its shares are worth $0.

The LPs turn to the GPs and say, "Wait a minute. I put in $300 million and all I am getting back is $180 million?" The GPs have to give the LPs the $20 million they took from the sale of the first portfolio firm. This giving back of early returns is called a **clawback**. When the economic downturn hit in 2008, a number of private equity firms faced significant clawbacks.

Clawbacks: The early returns from a private equity fund that have been paid to the general partners of the fund that must be returned to the investors if the later returns on the fund are at a lower rate of return than initial returns.

The private equity market is rather complicated, with its own vocabulary and complex structures. But why has it been considered in such a negative light in recent years? We turn next to some of the controversies that surround the private equity industry.

SECTION REVIEW

Q1) Sandy is confused about the terminology used in the private equity industry. How would you explain to her the differences between a limited partner and general partner in private equity?

Q2) "Waterfalls are pretty things in nature; it is water falling off a cliff. But how do they function in private equity?," asks your friend. How do you answer this question?

Q3) People who operate private equity funds can receive very high levels of compensation if the fund is able to sell its portfolio firms for a much higher price than what it paid for and invested in them. This return that is paid to the operators of private equity funds is called:

a. dividend payments.

b. earned income.

c. fixed compensation.

d. carried interest.

Private Equity Controversies

24-4

The private equity industry has long tried to keep a low profile. The industry, in its most recent form, dates back to the end of World War II, yet most people did not become familiar with it until the leveraged buyouts that occurred during the 1980s. During the height of the LBO craze, corporate raiders such as Carl Icahn, T. Boone Pickens, and Ron Perelman became household names. After the LBO craze died down, the private equity funds that continued in operation primarily focused on corporate buyouts and preferred to remain out of the limelight.

When former Massachusetts governor and former CEO of Bain Capital Mitt Romney decided to run for president of the United States in 2012, however, private equity was again in the spotlight. A question arose: How do people in the private equity industry get so rich? The answer is carried interest. But this led to only more questions and more controversy.

24-4a Capital Gains versus Income Tax Controversy

One of the most hotly debated issues in private equity is how very few taxes private equity LPs actually pay. The main reason is because the carried interest GPs earn is not considered earned income; it is considered a capital gain. Recall that private equity funds buy shares of corporations, hope to improve these companies, and then sell the shares at a much higher price than what they paid for them. Remember as well that the difference between the purchase price and the eventual selling price of the shares is a capital gain.

The federal tax rate on long-term capital gains is much lower than the tax rate on ordinary or earned income. For example, in 2015 the tax rate on longer-term capital gains in the United States is 0% for the 10% to 15% income tax bracket, 15% for the 25% to 35% income tax bracket, and 20% for the 39.6% income tax bracket. In 2015 the 15% tax bracket ends at $73,800 for a married couple filing jointly or $36,900 for single filers. So, if a private equity general partner took in less than $73,800 in earned income, she would pay no federal income tax on her carried interest. Depending on the performance of the fund, however, the carried interest in one year could be tens of millions of dollars.

Thus, many were shocked when it came to light during the presidential campaign of 2012 that Mitt Romney had an effective tax rate of only 14%.[12] That means that all Americans who were earning $37,000 or more a year were paying a higher tax rate than Mitt Romney, despite the fact he earned more than $42 million in 2010. Those in the media made the link between capital gains tax rates and the fact the GPs in private equity funds earn carried interest taxed at the capital gains rate.

Defenders of private equity argue that what the GPs do is legal—it is in keeping with the US tax code. The lower tax rates on long-term capital gains are designed to encourage investors to make long-term investments and not seek merely short-term returns. The debate rages on even as the 2012 presidential campaign becomes a distant memory.

24-4b Dumb Money versus Smart Money

The large sums made by some GPs in private equity partnerships have led many to "seek their fortune" in the private equity industry. Today it is not uncommon for business schools to offer courses that focus on nothing but the private equity industry. Several books about the industry have been written in the past few years to teach would-be GPs how to get "a piece of the action."

12 See Huma Khan, "Mitt Romney Made Nearly $22 Million in 2010, Paid Less Than 14 Percent in Taxes." abcNews.com, January 24, 2010. http://abcnews.go.com/Politics/OTUS/mitt-romney-made-42-million-paid-14-percent/story?id=15423615.

At the same time, many institutional investors who lack private equity investments in their portfolios look on with envy as private equity funds pay high returns to their investors. Successful private equity institutional investors such as David Swenson at the Yale University Investment Office have made other institutional investors very jealous.

This increase in the popularity of the industry has some inside the industry worrying about its future. They point out that to be successful a GP needs more than just money from institutional investors. Those who rush to become newly minted GPs and have little knowledge about the portfolio firms in which they are investing are called **dumb money**. These GPs have only money and very little insight to offer to portfolio firms. **Smart money**, on the other hand, represents GPs who come with a great deal of industry knowledge as well as LP money to invest in firms.

Dumb money: A private equity firm or investor who offers little more than a financial investment in a portfolio firm.

Smart money: A private equity firm or investor who, in addition to offering financial resources to a portfolio firm, can also offer insight, connections, and advice that will be of great assistance to the portfolio firm.

The results of private equity returns bear this out. The returns often are described as bimodal. Some private equity funds pay their LPs very high rates of returns, whereas a large number of funds lose everything. There are almost no private equity funds in between these two extremes. Swenson from the Yale Investment Office warns that "in the absence of truly superior fund-selection skills (or extraordinary luck) investors should stay far, far away from private equity investments."[13]

24-4c Job-Destroying Vulture Capitalism

While there is little doubt that large amounts of money can be earned by GPs in private equity, and that LPs can earn very high rates of return on their private equity investments, a hotly debated issue is just *how* these high returns are generated. One common strategy in buyouts is for private equity firms to use leverage to purchase the outstanding shares of a company and assign that debt to the firm. Since interest payments are deductible from a corporation's federal income tax, this is often referred to as the **corporate debt tax shield**.

Corporate debt tax shield: The interest a corporation pays on debt it issues is a tax-deductible expense.

During the early LBO craze, many corporate raiders set their sights on corporations with large amounts of cash. They would use debt to buy up outstanding shares and use the corporation's cash to pay interest on the debt while they sold off portions of the company to repay the debt. The raiders then would reduce costs in the firm, most often through reducing labor costs, and pay lower taxes via the corporate debt tax shield. Finally, the raiders would sell the newly restructured firm back to the public. Sometimes the troubled firm would be merged with other firms into a single firm to reduce overhead. These are referred to as **rollups**.

Private equity rollup: A practice used in the private equity industry whereby several small firms in the same market are purchased by private equity funds and merged into one single, larger firm.

In most buyouts jobs are eliminated, the salaries and wages of workers left behind are cut, and/or employee benefits are reduced. Proponents of buyouts claim that often this is the only

13 See Robert Lenzner, "The Economist Blasts Private Equity, Romney's Path to Fortune." *Forbes*, January 30, 2012. http://www.forbes.com/sites/robertlenzner/2012/01/30/the-economist-blasts-private-equity-romneys-path-to-fortune/.

way to save the company. Many of these corporations were poorly run in the past, costs were allowed to increase unchecked, and the private equity firm is seeking to turn the firm around.

Critics of buyouts, such as Matt Taibbi, writing for *Rolling Stone*, argue that this "turn around" technique has a long history—in organized crime.[14] It was called the "bust out." In organized crime a criminal organization takes over a restaurant or retail store, runs up huge amounts of debt in the firm's name, and then sets fire to the establishment to collect the insurance money. Taibbi quotes Wall Street traders describing private equity buyouts: "'It's the bust-out,' one Wall Street trader says with a laugh. 'That's all it is.'"

Thus the private equity industry has remained in the public spotlight, and often that spotlight has not been very flattering. It will be interesting to see how public opinion about the industry manifests itself in terms of public policy. Will GPs continue to enjoy the low capital gains tax rates? Or, will carried interest be considered earned income in the future? Other possible regulations the private equity industry might face in the future is an open question.

SECTION REVIEW

Q1) Why do general partners in private equity funds pay such a low rate of tax on the income they generate?

Q2) Robyn is an entrepreneur, and she is looking for a private equity firm to make an equity investment in her firm. How can Robyn tell the difference between the dumb money and smart money that various private equity firms are offering?

Q3) Private equity funds often earn high returns on their investments, in part because the interest that must be paid on debt issued by their portfolio firms can be used to reduce the amount of federal income tax the portfolio firms must pay. This is often referred to as making use of the:

a. progressive income tax.
b. corporate debt tax shield.
c. regressive debt tax.
d. carried interest tax deduction.

14 See Matt Taibbi, "Greed and Debt: The True Story of Mitt Romney and Bain Capital." *Rolling Stone*, August 29, 2012. http://www.rollingstone.com/politics/news/greed-and-debt-the-true-story-of-mitt-romney-and-bain-capital-20120829.

24-5 Conclusion

Investment banks and private equity are arguably two of the most controversial components of our financial markets. We have learned that investment banks evolved from being conservative financial market gatekeepers into large, global financial service providers. These very old financial institutions have created a great deal of controversy, especially in recent years, in terms of their incentives and their impact on public policy.

Private equity funds, while much younger than investment banks, also have created much controversy. Many in the private equity industry have tried to shun the public spotlight and undertake their long-term investments in relative anonymity. Over the past few years, however, as some former private equity executives have run for public office, more attention has been given to the waterfalls and carried interest in private equity transactions. In addition, larger questions of how exactly these returns are earned have been raised.

These two important yet controversial financial institutions will most likely continue to play an important role in the future development of our financial markets. It will be interesting to see how public perceptions of these institutions affect future government regulations of them.

IN THE NEWS. . .

The Vampire Squid Strikes Again: The Mega Banks' Most Devious Scam Yet

Banks are no longer just financing heavy industry. They are actually buying it up and inventing bigger, bolder and scarier scams than ever.

Matt Taibbi
Rolling Stone
February 12, 2014

Call it the loophole that destroyed the world. It's 1999, the tail end of the Clinton years. . . . Congress is feverishly crafting what could yet prove to be one of the most transformative laws in the history of our economy — a law that would make possible a broader concentration of financial and industrial power than we've seen in more than a century. . . .

A tiny provision in the bill [that would become the Financial Services Modernization Act of 1999, or the Gramm-Leach-Bliley Act] also permitted commercial banks to delve into any activity that is "complementary to a financial activity and does not pose a substantial risk to the safety or soundness of depository institutions or the financial system generally."

Complementary to a financial activity. What the hell did that mean?. . . "Nobody knew the reach it would have into the real economy," says Ohio Sen. Sherrod Brown. . . .

Today, banks like Morgan Stanley, JPMorgan Chase and Goldman Sachs own oil tankers, run airports and control huge quantities of coal, natural gas, heating oil, electric power and precious metals. They likewise can now be found exerting direct control over the supply of a whole galaxy of raw materials crucial to world industry and to society in general, including everything from food products to metals like zinc, copper, tin, nickel and, most infamously thanks to a recent high-profile scandal, aluminum. And they're doing it not just here but abroad as well: In Denmark, thousands took to the streets in protest in recent weeks, vampire-squid banners in hand, when news came out that Goldman Sachs was about to buy a 19 percent stake in Dong Energy, a national electric provider. The furor inspired mass resignations of ministers from the government's ruling coalition, as the Danish public wondered how an American investment bank could possibility hold so much influence over the state energy grid. . . .

This article points out that investment banks' activities in recent years have gone well beyond their traditional role of underwriting stocks and bonds. Investment banks (remember, most of them are now bank holding companies and thus are able to borrow funds from the Federal Reserve and get taxpayer-funded bailouts) are involved in a wide variety of "complimentary financial activities." What are the possible implications for financial markets as investment banks continue to expand their activities? Is this an efficient way for investment banks to diversify their activities? Or is it, as Taibbi suggests, an attempt by investment banks to corner markets that could result in the next global financial crisis?

A

Actuary: An applied statistician within an insurance company who calculates risks and premiums.

Adjustable-rate mortgage (ARM): A loan where real estate is used as collateral and the interest rate paid by the borrower may be changed by the lender under terms stated in the loan.

Adverse selection: A situation where undesirable results occur because the two parties in a transaction, the buyer and seller, have different amounts of information.

Aggregate supply: The relationship between the real level of output produced and the price level in a given time period.

Asset transformation: The process by which a financial institution creates a new asset from existing liabilities with different characteristics. Commercial banks take their liabilities (e.g., bank deposits), which are short term and generally small in size, and transform them into large, long-term assets (e.g., bank loans).

Asymmetric information: Information that is not equal or even.

B

Back-end load: A sales charge incurred when an investor sells mutual fund shares back to an investment company.

Bank charter: Permission issued, usually by a government or government agency, to establish and operate a depository institution.

Banker's acceptances: A common way to facilitate trade; a promise by one party to pay another party in the future, which is accepted or guaranteed by a bank.

Basel I: An international agreement among central banks and bank regulators that for the first time created standard definitions of bank capital and established risk-weighted bank capital levels. Basel I was issued in 1988.

Basel II: The second of the international banking regulation accords that was issued in 2004 and was designed to be implemented in 2008. Three pillars included (1) more flexible minimum bank capital levels, (2) changed supervisory review, and (3) increased dependence on market discipline via increased bank disclosures.

Basel III: The third and most recent international banking regulation accords, which were created in 2010 in the wake of the global financial crisis.

Beige Book: A document created eight times a year by the staff of the Board of Governors of the Federal Reserve that describes the current status of business conditions and of the US economy as a whole.

Best effort: An agreement between an underwriter of a security and the issuing entity whereby the underwriter promises to make a full-hearted attempt to sell as much of the security offering as possible to the public.

Bond: A written legal contract that is a promise to repay with interest; issued by a corporation, government, or government agency.

Bond covenants: A portion of a bond agreement that specifies what the borrower (the bond issuer) may or may not do during the life of the bond.

Bond discount: When the market price is less than its face value.

Bond premium: When the market price of a bond is above the face value.

C

Call provision: A clause in a bond contract that allows the issuer of the bond the right to buy back all or part of the bond issued before the bond's maturity date.

Call reports: Detailed quarterly reports of the operations and financial condition of a depository institution. Formally known as a "Consolidated Report of Condition and Income," commercial banks and thrifts must file them with the FDIC and credit unions must file them with the National Credit Union Association.

Capital budgeting: The process by which a firm determines whether to pursue a project. Projects include research and development of new products, continued production of an existing product, construction of a new facility, and continued operation of an existing facility, among others.

Carried interest: The portion of the profits from the liquidation of a private equity fund that is paid to the general partners of the fund.

Casualty or liability insurance: Insurance that provides payment for losses occurring due to negligent acts or actions that cause injury or damage to others.

Cease and desist order: Legal notice given to a financial institution by one of its regulators, or by the courts, requiring the financial institution to take actions or follow proscriptions in the order to stop unlawful, unsafe, or unsound financial practices.

Certificates of deposit: Bank savings accounts that must be left on deposit for a stated length of time. There are usually substantial penalties for early withdrawals.

Change in demand versus change in quantity demanded: *Change in demand* is a change in the price and quantity relationship from a buyer's perspective, whereas a *change in quantity demanded* comes about from a change in the price of the good or service.

Change in supply versus change in quantity supplied: *Change in supply* is a change in the price and quantity relationship from a seller's perspective, whereas a *change in quantity supplied* comes about from a change in the price of the good or service.

Clawbacks: The early returns from a private equity fund that have been paid to the general partners of the fund that must be returned to the investors if the later returns on the fund are at a lower rate of return than initial returns.

Commercial paper: Short-term, unsecured debt issued most often by well-established corporations. Maturity is typically less than 270 days.

Commodities trading: The buying and selling of financial instruments tied to commodities such as agricultural products and mineral resources; often a division or part of an investment bank.

Commodity money: Money that has some use other than being a medium of exchange, being a unit of account, and having a store of value.

Common stock: Shares of a corporation that entitle the holder to a claim on the corporation's assets at liquidation and where holders are paid a portion of the corporation's profits through dividends decided by the corporation's board of directors. Holders of common stock elect the board of directors and vote on corporate policy.

Compound interest: Interest earned on the principal plus interest.

Consumption smoothing: The idea that people do not like to have a low level of spending one period and a high level of spending the next period. Instead, they borrow and save to ensure that they have a relatively smooth level of consumption over time.

Convertible bonds: A bond where the bondholder can convert the bond into a specified number of shares of stock of the firm that issued the bond.

Co-pay: The amount of out-of-pocket expense an insured person must pay either per visit to a health care provider or per prescription purchased.

Corporate debt tax shield: The interest a corporation pays on debt it issues is a tax-deductible expense.

Coupon rate: The stated rate of interest that will be paid to the holder of the bond.

Crawling peg exchange rate system: An exchange rate system where the stated official exchange rate remains unchanged day to day, but the official exchange is changed by the government or central bank when economic conditions warrant a change.

Credit crunch: A reduction in the general availability of credit in financial markets most often seen as an irrational increase in risk aversion.

Credit products: The buying and selling of debt instruments including mortgage backed securities and bank loans.

Credit report: Also known as "credit history," a detailed report on how an individual has attained and used credit in the past. Credit reports also often include information on the person's employment history, past residential addresses, legal action taken against the person, and number of past credit report inquiries.

Credit risk: The risk that a borrower will not pay interest or premium as promised.

Credit score: A numerical value that is reportedly a measurement of how an individual has used credit in the past. Often it is used as a barometer of credit risk, where a higher credit score signals lower credit risk.

Currency appreciation: An increase in the market value of a currency.

Currency board: A foreign exchange regime where a central bank or national government pledges to convert or exchange its local currency to another anchor currency at any time at a stated fixed price.

Currency depreciation: A decrease in the market value of a currency.

Curtailment or prepayment risk: The risk that a borrower will repay a loan early or before the loan's final payment date.

Cyclical unemployment: Unemployment that occurs as a result of a downturn in the business cycle.

D

Default risk: The risk that a borrower will not pay interest or principal (or both) as promised.

Default risk premium: The rate at which a lender is compensated for taking on more default risk.

Default risk premium spread: The difference in yields between assets with different levels of default risk.

Defensive transactions: Open market operations designed to maintain a certain level of reserves.

DIDMCA: The Depository Institutions Deregulation Monetary Control Act of 1980. This act sought to increase the amount of competition in financial markets while also granting the Federal Reserve additional regulatory oversight.

Discount rate: The interest rate the Federal Reserve charges on loans it makes to member banks. These discount loans are made at the Fed's discount window.

Discount rate yield: A simple measure of a bond's return, using a 360-day year, that is calculated relative to the face value of the bond.

Disintermediation: The removal of funds from a financial intermediary (e.g., a bank) to invest them directly, as through a mutual fund.

Diversification: A means of reducing risk by holding a variety of assets.

Dollarization: The situation when market participants use another country's currency as money.

Double coincidence of wants: The situation where each party wants what the other has to offer for sale.

Down payment: The amount of the purchase price a buyer must provide out of their own financial resources.

Drawn down: When the general partners of a private equity fund request some of the funds an investor has pledged to invest in the fund.

Dual banking system: A banking system where bank charters are granted by the national government as well as state or provincial governments.

Dumb money: A private equity firm or investor who offers little more than a financial investment in a portfolio firm.

Duration (of a bond): The weighted average of time until repayment of the price of a bond with a fixed cash flow; also called "Maculay duration."

Dynamic transactions: Open market operations designed to change the level of reserves.

E

Economy of scale: As output increases, the cost per unit of output decreases.

Efficient market hypothesis: The idea that it is impossible for any one investor to earn a return above the average market return because the market is efficient in that market prices reflect all relevant information.

Equity trader: An investor in financial markets who buys and sells equities or stocks; often works as part of an investment bank.

Eurodollar account: A bank account that is denominated in a currency other than the currency of the country in which the depository institution resides.

Ex ante (real interest rate): Using the expected rate of inflation.

Ex post (real interest rate): Using the actual rate of inflation.

Exchange-traded fund: An investment fund that is traded on a stock exchange throughout the trading day and holds securities that trade at a price close to their net asset value.

Exclusive insurance agent: An insurance sales agent who sells insurance products from only one insurance company.

Explicit inflation target: A monetary policy where the central bank states an explicit desired inflation rate and the central bank pledges to use monetary policy to achieve that inflation rate.

F

Face value (of a bond): The original amount of money borrowed by a bond issuer. This is also sometimes called the bond principal.

Federal Home Loan (FHL) Bank system: A system of US government–sponsored banks designed to increase the amount of low-cost funds available to financial institutions for home mortgage loans, small-business loans, agricultural loans, and rural economic development loans.

Federal Insurance Office: A federal office, housed within the US Department of Treasury, designed to monitor the insurance industry and coordinate policies that pertain to the insurance industry.

Federal Open Market Committee (FOMC): The committee within the Federal Reserve that is responsible for setting monetary policy.

Federal Reserve: The central bank and monetary authority of the United States.

Fiat money: An asset that functions as money but has no intrinsic value.

Financial accelerator: A negative shock to the economy may be intensified by worsening financial market conditions.

Firm commitment: An agreement between an underwriter of a security and the issuing entity whereby the underwriter agrees to purchase all of the securities directly from the issuer for sale to the public at a specific price.

Fixed-income trading: The buying and selling of debt instruments; often a division or part of an investment bank.

Fixed-rate mortgage: A loan where real estate is used as collateral and the interest rate paid by the borrower does not change over the life of the loan.

Flight to liquidity: A situation in financial markets where investors move funds from less liquid financial assets into financial assets that offer a higher level of liquidity.

Flight to quality: Movement of financial resources from financial instruments with default risk to financial instruments with lower levels of default risk. Often occurs because of increased uncertainty over future economic or market conditions.

Foreign exchange intervention: An economic policy tool used by central banks and national governments to influence the exchange rate of a nation's currency.

Free-floating exchange rates: A foreign exchange regime where the exchange rate of currencies are determined purely by market forces.

Free-rider problem: A situation where some members of society benefit from the consumption of a good or service without paying for the good or service.

Frictional or short-term unemployment: Unemployment that lasts only a few weeks or a few months as unemployed workers are searching for jobs.

Front-end load: A sales charge for purchasing mutual fund shares that is charged to the investor when they make a purchase.

Full employment: The level of real output at which all resources are being efficiently and effectively used.

Fully funded pension: A retirement system that has sufficient assets to meet current and future liabilities.

Fully vested: The ability of an employee to take all of the employer's retirement contribution with them when the employee leaves the employment of the employer.

Future value: The nominal value of an asset, such as money, at some point in time in the future.

G

Garn-St. Germain Act of 1982: An act designed to reduce the amount of regulation over the Savings & Loan or thrift industry.

General obligation bond: A bond issued and backed by a state or local municipality to raise funds that will be used for a variety of public works projects.

Government rationing: Limitations, implemented by a government, on the amount of goods a person can purchase; in the past put in place because of wartime shortages of many goods.

Government-sponsored deposit insurance: Protection offered to depositors by a government agency that protects the depositors from losses that may occur if the depository institution becomes insolvent or fails.

H

Home mortgages: A loan for which residential real estate is used as collateral. The lender may take possession of the property if the borrower fails to repay the money.

I

Impact or effectiveness lag: When a policy implemented in the present does not affect the overall economy until well into the future. As a result, when the policy's impact is achieved, it may be the wrong policy for that time.

Implicit target: A policy where the central bank does not state an explicit target or goal, but rather has targets that are not well defined.

Indenture: A legal contract between the bond issuer and the bond holder or purchaser. The contract lays out the legal requirements of the borrower or bond issuer.

Independent insurance agent: An insurance sales agent who sells insurance products from a variety of different insurance companies.

Inflation gap: The difference between the actual rate of inflation and the inflation target set by the central bank or monetary authority.

Inflation targeting: A monetary policy where the central bank uses its tools to achieve a stated rate of inflation over time.

Information lag: When policymakers do not have what they need to undertake the optimal policy because of a lack of readily available information.

Initial public offering: Often referred to as an IPO, the first time a corporation offers its shares for sale to the public.

Insurance claims adjuster: A person within an insurance company who assesses claims on insurance policies submitted by parties who have incurred covered losses.

Insurance deductible: The amount of a loss that the insured must pay out of their own resources before an insurer pays for expenses related to the covered loss.

Insurance guarantee fund: A fund established and administered by state governments in the United States to protect insurance policyholders and beneficiaries in the event that an insurance company becomes insolvent or defaults on paying benefits.

Insurance policy premium: Fees paid by the insured to the insurer to compensate the insurer for bearing the risk of specific events that would negatively affect the insured.

Insurance underwriter: A person within an insurance company who decides whether insurance is issued and under what terms.

Intellectual capture: The widely held belief that what whatever benefits the financial industry must also be beneficial to all of society.

Interest rate gap analysis: The difference between the amount of assets and the amount of liabilities on which interest rates are due to reset during a specific time period.

Interest rate risk: The chance that the value of an asset will change because of a change in interest rates.

Investment bank roadshow: The management of a company that is issuing securities travels around the country, often with investment bank employees, to give presentations to potential investors and analysts in order to receive feedback on the offering.

Investment return yield: A measurement of a bond's return, using a 365-day year, that is calculated relative to the price paid for the bond by the bondholder.

L

Legal tender: Assets accepted for repayment of debt to the government as well as private transactions.

Leveraged buyout: The acquisition of a public or private company where the buyout is financed mostly by debt (leverage).

Life insurance policy cash value: The investment portion of some life insurance policies that accumulates over the term of the policy. The policyholder may be able to withdraw or borrow against the cash value of the policy.

Life insurance policy face value: The amount of life insurance coverage or the amount paid to beneficiaries upon the death of the insured.

Liquidation or salvage value: The total value of a company's fixed assets when the company ceases to operate. The company's intangible assets, such as reputation and good will, are excluded.

Liquidity: The ease and expense at which one asset can be converted into another asset.

Liquidity coverage ratio: The ratio of a financial firm's liquid assets to its projected net cash outflows.

Liquidity mismatch: A situation in which there is a lack of unity between the contractual amounts and dates of cash inflows and outflows.

Liquidity risk: The risk that a financial firm will not be able to meet its current and/or future cash needs.

Liquidity trap: A situation where expansionary monetary policy fails to stimulate the overall economy because of a high level of savings and lack of borrowing in financial markets.

Loan loss provision: A noncash expense that banks set aside as an allowance to cover losses on loans.

M

Managed float exchange rate: A foreign exchange rate regime where a central bank or national government undertakes an exchange rate intervention but generally does not announce the intervention ahead of time nor lay out specific conditions under which an intervention will take place.

Marginal propensity to consume (MPC): A change in the desired level of consumption brought about by a change in the level of disposal income.

Marginal propensity to import: A change in the purchase of imports brought about by a change in the amount of disposable income.

Market price of a bond: The present value of the cash flow the owner of the bond can expect to receive over the life of the bond.

Market risk: The risk of a loss occurring as a result of the decline in the market value of an asset.

Matched sale-purchases: An arrangement where the Federal Reserve sells government securities to a primary dealer or the central bank of another country with the agreement to purchase the security back within a short period of time, usually 1 to 15 days.

Medium of exchange: A good that is accepted by both sides in a transaction.

Monetary aggregates: Broad measurements of the total amount of money within an economic system. Also referred to as the money supply or money supplies.

Monetary base: Currency in circulation + bank reserves + US Treasury currency in circulation. It is one of the narrowest measurements of the money supply.

Monetization of public debt: Governments require commercial banks and/or central banks to purchase government bonds.

Money: Anything that is generally acceptable in exchange for goods and services and/or repayment of debt.

Money market: A segment of a financial market where short-term debt instruments with high levels of liquidity and low default risk are traded.

Moral hazard: One entity takes on an excessive amount of risk because it knows another entity will bear the burden of those risks.

Mortgage pass-through: A financial instrument created when mortgages are pooled together and shares or participation certificates in the pool are sold to investors. The shares or participation certificates pay to the holder the payments of principal, interest, and prepayments from the underlying mortgages. Thus the payments from the mortgages are passed through to the share or participation certificate holders.

Municipal (muni) bonds: Bonds or debt issued by state governments, local governments, and/or local municipalities.

Mutual fund annual management fee: The annual fee investment companies charge mutual fund investors for managing the mutual fund.

N

Named-peril insurance policy: An insurance policy that pays for damages incurred by the insured stemming from specific events.

Net stable funding ratio: The proportion of a bank's long-term assets funded by stable, long-term sources, including bank customer deposits, long-term bank borrowing, and bank capital.

Nonprofit financial institutions: Financial institutions that are designed to serve their customers and do not have a profit motive.

O

On-site examination: A periodic physical inspection of a bank's operations, including the quality of the bank's management, assets, lending policies, and compliance with banking regulations.

Open-end mutual fund: A fund operated by an investment company that does not limit the amount of shares the fund will issue.

Open-peril insurance policy: Also known as an all-risk policy, an insurance policy that pays for all damages incurred by the insured except for those due to specific events or circumstances.

Operational risk: The risk of loss resulting from an inadequate or failed internal process or external event.

Optimal or optimum currency area: The situation where economies could join together in a currency union and the result would be a maximization of economic efficiency.

Output gap: The difference between the actual level of real GDP and GDP potential.

P

Par: A situation when the market price of a bond equals the face value of the bond.

Pay off and liquidate: A policy used by bank regulators to deal with failed or failing institutions whereby the depositors are paid their deposit balances from the liquidation of the institution's assets.

Preferred stock: Shares of a corporation that entitle holders to a claim on the corporation's assets at liquidation senior to common stock holders. Holders are entitled to a fixed dividend payment that is paid before common stock dividends.

Price level targeting: A monetary policy where the central bank uses its tools to achieve a stated price index over time.

Primary credit: Healthy banks are allowed to borrow from the Federal Reserve for short periods of time, historically overnight.

Primary market: The initial sale of a bond.

Primary offering: The initial sale of a stock or bond by a corporation or a government or government agency.

Principle–agent problem: The problem of motivating one party (the agent) who has been hired by another party (the principle) to act in the best interests of the hiring party.

Private equity commitment: The size of an investment an investor pledges to a private equity fund.

Private equity management fee: The annual fee for managing the fund the general partners of a private equity fund charge to the investors in the fund.

Private equity rollup: A practice used in the private equity industry whereby several small firms in the same market are purchased by private equity funds and merged into one single, larger firm.

Private mortgage insurance: An insurance policy that pays the lender of the mortgage in the case of default by the borrower. The policy typically pays the lender a percentage of the outstanding loan principal, accrued interest, and expenses. State laws usually state this percentage may be no more than about 25% to 30% of the claimed amount.

Private placement: The sale of newly issued stocks or bonds that are not offered for sale to the general public. Most often the new stocks or bonds are sold to a single buyer or a limited number of buyers.

Prospectus: A legal document containing information about the issuer of stocks and bonds. This is required by the Securities and Exchange Commission from corporations and governments that want to sell their stocks and bonds to the public. A prospectus must include information that is designed to ensure investors have the information they need to make an informed investment decision.

Purchase and assume: A policy used by bank regulators to deal with failed or failing institutions whereby the regulator finds a solvent institution to purchase the performing assets of the failed or failing institution and the regulator assumes or takes over the nonperforming assets.

Purchasing power parity: The exchange rate between currencies that equalizes the purchasing power of each currency by eliminating the differences in price levels in each economy.

Pure expectations theory: A framework where long-term interest rates are based on the expectations of what short-term interest rates will be in the future.

Pure or insurable risk: Category or type of risk where the only possible outcomes are a loss or no loss.

Q

QE1: The first round of quantitative easing undertaken by the Federal Reserve began in November 2008 and lasted until March 2010.

QE2: The second round of quantitative easing, or extraordinary expansionary monetary policy, undertaken by the Federal Reserve from November 2010 to June 2011.

QE3: The third round of quantitative easing, or extraordinary expansionary monetary policy, undertaken by the Federal Reserve from late 2013 to late 2014.

Quantity theory of money: The concept that the quantity of money is directly proportional to the price level.

R

Rational market: A market where all available information is used to make correct predictions about the future and market participants learn from their mistakes. Thus mistakes are not repeated, or they are corrected by other market participants.

Real bills doctrine: Central banks should lend money to commercial banks if and only if the commercial banks use those funds to support "real" (as opposed to speculative) economic activity.

Real cost of debt: The burden of debt measured in constant terms.

Real realized rate of return: The rate of return earned after controlling for inflation.

Redlining: The act of denying financial services to people living in a particular area.

Registered investment advisor: A financial advisor registered with the Securities and Exchange Commission or state securities regulatory agency who has pledged to put their clients' interests ahead of their own.

Regulation Q: The interest rate on bank deposit accounts ceiling in effect from 1933 to 2011.

Regulator shopping: When banks and other financial institutions are allowed to choose their regulator, they may pit the regulators against each other and then choose the regulator that offers the most favorable regulations.

Repurchase agreement: A financial transaction where a primary dealer sells a security to the Federal Reserve with the agreement to buy it back at a set date in the future.

Required reserve ratio: The proportion of deposits banks must hold in the form of cash or reserves.

Residual claim: The amount that stockholders are paid at the liquidation of a corporation after taxes, debts, and other claims have been satisfied.

Resolution Trust Corporation: A government agency in operation from 1989 to 1996 that was in charge of liquidating insolvent thrift institutions and selling off the assets of the failed institutions. It also arranged mergers and bailouts for bankruptcy by still operating thrifts.

Revenue bond: A bond issued and backed by a state or local municipality to raise funds that will be used for a specific income-generating project.

S

Savings & Loan: A depository institution that focuses on taking deposits from households and individuals. Most loans are consumer loans, including home mortgages.

Search costs: The implicit and explicit costs involved in savers and borrowers looking for each other.

Seasonal credit: Credit given to a limited number of banks that experience unusually high swings in their levels of reserves during different seasons of the year.

Seasoned offering: The sale of stocks or bonds by a corporation, government, or government agency that has issued similar stocks or bonds in the past.

Secondary bond market: The market for bonds or other debt instruments that were previously issued.

Secondary credit: Banks suffering from financial difficulty can borrow from the Federal Reserve, but they must pay a penalty interest rate above the discount rate.

Segmented market theory: Also called the segmented markets theory or the market segmentation theory, a framework where the short-term, medium-term, and long-term bond markets are all different or segmented markets.

Settlement risk: In a securities transaction, the risk that the other side of the trade will not deliver the cash or the securities as promised.

Share buyback: When a corporation buys back shares it previously sold to investors; also called share repurchase.

Sinking fund: A pool of money set aside for the repayment of a bond.

Smart money: A private equity firm or investor who, in addition to offering financial resources to a portfolio firm, can also offer insight, connections, and advice that will be of great assistance to the portfolio firm.

Speculative risk: Category or type of risk where the possible outcomes are loss, no loss, or a gain.

Stagflation: An economic condition where an economy is suffering from a relatively high and often increasing inflation rate and stagnant economic growth often accompanied by an increasing unemployment rate.

Sterilized foreign exchange intervention: A foreign exchange intervention where the central bank or government undertake an offsetting policy to insulate their domestic money supply or financial markets from the foreign exchange intervention.

Stigma effect: A situation in which commercial banks fear that borrowing from the central bank will be considered as a sign of financial weakness.

Store of value: The ability of an asset that functions as money to retain its purchasing power over time.

Structural unemployment: Unemployment that occurs as some industries or sectors of the economy are contracting while others are expanding. People in the contracting industry(ies) may have difficulty finding jobs in the expanding industries.

Subprime mortgage loan: A home mortgage where the borrower has substandard qualifications.

T

Target zone regime: An exchange rate system where the central bank or government sets official upper and lower bounds for the market value of the country's currency. The market determines the exchange rate day to day, and the central bank or government pledges to undertake an intervention if the market rate approaches either the upper or lower bound.

Taylor Rule: A rule for monetary policy that suggests how much nominal interest rates should change in response to inflation, output levels, and financial market conditions.

Term premium theory: A framework where longer-term bonds have higher yields than shorter-term bonds as a way of creating an incentive for bond buyers to purchase the less desirable longer-term bonds.

Time preference: The rate at which a person will prefer to consume today as opposed to consuming in the future. A high time preference implies a person wants very much to consume now as opposed to in the future. A low time preference implies a person is indifferent between consuming now or in the future.

Time value of money: Money received today has a higher value than money received in the future.

Time-inconsistency problem: The situation in which a policymaker may prefer one policy in advance, but when it comes time to implement the policy the policymaker prefers a completely different policy.

Too big to fail (TBTF): A policy followed by bank regulators whereby some financial institutions are so important to the entire financial and economic system that these institutions will not be allowed to fail. That is, regulators will take action to ensure that these systemically important institutions continue in operation.

Total factor productivity: A measurement of how efficiently and intensely inputs are used in the production of goods and services.

Transaction deposit account: A liquid bank account most often used by depositors for transferring funds to another party.

U

Underfunded pension: A retirement system that has more liabilities than it does assets.

Underwriting gross spread: The difference between the price of a stock or bond the investment bank pays to the issuer and the price the investment bank charges its clients to buy the same stock or bond.

Underwriting syndicate: A group of investment banks that collectively work together to sell a stock or bond being issued.

Unit of account: An agreed-upon method of placing relative value on assets.

Unsterilized foreign exchange intervention: A foreign exchange intervention where the central bank or government have *not* insulated their domestic money supply or financial markets from the foreign exchange intervention. There is no offsetting policy action.

V

Velocity of money: Also known as the turnover rate of money, the number of times in a time period a unit of money is used.

W

Wage and price controls: Also called incomes policy, an economic policy where governments place legal limits on the amount of wage and price increases.

War bond: Debt issued by the federal government to fund the spending on wars. Done in the United States most recently during World War I and World War II.

Waterfall: The structure of repayments made to the investors of a private equity fund.

Y

Yield curve: Graph of the yields of bonds or debt at one point in time.

Z

Zombie institutions: Financial institutions that are insolvent but are allowed by bank regulators to continue operating.

Index

C

D

E

G

H

S